THE
FILM BUFF'S
BIBLE

of Motion Pictures (1915 - 1972)

edited by D. Richard Baer

HOLLYWOOD FILM ARCHIVE
HOLLYWOOD, CALIFORNIA

D1290721

Copyright © 1972 by D. Richard Baer.

All rights reserved. No part of this book may be reproduced in any manner whatsoever without written permission.

Critical ratings of motion pictures reprinted from other copyrighted sources as follows:

From MOVIES ON TV edited by Steven H. Scheuer. Copyright © 1958, 1961, 1966, 1968, 1969, 1971 by Bantam Books, Inc.

From TV MOVIES edited by Leonard Maltin. Copyright © 1969 by Leonard Maltin.

Published by

Hollywood Film Archive

Post Office Box 36553

Hollywood, California 90036

First Edition
First Printing, October 1972

Manufactured in the United States of America.

CONTENTS

APPENDIX

FOREWORD

THE FILM BUFF'S BIBLE is a comprehensive summary of information and critical appraisal of some 13,000 motion pictures with entries for films released as late as September, 1972; it includes silent films, short features, movies made for television, and movies which have never been shown on television. The book's main function is to give you a good idea as to whether or not a film is worth watching; it is intended to be used as a supplement to your television log (or theatre guide) in which you are more likely to find the credits and summaries we have necessarily had to omit for lack of space.

Although the films listed in this volume constitute only a fraction of all feature motion pictures ever made, we have tried to include almost all of those likely to be shown on television or reissued at your local theatre. Sorry if we missed one of your favorites; a letter of vehement protest might induce us to include it in the next edition.

NOTES

Titles. Titles are in alphabetical order. Abbreviated words are treated as if they were spelled out (e.g., a title beginning with "St. Louis" is alphabetized as "Saint Louis"). Initials are treated as if they were one-letter words (e.g., "C.C. and Company" is alphabetized at the beginning of the titles beginning with "c") except in cases where initials practically constitute a word (such as "FBI" or "M*A*S*H"). The abbreviation "Mrs." is always alphabetized immediately after "Mister" (or "Mr."). And in case you are looking for the title "08/15," it is alphabetized as "O EIGHT . . ."

We have tried to give each title as the producer intended it should appear. The television logs of many newspapers are notorious for being inaccurate in this regard; thus, "Woman of Devil's Island" may be called "Women of Devil's Island," or "Horse Feathers" may be contracted to read "Horsefeathers;" we have seen "The Lost Man" spelled "The Last Man" and we have probably made a few errors ourselves.

Names of actors are shown only when two or more films have the same or similar title (e.g., "The Lovemaker" and "The Love Makers" are considered similar). We have also tried to do this in cases in which a film in this book has the same or similar title as a feature not listed in this book (e.g., "Seven Keys to Baldpate" is the title of at least five different films — we have listed only one). However, lack of actors' names is no guarantee that there is not another film by the same or similar title.

Alternate Titles. Some films have two or more different titles; a few have several. Films with "a" to the left of the date have alternate titles (but the lack of this symbol is no guarantee that a film does not have an alternate title). See Appendix for a list of alternate titles.

Year. The date shown is the year in which the film was released, not necessarily the year in which it was completed. For example, the Japanese film **Men Who Tread on the Tiger's Tail** was completed in 1945, but was banned by the Japanese government and later by the Allied occupation forces until the early fifties.

Note: Foreign films often come to the U.S. years after they were released in their country of origin; while we have attempted to give the year of original release, there are a few cases in which that information was not available; thus the year shown may be the year the film was released in the U.S.

Running Time. In most cases, this is the original running time in minutes; in some cases, a film has been edited by the producer or distributor after its initial release, so we have tried to give the running time of the most popular version.

There are a few films of which no complete version exists. **Intolerance** (1916) originally ran about 3½ hours, but it is doubtful if any existing print is complete.

On rare occasions, television may actually improve a film by cutting irrelevant or boring scenes. In most cases, however, your TV station or network will cut a film simply to fit it into a shorter time slot; the resulting abortion is usually pretty sad. For example, some lazy, incompetent film editor may cut the first 30 minutes out of **The Chalk Garden** (106 minutes) in order to put it on a 90 minute program, commercials included of course. A few independent stations are notorious for breaking into the middle of a line of dialogue or a heavy scene for commercials. We also see more and more of the practice of showing parts of a picture on two or even three different days (and don't you appreciate it when they omit a half-hour of the second day to show the President making a speech that can be seen on the other six channels?). When public-be-damned stunts like that are pulled, you might write the sponsors, or better yet, telephone the station. If about ten people call any station and say that they are not going to watch a certain movie because it has obviously been cut, you can be sure that someone is going to start worrying about his Neilsen rating, which spells $$$$$$.

Critical Ratings. One glance at the numerical ratings in this book will usually tell you more about the quality of a movie than reading a three column review in a magazine or newspaper (although a few noteworthy films listed in this book have not been rated). In addition to our own rating, we have included the ratings of two of the most popular and presumably **honest** sources (but you will have to judge their **credibility** for yourself; they almost invariably give undeservedly high ratings to films of the Marx Brothers and to World War II pictures made during WW2). We know of other film critics who use the four-star rating system and similar systems; we don't accuse them of being dishonest, but we suspect some of them of being unduly influenced by a glamorous industry. Many readers will undoubtedly wonder why we did not include the ratings of Consumers Union, one of the most widely read and respected sources — the reason is that they wouldn't give us permission, so complain about it to them, not us. We have listed the ratings of the following sources:

- **Movies On TV** edited by Steven H. Scheuer, 6th edition (formerly published as "TV Key Movie Guide"). Available in paperback (Bantam) on most newsstands for $1.50. In addition to using the four-star rating system, this book gives the names of major stars and a one paragraph review of each of about 7,000 movies which have been shown on television (or are available to TV). Each new edition has deleted reviews of some films published in previous editions; although most of the films deleted are of inferior quality, we have tried to include all of the ratings given since the second edition; we have omitted a few entries of the first edition, mainly the Z-grade westerns of Roy Rogers, Rex Allen, Gene Autry, Tim Holt, etc. In addition to the note concerning credibility in the last paragraph, it is also our opinion that this book tends to overrate the films of W.C. Fields and Randolph Scott, as well as many of the early "classics."

- **TV Movies** edited by Leonard Maltin, first edition. Published in paperback (Signet) for $1.25, though you may have to write New American Library in order to obtain a copy. This book also uses the four-star rating system for all movies except some of those in the old series (who needs them?) such as Charlie Chan, Bulldog Drummond, Blondie, and The Bowery Boys. It gives the names of major and supporting actors, the director, and a one paragraph review of each of about 8,000 movies which have been shown on television. Although it has less of a tendency than Scheuer's book to overrate films, it still unnecessarily deifies many of the early "classics."

In a few instances, one of the aforementioned sources has given different ratings to the same film; this has occurred when a film with alternate titles was somehow given a different rating for each title. We have not tried to outguess whoever was responsible for these circumstances. We have just printed the ratings as they were given to each title.

We strongly recommend that you purchase both of the aforementioned books for names of actors and summaries.

● The editor and staff of **The Film Buff's Bible**. Ratings in this column are followed by an asterisk (*) if they have been viewed and rated by the editor and/or staff of **The Film Buff's Bible**. All other ratings in this column are based on our evaluation of a consensus of reviews by other responsible critics.

Our ratings are on a 1 to 10 scale, 10 being the highest; these ratings are based primarily on one factor, a film's modern entertainment value. A split rating (such as "5-6") means either a disagreement among the staff or the inability of the editor to make a Solomonic decision. A widely split rating (such as "6-8") indicates a wide disagreement among the staff. However, the editor has made the final decision on every FBB rating entered in this book. A film cannot receive a rating of 9 or 10 unless it has been seen by the editor.† (See **The Editor's Philosophy**.)

There is a sizable school of film enthusiasts who believe that knowing the name of a film's director is more valuable than any number of critical reviews or ratings in pre-judging its quality — we disagree; if a screenplay is a sow's ear, neither John Ford nor Alfred Hitchcock (or any other such demi-god) ever made it into a silk purse.

Although we have our preferences and prejudices, we have no sacred cows; if a Chaplin picture is lousy, that's that. Our ratings make no attempt to evaluate any film's "decency" or its suitability for children; we assume (rightly or wrongly) that the reader is an open-minded adult who can appreciate anything from G-rated **National Velvet** to X-rated **A Clockwork Orange**. And our rating does not necessarily indicate approval or disapproval of any film's content, lest anyone suspect that we sympathize with the beliefs and actions of characters like Joe Curran (played by actor Peter Boyle) in **Joe** (rated 8).

Distributor. This is the original theatrical distributor, if known, or the television distributor or production company. Sometimes a film is handled by two or more distributors, or the current distributor may not be the original one; distribution firms may merge or become defunct. Various sources of information often disagree as to who the distributor is; we have tried to use the best sources available. As a rule of thumb: the more important the film, the more likely that we have given the correct distributor.

---

†Only four films have received a 10 rating; they are **My Fair Lady, The Pawnbroker, Tom Jones,** and **Z.** There is no "zero" rating, but if there were, the prime candidate would be **Wind From The East.**

Comments. Space does not permit much of a comment on any film in this book, but in a few cases we have given an extra piece of information or a critical comment which may help the reader decide whether a film is worth watching. For instance, "SLOW BUILDUP" generally means that the movie gets better as it goes along. We may also put the nationality of the film in this space if there is a lack of room after the title.

In reference to the Academy Awards, we have put a notation on every picture receiving "BEST PICTURE AWARD" or "NOMINATED BEST PICTURE." The notation "BELIEVED LOST" means just that; there are a few films of which no prints are known to exist . . . sorry.

* * *

The Editor's Philosophy. It is no sin for a film to make a powerful social comment, teach a moral, illustrate the problems of our senior citizens, promote racial harmony or religious tolerance, or be the first to break various moral taboos; but none of these things will make a movie entertaining if the story is mediocre or the production is inferior. Therefore, do not conclude that the editor is unsympathetic to the plight of the mentally ill just because the FBB ratings tend to downgrade movies dealing with the subject of mental illness; most of such movies just aren't that good (**Charly** and **David and Lisa** are notable exceptions).

Movies have to be compared to other movies of the same type, so don't write us an angry letter asking how we can give the same rating to **A Funny Thing Happened on the Way to the Forum** (a light musical comedy) and **Diabolique** (a horror story).

Minimal consideration has been given to the era during which a film was made. The strict moral code of the late thirties and early forties may have severely restricted the content of films of that period, but that fact is of little consolation to a modern filmwatcher. Early "classics" such as **Grand Hotel, Public Enemy, Cleopatra** (1934), **Stagecoach** (1939), and **The Magnificent Ambersons** are typical of the phony stories and trite dialogue which characterized the first quarter-century of the sound era; historical significance should not be confused with artistic excellence.

Certain foreign films seem to have an effect similar to that of the emperor's new clothes on many film critics and those who value their opinions; as soon as one influential critic discovers an abstract esoteric meaning from some incomprehensible plotless nonsense, filmed on grainy stock, printed in a garage, with dialogue in Polish, Finnish or Hungarian (and half the titles superimposed on a white shirt or bedsheet), it is surprising how many others will mystically discover the same wonderful qualities. Congratulations to those who found something worthwhile in 8½ or **Ashes and Diamonds**; please forgive those of us who prefer pictures which have a beginning, middle and end.

The quality of each film, old or new, must be considered in comparison to all films; what may have been called excellent or fascinating at the time a movie was released may be humdrum today. This, of course, also means that the FBB ratings are neither infallible nor permanent; it is almost a certainty that as we watch new movies and re-watch old ones, we will reassess our ratings of a substantial number.

RATING GUIDE

Because our other sources use a rating system different from ours, the following chart gives their **approximate** equivalents:

Steven Scheuer's "Movies On TV" and Leonard Maltin's "TV Movies"	The Film Buff's Bible	Explanation
	10	All time great. Highest possible rating.
	9	Outstanding.
**** (4.0)	8	Excellent. Recommend for all movie watchers.
***½ (3.5)	7	Very Good. Definitely worth watching.
*** (3.0)	6	Good. Worth going to see in a theatre, or at least worth watching on TV.
	5	Passable. Maybe worth watching on TV, or perhaps in a theatre if the other feature is better.
**½ (2.5)		This is about the borderline between whether or not a film is worth watching.
	4	Mediocre. Probably not worth watching.
** (2.0)	3	Only Fair. Not worth watching.
*½ (1.5)	2	Poor. Definitely not worth watching.
* (1.0) "Bomb" in Maltin's book	1	Terrible. Reserved for the really miserable turkeys which are painful to watch.

NOTE: A dash (-) in place of a rating on the four-star scale means that the film was mentioned or reviewed in that book, but that no numerical rating was given.

ABBREVIATIONS

BR., BRIT.	British	DIST. CORP. OF AMER.	Distributors Corporation of America
DOC.	Documentary	FEATURE FILM CORP.	Feature Film Corporation of America
FR.	French		
GER.	German	FILMS AROUND THE WLD.	Films Around the World
IT., ITAL.	Italian	LANDAU/UNGER COM.UN.	Landau/Unger Commonwealth United
JAP.	Japanese	NAT'L FILM BOARD CAN.	National Film Board of Canada
SPAN.	Spanish	TURN OF CENT. FIGHTS	Turn of the Century Fights, Inc.
SWED.	Swedish	UN. MOTION PIC. ORG.	United Motion Picture Organization (UMPO)
T.V.	Movie made for Television		

TITLE (LEADING ACTORS SHOWN WHERE TWO OR MORE FILMS HAVE THE SAME OR SIMILAR TITLE)	YEAR RELEASED	RUNNING TIME IN MINUTES	CRITICAL RATINGS			DISTRIBUTOR	COMMENT
			THE FILM BUFF'S BIBLE ‡	STEVEN SCHEUER	LEONARD MALTIN		
A-HAUNTING WE WILL GO	1942	68		1.5	1.5	20th CENTURY FOX	
A.K.A. CASSIUS CLAY (DOCUMENTARY)	1970	79	5			UNITED ARTISTS	
A NOUS LA LIBERTE (FRENCH)	1932	95	3*			TOBIS	
AARON SLICK FROM PUNKIN CRICK	1952	95		2.0	2.0	PARAMOUNT	
ABANDON SHIP! (BRITISH)	a1957	95	6*	3.0	3.0	COLUMBIA	SLOW BUILDUP
ABANDONED	1949	79		2.5	1.5	UNIVERSAL	
ABBOTT & COSTELLO GO TO MARS	1953	77		2.0	2.0	UNIVERSAL	
ABBOTT & COSTELLO IN HOLLYWOOD	1945	84		1.5	2.0	M-G-M	
ABBOTT & COSTELLO IN THE FOREIGN LEGION	1950	79		2.0	2.0	UNIVERSAL	
ABBOTT & COSTELLO IN THE NAVY	a1941	85		2.5	2.5	UNIVERSAL	
ABBOTT & COSTELLO LOST IN ALASKA	a1952	76	2	2.5	2.0	UNIVERSAL	
ABBOTT & COSTELLO MEET CAPTAIN KIDD	1952	70		2.0	2.0	WARNER BROTHERS	
ABBOTT & COSTELLO MEET DR JEKYLL AND MR HYDE	1953	77		2.5	2.0	UNIVERSAL	
ABBOTT & COSTELLO MEET FRANKENSTEIN	1948	92	5	3.0	3.0	UNIVERSAL	
ABBOTT & COSTELLO MEET THE INVISIBLE MAN	1951	82		2.0	2.0	UNIVERSAL	
ABBOTT & COSTELLO MEET THE KEYSTONE COPS	1955	79		3.0	2.0	UNIVERSAL	
ABBOTT & COSTELLO MEET THE KILLER, BORIS KARLOFF	1949	84		2.0	2.5	UNIVERSAL	
ABBOTT & COSTELLO MEET THE MUMMY	1955	79		2.0	2.5	UNIVERSAL	
ABDUCTORS, THE (VICTOR MCLAGLEN, GEORGE MACREADY)	1957	80		2.5	1.5	20th CENTURY FOX	
ABDUCTORS, THE (CHERI CAFFARO, WILLIAM GRANNEL)	1972	95	1			JOSEPH BRENNER	
ABE LINCOLN IN ILLINOIS	1940	110	5*	4.0	4.0	RKO	
ABIE'S IRISH ROSE	1946	96		1.0	1.0	UNITED ARTISTS	
ABILENE TOWN	1946	89		3.0	3.0	UNITED ARTISTS	
ABOMINABLE DR PHIBES, THE (BRITISH)	a1971	93	2			AMERICAN-INTERNAT'L	
ABOMINABLE SNOWMAN OF THE HIMALAYAS, THE (BRIT.)	a1957	85		2.5	2.5	20th CENTURY FOX	
ABOUT FACE	1952	94		2.0	1.5	WARNER BROTHERS	
ABOUT MRS LESLIE	1954	104		2.5	3.0	PARAMOUNT	
ABOVE AND BEYOND	1953	122	5-6*	3.0	3.0	M-G-M	
ABOVE SUSPICION	1943	90		2.5	3.0	M-G-M	
ABOVE US THE WAVES (BRITISH)	1955	99		3.0	3.0	REPUBLIC	
ABRAHAM LINCOLN	1930	80		2.0	2.5	UNITED ARTISTS	
ABROAD WITH TWO YANKS	1944	80		3.0	2.5	UNITED ARTISTS	
ABSENT-MINDED PROFESSOR, THE	1961	97	6			BUENA VISTA	
ACCATTONE! (ITALIAN)	1961	120	6	3.0		BRANDON	
ACCENT ON YOUTH	1935	77		2.5	3.0	PARAMOUNT	
ACCIDENT (BRITISH)	1967	105	3*	3.5	3.5	CINEMA V	
ACCIDENTAL DEATH (BRITISH)	1963	57		2.0	2.5	AVCO-EMBASSY	
ACCOMPLICES, THE (ITALIAN)	1959	93			1.5	ARCHWAY	
ACCORDING TO MRS HOYLE	1951	60	1			MONOGRAM	
ACCOUNT RENDERED (BRITISH)	1957	61		2.0		J. ARTHUR RANK	
ACCURSED, THE (BRITISH)	1958	78		2.5	1.5	ALLIED ARTISTS	
ACCUSED, THE (LORETTA YOUNG, ROBERT CUMMINGS)	1948	101	6*	3.0	3.0	PARAMOUNT	
ACCUSED OF MURDER	1956	74		2.0	2.0	REPUBLIC	
ACE HIGH (ITALIAN)	1968	122	2			PARAMOUNT	
ACE IN THE HOLE	a1951	112	6*	4.0	3.0	PARAMOUNT	
ACROSS THE BRIDGE (BRITISH)	1957	103	4	3.0	2.5	J. ARTHUR RANK	
ACROSS THE PACIFIC	1942	97	5*	3.5	2.5	WARNER BROTHERS	
ACROSS THE RIVER	1965	85	4			DEBEMA PRODUCTION	
ACROSS THE WIDE MISSOURI	1951	78		2.0	2.5	M-G-M	
ACT OF LOVE	1954	108	6	3.5	3.0	UNITED ARTISTS	
ACT OF MURDER, AN (FREDRIC MARCH, EDMOND O'BRIEN)	1948	91	6*	3.5	3.0	UNIVERSAL	
ACT OF THE HEART, THE	1970	103	6			UNIVERSAL	
ACT OF VIOLENCE	1949	82		2.5	3.0	M-G-M	
ACT ONE	1963	110	4	3.0	2.5	WARNER BROTHERS	
ACTION FOR SLANDER (BRITISH)	1938	83		3.0		UNITED ARTISTS	
ACTION IN ARABIA	1944	75		2.5	2.5	RKO	
ACTION IN THE NORTH ATLANTIC	1943	127	4*	3.5	3.0	WARNER BROTHERS	
ACTION MAN (FRENCH)	1972	95				H.K. FILM DIST.	
ACTION OF THE TIGER (BRITISH)	1957	93	3	2.5	2.5	M-G-M	
ACTIVIST, THE	1969	86	4			REGIONAL	
ACTORS AND SIN	1952	85		3.0	2.5	UNITED ARTISTS	
ACTRESS, THE	1953	90		3.0	2.5	M-G-M	
ADA	1961	108		2.0	3.0	M-G-M	
ADALEN '31 (SWEDISH)	1969	115	6			PARAMOUNT	
ADAM AND EVALYN (BRITISH)	1949	92		2.5	2.5	UNIVERSAL	
ADAM AND EVE (MEXICAN)	1956	76	2			WILLIAM M. HORNE	NO DIALOGUE
ADAM AT SIX A.M.	1970	100	4			NATIONAL GENERAL	
ADAM HAD FOUR SONS	1941	81		3.0	3.0	COLUMBIA	
ADAM'S RIB (SILENT - MILTON SILLS)	1923	106				PARAMOUNT	
ADAM'S RIB (SPENCER TRACY, KATHARINE HEPBURN)	1949	101	6*	3.5	4.0	M-G-M	
ADDING MACHINE, THE (BRITISH)	1969	100	4*			REGIONAL	
ADDRESS UNKNOWN	1944	72		3.0	3.0	COLUMBIA	
ADELAIDE (FRENCH)	1968	86	3			SIGMA III	
ADIOS, GRINGO (ITALIAN)	1965	95		1.0		TRANS-LUX DIST.	
ADIOS, SABATA	1971	106	1			UNITED ARTISTS	
ADMIRABLE CRICHTON, THE (BRITISH)	a1957	93	5	3.0	2.0	COLUMBIA	
ADMIRAL WAS A LADY, THE	1950	87		2.0	2.0	UNITED ARTISTS	
ADORABLE CREATURES (FRENCH)	1952	106		3.0	2.0	CONTINENTAL	
ADORABLE JULIA (AUSTRIAN)	1962	94	4*	2.0	3.0	SEE-ART FILMS	
ADRIFT (CZECH)	1970	108	6			MPO VIDEOTRONICS	
ADVANCE TO THE REAR	1964	97		2.5	2.5	M-G-M	
ADVENTURE (CLARK GABLE, GREER GARSON)	1945	126		2.5	2.0	M-G-M	
ADVENTURE IN BALTIMORE	1949	89		2.0	2.0	RKO	
ADVENTURE IN DIAMONDS	1940	76		2.5	2.0	PARAMOUNT	

‡ An asterisk (*) in THE FILM BUFF'S BIBLE column indicates that the film has been rated by the editor and/or staff. All other ratings in this column are based on a consensus of reviews (see NOTES).

Column header notes: "a" TO LEFT OF YEAR INDICATES THAT FILM HAS AN ALTERNATE TITLE

TITLE (LEADING ACTORS SHOWN WHERE TWO OR MORE FILMS HAVE THE SAME OR SIMILAR TITLE)	YEAR RELEASED	RUNNING TIME IN MINUTES	THE FILM BUFF'S BIBLE ‡	STEVEN SCHEUER	LEONARD MALTIN	DISTRIBUTOR	COMMENT
ADVENTURE IN MANHATTAN	1936	75		2.5	2.5	COLUMBIA	
ADVENTURE IN WASHINGTON	1941	85		2.0	2.0	COLUMBIA	
ADVENTURE ISLAND	1947	67		2.0	2.0	PARAMOUNT	
ADVENTURER OF SEVILLE, THE (SPANISH)	1954	90		1.5			
ADVENTURERS, THE (BR.- JACK HAWKINS, DENNIS PRICE)	a1951	82		2.5	2.0	J. ARTHUR RANK	
ADVENTURERS, THE (BEKIM FEHMIU, ERNEST BORGNINE)	1970	171	2			PARAMOUNT	
ADVENTURES AT RUGBY	a1940	81		3.0	3.0	RKO	
ADVENTURES IN INDO-CHINA (FRENCH)	1961	85		1.0		AMERICAN-INTERNAT'L	
ADVENTURES IN SILVERADO	1948	75		3.0		COLUMBIA	
ADVENTURES OF A ROOKIE	1943	64		2.5		RKO	
ADVENTURES OF A YOUNG MAN	a1962	145		2.0	2.0	20th CENTURY FOX	
ADVENTURES OF ARSENE LUPIN, THE (FRENCH)	1956	103		2.0		RKO	
ADVENTURES OF BULLWHIP GRIFFIN, THE	1967	110	5			BUENA VISTA	
ADVENTURES OF CAPTAIN FABIAN	1951	100		1.5	1.5	REPUBLIC	
ADVENTURES OF CASANOVA	1948	83		1.5	2.0	EAGLE LION	
ADVENTURES OF CHICO (DOCUMENTARY)	1938	60		3.0		MONOGRAM	
ADVENTURES OF DON JUAN	1949	110	4*	2.0	3.0	WARNER BROTHERS	
ADVENTURES OF GALLANT BESS	1948	73		2.0	2.0	EAGLE LION	
ADVENTURES OF GIL BLAS, THE (FRENCH)	1955	95		1.0		TRANS-AMERICA	
ADVENTURES OF HAJJI BABA, THE	1954	93		1.5	2.5	20th CENTURY FOX	
ADVENTURES OF HUCKLEBERRY FINN, THE (M. ROONEY)	a1939	90		2.0	3.0	M-G-M	
ADVENTURES OF HUCKLEBERRY FINN, THE (TONY RANDALL)	a1960	107		2.5	3.0	M-G-M	
ADVENTURES OF ICHABOD AND MR TOAD	a1949	67	6			RKO	
ADVENTURES OF MANDERIN, THE (ITALIAN)	a1949	82		2.0		REPUBLIC	
ADVENTURES OF MARCO POLO, THE	1938	100		2.5	2.5	UNITED ARTISTS	
ADVENTURES OF MARK TWAIN, THE	1944	130		3.0	3.0	WARNER BROTHERS	
ADVENTURES OF MARTIN EDEN, THE	a1942	87		3.0	3.0	COLUMBIA	
ADVENTURES OF MICHAEL STROGOFF	a1937	85		3.0		RKO	
ADVENTURES OF MR WONDERBIRD (CARTOON)	1959	70		3.0		LIPPERT PRODS.	
ADVENTURES OF ROBIN HOOD, THE	1938	105	5*	3.0	3.5	WARNER BROTHERS	NOMINATED BEST PICTURE
ADVENTURES OF ROBINSON CRUSOE	a1954	90	6*	3.5	3.0	UNITED ARTISTS	
ADVENTURES OF SADIE, THE (BRITISH)	1955	88		3.0	2.5	20th CENTURY FOX	
ADVENTURES OF SCARAMOUCHE, THE (FRENCH)	1963	98		2.0	2.0	AVCO-EMBASSY	
ADVENTURES OF SHERLOCK HOLMES	1939	85	5*	3.0	-	20th CENTURY FOX	
ADVENTURES OF TARTU, THE (BRITISH)	a1943	103		2.5	2.5	M-G-M	
ADVENTURES OF TOM SAWYER, THE	1938	93		3.5	3.5	NEW TRENDS ASSOC.	
ADVENTURESS, THE (BRITISH)	1947	98	6*	4.0	3.5	EAGLE LION	
ADVISE AND CONSENT	1962	139	6*	4.0	3.0	COLUMBIA	
AFFAIR, THE	a1972	91	2			CAMBIST	
AFFAIR BLUM, THE (GERMAN)	1949	90	7			CENTRAL CINEMA CORP.	
AFFAIR IN HAVANA	1957	71		2.5	1.5	ALLIED ARTISTS	
AFFAIR IN MONTE CARLO (BRITISH)	1953	75		2.0	2.0	ALLIED ARTISTS	
AFFAIR IN RENO	1957	75		2.5	1.5	REPUBLIC	
AFFAIR IN TRINIDAD	1952	98		2.5	2.5	COLUMBIA	
AFFAIR OF THE SKIN, AN	1963	102	4			ZENITH INTERNATIONAL	
AFFAIR TO REMEMBER, AN	1957	119	4*	2.5	2.5	20th CENTURY FOX	
AFFAIR WITH A STRANGER	1953	89	4	3.0	2.5	RKO	
AFFAIRS IN VERSAILLES (FRENCH)	a1954	152		2.5	2.5	TIMES FILM CORP.	
AFFAIRS OF CELLINI	1934	80			3.0	UNITED ARTISTS	
AFFAIRS OF DOBIE GILLIS, THE	1953	74	4	2.5	3.0	M-G-M	
AFFAIRS OF DR HOLL (GERMAN)	a1952	88		2.0			
AFFAIRS OF GERALDINE	1946	68		2.0		REPUBLIC	
AFFAIRS OF JIMMY VALENTINE	a1942	72		3.5		REPUBLIC	
AFFAIRS OF MARTHA, THE	a1942	66		2.5		M-G-M	
AFFAIRS OF MESSALINA (ITALIAN)	a1952	108		2.5		COLUMBIA	
AFFAIRS OF SUSAN, THE	1945	110		2.5	2.5	PARAMOUNT	
AFFECTIONATELY YOURS	1941	90		2.0	2.0	WARNER BROTHERS	
AFRICA ADDIO (ITALIAN, DOCUMENTARY)	1966	120	4		3.0	RIZZOLI FILM	
AFRICA ADVENTURE (DOCUMENTARY)	1954	64	4			RKO	
AFRICA SCREAMS	1949	79		1.5	2.0	UNITED ARTISTS	
AFRICA - TEXAS STYLE! (BRITISH)	1967	109	4	2.5	2.5	PARAMOUNT	
AFRICAN ELEPHANT, THE (DOCUMENTARY)	a1971	92	5*			NATIONAL GENERAL	
AFRICAN FURY (BRITISH)	a1951	105	5*	3.5	3.5	UNITED ARTISTS	
AFRICAN LION, THE (DOCUMENTARY)	1955	75	6			BUENA VISTA	
AFRICAN MANHUNT	1955	65		2.0		REPUBLIC	
AFRICAN QUEEN, THE	1951	105	7*	4.0	4.0	UNITED ARTISTS	
AFRICAN SAFARI (DOCUMENTARY)	1969	98	6			CROWN INTERNATIONAL	
AFRICAN TREASURE	1952	70			-	MONOGRAM	
AFTER MIDNITE WITH BOSTON BLACKIE	1943	64		2.0	-	COLUMBIA	
AFTER OFFICE HOURS	1935	75		2.5	2.5	M-G-M	
AFTER THE BALL (BRITISH)	1957	89		2.0		ROMULUS FILMS	
AFTER THE FOX	1966	103		2.5	2.5	UNITED ARTISTS	
AFTER THE THIN MAN	1936	110	4*	3.0	-	M-G-M	
AGAINST ALL FLAGS	1952	83	2	2.0	2.5	UNIVERSAL	
AGAINST THE WIND (BRITISH)	1948	95		3.5		EAGLE LION	
AGE OF CONSENT (AUSTRALIAN)	1970	98	4			COLUMBIA	
AGE OF ILLUSIONS (HUNGARIAN)	1965	97	3			BRANDON	
AGENT FOR H.A.R.M.	1966	84	2	2.0		UNIVERSAL	
AGENT 008 3/4 (BRITISH)	1965	77	5	3.0	3.0	CONTINENTAL	
AGENT OF DOOM (FRENCH)	1963	90		2.5		G.R.K. FILMS	
AGENT 38-24-36 (THE WARMBLOODED SPY) (FRENCH)	a1964	105	1			SEVEN ARTS	
AGONY AND THE ECSTASY, THE	1965	140		2.5	2.5	20th CENTURY FOX	
AH, WILDERNESS	1935	101		3.5	3.0	M-G-M	
AIDA (ITALIAN)	1953	95	6			ITALIAN FILMS EXPORT	

‡ An asterisk (*) in THE FILM BUFF'S BIBLE column indicates that the film has been rated by the editor and/or staff. All other ratings in this column are based on a consensus of reviews (see NOTES).

TITLE (LEADING ACTORS SHOWN WHERE TWO OR MORE FILMS HAVE THE SAME OR SIMILAR TITLE) "a" TO LEFT OF YEAR INDICATES THAT FILM HAS AN ALTERNATE TITLE	YEAR RELEASED	RUNNING TIME IN MINUTES	CRITICAL RATINGS			DISTRIBUTOR	COMMENT
			THE FILM BUFF'S BIBLE ‡	STEVEN SCHEUER	LEONARD MALTIN		
AIN'T MISBEHAVIN'	1955	82		2.5	2.5	UNIVERSAL	
AIN'T NO TIME FOR GLORY	1957	90		2.0		SCREEN GEMS	
AIR CADET	1951	94		2.0	2.0	UNIVERSAL	
AIR FORCE	1943	124	3*	3.0	3.0	WARNER BROTHERS	
AIR MAIL	1932	83			3.0	UNIVERSAL	
AIR PATROL	1962	70	2			20th CENTURY FOX	
AIR RAID WARDENS	1943	67		1.5	2.0	M-G-M	
AIR STRIKE	1955	67		2.0		LIPPERT PRODS.	
AIRBORNE	1962	80	3	1.5		GILLMAN FILM DISTS.	
AIRPORT	1970	137	6*			PARAMOUNT	NOMINATED BEST PICTURE
AKU AKU (DOCUMENTARY)	1961	86		3.0	2.5	CONTINENTAL	
AL CAPONE	1959	105	5*	3.5	2.5	ALLIED ARTISTS	
AL JENNINGS OF OKLAHOMA	1951	79		2.0	2.0	COLUMBIA	
ALADDIN AND HIS LAMP	1952	67		1.5	1.5	MONOGRAM	
ALAKAZAM THE GREAT (CARTOON, JAPANESE)	1961	84	4	3.0	1.0	AMERICAN-INTERNAT'L	
ALAMO, THE	1960	192	4*	1.5		UNITED ARTISTS	NOMINATED BEST PICTURE
ALASKA PASSAGE	1959	71		1.5		20th CENTURY FOX	
ALASKA SEAS	1954	78		2.0	2.0	PARAMOUNT	
ALBERT SCHWEITZER (DOCUMENTARY)	1957	80	6	3.0		DE ROCHEMONT	
ALBUQUERQUE	1948	89		2.0	2.0	PARAMOUNT	
ALCATRAZ EXPRESS (T.V.)	1962	90	5*	2.5		DESILU	
ALEX IN WONDERLAND	1970	109	3			M-G-M	
ALEXANDER (FRENCH)	a1968	94	6			CINEMA V	
ALEXANDER HAMILTON	1931	73		3.5	2.0	WARNER BROTHERS	
ALEXANDER NEVSKY (RUSSIAN)	1938	92				AMKINO	
ALEXANDER THE GREAT	1956	141	5*	3.5	3.0	UNITED ARTISTS	
ALEXANDER'S RAGTIME BAND	1938	105		3.5	3.0	20th CENTURY FOX	NOMINATED BEST PICTURE
ALFIE (BRITISH)	1966	114	7	4.0	3.5	PARAMOUNT	NOMINATED BEST PICTURE
ALFRED NOBEL STORY, THE (GERMAN)	1955	91		2.5		TELEDYNAMICS	
ALFRED THE GREAT (BRITISH)	1969	122	3			M-G-M	
ALGIERS	1938	95		3.0	3.0	UNITED ARTISTS	
ALI BABA AND THE FORTY THIEVES (JON HALL)	1944	87		2.5	2.5	UNIVERSAL	
ALI BABA AND THE FORTY THIEVES (FR. - FERNANDEL)	1954	90		2.0		REPUBLIC	
ALI BABA AND THE SACRED CROWN (ITALIAN)	a1960	95		1.5		TELEWIDE SYSTEMS	
ALI BABA AND THE SEVEN SARACENS (ITALIAN)	1964	83		1.0		AMERICAN-INTERNAT'L	
ALI BABA GOES TO TOWN	1937	81		3.0	2.5	20th CENTURY FOX	
ALIAS A GENTLEMAN	1948	76		2.0	2.0	M-G-M	
ALIAS BULLDOG DRUMMOND (BRITISH)	1935	62			-	GAUMONT-BRITISH	
ALIAS FRENCH GERTIE	1930	71		1.0		RKO	
ALIAS JESSE JAMES	1959	92		3.0	3.0	UNITED ARTISTS	
ALIAS JOHN PRESTON (BRITISH)	1955	66		2.0		ASSOCIATED ARTISTS	
ALIAS MR TWILIGHT	1946	69		2.0		COLUMBIA	
ALIAS NICK BEAL	1949	93	5*	3.5	3.0	PARAMOUNT	
ALIAS SMITH AND JONES (T.V.)	1971	90		1.5		UNIVERSAL	
ALIAS THE CHAMP	1949	60		2.5		REPUBLIC	
ALIBI (CHESTER MORRIS, REGIS TOOMEY)	1929	90				UNITED ARTISTS	NOMINATED BEST PICTURE 1928/29
ALIBI IKE	1935	73	4*	3.0	3.0	WARNER BROTHERS	
ALICE ADAMS	1935	99	5*	3.5	3.5	RKO	NOMINATED BEST PICTURE
ALICE IN WONDERLAND (CHARLOTTE HENRY, W C FIELDS)	1933	90		3.0	2.5	PARAMOUNT	
ALICE IN WONDERLAND (BRITISH - CAROL MARSH)	1949	83		2.5	2.0	SOUVAINE SELECTIVE	
ALICE IN WONDERLAND (CARTOON)	1951	75	5			RKO	
ALICE'S RESTAURANT	1969	111	6*	4.0		UNITED ARTISTS	
ALIMONY	1949	71	2			EAGLE LION	
ALIVE AND KICKING (BRITISH)	1958	95		3.0		ASSOC. BRITISH-PATHE	
ALL ABOUT EVE	1950	138	7-8*	4.0	4.0	20th CENTURY FOX	BEST PICTURE AWARD
ALL AMERICAN, THE	1953	83		2.0	2.0	UNIVERSAL	
ALL ASHORE	1953	80		2.0	1.5	COLUMBIA	
ALL AT SEA (BRITISH - ALEC GUINESS, IRENE BROWNE)	1958	87	5	3.5	3.0	M-G-M	
ALL FALL DOWN	1962	110		2.5	3.0	M-G-M	
ALL FOR MARY (BRITISH)	1956	82		2.0		PAUL SOSKIN	
ALL HANDS ON DECK	1961	98		1.5	2.0	20th CENTURY FOX	
ALL I DESIRE	1953	70		2.5	2.5	UNIVERSAL	
ALL IN A NIGHT'S WORK	1961	94		3.0	2.5	PARAMOUNT	
ALL MINE TO GIVE	1958	102		2.5	2.5	UNIVERSAL	
ALL MY SONS	1948	94	4-5*	3.5	3.0	UNIVERSAL	
ALL NEAT IN BLACK STOCKINGS (BRITISH)	1969	99	2			NATIONAL GENERAL	
ALL NIGHT LONG (BRITISH)	1961	91		3.0	2.0	CONTINENTAL	
ALL OF ME	1934	75		2.0	2.0	PARAMOUNT	
ALL OVER THE TOWN (BRITISH)	1948	87		3.5		UNIVERSAL	
ALL QUIET ON THE WESTERN FRONT	1930	105	6*	4.0	4.0	UNIVERSAL	BEST PICTURE AWARD 1929/30
ALL RIGHT NOISES	1971	116				20th CENTURY FOX	
ALL THAT HEAVEN ALLOWS	1956	89		2.0	3.0	UNIVERSAL	
ALL THAT MONEY CAN BUY	a1941	112	7*	4.0	3.5	RKO	
ALL THE BROTHERS WERE VALIANT	1953	101		2.5	2.5	M-G-M	
ALL THE FINE YOUNG CANNIBALS	1960	112		2.0	1.5	M-G-M	
ALL THE KING'S HORSES	1935	87		1.5		PARAMOUNT	
ALL THE KING'S MEN	1949	109	8*	4.0	4.0	COLUMBIA	BEST PICTURE AWARD
ALL THE LOVING COUPLES	1969	85	1			U-M PRODS.	
ALL THE OTHER GIRLS DO (ITALIAN)	1964	90	3			HARLEQUIN INTERNAT'L	
ALL THE WAY HOME	1963	103	7	3.5	3.5	PARAMOUNT	
ALL THE YOUNG MEN	1960	87		2.5	2.5	COLUMBIA	
ALL THESE WOMEN (SWEDISH)	1964	80	3		2.5	JANUS FILMS	
ALL THIS AND HEAVEN TOO	1940	143	4*	3.0	3.0	WARNER BROTHERS	NOMINATED BEST PICTURE
ALL THROUGH THE NIGHT	1942	107		3.0	3.0	WARNER BROTHERS	

‡ An asterisk (*) in THE FILM BUFF'S BIBLE column indicates that the film has been rated by the editor and/or staff. All other ratings in this column are based on a consensus of reviews (see NOTES).

TITLE (LEADING ACTORS SHOWN WHERE TWO OR MORE FILMS HAVE THE SAME OR SIMILAR TITLE)	YEAR RELEASED	RUNNING TIME IN MINUTES	THE FILM BUFF'S BIBLE ‡	STEVEN SCHEUER	LEONARD MALTIN	DISTRIBUTOR	COMMENT
ALL WOMEN HAVE SECRETS	1940	74		1.5		PARAMOUNT	
ALLEGHANY UPRISING	1939	81		3.0	3.0	RKO	
ALLIGATOR NAMED DAISY, AN (BRITISH)	1955	88	4	2.5	2.5	J. ARTHUR RANK	
ALLIGATOR PEOPLE, THE	1959	74	2*	1.5	2.5	20th CENTURY FOX	
ALLOTMENT WIVES	1945	83			2.0	MONOGRAM	
ALMOST A BRIDE	a1949	88		1.0	2.0	UNITED ARTISTS	
ALMOST ANGELS	1962	93	7			BUENA VISTA	
ALOMA OF THE SOUTH SEAS	1941	77		1.5	2.0	PARAMOUNT	
ALONE AGAINST ROME (ITALIAN)	1962	100		1.5		MEDALLION	
ALONG CAME A SPIDER (T.V.)	1970	75		2.5		20th CENTURY FOX	
ALONG CAME JONES	1945	90		3.5	3.0	RKO	
ALONG CAME YOUTH	1931	48		1.0		PARAMOUNT	
ALONG THE GREAT DIVIDE	1951	88	4*	2.5	2.5	WARNER BROTHERS	
ALONG THE MOHAWK TRAIL	1956	89		1.5		SIGMUND NEUFELD	
ALPHABET MURDERS, THE (BRITISH)	1966	85		2.0	2.5	M-G-M	
ALPHAVILLE (FRENCH)	1965	100		2.5	2.0	PATHE CONTEMPARARY	
ALVAREZ KELLY	1966	116	5*	3.0	2.5	COLUMBIA	
ALWAYS A BRIDE (BRIT. - PEGGY CUMMINS, T. MORGAN)	1953	83		3.0		UNIVERSAL	
ALWAYS GOODBYE (BARBARA STANWYCK, H. MARSHALL)	1938	75		2.0	2.5	20th CENTURY FOX	
ALWAYS IN MY HEART	1942	92		2.5	1.5	WARNER BROTHERS	
ALWAYS LEAVE THEM LAUGHING	1949	116		2.5	2.5	WARNER BROTHERS	
ALWAYS TOGETHER	1948	78		2.5	2.5	WARNER BROTHERS	
AMAZING COLOSSAL MAN, THE	1956	80		2.0	2.5	AMERICAN-INTERNAT'L	
AMAZING DR CLITTERHOUSE, THE	1938	87	5*	3.5	3.0	WARNER BROTHERS	
AMAZING DR G., THE (ITALIAN)	1965	85		2.0		AMERICAN-INTERNAT'L	
AMAZING MR BEECHAM, THE (BRITISH)	a1949	85	5	3.0		EAGLE LION	
AMAZING MR WILLIAMS, THE	1939	80		3.0	2.5	COLUMBIA	
AMAZING MR X, THE	a1948	78		2.0	2.0	EAGLE LION	
AMAZING MRS HOLLIDAY, THE	1943	96		2.5	2.5	UNIVERSAL	
AMAZING MONSIEUR FABRE, THE	a1951	90	6			DISTINGUISHED FILMS	ENGLISH VERSION
AMAZING TRANSPARENT MAN, THE	1960	60		2.0	1.0	AMERICAN-INTERNAT'L	
AMAZONS OF ROME (FRENCH)	1963	93	1			CARLO BRAGAGLIA	
AMBASSADOR'S DAUGHTER, THE	1956	102		2.5	2.5	UNITED ARTISTS	
AMBUSH (ROBERT TAYLOR, ARLENE DAHL)	1950	89	4	2.0	2.5	M-G-M	
AMBUSH AT CIMARRON PASS	1958	73		2.0	2.0	20th CENTURY FOX	
AMBUSH AT TOMAHAWK GAP	1953	73	3	3.0	1.5	COLUMBIA	
AMBUSH BAY	1966	109		2.5	2.5	UNITED ARTISTS	
AMBUSH IN LEOPARD STREET (BRITISH)	1961	60		1.5	1.5	COLUMBIA	
AMBUSHERS, THE	1967	102		1.0	2.5	COLUMBIA	
AMELIE (FRENCH)	1960	111		2.0		UN. MOTION PIC. ORG.	
AMERICA, AMERICA	a1963	174	8	4.0		WARNER BROTHERS	NOMINATED BEST PICTURE
AMERICAN DREAM, AN	a1966	103	4	2.5	2.5	WARNER BROTHERS	
AMERICAN EMPIRE	1942	82			2.5	UNITED ARTISTS	
AMERICAN GUERRILLA IN THE PHILIPPINES	1950	105		2.0	2.5	20th CENTURY FOX	
AMERICAN IN PARIS, AN	1951	113	6*	4.0		M-G-M	BEST PICTURE AWARD
AMERICAN REVOLUTION 2	1969	80	6			CANNON RELEASING	
AMERICAN ROMANCE, AN	1944	122		2.5	2.5	M-G-M	
AMERICANIZATION OF EMILY, THE	1964	117	6-7*	3.0	3.5	M-G-M	
AMERICANO, THE	1955	85	3	2.5	2.5	RKO	
AMONG THE HEADHUNTERS (BRITISH)	1955	92		3.0		J. ARTHUR RANK	
AMONG THE LIVING	1941	68		2.5	2.5	PARAMOUNT	
AMOROUS ADVENTURES OF MOLL FLANDERS, THE (BRITISH)	1965	122	4	3.0	2.5	PARAMOUNT	
AMOROUS MR PRAWN, THE (BRITISH)	1962	89		2.5	2.5	TELEWIDE SYSTEMS	
AMPHIBIAN MAN, THE (RUSSIAN)	1964	86		1.0		NTA PICTURES	
ANASTASIA	1956	105	7*	3.5	4.0	20th CENTURY FOX	
ANATOMIST, THE (BRITISH)	1961	73		2.5	2.0	DAVID BADER	
ANATOMY OF A MARRIAGE (FRENCH)	1964	196	5		2.5	JANUS FILMS	TWO PARTS
ANATOMY OF A MURDER	1959	160	7*	3.5	3.0	COLUMBIA	NOMINATED BEST PICTURE
ANATOMY OF A PSYCHO	1961	75	2	1.0		BROOKE L. PETERS	
ANATOMY OF LOVE, THE (ITALIAN)	1953	97	7			KASSLER FILMS	FIVE STORIES
ANCHORS AWEIGH	1945	140		3.5	2.5	M-G-M	NOMINATED BEST PICTURE
AND BABY MAKES THREE	1949	84		2.0	2.0	COLUMBIA	
AND GOD CREATED WOMAN (FRENCH)	1957	90	6	2.5		KINGSLEY INTERNAT'L	
AND NOW FOR SOMETHING COMPLETELY DIFFERENT	1972	89		3.0		COLUMBIA	
AND NOW MIGUEL	1966	95	6	3.0	3.0	UNIVERSAL	
AND NOW TOMORROW	1944	85		2.5	2.5	PARAMOUNT	
AND QUIET FLOWS THE DON (RUSSIAN)	1957	107	6		3.0	UNITED ARTISTS	
AND SO THEY WERE MARRIED (MELVYN DOUGLAS)	1936	74		2.5	2.5	COLUMBIA	
AND SO THEY WERE MARRIED (SIMONE SIMON)	a1944	79		3.0	2.5	MONOGRAM	
AND SOON THE DARKNESS (BRITISH)	1970	99	3			LEVITT-PICKMAN	
AND SUDDEN DEATH	1936	68		1.5		PARAMOUNT	
. . . AND SUDDENLY IT'S MURDER! (ITALIAN)	1960	90	4		2.5	ROYAL FILMS INT'L	
AND THE ANGELS SING	1944	96		2.5	2.5	PARAMOUNT	
AND THE WILD, WILD WOMEN (ITALIAN)	1962	85		3.0		RIMA FILMS	
AND THEN THERE WERE NONE	1945	98	6*	4.0	3.5	20th CENTURY FOX	
AND THERE CAME A MAN (ITALIAN)	1965	90	2			BRANDON	
ANDERSON PLATOON, THE (FRENCH, DOCUMENTARY)	1967	65	4			PATHE CONTEMPARARY	
ANDERSON TAPES, THE	1971		4-5*			COLUMBIA	
ANDREA CHENIER (ITALIAN)	1956	110		2.0		ARCHWAY	
ANDROCLES AND THE LION	1953	98		2.0	3.0	RKO	
ANDROMEDA STRAIN, THE	1971	131	6*			UNIVERSAL	
ANDY	1965	86		2.5	3.0	UNIVERSAL	
ANDY HARDY COMES HOME	1958	80		2.5	-	M-G-M	
ANDY HARDY GETS SPRING FEVER	1939	85		2.5	-	M-G-M	

‡ An asterisk (*) in THE FILM BUFF'S BIBLE column indicates that the film has been rated by the editor and/or staff. All other ratings in this column are based on a consensus of reviews (see NOTES).

TITLE (LEADING ACTORS SHOWN WHERE TWO OR MORE FILMS HAVE THE SAME OR SIMILAR TITLE)	YEAR RELEASED	RUNNING TIME IN MINUTES	THE FILM BUFF'S BIBLE ‡	STEVEN SCHEUER	LEONARD MALTIN	DISTRIBUTOR	COMMENT
ANDY HARDY MEETS A DEBUTANTE	1940	86		2.5	-	M-G-M	
ANDY HARDY'S BLONDE TROUBLE	1944	107		2.0	-	M-G-M	
ANDY HARDY'S DOUBLE LIFE	1942	92		2.0	-	M-G-M	
ANDY HARDY'S PRIVATE SECRETARY	1941	101		2.5	-	M-G-M	
ANGEL	1937	98		2.0	2.0	PARAMOUNT	
ANGEL AND THE BADMAN	1946	100		3.5	3.0	REPUBLIC	
ANGEL, ANGEL, DOWN WE GO	a1969	93	2			AMERICAN-INTERNAT'L	
ANGEL BABY	1961	97	5	3.0	3.0	ALLIED ARTISTS	
ANGEL FACE	1953	90		2.5	2.5	RKO	
ANGEL FROM TEXAS, AN	1940	69		2.5		WARNER BROTHERS	
ANGEL IN EXILE	1948	90		3.0		REPUBLIC	
ANGEL IN MY POCKET	1968	105	5	2.5		UNIVERSAL	
ANGEL LEVINE, THE	1970	104	5			UNITED ARTISTS	
ANGEL ON EARTH (FRENCH)	1961	88		2.0		NTA PICTURES	
ANGEL ON MY SHOULDER	1946	101	6	3.0	3.0	UNITED ARTISTS	
ANGEL ON THE AMAZON	1948	86		1.5	1.5	REPUBLIC	
ANGEL UNCHAINED	1970	90	2			AMERICAN-INTERNAT'L	
ANGEL WHO PAWNED HER HARP, THE (BRITISH)	1956	73		3.0		ASSOCIATED ARTISTS	
ANGEL WITH A TRUMPET, THE, THE (BRITISH)	1949	99		3.5		KORDA	
ANGEL WORE RED, THE	1960	99		2.0	2.5	M-G-M	
ANGELA	1955	81	2			20th CENTURY FOX	
ANGEL'S ALLEY	1948	67			-	MONOGRAM	
ANGELS DIE HARD!	1971	87	1			NEW WORLD	
ANGELS HARD AS THEY COME	1971	90	1			NEW WORLD	
ANGELS IN DISGUISE	1949	63			-	MONOGRAM	
ANGELS IN THE OUTFIELD	1951	102	6	3.5	3.0	M-G-M	
ANGELS OF DARKNESS (ITALIAN)	1956	84		2.5	2.0	EXCELSIOR	
ANGELS ONE FIVE (BRITISH)	1952	98		3.0	2.0	STRATFORD PICS.	
ANGELS OVER BROADWAY	1940	80	5*	3.5	3.5	COLUMBIA	
ANGELS WASH THEIR FACES	1939	76		2.5	2.5	WARNER BROTHERS	
ANGELS WITH DIRTY FACES	1938	97	5*	3.5	3.0	WARNER BROTHERS	
ANGRY BREED, THE	1968	89	1			LANDAU/UNGER COM. UN.	
ANGRY HILLS, THE (BRITISH)	1959	105		2.5	2.5	M-G-M	
ANGRY RED PLANET, THE	1960	83	2	1.5		AMERICAN-INTERNAT'L	
ANGRY SILENCE, THE (BRITISH)	1960	95	4*	4.0	3.0	VALIANT	
ANIMAL CRACKERS	1930	100				PARAMOUNT	
ANIMAL FARM (BRITISH, CARTOON)	1954	72	7*	4.0	3.0	DE ROCHEMONT	
ANIMAL KINGDOM, THE	1932	90				RKO	
ANIMAL WORLD, THE (DOCUMENTARY)	1956	82	6			WARNER BROTHERS	
ANIMALS, THE (DOCUMENTARY)	1959	87	6*			FOUR STAR	
ANIMALS, THE (HENRY SILVA, KEENAN WYNN)	1971	86	3			LEVITT-PICKMAN	
ANN AND EVE (SWEDISH)	1970	89	2			CHEVRON	ENGLISH LANGUAGE
ANNA (ITALIAN)	1952	100		2.0	2.5	ITALIAN FILMS EXPORT	
ANNA AND THE KING OF SIAM	1946	128	6*	4.0	3.5	20th CENTURY FOX	
ANNA CHRISTIE	1930	86		4.0	3.0	M-G-M	
ANNA KARENINA (GRETA GARBO, FREDRIC MARCH)	1935	95	6*	3.5	4.0	M-G-M	
ANNA KARENINA (BRITISH - VIVIEN LEIGH)	1947	110		3.0	2.5	20th CENTURY FOX	
ANNA LUCASTA (PAULETTE GODDARD, OSCAR HOMOLKA)	1949	86	5			COLUMBIA	
ANNA LUCASTA (EARTHA KITT, SAMMY DAVIS JR)	1958	97	4	2.5	2.0	UNITED ARTISTS	
ANNAPOLIS STORY, AN	1955	81		2.0	2.0	ALLIED ARTISTS	
ANNAPURNA (BRITISH, DOCUMENTARY)	1953	60	6	4.0		KINGSLEY INTERNAT'L	
ANNE OF GREEN GABLES	1934	79		3.0	3.0	RKO	
ANNE OF THE INDIES	1951	81	4	2.5	2.5	20th CENTURY FOX	
ANNE OF THE THOUSAND DAYS (BRITISH)	1969	143	6-7*			UNIVERSAL	NOMINATED BEST PICTURE
ANNE OF WINDY POPLARS	1940	88		2.5	2.0	RKO	
ANNIE GET YOUR GUN	1950	107	4*	3.0	3.0	M-G-M	
ANNIE OAKLEY	1935	88	4*	3.0	3.0	RKO	
ANNIVERSARY, THE (BRITISH)	1968	95	3	1.5		20th CENTURY FOX	
ANONYMOUS VENETIAN, THE (ITALIAN)	1970	91	2			ALLIED ARTISTS	
ANOTHER DAWN	1937	73	3*	2.5	2.5	WARNER BROTHERS	
ANOTHER MAN'S POISON (BRITISH)	1951	89		3.0	2.0	UNITED ARTISTS	
ANOTHER PART OF THE FOREST	1948	107	6	3.0	3.0	UNIVERSAL	
ANOTHER THIN MAN	1939	105		3.0	-	M-G-M	
ANOTHER SHORE (BRITISH)	1948	77		3.0		J. ARTHUR RANK	
ANOTHER TIME, ANOTHER PLACE (BRITISH)	1958	98		2.0	2.5	PARAMOUNT	
ANTHONY ADVERSE	1936	136	6*	3.5	3.5	WARNER BROTHERS	NOMINATED BEST PICTURE
ANTIGONE (GREEK - IRENE PAPPAS, MANOS KATRAKIS)	1961	88	6			ELLIS FILMS	
ANY GUN CAN PLAY (ITALIAN)	1967	103	1	1.5		GOLDEN EAGLE	ENGLISH LANGUAGE
ANY NUMBER CAN PLAY	1949	112		3.0	2.0	M-G-M	
ANY NUMBER CAN WIN (FRENCH)	1963	110	5	2.5	2.5	M-G-M	
ANY WEDNESDAY	a1966	109		3.5	3.0	WARNER BROTHERS	
ANYONE CAN PLAY (ITALIAN)	1967	88	3			PARAMOUNT	
ANYTHING CAN HAPPEN	1952	107	6	3.5	2.0	PARAMOUNT	
ANYTHING GOES (BING CROSBY, ETHEL MERMAN)	a1936	92		2.5	2.5	PARAMOUNT	
ANYTHING GOES (BING CROSBY, JEANMARIE)	1956	106		2.5	2.0	PARAMOUNT	
ANZIO (ITALIAN)	a1968	117	3	2.0		COLUMBIA	ENGLISH VERSION
APACHE	1954	91	3*	2.0	2.0	UNITED ARTISTS	
APACHE AMBUSH	1955	68	2	2.0	2.0	COLUMBIA	
APACHE COUNTRY	1952	62	4			COLUMBIA	
APACHE DRUMS	1951	75	3	2.0	1.5	UNIVERSAL	
APACHE FURY (SPANISH)	1965	84		1.5		AMERICAN-INTERNAT'L	
APACHE GOLD (GERMAN)	1965	91	3		2.5	COLUMBIA	
APACHE RIFLES	1964	92		2.0	2.5	20th CENTURY FOX	
APACHE TERRITORY	1958	75		2.0	1.5	COLUMBIA	

‡ An asterisk (*) in THE FILM BUFF'S BIBLE column indicates that the film has been rated by the editor and/or staff. All other ratings in this column are based on a consensus of reviews (see NOTES).

TITLE (LEADING ACTORS SHOWN WHERE TWO OR MORE FILMS HAVE THE SAME OR SIMILAR TITLE)	YEAR RELEASED	RUNNING TIME IN MINUTES	THE FILM BUFF'S BIBLE ‡	STEVEN SCHEUER	LEONARD MALTIN	DISTRIBUTOR	COMMENT
APACHE TRAIL	1943	66		1.5		M-G-M	
APACHE UPRISING	1966	90	2	1.5		PARAMOUNT	
APACHE WAR SMOKE	1952	67		2.0	1.5	M-G-M	
APACHE WARRIOR	1957	74		2.0	2.0	20th CENTURY FOX	
APACHE WOMAN	1955	83		2.0		AMERICAN-INTERNAT'L	
APARAJITO (INDIAN)	a1956	113	6	4.0		HARRISON PICTURES	
APARTMENT, THE	1960	125	6*	4.0	4.0	UNITED ARTISTS	BEST PICTURE AWARD
APARTMENT FOR PEGGY	1948	98		3.0	3.0	20th CENTURY FOX	
APE, THE	1940	62			2.0	MONOGRAM	
APE MAN, THE	1943	64			2.0	MONOGRAM	
APE MAN OF THE JUNGLE (ITALIAN)	1962	80		1.0		AMERICAN-INTERNAT'L	
APE WOMAN, THE (ITALIAN)	1964	92	4	2.0		AVCO-EMBASSY	
APHRODITE, GODDESS OF LOVE (ITAL. - ISABEL CORY)	1962	86		1.5		AVCO-EMBASSY	
APPALOOSA, THE	1966	98		2.0	2.5	UNIVERSAL	
APPLAUSE	1929	87	3*		2.5	PARAMOUNT	
APPOINTMENT, THE	1969	100				M-G-M	
APPOINTMENT FOR LOVE	1941	89		3.0	2.5	UNIVERSAL	
APPOINTMENT IN BERLIN	1943	77		2.5	2.5	COLUMBIA	
APPOINTMENT IN HONDURAS	1953	79		2.5	2.5	RKO	
APPOINTMENT IN LONDON (BRITISH)	1953	96		3.5		ASSOCIATED ARTISTS	
APPOINTMENT WITH A SHADOW	1958	73		2.0	2.0	UNIVERSAL	
APPOINTMENT WITH DANGER	1951	89	5	3.0	3.0	PARAMOUNT	
APPOINTMENT WITH MURDER	1948	67			-	FILM CLASSICS	
APRIL FOOLS, THE	1969	95	6*	2.5		NATIONAL GENERAL	
APRIL IN PARIS	1953	101		2.5	2.5	WARNER BROTHERS	
APRIL LOVE	1957	97		2.5	2.5	20th CENTURY FOX	
APRIL SHOWERS	1948	94		2.5	2.0	WARNER BROTHERS	
AQUARIANS, THE (T.V.)	1970	100		2.5		UNIVERSAL	
ARABELLA	1969	91	3			UNIVERSAL	
ARABESQUE (BRITISH)	1966	105		2.5	3.0	UNIVERSAL	
ARABIAN NIGHTS	1942	86		2.0	2.0	UNIVERSAL	
ARCH OF TRIUMPH	1948	120		2.5	2.5	UNITED ARTISTS	
ARCHANGELS, THE (ITALIAN)	1965	102		2.0		AVCO-EMBASSY	
ARCTIC FLIGHT	1952	78	4	2.5		MONOGRAM	
ARCTIC MANHUNT	1949	69		1.5		UNIVERSAL	
ARE HUSBANDS NECESSARY?	1942	79		2.0	2.0	PARAMOUNT	
ARE PARENTS PEOPLE? (SILENT)	1925	73			2.5	PARAMOUNT	
ARE YOU WITH IT?	1948	90	4	3.0	2.5	UNIVERSAL	
ARENA	1953	83		2.0	2.0	M-G-M	
ARISE, MY LOVE	1940	113		2.0	3.0	PARAMOUNT	
ARISTOCATS, THE (CARTOON)	1970	78	6			BUENA VISTA	
ARIZONA	1940	127		2.5	2.5	COLUMBIA	
ARIZONA BUSHWACKERS	1968	86	3	2.0		PARAMOUNT	
ARIZONA MISSION	a1956	78		2.0	2.0	UNITED ARTISTS	
ARIZONA RAIDERS	1965	88	3		2.5	COLUMBIA	
ARKANSAS JUDGE	1941	72		1.5		REPUBLIC	
ARKANSAS TRAVELER, THE	1938	83		3.0		PARAMOUNT	
ARMORED ATTACK	a1943	105		2.5	2.5	RKO	
ARMORED CAR ROBBERY	1950	68		3.5	1.5	RKO	
ARMORED COMMAND	1961	99		2.0	2.0	ALLIED ARTISTS	
ARMY BOUND	1952	61	2	1.5		MONOGRAM	
ARMY SURGEON	1942	63		2.0		RKO	
ARNELO AFFAIR, THE	1947	86		1.5	2.0	M-G-M	
AROUND THE WORLD	1943	43		2.5		RKO	
AROUND THE WORLD IN 80 DAYS	1956	168	6*			UNITED ARTISTS	BEST PICTURE AWARD
AROUND THE WORLD UNDER THE SEA	1966	117		2.0	2.0	M-G-M	
AROUSED	1966	82	3			CAMBIST	
ARRANGEMENT, THE	1969	127	3			WARNER BROTHERS	
ARREST BULLDOG DRUMMOND	1939	57			-	PARAMOUNT	
ARRIVEDERCI, BABY! (BRITISH)	a1966	100	3*	3.0		PARAMOUNT	
ARROW IN THE DUST	1954	80		2.0	2.0	ALLIED ARTISTS	
ARROWHEAD	1953	105		2.5	2.5	PARAMOUNT	
ARROWSMITH	1931	108				UNITED ARTISTS	NOMINATED BEST PICTURE 1931/32
ARSENE LUPIN	1932	84		3.0	3.0	M-G-M	
ARSENIC AND OLD LACE	1944	118	7*	3.5	3.0	WARNER BROTHERS	
ARSON FOR HIRE	1959	67	1	1.5		ALLIED ARTISTS	
ART OF LOVE, THE	1965	99		2.5	2.0	UNIVERSAL	
ARTISTS AND MODELS (JACK BENNY, IDA LUPINO)	1937	97		3.0	2.5	PARAMOUNT	
ARTISTS AND MODELS (DEAN MARTIN, JERRY LEWIS)	1955	108		2.5	3.0	PARAMOUNT	
ARTISTS AND MODELS ABROAD	1938	90		3.0	3.0	PARAMOUNT	
ARTURO'S ISLAND (ITALIAN)	1962	90	6			M-G-M	
AS IF IT WERE RAINING (FRENCH)	1963	88		1.5	2.0	PARAMOUNT	
AS LONG AS THEY'RE HAPPY (BRITISH)	1955	91		2.5	1.5	J. ARTHUR RANK	
AS LONG AS YOU'RE NEAR ME (GERMAN)	1955	101		2.0		WARNER BROTHERS	
AS THE EARTH TURNS	1934	73		3.0		WARNER BROTHERS	
AS THE SEA RAGES (GERMAN)	1960	74		1.5	2.5	COLUMBIA	ENGLISH LANGUAGE
AS USUAL, UNKNOWN (ITALIAN)	1956	91		2.5			
AS YOU DESIRE ME	1932	71		3.0	3.0	M-G-M	
AS YOUNG AS WE ARE	1959	76	3	2.0		PARAMOUNT	
AS YOUNG AS YOU FEEL	1951	77	4	2.0	3.0	20th CENTURY FOX	
ASHES AND DIAMONDS (POLISH)	1959	109	3*	4.0	3.0	JANUS FILMS	
ASK ANY GIRL	1959	101	3*	2.5	3.0	M-G-M	
ASPHALT JUNGLE, THE	1950	112	5-6*	4.0	3.5	M-G-M	
ASSASSIN, THE (BRITISH - RICHARD TODD, EVA BARTOK)	1953	90	4	2.5	2.0	UNITED ARTISTS	

‡ An asterisk (*) in THE FILM BUFF'S BIBLE column indicates that the film has been rated by the editor and/or staff. All other ratings in this column are based on a consensus of reviews (see NOTES).

TITLE (LEADING ACTORS SHOWN WHERE TWO OR MORE FILMS HAVE THE SAME OR SIMILAR TITLE)	YEAR RELEASED	RUNNING TIME IN MINUTES	THE FILM BUFF'S BIBLE ‡	STEVEN SCHEUER	LEONARD MALTIN	DISTRIBUTOR	COMMENT
ASSASSIN, THE (ITALIAN - MARCELLO MASTROANNI)	1961	105			2.5	CONNOISSEUR	
ASSASSINATION BUREAU, THE (BRITISH)	1969	110	5	3.0		PARAMOUNT	
ASSAULT ON A QUEEN	1966	106		1.0	2.5	PARAMOUNT	
ASSAULT ON THE WAYNE (T.V.)	1971	90		1.5		PARAMOUNT	
ASSIGNMENT ABROAD	1955	73		1.0		TRIANGLE	
ASSIGNMENT IN BRITTANY	1943	96		2.0	2.0	M-G-M	
ASSIGNMENT K (BRITISH)	1968	97	3	2.0		COLUMBIA	
ASSIGNMENT OUTER SPACE	1962	79	2	1.5		AMERICAN-INTERNAT'L	
ASSIGNMENT - PARIS	1952	85		2.5	2.0	COLUMBIA	
ASSIGNMENT REDHEAD (BRITISH)	1956	79		1.5		UNITED ARTISTS	
ASSIGNMENT TO KILL	1969	102	2	1.5		WARNER BROTHERS	
ASTONISHED HEART, THE (BRITISH)	1949	92		2.5	2.5	UNIVERSAL	
ASTOUNDING SHE MONSTER, THE	1957	60		1.0		AMERICAN-INTERNAT'L	
ASTRO-ZOMBIES, THE	1969	90	1			GEMENI FILMS	
AT GUNPOINT	1955	81		2.5	2.5	REPUBLIC	
AT SWORD'S POINT	1952	81	4	3.0	2.5	RKO	
AT THE CIRCUS	a1939	87		2.5	2.5	M-G-M	
AT THE STROKE OF NINE (BRITISH)	1957	71		2.0		GRAND NATIONAL	
AT WAR WITH THE ARMY	1951	93		2.5	2.5	PARAMOUNT	
ATHENA	1954	96		2.0	2.5	M-G-M	
ATLANTIC CITY	1944	86		2.0		REPUBLIC	
ATLANTIC CONVOY	1942	66		2.5		COLUMBIA	
ATLANTIS, THE LOST CONTINENT	1961	90	2*	2.0	1.5	M-G-M	
ATLAS	1960	80	3	2.0		ALLIED ARTISTS	
ATLAS AGAINST THE CYCLOPS (ITALIAN)	1961	100		1.0		MEDALLION	
ATLAS AGAINST THE CZAR (ITALIAN)	1964	91		1.0		TELEWIDE SYSTEMS	
ATOM AGE VAMPIRE (ITALIAN)	1960	87		1.5		TOPAZ FILM CORP.	
ATOMIC AGENT (FRENCH)	1959	85		2.0		AMERICAN-INTERNAT'L	
ATOMIC CITY, THE	1952	85		3.0	2.5	PARAMOUNT	
ATOMIC KID, THE	1954	86		2.0	1.5	REPUBLIC	
ATOMIC MAN, THE (BRITISH)	1955	78		2.0	2.0	ALLIED ARTISTS	
ATOMIC RULERS OF THE WORLD (JAPANESE)	1964	80		1.0		TELEWORLD	
ATOMIC SUBMARINE, THE	1960	72		1.5	2.0	ALLIED ARTISTS	
ATRAGON (JAPANESE)	1964	88	2	1.5		AMERICAN-INTERNAT'L	
ATTACK!	1956	107	5*	4.0	3.0	UNITED ARTISTS	
ATTACK AND RETREAT (ITALIAN)	a1963	156		2.5	3.0	AVCO-EMBASSY	
ATTACK OF THE CRAB MONSTERS	1957	64		1.5	1.5	ALLIED ARTISTS	
ATTACK OF THE 50 FOOT WOMAN	1958	66		2.0	1.0	ALLIED ARTISTS	
ATTACK OF THE GIANT LEECHES	a1959	62		2.0		AMERICAN-INTERNAT'L	
ATTACK OF THE MAYAN MUMMY (MEXICAN)	1963	74		1.0		MEDALLION	
ATTACK OF THE MOORS (ITALIAN)	1960	80		1.0		AMERICAN-INTERNAT'L	
ATTACK OF THE MUSHROOM PEOPLE (JAPANESE)	1964	89		1.5		AMERICAN-INTERNAT'L	
ATTACK OF THE NORMANS (ITALIAN)	1961	79		1.5		AMERICAN-INTERNAT'L	
ATTACK OF THE PUPPET PEOPLE	1958	78		1.5	1.5	AMERICAN-INTERNAT'L	
ATTACK ON THE IRON COAST (BRITISH)	1968	89	2			UNITED ARTISTS	
ATTACK SQUADRON (JAPANESE)	1963	102		2.0		PARAMOUNT	
ATTEMPT TO KILL (BRITISH)	1961	57		1.0	2.0	ANGLO AMALGAMATED	
ATTILA (ITALIAN)	1955	79		2.0	1.5	ATTILA ASSOCIATES	
AU HAZARD BALTHAZAR (FRENCH)	1966	95	3*			NEW YORKER FILMS	
AUNT CLARA (BRITISH)	1954	84	5*	2.0		SHOWCORPORATION	
AUNTIE MAME	1958	143	5*	2.5	2.5	WARNER BROTHERS	NOMINATED BEST PICTURE
AUTOPSY OF A CRIMINAL (SPANISH)	1964	92		1.5		PARAMOUNT	
AUTUMN LEAVES	1956	108		2.5	2.5	COLUMBIA	
AVALANCHE	1946	70			1.5	PRODUCERS RELEASING	
AVENGER, THE (GERMAN - HEINZ DRACHE)	1960	102		1.5	2.5	UCC FILMS	
AVENGER, THE (ITALIAN - STEVE REEVES)	a1965	108	1			MEDALLION	
AVENGER OF THE SEVEN SEAS (ITALIAN)	1960	94		1.0		AMERICAN-INTERNAT'L	
AVENGER OF VENICE (ITALIAN)	1963	91		1.0		FOUR STAR	
AVENGERS, THE	1950	90		1.5		REPUBLIC	
AWAKENING, THE (ITALIAN)	1956	97	6	3.5		KINGSLEY INTERNAT'L	
AWAY ALL BOATS	1956	114		2.5	2.5	UNIVERSAL	
AWFUL DR ORLOFF, THE (SPANISH)	1961	90		1.0	2.0	SIGMA III	
AWFUL TRUTH, THE	1937	92		3.5	3.5	COLUMBIA	NOMINATED BEST PICTURE
B.F.'S DAUGHTER	1948	108	3	1.5	1.5	M-G-M	
B.S. I LOVE YOU	1971	99	2			20th CENTURY FOX	
BABBITT	1934	74		2.5	3.0	FIRST NATIONAL	
BABE RUTH STORY, THE	1948	106		2.0	2.0	ALLIED ARTISTS	
BABES IN ARMS	1939	97		3.0	3.0	M-G-M	
BABES IN BAGDAD	1952	79		1.0	1.0	UNITED ARTISTS	
BABES IN TOYLAND (LAUREL AND HARDY)	a1934	73			3.0	M-G-M	
BABES IN TOYLAND (ANNETTE FUNICELLO)	1961	105	3*			BUENA VISTA	
BABES ON BROADWAY	1941	118		2.5	2.5	M-G-M	
BABETTE GOES TO WAR (FRENCH)	1959	100	4		2.5	COLUMBIA	
BABY AND THE BATTLESHIP, THE (BRITISH)	1956	96		2.5	2.5	DIST. CORP. OF AMER.	
BABY DOLL	1956	114	6	3.5		WARNER BROTHERS	
BABY FACE NELSON	1957	85		3.0	2.0	UNITED ARTISTS	
BABY LOVE (BRITISH)	1969	93	2	2.0		AVCO-EMBASSY	
BABY MAKER, THE	1970	109	6			NATIONAL GENERAL	
BABY, THE RAIN MUST FALL	1965	100		2.0	3.0	COLUMBIA	
BABYSITTER, THE	1969	90	2			CROWN INTERNATIONAL	
BACCHANTES, THE	1961	102		2.0		TELEWIDE SYSTEMS	

‡ An asterisk (*) in THE FILM BUFF'S BIBLE column indicates that the film has been rated by the editor and/or staff. All other ratings in this column are based on a consensus of reviews (see NOTES).

TITLE (LEADING ACTORS SHOWN WHERE TWO OR MORE FILMS HAVE THE SAME OR SIMILAR TITLE)	YEAR RELEASED	RUNNING TIME IN MINUTES	THE FILM BUFF'S BIBLE ‡	STEVEN SCHEUER	LEONARD MALTIN	DISTRIBUTOR	COMMENT
BACHELOR AND THE BOBBY-SOXER, THE	1947	95	6	3.5	3.0	RKO	
BACHELOR APARTEMENT	1931	83		2.0	2.5	RKO	
BACHELOR FATHER	1931	90		2.0	2.5	RKO	
BACHELOR FLAT	1962	91		2.5	2.0	20th CENTURY FOX	
BACHELOR IN PARADISE	1961	109		3.0	2.5	M-G-M	
BACHELOR MOTHER	1939	81	6*	4.0	3.5	RKO	
BACHELOR OF HEARTS (BRITISH)	1958	97		2.5		CONTINENTAL	
BACHELOR PARTY, THE	1957	93	6*	3.5	3.0	UNITED ARTISTS	
BACHELOR'S DAUGHTERS, THE	1946	88	5	1.5		UNITED ARTISTS	
BACK AT THE FRONT	a1953	87		2.5	2.5	UNIVERSAL	
BACK DOOR TO HEAVEN	1939	85			2.0	PARAMOUNT	
BACK DOOR TO HELL	1964	68	1			20th CENTURY FOX	
BACK FROM ETERNITY	1956	97		2.5	2.5	RKO	
BACK FROM THE DEAD	1957	79	1		1.0	20th CENTURY FOX	
BACK STREET (IRENE DUNNE, JOHN BOLES)	1932	93				UNIVERSAL	
BACK STREET (CHARLES BOYER, MARGARET SULLAVAN)	1941	89		3.5	3.0	UNIVERSAL	
BACK STREET (SUSAN HAYWARD, JOHN GAVIN)	1961	107		2.0	2.5	UNIVERSAL	
BACK TO BATAAN	1945	95		3.0	3.0	RKO	
BACK TO GOD'S COUNTRY	1953	78		2.0	2.5	UNIVERSAL	
BACK TO THE WALL (FRENCH)	1958	94		3.5	2.5	ELLIS FILMS	
BACKFIRE (VIRGINIA MAYO, GORDON MACRAE)	1950	91		2.0	2.0	WARNER BROTHERS	
BACKFIRE (BRITISH - ALFRED BURKE, ZENA MARSHALL)	1961	59		1.5	2.0	ANGLO AMALGAMATED	
BACKFIRE (FR. - JEAN SEBERG, JEAN-PAUL BELMONDO)	1964	97	4			ROYAL FILMS INT'L	
BACKGROUND TO DANGER	1943	80		2.5	2.5	WARNER BROTHERS	
BACKLASH (RICHARD TRAVIS, JEAN ROGERS)	1947	66			2.0	20th CENTURY FOX	
BACKLASH (RICHARD WIDMARK, DONNA REED)	1956	84	3	2.5	2.5	UNIVERSAL	
BACKTRACK	1969	97	4			UNIVERSAL	
BAD AND THE BEAUTIFUL, THE	1952	118	5*	4.0	3.0	M-G-M	
BAD BASCOMB	1946	110		2.0	1.5	M-G-M	
BAD BLONDE	1953	80	1			LIPPERT PRODS.	
BAD BOY	1949	86		3.5	2.5	ALLIED ARTISTS	
BAD DAY AT BLACK ROCK	1955	81	6*	4.0	3.5	M-G-M	
BAD FOR EACH OTHER	1954	83	3	2.0	2.5	COLUMBIA	
BAD GIRL (JAMES DUNN, SALLY ELLERS)	1931	88				20th CENTURY FOX	NOMINATED BEST PICTURE 1931/32
BAD GIRL (BRITISH - ANNA NEAGLE, SYLVIA SYMS)	a1956	100		3.0	1.5	VALIANT	
BAD LORD BYRON, THE (BRITISH)	1949	85		1.5	2.5	J. ARTHUR RANK	
BAD MAN, THE (WALLACE BEERY, LIONEL BARRYMORE)	1941	70			2.5	M-G-M	
BAD MAN OF BRIMSTONE	1937	90		2.5	2.0	M-G-M	
BAD MEN OF MISSOURI	1941	74		3.0	3.0	WARNER BROTHERS	
BAD MEN OF TOMBSTONE	1949	75	3	1.5		ALLIED ARTISTS	
BAD SEED, THE	1956	129	6-7*	3.0	3.0	WARNER BROTHERS	
BAD SISTER (BRITISH)	a1947	90		2.0		UNIVERSAL	
BADGE OF MARSHAL BRENNAN, THE	1957	76		2.0	1.5	ALLIED ARTISTS	
BADLANDERS, THE	1958	83		2.5	3.0	M-G-M	
BADLANDS OF DAKOTA	1941	74			2.5	UNIVERSAL	
BADLANDS OF MONTANA	1957	75			1.5	20th CENTURY FOX	
BADMAN'S COUNTRY	1958	68		2.0	2.5	WARNER BROTHERS	
BADMAN'S TERRITORY	1946	97		3.0	3.0	RKO	
BAGDAD	1949	82		2.0	2.0	UNIVERSAL	
BAHAMA PASSAGE	1941	83		1.5	2.5	PARAMOUNT	
BAILOUT AT 43,000	1957	78	3*	2.0	2.0	UNITED ARTISTS	
BAIT (CLEO MOORE, HUGO HAAS)	1954	79		2.0	1.5	COLUMBIA	
BAL TABARIN	1952	84	2	1.5		REPUBLIC	
BALALAIKA	1939	102		2.0	2.0	M-G-M	
BALCONY, THE	1963	84	4	3.0		CONTINENTAL	
BALL OF FIRE	1941	111		3.5	3.5	RKO	
BALLAD OF A GUNFIGHTER	1964	84	1	1.0		PARAMOUNT	
BALLAD OF A SOLDIER (RUSSIAN)	1960	89	7*	4.0	3.0	ARTKINO	
BALLAD OF ANDY CROCKER, THE (T.V.)	1969	80		3.0		ABC FILMS	
BALLAD OF CABLE HOGUE, THE	1970	120	6			WARNER BROTHERS	
BALLAD OF JOSIE, THE	1968	102		1.5	2.5	UNIVERSAL	
BALLAD OF LOVE, A (RUSSIAN)	1965	45	7			ARTKINO	
BALLAD OF NARAYAMA, THE (JAPANESE)	1958	98	6			FILMS AROUND THE WLD.	
BALLERINA (FRENCH)	1953	78		2.0		LUX FILM AMERICA	
BAMBI (CARTOON)	1942	70	5*			RKO	
BAMBOLE! (ITALIAN)	a1965	111	4		2.0	ROYAL FILMS INT'L	FOUR STORIES
BAMBOO PRISON, THE	1955	80	3	3.0	2.0	COLUMBIA	
BAMBOO SAUCER	1968	100	1			WORLD ENTERTAINMENT	
BAMSE (SWEDISH)	a1969	110	3			CHEVRON	
BANANA PEEL (FRENCH)	1964	97	4			PATHE CONTEMPARARY	
BANANAS	1971	82	6			UNITED ARTISTS	
BAND OF ANGELS	1957	127		2.5	2.5	WARNER BROTHERS	
BAND OF OUTSIDERS (FRENCH)	1964	95	6			ROYAL FILMS INT'L	
BAND WAGON, THE	1953	112	4*	3.5	3.5	M-G-M	
BANDIDO	1956	92		2.5	2.5	UNITED ARTISTS	
BANDIT AND THE PRINCESS, THE (GERMAN)	1964	91		1.5		SCREEN GEMS	
BANDIT OF SHERWOOD FOREST, THE	1946	86			2.5	COLUMBIA	
BANDIT OF ZHOBE, THE (BRITISH)	1959	80		2.0	2.5	COLUMBIA	
BANDITS OF CORSICA, THE	1953	81		2.0	2.0	UNITED ARTISTS	
BANDITS OF ORGOSOLO (ITALIAN)	1963	98	6			PATHE CONTEMPARARY	
BANDOLERO!	1968	106	3	1.5		20th CENTURY FOX	
BANG, BANG	a1968	90	2			AJAY FILMS	
BANG BANG KID, THE	a1968	90	2			AJAY FILMS	
BANG, BANG, YOU'RE DEAD! (BRITISH)	a1966	92	3	2.0	2.5	AMERICAN-INTERNAT'L	

‡ An asterisk (*) in THE FILM BUFF'S BIBLE column indicates that the film has been rated by the editor and/or staff. All other ratings in this column are based on a consensus of reviews (see NOTES).

"a" TO LEFT OF YEAR INDICATES THAT FILM HAS AN ALTERNATE TITLE

TITLE (LEADING ACTORS SHOWN WHERE TWO OR MORE FILMS HAVE THE SAME OR SIMILAR TITLE)	YEAR RELEASED	RUNNING TIME IN MINUTES	THE FILM BUFF'S BIBLE ‡	STEVEN SCHEUER	LEONARD MALTIN	DISTRIBUTOR	COMMENT
BANJO	1947	68	2	2.0		RKO	
BANJO ON MY KNEE	1936	80		2.5	3.0	20th CENTURY FOX	
BANK DICK, THE	1940	74	6*	4.0	4.0	UNIVERSAL	
BANK RAIDERS, THE (BRITISH)	1958	61		2.5		J. ARTHUR RANK	
BANNERLINE	1951	88		2.0	2.0	M-G-M	
BANNING	1967	102	3	1.5	3.0	UNIVERSAL	
BANYON (T.V.)	a1971	100	5-6*	2.5		WARNER BROTHERS	
BAR SINISTER, THE	a1955	88		3.5	2.5	M-G-M	
BARABBAS (ITALIAN)	1961	144	5-6*	3.5	3.0	COLUMBIA	ENGLISH LANGUAGE
BARBARA	1970	91	3			OLYMPIA	
BARBARELLA (FRENCH)	1967	98	3*	3.0		PARAMOUNT	ENGLISH VERSION
BARBARIAN AND THE GEISHA, THE	1958	105		2.0	2.5	20th CENTURY FOX	
BARBARIAN KING, THE (BULGARIAN)	1964	89		1.5		FOUR STAR	
BARBARIANS, THE (ITALIAN)	1953	84		1.5		TELEDYNAMICS	
BARBARY COAST	1935	97	3*	2.0	3.5	UNITED ARTISTS	
BARBARY COAST GENT	1944	87		2.0	2.0	M-G-M	
BARBARY PIRATE	1949	65		1.5		COLUMBIA	
BARBER OF SEVILLE (ITAL. - FERRUCCIO TAGLIAVINI)	1945	92		3.0		EXCELSIOR	T. GOBBI WAS IN BOTH VERSIONS
BARBER OF SEVILLE (ITAL.- TITO GOBBI, IRENE GENNA)	1956	100		2.0		CITATION	T. GOBBI WAS IN BOTH VERSIONS
BAREFOOT BATTALION (GREEK)	1954	89				20th CENTURY FOX	
BAREFOOT CONTESSA, THE	1954	128	6*	3.0	3.0	UNITED ARTISTS	
BAREFOOT EXECUTIVE, THE	1971	95	4			BUENA VISTA	
BAREFOOT IN THE PARK	1967	106	6	3.5		PARAMOUNT	
BAREFOOT MAILMAN, THE	1951	83		2.5	2.0	COLUMBIA	
BAREFOOT SAVAGE, THE (ITALIAN)	a1954	72		2.0	2.0	ITALIAN FILMS EXPORT	
BARGAIN, THE	1931	70		3.0		FIRST NATIONAL	
BARKLEYS OF BROADWAY, THE	1949	109	6	3.5	3.0	M-G-M	
BARNACLE BILL (WALLACE BEERY)	1941	98		2.0	2.0	M-G-M	
BARON OF ARIZONA, THE	1950	90		2.0	2.5	LIPPERT PRODS.	
BARONESS AND THE BUTLER, THE	1938	75		2.0	2.0	20th CENTURY FOX	
BARON'S AFRICAN WAR, THE	1943	100		2.5	2.5	REPUBLIC	RE-EDITED SERIAL
BARQUERO	1970	115	4			UNITED ARTISTS	
BARREN LIVES (BRAZILIAN)	1963	100		3.5		PATHE CONTEMPARARY	
BARRETTS OF WIMPOLE STREET (NORMA SHEARER)	1934	110		3.5		M-G-M	NOMINATED BEST PICTURE
BARRETTS OF WIMPOLE STREET (JENNIFER JONES)	1957	105	5	2.5	2.5	M-G-M	
BARRICADE (ALICE FAYE, WARNER BAXTER)	1939	71		2.0	2.0	20th CENTURY FOX	
BARRICADE (DANE CLARK, RAYMOND MASSEY)	1950	75		2.0	2.0	WARNER BROTHERS	
BARRIER (POLISH)	1966	83	2*			JANUS FILMS	
BARRIER OF THE LAW (ITALIAN)	1950	81		1.5		ITALIAN FILMS EXPORT	
BARTLEBY (BRITISH)	1971	79	3			MARON FILMS, LTD.	
BASHFUL ELEPHANT, THE (GERMAN)	1962	82		2.0	1.0	ALLIED ARTISTS	
BAT, THE	1959	80		1.5	2.5	ALLIED ARTISTS	
BATAAN	1943	114		3.0	3.0	M-G-M	
BATHING BEAUTY	1944	101		2.0	2.5	M-G-M	
BATMAN	1966	105	2*		2.0	20th CENTURY FOX	
BATMEN OF AFRICA	1936	100		1.5	2.0	REPUBLIC	RE-EDITED SERIAL
BATTLE, THE (BRITISH)	a1935	79		2.5		UNITED ARTISTS	
BATTLE AT APACHE PASS	1952	85		2.5	2.5	UNIVERSAL	
BATTLE AT BLOODY BEACH	1961	83	2	2.0	2.5	20th CENTURY FOX	
BATTLE BENEATH THE EARTH (BRITISH)	1968	92	1			M-G-M	
BATTLE BEYOND THE SUN (GERMAN)	1963	75	3	1.5		AMERICAN-INTERNAT'L	
BATTLE CIRCUS	1953	90		2.0	2.0	M-G-M	
BATTLE CRY	1955	149		2.5	3.0	WARNER BROTHERS	
BATTLE FLAME	1959	78		2.0	1.5	ALLIED ARTISTS	
BATTLE HELL	1957	112	6	3.0		DIST. CORP. OF AMER.	
BATTLE HYMN	1957	108	6	3.0	3.0	UNIVERSAL	
BATTLE IN OUTER SPACE (JAPANESE)	1960	90		1.5	1.5	COLUMBIA	
BATTLE OF ALGIERS (FRENCH-ALGERIAN)	1966	125	6*	4.0		RIZZOLI FILM	
BATTLE OF AUSTERLITZ, THE (FRENCH)	a1960	123		2.0		20th CENTURY FOX	
BATTLE OF BLOOD ISLAND	1960	64		2.5		FILMGROUP	
BATTLE OF BRITAIN (BRITISH - LAURENCE OLIVIER)	1969	132	4			UNITED ARTISTS	
BATTLE OF NERETVA	1971	112	3			AMERICAN-INTERNAT'L	
BATTLE OF ROGUE RIVER	1954	71		2.0	2.0	COLUMBIA	
BATTLE OF THE BULGE	1966	163	4*	2.0		WARNER BROTHERS	
BATTLE OF THE CORAL SEA, THE	1959	80		2.0	2.5	COLUMBIA	
BATTLE OF THE RAILS (FRENCH, DOCUMENTARY)	1947	87		3.0		MAYER-BURSTYN	
BATTLE OF THE SEXES, THE (BRITISH)	1959	88	6	3.0	3.0	CONTINENTAL	
BATTLE OF THE VILLA FIORITA, THE (BRITISH)	1965	105		2.0	2.5	WARNER BROTHERS	
BATTLE OF THE WORLDS (ITALIAN)	1960	84		1.5		ULTRA PICTURES CORP.	
BATTLE STATIONS	1956	81		2.0	1.5	COLUMBIA	
BATTLE STRIPE	a1950	86	3*	4.0	3.5	UNITED ARTISTS	
BATTLE TAXI	1955	82		2.0	2.0	UNITED ARTISTS	
BATTLE ZONE	1952	82		2.0	2.0	ALLIED ARTISTS	
BATTLEAXE, THE (BRITISH)	1962	66		2.0	2.0	PARAMOUNT	
BATTLEGROUND	1949	118	5*	3.5	3.0	M-G-M	NOMINATED BEST PICTURE
BAY OF SAINT MICHEL, THE	a1963	73		3.0	2.0	J. ARTHUR RANK	
BAY OF THE ANGELS (FRENCH)	1963	85	4			PATHE CONTEMPARARY	
BAYOU	a1957	85	1			UNITED ARTISTS	
BE BEAUTIFUL BUT SHUT UP (FRENCH)	1957	94		1.5	2.0		
BEACH BALL	1965	83	3		2.0	PARAMOUNT	
BEACH BLANKET BINGO	1965	98		2.5	2.0	AMERICAN-INTERNAT'L	
BEACH CASSANOVA (ITALIAN)	1965	85		2.5		AMERICAN-INTERNAT'L	
BEACH GIRLS AND THE MONSTER	1965	70	1			U.S. FILMS	
BEACH PARTY	1963	101	2	2.0	2.0	AMERICAN-INTERNAT'L	

‡ An asterisk (*) in THE FILM BUFF'S BIBLE column indicates that the film has been rated by the editor and/or staff. All other ratings in this column are based on a consensus of reviews (see NOTES).

TITLE (LEADING ACTORS SHOWN WHERE TWO OR MORE FILMS HAVE THE SAME OR SIMILAR TITLE)	YEAR RELEASED	RUNNING TIME IN MINUTES	THE FILM BUFF'S BIBLE ‡	STEVEN SCHEUER	LEONARD MALTIN	DISTRIBUTOR	COMMENT
BEACH PARTY - ITALIAN STYLE (ITALIAN)	1963	95		1.5		BROGGI & LIABASSI	
BEACH RED	1967	105	6	3.0		UNITED ARTISTS	
BEACHCOMBER, THE (BRITISH - CHARLES LAUGHTON)	1938	80	6*	3.5	3.0	PARAMOUNT	
BEACHCOMBER, THE (BRITISH - ROBERT NEWTON)	1954	90	4	2.5	3.0	UNITED ARTISTS	
BEACHHEAD	1954	89	4	2.5	3.0	UNITED ARTISTS	
BEAR, THE (FRENCH)	1963	86		3.0		AVCO-EMBASSY	
BEAR AND THE DOLL, THE (FRENCH)	1971	89	1			PARAMOUNT	
BEAST FROM THE HAUNTED CAVE, THE	1959	75		1.5		ALLIED ARTISTS	
BEAST FROM 20,000 FATHOMS, THE	1953	80		2.5	2.0	WARNER BROTHERS	
BEAST IN THE CELLAR, THE (BRITISH)	1971	87	5			CANNON RELEASING	
BEAST OF BLOOD	1970	90	1			HEMISPHERE	
BEAST OF BUDAPEST, THE	1958	72		2.0	1.5	ALLIED ARTISTS	
BEAST OF HOLLOW MOUNTAIN, THE	1956	77		2.5	2.5	UNITED ARTISTS	
BEAST OF THE YELLOW NIGHT	1971	87	1			NEW WORLD	
BEAST WITH A MILLION EYES	1956	71		1.5		AMERICAN RELEASING	
BEAST WITH FIVE FINGERS, THE	1946	88		1.5	1.5	WARNER BROTHERS	
BEASTS OF MARSEILLES (BRITISH)	1959	70		3.0		LOPERT	
BEAT GENERATION, THE	a1959	95		1.5	1.5	M-G-M	
BEAT GIRL (BRITISH)	a1960	86		1.0	2.0	VICTORIA	
BEAT THE BAND	1947	67		2.0		RKO	
BEAT THE DEVIL	1954	92	4*	3.5	3.0	UNITED ARTISTS	
BEATNIKS, THE	1958	78		1.5		BAJUL INTERNATIONAL	
BEAU BRUMMELL (STEWART GRANGER, PETER USTINOV)	1954	111	5*	3.0	2.5	M-G-M	
BEAU GESTE (GARY COOPER, RAY MILLAND)	1939	120	6*	3.5	3.5	PARAMOUNT	
BEAU GESTE (GUY STOCKWELL, DOUG MCCLURE)	1966	103	3	2.5	2.5	UNIVERSAL	
BEAU JAMES	1957	105		3.0	3.0	PARAMOUNT	
BEAUTIES OF THE NIGHT (FRENCH)	1952	87	6	3.5	2.5	UNITED ARTISTS	
BEAUTIFUL BLONDE FROM BASHFUL BEND, THE	1949	77		2.0	2.5	20th CENTURY FOX	
BEAUTIFUL BUT DANGEROUS (ITALIAN)	1958	103	4			20th CENTURY FOX	
BEAUTY AND THE BEAST (FRENCH - JEAN MARAIS)	1946	90	4*			LOPERT	
BEAUTY AND THE BEAST (JOYCE TAYLOR, MARK DAMON)	1963	77	4			UNITED ARTISTS	
BEAUTY AND THE DEVIL (FRENCH)	1952	95	6			ARTHUR DAVIS ASSOC.	
BEAUTY ON PARADE	1950	66	3			COLUMBIA	
BEAVER VALLEY (DOCUMENTARY)	1951	32	5*			BUENA VISTA	
BEBO'S GIRL (ITALIAN)	1963	106		2.5	2.5	CONTINENTAL	
BECAUSE OF HIM	1946	88		3.0	3.0	UNIVERSAL	
BECAUSE OF YOU	1952	95	4	2.5	3.0	UNIVERSAL	
BECAUSE THEY'RE YOUNG	1960	102	4	2.5	2.5	COLUMBIA	
BECAUSE YOU'RE MINE	1952	103	5	3.0		M-G-M	
BECKET (BRITISH)	1964	148	8*	4.0	3.0	PARAMOUNT	NOMINATED BEST PICTURE
BECKET AFFAIR, THE (ITALIAN)	1966	95		1.0		OFFICIAL INDUSTRIES	
BECKY SHARP	1935	83			2.5	RKO	
BED, THE	1955	101	5			GETZ-KINGSLEY	FOUR STORIES
BED AND BOARD (FRENCH)	1971	95	7			COLUMBIA	
BED OF GRASS (GREEK)	1957	92	5			TRANS-LUX DIST.	
BED SITTING ROOM, THE (BRITISH)	1969	90	3			UNITED ARTISTS	
BEDAZZLED (BRITISH)	1967	103	6	3.5		20th CENTURY FOX	
BEDELIA (BRITISH)	1946	83		2.5		EAGLE LION	
BEDEVILLED	1955	85		2.0	2.0	M-G-M	
BEDFORD INCIDENT, THE (BRITISH)	1965	102	5-6*	3.0	3.0	COLUMBIA	
BEDKNOBS AND BROOMSTICKS	1971	117	6			BUENA VISTA	
BEDLAM	1946	79		3.0	3.0	RKO	
BEDTIME FOR BONZO	1951	82	4	2.0	2.0	UNIVERSAL	
BEDTIME STORY (MARLIN BRANDO, DAVID NIVEN)	1964	99		2.5	2.5	UNIVERSAL	
BEDTIME STORY, A (MAURICE CHEVALIER)	1933	87		2.5	2.5	PARAMOUNT	
BEDTIME STORY, A (FREDRIC MARCH, LORETTA YOUNG)	1941	85	6-7*	3.5	3.0	COLUMBIA	
BEEN DOWN SO LONG IT LOOKS LIKE UP TO ME	1971	92	2			PARAMOUNT	
BEFORE I HANG	1940	71	4*		2.5	COLUMBIA	
BEFORE WINTER COMES (BRITISH)	1969	103	5			COLUMBIA	
BEGGAR'S OPERA, THE (BRITISH)	1953	94	6			WARNER BROTHERS	
BEGINNING OF THE END	1957	73		1.5	2.0	REPUBLIC	
BEGINNING OR THE END, THE	1947	112	4*	2.5	3.0	M-G-M	
BEGUILED, THE	1971	109	3			UNIVERSAL	
BEHAVE YOURSELF	1951	81		2.5	2.0	RKO	
BEHIND GREEN LIGHTS	1946	64		2.5		20th CENTURY FOX	
BEHIND LOCKED DOORS	1948	62		3.0	2.0	EAGLE LION	
BEHIND THAT CURTAIN	1929	92				20th CENTURY FOX	
BEHIND THE FRONT (SILENT)	1926	62			2.5	PARAMOUNT	
BEHIND THE HIGH WALL	1956	85		1.5	2.0	UNIVERSAL	
BEHIND THE MASK (BORIS KARLOFF)	1932	70			2.0	COLUMBIA	
BEHIND THE MASK (BRITISH - MICHAEL REDGRAVE)	1958	99	3*	3.0		SHOWCORPORATION	
BEHIND THE MASK OF ZORRO (ITALIAN)	1964	85		1.5		NTA PICTURES	
BEHIND THE RISING SUN	1943	89		3.0	2.5	RKO	
BEHOLD A PALE HORSE	1964	118		2.5	2.5	COLUMBIA	
BEHOLD MY WIFE	1935	78		1.5	2.0	PARAMOUNT	
BELIEVE IN ME	1971	86	3			M-G-M	
BELL' ANTONIO (ITALIAN)	1960	101		3.0	2.5	AVCO-EMBASSY	
BELL, BOOK AND CANDLE	1958	103	5*	3.0	2.5	COLUMBIA	
BELL FOR ADANO, A	1945	103	6*	3.5	3.5	20th CENTURY FOX	
BELLBOY, THE	1960	72	4	2.0	3.0	PARAMOUNT	
BELLE DE JOUR (FRENCH)	1967	100	6			ALLIED ARTISTS	
BELLE LE GRAND	1951	90		1.5	1.5	REPUBLIC	
BELLE OF NEW YORK, THE	1952	82		2.0	2.5	M-G-M	
BELLE OF OLD MEXICO	1949	70	2	2.0		REPUBLIC	

‡ An asterisk (*) in THE FILM BUFF'S BIBLE column indicates that the film has been rated by the editor and/or staff. All other ratings in this column are based on a consensus of reviews (see NOTES).

TITLE (LEADING ACTORS SHOWN WHERE TWO OR MORE FILMS HAVE THE SAME OR SIMILAR TITLE)	YEAR RELEASED	RUNNING TIME IN MINUTES	THE FILM BUFF'S BIBLE ‡	STEVEN SCHEUER	LEONARD MALTIN	DISTRIBUTOR	COMMENT
BELLE OF THE NINETIES	1934	75		2.5	3.0	PARAMOUNT	
BELLE OF THE YUKON	1944	84		2.0	2.5	RKO	
BELLE SOMMERS	1962	62	2	2.0		COLUMBIA	
BELLE STARR	1941	87		2.5	2.5	20th CENTURY FOX	
BELLE STARR'S DAUGHTER	1948	86			2.0	20th CENTURY FOX	
BELLES AND BALLETS (FRENCH)	1960	92		2.5		EXCELSIOR	
BELLES OF ST TRINIAN'S, THE (BRITISH)	1954	90	4*	3.0	2.5	CONTINENTAL	
BELLES ON THEIR TOES	1952	89		2.5	3.0	20th CENTURY FOX	
BELLISSIMA (ITALIAN)	1951	100	5	2.5	2.5	ITALIAN FILMS EXPORT	
BELLS ARE RINGING	1960	127	6	3.0	3.0	M-G-M	
BELLS OF ST MARY'S, THE	1945	126		3.5	3.0	REPUBLIC	NOMINATED BEST PICTURE
BELOVED ENEMY	1936	90	4*	3.0	3.0	UNITED ARTISTS	
BELOVED INFIDEL	1959	123		2.5	2.0	20th CENTURY FOX	
BELOVED ROGUE, THE (SILENT)	1926	103	6*			UNITED ARTISTS	
BELOW THE BELT	1971	90	2			BOXOFFICE INTERNAT'L	
BELOW THE SAHARA (DOCUMENTARY)	1953	65	6	3.0		RKO	
BEN	1972	93	4			CINERAMA RELEASING	
BEN-HUR (SILENT - RAMON NOVARRO)	1926	133				M-G-M	
BEN-HUR (CHARLTON HESTON, STEPHEN BOYD)	1959	217	9*	4.0		M-G-M	BEST PICTURE AWARD
BEND OF THE RIVER	1952	91	5*	3.0	3.0	UNIVERSAL	
BENEATH THE PLANET OF THE APES	1970	95	4			20th CENTURY FOX	
BENEATH THE 12-MILE REEF	1953	102		2.5	2.5	20th CENTURY FOX	
BENEFIT OF THE DOUBT, THE (BRITISH)	1967	70			2.5		
BENGAL BRIGADE	1954	87		2.0		UNIVERSAL	
BENGAZI	1955	78	2		1.5	RKO	
BENJAMIN (FRENCH)	1968	100	5	3.0		PARAMOUNT	
BENNY GOODMAN STORY, THE	1956	116	4*	2.5	2.5	UNIVERSAL	
BERKELEY SQUARE	1933	87			3.0	20th CENTURY FOX	
BERLIN AFFAIR (T.V.)	1970	100		2.5		UNIVERSAL	
BERLIN CORRESPONDENT	1942	70		2.0	2.5	20th CENTURY FOX	
BERLIN EXPRESS	1948	86	5*	3.5	3.0	RKO	
BERMUDA AFFAIR (BRITISH)	1956	77	4	2.5		DIST. CORP. OF AMER.	
BERMUDA MYSTERY	1944	65		1.5	2.0	20th CENTURY FOX	
BERNADETTE OF LOURDES (FRENCH)	1960	105		3.0	2.5	JANUS FILMS	
BERNADINE	1957	95	2*	1.5	2.0	20th CENTURY FOX	
BERSERK (BRITISH)	1967	96	2	2.0	2.5	COLUMBIA	
BESPOKE OVERCOAT, THE (BRITISH)	1955	33	7			GEORGE K. ARTHUR	
BEST FOOT FORWARD	1943	95		3.0	3.0	M-G-M	
BEST HOUSE IN LONDON, THE (BRITISH)	1969	96	3	1.5		M-G-M	
BEST MAN, THE	1964	102	7*	4.0	3.0	UNITED ARTISTS	
BEST OF ENEMIES, THE (IT. - DAVID NIVEN, A. SORDI)	1961	104	7*	3.0	3.0	COLUMBIA	ENGLISH LANGUAGE
BEST OF EVERYTHING, THE	1959	127		2.5	3.0	20th CENTURY FOX	
BEST OF THE BADMEN	1951	84	4	2.5	2.5	RKO	
BEST THINGS IN LIFE ARE FREE, THE	1956	104		2.5	2.5	20th CENTURY FOX	
BEST YEARS OF OUR LIVES, THE	1946	172	7*	4.0	4.0	RKO	BEST PICTURE AWARD
BETRAYAL, THE (BRIT.- PHILIP FRIEND, DIANA BECKER)	1956	82		2.5		UNITED ARTISTS	
BETRAYAL FROM THE EAST	1945	82		2.0	2.0	RKO	
BETRAYED (KIM HUNTER)	a1944	67		3.5	2.0	MONOGRAM	
BETRAYED (CLARK GABLE, LANA TURNER)	1954	108		2.0	2.0	M-G-M	
BETRAYED WOMEN	1955	70		1.5	1.5	ALLIED ARTISTS	
BETTER A WIDOW (ITALIAN)	1968	101	2	1.5		UNIVERSAL	
BETWEEN HEAVEN AND HELL	1956	94		2.5	3.0	20th CENTURY FOX	
BETWEEN MIDNIGHT AND DAWN	1950	89		2.0	2.0	COLUMBIA	
BETWEEN TIME AND ETERNITY (GERMAN)	1956	84		2.0	2.5	UNIVERSAL	
BETWEEN TWO WOMEN (VAN JOHNSON, GLORIA DE HAVEN)	1944	83		2.0	-	M-G-M	
BETWEEN TWO WORLDS	1944	112		2.5	2.5	WARNER BROTHERS	
BETWEEN US GIRLS	1942	89			2.0	UNIVERSAL	
BEWARE, MY LOVELY	1952	77	4	2.5	2.5	RKO	
BEWARE OF BLONDIE	1950	66		2.0		COLUMBIA	
BEWARE OF CHILDREN (BRITISH)	1960	80		2.0	1.5	AMERICAN-INTERNAT'L	
BEWARE OF PITY (BRITISH)	1946	103			2.5	TWO CITIES	
BEWARE SPOOKS!	1939	68			2.0	COLUMBIA	
BEWARE! THE BLOB	1972	87	2			JACK H. HARRIS	
BEWITCHED	1945	65		2.5	2.5	M-G-M	
BEYOND A REASONABLE DOUBT	1956	80		2.0	3.0	RKO	
BEYOND ALL LIMITS	1961	115		2.0		SUTTON PICTURES	
BEYOND CONTROL	1971	89	1			WILLIAM MISHKIN	
BEYOND GLORY	1948	82		2.5	2.5	PARAMOUNT	
BEYOND LOVE AND EVIL	1971	90	1			ALLIED ARTISTS	
BEYOND MOMBASA (BRITISH)	1956	90	3*	2.0	2.0	COLUMBIA	
BEYOND THE BLUE HORIZON	1942	76		1.5	2.0	PARAMOUNT	
BEYOND THE CURTAIN (BRITISH)	1960	88		2.5		J. ARTHUR RANK	
BEYOND THE FOREST	1949	96		2.0	2.0	WARNER BROTHERS	
BEYOND THE LAW (RIP TORN, GEORGE PLIMPTON)	1968	110	6	3.5		GROVE PRESS	
BEYOND THE TIME BARRIER	1960	75		1.5	2.0	AMERICAN-INTERNAT'L	
BEYOND THE VALLEY OF THE DOLLS	1970	109	1			20th CENTURY FOX	
BEYOND TOMORROW	1940	84			2.5	RKO	
BHOWANI JUNCTION (BRITISH)	1956	110		2.5	3.0	M-G-M	
BIBLE, THE	1966	174	5			20th CENTURY FOX	
BICYCLE THIEF, THE (ITALIAN)	1949	90	6*	4.0	4.0	MAYER-BURSTYN	
BIG BEAT, THE	1958	82	3	2.0		UNIVERSAL	
BIG BIRD CAGE, THE	1972	92	1			NEW WORLD	
BIG BLUFF, THE	1955	70	2	1.5	2.0	TOWER	
BIG BOODLE, THE	1957	83		2.0	1.5	UNITED ARTISTS	

‡ An asterisk (*) in THE FILM BUFF'S BIBLE column indicates that the film has been rated by the editor and/or staff. All other ratings in this column are based on a consensus of reviews (see NOTES).

TITLE (LEADING ACTORS SHOWN WHERE TWO OR MORE FILMS HAVE THE SAME OR SIMILAR TITLE)	YEAR RELEASED	RUNNING TIME IN MINUTES	THE FILM BUFF'S BIBLE ‡	STEVEN SCHEUER	LEONARD MALTIN	DISTRIBUTOR	COMMENT
BIG BOUNCE, THE	1969	102	1			WARNER BROTHERS	
BIG BROADCAST, THE	1932	78		3.0	3.0	PARAMOUNT	
BIG BROADCAST OF 1936, THE	1935	97		2.5	3.0	PARAMOUNT	
BIG BROADCAST OF 1937, THE	1936	100		3.0	3.0	PARAMOUNT	
BIG BROADCAST OF 1938, THE	1938	90		3.0	2.0	PARAMOUNT	
BIG BROWN EYES	1936	77		1.5	2.5	PARAMOUNT	
BIG CAGE, THE	1933	76			2.5	UNIVERSAL	
BIG CAPER, THE	1957	84		2.0	2.5	UNITED ARTISTS	
BIG CARNIVAL, THE	a1951	112	6*	4.0	3.0	PARAMOUNT	
BIG CAT, THE	1949	75	5	3.0		EAGLE LION	
BIG CHANCE, THE (BRITISH)	1957	61		2.0		J. ARTHUR RANK	
BIG CIRCUS, THE	1959	108	5*	2.5	2.5	ALLIED ARTISTS	
BIG CITY, THE (SPENCER TRACY, LUISE RANIER)	a1937	80		2.0	2.5	M-G-M	
BIG CITY, THE (MARGARET O'BRIEN, ROBERT PRESTON)	1948	103	4	1.5	2.5	M-G-M	
BIG CITY, THE (INDIAN - MADHABI MUKHERJEE)	1964	125	6			HARRISON PICTURES	
BIG CITY BLUES	1932	65		2.5	2.5	WARNER BROTHERS	
BIG CLOCK, THE	1948	95	6*	3.5	3.0	PARAMOUNT	
BIG COMBO, THE	1955	89	4	2.5	2.5	ALLIED ARTISTS	
BIG COUNTRY, THE	1958	165	5-6*	3.0	3.0	UNITED ARTISTS	
BIG CUBE, THE	1969	98	2			WARNER BROTHERS	
BIG DEAL ON MADONNA STREET, THE (ITALIAN)	1958	91	5	4.0	3.5	UN. MOTION PIC. ORG.	
BIG DOLL HOUSE, THE	1971	93	1			NEW WORLD	
BIG FISHERMAN, THE	1959	180	5			BUENA VISTA	
BIG FRAME, THE (BRITISH)	1953	67		2.0		RKO	
BIG GAMBLE, THE (STEPHEN BOYD, JULIETTE GRECO)	1961	100		2.0	2.5	PATHE-RKO	
BIG GUNDOWN, THE (ITALIAN)	1967	90	3	2.0		COLUMBIA	
BIG GUSHER, THE	1951	68		2.0	1.5	COLUMBIA	
BIG GUY, THE	1940	78			2.0	UNIVERSAL	
BIG HAND FOR THE LITTLE LADY, A	1966	95	6	3.5	3.0	WARNER BROTHERS	
BIG HANGOVER, THE	1950	82		2.5	2.5	M-G-M	
BIG HEAT, THE	1953	90	4*	3.5	3.5	COLUMBIA	
BIG HOUSE, THE	1930	88		3.0	3.0	M-G-M	NOMINATED BEST PICTURE 1929/30
BIG HOUSE, U.S.A.	1955	82	4	3.0	2.5	UNITED ARTISTS	
BIG JACK	1949	85		2.5	2.0	M-G-M	
BIG JAKE	1971	110	4			NATIONAL GENERAL	
BIG JIM MCLAIN	1952	90		2.0	2.5	WARNER BROTHERS	
BIG KNIFE, THE	1955	111	6	3.5	3.0	UNITED ARTISTS	
BIG LAND, THE	1957	92		2.5	2.5	WARNER BROTHERS	
BIG LEAGUER, THE	1953	70		2.0	2.0	M-G-M	
BIG LIFT, THE	1950	120	5	2.0	2.5	20th CENTURY FOX	
BIG MONEY, THE (BRITISH)	1958	86		2.0		J. ARTHUR RANK	
BIG MOUTH, THE	1967	107		2.0	2.5	COLUMBIA	
BIG NIGHT, THE (JOHN BARRYMORE JR.)	1951	75	3	3.0	2.5	UNITED ARTISTS	
BIG NIGHT, THE (RANDY SPARKS)	1960	74	3	2.5		PARAMOUNT	
BIG NOISE, THE (LAUREL AND HARDY)	1944	74		1.5	1.0	20th CENTURY FOX	
BIG OPERATOR, THE	a1959	91		1.5	2.0	M-G-M	
BIG PARADE, THE (SILENT)	1925	128				M-G-M	
BIG PARADE OF COMEDY, THE	a1964	91	4*	3.5	2.5	M-G-M	
BIG POND, THE	1930	75			2.5	PARAMOUNT	
BIG PUNCH, THE	1948	80	3	2.0		WARNER BROTHERS	
BIG RED	1962	93	4			BUENA VISTA	
BIG RISK, THE (FRENCH)	1960	111			2.0	UNITED ARTISTS	
BIG SHAKEDOWN, THE	1934	64		2.5	2.0	FIRST NATIONAL	
BIG SHOT, THE (HUMPHREY BOGART, IRENE MANNING)	1942	82		2.5	2.5	WARNER BROTHERS	
BIG SHOW, THE (CLIFF ROBERTSON, ESTHER WILLIAMS)	1961	113		2.0	2.5	20th CENTURY FOX	
BIG SKY, THE	1952	140		3.0	2.0	RKO	
BIG SLEEP, THE	1946	114		3.0	3.0	WARNER BROTHERS	
BIG STEAL, THE	1949	71		2.0	2.5	RKO	
BIG STORE, THE	1941	80		3.0	2.0	M-G-M	
BIG STREET, THE	1942	88		2.5	2.5	RKO	
BIG T.N.T. SHOW, THE (DOCUMENTARY)	1966	93	2		2.0	AMERICAN-INTERNAT'L	
BIG TIMBER	1950	73	2			MONOGRAM	
BIG TIP OFF	1955	78		2.0		ALLIED ARTISTS	
BIG TOWN	1947	60	2	1.5	2.0	PARAMOUNT	
BIG TOWN AFTER DARK	a1947	69		2.5	2.0	PARAMOUNT	
BIG TOWN SCANDAL	1948	62		1.5		PARAMOUNT	
BIG TREES, THE	1952	89		2.0	2.5	WARNER BROTHERS	
BIG WAVE, THE (JAPANESE)	1962	73		2.5	1.5	ALLIED ARTISTS	
BIG WHEEL, THE	1949	92		2.5	2.5	UNITED ARTISTS	
BIGAMIST, THE (EDMOND O'BRIEN, JOAN FONTAINE)	1953	80		3.0	2.5	FILMMAKERS	
BIGAMIST, THE (ITALIAN - VITTORIO DE SICA)	1956	97	3			DIST. CORP. OF AMER.	
BIGFOOT	1971	95	3			ELLMAN ENTERPRISES	
BIGGER THAN LIFE	1956	95	4*	3.5	3.0	20th CENTURY FOX	
BIGGEST BUNDLE OF THEM ALL, THE	1967	110	3	2.0		M-G-M	
BIKINI BEACH	1964	100		2.5	2.0	AMERICAN-INTERNAT'L	
BILL AND COO	1947	61	3*	3.0	3.0	REPUBLIC	
BILL OF DIVORCEMENT, A (JOHN BARRYMORE)	1932	76		3.5	3.5	RKO	
BILL OF DIVORCEMENT, A (MAUREEN O'HARA)	a1940	74			2.5	RKO	
BILLIE	1965	87		2.0	2.5	UNITED ARTISTS	
BILLION DOLLAR BRAIN (BRITISH)	1967	108	3	2.0		UNITED ARTISTS	
BILLY BUDD (BRITISH)	1962	123	7*	3.5	4.0	ALLIED ARTISTS	
BILLY JACK	1971	112	6			WARNER BROTHERS	
BILLY LIAR (BRITISH)	1963	96	5-6*	3.5	3.5	CONTINENTAL	
BILLY ROSE'S DIAMOND HORSESHOE	a1945	104		3.0	3.0	20th CENTURY FOX	

‡ An asterisk (*) in THE FILM BUFF'S BIBLE column indicates that the film has been rated by the editor and/or staff. All other ratings in this column are based on a consensus of reviews (see NOTES).

TITLE (LEADING ACTORS SHOWN WHERE TWO OR MORE FILMS HAVE THE SAME OR SIMILAR TITLE)	YEAR RELEASED	RUNNING TIME IN MINUTES	THE FILM BUFF'S BIBLE ‡	STEVEN SCHEUER	LEONARD MALTIN	DISTRIBUTOR	COMMENT
BILLY ROSE'S JUMBO	1962	125		2.5	3.0	M-G-M	
BILLY THE KID (JOHNNY MACK BROWN, WALLACE BEERY)	1930	98		3.0	2.5	M-G-M	
BILLY THE KID (ROBERT TAYLOR, BRIAN DONLEVY)	1941	95		2.5	2.5	M-G-M	
BILLY THE KID VS DRACULA	1966	84		1.0		AVCO-EMBASSY	
BIMBO THE GREAT (GERMAN)	1958	92		2.0	1.5	WARNER BROTHERS	
BIOGRAPHY OF A BACHELOR GIRL	1935	82		2.5	2.5	M-G-M	
BIRD MAN OF ALCATRAZ	1962	147	7*	4.0	3.0	UNITED ARTISTS	
BIRD OF PARADISE	1951	100		2.0	2.0	20th CENTURY FOX	
BIRD WITH THE CRYSTAL PLUMAGE, THE	1970	98	3			UMC PICTURES	
BIRDS, THE	1963	120	5*	2.5	3.5	UNIVERSAL	
BIRDS AND THE BEES, THE	1956	94		2.0	2.0	PARAMOUNT	
BIRDS DO IT	1966	95	2		2.0	COLUMBIA	
BIRDS IN PERU (FRENCH)	1968	95	1	1.0		REGIONAL	
BIRDS, THE BEES AND THE ITALIANS, THE (ITALIAN)	1966	115	6			CLARIDGE	
BIRTH OF A NATION (SILENT)	1915	157	5*			UNITED ARTISTS	
BIRTH OF THE BLUES	1941	85		3.5	3.0	PARAMOUNT	
BIRTHDAY PARTY, THE (BRITISH)	1968	123	7	4.0		CONTINENTAL	
BIRTHDAY PRESENT (BRITISH)	1957	100		3.0		SHOWCORPORATION	
BISCUIT EATER, THE (EARL HOLLIMAN, PAT CROWLEY)	1972	92	4			BUENA VISTA	
BISHOP MISBEHAVES, THE	1935	86		3.0		M-G-M	
BISHOP'S WIFE, THE	1947	108	5*	3.0	3.0	RKO	NOMINATED BEST PICTURE
BITTER CREEK	1954	74		1.5	1.5	ALLIED ARTISTS	
BITTER HARVEST (BRITISH)	1963	96		2.0		CONTINENTAL	
BITTER REUNION (FRENCH)	1959	105		3.0		AJYM FILMS	
BITTER RICE (ITALIAN)	1949	107	6	3.0	3.0	LUX FILM AMERICA	
BITTER SPRINGS (AUSTRALIAN)	1950	86		3.5		J. ARTHUR RANK	
BITTER SWEET	1940	92		2.5	2.5	M-G-M	
BITTER TEA OF GENERAL YEN, THE	1933	89			2.5	COLUMBIA	
BITTER VICTORY (FRENCH)	1957	90		2.5	2.5	COLUMBIA	
BLACK ABBOT, THE (GERMAN)	1963	95		1.5	2.0	UCC FILMS	
BLACK ANGEL (DAN DURYEA, PETER LORRE)	1946	80		2.5	2.5	UNIVERSAL	
BLACK ANGELS (DES ROBERTS, LINDA JACKSON)	1970	92	1			MERRICK INT'L PICS.	
BLACK ARROW, THE	1948	76	5	3.0	3.0	COLUMBIA	
BLACK BART	1948	80	3		2.5	UNIVERSAL	
BLACK BEAUTY (MONA FREEMAN, RICHARD DENNING)	1946	74			2.5	NEW TRENDS ASSOC.	
BLACK BEAUTY (BRIT. - MARK LESTER, WALTER SLEZAK)	1971	108	4			PARAMOUNT	
BLACK BOOK, THE	a1949	89	4	3.0	3.0	EAGLE LION	
BLACK CAMEL	1931	71			-	20th CENTURY FOX	
BLACK CASTLE, THE	1952	81		2.0	2.0	UNIVERSAL	
BLACK CAT, THE (BORIS KARLOFF, BELA LUGOSI)	1934	65		2.0	3.0	UNIVERSAL	
BLACK CAT, THE (BRODERICK CRAWFORD, B. RATHBONE)	1941	70		2.5	2.5	UNIVERSAL	
BLACK CHAPEL, THE (FRENCH)	1962	88		2.0		SCREEN GEMS	
BLACK COBRA, THE (GERMAN)	1961	95		1.5		UCC FILMS	
BLACK CROSS (POLISH)	1960	175			2.0		
BLACK DAKOTAS, THE	1954	65		2.0	2.0	COLUMBIA	
BLACK DEVILS OF KALI, THE	a1955	72		1.0	1.5	REPUBLIC	
BLACK DRAGON OF MANZANAR	1943	100		2.5	2.5	REPUBLIC	RE-EDITED SERIAL
BLACK DUKE, THE (ITALIAN)	1961	90		1.5		PRODUCERS RELEASING	
BLACK FOX, THE (DOCUMENTARY)	1962	89	7*	3.0	3.5	CAPRI FILMS	
BLACK FRIDAY	1940	70			2.0	UNIVERSAL	
BLACK FURY	1935	92	5*	3.5	3.5	FIRST NATIONAL	
BLACK GIRL (FRENCH)	1966	60		3.5		NEW YORKER FILMS	
BLACK GLOVE, THE (BRITISH)	1954	84		2.5		LIPPERT PRODS.	
BLACK GOLD (ANTHONY QUINN)	1947	92	5	3.0		ALLIED ARTISTS	
BLACK GOLD (PHILIP CAREY, DIANE MCBAIN)	1963	98	3	2.0	2.5	WARNER BROTHERS	
BLACK HAND	1950	93		2.5	2.0	M-G-M	
BLACK HORSE CANYON	1954	81		2.5	2.5	UNIVERSAL	
BLACK ICE, THE (BRITISH)	1957	62		2.0		PARKSIDE PRODS.	
BLACK INVADERS, THE (ITALIAN)	1960	90		1.0		AMERICAN-INTERNAT'L	
BLACK JACK KETCHUM, DESPERADO	1956	76		2.0		COLUMBIA	
BLACK JESUS	1971	90	2			PLAZA PICTURES	
BLACK KNIGHT, THE (BRITISH)	1954	85	3	2.0	2.5	COLUMBIA	
BLACK LANCERS, THE (ITALIAN)	a1961	97		2.0	2.5	PARAMOUNT	
BLACK LEGION	1936	83	4*	2.5	3.0	WARNER BROTHERS	
BLACK LIKE ME	1964	107		2.5	2.5	CONTINENTAL	
BLACK MAGIC (SIDNEY TOLER)	a1944	67			-	MONOGRAM	
BLACK MAGIC (ORSON WELLES, AKIM TAMIROFF)	1949	105		2.0	2.5	UNITED ARTISTS	
BLACK MONOCLE, THE (FRENCH)	1961	85		1.5		OREX FILMS	
BLACK NARCISSUS (BRITISH)	1947	100	7	3.5	3.5	UNIVERSAL	
BLACK ON WHITE (IT. - ANITA SANDERS, TERRY CARTER)	1969	80	1			AUDUBON	
BLACK ORCHID, THE (SOPHIA LOREN, ANTHONY QUINN)	1959	96		2.5	2.5	PARAMOUNT	
BLACK ORPHEUS (BRAZILIAN)	1959	98	6*	4.0	3.5	LOPERT	
BLACK PANTHER OF RATANA, THE (GERMAN)	1962	94		1.0		UCC FILMS	
BLACK PARACHUTE	1944	65		2.0		COLUMBIA	
BLACK PATCH	1958	83		2.0	1.0	WARNER BROTHERS	
BLACK PIRATES, THE (MEXICAN)	1954	72			2.5	LIPPERT PRODS.	
BLACK PIT OF DR M (MEXICAN)	1959	72		1.0		AZTECA	
BLACK ROOM, THE	1935	67			2.5	COLUMBIA	
BLACK ROSE, THE (BRITISH)	1950	121		2.5	2.5	20th CENTURY FOX	
BLACK SABBATH (ITALIAN)	1964	99	3	3.0	2.5	AMERICAN-INTERNAT'L	THREE STORIES
BLACK SCORPION, THE	1957	88		1.0	1.5	WARNER BROTHERS	
BLACK SHIELD OF FALWORTH, THE	1954	99	5*	2.5	2.5	UNIVERSAL	
BLACK SLEEP, THE	1956	81	3		1.5	UNITED ARTISTS	
BLACK SPURS	1965	81	2		1.5	PARAMOUNT	

‡An asterisk (*) in THE FILM BUFF'S BIBLE column indicates that the film has been rated by the editor and/or staff. All other ratings in this column are based on a consensus of reviews (see NOTES).

TITLE (LEADING ACTORS SHOWN WHERE TWO OR MORE FILMS HAVE THE SAME OR SIMILAR TITLE)	YEAR RELEASED	RUNNING TIME IN MINUTES	THE FILM BUFF'S BIBLE ‡	STEVEN SCHEUER	LEONARD MALTIN	DISTRIBUTOR	COMMENT
BLACK SUNDAY (ITALIAN)	1960	83	2	2.0	2.5	AMERICAN-INTERNAT'L	
BLACK SWAN, THE	1942	85		3.0	3.0	20th CENTURY FOX	
BLACK TENT, THE (BRITISH)	1956	93			2.0	J. ARTHUR RANK	
BLACK TIDE (BRITISH)	1956	79		1.5		ASTOR	
BLACK TIGHTS (FRENCH)	1960	120	6			MAGNA PICTURES	FOUR STORIES
BLACK TORMENT, THE (BRITISH)	1964	85		2.5		GOVERNOR	
BLACK TUESDAY	1955	80	5	3.0	3.0	UNITED ARTISTS	
BLACK VEIL FOR LISA, A (ITALIAN-GERMAN)	1969	88	3			LANDAU/UNGER COM. UN.	
BLACK WATER GOLD (T.V.)	1970	75		2.0		ABC FILMS	
BLACK WHIP, THE	1956	77	3		1.5	20th CENTURY FOX	
BLACK WIDOW (GINGER ROGERS, VAN HEFLIN)	1954	95		2.5	2.5	20th CENTURY FOX	
BLACK ZOO	1963	88		2.0	1.0	ALLIED ARTISTS	
BLACKBEARD, THE PIRATE	1952	99		2.5	2.0	RKO	
BLACKBEARD'S GHOST	1968	107	4			BUENA VISTA	
BLACKBOARD JUNGLE, THE	1955	101	5*	4.0	3.5	M-G-M	
BLACKJACK KETCHUM, DESPERADO	1956	76			1.5	COLUMBIA	
BLACKMAIL (EDWARD G. ROBINSON, GENE LOCKHART)	1939	81		2.0	2.5	M-G-M	
BLACKMAIL (WILLIAM MARSHALL, ADELE MARA)	1947	67		2.0		REPUBLIC	
BLACKMAILED (BRIT. - MAI ZETTERLING, DIRK BOGARDE)	1950	85		2.0		BELL PICTURES	
BLACKMAILERS, THE (SPANISH)	1960	105		1.5		LANDAU/UNGER COM. UN.	
BLACKOUT (BRITISH - DANE CLARK, BELINDA LEE)	1954	87		2.0	2.0	LIPPERT PRODS.	
BLACKWELL'S ISLAND	1939	71		3.0	2.5	WARNER BROTHERS	
BLANCHE FURY (BRITISH)	1948	93		2.5	2.5	EAGLE LION	
BLANCHEVILLE MONSTER (ITALIAN)	1960	88		2.5		AMERICAN-INTERNAT'L	
BLAST OF SILENCE	1961	77	3	2.0		UNIVERSAL	•
BLAST-OFF (BRITISH)	a1967	95	3		2.0	AMERICAN-INTERNAT'L	
BLAZE OF NOON	1947	91		2.5	2.5	PARAMOUNT	
BLAZING FOREST, THE	1952	90		2.0	1.5	PARAMOUNT	
BLAZING SAND (ISRAELI)	1960	98		2.0		AVCO-EMBASSY	
BLESS THE BEASTS AND CHILDREN	1971	109	4*			COLUMBIA	
BLESSED EVENT	1932	84		3.0		WARNER BROTHERS	
BLIND ALIBI	1938	62		3.0		RKO	
BLIND ALLEY	1939	70		3.5		COLUMBIA	
BLIND GODDESS (BRITISH)	1949	88		2.5		UNIVERSAL	
BLIND JUSTICE (GERMAN)	a1961	97		2.5		PARAMOUNT	
BLIND SPOT (CHESTER MORRIS)	1947	73		3.0	3.0	COLUMBIA	
BLIND SPOT (BRITISH - ROBERT MACKENZIE)	1958	72		2.0		UCC FILMS	
BLINDFOLD	1966	102		3.0	2.5	UNIVERSAL	
BLINDMAN	1972	105	1			20th CENTURY FOX	
BLISS OF MRS BLOSSOM, THE (BRITISH)	1968	93	5	3.0		PARAMOUNT	
BLITZ ON BRITAIN (BRITISH)	1962	71		2.5		ANGLO-CONTINENTAL	
BLITZKRIEG - THE WAR FOR RUSSIA (GERMAN, DOC.)	1958	93		2.5		CONTINENTAL	
BLOB, THE	1958	86		1.5	2.0	PARAMOUNT	
BLOCK BUSTERS	1944	60			-	MONOGRAM	
BLOCK-HEADS	1938	55			3.0	M-G-M	
BLOCKADE	1938	85		3.5	3.0	UNITED ARTISTS	
BLONDE BAIT (BRITISH)	1956	71		1.5		M & A ALEXANDER	
BLONDE BLACKMAILER (BRITISH)	1958	58	2	1.0	1.0	ALLIED ARTISTS	
BLONDE CRAZY	1931	73		2.5	2.5	WARNER BROTHERS	
BLONDE DYNAMITE	1950	66			-	MONOGRAM	
BLONDE FEVER	1944	69		2.0	2.0	M-G-M	
BLONDE FROM BROOKLYN	1945	65		2.0		COLUMBIA	
BLONDE INSPIRATION	1941	72		2.5		M-G-M	
BLONDE RANSOM	1946	68		1.5		UNIVERSAL	
BLONDE VENUS	1932	80	4*	1.5	3.0	PARAMOUNT	
BLONDIE	1938	69		2.5	-	COLUMBIA	
BLONDIE BRINGS UP BABY	1939	67		2.5	-	COLUMBIA	
BLONDIE FOR VICTORY	1942	70		2.0		COLUMBIA	
BLONDIE GOES LATIN	1941	69		2.5	-	COLUMBIA	
BLONDIE GOES TO COLLEGE	1942	74		2.0		COLUMBIA	
BLONDIE HAS SERVANT TROUBLE	1940	70		2.5	-	COLUMBIA	
BLONDIE HITS THE JACKPOT	1949	66		1.5	-	COLUMBIA	
BLONDIE IN SOCIETY	1941	75		3.0	-	COLUMBIA	
BLONDIE IN THE DOUGH	1947	69		2.0	-	COLUMBIA	
BLONDIE JOHNSON	1933	69		2.5		FIRST NATIONAL	NOT IN THE BLONDIE SERIES
BLONDIE KNOWS BEST	1946	69		2.5	-	COLUMBIA	
BLONDIE MEETS THE BOSS	1939	58		2.5	-	COLUMBIA	
BLONDIE OF THE FOLLIES	1932	90		1.5	2.5	M-G-M	NOT IN THE BLONDIE SERIES
BLONDIE ON A BUDGET	1940	73		3.0	-	COLUMBIA	
BLONDIE PLAYS CUPID	1940	68		2.5	-	COLUMBIA	
BLONDIE TAKES A VACATION	1939	61		2.5	-	COLUMBIA	
BLONDIE'S ANNIVERSARY	1947	75		2.0	-	COLUMBIA	
BLONDIE'S BIG DEAL	1949	66		2.0	-	COLUMBIA	
BLONDIE'S BIG MOMENT	1947	69		2.0	-	COLUMBIA	
BLONDIE'S BLESSED EVENT	1942	69		3.0	-	COLUMBIA	
BLONDIE'S HERO	1949	67		1.5	-	COLUMBIA	
BLONDIE'S HOLIDAY	1947	67		2.0	-	COLUMBIA	
BLONDIE'S LUCKY DAY	1946	75		2.0	-	COLUMBIA	
BLONDIE'S REWARD	1948	67		2.0	-	COLUMBIA	
BLONDIE'S SECRET	1948	68		2.0	-	COLUMBIA	
BLOOD ALLEY	1955	115		2.0	2.5	WARNER BROTHERS	
BLOOD AND BLACK LACE (ITALIAN)	1965	88	2	2.0	1.5	ALLIED ARTISTS	
BLOOD AND DEFIANCE (ITALIAN)	1966	92		1.0		AVCO-EMBASSY	
BLOOD AND LACE	1971	87	1			AMERICAN-INTERNAT'L	

‡ An asterisk (*) in THE FILM BUFF'S BIBLE column indicates that the film has been rated by the editor and/or staff. All other ratings in this column are based on a consensus of reviews (see NOTES).

TITLE (LEADING ACTORS SHOWN WHERE TWO OR MORE FILMS HAVE THE SAME OR SIMILAR TITLE)	"a" TO LEFT OF YEAR INDICATES THAT FILM HAS AN ALTERNATE TITLE — YEAR RELEASED	RUNNING TIME IN MINUTES	CRITICAL RATINGS — THE FILM BUFF'S BIBLE ‡	STEVEN SCHEUER	LEONARD MALTIN	DISTRIBUTOR	COMMENT
BLOOD AND ROSES (ITALIAN)	1960	74		2.0	2.5	PARAMOUNT	
BLOOD AND SAND (SILENT - RUDOLPH VALENTINO)	1922	101	3*			PARAMOUNT	
BLOOD AND SAND (TYRONE POWER)	1941	123		2.0	3.0	20th CENTURY FOX	
BLOOD AND STEEL	1959	63		2.0	1.5	20th CENTURY FOX	
BLOOD ARROW	1958	75	2		1.5	20th CENTURY FOX	
BLOOD BATH	1966	69	1			AMERICAN-INTERNAT'L	
BLOOD BEAST FROM OUTER SPACE (BRITISH)	1965	84	2			WORLD ENTERTAINMENT	
BLOOD FEAST	1963	75	1			BOX OFFICE SPECTACS.	
BLOOD FROM THE MUMMY'S TOMB	1972	94	1			AMERICAN-INTERNAT'L	
BLOOD OF DRACULA	1957	68		1.0	1.5	AMERICAN-INTERNAT'L	
BLOOD OF DRACULA'S CASTLE	1969	84	1			CROWN INTERNATIONAL	
BLOOD OF NOSTRADAMUS, THE (MEXICAN)	1960	98		1.0		AZTECA	
BLOOD OF THE VAMPIRE (BRITISH)	1958	87	2		2.0	UNIVERSAL	
BLOOD ON HIS SWORD (FRENCH)	1961	126		2.0		AVCO-EMBASSY	
BLOOD ON SATAN'S CLAW, THE	1971	100	2			CANNON RELEASING	
BLOOD ON THE ARROW	1964	91	2	2.0	1.5	ALLIED ARTISTS	
BLOOD ON THE MOON	1948	88		3.0	3.0	RKO	
BLOOD ON THE SUN	1945	98	4*	3.0	3.0	UNITED ARTISTS	
BLOOD ROSE, THE	1970	92	1			ALLIED ARTISTS	
BLOODHOUNDS OF BROADWAY	1952	90		2.5	2.5	20th CENTURY FOX	
BLOODLUST	1961	68		1.0		PARAMOUNT	
BLOODY MAMA	1970	92	2			AMERICAN-INTERNAT'L	
BLOODY PIT OF HORROR (ITALIAN)	1965	74	1			PACEMAKER PICS.	
BLOODY VAMPIRE, THE (MEXICAN)	1963	98		1.0		AZTECA	
BLOSSOMS IN THE DUST	1941	100		3.0	3.0	M-G-M	NOMINATED BEST PICTURE
BLOW-UP (BRITISH)	1966	111	5-6*			PREMIER PICTURES	
BLOWING WILD	1953	90		2.5	2.0	WARNER BROTHERS	
BLUE	1968	113	2	1.0		PARAMOUNT	
BLUE ANGEL, THE (GERMAN - EMIL JANNINGS)	1930	95	6*			PARAMOUNT	
BLUE ANGEL, THE (CURT JURGENS, MAY BRITT)	1959	107	4	2.5	1.5	20th CENTURY FOX	
BLUE BEAST (JAPANESE)	1961	95	5			TOHO	
BLUE BIRD, THE	1940	88		2.5	2.5	20th CENTURY FOX	
BLUE BLOOD	1951	72		2.5	1.5	MONOGRAM	
BLUE CONTINENT (ITALIAN, DOCUMENTARY)	1954	95		2.0		GALATEA PRODS.	
BLUE DAHLIA, THE	1946	96	4*	3.0	3.0	PARAMOUNT	
BLUE DENIM	1959	89		2.5	3.0	20th CENTURY FOX	
BLUE GARDENIA, THE	1953	90		2.5	2.5	WARNER BROTHERS	
BLUE GRASS OF KENTUCKY	1950	71		2.5	2.0	MONOGRAM	
BLUE HAWAII	1961	101		2.0	2.5	PARAMOUNT	
BLUE LAGOON, THE (BRITISH)	1949	101		2.0	3.0	UNIVERSAL	
BLUE LAMP, THE (BRITISH)	1950	84	6	3.0	3.0	EAGLE LION	
BLUE MAX, THE (BRITISH)	1966	156	6*	2.5		20th CENTURY FOX	
BLUE MURDER AT ST TRINIAN'S (BRITISH)	1957	86		2.5	3.0	CONTINENTAL	
BLUE SEXTET	1972	90				UNISPHERE REL. CORP.	
BLUE SKIES	1946	104	6	3.0	3.0	PARAMOUNT	
BLUE VEIL, THE (JANE WYMAN, CHARLES LAUGHTON)	1951	113	6	2.5	3.0	RKO	
BLUE WATER, WHITE DEATH (DOCUMENTARY)	1971	100	3*			NATIONAL GENERAL	
BLUE, WHITE AND PERFECT	1942	78		2.5		20th CENTURY FOX	
BLUEBEARD (JOHN CARRADINE, JEAN PARKER)	1944	73		3.0	3.0	PRODUCERS RELEASING	
BLUEBEARD (FRENCH - CHARLES DENNER)	a1963	114		2.5	2.5	AVCO-EMBASSY	
BLUEBEARD (RICHARD BURTON, JOEY HEATHERTON)	1972	123	2			CINERAMA RELEASING	
BLUEBEARD'S EIGHTH WIFE	1938	87		4.0		PARAMOUNT	
BLUEBEARD'S TEN HONEYMOONS (BRITISH)	1960	92	2	2.5	2.0	ALLIED ARTISTS	
BLUEPRINT FOR MURDER, A	1953	76		2.0	2.5	20th CENTURY FOX	
BLUEPRINT FOR ROBBERY	1961	87	4			PARAMOUNT	
BLUES BUSTERS	1950	67			-	MONOGRAM	
BLUES IN THE NIGHT	1941	88		3.0	3.0	WARNER BROTHERS	
BOATNIKS, THE	1970	100	6			BUENA VISTA	
BOB AND CAROL AND TED AND ALICE	1969	104	5-6*	4.0		COLUMBIA	
BOB MATHIAS STORY, THE	1954	80	4*	2.5	3.0	ALLIED ARTISTS	
BOBBIKINS (BRITISH)	1959	90		2.5	2.0	20th CENTURY FOX	
BOBBY WARE IS MISSING	1955	67		2.5	1.5	ALLIED ARTISTS	
BOBO, THE (BRITISH)	1967	105	3*	2.0		WARNER BROTHERS	
BOCCACCIO '70 (ITALIAN)	1962	165	6	3.5	3.0	AVCO-EMBASSY	THREE STORIES
BODY, THE (BRITISH, DOCUMENTARY)	1970	112	4			M-G-M	
BODY AND SOUL	1947	104	7	4.0	4.0	UNITED ARTISTS	
BODY BENEATH, THE	1970	85				NOVA INTERNATIONAL	
BODY DISAPPEARS, THE	1941	72		2.0	2.0	WARNER BROTHERS	
BODY IS MISSING, THE (FRENCH)	a1962	95		1.5	2.0		
BODY SNATCHER, THE	1945	77		3.5	3.5	RKO	
BODY STEALERS, THE	1970	90	3			ALLIED ARTISTS	
BODYGUARD	1948	62		2.0	2.0	COLUMBIA	
BODYHOLD	1949	63		2.0	1.5	COLUMBIA	
BOEING, BOEING	1965	102		2.0	3.0	PARAMOUNT	
BOFORS GUN, THE (BRITISH)	1968	106	6	3.5		REGIONAL	
BOHEMIAN GIRL, THE	1936	70			3.0	M-G-M	
BOLD ADVENTURE, THE (FRENCH)	1956	87		2.0		UNITED ARTISTS	
BOLD AND THE BRAVE, THE	1956	87	5	3.5	3.0	RKO	
BOLERO (GEORGE RAFT, CAROLE LOMBARD)	1934	83		2.0	2.5	PARAMOUNT	
BOLSHOI BALLET '67	1966	75	6			PARAMOUNT	
BOMB AT 10:10 (YUGOSLAVIAN)	1966	86		2.0	2.0	WALTER READE	
BOMB FOR A DICTATOR, A (FRENCH)	a1957	73		2.0	2.0	MEDALLION	
BOMB IN HIGH STREET, THE (BRITISH)	1963	60		1.5	2.5	HEMISPHERE	
BOMBA AND THE HIDDEN CITY	1950	71			-	MONOGRAM	

‡ An asterisk (*) in **THE FILM BUFF'S BIBLE** column indicates that the film has been rated by the editor and/or staff. All other ratings in this column are based on a consensus of reviews (see **NOTES**).

TITLE (LEADING ACTORS SHOWN WHERE TWO OR MORE FILMS HAVE THE SAME OR SIMILAR TITLE)	YEAR RELEASED	RUNNING TIME IN MINUTES	THE FILM BUFF'S BIBLE ‡	STEVEN SCHEUER	LEONARD MALTIN	DISTRIBUTOR	COMMENT
BOMBA AND THE JUNGLE GIRL	a1952	70			-	MONOGRAM	
BOMBA ON PANTHER ISLAND	1949	76	2		-	MONOGRAM	
BOMBA, THE JUNGLE BOY	1949	70			-	MONOGRAM	
BOMBARDIER	1943	99		3.0	3.0	RKO	
BOMBAY TALKIE (INDIAN)	1971	110	4			DIA FILMS	
BOMBERS B-52	1957	106	4*	2.0	2.5	WARNER BROTHERS	
BOMBER'S MOON	1943	70		2.0		20th CENTURY FOX	
BOMBS OVER BURMA	1942	62			2.0	PRODUCERS RELEASING	
BOMBSHELL	a1933	91		3.0	3.5	M-G-M	
BON VOYAGE	1962	133	4			BUENA VISTA	
BONJOUR TRISTESSE (BRITISH)	1958	94	5*	2.5	3.0	COLUMBIA	
BONNIE AND CLYDE	1967	111	6*	4.0		WARNER BROTHERS	NOMINATED BEST PICTURE
BONNIE PARKER STORY, THE	1958	81	3*	2.0	2.5	AMERICAN-INTERNAT'L	
BONNIE SCOTLAND	1935	80			2.5	M-G-M	
BONZO GOES TO COLLEGE	1952	80		2.0	2.0	UNIVERSAL	
BOOBY TRAP, THE (BRITISH)	1957	72		2.5		EROS FILMS	
BOOM! (BRITISH)	1968	113	3	2.0		UNIVERSAL	
BOOM TOWN	1940	116		3.0	3.0	M-G-M	
BOOMERANG!	1947	88	7	4.0	4.0	20th CENTURY FOX	
BOOT POLISH (INDIAN)	a1954	90	6			HOFFBERG	
BOOTS MALONE	1952	103	5	3.0	3.0	COLUMBIA	
BORA BORA (ITALIAN)	1970	90	1			AMERICAN-INTERNAT'L	
BORDER INCIDENT	1949	92		2.5	2.0	M-G-M	
BORDER RIVER	1954	80		2.0	2.0	UNIVERSAL	
BORDERLINE (FRED MACMURRAY, CLAIRE TREVOR)	1950	88		2.0	2.5	UNIVERSAL	
BORDERTOWN	1935	90	5*	3.5	3.0	WARNER BROTHERS	
BORGIA STICK, THE	1967	100	5*	2.0	3.0	UNIVERSAL	
BORN FREE (BRITISH)	1966	95	7*	4.0	3.5	COLUMBIA	
BORN LOSERS	1967	112	3			AMERICAN-INTERNAT'L	
BORN RECKLESS	1959	79		1.5	2.0	WARNER BROTHERS	
BORN TO BE BAD (LORETTA YOUNG, CARY GRANT)	1934	61			2.0	UNITED ARTISTS	
BORN TO BE BAD (JOAN FONTAINE, ROBERT RYAN)	1950	94	5	3.0	3.0	RKO	
BORN TO BE LOVED	1959	82		2.0	2.0	UNIVERSAL	
BORN TO DANCE	1936	108		3.0	3.0	M-G-M	
BORN TO KILL	1947	92		1.5	2.0	RKO	
BORN TO SING	1942	82		2.0		M-G-M	
BORN TO WIN	1971	90	4			UNITED ARTISTS	
BORN WILD	1968	100	2			AMERICAN-INTERNAT'L	
BORN YESTERDAY	1950	103	6*	4.0	3.5	COLUMBIA	NOMINATED BEST PICTURE
BORSALINO (FRENCH)	1970	123	6			PARAMOUNT	
BOSS, THE	1956	89	4	3.0	3.0	UNITED ARTISTS	
BOSTON BLACKIE AND THE LAW	1946	69		2.5	-	COLUMBIA	
BOSTON BLACKIE BOOKED ON SUSPICION	1945	66			-	COLUMBIA	
BOSTON BLACKIE'S CHINESE VENTURE	1948	59			-	COLUMBIA	
BOSTON BLACKIE'S RENDEZVOUS	1945	64			-	COLUMBIA	
BOSTON STRANGLER, THE	1968	116	5	2.5		20th CENTURY FOX	
BOTANY BAY	1953	94		2.0	2.5	PARAMOUNT	
BOTH SIDES OF THE LAW (BRITISH)	a1954	94		3.0	3.0	UNIVERSAL	
BOTTOM OF THE BOTTLE, THE	1956	88		2.5	2.5	20th CENTURY FOX	
BOTTOMS UP (BRITISH)	1960	86		2.0		ASSOC. BRITISH-PATHE	
BOUNTY HUNTER, THE	1954	79		2.0	2.5	WARNER BROTHERS	
BOUNTY KILLER, THE	1965	92		1.5	2.5	AVCO-EMBASSY	
BOWERY, THE	1933	90		2.5	3.0	UNITED ARTISTS	
BOWERY AT MIDNIGHT	1942	63			2.0	MONOGRAM	
BOWERY BATALLION	1951	69			-	MONOGRAM	
BOWERY BLITZKRIEG	1941	62			-	MONOGRAM	
BOWERY BOMBSHELL	1946	65			-	MONOGRAM	
BOWERY BOYS MEET THE MONSTERS, THE	1954	66			-	ALLIED ARTISTS	
BOWERY BUCKAROOS	1947	66			-	MONOGRAM	
BOWERY CHAMPS	1944	62			-	MONOGRAM	
BOWERY TO BAGDAD	1955	64			-	ALLIED ARTISTS	
BOWERY TO BROADWAY	1944	94		2.5	2.5	UNIVERSAL	
BOXCAR BERTHA	1972	92	4			AMERICAN-INTERNAT'L	
BOY AND THE PIRATES, THE	1960	82		2.0	2.5	UNITED ARTISTS	
BOY CRIED MURDER, THE (BRITISH)	1966	86	3	2.5	2.5	UNIVERSAL	
BOY, DID I GET A WRONG NUMBER!	1966	99	2	1.0	1.0	UNITED ARTISTS	
BOY FRIEND (JANE WITHERS, RICHARD BOND)	1939	72		1.5		20th CENTURY FOX	
BOY FRIEND, THE (BRIT.- TWIGGY, CHRISTOPHER GABLE)	1971	108	6*			M-G-M	
BOY FROM INDIANA	1950	66	2		2.0	EAGLE LION	
BOY FROM OKLAHOMA, THE	1954	88		3.0	2.5	WARNER BROTHERS	
BOY FROM STALINGRAD	1943	70		2.0		COLUMBIA	
BOY MEETS GIRL	1938	80	2*	3.0	3.0	WARNER BROTHERS	
BOY NAMED CHARLIE BROWN, A (CARTOON)	1970	85	6			NATIONAL GENERAL	
BOY ON A DOLPHIN	1957	111		2.5	2.5	20th CENTURY FOX	
BOY SLAVES	1939	72		3.0		RKO	
BOY TEN FEET TALL, A (BRITISH)	a1963	128	5*	3.0	3.0	PARAMOUNT	
BOY WHO CAUGHT A CROOK, THE	1961	72		1.5	2.0	UNITED ARTISTS	
BOY WHO STOLE A MILLION, THE (BRITISH)	1960	84	4	2.0	2.0	PARAMOUNT	
BOY WITH THE GREEN HAIR, THE	1948	82	4*	3.0	3.0	RKO	
BOYS, THE (BRITISH)	1961	123		2.5	3.0	GALA	
BOYS FROM SYRACUSE, THE	1940	73		3.0	3.0	UNIVERSAL	
BOYS IN THE BAND, THE	1970	120	6			NATIONAL GENERAL	
BOYS' NIGHT OUT	1962	115	5	3.0	3.0	M-G-M	
BOYS OF PAUL STREET, THE (HUNGARIAN)	1968	104	6	3.0		20th CENTURY FOX	ENGLISH LANGUAGE

‡ An asterisk (*) in THE FILM BUFF'S BIBLE column indicates that the film has been rated by the editor and/or staff. All other ratings in this column are based on a consensus of reviews (see NOTES).

TITLE (LEADING ACTORS SHOWN WHERE TWO OR MORE FILMS HAVE THE SAME OR SIMILAR TITLE)	YEAR RELEASED	RUNNING TIME IN MINUTES	THE FILM BUFF'S BIBLE ‡	STEVEN SCHEUER	LEONARD MALTIN	DISTRIBUTOR	COMMENT
BOYS OF THE CITY	1940	65			-	MONOGRAM	
BOY'S RANCH	1946	97		2.5		M-G-M	
BOYS TOWN	1938	90		3.0	3.0	M-G-M	NOMINATED BEST PICTURE
BRAIN, THE (BRIT. - ANNE HEYWOOD, PETER VAN EYCK)	1964	83		2.5		GOVERNOR	
BRAIN, THE (DAVID NIVEN, JEAN-PAUL BELMONDO)	1969	100	5			PARAMOUNT	(FRENCH) ENGLISH VERSION
BRAIN EATERS, THE	1958	60	2	2.0		AMERICAN-INTERNAT'L	
BRAIN FROM PLANET AROUS	1958	70	1	1.5	2.0	HOWCO INTERNATIONAL	
BRAIN MACHINE, THE (BRITISH)	1954	83			2.0	RKO	
BRAIN OF BLOOD	1971	88				HEMISPHERE	
BRAIN THAT WOULDN'T DIE, THE	1962	81		1.5	1.5	AMERICAN-INTERNAT'L	
BRAINIAC, THE (MEXICAN)	1963	77		1.0		AZTECA	
BRAINSTORM	1965	114		2.5	2.0	WARNER BROTHERS	
BRAINWASHED (GERMAN)	1960	102		2.0	2.0	ALLIED ARTISTS	
BRAMBLE BUSH, THE	1960	105		2.0	2.5	WARNER BROTHERS	
BRAND X	1970	87	2			CMB FILMS	
BRANDED (ALAN LADD, MONA FREEMAN)	1951	104		2.5	2.5	PARAMOUNT	
BRANDY FOR THE FARSON (BRITISH)	1952	78	6	3.5		MAYER-KINGSLEY	
BRASHER DOUBLOON, THE	1947	74		1.5	2.0	20th CENTURY FOX	
BRASS BOTTLE, THE	1964	89	3	2.0	1.5	UNIVERSAL	
BRASS LEGEND, THE	1956	79		2.0	1.5	UNITED ARTISTS	
BRAVADOS, THE	1958	98		2.0	3.0	20th CENTURY FOX	
BRAVE BULLS, THE	1951	108	5*	4.0	3.0	COLUMBIA	
BRAVE DON'T CRY, THE (BRITISH)	1952	91		3.0		MAYER-KINGSLEY	
BRAVE ONE, THE	1956	100	6	3.0		UNIVERSAL	
BRAVE WARRIOR	1952	73		2.0	1.5	COLUMBIA	
BRAZEN WOMEN OF BALZAC	1971	80	1			GLOBE PICTURES	
BRAZIL	1944	91		2.5		REPUBLIC	
BREAD, LOVE AND DREAMS (ITALIAN)	1953	90	6	3.0	3.0	ITALIAN FILMS EXPORT	
BREAD PEDDLER, THE (FRENCH)	1963	122		2.0		EMERY PICTURES	
BREAK, THE (BRITISH)	1963	75	3			BRITISH-LION	
BREAK IN THE CIRCLE (BRITISH)	1955	91		1.5	1.5	20th CENTURY FOX	
BREAK OF HEARTS	1935	80		3.0	2.5	RKO	
BREAK TO FREEDOM (BRITISH)	1955	88		3.0	2.0	UNITED ARTISTS	
BREAKAWAY (BRITISH)	1956	72		2.0		ASSOCIATED ARTISTS	
BREAKDOWN (BRITISH)	1952	77		1.5		REALART	
BREAKFAST AT TIFFANY'S	1961	115	7*	3.5	3.5	PARAMOUNT	
BREAKFAST FOR TWO	1937	65		3.0	2.5	RKO	
BREAKFAST IN BED (GERMAN)	1963	90		2.0		SCREEN GEMS	
BREAKFAST IN HOLLYWOOD	1946	100			1.5	UNITED ARTISTS	
BREAKING POINT, THE (JOHN GARFIELD, PATRICIA NEAL)	1950	97		2.5	3.5	WARNER BROTHERS	
BREAKING THE SOUND BARRIER (BRITISH)	a1952	109	6*	4.0	3.5	UNITED ARTISTS	
BREAKOUT (BRITISH - RICHARD TODD)	a1959	99		2.5	2.5	CONTINENTAL	
BREAKOUT (BRITISH - LEE PATTERSON)	1959	62		2.0		ANGLO AMALGAMATED	
BREAKOUT (T.V. - JAMES DRURY)	1971	100	4*	2.0		UNIVERSAL	
BREAKTHROUGH (DAVID BRIAN, FRANK LOVEJOY)	1950	91	4	2.0	2.5	WARNER BROTHERS	
BREATH OF SCANDAL, A	1960	98		2.0	2.0	PARAMOUNT	
BREATHLESS (FRENCH)	1960	90	5		3.0	FILMS AROUND THE WLD.	
BRENNUS, ENEMY OF ROME (ITALIAN)	a1963	93		1.0		AMERICAN-INTERNAT'L	
BREWSTER MCCLOUD	1970	101	5			M-G-M	
BREWSTER'S MILLIONS	1945	79		2.5	2.5	UNITED ARTISTS	
BRIAN'S SONG (T.V.)	1971	75	6*			SCREEN GEMS	
BRIBE, THE	1949	98		2.0	2.0	M-G-M	
BRIDAL PATH, THE (BRITISH)	1959	95		2.5	2.5	KINGSLEY INTERNAT'L	
BRIDE AND THE BEAST, THE	1958	78		1.0	1.0	ALLIED ARTISTS	
BRIDE BY MISTAKE	1944	80		2.5		RKO	
BRIDE CAME C.O.D., THE	1941	92		3.0	2.5	WARNER BROTHERS	
BRIDE COMES HOME, THE	1935	82		2.5	2.5	PARAMOUNT	
BRIDE FOR FRANK, A (ITALIAN)	1958	90		2.0			
BRIDE FOR SALE	1949	87		2.5	2.5	RKO	
BRIDE GOES WILD, THE	1948	98		2.5	2.5	M-G-M	
BRIDE IS MUCH TOO BEAUTIFUL, THE (FRENCH)	1956	93		2.0	2.5	ELLIS FILMS	
BRIDE OF FRANKENSTEIN, THE	1935	80		3.0	3.0	UNIVERSAL	
BRIDE OF THE GORILLA	1951	76	1			REALART	
BRIDE OF THE MONSTER	1956	67		1.0		BANNER	
BRIDE OF VENGEANCE	1949	91		2.0	2.0	PARAMOUNT	
BRIDE WALKS OUT, THE	1936	75		2.0	2.0	RKO	
BRIDE WORE BLACK, THE (FRENCH)	1968	107	5			LOPERT	
BRIDE WORE BOOTS, THE	1946	86		1.5	2.0	PARAMOUNT	
BRIDE WORE RED, THE	1937	103		2.0	2.0	M-G-M	
BRIDES OF DRACULA, THE (BRITISH)	1960	85	4		2.5	UNIVERSAL	
BRIDES OF FU MANCHU, THE (BRITISH)	1966	91	3			SEVEN ARTS	
BRIDGE, THE (GERMAN)	1959	102	6*	4.0	3.0	ALLIED ARTISTS	
BRIDGE AT REMAGEN, THE	1969	115	4	2.5		UNITED ARTISTS	
BRIDGE OF SAN LUIS REY, THE	1944	85				UNITED ARTISTS	
BRIDGE ON THE RIVER KWAI, THE	1957	161	9*	4.0	4.0	COLUMBIA	BEST PICTURE AWARD
BRIDGE TO THE SUN	1961	113	6	3.5	3.0	M-G-M	
BRIDGES AT TOKO-RI, THE	1955	103	5*	3.5	3.5	PARAMOUNT	
BRIEF ENCOUNTER (BRITISH)	1945	86	6*	4.0	4.0	UNIVERSAL	
BRIGADOON	1954	108	6	3.5		M-G-M	
BRIGAND, THE	1952	94		2.5	2.0	COLUMBIA	
BRIGAND OF KANDAHAR, THE (BRITISH)	1965	81	4		2.5	COLUMBIA	
BRIGHAM YOUNG, FRONTIERSMAN	1940	114		3.0	2.0	20th CENTURY FOX	
BRIGHT EYES	1934	83			2.5	20th CENTURY FOX	
BRIGHT LEAF	1950	110	5-6*	2.5	2.5	WARNER BROTHERS	

‡ An asterisk (*) in THE FILM BUFF'S BIBLE column indicates that the film has been rated by the editor and/or staff. All other ratings in this column are based on a consensus of reviews (see NOTES).

TITLE (LEADING ACTORS SHOWN WHERE TWO OR MORE FILMS HAVE THE SAME OR SIMILAR TITLE)	YEAR RELEASED	RUNNING TIME IN MINUTES	THE FILM BUFF'S BIBLE ‡	STEVEN SCHEUER	LEONARD MALTIN	DISTRIBUTOR	COMMENT
BRIGHT LIGHTS	1935	83		2.0	2.0	FIRST NATIONAL	
BRIGHT ROAD	a1953	68	4	2.0	2.0	M-G-M	
BRIGHT VICTORY	1951	97	7	3.5	3.0	UNIVERSAL	
BRIGHTHAVEN EXPRESS (BRITISH)	1950	75		1.5		UNIVERSAL	
BRIGHTON STRANGLER, THE	1945	67		2.0	2.0	RKO	
BRIGHTY OF GRAND CANYON	1967	89	3			FEATURE FILM CORP.	
BRIMSTONE	1949	90	4	3.0	2.0	REPUBLIC	
BRING 'EM BACK ALIVE	1932	70		3.5		RKO	
BRING ME THE VAMPIRE (MEXICAN)	1965	80		1.0		TRANS-INTERNATIONAL	
BRING ON THE GIRLS	1945	92		2.5		PARAMOUNT	
BRING YOUR SMILE ALONG	1955	83	4	2.5		COLUMBIA	
BRINGING UP BABY	1938	102		3.0	3.0	RKO	
BRINK OF LIFE (SWEDISH)	1958	82	5			AJAY FILMS	
BRITISH AGENT	1934	81		2.5	2.5	FIRST NATIONAL	
BRITISH INTELLIGENCE	1940	62		2.0	2.0	WARNER BROTHERS	
BROAD COALITION, THE	1972	90				AUGUST FILMS	
BROAD-MINDED	1931	72		2.0	2.5	FIRST NATIONAL	
BROADWAY	1942	91		3.0	3.0	UNIVERSAL	
BROADWAY GONDOLIER	1935	98		2.0	2.5	WARNER BROTHERS	
BROADWAY LIMITED	1941	74		2.0	2.0	UNITED ARTISTS	
BROADWAY MELODY, THE	1929	110			2.5	M-G-M	BEST PICTURE AWARD 1928/29
BROADWAY MELODY OF 1936	1935	103		3.5	3.0	M-G-M	NOMINATED BEST PICTURE
BROADWAY MELODY OF 1938	1937	110		3.0	2.5	M-G-M	
BROADWAY MELODY OF 1940	1940	102		3.0	3.0	M-G-M	
BROADWAY MUSKETEERS	1938	62		2.0		FIRST NATIONAL	
BROADWAY RHYTHM	1944	114		2.5	2.5	M-G-M	
BROADWAY SERENADE	1939	114		1.5	2.0	M-G-M	
BROADWAY THRU A KEYHOLE	1933	85		2.0		UNITED ARTISTS	
BROKEN ARROW	1950	93	5*	3.0	3.0	20th CENTURY FOX	
BROKEN BLOSSOMS (SILENT)	1919	87				D.W. GRIFFITH PRODS.	
BROKEN HORSESHOE, THE (BRITISH)	1953	80		3.0		VIDEO ARTISTS	
BROKEN JOURNEY (BRITISH)	1948	89		3.0		EAGLE LION	
BROKEN LANCE	1954	96	5-6*	3.0	3.5	20th CENTURY FOX	
BROKEN LAND, THE	1962	60	3			20th CENTURY FOX	
BROKEN LULLABY	a1932	94		3.0	3.0	PARAMOUNT	
BROKEN WINGS, THE (LEBANESE - PIERRE BORDEY)	1964	90		2.5		CONTINENTAL	
BRONCO BUSTER	1952	81		2.5	1.5	UNIVERSAL	
BROTH OF A BOY (IRISH)	1959	77	4	3.0	2.5	KINGSLEY INTERNAT'L	
BROTHER JOHN	1971	94	3			COLUMBIA	
BROTHER ORCHID	1940	91		3.5	3.5	WARNER BROTHERS	
BROTHER RAT	1938	90	3*	3.5	3.0	WARNER BROTHERS	
BROTHER RAT AND A BABY	1940	87		2.0	2.5	WARNER BROTHERS	
BROTHERHOOD, THE	1968	98	2*	2.5		PARAMOUNT	
BROTHERHOOD OF SATAN, THE	1971	92	3			COLUMBIA	
BROTHERHOOD OF THE BELL, THE (T.V.)	1970	100	6*	2.5		CINEMA CENTER 100	
BROTHERLY LOVE	1970	112	2			M-G-M	
BROTHERS, THE (BRITISH)	1947	90		2.0		UNIVERSAL	
BROTHERS-IN-LAW (BRITISH)	1957	94	5	2.5		CONTINENTAL	
BROTHERS IN THE SADDLE	1949	60		3.5		RKO	
BROTHERS KARAMAZOV, THE (YUL BRYNNER, LEE J. COBB)	1958	146	5*	3.0	3.0	M-G-M	
BROTHERS RICO, THE	1957	92		2.5	2.5	COLUMBIA	
BROWNING VERSION, THE (BRITISH)	1951	90	6*	4.0	3.0	UNIVERSAL	
BRUSHFIRE	1962	80	1			PARAMOUNT	
BRUTE CORPS	1972	90				GENERAL FILM CORP.	
BRUTE FORCE	1947	98	5	3.5	3.5	UNIVERSAL	
BRUTE MAN, THE	1946	60			1.5	PRODUCERS RELEASING	
BUBBLE, THE	1967	112	3			ARCH OBOLER	
BUCCANEER, THE (FREDRIC MARCH, FRANCISKA GAAL)	1962	90				PARAMOUNT	
BUCCANEER, THE (YUL BRYNNER, CHARLTON HESTON)	1958	121		3.0	3.0	PARAMOUNT	
BUCCANEER'S GIRL	1950	77		2.0	2.0	UNIVERSAL	
BUCHANAN RIDES ALONE	1958	78	4	3.0	2.5	COLUMBIA	
BUCK AND THE PREACHER	1972	102	4			COLUMBIA	
BUCK BENNY RIDES AGAIN	1940	82	3*	2.5	2.0	PARAMOUNT	
BUCK PRIVATES	1941	84		3.5	2.5	UNIVERSAL	
BUCK PRIVATES COME HOME	1947	77		2.0	3.0	UNIVERSAL	
BUCKET OF BLOOD, A	1959	66		2.5	1.5	AMERICAN-INTERNAT'L	
BUCKSKIN	1968	97	2	1.5		PARAMOUNT	
BUCKSKIN LADY, THE	1957	66	1			UNITED ARTISTS	
BUDDENBROOKS (GERMAN)	1964	88		2.5		SCREEN GEMS	
BUFFALO BILL	1944	90		2.5	2.5	20th CENTURY FOX	
BUFFALO GUN	1962	72		1.0		ALLIED ARTISTS	
BUGLE SOUNDS, THE	1941	110		2.5	2.0	M-G-M	
BUGLES IN THE AFTERNOON	1952	85	3*	3.0	2.5	WARNER BROTHERS	
BULLDOG DRUMMOND	1929	90				UNITED ARTISTS	
BULLDOG DRUMMOND AT BAY (BRITISH - JOHN LODGE)	1937	62			-	REPUBLIC	
BULLDOG DRUMMOND AT BAY (RON RANDELL)	1947	70			-	COLUMBIA	
BULLDOG DRUMMOND COMES BACK	1937	64			-	PARAMOUNT	
BULLDOG DRUMMOND ESCAPES	1937	65			-	PARAMOUNT	
BULLDOG DRUMMOND IN AFRICA	1938	60			-	PARAMOUNT	
BULLDOG DRUMMOND STRIKES BACK (RONALD COLEMAN)	1934	83			-	UNITED ARTISTS	
BULLDOG DRUMMOND STRIKES BACK (RON RANDELL)	1947	65			-	COLUMBIA	
BULLDOG DRUMMOND'S BRIDE	1939	55			-	PARAMOUNT	
BULLDOG DRUMMOND'S PERIL	1938	66			-	PARAMOUNT	
BULLDOG DRUMMOND'S REVENGE	1937	60			-	PARAMOUNT	

‡ An asterisk (*) in THE FILM BUFF'S BIBLE column indicates that the film has been rated by the editor and/or staff. All other ratings in this column are based on a consensus of reviews (see NOTES).

TITLE (LEADING ACTORS SHOWN WHERE TWO OR MORE FILMS HAVE THE SAME OR SIMILAR TITLE)	YEAR RELEASED	RUNNING TIME IN MINUTES	THE FILM BUFF'S BIBLE ‡	STEVEN SCHEUER	LEONARD MALTIN	DISTRIBUTOR	COMMENT
BULLDOG DRUMMOND'S SECRET POLICE	1939	56			-	PARAMOUNT	
BULLET FOR A BADMAN	1964	80	3	2.0	2.5	UNIVERSAL	
BULLET FOR JOEY, A	1955	85		2.0	2.5	UNITED ARTISTS	
BULLET FOR PRETTY BOY, A	1970	91	2			AMERICAN-INTERNAT'L	
BULLET FOR SANDOVAL	1970	91	1			UMC PICTURES	
BULLET FOR STEFANO (ITALIAN)	1950	96			2.0	LUX FILM AMERICA	
BULLET FOR THE GENERAL, A (ITALIAN)	1967	115		1.0		AVCO-EMBASSY	
BULLET IS WAITING, A	1954	82		2.5	2.5	COLUMBIA	
BULLETS OR BALLOTS	1936	77	4*	3.0	3.0	FIRST NATIONAL	
BULLFIGHT (FRENCH, DOCUMENTARY)	1956	76		3.5		JANUS FILMS	
BULLFIGHTER AND THE LADY, THE	1951	87	6	3.5	3.0	REPUBLIC	
BULLFIGHTERS, THE	1945	61		1.5	2.0	20th CENTURY FOX	
BULLITT	1968	113	5*	4.0		WARNER BROTHERS	
BULLWHIP	1958	80		2.5	2.0	ALLIED ARTISTS	
BUNCO SQUAD	1950	67	4			RKO	
BUNDLE OF JOY	1956	98		2.5	2.0	RKO	
BUNNY LAKE IS MISSING (BRITISH)	1965	107		3.0	2.0	COLUMBIA	
BUNNY O'HARE	1971	92	3			AMERICAN-INTERNAT'L	
BUONA SERA, MRS CAMPBELL	1969	111	6	3.5		UNITED ARTISTS	
BUREAU OF MISSING PERSONS	1933	79		2.5	2.5	FIRST NATIONAL	
BURGLAR, THE (DAN DURYEA, JAYNE MANSFIELD)	1957	90		1.5	1.5	COLUMBIA	
BURGLARS, THE (FRENCH - JEAN-PAUL BELMONDO)	1971	120	4			COLUMBIA	
BURMA CONVOY	1941	72		2.0	2.5	UNIVERSAL	
BURMESE HARP, THE (JAPANESE)	1956	116	6			BRANDON	
BURN! (ITALIAN)	a1970	112	5	3.0		UNITED ARTISTS	
BURN 'EM UP O'CONNOR	1939	70		1.5		M-G-M	
BURN, WITCH, BURN (BRITISH)	1962	90	4	2.5	3.0	AMERICAN-INTERNAT'L	
BURNING HILLS, THE	1956	94		1.5	2.0	WARNER BROTHERS	
BURY ME AN ANGEL	1971		1			NEW WORLD	
BURY ME DEAD	1947	71		2.5		EAGLE LION	
BUS, THE (DOCUMENTARY)	1965	62	6			HARRISON PICTURES	
BUS IS COMING	1971	101				WM. THOMPSON, INT'L	
BUS RILEY'S BACK IN TOWN	1965	93		2.0	2.5	UNIVERSAL	
BUS STOP	a1956	96	5*	3.0	3.5	20th CENTURY FOX	
BUSH CHRISTMAS (AUSTRALIAN)	1947	76		3.0		UNIVERSAL	
BUSHBABY, THE	1970	101	3			M-G-M	
BUSHIDO (JAPANESE)	1963		5			TOHO	
BUSHWACKERS, THE	1951	70		1.0	1.5	REALART	
BUSSES ROAR	1942	61		2.0		WARNER BROTHERS	
BUSTER KEATON STORY, THE	1957	91	4*	2.0	1.5	PARAMOUNT	
BUSY BODY, THE	1967	90	4	2.5	2.5	PARAMOUNT	
BUT I DON'T WANT TO GET MARRIED (T.V.)	1970	75	4*	2.5		ABC FILMS	
BUT NOT FOR ME	1959	105		2.5	3.0	PARAMOUNT	
BUTCH CASSIDY AND THE SUNDANCE KID	1969	110	9*	4.0		20th CENTURY FOX	NOMINATED BEST PICTURE
BUTCH MINDS THE BABY	1942	76		2.5		UNIVERSAL	
BUTTERCUP CHAIN, THE (BRITISH)	1970	95	3			COLUMBIA	
BUTTERFIELD 8	1960	109	6*	2.5		M-G-M	
BUTTERFLIES ARE FREE	1972	93	7			COLUMBIA	
BUY ME THAT TOWN	1941	70		2.5		PARAMOUNT	
BWANA DEVIL	1953	79		1.5	1.5	UNITED ARTISTS	
BY LOVE POSSESSED	1961	115	4	2.5	3.0	UNITED ARTISTS	
BY THE LIGHT OF THE SILVERY MOON	1953	102		3.0	2.5	WARNER BROTHERS	
BYE BYE BIRDIE	1963	111		3.5	2.5	COLUMBIA	
BYE BYE BRAVERMAN	1968	94	4	3.0		WARNER BROTHERS	
C.C. AND COMPANY	1970	94	2			AVCO-EMBASSY	
C-MAN	1949	75			2.0	FOUR CONTINENTS	
CABARET (GERMAN - PAUL HENREID, EVA KERBLER)	1954	104				SAM BAKER ASSOCIATES	
CABARET (LIZA MINNELLI, MICHAEL YORK)	1972	120	9*			ALLIED ARTISTS	
CABIN IN THE COTTON	1932	77		2.5	2.5	FIRST NATIONAL	
CABIN IN THE SKY	1943	98		3.0		M-G-M	
CABINET OF CALIGARI, THE	1962	104		1.5	2.5	20th CENTURY FOX	
CABINET OF DR CALIGARI, THE (GERMAN, SILENT)	1919	81	2*			SAMUEL GOLDWYN	
CABIRIA (ITALIAN - GIULIETTA MASINA)	a1957	110	3*	3.5	3.5	LOPERT	
CACTUS FLOWER	1969	103	6-7*			COLUMBIA	
CACTUS IN THE SNOW	1972	90	5			GENERAL FILM CORP.	
CADDY, THE	1953	95		2.5	2.0	PARAMOUNT	
CADET GIRL	1941	69		1.0		20th CENTURY FOX	
CADETS ON PARADE	1942	63		2.0		COLUMBIA	
CAESAR AND CLEOPATRA (BRITISH)	1945	130	6	3.0	3.5	UNITED ARTISTS	
CAESAR THE CONQUERER (ITALIAN)	1962	103		1.5		TELEWIDE SYSTEMS	
CAFE METROPOLE	1937	83		3.0		20th CENTURY FOX	
CAFE SOCIETY	1939	83		2.5	2.5	PARAMOUNT	
CAGE OF EVIL	1960	70	3			UNITED ARTISTS	
CAGE OF GOLD (BRITISH)	1950	83	4	2.5		ELLIS FILMS	
CAGED	1950	96	6	3.5	3.0	WARNER BROTHERS	
CAGED FURY	1948	60	3			PARAMOUNT	
CAIN AND MABEL	1936	90		2.0	2.0	WARNER BROTHERS	
CAINE MUTINY, THE	1954	125	8*	3.5	4.0	COLUMBIA	NOMINATED BEST PICTURE
CAIN'S WAY	1971	95				FANFARE	
CAIRO (JEANETTE MACDONALD, ROBERT YOUNG)	1942	101		1.5	2.0	M-G-M	
CAIRO (GEORGE SANDERS, RICHARD JOHNSON)	1963	91	3			M-G-M	

‡ An asterisk (*) in THE FILM BUFF'S BIBLE column indicates that the film has been rated by the editor and/or staff. All other ratings in this column are based on a consensus of reviews (see NOTES).

TITLE (LEADING ACTORS SHOWN WHERE TWO OR MORE FILMS HAVE THE SAME OR SIMILAR TITLE)	YEAR RELEASED	RUNNING TIME IN MINUTES	THE FILM BUFF'S BIBLE ‡	STEVEN SCHEUER	LEONARD MALTIN	DISTRIBUTOR	COMMENT
CAIRO ROAD (BRITISH)	1950	90	3			CONTINENTAL	
CALAMITY JANE	1953	101		2.5	3.0	WARNER BROTHERS	
CALAMITY JANE AND SAM BASS	1949	85	3	1.5	1.5	UNIVERSAL	
CALCUTTA	1947	83		2.0	2.5	PARAMOUNT	
CALENDAR GIRL	1947	88		2.0		REPUBLIC	
CALIFORNIA (BARBARA STANWYCK, RAY MILLAND)	1947	97	3*	3.0	2.5	PARAMOUNT	
CALIFORNIA (JOCK MAHONEY, FAITH DOMERGUE)	1963	77		1.5		AMERICAN-INTERNAT'L	
CALIFORNIA CONQUEST	1952	79	3	2.5	2.5	COLUMBIA	
CALIFORNIA PASSAGE	1950	90	4	2.5		REPUBLIC	
CALIFORNIA STRAIGHT AHEAD	1937	67			2.0	UNIVERSAL	
CALL A MESSENGER	1939	65			-	UNIVERSAL	
CALL IT A DAY	1937	89		3.0	2.0	WARNER BROTHERS	
CALL ME BWANA (BRITISH)	1963	103		2.5	2.0	UNITED ARTISTS	
CALL ME GENIUS (BRITISH)	1961	105	4	2.5		CONTINENTAL	
CALL ME MADAM	1953	117	6	3.5	3.0	20th CENTURY FOX	
CALL ME MISTER	1951	95		2.5	2.5	20th CENTURY FOX	
CALL NORTHSIDE 777	a1948	111	6*	3.5	3.5	20th CENTURY FOX	
CALL OF THE SOUTH SEAS	1944	55		1.0		REPUBLIC	
CALL OF THE WILD	1935	95		3.0	3.0	UNITED ARTISTS	
CALL OUT THE MARINES	1942	67		2.5		RKO	
CALLAWAY WENT THATAWAY	1951	81		3.0	2.5	M-G-M	
CALLING ALL HUSBANDS	1940	64		1.5		WARNER BROTHERS	
CALLING BULLDOG DRUMMOND (BRITISH)	1951	80		2.5	-	M-G-M	
CALLING DR DEATH	1943	63		3.0	2.5	UNIVERSAL	
CALLING DR GILLESPIE	1942	82		2.0	-	M-G-M	
CALLING DR KILDARE	1939	86		2.5	-	M-G-M	
CALLING HOMICIDE	1956	61		2.5	1.5	ALLIED ARTISTS	
CALLING NORTHSIDE 777	a1948	111	6*	3.5	3.5	20th CENTURY FOX	
CALLING PHILO VANCE	1940	62				WARNER BROTHERS	
CALTIKI, THE IMMORTAL MONSTER (ITALIAN)	1959	76		2.0	2.0	ALLIED ARTISTS	
CALYPSO HEAT WAVE	1957	86		1.5		COLUMBIA	
CALYPSO JOE	1957	76	3	1.5		ALLIED ARTISTS	
CAMELOT	1967	179	6	3.0		WARNER BROTHERS	
CAMERAMAN, THE (SILENT)	1928	78		4.0		M-G-M	
CAMILLE	1936	108		3.5	3.5	M-G-M	
CAMILLE 2000	1969	115	3			AUDUBON	
CAMP ON BLOOD ISLAND, THE (BRITISH)	1958	81		2.0	2.0	COLUMBIA	
CAMPBELL'S KINGDOM (BRITISH)	1957	100		3.0	2.0	J. ARTHUR RANK	
CAN-CAN	1960	131	4*	2.5	2.5	20th CENTURY FOX	
CAN HEIRONYMUS MERKIN EVER FORGET MERCY HUMPPE AND FIND TRUE HAPPINESS? (BRITISH)	1969	104	3			REGIONAL	
CANADIAN PACIFIC	1949	95		2.5	2.5	20th CENTURY FOX	
CANADIANS, THE	1961	85	3*	1.5	2.5	20th CENTURY FOX	TITLE SONG IS GOOD
CANAL ZONE	1942	78		2.0		COLUMBIA	
CANARIS (MASTER SPY) (GERMAN)	a1954	92		2.5	2.0	DOMINANT PICTURES	
CANARY MURDER CASE	1929	81			-	PARAMOUNT	
CANDIDATE, THE (MAMIE VAN DOREN, JUNE WILKINSON)	a1964	84	1			ATLANTIC PICTURES	
CANDIDATE, THE (ROBERT REDFORD, PETER BOYLE)	1972	110	7			WARNER BROTHERS	
CANDIDATE FOR MURDER (BRITISH)	1962	60		2.0	2.5	SCHOENFELD FILM DIST.	
CANDIDE (FRENCH)	1961	90	4			UNION FILMS	
CANDY	1968	119	1	1.0		CINERAMA RELEASING	
CANGACIERO - THE STORY OF AN OUTLAW (BRAZILIAN)	1953	91		3.0		COLUMBIA	
CANNIBAL ATTACK	1954	69		1.5	-	COLUMBIA	
CANNON (T.V.)	1971	100	4*	2.5		QM PRODS.	
CANNON FOR CORDOBA	1970	104	3			UNITED ARTISTS	
CANON CITY	a1948	82	6	3.0		EAGLE LION	
CAN'T HELP SINGING	1944	89		2.5	2.5	UNIVERSAL	
CANTERVILLE GHOST, THE	1944	96		3.0	3.0	M-G-M	
CANYON CITY	a1948	82	6	3.0		EAGLE LION	
CANYON CROSSROADS	1955	83		2.5	2.5	UNITED ARTISTS	
CANYON PASSAGE	1946	90		3.0	3.0	UNIVERSAL	
CANYON RIVER	1956	80		1.5	1.5	ALLIED ARTISTS	
CAPE CANAVERAL MONSTERS, THE	1960	71		1.0		M & A ALEXANDER	
CAPE FEAR	1962	105	4*	3.0	3.0	UNIVERSAL	
CAPER OF THE GOLDEN BULLS, THE	a1967	103	4	2.5		AVCO-EMBASSY	
CAPRICE	1967	98	3	2.0		20th CENTURY FOX	
CAPRICE OF 'DEAR CAROLINE' (FRENCH)	1952	85		2.0		GALA-CAMEO-POLY	
CAPRICIOUS SUMMER (CZECH)	1968	75	5	3.0		SIGMA III	
CAPTAIN APACHE (BRITISH)	1971	94	1			SCOTIA INTERNATIONAL	
CAPTAIN BLACKJACK	1952	90	2	1.5		UNITED ARTISTS	
CAPTAIN BLOOD (ERROL FLYNN, OLIVIA DE HAVILLAND)	1935	119		3.5	3.5	FIRST NATIONAL	NOMINATED BEST PICTURE
CAPTAIN BLOOD (FRENCH - JEAN MARAIS)	1960	95			2.0	E.J. FANCEY	
CAPTAIN BOYCOTT (BRITISH)	1947	93	6*	3.5	3.5	UNIVERSAL	
CAPTAIN CAREY, U.S.A.	1950	83	4	2.5	2.5	PARAMOUNT	
CAPTAIN CAUTION	1940	85		2.0	2.0	UNITED ARTISTS	
CAPTAIN CHINA	1950	97		2.0	2.0	PARAMOUNT	
CAPTAIN EDDIE	1945	107		2.5	2.5	20th CENTURY FOX	
CAPTAIN FALCON (ITALIAN)	1958	97		1.5	1.5	AVCO-EMBASSY	
CAPTAIN FROM CASTILE	1947	140	4*	2.5	2.5	20th CENTURY FOX	
CAPTAIN FROM KOEPENICK (GERMAN)	1956	93	7	3.5		HAL ROACH	
CAPTAIN FURY	1939	91	4*	3.0	3.0	UNITED ARTISTS	
CAPTAIN HATES THE SEA	1934	92			2.0	COLUMBIA	
CAPTAIN HORATIO HORNBLOWER	1951	117	5*	3.5	3.0	WARNER BROTHERS	
CAPTAIN IS A LADY, THE	1940	63		2.0	2.0	M-G-M	

‡ An asterisk (*) in THE FILM BUFF'S BIBLE column indicates that the film has been rated by the editor and/or staff. All other ratings in this column are based on a consensus of reviews (see NOTES).

TITLE (LEADING ACTORS SHOWN WHERE TWO OR MORE FILMS HAVE THE SAME OR SIMILAR TITLE)	YEAR RELEASED	RUNNING TIME IN MINUTES	THE FILM BUFF'S BIBLE ‡	STEVEN SCHEUER	LEONARD MALTIN	DISTRIBUTOR	COMMENT
CAPTAIN JANUARY	1936	75		2.0	2.5	20th CENTURY FOX	
CAPTAIN JOHN SMITH AND POCAHONTAS	1953	75		1.5	1.5	UNITED ARTISTS	
CAPTAIN KIDD	1945	89		1.5	2.0	UNITED ARTISTS	
CAPTAIN KIDD AND THE SLAVE GIRL	1954	83		1.0	2.0	UNITED ARTISTS	
CAPTAIN LIGHTFOOT	1955	91		2.5	2.5	UNIVERSAL	
CAPTAIN MEPHISTO AND THE TRANSFORMATION MACHINE	1945	100		2.5	2.0	REPUBLIC	RE-EDITED SERIAL
CAPTAIN MILKSHAKE	1972	100	3			TWI NATIONAL	
CAPTAIN NEMO AND THE UNDERWATER CITY (BRITISH)	1969	106	3			M-G-M	
CAPTAIN NEWMAN, M.D.	1964	126	5*	3.0	3.0	UNIVERSAL	
CAPTAIN PIRATE	1952	85	4			COLUMBIA	
CAPTAIN SCARLETT	1953	75			1.5	UNITED ARTISTS	
CAPTAIN SINBAD	1963	85		1.0	2.5	M-G-M	
CAPTAIN TUGBOAT ANNIE	1945	60			2.0	REPUBLIC	
CAPTAINS COURAGEOUS	1937	116	6*	3.5	4.0	M-G-M	NOMINATED BEST PICTURE
CAPTAINS OF THE CLOUDS	1942	113		3.0	3.0	WARNER BROTHERS	
CAPTAIN'S PARADISE, THE (BRITISH)	1953	93	7*	4.0	3.0	UNITED ARTISTS	
CAPTAIN'S TABLE, THE (BRITISH)	1959	90	4*	2.5	2.0	20th CENTURY FOX	
CAPTIVE CITY, THE	1952	91	5	3.5		UNITED ARTISTS	
CAPTIVE GIRL	1950	73		1.5		COLUMBIA	
CAPTIVE HEART, THE (BRITISH)	1946	86	4*	4.0		UNIVERSAL	
CAPTIVE WILD WOMAN	1943	60		2.0		UNIVERSAL	
CAPTIVE WOMEN	1952	65	2	1.5		RKO	
CAPTURE, THE	1950	81	4	3.5	2.5	RKO	
CAPTURED	1933	72		2.5	2.5	WARNER BROTHERS	
CAR 99	1935	68		3.0		PARAMOUNT	
CARAVAN (LORETTA YOUNG, CHARLES BOYER)	1934	101			2.5	20th CENTURY FOX	
CARAVAN (BRITISH - STEWART GRANGER, JEAN KENT)	1946	80		2.5		EAGLE LION	
CARBINE WILLIAMS	1952	91		3.0	3.0	M-G-M	
CARDINAL, THE	1963	175	6	3.0	2.5	COLUMBIA	
CARDINAL RICHELIEU	1935	83			2.5	UNITED ARTISTS	
CAREER (ANTHONY FRANCIOSA, DEAN MARTIN)	1959	105	5*	3.5	3.0	PARAMOUNT	
CAREER GIRL (JUNE WILKINSON)	1960	61	2		1.5	ASTOR	
CAREFREE	1938	80		3.0	3.0	RKO	
CAREFUL - SOFT SHOULDER	1942	69		2.5		20th CENTURY FOX	
CARELESS YEARS, THE	1957	70	5			UNITED ARTISTS	
CARESSED	1965	81	2			JOSEPH BRENNER	
CARETAKERS, THE	a1963	97	4*	1.5	3.0	UNITED ARTISTS	
CAREY TREATMENT, THE	1972	100	4			M-G-M	
CARGO TO CAPETOWN	1950	80		2.5	1.5	COLUMBIA	
CARIB GOLD	1957	71		2.0		PREMIER PICTURES	
CARIBBEAN	1952	97		2.0	2.0	PARAMOUNT	
CARIBBEAN HAWK (SPANISH)	1964	115		1.5		TELEWIDE SYSTEMS	
CARIBBEAN MYSTERY	1945	65		2.0		20th CENTURY FOX	
CARIBOO TRAIL, THE	1950	81		2.5	2.5	20th CENTURY FOX	
CARMEN, BABY (YUGOSLAVIAN)	1967	90	1			AUDUBON	
CARMEN JONES	1954	105	5*	3.5		20th CENTURY FOX	
CARNAL KNOWLEDGE	1971	100	6*			AVCO-EMBASSY	
CARNATION FRANK (GERMAN)	1961	85		1.0			
CARNEGIE HALL	1947	154	4	2.0		UNITED ARTISTS	
CARNIVAL (BRITISH - SALLY GRAY, MICHAEL WILDING)	1946	93		3.0		J. ARTHUR RANK	
CARNIVAL IN COSTA RICA	1947	95		2.0	2.0	20th CENTURY FOX	
CARNIVAL IN FLANDERS (FRENCH)	1935	90	2*			INTERFILM CO.	
CARNIVAL OF SOULS	1962	80		2.5		HERTS-LION INT'L	
CARNIVAL STORY	1954	95		2.5	2.0	RKO	
CAROLINA BLUES	1944	81		2.0		COLUMBIA	
CAROLINA CANNONBALL	1955	74		1.5	1.5	REPUBLIC	
CAROUSEL	1956	128	6*	3.5		20th CENTURY FOX	
CARPET OF HORROR, THE (GERMAN)	1962	93		1.5		UCC FILMS	
CARPETBAGGERS, THE	1964	150		1.5	2.5	PARAMOUNT	
CARRIE	1952	118		3.5	2.5	PARAMOUNT	
CARRY IT ON (DOCUMENTARY)	a1970	80	6			MARON FILMS, LTD.	
CARRY ON ADMIRAL (BRITISH)	a1957	82	4		2.0	GEORGE K. ARTHUR	
CARRY ON CABBY (BRITISH)	1963	91	3			GOVERNOR	
CARRY ON CAMPING (BRITISH)	1969	88	4			AMERICAN-INTERNAT'L	
CARRY ON CLEO (BRITISH)	1965	92	4	2.5	2.5	GOVERNOR	
CARRY ON CONSTABLE (BRITISH)	1960	86	3	2.0		GOVERNOR	
CARRY ON CRUISING (BRITISH)	1962	87		2.0		GOVERNOR	
CARRY ON HENRY VIII (BRITISH)	1972	90	1			AMERICAN-INTERNAT'L	
CARRY ON NURSE (BRITISH)	1959	90		2.5	3.0	GOVERNOR	
CARRY ON REGARDLESS (BRITISH)	1961	87		2.0		GOVERNOR	
CARRY ON SERGEANT (BRITISH)	1958	83	4	2.5	2.0	GOVERNOR	
CARRY ON SPYING (BRITISH)	1964	83	4	2.5	2.5	GOVERNOR	
CARRY ON TEACHER (BRITISH)	1959	86	5	2.5		GOVERNOR	
CARRY ON TV (BRITISH)	a1963	88	3	1.5		GOVERNOR	
CARRY ON VENUS (BRITISH)	1964	87		2.5		GOVERNOR	
CARSON CITY	1952	87		2.5	2.0	WARNER BROTHERS	
CARTER'S ARMY (T.V.)	1970	80	5*	2.5		ABC FILMS	
CARTHAGE IN FLAMES (ITALIAN)	1959	93	2	2.0	2.0	COLUMBIA	
CARTOUCHE (ITALIAN - RICHARD BASEHART)	1954	73		2.0		RKO	
CARTOUCHE (FRENCH - JEAN-PAUL BELMONDO)	1962	115	5	3.0		AVCO-EMBASSY	
CARVE HER NAME WITH PRIDE (BRITISH)	1958	116		4.0		LOPERT	
CASA RICORDI (ITALIAN)	a1954	112		2.0	2.0	CONTINENTAL	
CASABLANCA	1943	102	8*	3.5	4.0	WARNER BROTHERS	BEST PICTURE AWARD
CASANOVA (ITALIAN - GABRIELE FERZETTI)	1955	90		1.5		ABC FILMS	

‡ An asterisk (*) in THE FILM BUFF'S BIBLE column indicates that the film has been rated by the editor and/or staff. All other ratings in this column are based on a consensus of reviews (see NOTES).

TITLE (LEADING ACTORS SHOWN WHERE TWO OR MORE FILMS HAVE THE SAME OR SIMILAR TITLE)	YEAR RELEASED	RUNNING TIME IN MINUTES	THE FILM BUFF'S BIBLE ‡	STEVEN SCHEUER	LEONARD MALTIN	DISTRIBUTOR	COMMENT
CASANOVA BROWN	1944	94		2.5	2.5	RKO	
CASANOVA IN BURLESQUE	1944	74		1.5	2.0	REPUBLIC	
CASANOVA '70 (ITALIAN)	1965	113	5	3.0		AVCO-EMBASSY	
CASANOVA'S BIG NIGHT	1954	86		2.0	2.5	PARAMOUNT	
CASBAH	1948	94	3	2.5	2.5	UNIVERSAL	
CASE AGAINST BROOKLYN, THE	1958	82		2.0	1.5	COLUMBIA	
CASE AGAINST MRS AMES, THE	1936	85		2.5	2.5	PARAMOUNT	
CASE OF DR LAURENT, THE (FRENCH)	1957	110	6	4.0	2.0	TRANS-LUX DIST.	
CASE OF LENA SMITH, THE (SILENT)	1929	80				PARAMOUNT	BELIEVED LOST
CASE OF MRS LORING, THE (BRITISH)	a1958	86		2.0	2.5	NTA PICTURES	
CASE OF THE MISSING SWITCHBOARD OPERATOR, THE	a1967	70	6			BRANDON	(YUGOSLAVIAN)
CASE OF THE MUKKINESE BATTLEHORN, THE (BRITISH)	1955	29	6			UNION FILMS	
CASE OF THE RED MONKEY (BRITISH)	1955	73		1.5	2.0	ALLIED ARTISTS	
CASE 33: ANTWERP (GERMAN)	1965	85		1.5		PARKSIDE PRODS.	
CASH MCCALL	1960	102		2.5	2.5	WARNER BROTHERS	
CASH ON DELIVERY (BRITISH)	1956	82			2.0	RKO	
CASH ON DEMAND (BRITISH)	1962	84	4			COLUMBIA	
CASINO DE PARIS (GERMAN)	1957	85		2.0		RIZZOLI FILM	
CASINO MURDER CASE	1935	85		2.5	-	M-G-M	
CASINO ROYALE (BRITISH)	1967	131	2*	2.5	2.5	COLUMBIA	
CASQUE D'OR (FRENCH)	a1952	96	5			DISCINA INTERNAT'L	
CASS TIMBERLANE	1948	119		2.5	2.5	M-G-M	
CAST A DARK SHADOW (BRITISH)	1955	82	4*	2.5	3.0	DIST. CORP. OF AMER.	
CAST A GIANT SHADOW	1966	142	4	2.5		UNITED ARTISTS	
CAST A LONG SHADOW	1959	82		1.5	1.5	UNITED ARTISTS	
CASTA DIVA	1954	100		2.0		CONTINENTAL	
CASTILIAN, THE (SPANISH)	1963	129	3	2.0	2.5	WARNER BROTHERS	
CASTLE, THE (GERMAN)	1968	93	3			CONTINENTAL	ENGLISH LANGUAGE
CASTLE IN THE AIR (BRITISH)	1952	92	4	2.5		STRATFORD PICS.	
CASTLE KEEP	1969	105	4*	2.5		COLUMBIA	
CASTLE OF BLOOD (ITALIAN)	a1964	85	3	2.0		WOOLNER BROTHERS	
CASTLE OF TERROR, THE (ITALIAN - BARBARA STEELE)	a1964	85	3	2.0		WOOLNER BROTHERS	
CASTLE OF TERROR, THE (ITALIAN - ROSSANA PODESTA)	a1965	82	3	1.5	2.5	ZODIAC FILMS	ENGLISH LANGUAGE
CASTLE OF THE LIVING DEAD (ITALIAN)	1964	90				AMERICAN-INTERNAT'L	
CASTLE ON THE HUDSON	1940	77	3*	2.5	3.0	WARNER BROTHERS	
CASTLES IN SPAIN (FRENCH)	1954	90		2.0			
CAT, THE (FR. - FRANCOISE ARNOUL, BERNARD BLIER)	1958	108	5	2.5		ELLIS FILMS	
CAT, THE (PEGGY ANN GARNER, ROGER PERRY)	1966	87		2.5	1.0	AVCO-EMBASSY	
CAT AND MOUSE (BRITISH - LEE PATTERSON)	1958	79		1.5		EROS FILMS	
CAT AND MOUSE (GERMAN - LARS BRANDT)	1970	92	3			GROVE PRESS	
CAT AND THE CANARY, THE (SILENT - LAURA LA PLANTE)	1927	86			3.0	UNIVERSAL	
CAT AND THE CANARY, THE (BOB HOPE, P. GODDARD)	1939	74		3.0		PARAMOUNT	
CAT AND THE FIDDLE, THE	1934	90		3.0	2.5	M-G-M	
CAT BALLOU	1965	96	8*	4.0	3.5	COLUMBIA	
CAT BURGLAR, THE	1961	65	3			UNITED ARTISTS	
CAT CREEPS, THE	1946	58		1.5	1.0	UNIVERSAL	
CAT GIRL (BRITISH)	1957	69		2.0	1.5	AMERICAN-INTERNAT'L	
CAT ON A HOT TIN ROOF	1958	108	7*	4.0	3.5	M-G-M	NOMINATED BEST PICTURE
CAT O'NINE TAILS, THE	1971	112	2	1.0		NATIONAL GENERAL	
CAT PEOPLE	1942	73		3.5	3.5	RKO	
CATCH-22	1970	121	5*			PARAMOUNT	
CATERED AFFAIR, THE	a1956	93	7*	3.0	3.0	M-G-M	
CATHERINE OF RUSSIA (GERMAN)	1962	105		2.0		NTA PICTURES	
CATHERINE THE GREAT (BRITISH)	1934	92		2.5	2.5	UNITED ARTISTS	
CATLOW	1971	103	4			M-G-M	
CATS, THE (SWEDISH)	1964	93	1			NAT'L SHOWMANSHIP	
CATTLE DRIVE	1951	77		2.5	2.5	UNIVERSAL	
CATTLE EMPIRE	1958	83		2.5	2.0	20th CENTURY FOX	
CATTLE KING	1963	88	3			M-G-M	
CATTLE QUEEN OF MONTANA	1954	88		2.0	2.5	RKO	
CATTLE TOWN	1952	71		2.0	2.0	WARNER BROTHERS	
CATWOMEN OF THE MOON	1954	65	1			ASTOR	
CAUGHT (JAMES MASON, BARBARA BEL GEDDES)	1949	88	5	3.0	3.0	M-G-M	
CAUGHT IN THE ACT (BRIGETTE EVANS, S. HOLLISTER)	1966	82	4			WILLIAM MISHKIN	
CAUGHT IN THE DRAFT	1941	82		3.5	3.0	PARAMOUNT	
CAULDRON OF BLOOD (SPANISH)	a1968	101				CANNON RELEASING	
CAUSE FOR ALARM	1951	74		2.0	2.5	M-G-M	
CAVALCADE	1933	109	5*		3.0	20th CENTURY FOX	BEST PICTURE AWARD 1932/33
CAVALIER IN THE DEVIL'S CASTLE (ITALIAN)	1962	87		1.5		TELEWIDE SYSTEMS	
CAVALLERIA RUSTICANA (ITALIAN - MARIO DEL MONICO)	1952	53		2.0		ASTOR	
CAVALRY COMMAND	1964	81	3	1.5		PARAMOUNT	
CAVALRY SCOUT	1951	78		1.5	2.0	MONOGRAM	
CAVE OF OUTLAWS	1951	75		2.0	2.0	UNIVERSAL	
CAVERN, THE	1965	83	2			20th CENTURY FOX	
CEASE FIRE	1954	75		3.0		PARAMOUNT	
CEILING ZERO	1935	95		3.5	3.0	WARNER BROTHERS	
CELEBRATION AT BIG SUR (DOCUMENTARY)	1971	82	4			20th CENTURY FOX	
CELL 2455, DEATH ROW	1955	77		2.5	2.0	COLUMBIA	
CENSORSHIP IN DENMARK (DOCUMENTARY)	1969	75	3			SHERPIX	
CENTENNIAL SUMMER	1946	102		2.0	2.5	20th CENTURY FOX	
CENTURION, THE (ITALIAN)	1961	78	1	1.5		PRODUCERS INTERNAT'L	
CEREMONY, THE (BRITISH)	1963	106		2.0	2.5	UNITED ARTISTS	
CERTAIN SMILE, A	1958	106		2.5	2.5	20th CENTURY FOX	
CHAD HANNA	1940	86		2.0	2.0	20th CENTURY FOX	

‡ An asterisk (*) in THE FILM BUFF'S BIBLE column indicates that the film has been rated by the editor and/or staff. All other ratings in this column are based on a consensus of reviews (see NOTES).

TITLE (LEADING ACTORS SHOWN WHERE TWO OR MORE FILMS HAVE THE SAME OR SIMILAR TITLE)	YEAR RELEASED	RUNNING TIME IN MINUTES	THE FILM BUFF'S BIBLE ‡	STEVEN SCHEUER	LEONARD MALTIN	DISTRIBUTOR	COMMENT
CHAFED ELBOWS	1967	63	5			IMPACT FILMS	
CHAIN LIGHTING	1950	94		2.5	2.0	WARNER BROTHERS	
CHAIN OF EVIDENCE	1957	64		2.0	1.5	ALLIED ARTISTS	
CHAINED	1934	71		2.0	2.5	M-G-M	
CHAIRMAN, THE (BRITISH)	1969	102	3	2.0		20th CENTURY FOX	
CHALK GARDEN, THE (BRITISH)	1964	106	7*	3.5	3.0	UNIVERSAL	
CHALLENGE, THE (TOM CONWAY, JUNE VINCENT)	1948	68	3			20th CENTURY FOX	
CHALLANGE, THE (BRITISH - JAYNE MANSFIELD)	a1960	89		1.5	2.0	VALIANT	
CHALLENGE, THE (T.V. - DARREN MCGAVIN)	1970	90	4*			20th CENTURY FOX	
CHALLENGE FOR ROBIN HOOD, A (BRITISH)	1968	85	4	3.0		20th CENTURY FOX	
CHALLENGE OF THE GLADIATOR (ITALIAN)	1964	90		1.5		AMERICAN-INTERNAT'L	
CHALLENGE TO LASSIE	1949	76		2.5	2.0	M-G-M	
CHALLENGERS, THE (T.V.)	1969	100		2.5		UNIVERSAL	
CHAMBER OF HORRORS (BRITISH - LESLIE BANKS)	1941	80			2.5	MONOGRAM	
CHAMBER OF HORRORS (PATRICK O'NEAL)	1966	99		2.0	1.5	WARNER BROTHERS	
CHAMP, THE	1931	86		4.0	3.0	M-G-M	NOMINATED BEST PICTURE 1931/32
CHAMP FOR A DAY	1953	90		3.0	2.0	REPUBLIC	
CHAMPAGNE FOR CAESAR	1950	99	7*	3.5	3.0	UNIVERSAL	
CHAMPAGNE MURDERS, THE (FRENCH)	1967	98	3	2.0	2.5	UNIVERSAL	ENGLISH LANGUAGE
CHAMPAGNE WALTZ	1937	85		3.0	2.5	PARAMOUNT	
CHAMPION	1949	99	6*	4.0	3.5	UNITED ARTISTS	
CHANCE MEETING (BR. - ODILE VERSOIS, DAVID KNIGHT)	a1954	96	5	2.5		PACEMAKER PICS.	
CHANCE MEETING (BRITISH - HARDY KRUGER)	1959	96		2.5	2.5	PARAMOUNT	
CHANDLER	1971	88	1			M-G-M	
CHANGE OF HABIT	1969	93	3			UNIVERSAL	
CHANGE OF HEART (JANET GAYNOR, CHARLES FARRELL)	1934	76				20th CENTURY FOX	
CHANGE OF HEART (GLORIA STUART, MICHAEL WHALEN)	1938	66		3.0		20th CENTURY FOX	
CHANGE OF HEART (JOHN CARROLL, SUSAN HAYWARD)	a1943	82		3.0		REPUBLIC	
CHANGE OF MIND	1969	96	3			CINERAMA RELEASING	
CHANGE PARTNERS (BRITISH)	1966	61		1.5		GOVERNOR	
CHANGES	1969	93	5			CINERAMA RELEASING	
CHAPMAN REPORT, THE	1963	125		2.5	2.5	WARNER BROTHERS	
CHAPPAQUA	1967	92	6	3.5		REGIONAL	
CHARADE (JAMES MASON, PAMELA KELLINO)	1952	86					THREE STORIES
CHARADE (AUDREY HEPBURN, CARY GRANT)	1963	114	7*	3.5	3.5	UNIVERSAL	
CHARGE AT FEATHER RIVER, THE	1953	96	3*	2.0	2.5	WARNER BROTHERS	
CHARGE OF THE BLACK LANCERS (ITALIAN)	a1961	97		2.0	2.5	PARAMOUNT	
CHARGE OF THE LANCERS	1954	74		2.0	2.0	COLUMBIA	
CHARGE OF THE LIGHT BRIGADE, THE (ERROL FLYNN)	1936	116	5*	3.5	3.0	WARNER BROTHERS	
CHARGE OF THE LIGHT BRIGADE, THE (TREVOR HOWARD)	1968	128	6	3.5		UNITED ARTISTS	
CHARLEY'S AUNT (JACK BENNY, KAY FRANCIS)	1941	81		3.0		20th CENTURY FOX	
CHARLIE BUBBLES (BRITISH)	1968	89	3*	3.5		UNIVERSAL	
CHARLIE CHAN AT MONTE CARLO	1937	71			-	20th CENTURY FOX	
CHARLIE CHAN AT THE CIRCUS	1936	72			-	20th CENTURY FOX	
CHARLIE CHAN AT THE OLYMPICS	1937	71			-	20th CENTURY FOX	
CHARLIE CHAN AT THE OPERA	1936	66			-	20th CENTURY FOX	
CHARLIE CHAN AT THE RACE TRACK	1936	70			-	20th CENTURY FOX	
CHARLIE CHAN AT THE WAX MUSEUM	1940	63			-	20th CENTURY FOX	
CHARLIE CHAN AT TREASURE ISLAND	1939	59			-	20th CENTURY FOX	
CHARLIE CHAN CARRIES ON	1931	76				20th CENTURY FOX	
CHARLIE CHAN IN CITY OF DARKNESS	1939	75			-	20th CENTURY FOX	
CHARLIE CHAN IN EGYPT	1935	65		2.0	-	20th CENTURY FOX	
CHARLIE CHAN IN HONOLULU	1938	65			-	20th CENTURY FOX	
CHARLIE CHAN IN LONDON	1934	79			-	20th CENTURY FOX	
CHARLIE CHAN IN PANAMA	1940	67			-	20th CENTURY FOX	
CHARLIE CHAN IN PARIS	1935	70			-	20th CENTURY FOX	
CHARLIE CHAN IN RENO	1939	70			-	20th CENTURY FOX	
CHARLIE CHAN IN RIO	1941	60			-	20th CENTURY FOX	
CHARLIE CHAN IN SHANGHAI	1935	70			-	20th CENTURY FOX	
CHARLIE CHAN IN THE SECRET SERVICE	1944	63			-	MONOGRAM	
CHARLIE CHAN ON BROADWAY	1937	68			-	20th CENTURY FOX	
CHARLIE CHAN'S CHANCE	1932	73				20th CENTURY FOX	
CHARLIE CHAN'S COURAGE	1934	72				20th CENTURY FOX	
CHARLIE CHAN'S GREATEST CASE	1933	71				20th CENTURY FOX	
CHARLIE CHAN'S MURDER CRUISE	1940	75			-	20th CENTURY FOX	
CHARLIE CHAN'S SECRET	1936	71				20th CENTURY FOX	
CHARLIE CHAPLIN CARNIVAL	1938	84	4*	4.0	4.0	RKO	FOUR SHORTS RELEASED 1916
CHARLIE CHAPLIN CAVALCADE	1938	81	4*	4.0	4.0	RKO	FOUR SHORTS RELEASED 1916
CHARLIE CHAPLIN FESTIVAL	1938	82	3*	4.0	4.0	RKO	FOUR SHORTS RELEASED 1917
CHARLIE, THE LONESOME COUGAR	1967	75	5			BUENA VISTA	
CHARLY	1968	106	7-8*	3.0		CINERAMA RELEASING	
CHARRO!	1969	98	1			NATIONAL GENERAL	
CHARTER PILOT	1940	70		2.0		20th CENTURY FOX	
CHARTROOSE CABOOSE	1960	75		2.0	2.0	UNIVERSAL	
CHASE, THE (MICHELE MORGAN, ROBERT CUMMINGS)	1946	86	3	3.0	2.0	UNITED ARTISTS	
CHASE, THE (MARLIN BRANDO, JANE FONDA)	1966	135	4	2.0		COLUMBIA	
CHASE A CROOKED SHADOW (BRITISH)	1958	87		2.5	2.5	WARNER BROTHERS	
CHASE ME CHARLIE	1932	61		3.0	2.0	CITATION	
CHASTITY	1969	85	2			AMERICAN-INTERNAT'L	
CHATO'S LAND	1972	110	4			UNITED ARTISTS	
CHATTERBOX (JOE E. BROWN, JUDY CANOVA)	1943	76		2.5	2.5	REPUBLIC	
CHE!	1969	96	2	1.0		20th CENTURY FOX	
CHEAPER BY THE DOZEN	1950	85	6	3.0	3.0	20th CENTURY FOX	
CHEATERS, THE (JOSEPH SCHILDKRAUT, BILLIE BURKE)	a1945	87		3.0	3.0	REPUBLIC	

‡ An asterisk (*) in THE FILM BUFF'S BIBLE column indicates that the film has been rated by the editor and/or staff. All other ratings in this column are based on a consensus of reviews (see NOTES).

TITLE (LEADING ACTORS SHOWN WHERE TWO OR MORE FILMS HAVE THE SAME OR SIMILAR TITLE)	YEAR RELEASED	RUNNING TIME IN MINUTES	THE FILM BUFF'S BIBLE ‡	STEVEN SCHEUER	LEONARD MALTIN	DISTRIBUTOR	COMMENT
CHEATERS, THE (FR. - PASCALE PETIT, J. CHARRIER)	1958	120	3	2.0		CONTINENTAL	
CHECK AND DOUBLE CHECK	1930	71		1.0		RKO	
CHECKPOINT (BRITISH)	1956	84	4			J. ARTHUR RANK	
CHEERS FOR MISS BISHOP	1941	95	4*	3.0	3.0	UNITED ARTISTS	
CHELSEA GIRLS, THE	1966	210	3			FILMMAKERS	
CHEROKEE STRIP (RICHARD DIX, FLORENCE RICE)	1940	84		2.0		PARAMOUNT	
CHERRY, HARRY AND RAQUEL	1969	71	1			EVE RELEASING CORP.	
CHETNICKS	1943	73		2.5		20th CENTURY FOX	
CHEYENNE	a1947	100		2.0	2.0	WARNER BROTHERS	
CHEYENNE AUTUMN	1964	156		3.5	2.5	WARNER BROTHERS	
CHEYENNE SOCIAL CLUB, THE	1970	103	4			NATIONAL GENERAL	
CHICAGO CALLING	1952	74	2	2.0	2.0	UNITED ARTISTS	
CHICAGO CONFIDENTIAL	1957	73		2.5	2.5	UNITED ARTISTS	
CHICAGO DEADLINE	1949	87		2.5	2.5	PARAMOUNT	
CHICAGO KID, THE	1945	68		3.0		REPUBLIC	
CHICAGO SYNDICATE	1955	83		2.0	2.0	COLUMBIA	
CHICKEN EVERY SUNDAY	1949	91	5	2.5	2.5	20th CENTURY FOX	
CHIEF CRAZY HORSE	1955	86		2.5	2.5	UNIVERSAL	
CHILD AND THE KILLER (BRITISH)	1959	64		2.0		LOPERT	
CHILD IN THE HOUSE (BRITISH)	1956	88		3.0		EROS FILMS	
CHILD IS BORN, A	1940	79		2.5	3.0	WARNER BROTHERS	
CHILD IS WAITING, A	1963	102	5*	3.0	3.0	UNITED ARTISTS	
CHILDREN OF PARADISE (FRENCH)	a1945	188	5*	4.0	3.5	TRICOLORE	
CHILDREN OF THE DAMNED (BRITISH)	1964	90	3		2.5	M-G-M	
CHILDREN SHOULDN'T PLAY WITH DEAD THINGS	1972	101				GENENI FILM CO.	
CHILDREN'S HOUR, THE	a1962	107	6-7*	2.5	2.5	UNITED ARTISTS	
CHILD'S PLAY (BRITISH)	1957	68		2.0		DIST. CORP. OF AMER.	
CHINA (ALAN LADD, LORETTA YOUNG)	1943	79		2.0	2.0	PARAMOUNT	
CHINA! (BRITISH, DOCUMENTARY)	1965	65	7			JANUS FILMS	
CHINA CLIPPER	1936	85		3.0	2.5	FIRST NATIONAL	
CHINA CORSAIR	1951	67		1.0	1.5	COLUMBIA	
CHINA DOLL	1958	88		1.5	1.5	UNITED ARTISTS	
CHINA GATE	1957	97		2.0	2.0	20th CENTURY FOX	
CHINA GIRL	1942	95		2.5	2.0	20th CENTURY FOX	
CHINA IS NEAR (ITALIAN)	1967	108	6	3.0		ROYAL FILMS INT'L	
CHINA SEAS	1935	90		3.0	3.0	M-G-M	
CHINA SKY	1945	78		2.0	2.0	RKO	
CHINA VENTURE	1953	83		2.5	1.5	COLUMBIA	
CHINA'S LITTLE DEVILS	1945	74			2.0	MONOGRAM	
CHINATOWN AT MIDNIGHT	1949	67	4	2.0		COLUMBIA	
CHINESE CAT, THE	1944	65			-	MONOGRAM	
CHINESE GIRL, THE (FRENCH)	a1967	95	6	4.0		LEACOCK-PENNEBAKER	
CHINESE RING, THE	1947	67			-	MONOGRAM	
CHINMOKU (JAPANESE)	a1972	126				TOHO	
CHIP OFF THE OLD BLOCK	1944	82		3.0	2.0	UNIVERSAL	
CHISUM	1970	111	6			WARNER BROTHERS	
CHITTY CHITTY, BANG BANG (BRITISH)	1968	142	5	2.5		UNITED ARTISTS	
CHOCOLATE SOLDIER, THE	1941	102		3.0	2.0	M-G-M	
CHOPPERS, THE	1962	70		1.5		FAIRWAY INTERNAT'L	
CHRISTA (DANISH)	a1971	100	2			AMERICAN-INTERNAT'L	PART ENGLISH DIALOGUE
CHRISTIAN LICORICE STORE, THE	1971	90	3			NATIONAL GENERAL	
CHRISTINE (FRENCH - ROMY SCHNEIDER, ALAIN DELON)	1955	100		2.5			
CHRISTINE JORGENSEN STORY, THE	1970	89	3			UNITED ARTISTS	
CHRISTMAS CAROL, A (REGINALD OWEN)	1938	69		3.0	3.0	M-G-M	
CHRISTMAS CAROL, A (BRITISH - ALASTAIR SIM)	a1951	86	6	3.5	3.0	UNITED ARTISTS	
CHRISTMAS EVE	a1947	90		1.5	1.5	UNITED ARTISTS	
CHRISTMAS HOLIDAY	1944	92		3.0	3.0	UNIVERSAL	
CHRISTMAS IN CONNECTICUT	1945	101		2.5	2.5	WARNER BROTHERS	
CHRISTMAS IN JULY	1940	70	6*	4.0	3.5	PARAMOUNT	
CHRISTMAS KID, THE	1967	90	2			PRODUCERS RELEASING	
CHRISTMAS TREE, THE (FRENCH - WILLIAM HOLDEN)	1969	110	5	2.0		CONTINENTAL	ENGLISH VERSION
CHRISTOPHER COLUMBUS (BRITISH)	1949	104		2.5	3.0	UNIVERSAL	
CHRISTOPHER STRONG	1933	77		3.0	2.5	RKO	
CHROME AND HOT LEATHER	1971	91	2			AMERICAN-INTERNAT'L	
CHRONICLE OF ANNA MAGDALENA BACH (ITALIAN-GERMAN)	1968	93		2.5		NEW YORKER FILMS	
CHUBASCO	1968	100	3			WARNER BROTHERS	
CHUKA	1967	105	4	1.5		PARAMOUNT	
CHUMP AT OXFORD, A	1940	63			2.5	UNITED ARTISTS	
CHUSHINGURA (JAPANESE)	1962	108	6			TOHO	
CIGARETTES, WHISKEY AND WILD WOMEN (FRENCH)	1958	90		1.5			
CIMARRON (RICHARD DIX, IRENE DUNNE)	1931	130				RKO	BEST PICTURE AWARD 1930/31
CIMARRON (GLENN FORD, MARIA SCHELL)	1961	147		2.5	2.5	M-G-M	
CIMARRON KID, THE	1952	84		2.0	2.0	UNIVERSAL	
CINCINNATI KID, THE	1965	113	5*	3.0	2.5	M-G-M	
CINDERELLA (CARTOON)	1950	74	6			RKO	
CINDERELLA (RUSSIAN - BOLSHOI BALLET)	1960	84	7			JANUS FILMS	
CINDERELLA JONES	1946	92		2.0	2.0	WARNER BROTHERS	
CINDERFELLA	1960	91		2.0	2.5	PARAMOUNT	
CINERAMA'S RUSSIAN ADVENTURE (DOCUMENTARY)	a1966	140	4			UNITED ROADSHOW	
CIRCLE, THE (BRITISH)	a1957	84		3.0	2.5	KASSLER FILMS	
CIRCLE OF DANGER (BRITISH)	1951	86	4	3.0	2.5	EAGLE LION	
CIRCLE OF DEATH (MEXICAN - SARITA MONTIEL)	1960	79		2.0			
CIRCLE OF DECEPTION (BRITISH)	1960	100		2.5	2.5	20th CENTURY FOX	
CIRCLE OF LOVE (FRENCH)	1964	105	3			COLUMBIA	

‡ An asterisk (*) in THE FILM BUFF'S BIBLE column indicates that the film has been rated by the editor and/or staff. All other ratings in this column are based on a consensus of reviews (see NOTES).

TITLE (LEADING ACTORS SHOWN WHERE TWO OR MORE FILMS HAVE THE SAME OR SIMILAR TITLE)	YEAR RELEASED	RUNNING TIME IN MINUTES	THE FILM BUFF'S BIBLE ‡	STEVEN SCHEUER	LEONARD MALTIN	DISTRIBUTOR	COMMENT
CIRCULAR TRIANGLE, THE (GERMAN)	1964	112		2.0		PARAMOUNT	
CIRCUMSTANTIAL EVIDENCE (MICHAEL O'SHEA, L. NOLAN)	1945	68		1.5	2.5	20th CENTURY FOX	
CIRCUMSTANTIAL EVIDENCE (BRITISH - PATRICK HOLT)	1952	61		2.0		PHIL BRANDON	
CIRCUS, THE (SILENT)	1928	71				UNITED ARTISTS	
CIRCUS CLOWN	1934	63		2.0	2.0	FIRST NATIONAL	
CIRCUS OF FEAR (BRITISH)	a1967	83	3	2.0		AMERICAN-INTERNAT'L	
CIRCUS OF HORRORS (BRITISH)	1960	89		2.5	2.5	AMERICAN-INTERNAT'L	
CIRCUS STARS (RUSSIAN, DOCUMENTARY)	1958	61	6			PARAMOUNT	
CIRCUS WORLD	1964	135		2.5	2.5	PARAMOUNT	
CISCO KID AND THE LADY, THE	1939	73		2.5		20th CENTURY FOX	
CISCO PIKE	1971	94	4			COLUMBIA	
CITADEL, THE (BRITISH)	1938	110		4.0	3.5	M-G-M	NOMINATED BEST PICTURE
CITIZEN KANE	1941	119	6-7*	4.0	4.0	RKO	NOMINATED BEST PICTURE
CITY, THE (DOCUMENTARY)	1939	45	5*			CIVIC FILMS	
CITY, THE (T.V. - ANTHONY QUINN)	1971	100	3*			UNIVERSAL	
CITY ACROSS THE RIVER	1949	90		2.5	2.5	UNIVERSAL	
CITY AFTER MIDNIGHT (BRITISH)	a1957	84		2.0	1.5	RKO	
CITY BENEATH THE SEA (ROBERT RYAN, ANTHONY QUINN)	1953	87	4	2.5	2.5	UNIVERSAL	
CITY BENEATH THE SEA (T.V. - STUART WHITMAN)	1971	100		2.5		20th CENTURY FOX	
CITY FOR CONQUEST	1940	101	6*	3.0	3.0	WARNER BROTHERS	
CITY LIGHTS (SILENT)	1931	87	7			UNITED ARTISTS	
CITY OF BAD MEN	1953	82		2.5	2.0	20th CENTURY FOX	
CITY OF FEAR (VINCE EDWARDS, LYLE TALBOT)	1959	81		2.5	1.5	COLUMBIA	
CITY OF FEAR (BRITISH - PAUL MAXWELL, TERRY MOORE)	1965	75		1.5	1.5	ALLIED ARTISTS	
CITY OF GOLD (CANADIAN, DOCUMENTARY)	1957	23	6			NAT'L FILM BOARD CAN.	
CITY OF SHADOWS	1955	70		2.0	1.5	REPUBLIC	
CITY ON A HUNT	a1953	76		2.0	1.5	UNITED ARTISTS	
CITY STANDS TRIAL, THE (ITALIAN)	1954	95		2.5		ITALIAN FILMS EXPORT	
CITY STREETS	1931	82		2.0	3.0	PARAMOUNT	
CITY THAT NEVER SLEEPS, THE	1953	90	3	3.0	2.0	REPUBLIC	
CLAIRE'S KNEE (FRENCH)	1971	103	3*			COLUMBIA	
CLAMBAKE	1967	99	3	1.0		UNITED ARTISTS	
CLANCY STREET BOYS	1943	66			.	MONOGRAM	
CLARENCE, THE CROSS-EYED LION	1965	98	4		2.5	M-G-M	
CLASH BY NIGHT (BARBARA STANWYCK, PAUL DOUGLAS)	1952	105		2.5	2.5	RKO	
CLASH OF STEEL (FRENCH)	1962	79		1.5	2.5	SCREEN GEMS	
CLASS OF '74	1972	82	2			GENERAL FILM CORP.	
CLAUDELLE INGLISH	a1961	99		2.0	2.5	WARNER BROTHERS	
CLAUDIA	1943	91	5	3.5	3.0	20th CENTURY FOX	
CLAUDIA AND DAVID	1946	78		3.0	3.0	20th CENTURY FOX	
CLAW MONSTERS, THE	1955	100		2.0	1.5	REPUBLIC	RE-EDITED SERIAL
CLAY PIGEON, THE (BILL WILLIAMS, BARBARA HALE)	1949	63	3	2.0		RKO	
CLAY PIGEON, THE (TOM STERN, TELLY SAVALAS)	1971	96	1			M-G-M	
CLEAR AND PRESENT DANGER, A (T.V.)	1970	100		2.5		UNIVERSAL	
CLEO FROM 5 TO 7 (FRENCH)	1961	90		2.5	3.0	ZENITH INTERNATIONAL	
CLEOPATRA (CLAUDETTE COLBERT, WARREN WILLIAM)	1934	101	3*	2.5	3.5	PARAMOUNT	NOMINATED BEST PICTURE
CLEOPATRA (ELIZABETH TAYLOR, RICHARD BURTON)	1963	243	5	3.0	3.0	20th CENTURY FOX	NOMINATED BEST PICTURE
CLEOPATRA'S DAUGHTER (ITALIAN)	1960	102		1.5	2.0	MEDALLION	
CLIMATS (FRENCH)	1962	100		2.5		J. ARTHUR RANK	
CLIMAX, THE (BORIS KARLOFF)	1944	86			3.0	UNIVERSAL	
CLIMAX, THE (ITALIAN - UGO TOGNAZZI)	1967	97	6			LOPERT	
CLIMBERS, THE	1964	85		1.0		PARAMOUNT	
CLIPPED WINGS	1953	65			.	ALLIED ARTISTS	
CLIVE OF INDIA	1935	90			2.5	UNITED ARTISTS	
CLOAK AND DAGGER	1946	106		3.0	3.0	WARNER BROTHERS	
CLOCK, THE	1945	90		2.5	3.5	M-G-M	
CLOCKWORK ORANGE, A (BRITISH)	1971	137	7*			WARNER BROTHERS	NOMINATED BEST PICTURE
CLOPORTES (FRENCH)	1965	102	6			INTERNAT'L CLASSICS	
CLOSE CALL FOR BOSTON BLACKIE, A	1946	60		1.5	.	COLUMBIA	
CLOSE CALL FOR ELLERY QUEEN	1942	67		2.0	.	COLUMBIA	
CLOSE TO MY HEART	1951	90	4	2.5	3.0	WARNER BROTHERS	
CLOSE-UP	1948	76		2.5		EAGLE LION	
CLOSELY WATCHED TRAINS (CZECH)	1966	89	6	3.5		SIGMA III	
CLOUDBURST (BRITISH)	1951	92		2.0	2.5	UNITED ARTISTS	
CLOUDED YELLOW, THE (BRITISH)	1950	96	6	3.0	3.0	COLUMBIA	
CLOUDS OVER EUROPE (BRITISH)	a1939	82	4*	3.5	3.0	COLUMBIA	
CLOUDS OVER ISRAEL (ISRAELI)	1962	85	6			HEMISPHERE	
CLOWN, THE	1953	92	4	3.0	2.5	M-G-M	
CLOWN AND THE KID, THE	1962	65	3			UNITED ARTISTS	
CLOWNS, THE (ITALIAN, DOCUMENTARY)	1971	90	6			LEVITT-PICKMAN	
CLUB HAVANA	1945	62			2.0	PRODUCERS RELEASING	
CLUE OF THE NEW PIN, THE (BRITISH)	1960	60		2.0	1.5	ANGLO AMALGAMATED	
CLUE OF THE SILVER KEY, THE (BRITISH)	1961	59		2.0	2.5	ANGLO AMALGAMATED	
CLUE OF THE TWISTED CANDLE, THE (BRITISH)	1960	61		2.0		SCHOENFELD FILM DIST.	
CLUNY BROWN	1946	100	5*	3.5	3.5	20th CENTURY FOX	
C'MON, LET'S LIVE A LITTLE	1967	85	1			PARAMOUNT	
COAST OF SKELETONS (BRITISH)	1965	90	3		2.5	SEVEN ARTS	
COBRA, THE (ITALIAN)	1967	93	3			AMERICAN-INTERNAT'L	
COBRA STRIKES, THE	1948	62			2.0	EAGLE LION	
COBRA WOMAN	1944	70		2.0	2.0	UNIVERSAL	
COBWEB, THE	1955	124		3.5	2.5	M-G-M	
COCK-EYED WORLD, THE	1929	115				20th CENTURY FOX	
COCKEYED COWBOYS OF CALICO COUNTY, THE	1970	99	3			UNIVERSAL	
COCKEYED MIRACLE, THE	1946	81		2.0	2.0	M-G-M	

‡ An asterisk (*) in THE FILM BUFF'S BIBLE column indicates that the film has been rated by the editor and/or staff. All other ratings in this column are based on a consensus of reviews (see NOTES).

TITLE (LEADING ACTORS SHOWN WHERE TWO OR MORE FILMS HAVE THE SAME OR SIMILAR TITLE)	YEAR RELEASED	RUNNING TIME IN MINUTES	CRITICAL RATINGS			DISTRIBUTOR	COMMENT
"a" TO LEFT OF YEAR INDICATES THAT FILM HAS AN ALTERNATE TITLE			THE FILM BUFF'S BIBLE ‡	STEVEN SCHEUER	LEONARD MALTIN		
COCKLESHELL HEROES, THE (BRITISH)	1955	98	4-5*	3.5	2.0	COLUMBIA	
COCOANUT GROVE	1938	85		2.0	2.0	PARAMOUNT	
COCOANUTS, THE	1929	96		3.0	3.0	PARAMOUNT	
CODE NAME - TIGER (FRENCH)	1964	80		1.5		FOUR STAR	
CODE OF SCOTLAND YARD (BRITISH)	1948	60			2.0	REPUBLIC	
CODE OF SILENCE (BRITISH)	a1958	78	3	1.5			
CODE 7, VICTIM 5	1965	88	2		2.5	COLUMBIA	
CODE 645	1947	100		1.5	2.0	REPUBLIC	RE-EDITED SERIAL
CODE TWO	1953	69		2.0	2.0	M-G-M	
COFFIN FROM HONG KONG, A (GERMAN)	1964	93		1.5		UCC FILMS	
COLD SUN, THE	1953	78		1.0		OFFICIAL INDUSTRIES	
COLD TURKEY	1971	102	5			UNITED ARTISTS	
COLD WIND IN AUGUST, A	1961	80	5		2.5	LOPERT	
COLDITZ STORY, THE (BRITISH)	1954	97	6	3.0	2.5	REPUBLIC	
COLE YOUNGER, GUNFIGHTER	1958	78		2.0	2.0	ALLIED ARTISTS	
COLLECTOR, THE (TERRENCE STAMP, SAMANTHA EGGAR)	1965	119	7*	3.5		COLUMBIA	
COLLECTOR, THE (FRENCH - PATRICK BAUCHAU)	a1967	88	5			PATHE CONTEMPARARY	
COLLEEN	1936	89		2.5	2.5	WARNER BROTHERS	
COLLEGE COACH	1933	75		2.5	2.5	WARNER BROTHERS	
COLLEGE CONFIDENTIAL	1960	91		1.5	1.5	UNIVERSAL	
COLLEGE HOLIDAY	1936	88		2.5	2.5	PARAMOUNT	
COLLEGE HUMOR	1933	80		2.5	3.0	PARAMOUNT	
COLLEGE SWING	1938	86		1.5	2.5	PARAMOUNT	
COLONEL BLIMP (BRITISH)	a1943	148		4.0	3.0	ARCHERS-GENERAL	
COLONEL EFFINGHAM'S RAID	1945	70		3.0	2.5	20th CENTURY FOX	
COLOR ME DEAD	1969	97	2			LANDAU/UNGER COM. UN.	
COLORADO TERRITORY	1949	94	4	3.0	2.5	WARNER BROTHERS	
COLOSSUS AND THE AMAZON QUEEN (ITALIAN)	1960	96		1.0		AMERICAN-INTERNAT'L	
COLOSSUS AND THE HEADHUNTERS (ITALIAN)	1962	79		1.0		AMERICAN-INTERNAT'L	
COLOSSUS AND THE HUNS (ITALIAN)	1960	90		1.5		AMERICAN-INTERNAT'L	
COLOSSUS OF NEW YORK, THE	1958	70		2.0	2.0	PARAMOUNT	
COLOSSUS OF RHODES, THE (ITALIAN)	1960	129	3	2.0		M-G-M	
COLOSSUS OF THE ARENA (ITALIAN)	1960	99		1.5		AMERICAN-INTERNAT'L	
COLOSSUS, THE FORBIN PROJECT	a1970	100	5-6*			UNIVERSAL	
COLT .45	a1950	74		2.5	2.5	WARNER BROTHERS	
COLUMN SOUTH	1953	85		2.0	2.0	UNIVERSAL	
COMANCHE	1956	87		2.0	2.0	UNITED ARTISTS	
COMANCHE STATION	1960	74	4	3.0	2.5	COLUMBIA	
COMANCHE TERRITORY	1950	76		2.0	2.0	UNIVERSAL	
COMANCHEROS, THE	1961	107	5*	3.0	3.0	20th CENTURY FOX	
COMBAT SQUAD	1953	72		2.0	1.5	COLUMBIA	
COME AND GET IT	1936	99	6-7*	3.0	3.5	UNITED ARTISTS	
COME BACK, AFRICA (SEMI-DOCUMENTARY)	1959	95	6			LIONEL ROGOSIN	
COME BACK, CHARLSTON BLUE	1972	100	3			WARNER BROTHERS	
COME BACK, LITTLE SHEBA	1952	99	7	4.0	3.5	PARAMOUNT	
COME BLOW YOUR HORN	1963	112		3.0	3.0	PARAMOUNT	
COME DANCE WITH ME (FRENCH - BRIGITTE BARDOT)	1959	91	4		2.5	KINGSLEY INTERNAT'L	
COME FILL THE CUP	1951	113		3.0	2.5	WARNER BROTHERS	
COME FLY WITH ME (BRITISH)	1963	109		2.0	2.5	M-G-M	
COME LIVE WITH ME	1941	86		2.0	2.5	M-G-M	
COME NEXT SPRING	1956	92	6	3.5	3.0	REPUBLIC	
COME ON, THE	1956	83	3		2.0	ALLIED ARTISTS	
COME OUT FIGHTING	1945	62			-	MONOGRAM	
COME SEPTEMBER	1961	112		2.5	3.0	UNIVERSAL	
COME SPY WITH ME	a1967	85	1		1.5	20th CENTURY FOX	
COME TO THE STABLE	1949	94	4*	3.0	3.0	20th CENTURY FOX	
COMEDIANS, THE	1967	160	4*	2.5		M-G-M	
COMEDY MAN, THE (BRITISH)	1964	82	6	4.0		CONTINENTAL	
COMEDY OF TERRORS, THE	1964	88	2			AMERICAN-INTERNAT'L	
COMETOGETHER	1971	90	2			ALLIED ARTISTS	
COMIC, THE	1969	94	5*	3.5		COLUMBIA	
COMIN' ROUND THE MOUNTAIN (BOB BURNS, UNA MERKEL)	1940	63		1.5		PARAMOUNT	
COMIN' ROUND THE MOUNTAIN (ABBOTT & COSTELLO)	1951	107	2	2.0	2.0	PARAMOUNT	
COMING APART	1969	110	3			KALEIDOSCOPE	
COMING OUT PARTY, A (BRITISH - JAMES R. JUSTICE)	1961	98		3.0	2.5	UNION FILMS	
COMMAND, THE	1954	88		2.0	2.0	WARNER BROTHERS	
COMMAND DECISION	1948	112	5*	3.5	3.5	M-G-M	
COMMANDO (ITALIAN)	1962	95		2.5	2.5	AMERICAN-INTERNAT'L	
COMMANDOS STRIKE AT DAWN	1943	98		3.0		COLUMBIA	
COMMITTEE, THE (PETER BONERZ, BARBARA BOSSON)	1969	90	6	2.0		LANDAU/UNGER COM. UN.	
COMPANEROS	1972	107				CINERAMA RELEASING	
COMPANIONS IN NIGHTMARE (T.V.)	1968	100	5*	2.5		UNIVERSAL	
COMPANY OF KILLERS	1971	84	3			UNIVERSAL	
COMPANY SHE KEEPS, THE	1951	81	4	3.0	2.5	RKO	
COMPULSION	1959	103	7	3.0	3.5	20th CENTURY FOX	
COMPUTER WORE TENNIS SHOES, THE	1970	90	5			BUENA VISTA	
COMRADE X	1940	90		3.0	2.5	M-G-M	
CONCERT FOR BANGLADESH, THE (DOCUMENTARY)	1972	100	5			20th CENTURY FOX	
CONCERT OF INTRIGUE (ITALIAN)	1954	93		1.5		HOWCO INTERNATIONAL	
CONCRETE JUNGLE, THE (BRITISH)	1960	86		2.0	2.5	FANFARE	
CONDEMNED	1929	86		2.0	2.0	UNITED ARTISTS	
CONDEMNED OF ALTONA, THE	1963	114	4-5*	3.0	2.5	20th CENTURY FOX	
CONEY ISLAND	1943	96		3.0	3.0	20th CENTURY FOX	
CONFESS, DR CORDA (GERMAN)	1958	101		-	2.0	PRESIDENT FILMS	

‡ An asterisk (*) in THE FILM BUFF'S BIBLE column indicates that the film has been rated by the editor and/or staff. All other ratings in this column are based on a consensus of reviews (see NOTES).

TITLE (LEADING ACTORS SHOWN WHERE TWO OR MORE FILMS HAVE THE SAME OR SIMILAR TITLE)	YEAR RELEASED	RUNNING TIME IN MINUTES	THE FILM BUFF'S BIBLE ‡	STEVEN SCHEUER	LEONARD MALTIN	DISTRIBUTOR	COMMENT
CONFESSION (BASIL RATHBONE, KAY FRANCIS)	1937	86		2.0	2.5	WARNER BROTHERS	
CONFESSION (DENNIS O'KEEFE)	a1957	74	5*			SCREEN GEMS	
CONFESSION, THE (FRENCH - YVES MONTAND)	1970	142	6*	4.0		PARAMOUNT	
CONFESSIONS OF A NAZI SPY	1939	102		3.0	3.0	WARNER BROTHERS	
CONFESSIONS OF AN OPIUM EATER	a1962	85		1.0	1.5	ALLIED ARTISTS	
CONFESSIONS OF BOSTON BLACKIE	1941	65		1.5	-	COLUMBIA	
CONFESSIONS OF FELIX KRULL (GERMAN)	1958	107	5	2.5	2.5	DIST. CORP. OF AMER.	
CONFIDENCE GIRL	1952	81	3			UNITED ARTISTS	
CONFIDENTIAL AGENT	1945	118		3.0	3.0	WARNER BROTHERS	
CONFIDENTIAL REPORT (BRITISH)	a1955	99		3.0	2.5	CARI	
CONFIDENTIALLY CONNIE	1953	74		2.0	2.5	M-G-M	
CONFIRM OR DENY	1941	73		2.5	2.5	20th CENTURY FOX	
CONFLICT	1945	86		3.0	2.5	WARNER BROTHERS	
CONFLICT OF WINGS (BRITISH)	1954	84		3.0		UNITED ARTISTS	
CONFORMIST, THE (ITALIAN)	1971	116	5*			PARAMOUNT	
CONGO CROSSING	1956	87		2.0	2.0	UNIVERSAL	
CONGO MAISIE	1940	70		2.0	-	M-G-M	
CONJUGAL BED, THE (ITALIAN)	1963	90	5	4.0	3.0	AVCO-EMBASSY	
CONNECTICUT YANKEE, A	1931	91				20th CENTURY FOX	
CONNECTICUT YANKEE IN KING ARTHUR'S COURT, A	1949	107	5*	3.0	2.5	PARAMOUNT	
CONNECTION, THE	1962	103	6			FILMS AROUND THE WLD.	
CONQUERED CITY (ITALIAN)	1965	91	3	2.5	2.0	AMERICAN-INTERNAT'L	
CONQUEROR, THE	1956	111	6			RKO	
CONQUEROR OF ATLANTIS (ITALIAN)	1963	93		1.0		ABC FILMS	
CONQUEROR OF MARACAIBO (ITALIAN)	1960	101		1.5		TELEWIDE SYSTEMS	
CONQUEROR OF THE DESERT (ITALIAN)	1958	110		1.5		FOUR STAR	
CONQUEROR OF THE ORIENT (ITALIAN)	1962	86		1.5		AVCO-EMBASSY	
CONQUEROR WORM, THE (BRITISH)	1968	87	1	1.0		AMERICAN-INTERNAT'L	
CONQUEST	1937	112		3.0	3.0	M-G-M	
CONQUEST OF COCHISE	1953	70		2.0	2.0	COLUMBIA	
CONQUEST OF EVEREST, THE (BRITISH, DOCUMENTARY)	1954	78	7	4.0		UNITED ARTISTS	
CONQUEST OF MYCENE (ITALIAN)	1963	102		1.5		AVCO-EMBASSY	
CONQUEST OF SPACE	1955	80		2.5	2.5	PARAMOUNT	
CONQUEST OF THE AIR (BRITISH, DOCUMENTARY)	1935	74		2.0		UNITED ARTISTS	DOCUMENTARY DRAMA
CONQUEST OF THE PLANET OF THE APES	1972	86	4			20th CENTURY FOX	
CONSPIRACY OF HEARTS (BRITISH)	1960	111	6	3.0	3.0	PARAMOUNT	
CONSPIRACY OF THE BORGIAS (ITALIAN)	1965	93		1.5		SCREEN GEMS	
CONSPIRATOR (BR.- ELIZABETH TAYLOR, ROBERT TAYLOR)	1949	87		2.5	2.5	M-G-M	
CONSPIRATORS, THE (HEDY LAMARR, PAUL HENRIED)	1944	101		1.0	2.5	WARNER BROTHERS	
CONSTANT HUSBAND, THE (BRITISH)	1955	84	5	3.0		SHOWCORPORATION	
CONSTANT NYMPH, THE	1943	112		3.0	3.0	WARNER BROTHERS	
CONSTANTINE AND THE CROSS (ITALIAN)	1960	120	3	1.5	3.0	AVCO-EMBASSY	
CONTEMPT (ITALIAN)	1964	103	2		2.5	AVCO-EMBASSY	
CONTEST GIRL (BRITISH)	1966	82		3.0	2.5	CONTINENTAL	
CONTRABAND SPAIN (BRITISH)	1955	81		2.0		STRATFORD PICS.	
CONVICTED (GLENN FORD, BRODERICK CRAWFORD)	1950	91		3.0	2.5	COLUMBIA	
CONVICTS FOUR	a1962	105		2.5	3.0	ALLIED ARTISTS	
COOGAN'S BLUFF	1968	94	3	2.0		UNIVERSAL	
COOL AND THE CRAZY, THE	1958	78	1	2.0	1.5	AMERICAN-INTERNAT'L	
COOL BREEZE	1972	101	2			M-G-M	
COOL HAND LUKE	1967	129	6	4.0		WARNER BROTHERS	
COOL ONES, THE	1967	95	2	1.0		WARNER BROTHERS	
COOL WORLD, THE	1964	105	6			CINEMA V	
COP, THE (FRENCH)	1971	100	5			AUDUBON	
COP HATER	1958	75	2			UNITED ARTISTS	
COP-OUT (BRITISH)	1967	95	2			CINERAMA RELEASING	
COPACABANA	1947	92	3		2.0	UNITED ARTISTS	
COPPER CANYON	1950	83		2.0	2.5	PARAMOUNT	
COPPER SKY	1957	77	1			20th CENTURY FOX	
CORN IS GREEN, THE	1945	114	5*	3.5	3.5	WARNER BROTHERS	
CORNERED	1945	102	4*	4.0	3.0	RKO	
CORONER CREEK	1948	93	5		2.0	COLUMBIA	
CORPSE CAME C.O.D., THE	1947	87		2.0	2.0	COLUMBIA	
CORPSE VANISHES, THE	1942	64			1.5	MONOGRAM	
CORREGIDOR	1943	73			2.0	PRODUCERS RELEASING	
CORRIDOR OF MIRRORS (BRITISH)	1948	96		3.0		UNIVERSAL	
CORRIDORS OF BLOOD (BRITISH)	1962	85	2	2.5		M-G-M	
CORRUPT ONES, THE (GERMAN)	a1966	92	3	2.0		WARNER BROTHERS	ENGLISH LANGUAGE
CORRUPTION (BRITISH)	1968	91	1			COLUMBIA	
CORSICAN BROTHERS, THE (DOUGLAS FAIRBANKS JR)	1941	112	4*	2.5	2.5	UNITED ARTISTS	
CORSICAN BROTHERS, THE (FRENCH - GEOFFREY HORNE)	1960	85		2.0		NTA PICTURES	
CORVETTE K-225	1943	99		3.5	3.0	UNIVERSAL	
COSMIC MAN, THE	1959	72		1.0	1.5	ALLIED ARTISTS	
COSMIC MONSTERS, THE (BRITISH)	1958	75		2.0		WARNER BROTHERS	
COSSACKS, THE (ITALIAN)	1959	113	2		2.0	UNIVERSAL	
COTTON COMES TO HARLEM	1970	97	5			UNITED ARTISTS	
COUCH, THE	1962	100	3	2.0	2.5	WARNER BROTHERS	
COUGAR COUNTRY (DOCUMENTARY)	1970	106	5			AMERICAN NAT'L ENTS.	
COUNT FIVE AND DIE (BRITISH)	1958	92	4	2.5	2.5	20th CENTURY FOX	
COUNT OF MONTE CRISTO, THE (ROBERT DONAT)	1933	113	6*	3.5		UNITED ARTISTS	
COUNT OF MONTE CRISTO, THE (FRENCH - JEAN MARAIS)	1954	183			2.5	SIRIUS	TWO PART STORY
COUNT OF MONTE CRISTO, THE (FRENCH - PIERRE WILM)	1955	180		1.5		WARNER BROTHERS	
COUNT OF MONTE CRISTO, THE (FR. - LOUIS JOURDAN)	a1962	132	3		2.5	WARNER BROTHERS	
COUNT THE HOURS	1953	74		2.0	2.0	RKO	

‡ An asterisk (*) in THE FILM BUFF'S BIBLE column indicates that the film has been rated by the editor and/or staff. All other ratings in this column are based on a consensus of reviews (see NOTES).

TITLE (LEADING ACTORS SHOWN WHERE TWO OR MORE FILMS HAVE THE SAME OR SIMILAR TITLE)	YEAR RELEASED	RUNNING TIME IN MINUTES	THE FILM BUFF'S BIBLE ‡	STEVEN SCHEUER	LEONARD MALTIN	DISTRIBUTOR	COMMENT
COUNT THREE AND PRAY	1955	102	4	3.5	2.5	COLUMBIA	
COUNT YORGA, VAMPIRE	1970	91	2			AMERICAN-INTERNAT'L	
COUNT YOUR BLESSINGS	1959	102		2.5	2.0	M-G-M	
COUNTDOWN	1968	101	3			WARNER BROTHERS	
COUNTER-ATTACK	1945	90		2.5	2.5	COLUMBIA	
COUNTERBLAST (BRITISH)	1948	99		2.0		BRITISH NATIONAL	
COUNTERFEIT CONSTABLE, THE (FRENCH)	1964	86	2			SEVEN ARTS	
COUNTERFEIT KILLER, THE	1968	95		1.0	2.0	UNIVERSAL	
COUNTERFEIT PLAN, THE (BRITISH)	1957	87		1.5	2.0	WARNER BROTHERS	
COUNTERFEIT TRAITOR, THE	1962	140	6*	3.5	3.5	PARAMOUNT	
COUNTERPLOT	1959	76		1.5	2.0	UNITED ARTISTS	
COUNTERPOINT	1968	107	5*	1.0	2.5	UNIVERSAL	
COUNTESS FROM HONG KONG, A (BRITISH)	1967	108	3*	2.5		UNIVERSAL	
COUNTESS OF MONTE CRISTO, THE	1948	77		1.5	2.0	UNIVERSAL	
COUNTRY CUZZINS	1972	90				BOXOFFICE INTERNAT'L	
COUNTRY DOCTOR, THE	1936	110		2.5		20th CENTURY FOX	
COUNTRY GIRL, THE	1954	104	6*	4.0	3.5	PARAMOUNT	NOMINATED BEST PICTURE
COUNTRY MUSIC HOLIDAY	1958	81	1	1.5		PARAMOUNT	
COUNTY FAIR	1950	76	4	2.5		MONOGRAM	
COURAGE OF BLACK BEAUTY	1957	77		2.0	2.0	20th CENTURY FOX	
COURAGE OF LASSIE	1946	92		2.5	2.5	M-G-M	
COURAGEOUS DR CHRISTIAN, THE	1940	67			2.0	RKO	
COURAGEOUS MR PENN (BRITISH)	a1942	78		3.0		HOFFBERG	
COURT JESTER, THE	1956	101	5*	3.0	3.5	PARAMOUNT	
COURT MARTIAL (BRITISH - DAVID NIVEN)	a1955	105		3.5	2.5	KINGSLEY INTERNAT'L	
COURT MARTIAL (GERMAN - KARL HEINZ BOEHM)	1959	82	4			UNITED ARTISTS	
COURT MARTIAL OF BILLY MITCHELL, THE	1955	100	5*	3.5	3.0	WARNER BROTHERS	
COURT MARTIAL OF MAJOR KELLER, THE (BRITISH)	1963	69		2.5		WARNER BROTHERS	
COURTNEY AFFAIR, THE (BRITISH)	1947	112		2.5		CONTINENTAL	
COURTSHIP OF ANDY HARDY, THE	1942	93		2.0	-	M-G-M	
COURTSHIP OF EDDIE'S FATHER, THE	1963	117		3.0	3.0	M-G-M	
COUSINS, THE (FRENCH)	1958	103	5	3.5	2.0	FILMS AROUND THE WLD	
COVENANT WITH DEATH, A	1967	97	3	2.0		WARNER BROTHERS	
COVER GIRL	1944	107		3.5	3.0	COLUMBIA	
COVER ME BABE	1970	89	3			20th CENTURY FOX	
COVER UP	1949	85	4	3.0		UNITED ARTISTS	
COVERED WAGON, THE (SILENT)	1923	105			2.5	PARAMOUNT	
COW AND I, THE (FRENCH)	1959	98		3.0	3.0	ZENITH INTERNATIONAL	
COW COUNTRY	1953	82		1.5	2.0	ALLIED ARTISTS	
COWARDS	1970	89	3			JAYLO INTERNATIONAL	
COWBOY (GLENN FORD, JACK LEMMON)	1958	92	6	3.0	3.0	COLUMBIA	
COWBOY, THE (DOCUMENTARY)	1954	69	5	3.5		LIPPERT PRODS.	
COWBOY AND THE BLONDE, THE	1941	68		1.5		20th CENTURY FOX	
COWBOY AND THE LADY, THE	1938	91		2.0	2.5	UNITED ARTISTS	
COWBOY FROM BROOKLYN, THE	1938	80		3.0	2.5	WARNER BROTHERS	
COWBOY IN MANHATTAN	1943	60		2.0		UNIVERSAL	
COWBOYS, THE (JOHN WAYNE, ROSCOE LEE BROWNE)	1972	128	5			WARNER BROTHERS	
CRACK IN THE MIRROR	1960	97	4*	2.0	3.0	20th CENTURY FOX	
CRACK IN THE WORLD	1965	96		2.5	2.5	PARAMOUNT	
CRACK-UP (PAT O'BRIEN, CLAIRE TREVOR)	1946	93	5	3.0	3.0	20th CENTURY FOX	
CRACKED NUTS	1941	61		1.5		UNIVERSAL	
CRACKSMAN, THE (BRITISH)	1963	112		2.0		WARNER BROTHERS	
CRAIG'S WIFE	1936	75		3.0	3.0	COLUMBIA	
CRANES ARE FLYING, THE (RUSSIAN)	1958	94	7		3.5	ARTKINO	
CRASH DIVE (TYRONE POWER, ANNE BAXTER)	1943	105		2.5	2.5	20th CENTURY FOX	
CRASH LANDING	1958	76		1.5	1.5	COLUMBIA	
CRASH OF SILENCE (BRITISH)	a1953	93	6	4.0	3.0	UNIVERSAL	
CRASHING LAS VEGAS	1956	62			-	ALLIED ARTISTS	
CRASHOUT	1955	90	3*	3.0	2.5	FILMMAKERS	
CRAWLING EYE, THE (BRITISH)	1957	85		2.0		UCC FILMS	
CRAWLING HAND, THE	1963	89		1.0		MEDALLION	
CRAZY DESIRE (ITALIAN)	1962	108	6	3.0	3.5	AVCO-EMBASSY	
CRAZY FOR LOVE (FRENCH)	1951	84		1.5		ELLIS FILMS	
CRAZY HOUSE	1943	80		2.5	3.0	UNIVERSAL	
CRAZY OVER HORSES	1951	65				MONOGRAM	
CRAZY PARADISE (DANISH)	1965	95	3			SHERPIX	
CRAZY QUILT	1966	75	5			CONTINENTAL	
CRAZY WORLD OF LAUREL AND HARDY, THE	1967	83	6			JOSEPH BRENNER	
CRAZYLEGS	1954	87		3.0	1.5	REPUBLIC	
CREATION OF THE HUMANOIDS	1962	75		1.0		EMERSON FILMS	
CREATURE FROM THE BLACK LAGOON	1954	79		2.5	2.0	UNIVERSAL	
CREATURE FROM THE HAUNTED SEA	1960	60		2.5		FILMGROUP	
CREATURE OF THE WALKING DEAD	1963	74		1.5		MEDALLION	
CREATURE WALKS AMONG US, THE	1956	78		1.5	2.0	UNIVERSAL	
CREATURE WITH THE BLUE HAND	1971	72	3			NEW WORLD	
CREATURE WITH THE ATOM BRAIN	1955	70		2.0	2.0	COLUMBIA	
CREATURES THE WORLD FORGOT (BRITISH)	1971	95	2			COLUMBIA	
CREEPER, THE	1948	64			2.0	20th CENTURY FOX	
CREEPING UNKNOWN, THE (BRITISH)	1956	78	3		2.0	UNITED ARTISTS	
CREST OF THE WAVE (BRITISH)	1954	90		2.5	2.5	M-G-M	
CRIME AGAINST JOE	1956	69	3	3.0	3.0	UNITED ARTISTS	
CRIME AND PUNISHMENT (EDWARD ARNOLD, PETER LORRE)	1935	88			3.0	COLUMBIA	
CRIME AND PUNISHMENT (FRENCH - JEAN GABIN)	a1956	111	6	3.0	3.0	KINGSLEY INTERNAT'L	
CRIME AND PUNISHMENT, USA (GEORGE HAMILTON)	1959	78		2.0	2.5	ALLIED ARTISTS	

‡ An asterisk (*) in THE FILM BUFF'S BIBLE column indicates that the film has been rated by the editor and/or staff. All other ratings in this column are based on a consensus of reviews (see NOTES).

TITLE (LEADING ACTORS SHOWN WHERE TWO OR MORE FILMS HAVE THE SAME OR SIMILAR TITLE)	YEAR RELEASED	RUNNING TIME IN MINUTES	CRITICAL RATINGS			DISTRIBUTOR	COMMENT
			THE FILM BUFF'S BIBLE ‡	STEVEN SCHEUER	LEONARD MALTIN		
CRIME BY NIGHT	1944	72		2.5	2.5	WARNER BROTHERS	
CRIME DOCTOR	1943	66		2.0	-	COLUMBIA	
CRIME DOCTOR'S COURAGE, THE	1945	70		1.5	-	COLUMBIA	
CRIME DOCTOR'S DIARY, THE	1949	61			-	COLUMBIA	
CRIME DOCTOR'S GAMBLE, THE	1947	66			-	COLUMBIA	
CRIME DOCTOR'S MANHUNT	1946	61			-	COLUMBIA	
CRIME DOCTOR'S STRANGEST CASE	1943	68		2.0	-	COLUMBIA	
CRIME DOCTOR'S WARNING, THE	1945	69		2.0	-	COLUMBIA	
CRIME DOES NOT PAY (FRENCH)	a1962	159	5		2.5	AVCO-EMBASSY	THREE STORIES
CRIME IN THE STREETS	1956	91		3.0	2.0	ALLIED ARTISTS	
CRIME OF DR CRESPI, THE	1935	63			2.0	REPUBLIC	
CRIME OF DR FORBES, THE	1936	75		3.0		20th CENTURY FOX	
CRIME OF PASSION	1957	84		2.5	2.0	UNITED ARTISTS	
CRIME SCHOOL	1938	86		2.5	2.0	WARNER BROTHERS	
CRIME WAVE	1954	74		2.0	2.0	WARNER BROTHERS	
CRIME WITHOUT PASSION	1934	80	6*	3.5	3.0	PARAMOUNT	
CRIMINAL LAWYER	1951	74		2.0	1.5	COLUMBIA	
CRIMSON BLADE, THE	1963	81	3			COLUMBIA	
CRIMSON CANARY	1945	64		2.5		UNIVERSAL	
CRIMSON CULT, THE	1970	87	2			AMERICAN-INTERNAT'L	
CRIMSON KIMONO, THE	1959	84		2.0	2.0	COLUMBIA	
CRIMSON PIRATE, THE	1952	104	5*	3.0	2.5	WARNER BROTHERS	
CRIPPLE CREEK	1952	78		2.0	2.5	COLUMBIA	
CRISIS	1950	95		2.5	2.5	M-G-M	
CRISS CROSS	1949	87		3.0	2.5	UNIVERSAL	
CRITIC'S CHOICE	1963	100		2.5	2.5	WARNER BROTHERS	
CROMWELL (BRITISH)	1970	139	8*			COLUMBIA	
CROOK, THE (FRENCH)	1971	120	6			UNITED ARTISTS	
CROOKED CIRCLE, THE	1957	72	1	1.5		REPUBLIC	
CROOKED ROAD, THE (BRIT.- ROBERT RYAN, S. GRANGER)	1964	90	2	1.0	2.5	SEVEN ARTS	
CROOKED SKY, THE (BRITISH)	1957	77		1.5		UNITED ARTISTS	
CROOKED WAY, THE	1949	90		2.0	2.0	UNITED ARTISTS	
CROOKED WEB, THE	1955	77		2.0	1.5	COLUMBIA	
CROOKS ANONYMOUS (BRITISH)	1962	87	4	2.0		JANUS FILMS	
CROSS AND THE SWITCHBLADE, THE	1970	106	4			DICK ROSS & ASSOC.	
CROSS COUNTRY ROMANCE	1940	68		2.0		RKO	
CROSS MY HEART	1947	83		2.0		PARAMOUNT	
CROSS OF LORRAINE, THE	1943	90	4*	3.0	3.5	M-G-M	
CROSS UP	a1955	83	3	2.0		UNITED ARTISTS	
CROSSED SWORDS (ITALIAN)	1954	86		1.5	1.5	UNITED ARTISTS	
CROSSFIRE (ROBERT YOUNG, ROBERT MITCHUM)	1947	86	5*	4.0	3.5	RKO	NOMINATED BEST PICTURE
CROSSROADS	1942	84		2.0	2.0	M-G-M	
CROSSROADS TO CRIME (BRITISH)	1960	57		2.0		ANGLO AMALGAMATED	
CROSSTRAP (BRITISH)	1961	62		2.0	1.5	UNIFILMS	
CROSSWINDS	1951	93		2.0	2.0	PARAMOUNT	
CROWD ROARS, THE (JAMES CAGNEY, JOAN BLONDELL)	1932	85		2.0	2.5	WARNER BROTHERS	
CROWD ROARS, THE (ROBERT TAYLOR, EDWARD ARNOLD)	1938	92		2.5	2.5	M-G-M	
CROWDED PARADISE	1955	94		2.5		TUDOR PICTURES	
CROWDED SKY, THE	1960	105	3	2.5	2.5	WARNER BROTHERS	
CROWHAVEN FARM (T.V.)	1970	90		2.5		ABC FILMS	
CROWNING EXPERIENCE, THE	1960	100	5	2.0		MORAL REARMAMENT	
CRUCIBLE, THE (FRENCH)	a1957	140	6	3.5	3.0	KINGSLEY INTERNAT'L	
CRUCIBLE OF HORROR (BRITISH)	1971	91	3			CANNON RELEASING	
CRUEL SEA, THE (BRITISH)	1952	126	5*	4.0	3.5	UNIVERSAL	
CRUEL SWAMP	a1955	73		1.5	1.5	WOOLNER BROTHERS	
CRUEL TOWER, THE	1957	80		3.0		ALLIED ARTISTS	
CRUISIN' DOWN THE RIVER	1953	81	3	2.0		COLUMBIA	
CRUSADES, THE	1935	123		2.5	3.0	PARAMOUNT	
CRY BABY KILLER, THE	1958	62		2.5		ALLIED ARTISTS	
CRY BLOOD, APACHE	1970	82	2			GOLDEN EAGLE INT'L	
CRY DANGER	1951	79	5	3.5	3.0	RKO	
CRY FOR HAPPY	1961	110		2.5	2.5	COLUMBIA	
CRY FROM THE STREETS, A (BRITISH)	1958	99	6	3.0	3.0	TUDOR PICTURES	
CRY HAVOC	1943	97		2.5	2.5	M-G-M	
CRY IN THE NIGHT, A	1956	75		2.0	2.5	WARNER BROTHERS	
CRY OF BATTLE	1963	99		2.0	2.5	ALLIED ARTISTS	
CRY OF THE BANSHEE (BRITISH)	1970	87	3			AMERICAN-INTERNAT'L	
CRY OF THE BEWITCHED (MEXICAN)	1957	80		1.5		FUTURAMIC	
CRY OF THE CITY	1948	95	4*	3.0	2.5	20th CENTURY FOX	
CRY OF THE HUNTED	1953	80		2.5	2.0	M-G-M	
CRY OF THE WEREWOLF	1944	63		1.5	2.0	COLUMBIA	
CRY TERROR	1958	96		2.5	3.0	M-G-M	
CRY, THE BELOVED COUNTRY (BRITISH)	a1951	105	5*	3.5	3.5	UNITED ARTISTS	
CRY TOUGH	1959	83		2.5	2.0	UNITED ARTISTS	
CRY UNCLE	1971	87	2			CAMBIST	
CRY VENGEANCE	1954	83	4	3.0	2.5	ALLIED ARTISTS	
CRY WOLF (ERROL FLYNN, BARBARA STANWYCK)	1947	83		2.0	2.0	WARNER BROTHERS	
CRYSTAL BALL, THE	1943	81		2.0	2.0	UNITED ARTISTS	
CUBAN FIREBALL	1951	78		2.0		REPUBLIC	
CUL-DE-SAC (BRITISH)	1966	110	6			SIGMA III	
CULPEPPER CATTLE COMPANY, THE	1972	92	4			20th CENTURY FOX	
CULT OF THE COBRA	1955	82		2.0	2.5	UNIVERSAL	
CULT OF THE DAMNED	a1969	93	2			AMERICAN-INTERNAT'L	
CURE FOR LOVE, THE (BRITISH)	1949	97		2.5		ASSOCIATED ARTISTS	

‡ An asterisk (*) in THE FILM BUFF'S BIBLE column indicates that the film has been rated by the editor and/or staff. All other ratings in this column are based on a consensus of reviews (see NOTES).

TITLE (LEADING ACTORS SHOWN WHERE TWO OR MORE FILMS HAVE THE SAME OR SIMILAR TITLE)	YEAR RELEASED	RUNNING TIME IN MINUTES	THE FILM BUFF'S BIBLE ‡	STEVEN SCHEUER	LEONARD MALTIN	DISTRIBUTOR	COMMENT
CURLEY	a1947	53			2.0	UNITED ARTISTS	
CURLY TOP	1935	75			2.5	20th CENTURY FOX	
CURSE OF DRACULA, THE	a1958	77		2.0	2.0	UNITED ARTISTS	
CURSE OF FRANKENSTEIN, THE (BRITISH)	1957	83	4*	2.0		WARNER BROTHERS	
CURSE OF NOSTRADAMUS, THE (MEXICAN)	1962	77		1.0		AZTECA	
CURSE OF THE AZTEC MUMMY, THE (MEXICAN)	1959	65		1.0		AZTECA	
CURSE OF THE CAT PEOPLE, THE	1944	70		3.0	3.0	RKO	
CURSE OF THE CRYING WOMAN, THE (MEXICAN)	1960	74		1.0		AZTECA	
CURSE OF THE DEMON (BRITISH)	a1957	82	4*	2.5	2.5	COLUMBIA	
CURSE OF THE DOLL PEOPLE (MEXICAN)	1961	81		1.0		TRANS-INTERNATIONAL	
CURSE OF THE FACELESS MAN	1958	66		1.0	1.0	UNITED ARTISTS	
CURSE OF THE FLY, THE (BRITISH)	1965	86	2		2.0	20th CENTURY FOX	
CURSE OF THE HIDDEN VAULT, THE (GERMAN)	1964	91		1.5		UCC FILMS	
CURSE OF THE LIVING CORPSE, THE	1964	84	1			20th CENTURY FOX	
CURSE OF THE MUMMY'S TOMB, THE (BRITISH)	1964	80	2	2.0	2.0	COLUMBIA	
CURSE OF THE STONE HAND	1964	72		1.0		MEDALLION	
CURSE OF THE UNDEAD	1959	79	2	2.0	2.0	UNIVERSAL	
CURSE OF THE VAMPIRES (PHILLIPINE)	1970	90	1			HEMISPHERE	
CURSE OF THE VOODOO (BRITISH)	1965	77	1	2.0	1.5	ALLIED ARTISTS	
CURSE OF THE WEREWOLF, THE (BRITISH)	1961	91	4	3.0	2.5	UNIVERSAL	
CURSE OF THE YELLOW SNAKE, THE (GERMAN)	1963	100		1.5	2.5	UCC FILMS	
CURTAIN CALL	1940	63		3.0		RKO	
CURTAIN CALL AT CACTUS CREEK	1950	86		2.5	2.5	UNIVERSAL	
CURTAIN UP (BRITISH)	1952	81		2.5	2.5	J. ARTHUR RANK	
CURUCU, BEAST OF THE AMAZON	1956	76		2.0	1.5	UNIVERSAL	
CUSTER OF THE WEST	1967	120	4	2.5		CINERAMA RELEASING	
CUSTOMS AGENT	1950	72		2.0		COLUMBIA	
CYCLE SAVAGES, THE	1970	82	1			AMERICAN-INTERNAT'L	
CYCLOPS, THE	1957	75		1.5	2.0	ALLIED ARTISTS	
CYCLOTRODE 'X'	1946	100		2.5	2.5	REPUBLIC	RE-EDITED SERIAL
CYNARA	1932	75		2.5	2.0	UNITED ARTISTS	
CYNTHIA	1947	98	3	2.0	1.5	M-G-M	
CYRANO DE BERGERAC	1950	112	8*	3.5	4.0	UNITED ARTISTS	
D.A. - CONSPIRACY TO KILL, THE (T.V.)	1970	100		1.5		UNIVERSAL	
D.A.: MURDER ONE, THE (T.V.)	1969	100	4*	2.5		UNIVERSAL	
D-DAY ON MARS	1945	100			2.0	REPUBLIC	RE-EDITED SERIAL
D-DAY, THE SIXTH OF JUNE	1956	106	5	3.0	3.0	20th CENTURY FOX	
D.I., THE	1957	106	4*	2.0	2.0	WARNER BROTHERS	
D.O.A.	1949	83	5	3.5	3.0	UNITED ARTISTS	
DADDY LONG LEGS	1955	126		3.5	2.5	20th CENTURY FOX	
DADDY-O	1959	74		1.0		AMERICAN-INTERNAT'L	
DADDY'S GONE A-HUNTING	1969	108	4	2.5		NATIONAL GENERAL	
DAGGERS DRAWN (FRENCH)	1964	85		1.5		PARAMOUNT	
DAGMAR'S HOT PANTS, INC.	1971	94	2			AMERICAN-INTERNAT'L	
DAGORA, THE SPACE MONSTER (JAPANESE)	1965	81		1.0		TOHAN	
DAISIES (CZECH)	1966	74	3			SIGMA III	
DAISY KENYON	1947	99	5	2.5	2.5	20th CENTURY FOX	
DAKOTA	1945	82		2.0	2.0	REPUBLIC	
DAKOTA INCIDENT	1956	88	4	2.5	2.5	REPUBLIC	
DAKOTA LIL	1950	88		2.5	2.0	20th CENTURY FOX	
DALEKS - INVASION EARTH 2150 A.D. (BRITISH)	a1966	84			2.5	CONTINENTAL	
DALLAS	1950	94		2.5	2.5	WARNER BROTHERS	
DALTON GIRLS, THE	1957	71	1	1.5	1.5	UNITED ARTISTS	
DAM BUSTERS, THE (BRITISH)	1955	102	6*	4.0	2.5	WARNER BROTHERS	
DAMES	1934	90		3.0	3.0	WARNER BROTHERS	
DAMN CITIZEN	1958	88		2.5	2.5	UNIVERSAL	
DAMN THE DEFIANT! (BRITISH)	a1962	101		3.0	3.0	COLUMBIA	
DAMN YANKEES	1958	110	5*	2.5	3.0	WARNER BROTHERS	
DAMNED, THE (ITAL. - DIRK BOGARDE, INGRID THULIN)	a1969	153	6			WARNER BROTHERS	ENGLISH LANGUAGE
DAMNED DON'T CRY, THE	1950	103		2.5	2.5	WARNER BROTHERS	
DAMON AND PYTHIAS (ITALIAN)	1962	99	2		2.0	M-G-M	
DAMSEL IN DISTRESS, A	1937	98		3.0	3.0	RKO	
DANCE, FOOLS, DANCE	1931	81		3.0	2.5	M-G-M	
DANCE, GIRL, DANCE	1940	90		2.5	2.5	RKO	
DANCE HALL (CESAR ROMERO, CAROLE LANDIS)	1941	74		1.5	1.5	20th CENTURY FOX	
DANCE HALL (BRITISH - PETULA CLARK, NATASHA PERRY)	1950	80		2.5		J. ARTHUR RANK	
DANCE, LITTLE LADY (BRITISH)	1954	87		2.5		TRANS-LUX DIST.	
DANCE OF DEATH (FRENCH)	1960	86		1.5		PARAMOUNT	
DANCE WITH ME, HENRY	1956	80		1.5	2.0	UNITED ARTISTS	
DANCERS IN THE DARK	1932	60			2.5	PARAMOUNT	
DANCING CO-ED	1939	84		2.0		M-G-M	
DANCING IN MANHATTAN	1944	60		2.5		COLUMBIA	
DANCING IN THE DARK	1950	92		3.0	2.5	20th CENTURY FOX	
DANCING LADY	1933	82	3*	3.0	2.5	M-G-M	
DANCING MASTERS, THE	1943	63		1.5	1.5	20th CENTURY FOX	
DANCING MOTHERS (SILENT)	1926	80			2.5	PARAMOUNT	
DANCING ON A DIME	1941	74		2.5	2.5	PARAMOUNT	
DANDY IN ASPIC, A (BRITISH)	1968	107	3	1.0		COLUMBIA	
DANGER BY MY SIDE (BRITISH)	1962	63		1.5	2.0	BUTCHER'S	
DANGER: DIABOLIK (ITALIAN)	1967	99	3	1.0		PARAMOUNT	
DANGER IN THE MIDDLE EAST (FRENCH)	1959	88		1.5		LUTETIA FILMS	

‡ An asterisk (*) in THE FILM BUFF'S BIBLE column indicates that the film has been rated by the editor and/or staff. All other ratings in this column are based on a consensus of reviews (see NOTES).

TITLE (LEADING ACTORS SHOWN WHERE TWO OR MORE FILMS HAVE THE SAME OR SIMILAR TITLE)	YEAR RELEASED	RUNNING TIME IN MINUTES	THE FILM BUFF'S BIBLE ‡	STEVEN SCHEUER	LEONARD MALTIN	DISTRIBUTOR	COMMENT
DANGER - LOVE AT WORK	1937	81		2.5	2.5	20th CENTURY FOX	
DANGER ON MY SIDE (BRITISH)	1961	72		1.5		UNITED PRODS. OF AMER	
DANGER ON THE RIVER	a1942	60		2.0		UNIVERSAL	
DANGER ROUTE (BRITISH)	1968	91	2			UNITED ARTISTS	
DANGER SIGNAL	1945	78		2.0	2.0	WARNER BROTHERS	
DANGER TOMORROW (BRITISH)	1960	61		2.0		ANGLO AMALGAMATED	
DANGEROUS	1935	78	5*	2.5	2.5	WARNER BROTHERS	
DANGEROUS AGE, A (CANADIAN)	1957	70		2.0		AJAY FILMS	
DANGEROUS AGENT (FRENCH)	1954	88		1.5		LUTETIA FILMS	
DANGEROUS ASSIGNMENT (BRITISH)	1950	58		1.5			
DANGEROUS BLONDES	1943	80		3.0		COLUMBIA	
DANGEROUS CARGO (BRITISH)	1954	61		2.0		MODERN SOUND PICS.	
DANGEROUS CHARTER	1962	76		1.5		CROWN INTERNATIONAL	
DANGEROUS CROSSING	1953	75		2.5	2.5	20th CENTURY FOX	
DANGEROUS DAYS OF KIOWA JONES, THE	1966	100		2.0	2.5	M-G-M	
DANGEROUS EXILE (BRITISH)	1957	90	4	2.5	2.0	J. ARTHUR RANK	
DANGEROUS FEMALE	a1931	80		2.0	2.0	WARNER BROTHERS	
DANGEROUS GAME, A (RICHARD ARLEN, ANDY DEVINE)	1941	60		1.5		UNIVERSAL	
DANGEROUS GAMES (FRENCH - JEAN SERVAIS)	1958	90		2.0		WARNER BROTHERS	
DANGEROUS JOURNEY	1944	73		2.5		20th CENTURY FOX	
DANGEROUS MISSION	1954	75		2.0	2.0	RKO	
DANGEROUS MONEY	1946	64		-		MONOGRAM	
DANGEROUS MOONLIGHT (BRITISH)	a1941	98		4.0	3.0	RKO	
DANGEROUS PARTNERS	1945	74		2.5	2.5	M-G-M	
DANGEROUS PASSAGE	1944	62		2.0		PARAMOUNT	
DANGEROUS PROFESSION, A	1949	79		2.0	2.0	RKO	
DANGEROUS TO KNOW	1938	70		1.5	2.5	PARAMOUNT	
DANGEROUS WHEN WET	1953	95		2.0	2.0	M-G-M	
DANGEROUS YEARS	1948	62		2.0		20th CENTURY FOX	
DANGEROUS YOUTH	1958	98	2	1.0		WARNER BROTHERS	
DANGEROUSLY THEY LIVE	1941	71		2.5	2.5	WARNER BROTHERS	
DANIEL BOONE, TRAIL BLAZER	1956	76		1.5	2.5	REPUBLIC	
DANTE'S INFERNO	1935	88			2.5	20th CENTURY FOX	
DANUBE, THE (DOCUMENTARY)	1961	30	5*			BUENA VISTA	
DARBY O'GILL AND THE LITTLE PEOPLE	1959	93	6			BUENA VISTA	
DARBY'S RANGERS	1958	121		2.0	2.5	WARNER BROTHERS	
DAREDEVILS OF THE CLOUDS	1948	60		2.0		REPUBLIC	
DARING GAME	1968	100	3	2.0		PARAMOUNT	
DARING YOUNG MAN	1942	73		2.0	2.0	COLUMBIA	
DARK ALIBI	1946	61			-	MONOGRAM	
DARK ANGEL, THE	1935	110	6*	3.0	3.0	UNITED ARTISTS	
DARK AT THE TOP OF THE STAIRS, THE	1960	123	6*	3.0	3.0	WARNER BROTHERS	
DARK CITY	1950	88		2.5	2.5	PARAMOUNT	
DARK COMMAND	1940	94	4*	3.5	3.0	REPUBLIC	
DARK CORNER, THE	1946	99		3.0	3.0	20th CENTURY FOX	
DARK DELUSION	1947	90	4	2.5	-	M-G-M	
DARK HAZARD	1934	72		3.0	2.0	FIRST NATIONAL	
DARK HORSE (WARREN WILLIAM, BETTE DAVIS)	1932	75		3.5	2.5	FIRST NATIONAL	
DARK HORSE, THE (PHILLIP TERRY, ANN SAVAGE)	1946	80		2.5		UNIVERSAL	
DARK INTRUDER	1965	59		2.0	2.0	UNIVERSAL	
DARK JOURNEY	1937	82	4*			UNITED ARTISTS	
DARK MAN, THE (BRITISH)	1951	73		2.5		J. ARTHUR RANK	
DARK MIRROR, THE	1946	85	6*	3.5	3.5	UNIVERSAL	
DARK OF THE SUN (BRITISH)	1968	101	3	2.0		M-G-M	
DARK PASSAGE	1947	106	6*	2.5	3.0	WARNER BROTHERS	
DARK PAST, THE	1949	75		3.0	3.0	COLUMBIA	
DARK PURPOSE (ITALIAN-FRENCH)	1964	97	2	1.0		UNIVERSAL	ENGLISH LANGUAGE
DARK VENTURE	1956	84		1.0		ALLIED ARTISTS	
DARK VICTORY	1939	106	6*	3.5	3.5	WARNER BROTHERS	NOMINATED BEST PICTURE
DARK WATERS	1944	90		2.5	2.0	UNITED ARTISTS	
DARKER THAN AMBER	1970	97	3			NATIONAL GENERAL	
DARLING (BRITISH)	1965	127	8*	4.0	3.5	AVCO-EMBASSY	NOMINATED BEST PICTURE
DARLING, HOW COULD YOU	1951	96		2.0	2.5	PARAMOUNT	
DARLING LILI	1970	130	5			PARAMOUNT	
DATE AT MIDNIGHT (BRITISH)	1959	57		2.0		WARNER BROTHERS	
DATE BAIT	1960	71		1.0		FILMGROUP	
DATE WITH DEATH, A	1959	81		1.0		PACIFIC INTERNAT'L	
DATE WITH DISASTER (BRITISH)	1957	61		1.5		ASTOR	
DATE WITH JUDY, A	1948	113		2.5	2.5	M-G-M	
DATE WITH THE FALCON, A	1941	63		2.0	-	RKO	
DAUGHTER, THE	a1970	85	1			CHEVRON	
DAUGHTER OF DARKNESS (BRITISH - SIOBHAN MCKENNA)	1947	92		3.0		SCREENCRAFT	
DAUGHTER OF DR JEKYLL	1957	71		1.0	1.5	ALLIED ARTISTS	
DAUGHTER OF ROSIE O'GRADY, THE	1950	104		2.5	2.5	WARNER BROTHERS	
DAUGHTER OF SHANGHAI	1937	63		2.0	2.0	PARAMOUNT	
DAUGHTER OF THE JUNGLE	1949	69		1.0		REPUBLIC	
DAUGHTER OF THE MIND (T.V.)	1969	90		2.5		20th CENTURY FOX	
DAUGHTERS COURAGEOUS	1939	103		3.0	3.0	WARNER BROTHERS	
DAUGHTERS OF DARKNESS (BELGIAN - DELPHINE SEYRIG)	1971	87	1			GEMINI	ENGLISH VERSION
DAUGHTERS OF DESTINY (FRENCH)	1954	54	4	2.0	2.0	ARLAN PICTURES	
DAVID AND BATHSHEBA	1952	116	4	2.5	2.0	20th CENTURY FOX	
DAVID AND GOLIATH (ITALIAN)	1959	95	3*	2.0	2.0	ALLIED ARTISTS	
DAVID AND LISA	1962	94	7*	4.0	3.0	CONTINENTAL	
DAVID COPPERFIELD (W. C. FIELDS, LIONEL BARRYMORE)	1935	133	5-6*	4.0	4.0	M-G-M	NOMINATED BEST PICTURE

‡ An asterisk (*) in THE FILM BUFF'S BIBLE column indicates that the film has been rated by the editor and/or staff. All other ratings in this column are based on a consensus of reviews (see NOTES).

TITLE (LEADING ACTORS SHOWN WHERE TWO OR MORE FILMS HAVE THE SAME OR SIMILAR TITLE)	YEAR RELEASED	RUNNING TIME IN MINUTES	THE FILM BUFF'S BIBLE ‡	STEVEN SCHEUER	LEONARD MALTIN	DISTRIBUTOR	COMMENT
DAVID COPPERFIELD (BRITISH - ROBIN PHILLIPS)	1970	118	6*			20th CENTURY FOX	
DAVID HARDING, COUNTERSPY	1950	71	4			COLUMBIA	
DAVID HARUM	1934	83		2.5	2.5	20th CENTURY FOX	
DAVY CROCKETT AND THE RIVER PIRATES	1956	85	5*			BUENA VISTA	
DAVY CROCKETT, INDIAN SCOUT	1950	71		2.0	2.0	UNITED ARTISTS	
DAVY CROCKETT, KING OF THE WILD FRONTIER	1955	95	5*			BUENA VISTA	
DAWN AT SOCORRO	1954	80	3	2.5	2.5	UNIVERSAL	
DAWN PATROL, THE (RICHARD BARTHELMESS)	a1930	112		2.5		FIRST NATIONAL	
DAWN PATROL, THE (ERROL FLYNN, DAVID NIVEN)	1938	103	5*	3.5	3.5	WARNER BROTHERS	
DAY AND THE HOUR, THE (FRENCH)	1963	115	6	3.0		M-G-M	
DAY AT THE RACES, A	1937	111		3.5	3.5	M-G-M	
DAY IN THE DEATH OF JOE EGG (BRITISH)	1972	100				COLUMBIA	
DAY IT RAINED, THE (GERMAN)	1959	85		1.0		PARAMOUNT	
DAY MARS INVADED EARTH, THE	1963	70	3			20th CENTURY FOX	
DAY OF ANGER (ITALIAN)	1969	109	3			NATIONAL GENERAL	
DAY OF FEAR (SPANISH)	1957	83		1.5		MARTIN GOSCH	ENGLISH LANGUAGE
DAY OF FURY, A	1956	78	4	2.0	3.0	UNIVERSAL	
DAY OF THE BADMAN	1958	81		2.0	2.0	UNIVERSAL	
DAY OF THE EVIL GUN	1968	95		2.5	2.0	M-G-M	
DAY OF THE OUTLAW	1959	90		2.0	2.0	UNITED ARTISTS	
DAY OF THE TRIFFIDS, THE	1963	93	4	3.0	2.5	ALLIED ARTISTS	
DAY OF WRATH (DANISH)	1943	96				GEORGE SCHAEFER	
DAY THE EARTH CAUGHT FIRE, THE (BRITISH)	1961	90	5*	3.5	3.0	UNIVERSAL	
DAY THE EARTH FROZE, THE	1964	69		1.5		AMERICAN-INTERNAT'L	
DAY THE EARTH STOOD STILL, THE	1951	92	5*	3.0	3.5	20th CENTURY FOX	
DAY THE FISH CAME OUT, THE (BRITISH)	1967	109	2*	1.0		INTERNAT'L CLASSICS	
DAY THE SKY EXPLODED, THE (ITALIAN)	1958	80	2	1.5	2.5	EXCELSIOR	
DAY THE WORLD ENDED, THE	1956	80		1.5	2.0	AMERICAN RELEASING	
DAY THEY ROBBED THE BANK OF ENGLAND, THE (BRITISH)	1960	85	3*	3.0		M-G-M	
DAY TO REMEMBER, A (BRITISH)	1953	92		2.5		REPUBLIC	
DAYBREAK (BRITISH - ERIC PORTMAN, ANN TODD)	1947	88		2.0	2.0	J. ARTHUR RANK	
DAYDREAMER, THE	1966	101		3.0		AVCO-EMBASSY	
DAYS OF GLORY	1944	86		2.5	2.5	RKO	
DAYS OF THRILLS AND LAUGHTER	1961	93	5*		4.0	20th CENTURY FOX	
DAYS OF WINE AND ROSES	1963	117	7*	3.5	3.5	WARNER BROTHERS	
DAYTIME WIFE	1939	71		2.5	2.0	20th CENTURY FOX	
DAYTON'S DEVILS	1968	101	3			LANDAU/UNGER COM. UN.	
DE SADE	1969	113	2			AMERICAN-INTERNAT'L	
DEAD ARE ALIVE, THE	1972	104	1			NATIONAL GENERAL	
DEAD END	1937	93	4*	3.5	3.5	UNITED ARTISTS	NOMINATED BEST PICTURE
DEAD EYES OF LONDON (GERMAN)	1961	104	1	1.5		MAGNA PICTURES	
DEAD HEAT ON A MERRY-GO-ROUND	1966	104	6*	3.5	3.0	COLUMBIA	
DEAD MAN'S CHEST (BRITISH)	1965	59		2.0		AVCO-EMBASSY	
DEAD MAN'S EYES	1944	64		1.5	2.0	UNIVERSAL	
DEAD OF NIGHT (BRITISH)	1945	104	6*	4.0	4.0	UNIVERSAL	
DEAD OF SUMMER	1971	89	3			PLAZA PICTURES	
DEAD RECKONING	1947	100	5-6*	3.0	3.0	COLUMBIA	
DEAD RINGER	1964	115	4	2.5	2.5	WARNER BROTHERS	
DEAD TO THE WORLD	1962	87	2	1.0		UNITED ARTISTS	
DEADFALL (BRITISH)	1968	120	2	1.5		20th CENTURY FOX	
DEADLIER THAN THE MALE (FRENCH - JEAN GABIN)	1957	104		2.5	2.0	CONTINENTAL	
DEADLIER THAN THE MALE (BRITISH - RICHARD JOHNSON)	1967	98		2.5		UNIVERSAL	
DEADLIEST SIN, THE (BRITISH)	1956	77		2.0	1.5	ALLIED ARTISTS	
DEADLINE AT DAWN	1946	83		2.5	2.5	RKO	
DEADLINE U.S.A.	1952	87	6	3.0	3.0	20th CENTURY FOX	
DEADLOCK (T.V. - LESLIE NIELSEN, HARI RHODES)	1969	100		3.0		UNIVERSAL	
DEADLY AFFAIR, THE (BRITISH)	1967	107	6	3.0	3.0	COLUMBIA	
DEADLY BEES, THE (BRITISH)	1967	83		2.5	2.0	PARAMOUNT	
DEADLY COMPANIONS, THE	1961	90	5*	3.0	2.5	PATHE-AMERICA	
DEADLY DECISION (GERMAN)	a1954	92		2.5	2.0	DOMINANT PICTURES	
DEADLY DECOY, THE (FRENCH)	1962	90		1.5		FOUR STAR	
DEADLY DUO	1962	70	3			UNITED ARTISTS	
DEADLY IS THE FEMALE	a1949	87	4	3.0		UNITED ARTISTS	
DEADLY MANTIS, THE	1957	78		2.5	2.0	UNIVERSAL	
DEADLY RECORD (BRITISH)	1959	59		2.0		ANGLO AMALGAMATED	
DEADWOOD '76	1964	110		1.0		FILMWAY INTERNAT'L	
DEALING	1972	88	3			WARNER BROTHERS	
DEAR BRAT	1951	82	4		2.5	PARAMOUNT	
DEAR BRIGITTE	1965	100		2.5	2.5	20th CENTURY FOX	
DEAR CAROLINE (FRENCH)	1951	90		2.0			
DEAR HEART	1965	114	3*	3.0	3.0	WARNER BROTHERS	
DEAR JOHN (SWEDISH)	1964	115	6			SIGMA III	
DEAR MURDERER (BRITISH)	1947	94		2.0		UNIVERSAL	
DEAR RUTH	1947	95	5	2.5	2.5	PARAMOUNT	
DEAR WIFE	1950	88		3.0	2.5	PARAMOUNT	
DEATH AND THE SKY ABOVE (BRITISH)	1959	60		2.0			
DEATH IN SMALL DOSES	1957	79		2.0	1.5	ALLIED ARTISTS	
DEATH IN VENICE (ITALIAN)	1971	121	2*			WARNER BROTHERS	ENGLISH LANGUAGE
DEATH IS A WOMAN (BRITISH)	1965	80		2.0		AMERICAN-INTERNAT'L	
DEATH OF A CHAMPION	1939	67		2.0		PARAMOUNT	
DEATH OF A GUNFIGHTER	1969	94	3	2.5		UNIVERSAL	
DEATH OF A JEW	1972	90				H.K. FILM DIST.	
DEATH OF A SALESMAN	1951	115	7	4.0	3.5	COLUMBIA	
DEATH OF A SCOUNDREL	1956	119		2.0	2.5	RKO	

‡ An asterisk (*) in THE FILM BUFF'S BIBLE column indicates that the film has been rated by the editor and/or staff. All other ratings in this column are based on a consensus of reviews (see NOTES).

TITLE (LEADING ACTORS SHOWN WHERE TWO OR MORE FILMS HAVE THE SAME OR SIMILAR TITLE)	YEAR RELEASED	RUNNING TIME IN MINUTES	THE FILM BUFF'S BIBLE ‡	STEVEN SCHEUER	LEONARD MALTIN	DISTRIBUTOR	COMMENT
DEATH OF TARZAN, THE (CZECH)	a1962	72	5	3.0		BRANDON	
DEATH OF THE APE-MAN (CZECH)	a1962	72	5	3.0		BRANDON	
DEATH RIDES A HORSE (ITALIAN)	1968	115	3			UNITED ARTISTS	
DEATH TAKES A HOLIDAY (FREDRIC MARCH, E. VENABLE)	1934	78	7*	3.5	3.5	PARAMOUNT	
DEATH TAKES A HOLIDAY (T.V. - YVETTE MIMEUX)	1971	90	4*			UNIVERSAL	
DEATH TRAP (BRITISH)	1962	56		2.0		ANGLO AMALGAMATED	
DEATHWATCH	1967	88	4			ALTURA FILMS	
DECAMERON, THE (ITALIAN)	1971	114	3			UNITED ARTISTS	EIGHT STORIES
DECAMERON NIGHTS (BRITISH)	1953	94		3.0	2.0	RKO	
DECEPTION	1946	112		2.5	3.5	COLUMBIA	
DECISION AGAINST TIME (BRITISH)	1957	87		2.5	2.5	M-G-M	
DECISION AT SUNDOWN	1957	95	4	3.5	2.0	COLUMBIA	
DECISION BEFORE DAWN	1951	119	6*	2.5	3.0	20th CENTURY FOX	NOMINATED BEST PICTURE
DECISION OF CHRISTOPHER BLAKE, THE	1948	75		2.5	2.5	WARNER BROTHERS	
DECKS RAN RED, THE	1958	84		2.0	2.5	M-G-M	
DECLINE AND FALL OF A BIRDWATCHER (BRITISH)	1968	113	3	2.0		20th CENTURY FOX	
DECOY (JEAN GILLIE, EDWARD NORRIS)	1946	76	3	3.0		MONOGRAM	
DEEP ADVENTURE	1957	46	3			WARNER BROTHERS	
DEEP BLUE SEA, THE (BRITISH)	1955	99		2.0	2.5	20th CENTURY FOX	
DEEP END	1971	87	4			PARAMOUNT	
DEEP IN MY HEART	1954	132		3.0	2.5	M-G-M	
DEEP SIX, THE	1958	105		2.0	2.5	WARNER BROTHERS	
DEEP VALLEY	1947	104	3*	3.0	3.0	WARNER BROTHERS	
DEEP WATERS	1948	85	4	2.0	2.0	20th CENTURY FOX	
DEERSLAYER, THE	1957	78		1.5	1.5	20th CENTURY FOX	
DEFEAT OF HANNIBAL, THE (ITALIAN)	1937	102		1.0		TELEWIDE SYSTEMS	
DEFEAT OF THE BARBARIANS, THE (ITALIAN)	1962	85		1.0		TRANS-AMERICA	
DEFECTOR, THE (FRENCH-GERMAN)	1966	68		3.5	2.5	SEVEN ARTS	
DEFIANT DAUGHTERS (SWISS)	1962	91		2.0		TIMES FILM CORP.	
DEFIANT ONES, THE	1958	97	6*	4.0	4.0	UNITED ARTISTS	NOMINATED BEST PICTURE
DELICATE DELINQUENT, THE	1957	100	3*	3.0	3.0	PARAMOUNT	
DELICIOUS	1931	106				20th CENTURY FOX	
DELIGHTFULLY DANGEROUS	1945	93		1.0	2.5	UNITED ARTISTS	
DELINQUENTS (GLORIA MARLEN, CHARLES THORNBRIDGE)	1950	55		1.0		OFFICIAL INDUSTRIES	
DELIVERANCE (JON VOIGHT, BURT REYNOLDS)	1972	109	6			WARNER BROTHERS	
DEMENTIA 13	a1963	81	3*	3.0		AMERICAN-INTERNAT'L	
DEMETRIUS AND THE GLADIATORS	1954	101		2.5	2.5	20th CENTURY FOX	
DEMON PLANET, THE (ITALIAN)	a1965	86	2	1.5	2.5	AMERICAN-INTERNAT'L	
DEMONIAQUE (FRENCH)	1957	97		3.5	2.5	UN. MOTION PIC. ORG.	
DENTIST IN THE CHAIR (BRITISH)	1960	84		1.5	2.0	AJAY FILMS	
DENVER AND RIO GRANDE, THE	1952	89		2.5	2.5	PARAMOUNT	
DEPARTURE, THE (BELGIAN)	a1967	90	4			PATHE CONTEMPARARY	
DEPORTED	1950	80		2.5	2.5	UNIVERSAL	
DER ROSENKAVALIER (GERMAN - ELISABETH SCHWARZKOPF)	1962	192	7			SHOWCORPORATION	
DERBY (DOCUMENTARY)	a1971	91	5			CINERAMA RELEASING	
DERBY DAY (BRITISH)	a1952	84		3.0	2.5	CONTINENTAL	
DESERT ATTACK (BRITISH)	a1958	76		3.0	3.0	20th CENTURY FOX	
DESERT DESPERADOES (ITALIAN)	a1959	81		1.5	1.0	RKO	
DESERT FIGHTERS (FRENCH)	1960	85		1.5		AMERICAN-INTERNAT'L	
DESERT FOX, THE	1951	88	5*	3.5	3.0	20th CENTURY FOX	
DESERT FURY	1947	95		2.0	2.5	PARAMOUNT	
DESERT HAWK, THE	1950	77		2.0	2.0	UNIVERSAL	
DESERT HELL	1958	82		1.5	2.0	20th CENTURY FOX	
DESERT LEGION	1953	86		2.0	2.0	UNIVERSAL	
DESERT PATROL (BRITISH)	a1958	78	5		2.5	UNIVERSAL	
DESERT PURSUIT	1952	71	2	2.0		MONOGRAM	
DESERT RAIDERS (ITALIAN)	1963	87		1.0			
DESERT RATS, THE	1953	88	6*	3.0	3.0	20th CENTURY FOX	
DESERT SANDS	1955	87	3			UNITED ARTISTS	
DESERT SONG, THE (DENNIS MORGAN, IRENE MANNING)	1944	96		2.5		WARNER BROTHERS	
DESERT SONG, THE (KATHRYN GRAYSON, GORDON MACRAE)	1953	110		2.0	2.5	WARNER BROTHERS	
DESERT WAR (ITALIAN)	1960	83		1.5		AMERICAN-INTERNAT'L	
DESERT WARRIOR, THE (SPANISH)	1956	87		2.0		MEDALLION	
DESERTER, THE (BEKIM FEHMIU, JOHN HUSTON)	1971	99	3			PARAMOUNT	
DESIGN FOR LIVING	1933	90		2.5	3.5	PARAMOUNT	
DESIGN FOR LOVING (BRITISH)	1960	68		1.5		COLUMBIA	
DESIGN FOR SCANDAL	1941	85		2.5	2.5	M-G-M	
DESIGNING WOMAN	1957	118	6	3.0	3.0	M-G-M	
DESIRABLE	1934	68		3.0		WARNER BROTHERS	
DESIRE	1936	89	5*	3.0	3.0	PARAMOUNT	
DESIRE IN THE DUST	1960	102		2.0	2.5	20th CENTURY FOX	
DESIRE ME	1947	91		2.0	2.0	M-G-M	
DESIRE UNDER THE ELMS	1958	114	5	2.5	2.5	PARAMOUNT	
DESIREE	1954	110	5*	2.5	2.5	20th CENTURY FOX	
DESK SET	1957	103	5*	3.5	3.5	20th CENTURY FOX	
DESPERADO, THE (WAYNE MORRIS)	1954	81		1.5		ALLIED ARTISTS	
DESPERADOES, THE (GLENN FORD, RANDOLPH SCOTT)	1943	85		3.0	3.0	COLUMBIA	
DESPERADOES, THE (VINCE EDWARDS, JACK PALANCE)	1969	90	2			COLUMBIA	
DESPERADOS ARE IN TOWN, THE	1956	73			1.5	20th CENTURY FOX	
DESPERATE	1947	73	5	3.0		RKO	
DESPERATE CHARACTERS	1971	88	2*			PARAMOUNT	
DESPERATE HOURS, THE	1955	112	7	3.5	3.5	PARAMOUNT	
DESPERATE JOURNEY	1942	107		2.5	3.0	WARNER BROTHERS	
DESPERATE MAN, THE (BRITISH)	1959	57		2.0	1.5	ANGLO AMALGAMATED	

‡ An asterisk (*) in THE FILM BUFF'S BIBLE column indicates that the film has been rated by the editor and/or staff. All other ratings in this column are based on a consensus of reviews (see NOTES).

TITLE (LEADING ACTORS SHOWN WHERE TWO OR MORE FILMS HAVE THE SAME OR SIMILAR TITLE)	YEAR RELEASED	RUNNING TIME IN MINUTES	THE FILM BUFF'S BIBLE ‡	STEVEN SCHEUER	LEONARD MALTIN	DISTRIBUTOR	COMMENT
DESPERATE MISSION (ITALIAN - GERMAN COBBS)	a1964	112		1.0		WARNER BROTHERS	
DESPERATE MISSION (T.V. - RICARDO MONTALBAN)	1971	100				20th CENTURY FOX	
DESPERATE MOMENT (BRITISH)	1953	88	6*	3.5	2.5	UNIVERSAL	
DESPERATE ONES, THE	1968	104	4			AMERICAN-INTERNAT'L	
DESPERATE SEARCH	1953	73		2.5	2.5	M-G-M	
DESPERATE SIEGE	a1951	86		2.5	2.5	20th CENTURY FOX	
DESTINATION BIG HOUSE	1950	60		2.0		REPUBLIC	
DESTINATION DEATH (GERMAN)	1963	93		2.0		ALLIED ARTISTS	
DESTINATION FURY (FRENCH)	1961	88		2.0	2.0	AMERICAN-INTERNAT'L	
DESTINATION GOBI	1953	89		2.5	2.5	20th CENTURY FOX	
DESTINATION INNER SPACE	1966	83	3		2.0	MAGNA PICTURES	
DESTINATION MOON	1950	90		3.0	2.5	EAGLE LION	
DESTINATION 60,000	1957	65		1.5	1.0	ALLIED ARTISTS	
DESTINATION TOKYO	1943	135	2*	3.5	3.0	WARNER BROTHERS	
DESTINATION UNKNOWN	1942	61		1.5		UNIVERSAL	
DESTINY (GLORIA JEAN, ALAN CURTIS)	1944	65		2.0	2.0	UNIVERSAL	
DESTINY OF A SPY (T.V.)	1969	100		2.5		UNIVERSAL	
DESTROY ALL MONSTERS (JAPANESE)	1968	88	1			AMERICAN-INTERNAT'L	
DESTROYER	1943	99		2.5	2.5	COLUMBIA	
DESTRUCTORS, THE	1968	97	3		2.0	FEATURE FILM CORP.	
DESTRY	1955	95		2.5	2.5	UNIVERSAL	
DESTRY RIDES AGAIN	1939	94		4.0	3.5	UNIVERSAL	
DETECTIVE, THE (BRITISH - ALEC GUINESS)	1955	91	6*	3.0	3.0	COLUMBIA	
DETECTIVE, THE (FRANK SINATRA, LEE REMICK)	1968	114	6	3.0		20th CENTURY FOX	
DETECTIVE BELLI	1971	103	3			PLAZA PICTURES	
DETECTIVE KITTY O'DAY	1944	63			2.0	MONOGRAM	
DETECTIVE STORY	1951	103	6*	4.0	3.5	PARAMOUNT	
DETOUR (TOM NEAL, ANN SAVAGE)	1945	69		3.0		PRODUCERS RELEASING	
DETOUR (BULGARIAN - IVAN ANDONOV)	1967	90	4			BRANDON	
DEVI (INDIAN)	1961	96	6			HARRISON PICTURES	
DEVIL AND DANIEL WEBSTER, THE	a1941	112	7*	4.0	3.5	RKO	
DEVIL AND MISS JONES, THE	1941	90	5-6*	3.0	3.0	RKO	
DEVIL AND THE DEEP	1932	78		3.0	2.5	PARAMOUNT	
DEVIL AND THE TEN COMMANDMENTS, THE (FRENCH)	1962	143	4		2.5	UNION FILMS	EIGHT EPISODES
DEVIL AT 4 O'CLOCK, THE	1961	126	4*	2.5	2.5	COLUMBIA	
DEVIL AT MY HEELS (FRENCH)	1966	88		1.5		OFFICIAL INDUSTRIES	
DEVIL BAT	1941	69			2.0	PRODUCERS RELEASING	
DEVIL BAT'S DAUGHTER	1946	66			2.0	PRODUCERS RELEASING	
DEVIL BY THE TAIL, THE (FRENCH)	1968	93	6			LOPERT	
DEVIL COMMANDS, THE	1941	65			2.0	COLUMBIA	
DEVIL DOGS OF THE AIR	1935	86	4*	3.0		WARNER BROTHERS	
DEVIL DOLL (BRITISH - BRYANT HALIDAY)	1964	70	2.0		3.0	ASSOC'D FILM DISTS.	
DEVIL DOLL, THE (LIONEL BARRYMORE)	1936	79		2.5	3.0	M-G-M	
DEVIL GIRL FROM MARS	1955	75		1.0		DIST. CORP. OF AMER.	
DEVIL GODDESS	1955	70		1.5		COLUMBIA	
DEVIL IN LOVE, THE (ITALIAN)	1966	97	1			WARNER BROTHERS	
DEVIL IN THE FLESH (FRENCH)	1947	110		3.5	3.5	A.F.E. CORP.	
DEVIL IS A SISSY	1936	92		2.5	2.5	M-G-M	
DEVIL IS A WOMAN, THE (MARLENE DIETRICH)	1935	85		2.0	2.5	PARAMOUNT	
DEVIL MADE A WOMAN, THE (ITALIAN)	1960	87		1.5			
DEVIL MAKES THREE, THE	1952	96		2.5	2.0	M-G-M	
DEVIL OF THE DESERT AGAINST THE SON OF HERCULES	1964	93		1.5		AVCO-EMBASSY	(ITALIAN)
DEVIL ON HORSEBACK (BRITISH)	1954	88		2.0		BRITISH-LION	
DEVIL PAYS OFF, THE	1941	56		3.0	2.0	REPUBLIC	
DEVIL RIDER	1971		1			GOLDSTONE FILM ENT.	
DEVIL-SHIP PIRATES (BRITISH)	1964	86	4		2.5	COLUMBIA	
DEVIL STRIKES AT NIGHT, THE (GERMAN)	1958	97	6	3.0		ZENITH INTERNATIONAL	
DEVIL THUMBS A RIDE, THE	1947	65	3	2.5		RKO	
DEVIL TO PAY, THE	1931	65		2.0	2.5	UNITED ARTISTS	
DEVILS, THE (BRITISH)	1971	109	4*			WARNER BROTHERS	
DEVIL'S AGENT, THE (BRITISH)	1964	77		2.0		BRITISH-LION	
DEVIL'S ANGELS	1967	84	2			AMERICAN-INTERNAT'L	
DEVIL'S BAIT (BRITISH)	1959	58			1.5		
DEVIL'S BEDROOM, THE	1963	72		1.0		ALLIED ARTISTS	
DEVIL'S BRIDE, THE (BRITISH)	1968	95	2			20th CENTURY FOX	
DEVIL'S BRIGADE, THE	1968	130	4	2.5		UNITED ARTISTS	
DEVIL'S BROTHER, THE	a1933	88			3.0	M-G-M	
DEVIL'S CANYON	1953	92		2.5	2.0	RKO	
DEVIL'S CARGO	1948	61			-	FILM CLASSICS	
DEVIL'S CAVALIERS, THE (ITALIAN)	1958	92		1.5		TRANS-AMERICA	
DEVIL'S DAFFODIL, THE (BRITISH)	a1962	86	2		2.0	GOLDSTONE FILM ENT.	
DEVIL'S DISCIPLE, THE (BRITISH)	1959	82		3.5	2.5	UNITED ARTISTS	
DEVIL'S DOORWAY	1950	84		3.0	3.0	M-G-M	
DEVIL'S EIGHT, THE	1969	97	1			AMERICAN-INTERNAT'L	
DEVIL'S EYE, THE (SWEDISH)	1960	90	4		2.5	JANUS FILMS	
DEVIL'S GENERAL, THE (GERMAN)	1955	120	6	3.5		DIST. CORP. OF AMER.	
DEVIL'S HAIRPIN, THE	1957	82		2.5	2.5	PARAMOUNT	
DEVIL'S HAND, THE (LINDA CHRISTIAN, ROBERT ALDA)	1961	71		1.0		CROWN INTERNATIONAL	
DEVIL'S HENCHMAN, THE	1949	69		2.0	2.0	COLUMBIA	
DEVIL'S ISLAND	1939	62		2.5	2.5	WARNER BROTHERS	
DEVIL'S MASK, THE	1946	66			2.0	COLUMBIA	
DEVIL'S MESSENGER, THE (SWEDISH)	1961	72		1.5	1.5	HERTS-LION INT'L	
DEVILS OF DARKNESS (BRITISH)	1965	88	1*			20th CENTURY FOX	
DEVIL'S OWN, THE (BRITISH)	a1966	90	4	2.5		20th CENTURY FOX	

‡ An asterisk (*) in **THE FILM BUFF'S BIBLE** column indicates that the film has been rated by the editor and/or staff. All other ratings in this column are based on a consensus of reviews (see NOTES).

TITLE (LEADING ACTORS SHOWN WHERE TWO OR MORE FILMS HAVE THE SAME OR SIMILAR TITLE)	YEAR RELEASED	RUNNING TIME IN MINUTES	THE FILM BUFF'S BIBLE ‡	STEVEN SCHEUER	LEONARD MALTIN	DISTRIBUTOR	COMMENT
DEVIL'S PARTNER, THE	1960	61		2.0		FILMGROUP	
DEVIL'S PIPELINE, THE	1940	65		2.5		UNIVERSAL	
DEVIL'S PLAYGROUND	1937	74		2.0	2.5	COLUMBIA	
DEVIL'S TRAP (CZECH)	1964	85	6			EDWARD SALISBURY	
DEVIL'S WANTON, THE (SWEDISH)	1949	80		2.5	2.5	AVCO-EMBASSY	
DEVOTION (OLIVIA DE HAVILLAND, IDA LUPINO)	1946	107		2.5	2.5	WARNER BROTHERS	
DIABOLIQUE (FRENCH)	a1955	107	7*			UN. MOTION PIC. ORG.	
DIAL M FOR MURDER	1954	105	7*	3.5	3.0	WARNER BROTHERS	
DIAL 1119	1950	75	4	2.5	2.0	M-G-M	
DIAL RED 0	1955	63	3	2.5		ALLIED ARTISTS	
DIAMOND EARRINGS, THE (FRENCH)	a1953	102		2.0	2.0	ARLAN PICTURES	
DIAMOND HEAD	1963	107		2.0	2.5	COLUMBIA	
DIAMOND HORSESHOE	a1945	104		3.0	3.0	20th CENTURY FOX	
DIAMOND JIM	1935	93		3.0	3.0	UNIVERSAL	
DIAMOND QUEEN, THE	1953	80	2	2.5	2.5	WARNER BROTHERS	
DIAMOND SAFARI	1958	67	3	1.5		20th CENTURY FOX	
DIAMOND WIZARD, THE (BRITISH)	1954	83		2.5	2.0	UNITED ARTISTS	
DIAMONDS ARE FOREVER (BRITISH)	1971	119	5			UNITED ARTISTS	
DIAMONDS OF THE NIGHT (CZECH)	1964	75	4			IMPACT FILMS	
DIANE	1956	110		2.0	2.5	M-G-M	
DIARY OF A BACHELOR	1964	88			1.5	AMERICAN-INTERNAT'L	
DIARY OF A CHAMBERMAID, THE (BURGESS MEREDITH)	1946	86		2.5	2.5	UNITED ARTISTS	
DIARY OF A CHAMBERMAID, THE (FR. - JEANNE MOREAU)	1964	97	4			INTERNAT'L CLASSICS	
DIARY OF A HIGH SCHOOL BRIDE	1959	80	3	2.0		AMERICAN-INTERNAT'L	
DIARY OF A MAD HOUSEWIFE	1970	94	4*			UNIVERSAL	
DIARY OF A MADMAN	1963	96	3		2.5	UNITED ARTISTS	
DIARY OF A SCHIZOPHRENIC GIRL (ITALIAN)	1969	108	6			ALLIED ARTISTS	
DIARY OF ANNE FRANK, THE	1959	170	6*	3.5	3.5	20th CENTURY FOX	NOMINATED BEST PICTURE
DICK TRACY	1945	62		2.0	2.0	RKO	
DICK TRACY MEETS GRUESOME	1947	65		2.5	2.0	RKO	
DICK TRACY VERSUS CUEBALL	1946	62		2.0	2.0	RKO	
DICK TRACY'S DILEMMA	1947	60		2.0	2.0	RKO	
DID YOU HEAR THE ONE ABOUT THE TRAVELING SALESLADY	1968	97		1.0	2.0	UNIVERSAL	
DIE! DIE! MY DARLING! (BRITISH)	1965	97	4	2.5	2.5	COLUMBIA	
DIE, MONSTER, DIE (BRITISH)	a1965	81	2	2.0	2.0	AMERICAN-INTERNAT'L	
DIG THAT URANIUM	1956	61				ALLIED ARTISTS	
DILLINGER	1945	89		2.5	3.0	MONOGRAM	
DIME WITH A HALO	1963	94	4			M-G-M	
DIMENSION 5	1966	92	1			FEATURE FILM CORP.	
DIMPLES	1936	78		2.5	2.5	20th CENTURY FOX	
DINAH EAST	1970	87	3			EMERSON FILMS	
DING DONG WILLIAMS	1946	62		1.5		RKO	
DINGAKA (SOUTH AFRICAN)	1965	97	4	2.5	2.5	AVCO-EMBASSY	
DINKY	1935	65		2.0	2.0	WARNER BROTHERS	
DINNER AT EIGHT	1933	113		3.5	4.0	M-G-M	
DINNER AT THE RITZ (BRITISH)	1937	77		2.5	2.5	20th CENTURY FOX	
DINO	1957	94	4	3.0	2.5	ALLIED ARTISTS	
DINOSAURUS	1960	85		2.5	2.5	UNIVERSAL	
DIONYSUS IN '69	1969	90	2			SIGMA III	
DIPLOMATIC CORPSE (BRITISH)	1957	65		2.0		J. ARTHUR RANK	
DIPLOMATIC COURIER	1952	97		2.5	3.0	20th CENTURY FOX	
DIRTY DINGUS MAGEE	1970	91	3			M-G-M	
DIRTY DOZEN, THE	1967	149	5*	3.5		M-G-M	
DIRTY GAME, THE (FRENCH)	a1965	87	3	2.5	2.5	AMERICAN-INTERNAT'L	
DIRTY HANDS (FRENCH)	1951	103	6			MACDONALD	
DIRTY HARRY	1971	103	6*			WARNER BROTHERS	
DIRTY OUTLAWS, THE	1971	103				TRANSVUE PICTURES	
DIRTYMOUTH	a1970	102	4			CHEVRON	
DISASTER	1948	60		2.0		PARAMOUNT	
DISC JOCKEY	1951	77	2	1.5		ALLIED ARTISTS	
DISEMBODIED, THE	1957	65	2	2.0	1.5	ALLIED ARTISTS	
DISHONERABLE DISCHARGE (FRENCH)	1958	105		2.0	2.0	PARAMOUNT	
DISHONORED (MARLENE DIETRICH, VICTOR MCLAGLEN)	1931	91		2.5	2.5	PARAMOUNT	
DISHONORED LADY	1947	85	2	1.0	1.5	UNITED ARTISTS	
DISOBEDIENT (BRITISH)	a1953	85		1.5		CARROLL PICTURES	
DISORDER (ITALIAN)	1962	105		1.5		PATHE CONTEMPARARY	
DISORDERLY ORDERLY, THE	1964	90		2.0	2.5	PARAMOUNT	
DISPATCH FROM REUTERS, A	1940	89		3.0	2.5	WARNER BROTHERS	
DISPUTED PASSAGE	1939	87		2.0	2.5	PARAMOUNT	
DISRAELI (GEORGE ARLISS, JOAN BENNETT)	1929	89	5*		2.5	WARNER BROTHERS	NOMINATED BEST PICTURE 1929/30
DISTANT DRUMS	1951	101		3.0	2.5	WARNER BROTHERS	
DISTANT TRUMPET, A (TROY DONAHUE, S. PLESHETTE)	1964	117		2.0	2.5	WARNER BROTHERS	
DIVE BOMBER	1941	133		3.0	3.0	WARNER BROTHERS	
DIVIDED HEART, THE (BRITISH)	1954	89	6	3.0	3.0	REPUBLIC	
DIVORCE	1945	71			2.0	MONOGRAM	
DIVORCE, AMERICAN STYLE	1967	109	7*	3.5	3.0	COLUMBIA	
DIVORCE, ITALIAN STYLE (ITALIAN)	1961	104	8*	4.0	3.5	AVCO-EMBASSY	
DIVORCE OF LADY X, THE (BRITISH)	1938	90		3.0	3.0	UNITED ARTISTS	
DIVORCEE, THE	1930	80		2.0		M-G-M	NOMINATED BEST PICTURE 1929/30
DIXIE	1943	89		2.5	3.0	PARAMOUNT	
DO NOT DISTURB	1965	102		2.0	2.5	20th CENTURY FOX	
DO YOU KNOW THIS VOICE? (BRITISH)	1964	80		2.5		SCREEN GEMS	
DO YOU LOVE ME?	1946	91		2.5	2.5	20th CENTURY FOX	
DO YOU TAKE THIS STRANGER? (T.V.)	1970	100		1.0		UNIVERSAL	

‡ An asterisk (*) in THE FILM BUFF'S BIBLE column indicates that the film has been rated by the
   editor and/or staff. All other ratings in this column are based on a consensus of reviews (see NOTES).

TITLE (LEADING ACTORS SHOWN WHERE TWO OR MORE FILMS HAVE THE SAME OR SIMILAR TITLE)	YEAR RELEASED	RUNNING TIME IN MINUTES	THE FILM BUFF'S BIBLE ‡	STEVEN SCHEUER	LEONARD MALTIN	DISTRIBUTOR	COMMENT
DOBERMAN GANG, THE	1972	87	4			DIMENSION PICTURES	
DOC	1971	96	3			UNITED ARTISTS	
DOCK BRIEF, THE (BRITISH)	1962	88			2.5	M-G-M	
DOCKS OF NEW ORLEANS	1948	64			-	MONOGRAM	
DOCKS OF NEW YORK (GLORIA POPE, BOWERY BOYS)	1945	61			-	MONOGRAM	
DOCTOR AND THE GIRL, THE	1949	98		2.5	2.5	M-G-M	
DOCTOR AT LARGE (BRITISH)	1957	104		2.5	2.5	UNIVERSAL	
DOCTOR AT SEA (BRITISH)	1955	93		3.0	2.5	REPUBLIC	
DR BLOOD'S COFFIN (BRITISH)	1961	92	2		2.5	UNITED ARTISTS	
DR BROADWAY	1942	67		3.0		PARAMOUNT	
DR CHRISTIAN MEETS THE WOMEN	1940	68			2.0	RKO	
DR COOKS GARDEN (T.V.)	1971	90		3.0		PARAMOUNT	
DOCTOR COPPELIUS	1967	97	4			CHILDHOOD PRODS.	
DR CRIPPEN (BRITISH)	1963	97	3	2.5		WARNER BROTHERS	
DR CYCLOPS	1940	77		1.5	2.5	PARAMOUNT	
DOCTOR DOLITTLE	1967	138	6	3.0		20th CENTURY FOX	NOMINATED BEST PICTURE
DR EHRLICH'S MAGIC BULLET	a1940	103		4.0	4.0	WARNER BROTHERS	
DOCTOR FAUSTUS (BRITISH)	1967	93	3	1.5		COLUMBIA	
DR FRANKENSTEIN ON CAMPUS	1971	83	2			MEDFORD	
DR GILLESPIE'S CRIMINAL CASE	1943	89		2.0	-	M-G-M	
DR GILLESPIE'S NEW ASSISTANT	1942	87		2.0	-	M-G-M	
DR GLAS (DANISH)	1968	83	5			20th CENTURY FOX	
DR GOLDFOOT AND THE BIKINI MACHINE	1965	90	3			AMERICAN-INTERNAT'L	
DR GOLDFOOT AND THE GIRL BOMBS	1966	85	1			AMERICAN-INTERNAT'L	
DOCTOR IN DISTRESS (BRITISH)	1963	103	4	3.0		GOVERNOR	
DOCTOR IN LOVE (BRITISH)	1960	93		2.0	2.0	GOVERNOR	
DOCTOR IN THE HOUSE (BRITISH)	1954	91	6	3.0	3.0	REPUBLIC	
DR JEKYLL AND MR HYDE (FREDRIC MARCH)	1932	90		3.0		PARAMOUNT	
DR JEKYLL AND MR HYDE (SPENCER TRACY)	1941	123		3.0	3.0	M-G-M	
DR JEKYLL AND SISTER HYDE (BRITISH)	1971	97	3			AMERICAN-INTERNAT'L	
DR KILDARE GOES HOME	1940	78		2.0	-	M-G-M	
DR KILDARE'S CRISIS	1940	75		2.0	-	M-G-M	
DR KILDARE'S STRANGE CASE	1940	76		2.0	-	M-G-M	
DR KILDARE'S VICTORY	1941	92		2.0	-	M-G-M	
DR KILDARE'S WEDDING DAY	1941	82		2.0	-	M-G-M	
DR MABUSE VS SCOTLAND YARD (GERMAN)	1964	90		1.5		SCREEN GEMS	
DR MORELLE (BRITISH)	1949	73		1.5		EROS FILMS	
DR NO (BRITISH)	1962	105	5*	4.0	3.5	UNITED ARTISTS	
DOCTOR OF DOOM (MEXICAN)	1960	77		1.0		TRANS-INTERNATIONAL	
DOCTOR PAUL JOSEPH GOEBBELS (DOCUMENTARY)	1962	88		2.5		MONOGRAM	
DR PHIBES (BRITISH)	a1971	93	2			AMERICAN-INTERNAT'L	
DR PHIBES RISES AGAIN	1972	89	3			AMERICAN-INTERNAT'L	
DR RENAULT'S SECRET	1942	58		2.0		20th CENTURY FOX	
DR RHYTHM	1938	80		2.5	2.5	PARAMOUNT	
DOCTOR SATAN'S ROBOT	1940	100		2.5	2.5	REPUBLIC	RE-EDITED SERIAL
DR SOCRATES	1935	70		3.5	2.5	WARNER BROTHERS	
DR STRANGELOVE (BRITISH)	1964	93	9*	4.0	3.5	COLUMBIA	NOMINATED BEST PICTURE
DOCTOR TAKES A WIFE, THE	1940	89		3.0	3.0	COLUMBIA	
DR TERROR'S HOUSE OF HORRORS (BRITISH)	1965	98	4		2.5	PARAMOUNT	
DR WHO AND THE DALEKS (BRITISH)	1965	83	3	2.5	2.5	CONTINENTAL	
DOCTOR WITHOUT SCRUPLES (GERMAN)	1960	96		2.0		EMERY PICTURES	
DOCTOR X	1932	80		2.0	3.5	FIRST NATIONAL	
DOCTOR, YOU'VE GOT TO BE KIDDING	1967	94	3	1.0		M-G-M	
DOCTOR ZHIVAGO	1965	197	6*	3.5		M-G-M	NOMINATED BEST PICTURE
DOCTORS, THE (FRENCH)	1956	92	5	3.0		KINGSLEY INTERNAT'L	
DOCTOR'S DILEMMA, THE	1958	99	6	3.5	3.0	M-G-M	
DOCTORS' WIVES (RICHARD CRENNA, DYAN CANNON)	1971	100	2*			COLUMBIA	
DODES'KA-DEN (JAPANESE)	1970	140	1*			TOHO	
DODGE CITY	1939	105		3.0	3.0	WARNER BROTHERS	
DODSWORTH	1936	90			3.5	UNITED ARTISTS	NOMINATED BEST PICTURE
DOES, THE (FRENCH)	a1968	104	3			JACK H. HARRIS	
DOG OF FLANDERS, A (FRANKIE THOMAS, HELEN PARRISH)	1935	72		2.5		RKO	
DOG OF FLANDERS, A (DAVID LADD, DONALD CRISP)	1960	96	4-5*	3.5	2.0	20th CENTURY FOX	
DOG'S BEST FRIEND, A	1960	70	3			UNITED ARTISTS	
DOLL, THE (SWEDISH - PER OSCARSSON)	1962	96	6			KANAWHA FILMS LTD.	
DOLL FACE	1945	80		2.5	2.5	20th CENTURY FOX	
DOLL THAT TOOK THE TOWN, THE (ITALIAN)	1957	81		1.5		TELEWIDE SYSTEMS	
DOLLARS	a1971	120	5			COLUMBIA	
DOLLY SISTERS, THE	1945	114		2.5	2.5	20th CENTURY FOX	
DOLWYN (BRITISH)	a1949	95	4*	3.5	2.5	LOPERT	
DOMINO KID, THE	1957	73		1.5	1.5	COLUMBIA	
DON GIOVANNI (ITALIAN)	1955	170	6			DIST. CORP. OF AMER.	
DON JUAN (AUSTRIAN - CESARE DANOVA)	1954	89	4			TIMES FILM CORP.	
DON JUAN QUILLIGAN	1945	75		2.5	2.5	20th CENTURY FOX	
DON QUIXOTE (RUSSIAN - NIKOLAI CHERKASOV)	1957	106	7*			M-G-M	
DONDI	1961	100	2*	1.5	1.0	ALLIED ARTISTS	
DONOVAN'S BRAIN	1953	83	4	3.0	2.5	UNITED ARTISTS	
DONOVAN'S REEF	1963	109	5	3.0	3.0	PARAMOUNT	
DON'T BLAME THE STORK (BRITISH)	1953	80		2.0			
DON'T BOTHER TO KNOCK (RICHARD WIDMARK, M. MONROE)	1952	76	4	2.0	2.5	20th CENTURY FOX	
DON'T BOTHER TO KNOCK (BRITISH - RICHARD TODD)	a1961	88		2.0	1.5	SEVEN ARTS	
DON'T DRINK THE WATER	1969	98	4			AVCO-EMBASSY	
DON'T GET PERSONAL	1942	60		2.0		UNIVERSAL	
DON'T GIVE UP THE SHIP	1959	89		2.0	3.0	PARAMOUNT	

‡ An asterisk (*) in THE FILM BUFF'S BIBLE column indicates that the film has been rated by the editor and/or staff. All other ratings in this column are based on a consensus of reviews (see NOTES).

TITLE (LEADING ACTORS SHOWN WHERE TWO OR MORE FILMS HAVE THE SAME OR SIMILAR TITLE)	YEAR RELEASED	RUNNING TIME IN MINUTES	THE FILM BUFF'S BIBLE ‡	STEVEN SCHEUER	LEONARD MALTIN	DISTRIBUTOR	COMMENT
DON'T GO NEAR THE WATER	1957	107	4*	2.5	1.5	M-G-M	
DON'T JUST STAND THERE	1968	100		2.0	2.5	UNIVERSAL	
DON'T KNOCK THE ROCK	1957	84		1.5		COLUMBIA	
DON'T KNOCK THE TWIST	1962	87	3	1.5		COLUMBIA	
DON'T LOOK BACK (DOCUMENTARY)	1967	96	6	3.5		LEACOCK-PENNEBAKER	
DON'T LOOK NOW . . . WE'RE BEING SHOT AT (FRENCH)	1967	105				CINEPIX	
DON'T MAKE WAVES	1967	97	2	1.0		M-G-M	
DON'T RAISE THE BRIDGE, LOWER THE RIVER (BRITISH)	1968	99	3	2.0		COLUMBIA	
DON'T TAKE IT TO HEART (BRITISH)	1944	90	3*	3.5	3.0	EAGLE LION	
DON'T TEMPT THE DEVIL (FRENCH)	1963	106	6			UN. MOTION PIC. ORG.	
DON'T TRUST YOUR HUSBAND	a1948	90	4	2.0	2.0	UNITED ARTISTS	
DON'T TURN 'EM LOOSE	1936	65		2.5		RKO	
DON'T WORRY, WE'LL THINK OF A TITLE	1966	83	1		1.0	UNITED ARTISTS	
DOOLINS OF OKLAHOMA, THE	1949	90		2.0	2.5	COLUMBIA	
DOOMSDAY FLIGHT, THE (T.V.)	1966	100		2.5	2.5	UNIVERSAL	
DOOR-TO-DOOR MANIAC	a1962	74	1			AMERICAN-INTERNAT'L	
DOOR WITH SEVEN LOCKS, THE (GERMAN - EDDIE ARENT)	1962	96		1.5	2.5	UCC FILMS	
DORIAN GRAY	1970	95	1			AMERICAN-INTERNAT'L	
DOUBLE, THE (BRITISH)	1963	56		2.0	2.0	ANGLO AMALGAMATED	
DOUBLE AGENTS, THE (FRENCH)	1962	80		2.0		ALLIED ARTISTS	
DOUBLE ALIBI	1940	60		2.0		UNIVERSAL	
DOUBLE BUNK (BRITISH)	1961	92		2.5	1.5	SHOWCORPORATION	
DOUBLE CONFESSION (BRITISH)	1950	85		2.0	2.0	STRATFORD PICS.	
DOUBLE CROSS (KANE RICHMOND, PAULINE MOORE)	1941	66			1.5	PRODUCERS RELEASING	
DOUBLE CROSS (ITALIAN - VITTORIO GASSMAN)	1949	77			2.5	ITALIAN FILMS EXPORT	
DOUBLE CROSS (BRITISH - DONALD HOUSTON)	1956	71		2.0	2.0	EROS FILMS	
DOUBLE CROSSBONES	1951	75		2.5	2.0	UNIVERSAL	
DOUBLE DANGER	1938	62		2.0		RKO	
DOUBLE DEAL	1950	65		2.0		RKO	
DOUBLE DECEPTION (FRENCH)	1960	101		2.0		UN. MOTION PIC. ORG.	
DOUBLE DYNAMITE	1951	80		2.5	2.0	RKO	
DOUBLE EXPOSURE (CHESTER MORRIS, NANCY KELLY)	1944	63		2.5	2.0	PARAMOUNT	
DOUBLE EXPOSURE (BRITISH - JOHN BENTLEY)	1954	63		2.5		J. ARTHUR RANK	
DOUBLE IDENTITY (DENNIS MORGAN, VICTOR JORY)	a1940	69		2.0		WARNER BROTHERS	
DOUBLE IDENTITY (RAY MIDDLETON, JANE WYATT)	a1941	69		2.0		REPUBLIC	
DOUBLE INDEMNITY	1944	106	7*	4.0	4.0	PARAMOUNT	NOMINATED BEST PICTURE
DOUBLE JEOPARDY (ROD CAMERON, DALE ROBBINS)	1955	70		2.0		REPUBLIC	
DOUBLE LIFE, A	1947	104	6*	4.0	4.0	UNIVERSAL	
DOUBLE MAN, THE (BRITISH)	1967	105	4	3.0		WARNER BROTHERS	
DOUBLE OR NOTHING	1937	95		2.5	2.5	PARAMOUNT	
DOUBLE TROUBLE	1967	90	3	2.0		M-G-M	
DOUBLE VERDICT (FRENCH)	1961	102		2.0		PARAMOUNT	
DOUBLE WEDDING	1937	87		2.5	3.0	M-G-M	
DOUGHGIRLS, THE	1944	102		3.0	2.5	WARNER BROTHERS	
DOWN AMONG THE SHELTERING PALMS	1953	87		2.0	2.0	20th CENTURY FOX	
DOWN ARGENTINE WAY	1940	94		2.0	2.5	20th CENTURY FOX	
DOWN IN SAN DIEGO	1941	70		2.5		M-G-M	
DOWN MEMORY LANE	1949	72	3		2.5	EAGLE LION	
DOWN THREE DARK STREETS	1954	85		3.0	2.5	UNITED ARTISTS	
DOWN TO EARTH	1947	101	5	3.0	3.0	COLUMBIA	
DOWN TO THE SEA IN SHIPS	1949	120	5*	3.0	3.0	20th CENTURY FOX	
DOWNFALL (BRITISH)	1963	58		2.0		AVCO-EMBASSY	
DOWNHILL RACER	1969	102	5-6*			PARAMOUNT	
DRACULA (BELA LUGOSI, DAVID MANNERS)	1931	84	3*	2.5	3.5	UNIVERSAL	
DRACULA - PRINCE OF DARKNESS (BRITISH)	1966	90	3			20th CENTURY FOX	
DRACULA'S DAUGHTER	1936	72		3.0	3.0	UNIVERSAL	
DRAEGERMAN COURAGE	1937	58		3.0		WARNER BROTHERS	
DRAGNET (JACK WEBB, BEN ALEXANDER)	1954	89	5	2.5		SCREEN GUILD	
DRAGNET (JACK WEBB, HARRY MORGAN)	1969	100		2.5		UNIVERSAL	
DRAGON MURDER CASE	1934	68		2.0	-	FIRST NATIONAL	
DRAGON SEED	1944	145		3.0	2.5	M-G-M	
DRAGONFLY SQUADRON	1954	82	3	2.5	2.0	ALLIED ARTISTS	
DRAGON'S BLOOD, THE (ITALIAN)	1963	97		1.5		TRANS-AMERICA	
DRAGON'S GOLD	1953	70		1.0		UNITED ARTISTS	
DRAGONWYCK	1946	103		2.0	2.5	20th CENTURY FOX	
DRAGOON WELLS MASSACRE	1957	88		3.0	2.0	ALLIED ARTISTS	
DRAGSTRIP GIRL	1957	69		1.5		AMERICAN-INTERNAT'L	
DRAGSTRIP RIOT	1958	68	3	1.5		AMERICAN-INTERNAT'L	
DRAMA OF JEALOUSY AND OTHER THINGS, A (ITALIAN)	a1970	95	6			WARNER BROTHERS	
DRAMATIC SCHOOL	1938	80		2.0	2.5	M-G-M	
DRANGO	1957	92	2*	2.5	2.0	UNITED ARTISTS	
DREAM GIRL	1948	85	4	2.0	2.0	PARAMOUNT	
DREAM MAKER, THE (BRITISH)	1963	86	2	1.5		UNIVERSAL	
DREAM OF KINGS, A	1969	107	5			NATIONAL GENERAL	
DREAM WIFE	1953	101		2.5	1.5	M-G-M	
DREAMBOAT	1952	83		2.5	3.0	20th CENTURY FOX	
DREAMER, THE (ISRAELI)	1970	86	4			CANNON RELEASING	
DREAMS (SWEDISH)	1955	86	6			JANUS FILMS	
DREAMS OF GLASS	1970	83	6			UNIVERSAL	
DRESSED TO KILL (LLOYD NOLAN)	1941	74		2.5	-	20th CENTURY FOX	
DRIFTER, THE	1966	74	5			FILMMAKERS	
DRIVE A CROOKED ROAD	1954	82		3.5	2.0	COLUMBIA	
DRIVE, HE SAID	1971	90	3			COLUMBIA	
DRUM BEAT	1954	111		2.5	2.0	WARNER BROTHERS	

‡ An asterisk (*) in THE FILM BUFF'S BIBLE column indicates that the film has been rated by the editor and/or staff. All other ratings in this column are based on a consensus of reviews (see NOTES).

			CRITICAL RATINGS				
TITLE (LEADING ACTORS SHOWN WHERE TWO OR MORE FILMS HAVE THE SAME OR SIMILAR TITLE) "a" TO LEFT OF YEAR INDICATES THAT FILM HAS AN ALTERNATE TITLE	YEAR RELEASED	RUNNING TIME IN MINUTES	THE FILM BUFF'S BIBLE ‡	STEVEN SCHEUER	LEONARD MALTIN	DISTRIBUTOR	COMMENT
DRUMS (BRITISH)	1938	99		3.0	3.0	UNITED ARTISTS	
DRUMS ACROSS THE RIVER	1954	78		2.0	2.0	UNIVERSAL	
DRUMS ALONG THE MOHAWK	1939	103		3.5	3.0	20th CENTURY FOX	
DRUMS IN THE DEEP SOUTH	1951	87		2.5	2.0	RKO	
DRUMS OF AFRICA	1963	92	2			M-G-M	
DRUMS OF TAHITI	1954	73		2.0	1.0	COLUMBIA	
DUBARRY WAS A LADY	1943	101		3.5	3.0	M-G-M	
DUBLIN NIGHTMARE (BRITISH)	1958	64		2.0		J. ARTHUR RANK	
DUCHESS OF IDAHO	1950	98		2.0	2.5	M-G-M	
DUCK SOUP	1933	70	3*	3.5	4.0	PARAMOUNT	
DUCK, YOU SUCKER (ITALIAN)	1972	138	4			UNITED ARTISTS	ENGLISH LANGUAGE
DUDE GOES WEST, THE	1948	87		2.0	2.0	ALLIED ARTISTS	
DUEL (T.V.)	1971	75	4-5*			UNIVERSAL	
DUEL AT APACHE WELLS	1957	70		2.0	1.5	REPUBLIC	
DUEL AT DIABLO	1966	103	5	3.0	3.0	UNITED ARTISTS	
DUEL AT SILVER CREEK, THE	1952	77		1.5	1.5	UNIVERSAL	
DUEL AT THE RIO GRANDE (ITALIAN)	1962	91			2.0	TELEWORLD	
DUEL IN DURANGO	a1957	73		2.0	2.0	UNITED ARTISTS	
DUEL IN THE FOREST	1959	112		2.5			
DUEL IN THE JUNGLE (BRITISH)	1954	102		1.5	2.5	WARNER BROTHERS	
DUEL IN THE SUN	1946	138	6*	3.5	3.0	SELZNICK RELEASING	
DUEL OF CHAMPIONS (ITALIAN)	1961	105		2.0	2.0	MEDALLION	
DUEL OF FIRE (ITALIAN)	1960	85		1.5		AMERICAN-INTERNAT'L	
DUEL OF THE TITANS (ITALIAN)	1961	90		1.0	2.0	PARAMOUNT	
DUEL ON THE MISSISSIPPI	1955	72	3	2.0		COLUMBIA	
DUEL WITH DEATH (GERMAN)	1960	103		2.0		EMERY PICTURES	
DUET FOR CANNIBALS (SWEDISH)	1969	105	4			GROVE PRESS	
DUFFY (BRITISH)	1968	101	3	2.0		COLUMBIA	
DUFFY OF SAN QUENTIN	1954	78	4		2.5	WARNER BROTHERS	
DUFFY'S TAVERN	1945	98		3.0	1.0	PARAMOUNT	
DUKE OF CHICAGO	1949	59		2.0		REPUBLIC	
DUKE OF WEST POINT, THE	1938	96		2.5	2.5	UNITED ARTISTS	
DULCIMER STREET (BRITISH)	a1948	110		4.0	2.5	UNIVERSAL	
DULCY	1940	64		1.5	1.5	M-G-M	
DUNGEONS OF HORROR	1962	80		1.0		NTA PICTURES	
DUNKIRK (BRITISH)	1958	113	4*	3.5	2.5	M-G-M	
DUNWICH HORROR, THE	1970	90	2			AMERICAN-INTERNAT'L	
DURANT AFFAIR, THE (BRITISH)	1962	73		2.0	1.5	PARAMOUNT	
DUST BE MY DESTINY	1939	88		2.5	2.5	WARNER BROTHERS	
DUSTY AND SWEETS MCGEE (DOCUMENTARY)	1971	90	3			WARNER BROTHERS	
DUTCHMAN (BRITISH)	1967	55	6			CONTINENTAL	
DYNAMITE (CONRAD NAGLE, KAY JOHNSON)	1929	129		1.0	1.5	PATHE	
DYNAMITERS, THE (BRITISH)	1956	74		2.0		ASTOR	
EACH DAWN I DIE	1939	92	4*	2.5	3.0	WARNER BROTHERS	
EAGLE AND THE HAWK, THE (FREDRIC MARCH)	1933	68		3.0	3.5	PARAMOUNT	
EAGLE AND THE HAWK, THE (JOHN PAYNE)	1950	104		2.5	2.5	PARAMOUNT	
EAGLE IN A CAGE	1972	98	3			NATIONAL GENERAL	
EAGLE SQUADRON	1942	109		3.0	2.5	UNIVERSAL	
EARL CARROLL SKETCHBOOK	1946	90		1.5		REPUBLIC	
EARL CARROLL VANITIES	1945	91		2.5	2.5	REPUBLIC	
EARL OF CHICAGO, THE	1940	85		3.5	3.0	M-G-M	
EARLY TO BED	1936	75		2.0	2.5	PARAMOUNT	
EARRINGS OF MADAME DE, THE (FRENCH)	a1953	102		2.0	2.0	ARLAN PICTURES	
EARTH CRIES OUT, THE (ITALIAN)	1949	79		2.0		PREMIER PICTURES	
EARTH DIES SCREAMING, THE (BRITISH)	1965	62	3		2.5	20th CENTURY FOX	
EARTH II (T.V.)	1971	100	3*			ABC-TV	
EARTH VS THE FLYING SAUCERS	1956	83		1.5	2.0	COLUMBIA	
EARTHBOUND	1940	67		2.0		20th CENTURY FOX	
EARTHWORM TRACTORS	1936	63		2.5	2.5	FIRST NATIONAL	
EAST LYNNE	1931	102				20th CENTURY FOX	NOMINATED BEST PICTURE 1930/31
EAST OF EDEN	1955	115	6*	4.0	3.5	WARNER BROTHERS	
EAST OF KILIMANJARO	1962	75	3	1.5		PARAMOUNT	
EAST OF SUDAN (BRITISH)	1964	84	3	2.5		COLUMBIA	
EAST OF SUMATRA	1953	82	4	2.5	2.5	UNIVERSAL	
EAST OF THE RIVER	1940	73		2.5	2.5	WARNER BROTHERS	
EAST SIDE OF HEAVEN	1939	90		3.0	2.5	UNIVERSAL	
EAST SIDE, WEST SIDE	1950	108		2.5	2.5	M-G-M	
EASTER PARADE	1948	103	5*	3.5	3.5	M-G-M	
EASY COME, EASY GO (BARRY FITZGERALD)	1947	77		2.5	2.5	PARAMOUNT	
EASY COME, EASY GO (ELVIS PRESLY)	1967	95	4	2.0		PARAMOUNT	
EASY LIFE, THE (ITALIAN)	1962	105	6	4.0	3.0	AVCO-EMBASSY	
EASY LIVING (JEAN ARTHUR, EDWARD ARNOLD)	1937	90		3.0	3.0	PARAMOUNT	
EASY LIVING (VICTOR MATURE, LUCILLE BALL)	1949	77		3.0	2.0	RKO	
EASY MONEY (BRITISH)	1947	94		2.5		EAGLE LION	
EASY RIDER	1969	94	7-8*	4.0		COLUMBIA	
EASY TO LOOK AT	1945	65		2.0		UNIVERSAL	
EASY TO LOVE (ESTHER WILLIAMS, VAN JOHNSON)	1953	96		2.0	2.5	M-G-M	
EASY TO WED	1946	110		3.0	2.5	M-G-M	
EASY WAY, THE	a1952	98	6	3.5	3.0	WARNER BROTHERS	
EBB TIDE	1937	94		2.0	2.5	PARAMOUNT	
ECCO (ITALIAN, DOCUMENTARY)	1963	100	3			CRESA ROMA	

‡ An asterisk (*) in THE FILM BUFF'S BIBLE column indicates that the film has been rated by the editor and/or staff. All other ratings in this column are based on a consensus of reviews (see NOTES).

TITLE (LEADING ACTORS SHOWN WHERE TWO OR MORE FILMS HAVE THE SAME OR SIMILAR TITLE)	YEAR RELEASED	RUNNING TIME IN MINUTES	THE FILM BUFF'S BIBLE ‡	STEVEN SCHEUER	LEONARD MALTIN	DISTRIBUTOR	COMMENT
ECHOES OF SILENCE	1967	74	4			FILMMAKERS	
ECLIPSE, THE (ITALIAN)	1962	123	4			TIMES FILM CORP.	
EDDIE CANTOR STORY, THE	1954	116	3	2.0	1.5	WARNER BROTHERS	
EDDY DUCHIN STORY, THE	1956	123	4	2.5	2.0	COLUMBIA	
EDGE, THE	1968	100	5	3.0		FILMMAKERS	
EDGE OF DARKNESS	1943	120		3.0	3.0	WARNER BROTHERS	
EDGE OF DOOM	1950	99	4	2.0	2.0	RKO	
EDGE OF ETERNITY	1959	80		3.0	2.0	COLUMBIA	
EDGE OF FEAR (SPANISH)	1964	90		1.5		AVCO-EMBASSY	
EDGE OF HELL	1956	76		1.0	1.5	UNIVERSAL	
EDGE OF THE CITY	1957	85	6*	3.5	4.0	M-G-M	
EDISON, THE MAN	1940	107		3.0	3.0	M-G-M	
EDWARD, MY SON (BRITISH)	1948	112	6	3.0	3.0	M-G-M	
EEGAH	1963	90	1	1.0		FAIRWAY INTERNAT'L	
EGG AND I, THE	1947	108		3.0	3.0	UNIVERSAL	
EGYPTIAN, THE	1954	140	5*	2.0	2.5	20th CENTURY FOX	
8 1/2 (ITALIAN)	1963	135	3*	4.0	3.0	AVCO-EMBASSY	
800 LEAGUES OVER THE AMAZON (MEXICAN)	1960	78		1.5		CLASA-MOHME	
EIGHT IRON MEN	1952	80	4	3.5	2.5	COLUMBIA	
EIGHT O'CLOCK WALK (BRITISH)	1954	87	4*	3.0	2.5	ASSOCIATED ARTISTS	
EIGHT ON THE LAM	1967	106	3	1.0		UNITED ARTISTS	
EIGHTEEN AND ANXIOUS	1957	57		2.0	2.0	REPUBLIC	
8TH DAY OF THE WEEK, THE (POLISH)	1958	84		4.0		CONTINENTAL	
80 STEPS TO JONAH	1969	107	4			WARNER BROTHERS	
80,000 SUSPECTS (BRITISH)	1963	113		3.0	2.0	CONTINENTAL	
EL ALAMEIN	1953	67		2.0	2.0	COLUMBIA	
EL CID	1961	184	6*	2.5	3.0	ALLIED ARTISTS	
EL CONDOR	1970	102	1			NATIONAL GENERAL	
EL DORADO (JOHN WAYNE, CHARLENE HOLT)	1967	126	4*	3.5		PARAMOUNT	
EL GRECO (ITALIAN)	1964	94		2.0	2.0	20th CENTURY FOX	
EL PASO	1949	92		2.0	2.0	PARAMOUNT	
EL TOPO (SPANISH)	1971	123	4			ABKCO FILMS	
ELEANOR ROOSEVELT STORY, THE (DOCUMENTARY)	1966	91	6*	4.0	3.5	LANDAU/UNGER COM. UN.	
ELECTRA (GREEK)	1962	110	7			LOPERT	
ELECTRONIC MONSTER, THE (BRITISH)	1958	72	2	2.0	1.5	COLUMBIA	
ELEPHANT BOY (BRITISH)	1937	82		3.0	3.0	UNITED ARTISTS	
ELEPHANT CALLED SLOWLY, AN (BRITISH)	1969	91	6			CONTINENTAL	
ELEPHANT FURY (GERMAN)	1955	83		1.5		TELEDYNAMICS	
ELEPHANT GUN	1959	84	5		2.0	LOPERT	
ELEPHANT STAMPEDE	a1951	71			.	MONOGRAM	
ELEPHANT WALK	1954	103	4	2.5	2.0	PARAMOUNT	
ELIZABETH THE QUEEN	a1939	106	5-6*	3.5	3.5	WARNER BROTHERS	
ELLA CINDERS (SILENT)	1926	73			3.0	FIRST NATIONAL	
ELLERY QUEEN AND THE MURDER RING	1941	65		1.5	-	COLUMBIA	
ELLERY QUEEN AND THE PERFECT CRIME	1941	68		1.5	-	COLUMBIA	
ELLERY QUEEN, MASTER DETECTIVE	1940	66		2.0	-	COLUMBIA	
ELLERY QUEEN'S PENTHOUSE MYSTERY	1941	69		1.5	-	COLUMBIA	
ELMER GANTRY	1960	146	9*	4.0	3.5	UNITED ARTISTS	NOMINATED BEST PICTURE
ELMER THE GREAT	1933	74		2.5	3.0	FIRST NATIONAL	
ELOPEMENT	1951	82		2.0	2.0	20th CENTURY FOX	
ELUSIVE CORPORAL, THE (FRENCH)	1962	108	5		2.5	PATHE CONTEMPARARY	
ELVIRA MADIGAN (SWEDISH)	1967	89	7-8*	4.0		CINEMA V	
ELVIS - THAT'S THE WAY IT IS (DOCUMENTARY)	1970	108	5			M-G-M	
EMBALMER, THE (ITALIAN)	1964	83	1			EUROPIX-CONSOLIDATED	
EMBEZZLED HEAVEN (AUSTRIAN)	1958	91	5	2.0		DE ROCHEMONT	
EMBEZZLER, THE (BRITISH)	1954	61	.	2.0		J. ARTHUR RANK	
EMBRACEABLE YOU	1948	80		2.0	2.0	WARNER BROTHERS	
EMERGENCY (BRITISH)	1962	63			2.0	BUTCHER'S	
EMERGENCY WEDDING	1950	78		2.0	2.0	COLUMBIA	
EMIL AND THE DETECTIVES	1964	99	5			BUENA VISTA	
EMMA	1932	73		3.0	2.0	M-G-M	
EMPEROR WALTZ, THE	1948	106		3.0	2.5	PARAMOUNT	
EMPEROR'S CANDLESTICKS, THE	1937	89		3.0	2.5	M-G-M	
EMPEROR'S NIGHTINGALE, THE (CZECH)	1949	72		2.0		REMBRANDT	
EMPIRE IN THE SUN (ITALIAN, DOCUMENTARY)	1956	90		3.0		COM. UNITED T.V.	
EMPTY CANVAS, THE	1964	118	2	1.5		AVCO-EMBASSY	
ENCHANTED APRIL	1935	66		2.0	2.0	RKO	
ENCHANTED COTTAGE, THE	1945	91		3.5	2.5	RKO	
ENCHANTED FOREST	1945	78			2.5	PRODUCERS RELEASING	
ENCHANTED ISLAND	1958	94		1.5	1.5	WARNER BROTHERS	
ENCHANTMENT	1948	102	6	3.0	3.0	RKO	
ENCORE (BRITISH)	1951	89	6*	4.0	3.0	PARAMOUNT	THREE STORIES
END OF DESIRE (FRENCH)	1958	86		2.5	2.0	CONTINENTAL	
END OF THE AFFAIR, THE (BRITISH)	1955	106		3.0	2.5	COLUMBIA	
END OF THE BELLE, THE (FRENCH)	a1961	91	6	3.0		TRANS-LUX DIST.	
END OF THE LINE (BRITISH)	1958	66		2.0		EROS FILMS	
END OF THE RIVER, THE (BRITISH)	1947	80		1.5	2.0	UNIVERSAL	
END OF THE ROAD (STACY KEACH, JAMES EARL JONES)	1970	110	1*			ALLIED ARTISTS	
END OF THE ROAD, THE (BRITISH - FINLAY CURRIE)	1954	76		2.5		DIST. CORP. OF AMER.	
ENDLESS SUMMER, THE (DOCUMENTARY)	1966	95	8*	3.5	3.0	CINEMA V	
ENEMY AGENTS MEET ELLERY QUEEN	1942	65		1.5	-	COLUMBIA	
ENEMY BELOW, THE	1958	98	5*	3.0	3.0	20th CENTURY FOX	
ENEMY FROM SPACE (BRITISH)	1957	84	3	1.0	2.0	UNITED ARTISTS	
ENEMY GENERAL, THE	1960	74		2.0	2.5	COLUMBIA	

At top of table:
"a" TO LEFT OF YEAR INDICATES THAT FILM HAS AN ALTERNATE TITLE →

CRITICAL RATINGS

‡ An asterisk (*) in THE FILM BUFF'S BIBLE column indicates that the film has been rated by the editor and/or staff. All other ratings in this column are based on a consensus of reviews (see NOTES).

TITLE (LEADING ACTORS SHOWN WHERE TWO OR MORE FILMS HAVE THE SAME OR SIMILAR TITLE)	YEAR RELEASED	RUNNING TIME IN MINUTES	THE FILM BUFF'S BIBLE ‡	STEVEN SCHEUER	LEONARD MALTIN	DISTRIBUTOR	COMMENT
ENFORCER, THE	1951	87	6*	3.0	3.0	WARNER BROTHERS	
ENOUGH ROPE (FRENCH)	1963	104	3			ARTIXO PRODS.	
ENSIGN PULVER	1964	104		2.0	2.0	WARNER BROTHERS	
ENTER ARSENE LUPIN	1944	72			2.0	UNIVERSAL	
ENTER LAUGHING	1967	112	5*	3.0	3.0	COLUMBIA	
ENTER MADAME	1935	83		2.5	2.5	PARAMOUNT	
ENTERTAINER, THE (BRITISH)	1960	97	6*	4.0	3.5	CONTINENTAL	
ENTERTAINING MR SLOANE (BRITISH)	1970	94	6			CONTINENTAL	
EQUINOX	1971	81	1			VIP DISTRIBUTORS	
ERIC SOYA'S 17 (DANISH)	1965	87	3			PEPPERCORN-WORMSER	
ERIK THE CONQUEROR (ITALIAN)	1961	90	1	1.5	2.0	AMERICAN-INTERNAT'L	
ERRAND BOY, THE	1962	92	4	2.5	2.5	PARAMOUNT	
ESCAPADE (BRITISH - JOHN MILLS, YVONNE MITCHELL)	1955	87		2.0	2.0	DIST. CORP. OF AMER.	
ESCAPADE IN JAPAN	1957	92	4*	3.0	2.0	UNIVERSAL	
ESCAPADE (NORMA SHEARER, ROBERT TAYLOR)	1940	104		3.0	3.0	M-G-M	
ESCAPE (BRITISH - REX HARRISON, PEGGY CUMMINS)	1948	79		3.0	3.0	20th CENTURY FOX	
ESCAPE (T.V. - CHRISTOPHER GEORGE, MARILYN MASON)	1971	90		1.5		PARAMOUNT	
ESCAPE BY NIGHT (WILLIAM HALL, ANNE NAGEL)	1937	64		2.0		REPUBLIC	
ESCAPE BY NIGHT (BONAR COLLEANO, SIMONE SILVA)	1952	78		3.0		EROS FILMS	(BRITISH)
ESCAPE BY NIGHT (ITALIAN - LEO GENN)	a1960	82	4	2.5		ALLIED ARTISTS	
ESCAPE FROM CRIME	1942	60		1.5		WARNER BROTHERS	
ESCAPE FROM EAST BERLIN	a1962	94		2.5	2.0	M-G-M	
ESCAPE FROM FORT BRAVO	1953	98	5	3.0	3.0	M-G-M	
ESCAPE FROM HELL ISLAND	1964	80		2.0		CROWN INTERNATIONAL	
ESCAPE FROM HONG KONG	1942	60		1.5		UNIVERSAL	
ESCAPE FROM RED ROCK	1958	75	1		1.5	20th CENTURY FOX	
ESCAPE FROM SAHARA (GERMAN)	1963	95		2.0		MEDALLION	
ESCAPE FROM SAIGON (FRENCH)	1960	85		3.0		AMERICAN-INTERNAT'L	
ESCAPE FROM SAN QUENTIN	1957	81	1		1.0	COLUMBIA	
ESCAPE FROM TERROR	1960	81		1.0		COOGAN-ROGERS	
ESCAPE FROM THE PLANET OF THE APES	1971	98	4			20th CENTURY FOX	
ESCAPE FROM ZAHRAIN	1962	93		2.5	1.5	PARAMOUNT	
ESCAPE IN THE DESERT	1945	81		2.5	2.0	WARNER BROTHERS	
ESCAPE IN THE FOG	1945	65		2.0	2.0	COLUMBIA	
ESCAPE ME NEVER (IDA LUPINO, ERROL FLYNN)	1947	104		1.5	2.0	UNITED ARTISTS	
ESCAPE TO BURMA	1955	87	3	1.5		RKO	
ESCAPE TO GLORY	1940	74		2.5	2.5	COLUMBIA	
ESCAPE TO MINDANAO	1968	100		2.5		UNIVERSAL	
ESCORT FOR HIRE (BRITISH)	1960	66		2.0	2.0	M-G-M	
ESCORT WEST	1959	75	4			UNITED ARTISTS	
ESKIMO	1934	117		2.5		M-G-M	
ESPIONAGE AGENT	1939	83		2.0	2.0	WARNER BROTHERS	
ESTHER AND THE KING	1960	109		1.5	2.5	20th CENTURY FOX	
ESTHER WATERS (BRITISH)	a1948	108		2.0	2.5	J. ARTHUR RANK	
ETERNAL CHAIN, THE (ITALIAN)	1952	85		2.0			
ETERNAL SEA, THE	1955	103		2.5	2.5	REPUBLIC	
ETERNAL WALTZ, THE (GERMAN)	1954	99		2.0		BAKROS INTERNATIONAL	
ETERNALLY YOURS	1939	95		2.0	2.5	UNITED ARTISTS	
EUGENIE...THE STORY OF HER JOURNEY INTO PERVERSION	1970	91	1			DISTINCTION FILMS	
EUREKA STOCKADE (AUSTRALIAN)	a1948	103	5*	3.0		J. ARTHUR RANK	
EVA (FRENCH-ITALIAN)	1962	111	4		3.0	TIMES FILM CORP.	ENGLISH LANGUAGE
EVE (BRITISH)	1968	97	1	1.5		LANDAU/UNGER COM. UN.	
EVE AND THE HANDYMAN	1961	64	3			PAD-RAM ENTERPRISES	
EVE KNEW HER APPLES	1945	64		2.0	2.5	COLUMBIA	
EVE OF ST MARK, THE	1944	96	2*	3.0	3.0	20th CENTURY FOX	
EVEL KNIEVEL	1971	94	3			FANFARE	
EVELYN PENTICE	1934	80		2.5	3.0	M-G-M	
EVENING WITH THE ROYAL BALLET, AN (BRITISH, DOC.)	1964	85	8			SIGMA III	
EVENT, AN (YUGOSLAVIAN)	1969	88		3.5		CONTINENTAL	
EVER SINCE EVE	1937	79			2.5	WARNER BROTHERS	
EVERY BASTARD A KING	1970	93	1			CONTINENTAL	
EVERY DAY IS A HOLIDAY (SPANISH - ANGEL PERALTA)	1966	76	3			COLUMBIA	
EVERY DAY'S A HOLIDAY (MAE WEST, EDMUND LOWE)	1937	80		1.5	2.5	PARAMOUNT	
EVERY GIRL SHOULD BE MARRIED	1948	85		2.5	2.5	RKO	
EVERY LITTLE CROOK AND NANNY	1972	100	4			M-G-M	
EVERY MAN'S WOMAN (ITALIAN)	a1966	107	2			ROYAL FILMS INT'L	
EVERY MINUTE COUNTS (FRENCH)	1960	95		1.5		UNIFILMS	
EVERYBODY DOES IT	1949	98	4*	3.5	3.5	20th CENTURY FOX	
EVERYBODY GO HOME (ITALIAN)	1960	115	6			ROYAL FILMS INT'L	
EVERYBODY SING	1938	80		2.0	2.5	M-G-M	
EVERYBODY'S BABY	1939	62		2.5		20th CENTURY FOX	
EVERYTHING BUT THE TRUTH	1956	83	4		2.0	UNIVERSAL	
EVERYTHING HAPPENS AT NIGHT	1939	77		3.0	3.0	20th CENTURY FOX	
EVERYTHING I HAVE IS YOURS	1952	92		2.5	2.0	M-G-M	
EVERYTHING YOU ALWAYS WANTED TO KNOW ABOUT SEX BUT WERE AFRAID TO ASK	1972	88	4			UNITED ARTISTS	
EVERYTHING'S DUCKY	1961	81		2.0	2.0	COLUMBIA	
EVIL EYE, THE (ITALIAN)	1964	92	2	2.5	2.5	AMERICAN-INTERNAT'L	
EVIL OF FRANKENSTEIN, THE (BRITISH)	1964	86		2.0	2.0	UNIVERSAL	
EX-CHAMP	1939	64		2.5	2.0	UNIVERSAL	
EX-LADY	1933	65		2.0	2.0	WARNER BROTHERS	
EX-MRS BRADFORD, THE	1936	80	5*	3.5	3.0	RKO	
EXCLUSIVE	1937	85		2.0	2.5	PARAMOUNT	
EXCUSE MY DUST	1951	82		2.5	2.5	M-G-M	

‡ An asterisk (*) in THE FILM BUFF'S BIBLE column indicates that the film has been rated by the editor and/or staff. All other ratings in this column are based on a consensus of reviews (see NOTES).

TITLE (LEADING ACTORS SHOWN WHERE TWO OR MORE FILMS HAVE THE SAME OR SIMILAR TITLE)	YEAR RELEASED	RUNNING TIME IN MINUTES	CRITICAL RATINGS			DISTRIBUTOR	COMMENT
			THE FILM BUFF'S BIBLE ‡	STEVEN SCHEUER	LEONARD MALTIN		
EXECUTIONER, THE (GEORGE PEPPARD, JOAN COLLINS)	1970	107	4			COLUMBIA	(BRITISH)
EXECUTIONERS, THE (DOCUMENTARY)	a1958	78	5	2.5		VITALITE	
EXECUTIVE SUITE	1954	104	6*	3.0	3.0	M-G-M	
EXILE, THE	1947	95	4		2.5	UNIVERSAL	
EXIT SMILING (SILENT)	1926	72		4.0		M-G-M	
EXODUS	1960	213	7*	3.5	3.0	UNITED ARTISTS	
EXOTIC DREAMS OF CASANOVA, THE	1971	90				BOXOFFICE INTERNAT'L	
EXPERIMENT IN TERROR	a1962	123	5*	3.0	3.0	COLUMBIA	
EXPERIMENT PERILOUS	1944	91		3.0	2.5	RKO	
EXPLOSIVE GENERATION, THE	1961	89	3	3.0	2.0	UNITED ARTISTS	
EXPRESSO BONGO (BRITISH)	1959	111	6*	4.0	3.0	CONTINENTAL	
EXTERMINATING ANGEL, THE (MEXICAN)	1962	91	5			ALTURA FILMS	
EXTRA DAY, THE (BRITISH)	1956	83		3.0		UNITED ARTISTS	
EXTRA GIRL, THE (SILENT)	1923	63	3*			PATHE	
EXTRAORDINARY SEAMAN, THE	1969	80	3			M-G-M	
EYE FOR AN EYE, AN (ROBERT LANSING, PAT WAYNE)	1966	92	3	2.5	2.0	AVCO-EMBASSY	
EYE OF THE CAT	1969	102	4	2.5		UNIVERSAL	
EYE OF THE DEVIL (BRITISH)	1967	92	3	1.5		M-G-M	
EYE OF THE MONOCLE, THE (FRENCH)	1962	102		1.5		PARKSIDE PRODS.	
EYE WITNESS (BRITISH - ROBERT MONTGOMERY)	1950	104		3.0	2.5	EAGLE LION	
EYES IN THE NIGHT	1942	80		2.0	2.0	M-G-M	
EYES OF ANNIE JONES, THE (BRITISH)	1963	71	1	1.0		20th CENTURY FOX	
EYES OF THE SAHARA (FRENCH)	1957	79		2.0		AMERICAN-INTERNAT'L	
EYES OF THE UNDERWORLD	1943	61		2.5	2.5	UNIVERSAL	
FABIOLA (ITALIAN)	1949	97	4	2.0	4.0	20th CENTURY FOX	
FABULOUS DORSEYS, THE	1947	88		2.0	2.0	UNITED ARTISTS	
FABULOUS JOE, THE	1947	60			2.0	UNITED ARTISTS	
FABULOUS SENORITA, THE	1952	80		2.0		REPUBLIC	
FABULOUS SUZANNE, THE	1946	71			2.0	REPUBLIC	
FABULOUS TEXAN, THE	1947	95	4	2.0		REPUBLIC	
FABULOUS WORLD OF JULES VERNE, THE (CZECH)	1958	83		3.0	3.0	WARNER BROTHERS	
FACE BEHIND THE MASK, THE	1941	69			2.5	COLUMBIA	
FACE IN THE CROWD, A	1957	125	7	3.5	3.5	WARNER BROTHERS	
FACE IN THE RAIN, A	1963	91	4	3.0	2.5	AVCO-EMBASSY	
FACE OF A FUGITIVE	1959	81		2.5	2.0	COLUMBIA	
FACE OF FIRE	1959	83	4	2.5	3.0	ALLIED ARTISTS	
FACE OF FU MANCHU, THE (BRITISH)	1965	94	5		3.0	SEVEN ARTS	
FACE OF MARBLE	1946	70			2.0	MONOGRAM	
FACE OF THE FROG (GERMAN)	1959	92			2.0	UCC FILMS	
FACE OF WAR, A (DOCUMENTARY)	1968	72	7	4.0		LANDAU/UNGER COM. UN	VIET NAM WAR
FACE OF WAR, THE (SWEDISH, DOCUMENTARY)	1962	105	5			JANUS FILMS	WW1, WW2, & KOREAN WAR TWO STORIES
FACE TO FACE	1952	92		3.5	2.5	RKO	
FACES	1968	129	3*	4.0		CONTINENTAL	
FACTS OF LIFE, THE	1960	103	5	3.0	3.0	UNITED ARTISTS	
FACTS OF MURDER, THE (ITALIAN)	1960	100		3.0		WARNER BROTHERS	
FAHRENHEIT 451 (BRITISH)	1966	112	6*	3.0	2.0	UNIVERSAL	
FAIL-SAFE	1964	111	7*	3.5	3.0	COLUMBIA	
FAILING OF RAYMOND, THE (T.V.)	1971	75	4*			UNIVERSAL	
FAIR WIND TO JAVA	1953	92	4	3.0	2.5	REPUBLIC	
FAITHFUL CITY (ISRAELI)	1952	86		3.0		RKO	
FAITHFUL IN MY FASHION	1946	81		3.0	2.0	M-G-M	
FAITHLESS	1932	76		1.5	2.5	M-G-M	
FAKE, THE (BRITISH)	1953	80		2.5	2.0	UNITED ARTISTS	
FALCON AND THE CO-EDS, THE	1943	68		3.0	-	RKO	
FALCON IN DANGER, THE	1943	73		2.5	-	RKO	
FALCON IN HOLLYWOOD, THE	1944	67		2.5	-	RKO	
FALCON IN MEXICO, THE	1944	70		2.5	-	RKO	
FALCON IN SAN FRANCISCO, THE	1945	66		2.5	-	RKO	
FALCON OUT WEST, THE	1944	64		2.5	-	RKO	
FALCON STRIKES BACK, THE	1943	66		2.5	-	RKO	
FALCON TAKES OVER, THE	1942	63		2.5	-	RKO	
FALCON'S ADVENTURE, THE	1946	61		2.0	-	RKO	
FALCON'S ALIBI, THE	1946	62		2.5	-	RKO	
FALCON'S BROTHER, THE	1942	63		2.0	-	RKO	
FALL OF ROME, THE (ITALIAN)	1960	89		2.0		TELEWIDE SYSTEMS	
FALL OF THE ROMAN EMPIRE	1964	188	4	1.5	3.5	PARAMOUNT	
FALLEN ANGEL (DANA ANDREWS, ALICE FAYE)	1945	97		2.5	2.5	20th CENTURY FOX	
FALLEN IDOL, THE (BRITISH)	1948	94	7*	4.0	3.5	SELZNICK RELEASING	
FALLEN SPARROW, THE	1943	94		3.5	3.0	RKO	
FALSTAFF (SPANISH)	1966	115	6			PEPPERCORN-WORMSER	
FAME IS THE NAME OF THE GAME (T.V.)	1966	100		2.0	2.5	UNIVERSAL	
FAME IS THE SPUR (BRITISH)	1946	116		3.5	2.5	OXFORD FILMS	
FAMILY AFFAIR (BRITISH - BEN LYON, BEBE DANIELS)	1954	65		2.0			
FAMILY AFFAIR, A (LIONEL BARRYMORE, MICKEY ROONEY)	1937	69		2.5	-	M-G-M	
FAMILY DIARY (ITALIAN)	1962	115	6			M-G-M	
FAMILY HONEYMOON	1949	80		2.5	2.5	UNIVERSAL	
FAMILY JEWELS, THE	1965	100	3	2.0		PARAMOUNT	
FAMILY SECRET, THE	1951	85		2.5	2.5	COLUMBIA	
FAMILY WAY, THE (BRITISH)	1966	115	5			WARNER BROTHERS	
FAN, THE	1949	89		2.5	2.0	20th CENTURY FOX	
FANATICS, THE (FRENCH - PIERRE FRESNAY)	a1957	85		2.0	2.0	MEDALLION	

‡ An asterisk (*) in THE FILM BUFF'S BIBLE column indicates that the film has been rated by the editor and/or staff. All other ratings in this column are based on a consensus of reviews (see NOTES).

TITLE (LEADING ACTORS SHOWN WHERE TWO OR MORE FILMS HAVE THE SAME OR SIMILAR TITLE)	YEAR RELEASED	RUNNING TIME IN MINUTES	THE FILM BUFF'S BIBLE ‡	STEVEN SCHEUER	LEONARD MALTIN	DISTRIBUTOR	COMMENT
FANATICS, THE (BRITISH - CRAIG STEVENS)	1963	87		2.0		TRANSCONTINENTAL	
FANCY PANTS	1950	92	5*	3.0	3.0	PARAMOUNT	
FANDO AND LIS (MEXICAN)	1969	82	1			CANNON RELEASING	
FANFAN THE TULIP (FRENCH)	a1952	96	6		3.0	UNITED ARTISTS	
FANG AND CLAW (DOCUMENTARY)	1935	74		3.0		RKO	
FANGS OF THE ARCTIC	1953	63		1.0		ALLIED ARTISTS	
FANNY (LESLIE CARON, HORST BUCHHOLZ)	1961	133	7*	3.0	3.0	WARNER BROTHERS	NOMINATED BEST PICTURE
FANNY HILL (LETITIA ROMAN, MIRIAM HOPKINS)	1965	105	1			PAN WORLD	
FANTASIA (CARTOON)	1940	135	6*			RKO	
FANTASTIC PLASTIC MACHINE, THE (DOCUMENTARY)	1969	93	5			CROWN INTERNATIONAL	
FANTASTIC VOYAGE	1966	100	6*	4.0	3.5	20th CENTURY FOX	
FANTOMAS (AGAINST SCOTLAND YARD) (FRENCH)	1966	105			2.5	LOPERT	
FAR COUNTRY, THE	1955	97	5	3.0	3.0	UNIVERSAL	
FAR FROM THE MADDING CROWD (BRITISH)	1967	168	5*	3.0		M-G-M	
FAR FROM VIETNAM (FRENCH)	1967	90		3.5		NEW YORKER FILMS	
FAR HORIZONS, THE	1955	108		2.5	2.5	PALESTINE	
FAREWELL AGAIN (BRITISH)	1937	81		3.0	2.5	UNITED ARTISTS	
FAREWELL, MY LOVELY	a1944	95		3.5	2.5	RKO	
FAREWELL TO ARMS, A (HELEN HAYES, GARY COOPER)	1932	78		3.5		PARAMOUNT	NOMINATED BEST PICTURE 1932/33
FAREWELL TO ARMS, A (JENNIFER JONES, ROCK HUDSON)	1957	150		2.5	2.5	20th CENTURY FOX	
FARGO	1952	69		2.0		MONOGRAM	
FARMER TAKES A WIFE, THE (JANET GAYNOR, H. FONDA)	1935	91			2.5	20th CENTURY FOX	
FARMER TAKES A WIFE, THE (BETTY GRABLE)	1953	81		2.0	2.0	20th CENTURY FOX	
FARMER'S DAUGHTER, THE (MARTHA RAYE)	1940	60		1.5	2.0	PARAMOUNT	
FARMER'S DAUGHTER, THE (LORETTA YOUNG)	1947	97	7	4.0	3.5	RKO	
FASCIST, THE (ITALIAN)	a1965	102	6	3.0		AVCO-EMBASSY	
FASHIONS (OF 1934)	1934	78		3.0	3.0	FIRST NATIONAL	
FAST AND FURIOUS	1939	73		2.0		M-G-M	
FAST AND LOOSE (MIRIAM HOPKINS, FRANK MORGAN)	1930	75			1.5	PARAMOUNT	
FAST AND LOOSE (ROBERT MONTGOMERY, R. RUSSELL)	1939	80		2.5	2.5	M-G-M	
FAST AND LOOSE (BRIT. - KAY KENDALL, BRIAN REECE)	1954	75		2.5		J. ARTHUR RANK	
FAST AND SEXY (ITALIAN)	1957	98		2.0	2.5	COLUMBIA	
FAST AND THE FURIOUS, THE	1954	73	3		2.0	AMERICAN RELEASING	
FAST COMPANY (HOWARD KEEL, NINA FOCH)	1953	68		2.5	2.0	M-G-M	
FASTEST GUITAR ALIVE, THE	1967	85	3	2.0		M-G-M	
FASTEST GUN ALIVE, THE	1956	92	4	2.5	3.0	M-G-M	
FAT CITY	1972	96	6			COLUMBIA	
FAT MAN, THE	1951	77		2.0	2.5	UNIVERSAL	
FAT SPY, THE	1966	75	1			MAGNA PICTURES	
FATAL DESIRE (ITALIAN)	1953	80			2.0	ULTRA PICTURES CORP.	
FATAL WITNESS, THE	1945	59		2.0	1.5	REPUBLIC	
FATE IS THE HUNTER	1964	106	4	2.5		20th CENTURY FOX	
FATE OF A MAN (RUSSIAN)	1959	101	6			ARTKINO	
FATE TAKES A HAND (BRITISH)	1961	72		1.5	2.5	M-G-M	
FATHER (HUNGARIAN)	1966	95	3			CONTINENTAL	
FATHER GOOSE	1965	115		2.5	3.0	UNIVERSAL	
FATHER IS A BACHELOR	1950	84		2.0	2.0	COLUMBIA	
FATHER MAKES GOOD	1950	61	3		1.5	MONOGRAM	
FATHER OF A SOLDIER (RUSSIAN)	1965	83	6			ARTKINO	
FATHER OF THE BRIDE	1950	93	7	4.0	4.0	M-G-M	NOMINATED BEST PICTURE
FATHER TAKES A WIFE	1941	79		2.5	2.0	RKO	
FATHER TAKES THE AIR	1951	61	3		1.5	MONOGRAM	
FATHER WAS A FULLBACK	1949	84	4*	2.0	2.5	20th CENTURY FOX	
FATHER'S DILEMMA (ITALIAN)	1952	88		4.0		ARTHUR DAVIS ASSOC.	
FATHER'S LITTLE DIVIDEND	1951	82	7	3.5	4.0	M-G-M	
FATHER'S WILD GAME	1950	61			1.5	MONOGRAM	
FATHOM (BRITISH)	1967	99	3	2.5	3.0	20th CENTURY FOX	
FAUST AND THE DEVIL (ITALIAN)	1950	87	6	2.5		COLUMBIA	
FBI CODE 98	1964	94	3			WARNER BROTHERS	
FBI GIRL	1951	74	3		2.0	LIPPERT PRODS.	
FBI STORY, THE	1959	149		2.0	3.0	WARNER BROTHERS	
FBI 99	1945	100			2.0	REPUBLIC	RE-EDITED SERIAL
FEAR (PETER COOKSON, WARREN WILLIAM)	1946	68			1.5	MONOGRAM	
FEAR (GERMAN - INGRID BERGMAN)	1955	84		2.0		ASTOR	
FEAR, THE (GREEK - ELLI FOTIOU, ANESTIS VLACHOS)	1966	110	3			TRANS-LUX DIST.	
FEAR IN THE NIGHT	1947	72	4	3.0	2.0	PARAMOUNT	
FEAR NO EVIL (T.V.)	1969	100		3.0		UNIVERSAL	
FEAR NO MORE	1961	87	5	2.0		SUTTON PICTURES	
FEAR STRIKES OUT	1957	100	5*	4.0	3.0	PARAMOUNT	
FEARLESS FAGAN	1952	79	4			M-G-M	
FEARLESS FRANK	a1969	78	2			AMERICAN-INTERNAT'L	
FEARLESS VAMPIRE KILLERS (BRITISH)	1967	98	1			M-G-M	
FEARMAKERS, THE	1958	83		2.0	2.5	UNITED ARTISTS	
FEATHERED SERPENT, THE	1948	61			-.	MONOGRAM	
FEDRA, THE DEVIL'S DAUGHTER (SPANISH)	1957	102	5			TIMES FILM CORP.	
FELLINI SATYRICON (ITALIAN)	a1969	127	1*			UNITED ARTISTS	
FEMALE, THE (FRENCH - BRIGITTE BARDOT)	a1958	100	2			LOPERT	
FEMALE, THE (ARGENTINE - ISABEL SARLI)	a1962	89	1			CAMBIST	
FEMALE ANIMAL (SPANISH - ARLENE TIGER)	1970	75	1			CINEMATION INDUS.	ENGLISH VERSION
FEMALE ANIMAL, THE (HEDY LAMARR, JANE POWELL)	1958	84	4		2.5	UNIVERSAL	
FEMALE BUNCH, THE	1971	86	1			DALIA PRODS.	
FEMALE JUNGLE	1956	56			2.0	AMERICAN-INTERNAT'L	
FEMALE ON THE BEACH	1955	97	4	2.5	3.0	UNIVERSAL	
FEMININE TOUCH, THE (ROSALIND RUSSELL, DON AMECHE)	1941	97		2.5	2.5	M-G-M	

‡ An asterisk (*) in THE FILM BUFF'S BIBLE column indicates that the film has been rated by the editor and/or staff. All other ratings in this column are based on a consensus of reviews (see NOTES).

TITLE (LEADING ACTORS SHOWN WHERE TWO OR MORE FILMS HAVE THE SAME OR SIMILAR TITLE)	YEAR RELEASED	RUNNING TIME IN MINUTES	THE FILM BUFF'S BIBLE ‡	STEVEN SCHEUER	LEONARD MALTIN	DISTRIBUTOR	COMMENT
			CRITICAL RATINGS				
FEMINIST AND THE FUZZ, THE (T.V.)	1971	90		1.5		SCREEN GEMS	
FERNANDEL THE DRESSMAKER (FRENCH)	1956	92		2.5	2.5	UNION FILMS	
FERRY CROSS THE MERSEY (BRITISH)	1965	86	3			UNITED ARTISTS	
FERRY TO HONG KONG (BRITISH)	1959	103		2.0	2.5	20th CENTURY FOX	
FESTIVAL (DOCUMENTARY)	1967	95	6			PEPPERCORN-WORMSER	
FEUDIN' FOOL	1952	63			-	MONOGRAM	
FEUDIN', FUSSIN', AND A-FIGHTIN'	1948	78		2.0	2.0	UNIVERSAL	
FEVER HEAT (NICK ADAMS, JEANNINE RILEY)	1968	105	1			PARAMOUNT	
FEVER IN THE BLOOD, A	1961	117		2.5	2.5	WARNER BROTHERS	
FIANCES, THE (ITALIAN)	1963	84	6			JANUS FILMS	
FICKLE FINGER OF FATE, THE	1967	91	2			PRODUCERS RELEASING	
FIDDLER ON THE ROOF	1971	178	6*			UNITED ARTISTS	NOMINATED BEST PICTURE
FIEND WHO WALKED THE WEST, THE	1958	101	3		3.0	20th CENTURY FOX	
FIEND WITHOUT A FACE (BRITISH)	1958	74	2	2.0	1.5	M-G-M	
FIERCEST HEART, THE	1961	91	4		2.0	20th CENTURY FOX	
FIESTA	1947	104	4	2.0	2.0	M-G-M	
15 FROM ROME (ITALIAN)	1963	87	2			MCABEE PICTURES	
15 MAIDEN LANE	1936	65		2.0	2.0	20th CENTURY FOX	
FIFTH AVENUE GIRL	1939	83		2.0	2.5	RKO	
FIFTH HORSEMAN IS FEAR, THE (CZECH)	1966	100	7	4.0		SIGMA III	
55 DAYS AT PEKING	1963	154		2.5	3.0	ALLIED ARTISTS	
FIFTY MILLION FRENCHMEN	1931	74		2.0		WARNER BROTHERS	
FIFTY ROADS TO TOWN	1937	81		2.0	2.0	20th CENTURY FOX	
FIFTY YEARS BEFORE YOUR EYES (DOCUMENTARY)	1950	73	6			WARNER BROTHERS	
FIGHTER, THE	1952	78		3.5	2.5	UNITED ARTISTS	
FIGHTER ATTACK	1953	80		2.5	2.0	ALLIED ARTISTS	
FIGHTER SQUADRON	1948	96		2.0	2.0	WARNER BROTHERS	
FIGHTING CHANCE, THE	1955	70	2	2.0	2.0	REPUBLIC	
FIGHTING COAST GUARD	1951	86	3	2.5	2.5	REPUBLIC	
FIGHTING FATHER DUNNE	1948	93		3.5	2.5	RKO	
FIGHTING FOOLS	1949	69			-	MONOGRAM	
FIGHTING GUARDSMAN	1945	84			2.0	COLUMBIA	
FIGHTING KENTUCKIAN, THE	1949	100		2.5	2.5	REPUBLIC	
FIGHTING LAWMAN, THE	1953	71	2	2.0	1.5	ALLIED ARTISTS	
FIGHTING MAD (JOE KIRKWOOD JR)	a1948	75	2			MONOGRAM	
FIGHTING MAN OF THE PLAINS	1949	94		2.5	2.5	20th CENTURY FOX	
FIGHTING O'FLYNN, THE	1949	94	4		2.5	UNITED ARTISTS	
FIGHTING PRINCE OF DONEGAL, THE (BRITISH)	1966	104	4			BUENA VISTA	
FIGHTING RATS OF TOBRUK (AUSTRALIAN)	1945	71		2.5		RENOWN PICTURES	
FIGHTING SEABEES, THE	1944	100		3.5	3.0	REPUBLIC	
FIGHTING 69TH, THE	1940	89		3.5	3.0	WARNER BROTHERS	
FIGHTING TROUBLE	1956	61			-	ALLIED ARTISTS	
FIGHTING WILDCATS, THE (BRITISH)	1957	74		2.0	1.5	REPUBLIC	
FIGURES IN A LANDSCAPE (BRITISH)	1971	111	5			NATIONAL GENERAL	
FILE OF THE GOLDEN GOOSE, THE (BRITISH)	1970	105	3			UNITED ARTISTS	
FILE ON THELMA JORDAN, THE	a1949	100	4	3.0	2.5	PARAMOUNT	
FILLMORE	1972	105	3			20th CENTURY FOX	
FINAL COMEDOWN, THE	1972	85	3			NEW WORLD	
FINAL TEST, THE (BRITISH)	1953	91		3.5	2.5	J. ARTHUR RANK	
FIND THE BLACKMAILER	1943	55		2.0		WARNER BROTHERS	
FIND THE LADY (BRITISH)	1956	56		2.0		J. ARTHUR RANK	
FINDERS KEEPERS (BRITISH)	1966	94	3	2.5	2.5	UNITED ARTISTS	
FINDERS KEEPERS, LOVERS WEEPERS	1968	71	3			EVE RELEASING CORP.	
FINE MADNESS, A	1966	104	3*	3.5	3.0	WARNER BROTHERS	
FINE PAIR, A (ITALIAN)	1968	89	1			NATIONAL GENERAL	ENGLISH LANGUAGE
FINEST HOURS, THE (BRITISH, DOCUMENTARY)	1964	116	6			COLUMBIA	
FINGER MAN	1955	82		2.5	2.0	ALLIED ARTISTS	
FINGER OF GUILT (BRITISH)	1956	84		-	2.0	RKO	
FINGER ON THE TRIGGER	1965	87	2		1.0	ALLIED ARTISTS	
FINGER POINTS, THE	1931	90		3.0		FIRST NATIONAL	
FINGERS AT THE WINDOW	1942	80		1.5	2.5	M-G-M	
FINIAN'S RAINBOW	1968	145	6			WARNER BROTHERS	
FINNEY	1969	72	1			GOLD COAST	
FIRE AND ICE (FRENCH)	1963	105		3.0		PARAMOUNT	
FIRE DOWN BELOW	1957	116	5*	3.0	2.5	COLUMBIA	
FIRE OVER AFRICA	1954	84		2.0	2.0	COLUMBIA	
FIRE OVER ENGLAND (BRITISH)	1937	89			3.0	UNITED ARTISTS	
FIRE WITHIN, THE (FRENCH)	1963	110	6			GOVERNOR	
FIREBALL, THE	1950	84		2.0	3.0	20th CENTURY FOX	
FIREBALL 500	1966	92	3			AMERICAN-INTERNAT'L	
FIREBRAND, THE	1962	63	3			20th CENTURY FOX	
FIRECREEK	1968	104	4	2.5		WARNER BROTHERS	
FIREFLY, THE	1937	138		2.5	2.5	M-G-M	
FIREMAN, SAVE MY CHILD (JOE E. BROWN)	1932	67		2.5	2.0	FIRST NATIONAL	
FIREMAN, SAVE MY CHILD (SPIKE JONES)	1954	80		2.0	1.5	UNIVERSAL	
FIREMAN'S BALL, THE (CZECH)	1967	73	6	4.0		CINEMA V	
FIRST COMES COURAGE	1943	88			2.5	COLUMBIA	
FIRST LADY	1937	82		3.5		WARNER BROTHERS	
FIRST LEGION, THE	1951	86		4.0	3.0	UNITED ARTISTS	
FIRST LOVE (DEANNA DURBIN, ROBERT STACK)	1939	84		3.5	3.0	UNIVERSAL	
FIRST LOVE (ITALIAN - CARLA GRAVINA)	1958	103			2.0	GALA	
FIRST LOVE (JOHN MOULDER BROWN, DOMINIQUE SANDA)	1970	90	4			UMC PICTURES	
FIRST MAN INTO SPACE (BRITISH)	1959	77		2.0	1.5	M-G-M	
FIRST MEN IN THE MOON (BRITISH)	1964	103	5	3.0	3.0	COLUMBIA	

"a" TO LEFT OF YEAR INDICATES THAT FILM HAS AN ALTERNATE TITLE

‡ An asterisk (*) in THE FILM BUFF'S BIBLE column indicates that the film has been rated by the editor and/or staff. All other ratings in this column are based on a consensus of reviews (see NOTES).

TITLE (LEADING ACTORS SHOWN WHERE TWO OR MORE FILMS HAVE THE SAME OR SIMILAR TITLE)	YEAR RELEASED	RUNNING TIME IN MINUTES	THE FILM BUFF'S BIBLE ‡	STEVEN SCHEUER	LEONARD MALTIN	DISTRIBUTOR	COMMENT
FIRST SPACESHIP ON VENUS (GERMAN)	1960	78	2	1.0	1.5	CROWN INTERNATIONAL	
FIRST TEXAN, THE	1956	82		2.0	2.5	ALLIED ARTISTS	
FIRST TIME, THE (ROBERT CUMMINGS, BARBARA HALE)	1952	89		3.0	2.0	COLUMBIA	
FIRST TIME, THE (JACQUELINE BISSET, WES STERN)	1969	90	4			UNITED ARTISTS	
FIRST TO FIGHT	1967	97		1.5	2.5	WARNER BROTHERS	
FIRST TRAVELING SALESLADY, THE	1956	92		2.0	2.0	RKO	
FIRST YANK INTO TOKYO	1945	82		2.0	2.0	RKO	
FIST IN HIS POCKET (ITALIAN)	1965	105	6	3.5		PEPPERCORN-WORMSER	
FISTFUL OF DOLLARS, A (ITALIAN)	1964	96	3			UNITED ARTISTS	
FITZWILLY	1967	102	5			UNITED ARTISTS	
FIVE	1951	93	5	2.5	2.5	COLUMBIA	
FIVE AGAINST THE HOUSE	1955	84	3*	3.5	3.0	COLUMBIA	
FIVE BLOODY GRAVES	1970	88				INDEPENDENT INT'L	
FIVE BOLD WOMEN	1959	82		1.5		CITATION	
FIVE BRANDED WOMEN	1960	101	5*	2.0	2.0	PARAMOUNT	
FIVE CAME BACK	1939	75		3.0	2.0	RKO	
FIVE CARD STUD	1968	103	4	2.5		PARAMOUNT	
FIVE DAY LOVER, THE (FRENCH)	1961	86	5			KINGSLEY INTERNAT'L	
FIVE EASY PIECES	1970	95	7*			COLUMBIA	NOMINATED BEST PICTURE
FIVE FINGER EXERCISE	1962	109		2.0	2.5	COLUMBIA	
FIVE FINGERS	1952	108	5*	4.0	3.0	20th CENTURY FOX	
FIVE GATES TO HELL	1959	98		1.0	1.5	20th CENTURY FOX	
FIVE GOLDEN DRAGONS (BRITISH)	1967	70			2.0	COM. UNITED T.V.	
FIVE GOLDEN HOURS (BRITISH)	1960	90	4	2.5	2.5	COLUMBIA	
FIVE GRAVES TO CAIRO	1943	96	6*	2.5	3.5	PARAMOUNT	
FIVE GUNS TO TOMBSTONE	1961	71	1			UNITED ARTISTS	
FIVE GUNS WEST	1955	78	3		2.0	AMERICAN RELEASING	
FIVE MAN ARMY, THE (ITALIAN)	1970	107	3			M-G-M	
FIVE MILES TO MIDNIGHT (FRENCH-ITALIAN)	1963	110		2.0	2.5	UNITED ARTISTS	ENGLISH LANGUAGE
FIVE MILLION YEARS TO EARTH (BRITISH)	1967	98	3	3.0		20th CENTURY FOX	
FIVE OF A KIND	1938	85		1.5		20th CENTURY FOX	
FIVE PENNIES, THE	1959	117	6	3.0	2.5	PARAMOUNT	
FIVE STAR FINAL	1931	89	4*	2.5	3.0	FIRST NATIONAL	NOMINATED BEST PICTURE 1931/32
FIVE STEPS TO DANGER	1957	80		2.0	2.0	UNITED ARTISTS	
5000 FINGERS OF DR T, THE	1953	88	4*	4.0	3.5	COLUMBIA	
FIVE WEEKS IN A BALLOON	1962	101	4			20th CENTURY FOX	
FIXED BAYONETS	1951	92		2.5	2.5	20th CENTURY FOX	
FIXER, THE	1968	132	5			M-G-M	
FIXER DUGAN	1939	68		2.0		RKO	
FLAME, THE	1947	97		3.0	2.0	REPUBLIC	
FLAME AND THE ARROW, THE	1950	88	5*	3.0	3.0	WARNER BROTHERS	
FLAME AND THE FLESH, THE	1954	104		2.0	2.0	M-G-M	
FLAME BARRIER, THE	1958	70		2.0	1.5	UNITED ARTISTS	
FLAME IN THE STREETS (BRITISH)	1961	93	6			ATLANTIC PICTURES	
FLAME OF ARABY	1952	77	3	1.5	2.5	UNIVERSAL	
FLAME OF CALCUTTA	1953	70		1.0	1.5	COLUMBIA	
FLAME OF NEW ORLEANS, THE	1941	78		3.0	3.0	UNIVERSAL	
FLAME OF STAMBOUL	1951	68		2.0	1.5	COLUMBIA	
FLAME OF THE BARBARY COAST	1945	91		2.5	2.5	REPUBLIC	
FLAME OF THE ISLANDS	1955	90		2.5	2.0	REPUBLIC	
FLAME OF YOUTH	1949	60	1			REPUBLIC	
FLAME OVER INDIA (BRITISH)	1959	130	4*	3.5	3.0	20th CENTURY FOX	
FLAME WITHIN, THE	1935	71			2.0	M-G-M	
FLAMING FEATHER	1952	77	4		3.0	PARAMOUNT	
FLAMING FRONTIER (BRUCE BENNETT, JIM DAVIS)	1958	70	2		1.5	20th CENTURY FOX	
FLAMING FRONTIER (GERMAN - STEWART GRANGER)	1965	93	3	1.5		WARNER BROTHERS	ENGLISH LANGUAGE
FLAMING FURY	1949	60		2.5		REPUBLIC	
FLAMING STAR	1960	101	4	3.0	2.5	20th CENTURY FOX	
FLAMINGO ROAD	1949	94		2.5	3.0	WARNER BROTHERS	
FLAP	1970	105	4			WARNER BROTHERS	
FLAREUP	1969	100	1			M-G-M	
FLAT TOP	1952	83		2.0	2.5	ALLIED ARTISTS	
FLAXY MARTIN	1949	86	2	2.0	2.5	WARNER BROTHERS	
FLEA IN HER EAR, A	1968	94	3	2.0		20th CENTURY FOX	
FLEET'S IN, THE	1942	93		2.5	2.5	PARAMOUNT	
FLESH (WALLACE BEERY, KAREN MORLEY)	1932	95		2.5	3.0	M-G-M	
FLESH AND BLOOD (BRITISH)	1949	102		2.0	2.0	SHOWCORPORATION	
FLESH AND DESIRE (ITALIAN)	1955	94		2.0		ELLIS FILMS	
FLESH AND FANTASY	1943	93		3.5	3.0	UNIVERSAL	
FLESH AND FLAME	a1959	96	2	1.0	1.5	M-G-M	
FLESH AND FURY	1952	82		2.5	2.5	UNIVERSAL	
FLESH AND THE FIENDS, THE (BRITISH)	a1960	97	3	3.0		VALIANT	
FLESH AND THE WOMAN (FRENCH)	1958	102		2.0	2.0	DOMINANT PICTURES	
FLESH EATERS	1964	87	3			CINEMA DISTS. OF AMER	
FLIGHT ANGELS	1940	74		2.0		WARNER BROTHERS	
FLIGHT COMMAND	1940	110		1.5	2.0	M-G-M	
FLIGHT COMMANDER (R. BARTHELMESS, D. FAIRBANKS JR)	a1930	112		2.5		FIRST NATIONAL	
FLIGHT FOR FREEDOM	1943	99		2.5	2.5	RKO	
FLIGHT FROM ASHIYA	1964	100	3	2.0	2.0	UNITED ARTISTS	
FLIGHT FROM DESTINY	1941	73		3.0	3.0	WARNER BROTHERS	
FLIGHT FROM TREASON (BRITISH)	1960	60		2.0		20th CENTURY FOX	
FLIGHT FROM VIENNA (BRITISH)	1955	58		1.5		E. J. FANCEY	
FLIGHT LIEUTENANT	1942	80		2.0	1.5	COLUMBIA	
FLIGHT NURSE	1954	90		2.0	2.0	REPUBLIC	

‡ An asterisk (*) in THE FILM BUFF'S BIBLE column indicates that the film has been rated by the editor and/or staff. All other ratings in this column are based on a consensus of reviews (see NOTES).

TITLE (LEADING ACTORS SHOWN WHERE TWO OR MORE FILMS HAVE THE SAME OR SIMILAR TITLE)	YEAR RELEASED	RUNNING TIME IN MINUTES	THE FILM BUFF'S BIBLE ‡	STEVEN SCHEUER	LEONARD MALTIN	DISTRIBUTOR	COMMENT
FLIGHT OF THE DOVES (BRITISH)	1971	101	6			COLUMBIA	
FLIGHT OF THE LOST BALLOON, THE	1961	91		1.5	1.5	WOOLNER BROTHERS	
FLIGHT OF THE PHOENIX, THE	1965	147	7*	3.5	3.5	20th CENTURY FOX	SLOW BUILDUP
FLIGHT THAT DISAPPEARED, THE	1961	71	2			UNITED ARTISTS	
FLIGHT TO HONG KONG	1956	88		2.0	2.0	UNITED ARTISTS	
FLIGHT TO MARS	1951	72		2.0	2.0	MONOGRAM	
FLIGHT TO NOWHERE	1946	75		1.0	1.0	SCREEN GUILD	
FLIGHT TO TANGIER	1953	90	4		2.5	PARAMOUNT	
FLIM-FLAM MAN, THE	a1967	104	7*	2.5	3.0	20th CENTURY FOX	
FLIPPER	1963	90		2.5	2.5	M-G-M	
FLIPPER'S NEW ADVENTURE	a1964	103	4			M-G-M	
FLIRTATION WALK	1934	97		2.5	2.5	FIRST NATIONAL	NOMINATED BEST PICTURE
FLIRTING WITH FATE	1938	69			2.5	M-G-M	
FLOOD TIDE (GEORGE NADER, CORNELL BORCHERS)	1958	82		2.0	2.5	UNIVERSAL	
FLOODS OF FEAR (BRITISH)	1958	82		2.5	2.0	UNIVERSAL	
FLORIAN	1940	91		2.0	2.0	M-G-M	
FLORIDA SPECIAL	1936	70		2.0	2.0	PARAMOUNT	
FLOWER DRUM SONG	1961	133		3.0	2.0	UNIVERSAL	
FLOWING GOLD	1940	82		2.5	2.5	WARNER BROTHERS	
FLUFFY	1965	92		2.0	2.0	UNIVERSAL	
FLUTE AND THE ARROW, THE (SWEDISH)	1958	78	6			JANUS FILMS	
FLY, THE	1958	94	5*	3.0	3.0	20th CENTURY FOX	
FLY BY NIGHT	1943	68		2.5		PARAMOUNT	
FLYING CADETS	1941	60		2.5		UNIVERSAL	
FLYING DEUCES, THE	1939	65			2.5	RKO	
FLYING DOWN TO RIO	1933	89		3.0	3.0	RKO	
FLYING FONTAINES, THE	1959	84		2.0	2.5	COLUMBIA	
FLYING FORTRESS (BRITISH)	1942	68		2.0		WARNER BROTHERS	
FLYING IRISHMAN, THE	1939	72		3.0	2.0	RKO	
FLYING LEATHERNECKS	1951	102		2.0	3.0	RKO	
FLYING MATCHMAKER, THE (ISRAELI)	1970	104	3			NAT'L SHOWMANSHIP	
FLYING MISSILE, THE	1951	93		2.0	2.0	COLUMBIA	
FLYING SAUCER, THE (MIKEL CONRAD, PAT GARRISON)	1950	69		2.5	1.5	FILM CLASSICS	
FLYING SAUCER, THE (ITALIAN - ALBERTO SORDI)	1965	95		2.0		AVCO-EMBASSY	
FLYING SERPENT, THE	1946	59			2.0	PRODUCERS RELEASING	
FLYING TIGERS	1942	102		3.5	2.5	REPUBLIC	
FLYING WILD	1941	62				MONOGRAM	
FOG ISLAND	1945	72			1.5	PRODUCERS RELEASING	
FOG OVER FRISCO	1934	68		2.0	2.0	FIRST NATIONAL	
FOLIES BERGERE (MAURICE CHEVALIER, ANN SOTHERN)	1935	84			2.5	UNITED ARTISTS	
FOLIES BERGERE (FRENCH - JEANMARIE, E CONSTANTINE)	1958	90		2.0	2.0	FILMS AROUND THE WLD.	
FOLLOW A STAR (BRITISH)	1959	102		2.5	1.5	ZENITH INTERNATIONAL	
FOLLOW ME, BOYS	1966	131	5			BUENA VISTA	
FOLLOW ME QUIETLY	1949	59	4	3.0		RKO	
FOLLOW THAT DREAM	1962	110		2.5	2.5	UNITED ARTISTS	
FOLLOW THAT WOMAN	1945	69		2.0	2.0	PARAMOUNT	
FOLLOW THE BOYS (GEORGE RAFT, W. C. FIELDS)	1944	122		3.0	3.0	UNIVERSAL	
FOLLOW THE BOYS (CONNIE FRANCIS, PAULA PRENTISS)	1963	95	3		2.0	M-G-M	
FOLLOW THE FLEET	1936	110		4.0	4.0	RKO	
FOLLOW THE LEADER	1944	64				MONOGRAM	
FOLLOW THE SUN	1951	93	5	2.5	2.5	20th CENTURY FOX	
FOLLY TO BE WISE (BRITISH)	1952	91	4*	3.5	3.0	FINE ARTS	
FOOL KILLER, THE	1965	99		2.5	3.0	LANDAU/UNGER COM. UN.	
FOOLS	1970	93	3			CINERAMA RELEASING	
FOOLS FOR SCANDAL	1938	81		2.5	2.5	WARNER BROTHERS	
FOOLS' PARADE	a1971	98	4*			COLUMBIA	
FOOLS RUSH IN (BRITISH)	1948	82		2.0		J. ARTHUR RANK	
FOOTLIGHT PARADE	1933	102	5*		3.5	WARNER BROTHERS	
FOOTLIGHT SERENADE	1942	80		2.5	2.5	20th CENTURY FOX	
FOOTLIGHT VARITIES	1951	61		2.0		RKO	
FOOTSTEPS IN THE DARK	1941	96		2.5	2.5	WARNER BROTHERS	
FOOTSTEPS IN THE FOG (BRITISH)	1955	90	4	2.0	2.0	COLUMBIA	
FOOTSTEPS IN THE NIGHT	1957	62		2.5	1.5	ALLIED ARTISTS	
FOR A FEW DOLLARS MORE (ITALIAN)	1966	130	4			UNITED ARTISTS	
FOR BETTER FOR WORSE (BRITISH - DIRK BOGARDE)	1954	81			2.5	STRATFORD PICS.	
FOR HEAVEN'S SAKE	1950	92	3*	2.5	2.5	20th CENTURY FOX	
FOR LOVE OF IVY	1968	101	5	2.5		CINERAMA RELEASING	
FOR LOVE OR MONEY	1963	108		2.5	2.5	SHOCHIKU	
FOR ME AND MY GAL	1942	104		3.0	2.5	M-G-M	
FOR MEN ONLY	a1952	93		3.5	2.0	LIPPERT PRODS.	
FOR PETE'S SAKE	1967	90	4			WORLD WIDE PICS.	
FOR SINGLES ONLY	1968	91	2			COLUMBIA	
FOR THE FIRST TIME	1959	97	4			M-G-M	
FOR THE LOVE OF MARY	1948	90		2.5	2.5	UNIVERSAL	
FOR THE LOVE OF MIKE (RICHARD BASEHART, S. ERWIN)	a1960	84				20th CENTURY FOX	
FOR THOSE WHO THINK YOUNG	1964	96	3	1.0	2.0	UNITED ARTISTS	
FOR WHOM THE BELL TOLLS	1943	170	6*	4.0	3.5	PARAMOUNT	NOMINATED BEST PICTURE
FORBIDDEN (BRITISH - DOUGLASS MONTGOMERY)	1948	87		1.5		LONDON FILMS	
FORBIDDEN (JOANNE DRU, TONY CURTIS)	1954	85		2.0	2.0	UNIVERSAL	
FORBIDDEN (ITALIAN - MEL FERRER, LEA MASSARI)	1956	90		2.0		DOCUMENTO FILMS	
FORBIDDEN CARGO (BRITISH)	1954	85		3.0	2.0	FINE ARTS	
FORBIDDEN DESERT	1957	45	5			WARNER BROTHERS	SEMI-TRAVELOUGE
FORBIDDEN FRUIT (FRENCH)	1952	97		2.5	2.5	FILMS AROUND THE WLD	
FORBIDDEN GAMES (FRENCH)	1951	87	5*	4.0	3.0	TIMES FILM CORP.	

‡ An asterisk (*) in THE FILM BUFF'S BIBLE column indicates that the film has been rated by the editor and/or staff. All other ratings in this column are based on a consensus of reviews (see NOTES).

TITLE (LEADING ACTORS SHOWN WHERE TWO OR MORE FILMS HAVE THE SAME OR SIMILAR TITLE)	YEAR RELEASED	RUNNING TIME IN MINUTES	THE FILM BUFF'S BIBLE ‡	STEVEN SCHEUER	LEONARD MALTIN	DISTRIBUTOR	COMMENT
FORBIDDEN ISLAND	1959	66		1.5	1.5	COLUMBIA	
FORBIDDEN PLANET	1956	98	4	2.5	3.0	M-G-M	
FORBIDDEN STREET, THE	1949	91		2.0	2.0	20th CENTURY FOX	
FORBIN PROJECT, THE	a1970	100	5-6*			UNIVERSAL	
FORCE OF ARMS	1951	100		2.5	2.5	WARNER BROTHERS	
FORCE OF EVIL	1949	78	6	3.0	3.0	M-G-M	
FOREIGN AFFAIR, A	1948	116		3.0	3.5	PARAMOUNT	
FOREIGN CORRESPONDENT	1940	119		3.0	4.0	UNITED ARTISTS	NOMINATED BEST PICTURE
FOREIGN EXCHANGE (T.V.)	1970	90		2.0		ABC FILMS	
FOREIGN INTRIGUE	1956	100	4	3.0	2.5	UNITED ARTISTS	
FOREMAN WENT TO FRANCE, THE (BRITISH)	1942	88		3.5	2.5	UNITED ARTISTS	
FOREST RANGERS, THE	1942	87		2.5	2.5	PARAMOUNT	
FOREVER AMBER	1947	140		2.5	2.5	20th CENTURY FOX	
FOREVER AND A DAY	1943	104		4.0	4.0	RKO	
FOREVER DARLING	1956	96		2.0	2.5	M-G-M	
FOREVER FEMALE	1953	93	6		3.5	PARAMOUNT	
FOREVER MY LOVE (AUSTRIAN)	1962	167	4		2.5	PARAMOUNT	
FORGER OF LONDON (GERMAN)	1961	91			2.0	UCC FILMS	
FORGIVEN SINNER, THE (FRENCH)	1961	101		3.5	2.5		
FORGOTTEN WOMAN	1939	63			2.5	UNIVERSAL	
FORSAKING ALL OTHERS	1935	84		2.5	2.5	M-G-M	
FORT ALGIERS	1953	78	2	1.5	2.0	UNITED ARTISTS	
FORT APACHE	1948	127	5	3.0	3.0	RKO	
FORT BOWIE	1958	80	2			UNITED ARTISTS	
FORT COURAGEOUS	1965	72	3			20th CENTURY FOX	
FORT DEFIANCE	1951	81	4	3.0	2.5	UNITED ARTISTS	
FORT DOBBS	1958	90		2.0	2.0	WARNER BROTHERS	
FORT MASSACRE	1958	80		2.0	2.0	UNITED ARTISTS	
FORT OSAGE	1952	72		2.0	1.0	MONOGRAM	
FORT TI	1953	73		2.0	2.0	COLUMBIA	
FORT UTAH	1967	83	1			PARAMOUNT	
FORT VENGEANCE	1953	75		2.0	1.5	ALLIED ARTISTS	
FORT WORTH	1951	80		2.5	2.0	WARNER BROTHERS	
FORT YUMA	1955	78	2		2.0	UNITED ARTISTS	
FORTRESS OF THE DEAD	1965	78		2.5		COM. UNITED T.V.	
FORTUNE AND MEN'S EYES	1971	102	5			M-G-M	
FORTUNE COOKIE, THE	a1966	125	6*	3.5	3.0	UNITED ARTISTS	
FORTUNE IN DIAMONDS (BRITISH)	a1951	82		2.5	2.0	J. ARTHUR RANK	
FORTUNES OF CAPTAIN BLOOD	1950	91		2.5	2.0	COLUMBIA	
48 HOURS TO LIVE (SWEDISH)	a1959	75		1.5		MEDALLION	
FORTY GUNS	1957	80		2.5	2.5	20th CENTURY FOX	
FORTY GUNS TO APACHE PASS	1967	95	3			COLUMBIA	
FORTY LITTLE MOTHERS	1940	90		2.5	2.5	M-G-M	
FORTY-NINERS, THE	1954	71		2.5		ALLIED ARTISTS	
49TH MAN, THE	1953	73		2.5	2.0	COLUMBIA	
FORTY NAUGHTY GIRLS	1937	63		3.0		RKO	
FORTY-NINTH PARALLEL, THE (BRITISH)	a1941	105	6*	3.5	3.5	COLUMBIA	NOMINATED BEST PICTURE 1942
40 POUNDS OF TROUBLE	1963	106	4*	2.0	2.5	UNIVERSAL	
FORTY-SECOND STREET	1933	98	5*	3.5	3.5	WARNER BROTHERS	NOMINATED BEST PICTURE 1932/33
FORTY THOUSAND HORSEMEN (AUSTRALIAN)	1941	89		3.0		SHERMAN S. KRELLBERG	
FOUNTAIN, THE	1934	83		2.5	2.5	RKO	
FOUNTAIN OF LOVE, THE (AUSTRIAN)	1969	83	2			CROWN INTERNATIONAL	
FOUNTAINHEAD, THE	1949	114	5-6*	2.5	2.5	WARNER BROTHERS	
FOUR BAGS FULL (FRENCH)	1956	84		3.0	2.5	TRANS-LUX DIST.	
4-D MAN	a1959	85	4		2.5	UNIVERSAL	
FOUR DAUGHTERS	1938	90		4.0	3.5	WARNER BROTHERS	NOMINATED BEST PICTURE
FOUR DAYS IN NOVEMBER (DOCUMENTARY)	1964	120	7			UNITED ARTISTS	
FOUR DAYS IN PARIS (FRENCH)	1955	90		1.5			
FOUR DAYS' LEAVE (SWISS)	1950	98		2.5	2.0	FILM CLASSICS	
FOUR DAYS OF NAPLES, THE (ITALIAN)	1962	116	7			M-G-M	
FOUR DESPERATE MEN (AUSTRALIAN)	1959	104	4	3.0	2.5	CONTINENTAL	
FOUR FACES WEST	1948	90		2.5	2.5	UNITED ARTISTS	
FOUR FAST GUNS	1959	72		1.5	1.5	UNIVERSAL	
FOUR FEATHERS (BRITISH)	1939	115		3.5	3.5	UNITED ARTISTS	
FOUR FLIES ON GREY VELVET	1972	102	2			PARAMOUNT	
FOUR FOR TEXAS	1963	124		1.5	3.0	WARNER BROTHERS	
FOUR FRIGHTENED PEOPLE	1934	78			2.5	PARAMOUNT	
FOUR GIRLS IN TOWN	1957	85	5	3.5	3.0	UNIVERSAL	
FOUR GUNS TO THE BORDER	1954	82	3	2.0	2.5	UNIVERSAL	
FOUR HORSEMEN OF THE APOCALYPSE, THE (GLENN FORD)	1962	153		2.5	2.5	M-G-M	
400 BLOWS, THE (FRENCH)	1958	94	4*	4.0	4.0	ZENITH INTERNATIONAL	
FOUR IN A JEEP (SWISS)	1951	96		4.0	2.5	UNITED ARTISTS	
FOUR JACKS AND A JILL	1942	68		2.0		RKO	
FOUR JILLS IN A JEEP	1944	89		2.0	2.0	20th CENTURY FOX	
FOUR MEN AND A PRAYER	1938	85		3.0	3.5	20th CENTURY FOX	
FOUR MOTHERS	1941	86		2.0	2.5	WARNER BROTHERS	
491 (SWEDISH)	1964	110	3			PEPPERCORN-WORMSER	
FOUR POSTER, THE	1953	103	5*	3.0	3.5	COLUMBIA	
FOUR SKULLS OF JONATHAN DRAKE, THE	1959	70		1.0	2.0	UNITED ARTISTS	
FOUR SONS	1940	89		2.5	2.5	20th CENTURY FOX	
FOUR WAYS OUT (ITALIAN)	1954	77		2.0	2.5	CARROLL PICTURES	
FOUR WIVES	1939	110		2.5	2.5	WARNER BROTHERS	
FOUR'S A CROWD	1938	91		2.5	2.5	WARNER BROTHERS	
FOURTEEN HOURS	1951	92	5*	3.0	3.0	20th CENTURY FOX	

‡ An asterisk (*) in THE FILM BUFF'S BIBLE column indicates that the film has been rated by the editor and/or staff. All other ratings in this column are based on a consensus of reviews (see NOTES).

TITLE (LEADING ACTORS SHOWN WHERE TWO OR MORE FILMS HAVE THE SAME OR SIMILAR TITLE)	YEAR RELEASED	RUNNING TIME IN MINUTES	THE FILM BUFF'S BIBLE ‡	STEVEN SCHEUER	LEONARD MALTIN	DISTRIBUTOR	COMMENT
FOURTH FOR MARRIAGE, A	a1964	87	3	1.0		FAIRWAY INTERNAT'L	
FOURTH SQUARE, THE (BRITISH)	1961	58		2.0		ANGLO AMALGAMATED	
FOX, THE	1968	110	4*	3.0		CLARIDGE	
FOXES OF HARROW, THE	1947	117	5*	3.0	2.5	20th CENTURY FOX	
FOXFIRE	1955	92	4	2.5	3.0	UNIVERSAL	
FOXHOLE IN CAIRO (BRITISH)	1960	79		2.0	2.5	PARAMOUNT	
FOXIEST GIRL IN PARIS, THE (FRENCH)	1957	96		2.5	2.5	TIMES FILM CORP.	
FRAGMENT OF FEAR (BRITISH)	1970	95	3			COLUMBIA	
FRAMED	1947	82		3.0	2.0	COLUMBIA	
FRANCIS	1950	91	5	2.5	·	UNIVERSAL	
FRANCIS COVERS THE BIG TOWN	1953	86		2.5	·	UNIVERSAL	
FRANCIS GOES TO THE RACES	1951	88	5	2.5	·	UNIVERSAL	
FRANCIS GOES TO WEST POINT	1952	81		2.5	·	UNIVERSAL	
FRANCIS IN THE HAUNTED HOUSE	1956	80		2.0	·	UNIVERSAL	
FRANCIS IN THE NAVY	1955	80	3*	2.0	·	UNIVERSAL	
FRANCIS JOINS THE WACS	1954	94		2.5	·	UNIVERSAL	
FRANCIS OF ASSISI	1961	106		2.0	2.5	20th CENTURY FOX	
FRANKENSTEIN	1931	71	4*	3.0	3.0	UNIVERSAL	
FRANKENSTEIN CONQUERS THE WORLD (JAPANESE)	1964	87	2	1.5	2.0	AMERICAN-INTERNAT'L	
FRANKENSTEIN CREATED WOMAN (BRITISH)	1967	86	3			20th CENTURY FOX	
FRANKENSTEIN MEETS THE SPACE MONSTER	a1965	78		1.0	1.5	ALLIED ARTISTS	
FRANKENSTEIN MEETS THE WOLF MAN	1943	72		2.5	2.5	UNIVERSAL	
FRANKENSTEIN MUST BE DESTROYED! (BRITISH)	1970	97	3			WARNER BROTHERS	
FRANKENSTEIN - 1970	1958	83		2.0	1.0	ALLIED ARTISTS	
FRANKENSTEIN'S DAUGHTER	1958	85		1.0	1.5	ASTOR	
FRANKIE AND JOHNNY	1966	87		1.0	2.5	UNITED ARTISTS	
FRANTIC (FRENCH)	1958	90		2.5	1.5	TIMES FILM CORP.	
FRAULEIN	1958	98	3	1.5	2.0	20th CENTURY FOX	
FRAULEIN DOKTOR (ITALIAN)	1968	102	3			PARAMOUNT	ENGLISH LANGUAGE
FREAKS	1932	64				M-G-M	
FRECKLES	1960	84		2.0	1.5	20th CENTURY FOX	
FREE AND EASY	a1930	75			2.5	M-G-M	
FREE, BLONDE AND TWENTY-ONE	1940	67		2.0	1.5	20th CENTURY FOX	
FREE FOR ALL	1949	83		2.0	2.0	UNIVERSAL	
FREE SOUL, A	1931	91		2.0	3.0	M-G-M	
FREE, WHITE AND 21	1963	102	2			AMERICAN-INTERNAT'L	
FREEDOM TO DIE (BRITISH)	1961	61		1.5		BUTCHER'S	
FREEDOM TO LOVE (GERMAN, DOCUMENTARY)	1970	96	2			GROVE PRESS	
FRENCH CONNECTION, THE	1971	104	8*	3.0	2.5	20th CENTURY FOX	BEST PICTURE AWARD
FRENCH KEY, THE	1946	64		3.0	2.5	REPUBLIC	
FRENCH LINE, THE	1954	102		2.0	2.0	RKO	
FRENCH MISTRESS, A (BRITISH)	1960	98	4			FILMS AROUND THE WLD.	
FRENCH THEY ARE A FUNNY RACE, THE (BRITISH)	1957	83	4	2.5	2.0	CONTINENTAL	
FRENCH WITHOUT TEARS (BRITISH)	1940	67		1.5	2.5	PARAMOUNT	
FRENCHIE	1951	81		2.0	2.5	UNIVERSAL	
FRENCHMAN'S CREEK	1944	113		3.0	3.0	PARAMOUNT	
FRENZY (BRITISH - JON FINCH, BARRY FOSTER)	1972	116	6*			UNIVERSAL	
FRESH FROM PARIS	1955	70		1.5	1.5	20th CENTURY FOX	
FRESHMAN, THE (SILENT)	1925	76				PATHE	
FREUD	1962	139	6*	3.0	3.5	UNIVERSAL	
FRIEDA (BRITISH)	1947	98	6	3.5	3.0	UNIVERSAL	
FRIEND OF THE FAMILY (FRENCH)	1965	95	6			INTERNAT'L CLASSICS	
FRIENDLY ENEMIES	1942	95		2.0	2.5	UNITED ARTISTS	
FRIENDLY PERSUASION	1956	139	6*	4.0	3.0	ALLIED ARTISTS	NOMINATED BEST PICTURE
FRIENDS	1971	102	3			PARAMOUNT	
FRIENDS AND LOVERS (ANNE LINDEN, MARY KAHN)	a1969	82	3			STRATFORD PICS.	
FRIGHT (ERIC FLEMING, NANCY MALONE)	1956	81		1.5		ALLIED ARTISTS	
FRIGHT (BRITISH - SUSAN GEORGE, HONOR BLACKMAN)	1971	87	2			ALLIED ARTISTS	
FRIGHTENED BRIDE, THE (BRITISH)	1952	75		2.5	2.0	BEVERLY	
FRIGHTENED CITY, THE (BRITISH)	1961	97		1.5	2.5	ALLIED ARTISTS	
FRISCO KID	1935	77		3.0	2.0	WARNER BROTHERS	
FRISCO SAL	1945	63		2.5	2.0	UNIVERSAL	
FRISKY (ITALIAN)	1955	98		2.5	2.5	DIST. CORP. OF AMER.	
FRITZ THE CAT (CARTOON)	1972	78	3			CINEMATION INDUS.	
FROGMEN, THE	1951	96	4*	2.5	3.0	20th CENTURY FOX	
FROGS	1972	91	3			AMERICAN-INTERNAT'L	
FROM A ROMAN BALCONY (ITALIAN)	1961	84	5			CONTINENTAL	
FROM EAR TO EAR	1971	81	1			CINEMATION INDUS.	
FROM HELL IT CAME	1957	71		1.0	1.5	ALLIED ARTISTS	
FROM HELL TO BORNEO	1964	96		2.0	2.0	COM. UNITED T.V.	
FROM HELL TO TEXAS	a1958	100		2.5	2.5	20th CENTURY FOX	
FROM HERE TO ETERNITY	1953	118	7*	4.0	4.0	COLUMBIA	BEST PICTURE AWARD
FROM ISTANBUL - ORDERS TO KILL	1965	82		1.5		SIGMA III	
FROM RUSSIA WITH LOVE (BRITISH)	1964	118	6*	3.5	3.5	UNITED ARTISTS	
FROM THE EARTH TO THE MOON	1958	100		2.5	2.5	WARNER BROTHERS	
FROM THE TERRACE	1960	144	6*	3.0	3.0	20th CENTURY FOX	
FROM THIS DAY FORWARD	1946	95		3.0	3.0	RKO	
FRONT PAGE, THE	1931	101	6*			UNITED ARTISTS	NOMINATED BEST PICTURE 1930/31
FRONT PAGE STORY (BRITISH)	1954	95	4	3.5	2.5	ASSOCIATED ARTISTS	
FRONT PAGE WOMAN	1935	82		3.0	2.5	WARNER BROTHERS	
FRONTIER BADMAN	1943	77		2.5		UNIVERSAL	
FRONTIER GAL	1945	84		3.0	2.5	UNIVERSAL	
FRONTIER GAMBLER	1956	76		2.0		ASSOC'D FILM DISTS.	
FRONTIER GUN	1958	70		1.5	2.0	20th CENTURY FOX	

‡ An asterisk (*) in THE FILM BUFF'S BIBLE column indicates that the film has been rated by the editor and/or staff. All other ratings in this column are based on a consensus of reviews (see NOTES).

TITLE (LEADING ACTORS SHOWN WHERE TWO OR MORE FILMS HAVE THE SAME OR SIMILAR TITLE)	YEAR RELEASED	RUNNING TIME IN MINUTES	THE FILM BUFF'S BIBLE ‡	STEVEN SCHEUER	LEONARD MALTIN	DISTRIBUTOR	COMMENT
FRONTIER HELLCAT (GERMAN)	1964	98			2.5	COLUMBIA	
FRONTIER UPRISING	1961	68		1.5	1.5	UNITED ARTISTS	
FRONTIER WOLF (ITALIAN)	1950	76		1.5		TRANS-AMERICA	
FROZEN ALIVE (GERMAN)	1964	63	2	1.5		COM. UNITED T.V.	ENGLISH VERSION
FROZEN DEAD, THE (BRITISH)	1967	95	2		2.5	WARNER BROTHERS	
FROZEN GHOST, THE	1945	61		2.0	2.0	UNIVERSAL	
FRUITS OF SUMMER, THE (FRENCH)	1954	101	4			ELLIS FILMS	
FUEGO (SPANISH)	1969	81	1			HAVEN INTERNATIONAL	
FUGITIVE, THE	1947	104		4.0	3.5	RKO	
FUGITIVE FROM A PRISON CAMP	1940	59		1.5		COLUMBIA	
FUGITIVE FROM JUSTICE	1940	53		1.5		WARNER BROTHERS	
FUGITIVE IN SAIGON (FRENCH)	a1957	100		2.0		J. ARTHUR RANK	
FUGITIVE KIND, THE	1960	135	5*	3.0	2.5	UNITED ARTISTS	
FUGITIVE LADY	1951	78	2			REPUBLIC	
FULL CONFESSION	1939	73		3.0	2.0	RKO	
FULL HEARTS AND EMPTY POCKETS (GERMAN)	1964	88		2.5		SCREEN GEMS	
FULL OF LIFE	1957	91	4*	3.5	3.0	COLUMBIA	
FULLER BRUSH GIRL, THE	1950	85		3.0	2.0	COLUMBIA	
FULLER BRUSH MAN, THE	1948	93		3.0	2.5	COLUMBIA	
FUN AND FANCY FREE (CARTOON)	1947	73	6			RKO	
FUN IN ACAPULCO	1963	97		2.0	2.5	PARAMOUNT	
FUN ON A WEEKEND	1947	93		1.5	2.0	UNITED ARTISTS	
FUNERAL IN BERLIN (BRITISH)	1966	102	4*			PARAMOUNT	
FUNNY FACE	1957	103	6*	4.0	3.5	PARAMOUNT	
FUNNY GIRL	1968	151	7	4.0		COLUMBIA	NOMINATED BEST PICTURE
FUNNY THING HAPPENED ON THE WAY TO THE FORUM, A	1966	99	7*	4.0		UNITED ARTISTS	
FURIES, THE	1950	109	4*	2.5	3.0	PARAMOUNT	
FURIOUS ENCOUNTER (MEXICAN)	1962	74		1.0		COM. UNITED T.V.	
FURTHER PERILS OF LAUREL AND HARDY	1967	99	6	3.5		20th CENTURY FOX	
FURY	1936	90	8*	4.0	3.5	M-G-M	
FURY AT FURNACE CREEK	1948	88	4	2.0	2.0	20th CENTURY FOX	
FURY AT GUNSIGHT PASS	1956	68		2.0	2.0	COLUMBIA	
FURY AT SHOWDOWN	1957	75		1.5	1.5	UNITED ARTISTS	
FURY AT SMUGGLER'S BAY (BRITISH)	1961	92	2	2.0	2.0	AVCO-EMBASSY	
FURY IN PARADISE (MEXICAN)	1955	77		1.0		FILMMAKERS	
FURY OF ACHILLES (ITALIAN)	1962	116		1.5		AMERICAN-INTERNAT'L	
FURY OF HERCULES, THE (ITALIAN)	1961	95		1.5	2.0	TELEWIDE SYSTEMS	
FURY OF THE CONGO	1951	69		1.5	-	COLUMBIA	
FURY OF THE PAGANS (ITALIAN)	1960	86	1	1.5	2.0	COLUMBIA	
FUZZ	1972	92	3			UNITED ARTISTS	
FUZZY PINK NIGHTGOWN, THE	1957	87		2.0	2.0	UNITED ARTISTS	
FX 18, SECRET AGENT (FRENCH)	1964	95		1.0		PARAMOUNT	
G.I. BLUES	1960	104		2.5	3.0	PARAMOUNT	
G-MEN, THE	1935	85		3.0	3.0	WARNER BROTHERS	
GABRIEL OVER THE WHITE HOUSE	1933	87		2.0	2.5	M-G-M	
GABY	1956	97		2.5	2.5	M-G-M	
GAILY, GAILY	a1969	106	5			UNITED ARTISTS	
GAL WHO TOOK THE WEST, THE	1949	84		2.0	2.0	UNIVERSAL	
GALIA (FRENCH)	1965	105	4			ZENITH INTERNATIONAL	
GALLANT BESS	1946	101		2.0	2.0	M-G-M	
GALLANT BLADE, THE	1948	81	4		2.0	COLUMBIA	
GALLANT HOURS, THE	1960	111		2.5	3.0	UNITED ARTISTS	
GALLANT JOURNEY	1946	85		2.5	2.5	COLUMBIA	
GALLANT LEGION, THE	1948	88		3.0		REPUBLIC	
GALLANT SONS	1940	70		2.0		M-G-M	
GALLOPING MAJOR, THE (BRITISH)	1950	82		3.0	2.0	SOUVAINE SELECTIVE	
GAMBIT	1966	109	6*	3.0	3.0	UNIVERSAL	
GAMBLER, THE (BRITISH - MAURICE ROEVES)	1970	93	5*			TIME-LIFE FILMS	
GAMBLER AND THE LADY, THE (BRITISH)	1952	74		1.5	1.5	LIPPERT PRODS.	
GAMBLER FROM NATCHEZ, THE	1954	88		2.0	2.0	20th CENTURY FOX	
GAMBLER'S CHOICE	1944	66		2.0	2.0	PARAMOUNT	
GAMBLING HOUSE	1951	80		2.0	2.0	RKO	
GAMBLING LADY	1934	66		2.0	2.5	WARNER BROTHERS	
GAMBLING ON THE HIGH SEAS	1940	56		2.0		WARNER BROTHERS	
GAME FOR THREE LOSERS (BRITISH)	1964	56		2.0		AVCO-EMBASSY	
GAME IS OVER, THE (FRENCH)	1966	98	4			ROYAL FILMS INT'L	ENGLISH VERSION
GAME OF DANGER (BRITISH)	a1954	88		2.5	2.5	ASSOCIATED ARTISTS	
GAME OF DEATH, A	1946	72		2.5	1.5	RKO	
GAME OF LOVE (FRENCH - NICOLE BERGER)	1954	108	6			TIMES FILM CORP.	
GAMES (SIMONE SIGNORET, JAMES CAAN)	1967	100	5	3.0	3.0	UNIVERSAL	
GAMES, THE (BR. - MICHAEL CRAWFORD, STANLEY BAKER)	1970	95	3			20th CENTURY FOX	
GAMES MEN PLAY, THE (ARGENTINE)	1963	92	1			JOSEPH BRENNER	
GAMES OF DESIRE (GERMAN)	1964	90	1			TIMES FILM CORP.	
GAMMA PEOPLE, THE (BRITISH)	1956	79		2.0	2.0	COLUMBIA	
GANG THAT COULDN'T SHOOT STRAIGHT, THE	1971	96	3			M-G-M	
GANG WAR (CHARLES BRONSON, KENT TAYLOR)	1958	75	3	2.5	2.5	20th CENTURY FOX	
GANG WAR (BRITISH - SEAN KELLY, EIRA HEATH)	1962	65			2.0	UNITED ARTISTS	
GANGBUSTERS (MYRON HEALEY, DON C. HARVEY)	1955	78		1.5	2.0	VISUAL DRAMA, INC.	
GANG'S ALL HERE, THE	1943	103		2.5	2.5	20th CENTURY FOX	
GANGSTER, THE	1947	84		3.0	3.0	ALLIED ARTISTS	
GANGSTER BOSS (FRENCH)	1959	100		2.0	2.0	EMERY PICTURES	

‡ An asterisk (*) in THE FILM BUFF'S BIBLE column indicates that the film has been rated by the editor and/or staff. All other ratings in this column are based on a consensus of reviews (see NOTES).

TITLE (LEADING ACTORS SHOWN WHERE TWO OR MORE FILMS HAVE THE SAME OR SIMILAR TITLE)	YEAR RELEASED	RUNNING TIME IN MINUTES	THE FILM BUFF'S BIBLE ‡	STEVEN SCHEUER	LEONARD MALTIN	DISTRIBUTOR	COMMENT
GANGSTER STORY	1959	65		1.0	2.5	REPUBLIC	
GANGWAY FOR TOMORROW	1943	69		2.0		RKO	
GARDEN OF ALLAH, THE	1936	85		3.0	3.0	UNITED ARTISTS	
GARDEN OF DELIGHTS (SPANISH)	1971	95	6			ALTURA FILMS	
GARDEN OF EVIL	1954	100	4*	2.5	2.5	20th CENTURY FOX	
GARDEN OF THE FINZI CONTINIS, THE (ITALIAN)	1971	94	5*			CINEMA V	
GARDEN OF THE MOON	1938	94		3.0	2.5	WARNER BROTHERS	
GARIBALDI (ITALIAN)	1961	110		2.0		TRANS-AMERICA	
GARMENT JUNGLE, THE	1957	88	4	3.0	2.5	COLUMBIA	
GAS-OIL (FRENCH)	a1955	95		2.0		INTERMONDIA FILMS	
GAS-S-S-S!	1970	80	3			AMERICAN-INTERNAT'L	
GASLIGHT (INGRID BERGMAN, CHARLES BOYER)	1944	114	6*	3.0	3.5	M-G-M	NOMINATED BEST PICTURE
GASLIGHT FOLLIES	1945	110		2.0	1.5	AVCO-EMBASSY	
GATE OF HELL (JAPANESE)	1953	90	7	3.5	3.5	HARRISON PICTURES	
GATES OF PARIS (FRENCH)	1957	103		3.5	2.5	LOPERT	
GATEWAY	1938	73		2.0	2.0	20th CENTURY FOX	
GATHERING OF EAGLES, A	1963	115	5	2.5	3.5	UNIVERSAL	
GAY ADVENTURE, THE (BRITISH)	1953	87			3.0	UNITED ARTISTS	
GAY BLADES	a1946	67		2.5		REPUBLIC	
GAY BRIDE, THE	1934	80		2.0	1.5	M-G-M	
GAY CABALLERO, THE	1940	57		2.5		20th CENTURY FOX	
GAY DECEIVERS, THE	1969	91	3	1.0		FANFARE	
GAY DESPERADO, THE	1936	85		2.5	3.0	UNITED ARTISTS	
GAY DIVORCEE, THE	1934	107	3*	4.0	3.5	RKO	NOMINATED BEST PICTURE
GAY FALCON, THE	1941	67		2.5	-	RKO	
GAY LADY, THE (BRITISH)	a1949	91		3.0	2.5	EAGLE LION	
GAY PURR-EE (CARTOON)	1962	86		2.5	2.5	WARNER BROTHERS	
GAY SENORITA, THE	1946	69		2.0		COLUMBIA	
GAY SISTERS, THE	1942	108		2.0	2.0	WARNER BROTHERS	
GAY VAGABOND, THE	1941	66		2.0		REPUBLIC	
GAZEBO, THE	1960	100	6*	3.0	3.0	M-G-M	
GEISHA BOY, THE	1958	98	4*	2.5	2.5	PARAMOUNT	
GENE KRUPA STORY, THE	a1959	101	4	2.0	2.5	COLUMBIA	
GENERAL, THE (SILENT)	1927	83	6*			UNITED ARTISTS	
GENERAL DELLA ROVERE (ITALIAN)	1959	139	5*	3.5	3.5	CONTINENTAL	
GENERAL DIED AT DAWN, THE	1936	97	5*	3.5	3.5	PARAMOUNT	
GENERATION	1969	104	4			AVCO-EMBASSY	
GENEVIEVE (BRITISH)	1953	86	6*	4.0	3.5	UNIVERSAL	
GENGHIS KHAN (PHILIPPINE - MANUEL CONDE)	1952	88		3.0		UNITED ARTISTS	
GENGHIS KHAN (OMAR SHARIF, STEPHEN BOYD)	1965	124		2.0	2.5	COLUMBIA	
GENIUS AT WORK	1946	61		1.0		RKO	
GENTLE ANNIE	1944	80		2.5	2.0	M-G-M	
GENTLE GIANT	1967	93	5	2.5		PARAMOUNT	'GENTLE BEN' TV SERIES PILOT
GENTLE GUNMAN, THE (BRITISH)	1952	86		3.0	3.0	UNIVERSAL	
GENTLE SEX, THE (BRITISH)	1943	89		2.5		TWO CITIES	
GENTLE TOUCH, THE (BRITISH)	1955	86			2.0	J. ARTHUR RANK	
GENTLEMAN AFTER DARK	1942	77		1.5	2.0	UNITED ARTISTS	
GENTLEMAN AT HEART, A	1942	66		2.5	2.0	20th CENTURY FOX	
GENTLEMAN JIM	1942	104	6*	3.5	3.5	WARNER BROTHERS	
GENTLEMAN'S AGREEMENT	1947	118	7*	4.0	3.0	20th CENTURY FOX	BEST PICTURE AWARD
GENTLEMEN MARRY BRUNETTES	1955	97		2.5	2.0	UNITED ARTISTS	
GENTLEMEN OF THE NIGHT	1963	99		1.5		PARAMOUNT	
GENTLEMEN PREFER BLONDES (SILENT - RUTH TAYLOR)	1928	76				PARAMOUNT	BELIEVED LOST
GENTLEMEN PREFER BLONDES (MARILYN MONROE)	1953	91		3.0	2.5	20th CENTURY FOX	
GEORGE RAFT STORY, THE	1961	106		2.5	2.5	ALLIED ARTISTS	
GEORGE WASHINGTON SLEPT HERE	1942	93		3.0	2.5	WARNER BROTHERS	
GEORGE WHITE'S SCANDALS	1945	95			2.0	RKO	
GEORGIA, GEORGIA	1972	91	3			CINERAMA RELEASING	
GEORGY GIRL (BRITISH)	1966	99	7*	4.0	3.5	COLUMBIA	
GERALDINE	1954	90	3	2.0		REPUBLIC	
GERMANY, YEAR ZERO (GERMAN)	1947	75	7			SUPERFILM	
GERONIMO (PRESTON FOSTER, ELLEN DREW)	1939	89		2.0	2.0	PARAMOUNT	
GERONIMO (CHUCK CONNERS, KAMALA DEVI)	1962	101		2.5	2.5	UNITED ARTISTS	
GERTRUD (DANISH)	1964	120	3			PATHE CONTEMPARARY	
GERVAISE (FRENCH)	1956	116	6	3.0	3.0	CONTINENTAL	
GET-AWAY, THE	1941	89		1.5		M-G-M	
GET CARTER (BRITISH)	1971	111	4			M-G-M	
GET HEP TO LOVE	1942	71		2.0	1.5	UNIVERSAL	
GET ON WITH IT (BRITISH)	a1963	88	3	1.5		GOVERNOR	
GET OUT OF TOWN	1961	65		1.5	2.0	ALLIED ARTISTS	
GET TO KNOW YOUR RABBIT	1972	91	3			WARNER BROTHERS	
GET YOURSELF A COLLEGE GIRL	a1964	86	2			M-G-M	
GETTING GERTIE'S GARTER	1945	72		2.5	2.5	UNITED ARTISTS	
GETTING STRAIGHT	1970	124	5			COLUMBIA	
GHIDRAH, THE THREE-HEADED MONSTER (JAPANESE)	1965	85	2	1.5	2.5	CONTINENTAL	
GHOST, THE (ITALIAN)	1963	96	1			MAGNA PICTURES	
GHOST AND MR CHICKEN, THE	1966	90		2.0	2.5	UNIVERSAL	
GHOST AND MRS MUIR, THE	1947	104	5*	3.0	3.5	20th CENTURY FOX	
GHOST BREAKERS, THE	1940	82		3.0	3.0	PARAMOUNT	
GHOST CATCHERS	1944	67		2.5	2.5	UNIVERSAL	
GHOST CHASERS	1951	69			-	MONOGRAM	
GHOST COMES HOME, THE	1940	79		2.0	2.0	M-G-M	
GHOST DIVER	1957	76			1.5	20th CENTURY FOX	
GHOST GOES WEST, THE (BRITISH)	1935	78		3.5	3.0	UNITED ARTISTS	

‡ An asterisk (*) in THE FILM BUFF'S BIBLE column indicates that the film has been rated by the
editor and/or staff. All other ratings in this column are based on a consensus of reviews (see NOTES).

TITLE (LEADING ACTORS SHOWN WHERE TWO OR MORE FILMS HAVE THE SAME OR SIMILAR TITLE)	YEAR RELEASED	RUNNING TIME IN MINUTES	CRITICAL RATINGS			DISTRIBUTOR	COMMENT
			THE FILM BUFF'S BIBLE	STEVEN SCHEUER	LEONARD MALTIN		
GHOST IN THE INVISIBLE BIKINI	1966	82		1.5	2.0	AMERICAN-INTERNAT'L	
GHOST OF DRAGSTRIP HOLLOW, THE	1959	65		1.5	1.0	AMERICAN-INTERNAT'L	
GHOST OF FRANKENSTEIN, THE	1942	68			2.5	UNIVERSAL	
GHOST OF THE CHINA SEA	1958	79		1.5	2.0	COLUMBIA	
GHOST OF ZORRO	1949	69		1.5	2.0	REPUBLIC	
GHOST SHIP (BRITISH - DERMOT WALSH, HAZEL COURT)	1952	69		2.0	2.0	LIPPERT PRODS.	
GHOST SHIP, THE (RICHARD DIX, RUSSEL WADE)	1943	69		3.0		RKO	
GHOST TOWN	1956	75		1.5		UNITED ARTISTS	
GHOSTS - ITALIAN STYLE (ITALIAN)	1968	92	1			M-G-M	ENGLISH LANGUAGE
GHOSTS OF ROME (ITALIAN)	1961	105		3.0	2.5	TELEWORLD	
GHOSTS ON THE LOOSE	1943	65				MONOGRAM	
GIANT	1956	198	7-8*	3.5		WARNER BROTHERS	NOMINATED BEST PICTURE
GIANT BEHEMOTH, THE (BRITISH)	1959	79		2.0	2.0	ALLIED ARTISTS	
GIANT CLAW, THE	1957	76		2.0	1.5	COLUMBIA	
GIANT FROM THE UNKNOWN	1958	80		2.0		ASTOR	
GIANT GILA MONSTER, THE	1959	74		1.5	2.0	MCLENDON	
GIANT OF MARATHON, THE (ITALIAN)	1959	92	3			M-G-M	
GIANT OF METROPOLIS, THE (ITALIAN)	1962	92	1	1.5	2.0	WARNER BROTHERS	
GIANT OF THE EVIL ISLAND (ITALIAN)	1964	80		1.0		ROMANA FILMS	
GIANTS OF THESSALY, THE (ITALIAN)	1960	86		1.5	2.0	TELEWIDE SYSTEMS	
GIDEON OF SCOTLAND YARD (BRITISH)	1958	91	4	3.0	2.5	COLUMBIA	
GIDGET	1959	95		2.0	2.5	COLUMBIA	
GIDGET GOES HAWAIIAN	1961	102	3*	2.0	2.0	COLUMBIA	
GIDGET GOES TO ROME	1963	101		2.0	2.0	COLUMBIA	
GIDGET GROWS UP (T.V.)	1969	75		2.5		SCREEN GEMS	
GIFT FOR HEIDI, A	1958	71		1.5		RKO	
GIFT OF LOVE, THE	1958	105	4	2.0	2.5	20th CENTURY FOX	
GIGANTIS, THE FIRE MONSTER (JAPANESE)	1955	78	2	2.0	2.0	WARNER BROTHERS	
GIGI (FRENCH - DANIELE DELORME, FRANCK VILLARD)	1948	85	6			SPALTER INTERNAT'L	
GIGI (LESLIE CARON, LOUIS JOURDAN)	1958	116	6*	4.0	4.0	M-G-M	BEST PICTURE AWARD
GIGOT	1962	104	6*	2.5	3.0	20th CENTURY FOX	
GILBERT AND SULLIVAN (BRITISH)	a1954	109	6	3.5	3.5	UNITED ARTISTS	
GILDA	1946	110		2.5	3.0	COLUMBIA	
GILDED LILY, THE	1935	80		3.0	3.0	PARAMOUNT	
GILDERSLEEVE'S GHOST	1944	64			2.0	RKO	
GIMME SHELTER (DOCUMENTARY)	1971	91	6			CINEMA V	
GINA (FRENCH)	1959	90		2.0		SUTTON PICTURES	
GINGER (CHERI CAFFARO, CINDY BARNETT)	1971	102	1			JOSEPH BRENNER	
GIRL, A GUY, AND A GOB, A	1941	91		3.0	2.0	RKO	
GIRL AGAINST NAPOLEON, A (SPANISH)	1960	87		2.0		TELEWIDE SYSTEMS	
GIRL AND THE GENERAL, THE (ITALIAN)	1967	105	4			M-G-M	
GIRL AND THE LEGEND, THE (GERMAN)	1962	90		2.0			
GIRL AND THE RIVER, THE (FRENCH)	1958	98		2.0		CONTINENTAL	
GIRL CAN'T HELP IT, THE	1956	99	4	2.5	3.0	20th CENTURY FOX	
GIRL CRAZY	1943	99		3.5	3.5	M-G-M	
GIRL FROM AVENUE A	1940	73		1.5		20th CENTURY FOX	
GIRL FROM FLANDERS, THE (GERMAN)	1963	105		2.0		SCREEN GEMS	
GIRL FROM HAVANA	1940	69		1.5		REPUBLIC	
GIRL FROM HONG KONG, THE (GERMAN)	1963	95		1.5		NTA PICTURES	
GIRL FROM JONES BEACH, THE	1949	78		2.5	2.0	WARNER BROTHERS	
GIRL FROM MANHATTAN, THE	1948	81		1.5	2.0	UNITED ARTISTS	
GIRL FROM MISSOURI, THE	1934	75		2.5	2.5	M-G-M	
GIRL FROM 10TH AVENUE	1935	69		3.0		FIRST NATIONAL	
GIRL-GETTERS, THE (BRITISH)	a1964	93	6	3.0	3.0	AMERICAN-INTERNAT'L	
GIRL HAPPY	1965	96		2.0	2.5	M-G-M	
GIRL HE LEFT BEHIND, THE	1956	103		2.0	2.5	WARNER BROTHERS	
GIRL HUNTERS, THE (BRITISH)	1963	97		2.0	2.5	COLORAMA FEATURES	
GIRL IN A MILLION, A (BRITISH)	1945	81		2.0	2.0	DISTINGUISHED FILMS	
GIRL IN BLACK, A (GREEK)	1955	104	6			KINGSLEY INTERNAT'L	
GIRL IN BLACK STOCKINGS, THE	1957	73		2.5	2.0	UNITED ARTISTS	
GIRL IN EVERY PORT, A	1952	86		2.0	2.0	RKO	
GIRL IN HIS POCKET (FRENCH)	1957	82		2.0	2.5	MEDELEINE FILMS	
GIRL IN LOVER'S LANE, THE	1960	80		1.0		FUTURAMIC	
GIRL IN ROOM 13, THE	1961	97		1.5	1.5	ASTOR	
GIRL IN THE BIKINI, THE (FRENCH)	1952	78	2	1.5		ATLANTIS FILMS	
GIRL IN THE CASE, THE	1944	64		2.0		COLUMBIA	
GIRL IN THE KREMLIN, THE	1957	81		1.5	2.0	UNIVERSAL	
GIRL IN THE NEWS (BRITISH)	1940	78		2.5		20th CENTURY FOX	
GIRL IN THE PAINTING, THE (BRITISH)	a1948	89		3.0	3.0	UNIVERSAL	
GIRL IN THE RED VELVET SWING, THE	1955	109		2.5	2.5	20th CENTURY FOX	
GIRL IN THE WOODS	1958	71		2.0	1.5	REPUBLIC	
GIRL IN WHITE, THE	1952	93	4	2.0	2.0	M-G-M	
GIRL MOST LIKELY, THE	1958	98	5	3.0	3.0	UNIVERSAL	
GIRL NAMED TAMIKO, A	1963	110		2.5	2.5	PARAMOUNT	
GIRL NEXT DOOR, THE	1953	92		2.0	2.5	20th CENTURY FOX	
GIRL OF THE GOLDEN WEST, THE (JEANETTE MACDONALD)	1938	120		2.0	2.5	M-G-M	
GIRL OF THE LIMBERLOST (DORINDA CLIFTON)	1945	60	3*	1.0		COLUMBIA	
GIRL OF THE NIGHT	1960	93		1.0	2.5	WARNER BROTHERS	
GIRL ON A MOTORCYCLE, THE (BRITISH)	1968	91	2	1.0		CLARIDGE	
GIRL ON APPROVAL (BRITISH)	1962	75		2.0		CONTINENTAL	
GIRL ON THE BRIDGE	1951	77		1.5	1.0	20th CENTURY FOX	
GIRL RUSH (ROBERT MITCHUM)	1944	65		2.0		RKO	
GIRL RUSH, THE (ROSALIND RUSSELL)	1955	85		2.0	2.5	PARAMOUNT	
GIRL TROUBLE	1942	82		2.0	2.0	20th CENTURY FOX	

‡ An asterisk (*) in THE FILM BUFF'S BIBLE column indicates that the film has been rated by the editor and/or staff. All other ratings in this column are based on a consensus of reviews (see NOTES).

TITLE (LEADING ACTORS SHOWN WHERE TWO OR MORE FILMS HAVE THE SAME OR SIMILAR TITLE)	YEAR RELEASED	RUNNING TIME IN MINUTES	THE FILM BUFF'S BIBLE ‡	STEVEN SCHEUER	LEONARD MALTIN	DISTRIBUTOR	COMMENT
GIRL WHO COULDN'T SAY NO, THE	1969	83	1			20th CENTURY FOX	ENGLISH VERSION
GIRL WHO DARED	1944	56		1.5		REPUBLIC	
GIRL WHO HAD EVERYTHING, THE	1953	69		2.0	2.5	M-G-M	
GIRL WHO KNEW TOO MUCH, THE	1969	96	1			LANDAU/UNGER COM. UN.	
GIRL WITH A SUITCASE, THE (ITALIAN)	1961	108	6	3.5	3.5	ELLIS FILMS	
GIRL WITH GREEN EYES (BRITISH)	1964	91	7			LOPERT	
GIRL WITH THE GOLDEN EYES (FRENCH)	1961	90	4			KINGSLEY INTERNAT'L	
GIRL WITH THREE CAMELS, THE (CZECH)	1968	98	6			CONTINENTAL	
GIRLS AT SEA (BRITISH)	1958	80		1.5		WARNER BROTHERS	
GIRLS' DORMITORY (HERBERT MARSHALL)	1936	66		2.5	2.5	20th CENTURY FOX	
GIRLS! GIRLS! GIRLS!	1962	106		2.0	2.5	PARAMOUNT	
GIRLS IN PRISON	1956	87		1.5	1.5	AMERICAN-INTERNAT'L	
GIRLS IN THE NIGHT	1953	83		1.5	2.0	UNIVERSAL	
GIRLS OF PLEASURE ISLAND, THE	1953	95		2.0	2.5	PARAMOUNT	
GIRLS OF THE NIGHT (FRENCH)	1957	114	2	2.0	2.5	CONTINENTAL	
GIRLS ON THE BEACH	1965	80	1			PARAMOUNT	
GIRLS ON THE LOOSE	1958	78		2.0	2.0	UNIVERSAL	
GIRLS' SCHOOL (ANN SHIRLEY, RALPH BELLAMY)	1938	73		2.5		COLUMBIA	
GIRLS' SCHOOL (JOYCE REYNOLDS, ROSS FORD)	1950	62	1			COLUMBIA	
GIRLS' TOWN	1959	92		1.0	1.5	M-G-M	
GIRLY (BRITISH)	a1970	101	3			CINERAMA RELEASING	
GIT!	1965	90		2.0		AVCO-EMBASSY	
GIUSEPPE VERDI (ITALIAN)	1953	105		2.0		CITATION	
GIVE A GIRL A BREAK	1954	82	4	2.5	2.5	M-G-M	
GIVE 'EM HELL (FRENCH)	a1954	90		1.5	2.5	PARAMOUNT	
GIVE HER THE MOON	1970	92	6			UNITED ARTISTS	
GIVE ME A SAILOR	1938	80		2.5	2.5	PARAMOUNT	
GIVE ME YOUR HEART	a1936	87		3.0	2.5	WARNER BROTHERS	
GIVE MY REGARDS TO BROADWAY	1948	89	4	2.0	2.0	20th CENTURY FOX	
GIVE US WINGS	1940	62		2.5	-	UNIVERSAL	
GIVEN WORD, THE (BRAZILIAN)	1962	98	6			LIONEX	
GLADIATOR, THE	1938	70			2.5	COLUMBIA	
GLADIATOR OF ROME (ITALIAN)	a1962	100		1.5		TELEWIDE SYSTEMS	
GLADIATORS SEVEN (ITALIAN)	1964	92	2			M-G-M	
GLAMOUR BOY	1941	80		2.5		PARAMOUNT	
GLAMOUR FOR SALE	1940	57		1.5		COLUMBIA	
GLASS ALIBI, THE	1946	70		2.5	2.0	REPUBLIC	
GLASS BOTTOM BOAT, THE	1966	110		1.5	3.0	M-G-M	
GLASS CAGE, THE (JOHN HOYT, ARLINE SAX)	a1964	78		2.0	1.5	FUTURAMIC	
GLASS KEY, THE (EDWARD ARNOLD, GEORGE RAFT)	1935	77		3.0		PARAMOUNT	
GLASS KEY, THE (ALAN LADD, BRIAN DONLEVY)	1942	85	4*	3.0	3.5	PARAMOUNT	
GLASS HOUSES	1971	90	1			COLUMBIA	
GLASS MANAGERIE, THE	1950	107	7	4.0	3.0	WARNER BROTHERS	
GLASS MOUNTAIN, THE (BRITISH)	1948	94		3.5	3.0	EAGLE LION	
GLASS SLIPPER, THE	1955	94		3.0	2.5	M-G-M	
GLASS TOMB, THE (BRITISH)	1955	59		2.5	2.0	LIPPERT PRODS.	
GLASS TOWER, THE (GERMAN)	1957	104		2.0	2.5	ELLIS FILMS	
GLASS WALL, THE	1953	82		3.0	2.0	COLUMBIA	
GLASS WEB, THE	1953	81	4	2.5	3.0	UNIVERSAL	
GLEN AND RANDA	1971	94	1			UMC PICTURES	
GLENN MILLER STORY, THE	1954	116		3.0	3.0	UNIVERSAL	
GLOBAL AFFAIR, A	1964	84	3	2.0	2.5	M-G-M	
GLORIOUS AVENGER (ITALIAN)	1950	105		1.5		UNITED ARTISTS	
GLORY	1956	100		1.5	2.0	RKO	
GLORY ALLEY	1952	79		2.5	2.5	M-G-M	
GLORY AT SEA (BRITISH)	1952	88	3*	3.0		M & A ALEXANDER	
GLORY BOY	a1971	93	4			CINERAMA RELEASING	
GLORY BRIGADE, THE	1953	82		3.0	2.0	20th CENTURY FOX	
GLORY GUYS, THE	1965	112	3		2.0	UNITED ARTISTS	
GLORY STOMPERS, THE	1967	85	2	1.0		AMERICAN-INTERNAT'L	
GLORIFYING THE AMERICAN GIRL	1929	86	2*			PARAMOUNT	
GNOME-MOBILE, THE	1967	90	5			BUENA VISTA	
GO-BETWEEN, THE (BRITISH)	1971	116	4*			COLUMBIA	
GO FOR BROKE	1951	92	4*	3.0	3.0	M-G-M	
GO GETTER, THE	1937	92		3.0		WARNER BROTHERS	
GO GO MANIA (BRITISH, DOCUMENTARY)	1965	70	2	1.5		AMERICAN-INTERNAT'L	
GO INTO YOUR DANCE	1935	89		3.5	2.5	FIRST NATIONAL	
GO, JOHNNY, GO!	1958	75	3	1.5		VALIANT	
GO, MAN, GO!	1954	82		2.5	2.5	UNITED ARTISTS	
GO NAKED IN THE WORLD	1961	103	4		2.0	M-G-M	
GO WEST	a1940	81		3.0	2.0	M-G-M	
GO WEST, YOUNG LADY	1941	70		2.5		COLUMBIA	
GO WEST, YOUNG MAN	1936	82		2.5	2.5	PARAMOUNT	
GOAL! (BRITISH, DOCUMENTARY)	1966	107	6			ROYAL FILMS INT'L	
GOBS AND GALS	1952	86		2.0		REPUBLIC	
GOD FORGIVES - I DON'T	1969	97	1			AMERICAN-INTERNAT'L	
GOD IS MY CO-PILOT	1945	90		2.5	2.5	WARNER BROTHERS	
GOD IS MY PARTNER	1957	80		2.0	2.0	20th CENTURY FOX	
GODDESS, THE	1958	105	5*	3.5	3.0	COLUMBIA	
GODDESS OF LOVE, THE	1960	68		1.0	1.5	20th CENTURY FOX	
GODFATHER, THE	1972	177	8*			PARAMOUNT	
GOD'S COUNTRY	1946	62			2.0	SCREEN GUILD	
GOD'S COUNTRY AND THE WOMAN	1936	80		2.5	2.0	WARNER BROTHERS	
GOD'S LITTLE ACRE	1958	110	4*	2.5	3.0	UNITED ARTISTS	

‡ An asterisk (*) in THE FILM BUFF'S BIBLE column indicates that the film has been rated by the editor and/or staff. All other ratings in this column are based on a consensus of reviews (see NOTES).

TITLE (LEADING ACTORS SHOWN WHERE TWO OR MORE FILMS HAVE THE SAME OR SIMILAR TITLE)	YEAR RELEASED	RUNNING TIME IN MINUTES	THE FILM BUFF'S BIBLE ‡	STEVEN SCHEUER	LEONARD MALTIN	DISTRIBUTOR	COMMENT
GODSON, THE	1971	92	4			BOXOFFICE INTERNAT'L	
GODZILLA (KING OF THE MONSTERS) (JAPANESE)	1955	80		1.5	2.5	AVCO-EMBASSY	
GODZILLA VS THE SEA MONSTER (JAPANESE)	1966	88		2.0		TOHO	
GODZILLA VS THE SMOG MONSTER (JAPANESE)	1972	87	2			AMERICAN-INTERNAT'L	
GODZILLA VS THE THING (JAPANESE)	1964	90	3		2.5	AMERICAN-INTERNAT'L	
GOG	1954	85		2.0	2.0	UNITED ARTISTS	
GOIN' DOWN THE ROAD	1970	90	6			CHEVRON	
GOIN' TO TOWN (MAE WEST, PAUL CAVANAUGH)	1935	74		1.5	3.0	PARAMOUNT	
GOIN' TO TOWN (LUM AND ABNER)	1944	69				RKO	
GOING HOME	1971	97	4			M-G-M	
GOING MY WAY	1944	130	5*	4.0	3.5	PARAMOUNT	BEST PICTURE AWARD
GOING PLACES	1938	84		2.5	2.0	WARNER BROTHERS	
GOING STEADY	1958	79		2.5	1.5	COLUMBIA	
GOLD DIGGERS IN PARIS	1938	95		3.0		WARNER BROTHERS	
GOLD DIGGERS OF BROADWAY	1929	98				WARNER BROTHERS	
GOLD DIGGERS OF 1933	1933	96		3.0	3.5	WARNER BROTHERS	
GOLD DIGGERS OF 1935	1935	95		3.0	3.0	FIRST NATIONAL	
GOLD DIGGERS OF 1937	1936	100		3.0	2.5	FIRST NATIONAL	
GOLD EXPRESS (BRITISH)	1955	58		2.0		J. ARTHUR RANK	
GOLD FEVER	1953	63	3	2.5		MONOGRAM	
GOLD FOR THE CAESARS (ITALIAN)	1962	66	2			M-G-M	
GOLD IS WHERE YOU FIND IT	1938	90		2.5	2.5	WARNER BROTHERS	
GOLD OF NAPLES (ITALIAN)	1955	107		3.5	2.0	DIST. CORP. OF AMER.	FOUR STORIES
GOLD OF THE SEVEN SAINTS	1961	88	3			WARNER BROTHERS	
GOLD RAIDERS	1951	56		1.5	1.5	UNITED ARTISTS	
GOLD RUSH, THE (SILENT)	1925	95	7*			UNITED ARTISTS	
GOLD RUSH MAISIE	1940	82		1.5		M-G-M	
GOLDBERGS, THE	a1950	83		2.5	2.5	PARAMOUNT	
GOLDEN AGE OF COMEDY, THE	1958	78	5*	4.0	4.0	DIST. CORP. OF AMER.	SILENT FILM CLIPS
GOLDEN ARROW, THE (BETTE DAVIS, GEORGE BRENT)	1936	68		3.0	2.5	FIRST NATIONAL	
GOLDEN ARROW, THE (ITAL. - TAB HUNTER, R. PODESTA)	1962	91	2			M-G-M	
GOLDEN BLADE, THE	1953	81		2.0	2.5	UNIVERSAL	
GOLDEN BOY	1939	99	4*	3.0	2.5	COLUMBIA	
GOLDEN COACH, THE (ITALIAN)	1952	100		3.5	2.0	ITALIAN FILMS EXPORT	ENGLISH LANGUAGE
GOLDEN DEMON, THE (JAPANESE)	1956	95		2.5		HARRISON PICTURES	
GOLDEN EARRINGS	1947	95	3*	2.5	2.5	PARAMOUNT	
GOLDEN EYE, THE	1948	69			-	MONOGRAM	
GOLDEN FISH, THE (SHORT FEATURE)	1959	19	6*			COLUMBIA	
GOLDEN GIRL	1951	108		2.5	2.5	20th CENTURY FOX	
GOLDEN GLOVES STORY, THE	1950	76	3		1.5	EAGLE LION	
GOLDEN GODDESS OF RIO BENI (GERMAN)	1964	93		1.5		CASINO FILMS	
GOLDEN HANDS OF KURIGAL	1949	100		1.5	1.5	REPUBLIC	RE-EDITED SERIAL
GOLDEN HAWK, THE	1952	83	2	2.0	2.0	COLUMBIA	
GOLDEN HORDE, THE	1951	77		2.0	2.0	UNIVERSAL	
GOLDEN IDOL, THE	1954	71				ALLIED ARTISTS	
GOLDEN MADONNA, THE (BRITISH)	1949	88		3.0	2.5	STRATFORD PICS.	
GOLDEN MASK, THE (BRITISH)	1954	88		2.5	2.5	UNITED ARTISTS	
GOLDEN MISTRESS, THE	1954	82		2.5	2.0	UNITED ARTISTS	
GOLDEN PATSY, THE (GERMAN)	1962	84		2.0			
GOLDEN SALAMANDER, THE (BRITISH)	1950	96		3.0	3.0	EAGLE LION	
GOLDEN TWENTIES, THE (DOCUMENTARY)	1950	68	6			RKO	
GOLDFINGER (BRITISH)	1964	109	5-6*	3.0	3.5	UNITED ARTISTS	
GOLDSTEIN	1965	82	3			ALTURA FILMS	
GOLDWYN FOLLIES, THE	1938	115		2.0	2.5	UNITED ARTISTS	
GOLEM, THE (GERMAN, SILENT - ALBERT STEINRUECK)	1920	97				UFA	
GOLEM, THE (CZECH - HARRY BAUR, ROGER KARL)	1936	91				UNITED ARTISTS	
GOLIATH AGAINST THE GIANTS (ITALIAN)	1961	90		1.0	1.5	TELEWIDE SYSTEMS	
GOLIATH AND THE BARBARIANS (ITALIAN)	1959	86	2	1.5	2.0	AMERICAN-INTERNAT'L	
GOLIATH AND THE DRAGON (ITALIAN)	1960	87		1.5	1.0	AMERICAN-INTERNAT'L	
GOLIATH AND THE REBEL SLAVE (ITALIAN)	1963	86		1.5			
GOLIATH AND THE SINS OF BABYLON (ITALIAN)	1963	80	1			AMERICAN-INTERNAT'L	
GOLIATH AND THE VAMPIRES (ITALIAN)	1961	92			1.5	AMERICAN-INTERNAT'L	
GOLIATH AT THE CONQUEST OF DAMASCUS (ITALIAN)	1964	86		1.0		AMERICAN-INTERNAT'L	
GONE ARE THE DAYS	1963	97	6*	3.0	3.0	TRANS-LUX DIST.	
GONE WITH THE WIND	1939	219	9*			M-G-M	BEST PICTURE AWARD
GOOD DAME	1934	74		2.0	2.5	PARAMOUNT	
GOOD DAY FOR A HANGING	1959	85		2.0	2.5	COLUMBIA	
GOOD DIE YOUNG, THE (BRITISH)	1954	98		2.5	2.0	UNITED ARTISTS	
GOOD EARTH, THE	1937	138	6*	4.0	4.0	M-G-M	NOMINATED BEST PICTURE
GOOD FAIRY, THE	1935	90			2.5	UNIVERSAL	
GOOD FELLOWS, THE	1943	70		2.0		PARAMOUNT	
GOOD GIRLS GO TO PARIS	1939	75		2.5	2.5	COLUMBIA	
GOOD GUYS AND THE BAD GUYS, THE	1969	91	4			WARNER BROTHERS	
GOOD HUMOR MAN, THE	1950	79	4	3.0	2.5	COLUMBIA	
GOOD LUCK, MR YATES	1943	70		2.0		COLUMBIA	
GOOD MORNING AND GOODBYE!	1968	80	2	1.0		EVE RELEASING CORP.	
GOOD MORNING, MISS DOVE	1955	107		2.5	3.0	20th CENTURY FOX	
GOOD NEIGHBOR SAM	1964	130	5	2.0	3.0	COLUMBIA	
GOOD NEWS (PETER LAWFORD, JUNE ALLYSON)	1947	95		3.0	2.5	M-G-M	
GOOD SAM	1948	113	4	2.0	2.0	RKO	
GOOD SOLDIER SCHWEIK, THE (GERMAN)	1961	98	6			LIONEX	
GOOD, THE BAD AND THE UGLY, THE (ITALIAN)	1966	161	4	2.0		UNITED ARTISTS	ENGLISH LANGUAGE
GOOD TIME GIRL (BRITISH)	1948	81		1.0	1.5	FILM CLASSICS	
GOOD TIMES	1967	91	4	3.0		COLUMBIA	

‡ An asterisk (*) in THE FILM BUFF'S BIBLE column indicates that the film has been rated by the editor and/or staff. All other ratings in this column are based on a consensus of reviews (see NOTES).

TITLE (LEADING ACTORS SHOWN WHERE TWO OR MORE FILMS HAVE THE SAME OR SIMILAR TITLE)	YEAR RELEASED	RUNNING TIME IN MINUTES	THE FILM BUFF'S BIBLE ‡	STEVEN SCHEUER	LEONARD MALTIN	DISTRIBUTOR	COMMENT
GOODBYE AGAIN (INGRID BERGMAN, ANTHONY PERKINS)	1961	120		2.0	3.0	UNITED ARTISTS	
GOODBYE, CHARLIE	1964	117	2	1.0	1.5	20th CENTURY FOX	
GOODBYE, COLUMBUS	1969	105	6*			PARAMOUNT	
GOODBYE GEMINI (BRITISH)	1970	80	2			CINERAMA RELEASING	
GOODBYE MR CHIPS (ROBERT DONAT, GREER GARSON)	1939	114		4.0		M-G-M	NOMINATED BEST PICTURE
GOODBYE, MR CHIPS (PETER O'TOOLE, PETULA CLARK)	1969	147	6			M-G-M	(BRITISH)
GOODBYE, MY FANCY	1951	107	6*	2.5	3.0	WARNER BROTHERS	
GOODBYE, MY LADY	1956	95		2.5	2.5	WARNER BROTHERS	
GOODBYE RAGGEDY ANN (T.V.)	1971	75	2*			CBS-TV	
GOODNIGHT SWEETHEART	1944	67		2.5		REPUBLIC	
GOOSE AND THE GANDER, THE	1935	65		2.0	2.0	WARNER BROTHERS	
GORGEOUS HUSSY, THE	1936	102		2.0	2.5	WARNER BROTHERS	
GORGO (BRITISH)	1961	76	4	3.0	2.5	M-G-M	
GORGON, THE (BRITISH)	1964	83	3	2.5	2.5	COLUMBIA	
GORILLA, THE (RITZ BROTHERS, PATSY KELLY)	1939	66		2.5		20th CENTURY FOX	
GORILLA AT LARGE	1954	84	3	2.0	3.0	20th CENTURY FOX	
GORILLA MAN, THE	1942	64		1.5	2.0	WARNER BROTHERS	
GOSPEL ACCORDING TO ST MATTHEW, THE (ITALIAN)	1964	135	7			CONTINENTAL	
GOVERNMENT GIRL	1943	94		2.5	2.5	RKO	
GRACIE ALLEN MURDER CASE, THE	1939	74		2.5	.	PARAMOUNT	
GRADUATE, THE	1967	105	9*	4.0	4.0	AVCO-EMBASSY	NOMINATED BEST PICTURE
GRAND CENTRAL MURDER	1942	72		3.0		M-G-M	
GRAND HOTEL	1932	115	5*	4.0	4.0	M-G-M	BEST PICTURE AWARD 1931/32
GRAND ILLUSION (FRENCH)	1937	95	6*	4.0	4.0	WORLD PICTURES	NOMINATED BEST PICTURE 1938
GRAND MANEUVER, THE (FRENCH)	1956	107	6			UN. MOTION PIC. ORG.	
GRAND OLYMPICS, THE (ITALIAN, DOCUMENTARY)	1961	120	6			TIMES FILM CORP.	
GRAND PRIX	1966	179	5	2.5		M-G-M	
GRAND SLAM (ITALIAN - JANET LEIGH, ROBERT HOFFMAN)	1967	121	4*	3.0		PARAMOUNT	ENGLISH VERSION
GRANNY GET YOUR GUN	1940	56		2.0		WARNER BROTHERS	
GRAPES OF WRATH, THE	1940	128	6*	4.0	4.0	20th CENTURY FOX	NOMINATED BEST PICTURE
GRASS IS GREENER, THE	1960	105		3.0	3.0	UNIVERSAL	
GRASSHOPPER, THE	1970	95	4			NATIONAL GENERAL	
GRAZIE ZIA (ITALIAN)	1968	93	4			AVCO-EMBASSY	
GREAT ADVENTURE, THE (SWEDISH)	1953	73	5*			DE ROCHEMONT	
GREAT AMERICAN BROADCAST, THE	1941	92		3.0	2.5	20th CENTURY FOX	
GREAT AMERICAN PASTIME, THE	1956	89	4		2.0	M-G-M	
GREAT BANK ROBBERY, THE	1969	97	3			WARNER BROTHERS	
GREAT BRITISH TRAIN ROBBERY, THE (GERMAN)	1966	104	3			PEPPERCORN-WORMSER	ENGLISH LANGUAGE
GREAT CARUSO, THE	1951	109		3.5	3.0	M-G-M	
GREAT CATHERINE (BRITISH)	1968	99	2			WARNER BROTHERS	
GREAT CHASE, THE	1962	77	5*	2.5	3.5	CONTINENTAL	SILENT FILM CLIPS
GREAT DAN PATCH, THE	1949	94		2.0	2.5	UNITED ARTISTS	
GREAT DAY (BRITISH)	1945	80		2.0	2.5	RKO	
GREAT DAY IN THE MORNING	1956	92		2.5	2.0	RKO	
GREAT DIAMOND ROBBERY, THE	1954	69		2.0	2.0	M-G-M	
GREAT DICTATOR, THE	1940	126	5*			UNITED ARTISTS	NOMINATED BEST PICTURE
GREAT ESCAPE, THE	1963	168	6-7*	4.0	3.5	UNITED ARTISTS	
GREAT EXPECTATIONS (JANE WYATT, PHILLIPS HOLMES)	1934	100			2.5	UNIVERSAL	
GREAT EXPECTATIONS (BRITISH - JOHN MILLS)	1946	118	6*	4.0	4.0	UNIVERSAL	NOMINATED BEST PICTURE 1947
GREAT FLAMARION, THE	1945	78		2.5	2.5	REPUBLIC	
GREAT GAMBINI, THE	1937	70		3.0	2.5	PARAMOUNT	
GREAT GARRICK, THE	1937	89		3.0	2.5	WARNER BROTHERS	
GREAT GATSBY, THE	1949	92	5	3.0	3.0	PARAMOUNT	
GREAT GILBERT AND SULLIVAN, THE (BRITISH)	a1953	109	6	3.5	3.5	UNITED ARTISTS	
GREAT GUNS	1941	74		1.5	2.0	20th CENTURY FOX	
GREAT GUY	1936	75		2.0	2.0	GRAND NATIONAL	
GREAT IMPERSONATION, THE	1935	67		2.0		UNIVERSAL	
GREAT IMPOSTER, THE	1961	112	5*	2.5	3.0	UNIVERSAL	
GREAT JESSE JAMES RAID, THE	1953	74	3	2.5	2.5	LIPPERT PRODS.	
GREAT JEWEL ROBBERY, THE	1950	91	3	1.5	2.0	WARNER BROTHERS	
GREAT JOHN L., THE	1945	96		3.0	2.5	UNITED ARTISTS	
GREAT LIE, THE	1941	107	4*	2.5	3.0	WARNER BROTHERS	
GREAT LOCOMOTIVE CHASE, THE	1956	85	5-6*			BUENA VISTA	
GREAT LOVER, THE (BOB HOPE, RHONDA FLEMING)	1949	49	5	3.0	3.0	PARAMOUNT	
GREAT MAN, THE	1957	92	6	3.0	3.5	UNIVERSAL	
GREAT MAN VOTES, THE	1939	70		4.0	3.5	RKO	
GREAT MANHUNT, THE (BRITISH)	a1950	97	4*	4.0	3.0	COLUMBIA	
GREAT MAN'S LADY, THE	1942	90		2.5	2.5	PARAMOUNT	
GREAT MCGINTY, THE	1940	81		4.0	3.0	PARAMOUNT	
GREAT MIKE, THE	1944	70			2.0	PRODUCERS RELEASING	
GREAT MISSOURI RAID, THE	1951	83		2.0	2.0	PARAMOUNT	
GREAT MR NOBODY, THE	1941	70		2.5		WARNER BROTHERS	
GREAT MOMENT, THE	1944	83		2.5	2.0	PARAMOUNT	
GREAT NORTHFIELD, MINNESOTA RAID, THE	1972	91	4*			UNIVERSAL	
GREAT O'MALLEY, THE	1937	71		3.0	1.5	WARNER BROTHERS	
GREAT PROFILE, THE	1940	82		2.0	2.5	20th CENTURY FOX	
GREAT RACE, THE	1965	150	5*	2.5	2.5	WARNER BROTHERS	
GREAT RUPERT, THE	1950	86		2.5	2.5	EAGLE LION	
GREAT ST LOUIS BANK ROBBERY, THE	1959	86		2.0	1.5	UNITED ARTISTS	
GREAT SINNER, THE	1949	110		2.5	2.5	M-G-M	
GREAT SIOUX MASSACRE, THE	1965	91		2.0	2.5	COLUMBIA	
GREAT SIOUX UPRISING, THE	1953	80		2.0	2.5	UNIVERSAL	
GREAT SPY CHASE, THE (FRENCH)	1964	87	2			AMERICAN-INTERNAT'L	
GREAT SPY MISSION, THE	a1965	116	6			M-G-M	

‡ An asterisk (*) in THE FILM BUFF'S BIBLE column indicates that the film has been rated by the editor and/or staff. All other ratings in this column are based on a consensus of reviews (see NOTES).

TITLE (LEADING ACTORS SHOWN WHERE TWO OR MORE FILMS HAVE THE SAME OR SIMILAR TITLE)	YEAR RELEASED	RUNNING TIME IN MINUTES	THE FILM BUFF'S BIBLE ‡	STEVEN SCHEUER	LEONARD MALTIN	DISTRIBUTOR	COMMENT
GREAT TRAIN ROBBERY, THE (BOB STEELE, C. CARLETON)	1940	61		2.0		REPUBLIC	
GREAT VAN ROBBERY, THE (BRITISH)	1958	73	3			UNITED ARTISTS	
GREAT VICTOR HERBERT, THE	1939	84		3.0	2.5	PARAMOUNT	
GREAT WALTZ, THE	1938	102		2.0	2.5	M-G-M	
GREAT WAR, THE (ITALIAN)	1959	118		3.5	2.0	UNITED ARTISTS	
GREAT WHITE HOPE, THE	1970	106	4*	3.5		20th CENTURY FOX	
GREAT ZIEGFELD, THE	1936	184	6*	4.0	3.5	M-G-M	BEST PICTURE AWARD
GREATEST LOVE, THE (ITALIAN)	a1952	116	3		1.5	ITALIAN FILMS EXPORT	
GREATEST SHOW ON EARTH, THE	1952	153	6*	4.0	3.5	PARAMOUNT	BEST PICTURE AWARD
GREATEST STORY EVER TOLD, THE	1965	195	6			UNITED ARTISTS	
GREED (SILENT)	1925	112				METRO-GOLDWYN	
GREEKS HAD A WORD FOR THEM, THE	a1932	79			3.0	UNITED ARTISTS	
GREEN ARCHER, THE (GERMAN)	1961	95		1.5	2.5	CASINO FILMS	
GREEN BERETS, THE	1968	141		1.0		WARNER BROTHERS	
GREEN CARNATION, THE (BRITISH)	a1960	123	6			KINGSLEY INTERNAT'L	
GREEN DOLPHIN STREET	1947	141	4	1.5	2.5	M-G-M	
GREEN-EYED BLONDE, THE	1957	76		1.0	2.0	WARNER BROTHERS	
GREEN FINGERS (BRITISH)	1947	83		3.0		ANGLO-AMERICAN	
GREEN FIRE	1955	100		2.5	2.5	M-G-M	
GREEN FOR DANGER (BRITISH)	1947	93	6*	3.5	3.0	EAGLE LION	
GREEN GLOVE, THE	1952	88		2.5	2.5	UNITED ARTISTS	
GREEN GODDESS, THE	1930	80			2.0	WARNER BROTHERS	
GREEN GRASS OF WYOMING	1948	89		3.0	2.5	20th CENTURY FOX	
GREEN GROW THE RUSHES (BRITISH)	1951	77		3.5	3.0	MONARCH	
GREEN HELL	1940	87		2.0	2.5	UNIVERSAL	
GREEN HELMET, THE	1961	88	3			M-G-M	
GREEN LIGHT	1937	85		3.0	2.5	WARNER BROTHERS	
GREEN MAGIC (ITALIAN, DOCUMENTARY)	1955	85	6			ITALIAN FILMS EXPORT	
GREEN MAN, THE (BRITISH)	1956	80	6*	3.0	3.0	DIST. CORP. OF AMER.	
GREEN MANSIONS	1959	101		2.5	2.5	M-G-M	
GREEN MARE (FRENCH)	1959	93	5			ZENITH INTERNATIONAL	
GREEN PASTURES, THE	1936	93		4.0	3.5	WARNER BROTHERS	
GREEN PROMISE, THE	1949	93		2.0	2.5	RKO	
GREEN SCARF, THE (BRITISH)	1954	96	5*	3.5	3.0	ASSOCIATED ARTISTS	
GREEN SLIME, THE	1969	90	2			M-G-M	
GREEN WALL, THE (PERUVIAN)	1969	110	6			ALTURA FILMS	ENGLISH VERSION
GREEN YEARS, THE	1946	127		3.0	3.0	M-G-M	
GREENE MURDER CASE, THE	1929	69			-	PARAMOUNT	
GREENWICH VILLAGE	1944	82		2.0	2.0	20th CENTURY FOX	
GREENWICH VILLAGE STORY	1963	95	6			SHAWN INTERNATIONAL	
GREETINGS	1968	88	5			SIGMA III	
GREYFRIARS BOBBY (BRITISH)	1961	90	6			BUENA VISTA	
GRIMM'S FAIRY TALES FOR ADULTS ONLY	1971	76				CINEMATION INDUS.	
GRISBI (FRENCH)	a1954	95		3.0	2.5	UN. MOTION PIC. ORG.	
GRISSLY'S MILLIONS	1945	54		3.0	2.5	REPUBLIC	
GRISSOM GANG, THE	1971	127	3			CINERAMA RELEASING	
GROOM WORE SPURS, THE	1951	80		1.0	2.0	UNIVERSAL	
GROUNDS FOR MARRIAGE	1950	91		2.5	2.5	M-G-M	
GROUNDSTAR CONSPIRACY, THE	1972	96	5			UNIVERSAL	
GROUP, THE	1966	150	3*	3.0		UNITED ARTISTS	
GROUPIES (DOCUMENTARY)	1970	92	2			MARON FILMS, LTD.	
GUADALCANAL DIARY	1943	93	3*	3.5	3.5	20th CENTURY FOX	
GUARDSMAN, THE	1931	83		3.5		M-G-M	
GUENDALINA (ITALIAN)	1956	95		2.5		LOPERT	
GUERILLA GIRL	1953	81		1.5		UNITED ARTISTS	
GUERILLAS IN PINK LACE	1964	96		2.0	1.5	COM. UNITED T.V.	
GUESS WHAT WE LEARNED IN SCHOOL TODAY?	1971	96	4			CANNON RELEASING	
GUESS WHO'S COMMING TO DINNER	1967	108	7*	3.5		COLUMBIA	NOMINATED BEST PICTURE
GUEST, THE (BRITISH)	1964	105	5			JANUS FILMS	
GUEST IN THE HOUSE	1944	121		2.5	2.5	UNITED ARTISTS	
GUEST WIFE	1945	90		3.0	2.5	UNITED ARTISTS	
GUESTS ARE COMING (POLISH)	1964	110	6			MITCHELL KOWAL	
GUIDE, THE	1965	120	6			STRATTON INTERNAT'L	
GUIDE FOR THE MARRIED MAN, A	1967	89	6	3.0	3.5	20th CENTURY FOX	
GUILT (SWEDISH)	1965	90	1			CROWN INTERNATIONAL	
GUILT IS MY SHADOW (BRITISH)	1950	85	4			STRATFORD PICS.	
GUILT OF JANET AMES, THE	1947	83	5	3.0	3.0	COLUMBIA	
GUILTY (BRITISH - JOHN JUSTIN, BARBARA LAAGE)	1956	93		2.0		SHOWCORPORATION	
GUILTY, THE (BONITA GRANVILLE, DON CASTLE)	1947	70		2.5	2.5	MONOGRAM	
GUILTY BYSTANDER	1950	92	4	3.0	2.5	FILM CLASSICS	
GUILTY HANDS	1931	68		3.0		M-G-M	
GUILTY OF TREASON	1950	86	4		2.5	EAGLE LION	
GULLIVER'S TRAVELS	1939	74		3.0	2.5	PARAMOUNT	
GULLIVER'S TRAVELS BEYOND THE MOON (JAP., CARTOON)	1965	85		3.5		CONTINENTAL	ENGLISH LANGUAGE
GUMSHOE (BRITISH)	1972	84	5			COLUMBIA	
GUN BATTLE AT MONTEREY	1957	67	2	2.5	1.5	ALLIED ARTISTS	
GUN BELT	1953	77	3	2.5	2.5	UNITED ARTISTS	
GUN BROTHERS	1956	79		2.0	2.0	UNITED ARTISTS	
GUN CRAZY	a1949	87	4	3.0		UNITED ARTISTS	
GUN DUEL IN DURANGO	a1957	73		2.0	2.0	UNITED ARTISTS	
GUN FEVER	1958	81	2			UNITED ARTISTS	
GUN FOR A COWARD	1957	73		2.0	2.5	UNIVERSAL	
GUN FURY	1953	83		2.5	1.5	COLUMBIA	
GUN GLORY	1957	89		2.0	2.0	M-G-M	

‡ An asterisk (*) in THE FILM BUFF'S BIBLE column indicates that the film has been rated by the editor and/or staff. All other ratings in this column are based on a consensus of reviews (see NOTES).

TITLE (LEADING ACTORS SHOWN WHERE TWO OR MORE FILMS HAVE THE SAME OR SIMILAR TITLE)	YEAR RELEASED	RUNNING TIME IN MINUTES	THE FILM BUFF'S BIBLE ‡	STEVEN SCHEUER	LEONARD MALTIN	DISTRIBUTOR	COMMENT
GUN HAWK, THE	1963	92		2.0	2.5	ALLIED ARTISTS	
GUN OF ZANGARA	1959	90	5*	2.5		DESILU	
GUN RUNNERS, THE (AUDIE MURPHY, EDDIE ALBERT)	1958	83		2.5	2.0	UNITED ARTISTS	
GUN THAT WON THE WEST, THE	1955	71		2.0	2.0	COLUMBIA	
GUN THE MAN DOWN	a1956	78		2.0	2.0	UNITED ARTISTS	
GUNBELT	1953	77		2.5		UNITED ARTISTS	
GUNFIGHT, A (KIRK DOUGLAS, JOHNNY CASH)	1971	90	5			PARAMOUNT	
GUNFIGHT AT COMANCHE CREEK	1963	90	3			ALLIED ARTISTS	
GUNFIGHT AT DODGE CITY, THE	1959	81		2.0	2.0	UNITED ARTISTS	
GUNFIGHT AT INDIAN GAP	1957	70		1.5	1.5		
GUNFIGHT AT RED SANDS (SPANISH)	1965	97		2.0		SCREEN GEMS	
GUNFIGHT AT THE O.K. CORRAL	1957	122	7*	3.5	3.0	PARAMOUNT	
GUNFIGHT IN ABILENE	1967	86	2	1.5	2.5	UNIVERSAL	
GUNFIGHTER, THE (GREGORY PECK)	1950	84	5*	4.0	3.5	20th CENTURY FOX	
GUNFIGHTERS (RANDOLPH SCOTT)	1947	87	4	3.0	2.5	COLUMBIA	
GUNFIGHTERS OF ABILENE	1960	122	1			UNITED ARTISTS	
GUNFIGHTERS OF CASA GRANDE	1965	92	1			M-G-M	
GUNFIRE	1950	60			1.5	LIPPERT PRODS.	
GUNG HO!	1943	88		2.5	3.0	UNIVERSAL	
GUNGA DIN	1939	117	6*	4.0	4.0	RKO	
GUNMAN'S WALK	1958	97	3	3.0	3.0	COLUMBIA	
GUNMEN FROM LAREDO	1959	67		2.0	1.0	COLUMBIA	
GUNMEN OF THE RIO GRANDE (ITALIAN)	1965	86	3		2.0	ALLIED ARTISTS	
GUNN	1967	95	3	2.5		PARAMOUNT	
GUNPOINT	1966	86	3		2.0	UNIVERSAL	
GUNS AT BATASI (BRITISH)	1964	103		3.5	2.5	20th CENTURY FOX	
GUNS FOR SAN SEBASTIAN (FRENCH)	1967	111	3	2.0		M-G-M	ENGLISH LANGUAGE
GUNS, GIRLS AND GANGSTERS	1959	70	3			UNITED ARTISTS	
GUNS OF AUGUST, THE (DOCUMENTARY)	1964	100		3.5		UNIVERSAL	
GUNS OF DARKNESS (BRITISH)	1962	103		2.0	2.5	WARNER BROTHERS	
GUNS OF FORT PETTICOAT, THE	1957	82		2.5	3.0	COLUMBIA	
GUNS OF HATE	a1948	62	2			RKO	
GUNS OF JUANA GALLO, THE (MEXICAN)	a1958	91		2.0		AZTECA	
GUNS OF NAVARONE, THE	1961	159	8*	4.0	3.5	COLUMBIA	NOMINATED BEST PICTURE
GUNS OF THE BLACK WITCH (ITALIAN)	1961	81	1	1.5	2.0	AMERICAN-INTERNAT'L	
GUNS OF THE MAGNIFICENT SEVEN	1969	106	3			UNITED ARTISTS	
GUNS OF THE TIMBERLAND	1960	91		2.0	2.5	WARNER BROTHERS	
GUNSIGHT RIDGE	1957	85		2.0	2.0	UNITED ARTISTS	
GUNSLINGER, THE	1956	83		1.5	1.5	AMERICAN-INTERNAT'L	
GUNSMOKE (AUDIE MURPHY, SUSAN CABOT)	1953	75		2.0	2.5	UNIVERSAL	
GUNSMOKE IN TUCSON	1958	80		1.5	2.5	ALLIED ARTISTS	
GURU, THE	1969	112	5	3.0		20th CENTURY FOX	
GURU THE MAD MONK	1970	62				NOVA INTERNATIONAL	
GUY CALLED CAESAR, A (BRITISH)	1962	62			1.5	COLUMBIA	
GUY NAMED JOE, A	1943	118		2.5	2.5	M-G-M	
GUY WHO CAME BACK, THE	1951	91		2.0	2.0	20th CENTURY FOX	
GUYS AND DOLLS	1955	138	7-8*	3.0	3.0	M-G-M	
GYPSY	1962	149		3.0	2.5	WARNER BROTHERS	
GYPSY AND THE GENTLEMAN, THE (BRITISH)	1958	89		2.0	2.5	J. ARTHUR RANK	
GYPSY COLT	1954	72	5		2.5	M-G-M	
GYPSY FURY	1951	63			2.0	MONOGRAM	
GYPSY GIRL (BRITISH)	1966	102		3.0	2.5	CONTINENTAL	
GYPSY MOTHS, THE	1969	106	5			M-G-M	
GYPSY WILDCAT	1944	75		2.0	2.0	UNIVERSAL	
H.M. PULHAM, ESQ.	1941	120		3.5	3.5	M-G-M	
H-MAN, THE (JAPANESE)	1958	79		1.0	2.0	COLUMBIA	
HAGBARD AND SIGNE (DANISH)	a1967	92	6	3.5		PRENTOULIS FILMS	
HAIL, HERO!	1969	100	5			NATIONAL GENERAL	
HAIL! MAFIA (FRENCH)	1965	90	1			GOLDSTONE FILM ENT.	
HAIL THE CONQUERING HERO	1944	101	6-7*	4.0	4.0	PARAMOUNT	
HAIRY APE, THE	1944	90		3.0	3.0	UNITED ARTISTS	
HAL ROACH COMEDY CARNIVAL, THE	a1947	53			2.0	UNITED ARTISTS	
HALF A HERO	1953	71		2.0	2.5	M-G-M	
HALF A SIXPENCE (BRITISH)	1967	148	5			PARAMOUNT	
HALF ANGEL (LORETTA YOUNG, JOSEPH COTTON)	1951	77	4	2.0	2.5	20th CENTURY FOX	
HALF-BREED, THE	1952	81		2.0	2.0	RKO	
HALF HUMAN (JAPANESE)	1955	70		2.0	1.5	DIST. CORP. OF AMER.	
HALFWAY HOUSE, THE (BRITISH)	1944	95			2.5	A.F.E. CORP.	
HALFWAY TO SHANGHAI	1942	62		2.0		UNIVERSAL	
HALLELUJAH!	1929	109		3.0		M-G-M	
HALLELUJAH THE HILLS	1963	82	1			NEW YORK CINEMA CO.	
HALLELUJAH TRAIL, THE	1965	165	3	1.0	2.5	UNITED ARTISTS	
HALLIDAY BRAND, THE	1957	77		2.5	2.5	UNITED ARTISTS	
HALLS OF ANGER	1970	98	5			UNITED ARTISTS	
HALLS OF MONTEZUMA, THE	1951	113	5	2.5	2.5	20th CENTURY FOX	
HALLUCINATION GENERATION	1967	90	1			TRANS-AMERICA	
HAMLET (BRITISH - LAURENCE OLIVIER)	1948	153	8*	4.0	4.0	UNIVERSAL	BEST PICTURE AWARD
HAMLET (RUSSIAN - INNOKENTI SMOKTUNOVSKY)	1964	148	7			UNITED ARTISTS	
HAMLET (BRITISH - NICOL WILLIAMSON)	1969	114	6			COLUMBIA	
HAMMERHEAD (BRITISH)	1968	99	1	1.0		COLUMBIA	
HAMMERSMITH IS OUT	1972	108	4			J. CORNELIUS CREAN	

‡ An asterisk (*) in THE FILM BUFF'S BIBLE column indicates that the film has been rated by the editor and/or staff. All other ratings in this column are based on a consensus of reviews (see NOTES).

TITLE (LEADING ACTORS SHOWN WHERE TWO OR MORE FILMS HAVE THE SAME OR SIMILAR TITLE)	YEAR RELEASED	RUNNING TIME IN MINUTES	THE FILM BUFF'S BIBLE ‡	STEVEN SCHEUER	LEONARD MALTIN	DISTRIBUTOR	COMMENT
HAND, THE (BRITISH)	1960	60		2.5	1.5	AMERICAN-INTERNAT'L	
HAND IN HAND (BRITISH)	1960	80	6		2.5	COLUMBIA	
HAND OF DEATH	1962	60	1			20th CENTURY FOX	
HANDLE WITH CARE (DEAN JONES, JOAN O'BRIEN)	1958	82		2.0	2.5	M-G-M	
HANDLE WITH CARE (ROBERT MARK, LUISA RIVELLI)	1972	90				H.K. FILM DIST.	
HANDS ACROSS THE TABLE	1935	80		3.0	3.0	PARAMOUNT	
HANDS OF A STRANGER	1962	86		2.0	2.5	ALLIED ARTISTS	
HANDS OF A STRANGLER (FRENCH)	a1961	77	2	1.5		CONTINENTAL	
HANDS OF ORLAC, THE (FRENCH)	a1961	77	2	1.5		CONTINENTAL	
HANG 'EM HIGH	1968	114	4	2.5		UNITED ARTISTS	
HANGED MAN, THE (T.V.)	1964	110		2.0	2.5	UNIVERSAL	
HANGING TREE, THE	1959	106	5*	3.5	3.0	WARNER BROTHERS	
HANGMAN, THE	1959	86		2.0	2.0	PARAMOUNT	
HANGMAN'S KNOT	1952	81		3.0	2.0	COLUMBIA	
HANGMEN ALSO DIE	1943	131		3.0	2.5	UNITED ARTISTS	
HANGOVER SQUARE	1945	77		2.0	3.0	20th CENTURY FOX	
HANNAH LEE	a1954	74	4	2.5		REALART	
HANNIBAL (ITALIAN)	1960	103	3*	2.0	2.0	WARNER BROTHERS	
HANNIBAL BROOKS (BRITISH)	1969	101	3	1.0		UNITED ARTISTS	
HANNIE CAULDER (BRITISH)	1971	85	2			PARAMOUNT	
HANS CHRISTIAN ANDERSEN	1952	120		3.0	2.5	RKO	
HANSEL AND GRETEL (PUPPETS)	1954	75	6	3.0		RKO	
HAPPENING, THE	1967	92	3	2.5		COLUMBIA	
HAPPIEST DAYS OF YOUR LIFE, THE (BRITISH)	1950	81	5*	4.0	3.0	LONDON FILM	
HAPPIEST MILLIONAIRE, THE	1967	159	6			BUENA VISTA	
HAPPINESS AHEAD	1934	86		3.0		FIRST NATIONAL	
HAPPINESS CAGE, THE	1972	94	4			CINERAMA RELEASING	
HAPPINESS OF US, ALONE (JAPANESE)	1960	114	6			TOHO	
HAPPY ANNIVERSARY	1959	81		3.0	2.5	UNITED ARTISTS	
HAPPY BIRTHDAY, WANDA JUNE	1971	105	4			COLUMBIA	
HAPPY END (CZECH)	1967	73		3.5		CONTINENTAL	
HAPPY ENDING, THE	1969	112	5			UNITED ARTISTS	
HAPPY GO LOVELY (BRITISH)	1951	88		3.0	2.0	RKO	
HAPPY GO LUCKY	1943	81		2.5	2.5	PARAMOUNT	
HAPPY IS THE BRIDE (BRITISH)	1958	84		3.0	2.0	KASSLER FILMS	
HAPPY LAND	1943	73		2.5	2.5	20th CENTURY FOX	
HAPPY LANDING, THE	1938	102		2.5	2.5	20th CENTURY FOX	
HAPPY ROAD, THE	1957	100	4*			M-G-M	
HAPPY THIEVES, THE	1962	88		2.0	2.5	UNITED ARTISTS	
HAPPY TIME, THE	1952	94	4	3.5	2.5	COLUMBIA	
HAPPY YEARS, THE	1950	110	6	4.0	3.0	M-G-M	
HARAKIRI (JAPANESE)	1962	135	6			TOHO	
HARBOR LIGHTS	1963	68	1		1.0	20th CENTURY FOX	
HARBOR OF MISSING MEN	1950	60			1.5	REPUBLIC	
HARD-BOILED MAHONEY	1947	63			·	MONOGRAM	
HARD CONTRACT	1969	106	5			20th CENTURY FOX	
HARD DAY'S NIGHT, A (BRITISH)	1964	85	2*	4.0	4.0	UNITED ARTISTS	
HARD, FAST AND BEAUTIFUL	1951	79	4		2.0	RKO	
HARD MAN, THE	1957	80		2.5	2.0	COLUMBIA	
HARD RIDE, THE	1971	93	3			AMERICAN-INTERNAT'L	
HARD TO GET	1938	80		2.5	2.5	WARNER BROTHERS	
HARD TO HANDLE	1933	75		2.0	2.5	WARNER BROTHERS	
HARD WAY, THE	1942	109		2.5	3.0	WARNER BROTHERS	
HARDER THEY FALL, THE	1956	109	6*	3.5	3.0	COLUMBIA	
HARDYS RIDE HIGH, THE	1939	80		2.5	·	M-G-M	
HAREM GIRL	1952	70		1.5	2.0	COLUMBIA	
HARLEM GLOBETROTTERS, THE	1951	80		2.5	2.0	COLUMBIA	
HARLOW (CARROLL BAKER, PETER LAWFORD)	1965	125		2.0	2.5	PARAMOUNT	
HARLOW (CAROL LYNLEY, EFREM ZIMBALIST, JR)	1965	108	2		2.0	MAGNA PICTURES	
HARNESS, THE (T.V.)	1971	100	4*			UNIVERSAL	
HAROLD AND MAUDE	1971	90	4			PARAMOUNT	
HAROLD LLOYD'S WORLD OF COMEDY	1962	94	6		4.0	COLUMBIA	FILM CLIPS
HARPER	1966	121	4*	3.5	3.5	WARNER BROTHERS	
HARPY (T.V.)	1971	100	3*	1.0		CINEMA CENTER 100	
HARRIET CRAIG	1950	94	5*	3.0	3.0	COLUMBIA	
HARRIGAN'S KID	1943	80		2.0		M-G-M	
HARRY BLACK AND THE TIGER (BRITISH)	a1958	107	3	2.0	1.0	20th CENTURY FOX	
HARUM SCARUM	1965	95		1.0	2.5	M-G-M	
HARVEST, THE (FRENCH - GABRIEL GABRIO, FERNANDEL)	1939	80				FRENCH CINEMA CENTER	
HARVEY	1950	104	7	4.0	3.5	UNIVERSAL	
HARVEY GIRLS, THE	1946	104		3.0	3.5	M-G-M	
HARVEY MIDDLEMAN, FIREMAN	1965	75	4			COLUMBIA	
HAS ANYBODY SEEN MY GAL	1952	89		2.5	2.0	UNIVERSAL	
HASTY HEART, THE	1949	99		3.5	3.5	WARNER BROTHERS	
HATARI	1962	159	5	3.0	3.5	PARAMOUNT	
HATCHET MAN, THE	1932	74			1.5	FIRST NATIONAL	
HATFUL OF RAIN, A	1957	109	7*	4.0	3.0	20th CENTURY FOX	
HATTER'S CASTLE (BRITISH)	1948	105		2.0	2.5	PARAMOUNT	COMPLETED IN 1941
HAUNTED HONEYMOON (BRITISH)	1940	83		2.5	2.5	M-G-M	
HAUNTED PALACE, THE	1964	85	3			AMERICAN-INTERNAT'L	
HAUNTED STRANGLER, THE (BRITISH)	1958	81	2	2.0	2.5	M-G-M	
HAUNTING, THE (BRITISH)	1963	112		3.0	3.0	M-G-M	
HAUSER'S MEMORY	1970	100		2.5		UNIVERSAL	
HAVANA ROSE	1951	77		2.0		REPUBLIC	

‡ An asterisk (*) in THE FILM BUFF'S BIBLE column indicates that the film has been rated by the editor and/or staff. All other ratings in this column are based on a consensus of reviews (see NOTES).

TITLE (LEADING ACTORS SHOWN WHERE TWO OR MORE FILMS HAVE THE SAME OR SIMILAR TITLE)	YEAR RELEASED	RUNNING TIME IN MINUTES	THE FILM BUFF'S BIBLE ‡	STEVEN SCHEUER	LEONARD MALTIN	DISTRIBUTOR	COMMENT
HAVE ROCKET, WILL TRAVEL	1959	76	2	1.5	2.0	COLUMBIA	
HAVE YOU HEARD OF THE SAN FRANCISCO MIME TROUPE?	1968	60		3.5		FILMMAKERS	
HAVING A WILD WEEKEND	1965	91	3	2.5		WARNER BROTHERS	
HAVING WONDERFUL CRIME	1945	70		3.0	3.0	RKO	
HAVING WONDERFUL TIME	1938	71		2.5	2.5	RKO	
HAWAII	1966	186	6			UNITED ARTISTS	
HAWAIIANS, THE	a1970	134	5			UNITED ARTISTS	
HAWKS AND THE SPARROWS, THE (ITALIAN)	1966	91	6			BRANDON	
HAZARD	1948	95		2.0	2.0	PARAMOUNT	
HE LAUGHED LAST	1956	77	4	2.0		COLUMBIA	
HE MARRIED HIS WIFE	1940	83		2.0	2.0	20th CENTURY FOX	
HE RAN ALL THE WAY	1951	77	4	3.0	2.5	UNITED ARTISTS	
HE RIDES TALL	1964	84		2.0	2.5	UNIVERSAL	
HE STAYED FOR BREAKFAST	1940	89		2.0	2.0	COLUMBIA	
HE WALKED BY NIGHT	1948	79		3.5	3.0	EAGLE LION	
HE WAS HER MAN	1934	70		3.0	2.0	WARNER BROTHERS	
HE WHO MUST DIE (FRENCH)	1957	129	8*			LOPERT	
HE WHO RIDES A TIGER (BRITISH)	1966	103	5	3.5		SIGMA III	
HEAD (THE MONKEES, ANNETTE FUNICELLO)	1968	86	3			COLUMBIA	
HEAD, THE (GERMAN - HORST FRANK, KARIN KERNKE)	1959	92	2	2.0	2.0	TRANS-LUX DIST.	
HEAD OF A TYRANT (ITALIAN)	1959	94	3		2.0	UNIVERSAL	
HEADING FOR HEAVEN	1947	71		2.0	1.5	EAGLE LION	
HEADLESS GHOST, THE (BRITISH)	1959	63	2	2.0	2.0	AMERICAN-INTERNAT'L	
HEADLINE HUNTERS (ROD CAMERON, JULIE BISHOP)	1955	70		2.0	2.0	REPUBLIC	
HEADLINES OF DESTRUCTION (FRENCH)	1955	85		2.0	2.0	AMERICAN-INTERNAT'L	
HEADQUARTERS STATE SECRET (GERMAN)	1962	103		2.0		TELEWIDE SYSTEMS	
HEAR ME GOOD	1957	80	3	3.0	1.5	PARAMOUNT	
HEART IS A LONELY HUNTER, THE	1968	124	6*	4.0		WARNER BROTHERS	
HEART OF A CHILD (BRITISH)	1958	76		3.0		UNITED ARTISTS	
HEART OF A MAN (BRITISH)	1959	92		1.5		CONTINENTAL	
HEART OF THE MATTER, THE (BRITISH)	1953	105	6	3.5	3.0	ASSOCIATED ARTISTS	
HEART OF VIRGINIA	1948	55		1.5		REPUBLIC	
HEART WITHIN, THE (BRITISH)	1957	61		2.0		J. ARTHUR RANK	
HEARTBEAT	1946	102		3.0	2.0	RKO	
HEARTS DIVIDED	1936	87		2.5	2.0	FIRST NATIONAL	
HEAT WAVE (BRITISH)	1954	68		2.0	1.5	LIPPERT PRODS.	
HEAT'S ON, THE	1943	80		2.0		COLUMBIA	
HEAVEN CAN WAIT	1943	113	7*	3.0	3.5	20th CENTURY FOX	NOMINATED BEST PICTURE
HEAVEN KNOWS, MR ALLISON	1957	107	5*	3.0	3.0	20th CENTURY FOX	
HEAVEN ON EARTH (ITALIAN)	1960	84		2.0		JB FILM ENTERPRISES	
HEAVEN ONLY KNOWS	a1947	95		2.5	2.5	UNITED ARTISTS	
HEAVEN WITH A BARBED WIRE FENCE	1939	62		2.5	2.5	20th CENTURY FOX	
HEAVEN WITH A GUN	1969	101	4	2.5		M-G-M	
HEAVENLY BODY, THE	1943	95		2.0	2.0	M-G-M	
HEAVENLY DAYS	1944	71		2.0	2.0	RKO	
HEAVENS ABOVE! (BRITISH)	1963	105	6	3.5	3.0	JANUS FILMS	
HEIDI (SHIRLEY TEMPLE, JEAN HERSHOLT)	1937	88	5*	3.0	2.5	20th CENTURY FOX	
HEIDI (SWISS - ELSBETH SIGMUND, HEINRICH GRETLER)	1952	85	6	3.0	3.0	UNITED ARTISTS	
HEIDI AND PETER (SWISS)	1955	89		2.0	2.5	UNITED ARTISTS	
HEIRESS, THE	1949	115	7*	4.0	4.0	PARAMOUNT	NOMINATED BEST PICTURE
HELEN MORGAN STORY, THE	1957	118		2.5	2.5	WARNER BROTHERS	
HELEN OF TROY (ROSSANA PODESTA, STANLEY BAKER)	1956	118	4	2.0	2.0	WARNER BROTHERS	
HELGA (GERMAN)	1967	76	2	2.0		AMERICAN-INTERNAT'L	DOCUMENTARY DRAMA
HELGA UND MICHAEL (GERMAN)	a1968	87	3			AMERICAN-INTERNAT'L	
HELL AND HIGH WATER (RICHARD WIDMARK, DAVID WAYNE)	1954	103		2.5	2.5	20th CENTURY FOX	
HELL BELOW	1933	105		2.0	2.5	M-G-M	
HELL BELOW ZERO (BRITISH)	1954	91		2.0	2.0	M-G-M	
HELL BENT FOR LEATHER	1960	82	4	2.5	2.5	UNIVERSAL	
HELL BOATS (BRITISH)	1970	95	3			UNITED ARTISTS	
HELL CANYON OUTLAWS	1957	72		2.5	2.0	REPUBLIC	
HELL DIVERS	1931	113		2.5		M-G-M	
HELL DRIVERS (BRITISH)	1957	91			2.5	J. ARTHUR RANK	
HELL IN KOREA (BRITISH)	1956	82		3.0		DIST. CORP. OF AMER.	
HELL IN THE PACIFIC	1969	103	4			CINERAMA RELEASING	
HELL IS A CITY (BRITISH)	1960	96	4			COLUMBIA	
HELL IS FOR HEROES	1962	90	5	3.0	3.0	PARAMOUNT	
HELL OF LOST PILOTS, THE (FRENCH)	1949	90		2.0			
HELL ON DEVIL'S ISLAND	1957	74			1.5	20th CENTURY FOX	
HELL ON FRISCO BAY	1956	98	3	2.5	2.5	WARNER BROTHERS	
HELL ON WHEELS	1967	96	1			CROWN INTERNATIONAL	
HELL RAIDERS OF THE DEEP (ITALIAN)	1954	93	5			ITALIAN FILMS EXPORT	
HELL SHIP MUTINY	1957	66		1.5	1.5	REPUBLIC	
HELL SQUAD	1958	64	3	2.5		AMERICAN-INTERNAT'L	
HELL TO ETERNITY	1960	132		3.0	2.5	ALLIED ARTISTS	
HELL WITH HEROES, THE	1968	102		2.0	2.5	UNIVERSAL	
HELLBENDERS, THE (ITALIAN)	1966	92	2	2.0		AVCO-EMBASSY	
HELLCATS, THE	1968	90	3			CROWN INTERNATIONAL	
HELLCATS OF THE NAVY	1957	82		2.0	2.5	COLUMBIA	
HELLER IN PINK TIGHTS	1960	100		2.5	2.5	PARAMOUNT	
HELLFIGHTERS	1968	121	3	1.0		UNIVERSAL	
HELLFIRE	1949	90		2.5		REPUBLIC	
HELLFIRE CLUB, THE (BRITISH)	1963	93	3	1.5		AVCO-EMBASSY	
HELLGATE	1952	87		2.5	2.5	LIPPERT PRODS.	
HELLIONS, THE (BRITISH)	1961	80		2.0	2.5	COLUMBIA	

‡ An asterisk (*) in THE FILM BUFF'S BIBLE column indicates that the film has been rated by the editor and/or staff. All other ratings in this column are based on a consensus of reviews (see NOTES).

TITLE (LEADING ACTORS SHOWN WHERE TWO OR MORE FILMS HAVE THE SAME OR SIMILAR TITLE)	YEAR RELEASED	RUNNING TIME IN MINUTES	THE FILM BUFF'S BIBLE ‡	STEVEN SCHEUER	LEONARD MALTIN	DISTRIBUTOR	COMMENT
HELLO, DOLLY!	1969	148	7*	3.5		20th CENTURY FOX	NOMINATED BEST PICTURE
HELLO DOWN THERE	1969	98	2			PARAMOUNT	
HELLO ELEPHANT (ITALIAN)	a1952	83		2.0	1.5	ARLAN PICTURES	
HELLO, FRISCO, HELLO	1943	98		1.5	2.0	20th CENTURY FOX	
HELLO-GOODBYE	1970	107	3			20th CENTURY FOX	
HELLO SUCKER	1941	60		1.5	1.5	UNIVERSAL	
HELL'S ANGELS	1930	135				UNITED ARTISTS	
HELL'S ANGELS ON WHEELS	1967	95	1			U.S. FILMS	
HELL'S ANGELS '69	1969	97	1			AMERICAN-INTERNAT'L	
HELL'S BELLES	1969	98	3			AMERICAN-INTERNAT'L	
HELL'S BLOODY DEVILS	1970	92	1			INDEPENDENT INT'L	
HELL'S CROSSROADS	1957	73		2.0	2.0	REPUBLIC	
HELL'S FIVE HOURS	1958	73		2.5	2.0	ALLIED ARTISTS	
HELL'S HALF ACRE	1954	91		2.5	1.5	REPUBLIC	
HELL'S HIGHWAY	1932	80		3.0		RKO	
HELL'S HORIZON	1955	80		2.0	2.0	COLUMBIA	
HELL'S ISLAND	1955	84	3	3.0	1.5	PARAMOUNT	
HELL'S KITCHEN	1939	81		2.5	2.5	WARNER BROTHERS	
HELL'S LONG ROAD (ITALIAN)	1963	89			2.5		
HELL'S OUTPOST	1954	90		2.0	2.0	REPUBLIC	
HELLSTROM CHRONICLE, THE (DOCUMENTARY)	1971	90	6-7*			CINEMA V	
HELLZAPOPPIN	1941	84		3.5	3.0	UNIVERSAL	
HELP! (BRITISH)	1965	92	4	3.0	3.5	UNITED ARTISTS	
HEMINGWAY'S ADVENTURES OF A YOUNG MAN	a1962	145		2.0	2.0	20th CENTURY FOX	
HENRY ALDRICH, BOY SCOUT	1944	66		2.5		PARAMOUNT	
HENRY ALDRICH, EDITOR	1942	72		2.0		PARAMOUNT	
HENRY ALDRICH FOR PRESIDENT	1941	70		2.0		PARAMOUNT	
HENRY ALDRICH GETS GLAMOUR	1943	72		2.0		PARAMOUNT	
HENRY ALDRICH HAUNTS A HOUSE	1943	73		2.0		PARAMOUNT	
HENRY ALDRICH PLAYS CUPID	1944	65		2.0		PARAMOUNT	
HENRY ALDRICH SWINGS IT	1943	65		1.5		PARAMOUNT	
HENRY ALDRICH'S LITTLE SECRET	1944	74		2.0		PARAMOUNT	
HENRY AND DIZZY	1942	71		2.0		PARAMOUNT	
HENRY GOES ARIZONA	1939	67		2.0		M-G-M	
HENRY, THE RAINMAKER	1949	64			1.5	MONOGRAM	
HENRY V (BRITISH)	a1944	137	8*			J. ARTHUR RANK	NOMINATED BEST PICTURE 1946
HER ADVENTUROUS NIGHT	1946	76		2.5	2.5	UNIVERSAL	
HER CARDBOARD LOVER	1942	93		1.5	1.5	M-G-M	
HER FAVORITE PATIENT	a1945	70		2.0		UNITED ARTISTS	
HER FIRST ROMANCE	1951	73		2.0	1.5	COLUMBIA	
HER HIGHNESS AND THE BELLBOY	1945	112		2.0	2.5	M-G-M	
HER HUSBAND'S AFFAIRS	1947	82	3	1.5	1.5	COLUMBIA	
HER JUNGLE LOVE	1938	81		1.5	2.5	PARAMOUNT	
HER KIND OF MAN	1946	78		2.0	2.0	WARNER BROTHERS	
HER LUCKY NIGHT	1945	63		1.5	2.0	UNIVERSAL	
HER MAJESTY, LOVE	1931	75		3.0	1.5	20th CENTURY FOX	
HER MAN GILBEY (BRITISH)	1948	89			2.5	UNIVERSAL	
HER PANELLED DOOR (BRITISH)	1951	84		3.0	3.0	SOUVAINE SELECTIVE	
HER PRIMITIVE MAN	1944	79			1.5	UNIVERSAL	
HER SISTER'S SECRET	1946	86			2.5	PRODUCERS RELEASING	
HER TWELVE MEN	1954	91		2.5	2.0	M-G-M	
HERCULE (FRENCH - FERNANDEL)	1960	90		1.5			
HERCULES (ITALIAN - STEEVE REEVES)	1957	107	3	2.0	2.5	WARNER BROTHERS	
HERCULES AGAINST ROME (ITALIAN)	1960	87		1.0	2.0	AMERICAN-INTERNAT'L	
HERCULES AGAINST THE BARBARIANS (ITALIAN)	1960	91		1.0		AMERICAN-INTERNAT'L	
HERCULES AGAINST THE MONGOLS (ITALIAN)	1960	90		1.0		AMERICAN-INTERNAT'L	
HERCULES AGAINST THE MOON MEN (ITALIAN)	1965	88		1.0	2.0	GOVERNOR	
HERCULES AGAINST THE SONS OF THE SUN (ITALIAN)	1964	89		1.0	2.0	SCREEN GEMS	
HERCULES AND THE BLACK PIRATES (ITALIAN)	1960	91		1.0		AMERICAN-INTERNAT'L	
HERCULES AND THE CAPTIVE WOMEN (ITALIAN)	1963	87		2.0	2.0	WOOLNER BROTHERS	
HERCULES AND THE MASKED RIDER (ITALIAN)	1960	86		1.0		AMERICAN-INTERNAT'L	
HERCULES AND THE TEN AVENGERS (ITALIAN)	1964	90		1.0			
HERCULES AND THE TREASURE OF THE INCAS (ITALIAN)	1960	90		1.0		AMERICAN-INTERNAT'L	
HERCULES AND THE TYRANTS OF BABYLON (ITALIAN)	1964	86		1.0		AMERICAN-INTERNAT'L	
HERCULES IN THE HAUNTED WORLD (ITALIAN)	1961	89		1.0	2.0	WOOLNER BROTHERS	
HERCULES IN THE VALE OF WOE (ITALIAN)	a1964	95		1.5		AVCO-EMBASSY	
HERCULES OF THE DESERT (ITALIAN)	1964	80		1.0			
HERCULES, PRISONER OF EVIL (ITALIAN)	1964	90		1.0		AMERICAN-INTERNAT'L	
HERCULES, SAMSON AND ULYSSES (ITALIAN)	1965	85			2.0	M-G-M	
HERCULES UNCHAINED (ITALIAN)	1959	101		2.0	2.0	WARNER BROTHERS	
HERCULES VS ULYSSES (ITALIAN)	1962	99		1.5		AVCO-EMBASSY	
HERE COME THE CO-EDS	1945	87			2.5	UNIVERSAL	
HERE COME THE GIRLS	1953	78		2.5	2.5	PARAMOUNT	
HERE COME THE JETS	1959	71	1			20th CENTURY FOX	
HERE COME THE MARINES	1952	66	4		.	MONOGRAM	
HERE COME THE NELSONS	a1952	76	4		2.0	UNIVERSAL	
HERE COME THE WAVES	1944	99		3.0	3.0	PARAMOUNT	
HERE COMES COOKIE	1935	65		2.5		PARAMOUNT	
HERE COMES MR JORDAN	1941	93	6*	4.0	3.5	COLUMBIA	NOMINATED BEST PICTURE
HERE COMES THE GROOM	1951	113	6	3.0	3.0	PARAMOUNT	
HERE COMES THE NAVY	1934	86		3.0	2.5	WARNER BROTHERS	NOMINATED BEST PICTURE
HERE IS MY HEART	1934	77		3.5	2.5	PARAMOUNT	
HERE WE GO AGAIN	1942	76		2.0		RKO	
HERE WE GO ROUND THE MULBERRY BUSH (BRITISH)	1968	96	3	1.5		LOPERT	

‡ An asterisk (*) in THE FILM BUFF'S BIBLE column indicates that the film has been rated by the editor and/or staff. All other ratings in this column are based on a consensus of reviews (see NOTES).

TITLE (LEADING ACTORS SHOWN WHERE TWO OR MORE FILMS HAVE THE SAME OR SIMILAR TITLE)	YEAR RELEASED	RUNNING TIME IN MINUTES	THE FILM BUFF'S BIBLE ‡	STEVEN SCHEUER	LEONARD MALTIN	DISTRIBUTOR	COMMENT
HERE'S YOUR LIFE (SWEDISH)	1967	110	5	2.5		BRANDON	
HERO, THE (BRIT. - RICHARD HARRIS, ROMY SCHNEIDER)	1972	97				AVCO-EMBASSY	
HERO OF BABYLON (ITALIAN)	1963	98		1.5		AVCO-EMBASSY	
HERO OF ROME (ITALIAN)	1963	90		1.5		AVCO-EMBASSY	
HEROD THE GREAT (ITALIAN)	1959	93	2	2.0	1.5	ALLIED ARTISTS	
HEROES AND SINNERS (FRENCH)	1955	105	5			JANUS FILMS	
HEROES DIE YOUNG	1960	76	2	1.5		ALLIED ARTISTS	
HEROES FOR SALE	1933	73		1.5	2.5	FIRST NATIONAL	
HEROES OF TELEMARK, THE (BRITISH)	1965	131		2.5	2.5	COLUMBIA	
HERO'S ISLAND	1962	94		1.5	2.5	UNITED ARTISTS	
HERS TO HOLD	1943	94			2.0	UNIVERSAL	
HE'S A COCKEYED WONDER	1950	77		2.5	1.5	COLUMBIA	
HEY BOY! HEY GIRL!	1959	81	3		1.5	COLUMBIA	
HEY, LET'S TWIST!	1961	80	2		1.0	PARAMOUNT	
HEY, PINEAPPLE! (JAPANESE)	1963	97		1.5		PARAMOUNT	
HEY, ROOKIE	1944	77		2.5	2.5	COLUMBIA	
HEY THERE, IT'S YOGI BEAR (CARTOON)	1964	89	4		2.0	COLUMBIA	
HI DIDDLE DIDDLE	a1943	72		2.0	2.5	UNITED ARTISTS	
HI-JACK HIGHWAY (FRENCH)	a1955	95		2.0		INTERMONDIA FILMS	
HI, MOM!	1970	87	5			SIGMA III	
HI, NELLIE	1934	75		3.0	2.5	WARNER BROTHERS	
HI YA, SAILOR	1943	63		1.5		UNIVERSAL	
HIAWATHA	1952	80		2.0	1.5	ALLIED ARTISTS	
HICKEY AND BOGGS	1972	111				UNITED ARTISTS	
HIDDEN EYE, THE	1945	69		3.0	2.5	M-G-M	
HIDDEN FEAR	1957	83		2.0	1.5	UNITED ARTISTS	
HIDDEN GUNS	1956	66	1			REPUBLIC	
HIDDEN HOMICIDE (BRITISH)	1959	70		1.0	1.5	REPUBLIC	
HIDDEN ROOM, THE (BRITISH)	a1949	98	6	3.5	3.0	EAGLE LION	
HIDE AND SEEK (BRITISH)	1964	90	4	2.5		UNIVERSAL	
HIDEOUS SUN DEMON	1955	74		1.0		CLARKE-KING	
HIDE-OUT (ROBERT MONTGOMERY, MAUREEN O'SULLIVAN)	1934	82		3.0		M-G-M	
HIDEOUT, THE (BRITISH - HOWARD KEEL)	a1949	67		3.0		WALTER READE	
HIDEOUT, THE (LLOYD BRIDGES, ADRIAN BOOTH)	1949	59		2.5		REPUBLIC	
HIDE-OUT, THE (BRITISH - RONA ANDERSON)	1956	57		2.0		J. ARTHUR RANK	
HIDEOUT, THE (FRENCH - MARCEL MOULOUDJI)	1961	80			2.5	MIRACLE	
HIGH (CANADIAN)	1967	82	1			JOSEPH BRENNER	
HIGH AND DRY (BRITISH)	a1954	93		3.0	2.5	UNIVERSAL	
HIGH AND HAPPY	a1947	90		2.0		REPUBLIC	
HIGH AND LOW (JAPANESE)	1962	142	6	4.0	3.0	CONTINENTAL	
HIGH AND THE MIGHTY, THE	1954	147	6	3.5	3.0	WARNER BROTHERS	
HIGH BARBAREE	1947	91		1.5	1.5	M-G-M	
HIGH COMMISSIONER, THE (BRITISH)	a1968	93	4	2.5		CINERAMA RELEASING	
HIGH COST OF LOVING, THE	1958	87	6			M-G-M	
HIGH FLIGHT (BRITISH)	1957	89		2.5	1.5	COLUMBIA	
HIGH FURY	1948	71			2.0	UNITED ARTISTS	
HIGH HELL (BRITISH)	1958	87		1.5	2.5	PARAMOUNT	
HIGH INFIDELITY (ITALIAN)	1965	120	6			MAGNA PICTURES	
HIGH LONESOME	1950	81		3.0	2.0	EAGLE LION	
HIGH NOON	1952	85	9*	4.0	4.0	UNITED ARTISTS	NOMINATED BEST PICTURE
HIGH-POWERED RIFLE, THE	1960	60	1	1.5		20th CENTURY FOX	
HIGH SCHOOL (JANE WITHERS, JOE BROWN JR)	1940	74		1.5		20th CENTURY FOX	
HIGH SCHOOL (DOCUMENTARY)	1969	75	6			OSTI FILMS	
HIGH SCHOOL BIG SHOT	1959	70	3	1.5		SPARTA	
HIGH SCHOOL CAESAR	1960	63		1.0		FILMGROUP	
HIGH SCHOOL CONFIDENTIAL	a1958	85		1.0	1.5	M-G-M	
HIGH SCHOOL HELLCATS	1958	68		1.5		AMERICAN-INTERNAT'L	
HIGH SIERRA	1941	100	5*	3.5	3.0	WARNER BROTHERS	
HIGH SOCIETY (BOWERY BOYS)	1955	61			-	ALLIED ARTISTS	
HIGH SOCIETY (BING CROSBY, GRACE KELLY)	1956	107	6	3.0	3.0	M-G-M	
HIGH TERRACE (BRITISH)	1956	82			2.0	ALLIED ARTISTS	
HIGH TIDE	1947	72			2.5	MONOGRAM	
HIGH TIME	1960	130	4	3.0	2.5	20th CENTURY FOX	
HIGH TREASON (BRITISH)	1951	93		3.5	2.5	J. ARTHUR RANK	
HIGH WALL	1948	99	5*	3.0	3.0	M-G-M	
HIGH, WIDE, AND HANDSOME	1937	112		3.0	2.5	PARAMOUNT	
HIGH, WILD AND FREE (DOCUMENTARY)	1968	105	4			AMERICAN-INTERNAT'L	
HIGH WIND IN JAMAICA, A (BRITISH)	1965	103	4*	3.5	3.0	20th CENTURY FOX	
HIGHER AND HIGHER	1943	90	5*	3.0	3.0	RKO	
HIGHLY DANGEROUS (BRITISH)	1951	88		3.0	2.5	LIPPERT PRODS.	
HIGHWAY DRAGNET	1954	71		2.0	2.0	ALLIED ARTISTS	
HIGHWAY 301	1951	83		2.0	2.0	WARNER BROTHERS	
HIGHWAY TO BATTLE (BRITISH)	1960	71		2.0	2.0	PARAMOUNT	
HIGHWAY WEST	1941	63		2.5		WARNER BROTHERS	
HIGHWAYMAN, THE	1951	82	4		2.5	ALLIED ARTISTS	
HIGHWAYS BY NIGHT	1942	63		2.5		RKO	
HILDA CRANE	1956	87		1.5	2.5	20th CENTURY FOX	
HILL, THE (BRITISH)	1965	123	3*	3.5	3.0	M-G-M	
HILL 24 DOESN'T ANSWER (ISRAELI)	1955	100	4*	3.5	3.0	CONTINENTAL	
HILLS OF HOME	1948	97	5	3.0	3.0	M-G-M	
HILLS RUN RED, THE (ITALIAN)	1967	89	3			UNITED ARTISTS	
HIPPODROME (GERMAN)	1961	96	4	-	2.5	CONTINENTAL	
HIRED GUN, THE	1957	63		2.0	2.5	M-G-M	
HIRED HAND, THE	1971	93	3			UNIVERSAL	

‡ An asterisk (*) in THE FILM BUFF'S BIBLE column indicates that the film has been rated by the editor and/or staff. All other ratings in this column are based on a consensus of reviews (see NOTES).

TITLE (LEADING ACTORS SHOWN WHERE TWO OR MORE FILMS HAVE THE SAME OR SIMILAR TITLE)	YEAR RELEASED	RUNNING TIME IN MINUTES	THE FILM BUFF'S BIBLE ‡	STEVEN SCHEUER	LEONARD MALTIN	DISTRIBUTOR	COMMENT
HIRED KILLER, THE	1967	95	4			PARAMOUNT	
HIRED WIFE	1940	93		3.0	3.0	UNIVERSAL	
HIROSHIMA, MON AMOUR (FRENCH)	1959	88	6*	4.0	3.5	ZENITH INTERNATIONAL	
HIS BROTHER'S WIFE	1936	90		2.0	2.0	M-G-M	
HIS BUTLER'S SISTER	1943	94		3.0	2.5	UNIVERSAL	
HIS DOUBLE LIFE	1934	68		3.0		PARAMOUNT	
HIS GIRL FRIDAY	1940	92	5*	4.0	4.0	COLUMBIA	
HIS KIND OF WOMAN	1951	120	4	3.0	2.5	RKO	
HIS MAJESTY O'KEEFE	1954	90		3.0	2.5	WARNER BROTHERS	
HIS WOMAN	1931	80		1.5	2.0	PARAMOUNT	
HISTORY IS MADE AT NIGHT	1937	97		2.5	3.0	UNITED ARTISTS	
HISTORY OF MR POLLY, THE (BRITISH)	1949	96		3.5	3.0	INT'L RELEASING ORG.	
HIT AND RUN	1957	84		1.5	1.0	UNITED ARTISTS	
HIT PARADE OF 1951	1950	85	2	2.0		REPUBLIC	
HIT THE DECK	1955	112	5			M-G-M	
HIT THE ICE	1943	82			2.0	UNIVERSAL	
HITCH HIKE TO HAPPINESS	1945	72		2.0		REPUBLIC	
HITCH-HIKER, THE (EDMOND O'BRIEN, FRANK LOVEJOY)	1953	71	6	3.5	3.0	RKO	
HITCHHIKERS, THE (MISTY ROWE, NORMAN KLAR)	1972	93	3			ENTERTAINM'T VENTURES	
HITLER	1962	107	3	2.0	2.0	ALLIED ARTISTS	
HITLER - DEAD OR ALIVE	1943	70			2.0	BEN JUDELL	
HITLER GANG, THE	1944	101	5*	2.0	2.5	PARAMOUNT	
HITLER'S CHILDREN	1943	83		3.0	3.0	RKO	
HITLER'S EXECUTIONERS (GERMAN, DOCUMENTARY)	a1958	78	5	2.0		VITALITE	
HITLER'S HANGMAN	a1943	84			2.5	M-G-M	
HITLER'S MADMAN	a1943	84			2.5	M-G-M	
HITTING A NEW HIGH	1937	60		3.0	2.5	RKO	
HOA BINH (FRENCH)	1970	93	7			TRANSVUE PICTURES	
HOAXTERS, THE (DOCUMENTARY)	1953	36	4			M-G-M	
HOBSON'S CHOICE (BRITISH)	1954	107	7	4.0	3.0	UNITED ARTISTS	
HOLD BACK THE DAWN	1941	115	6*	3.5	3.5	PARAMOUNT	NOMINATED BEST PICTURE
HOLD BACK THE NIGHT	1956	80		2.5	2.5	ALLIED ARTISTS	
HOLD BACK TOMORROW	1955	75		1.0	1.5	UNIVERSAL	
HOLD ON	1966	85	2	1.5	2.5	M-G-M	
HOLD THAT BABY	1949	64			-	MONOGRAM	
HOLD THAT BLONDE	1945	76		2.0	2.0	PARAMOUNT	
HOLD THAT CO-ED	1938	80		3.5	3.0	20th CENTURY FOX	
HOLD THAT GHOST	1941	86			3.0	UNIVERSAL	
HOLD THAT HYPNOTIST	1957	61			-	ALLIED ARTISTS	
HOLD THAT LINE	1952	64			-	MONOGRAM	
HOLD YOUR MAN	1933	89		2.5	3.0	M-G-M	
HOLE IN THE HEAD, A	1959	120	4*	3.0	2.0	UNITED ARTISTS	
HOLIDAY (ANN HARDING, MARY ASTOR)	1930	89				PATHE-RKO	
HOLIDAY (KATHARINE HEPBURN, CARY GRANT)	1938	93	6*	3.5	3.5	COLUMBIA	
HOLIDAY AFFAIR	1949	87		2.5	3.0	RKO	
HOLIDAY CAMP (BRITISH)	1947	97	5	2.5	2.5	UNIVERSAL	
HOLIDAY FOR HENRIETTA (FRENCH)	1955	103	6			ARDEE FILMS	
HOLIDAY FOR LOVERS	1959	103		2.0	2.5	20th CENTURY FOX	
HOLIDAY FOR SINNERS	1952	72	4	3.0	2.5	M-G-M	
HOLIDAY IN HAVANA	1949	73	2	2.0		COLUMBIA	
HOLIDAY IN MEXICO	1946	127		3.0	3.0	M-G-M	
HOLIDAY INN	1942	101		3.5	3.0	PARAMOUNT	
HOLIDAY RHYTHM	1950	60				LIPPERT PRODS.	
HOLIDAY WEEK (BRITISH)	1957	88		1.0		MONARCH	
HOLLOW TRIUMPH	a1948	83	5	3.0	3.0	EAGLE LION	
HOLLY AND THE IVY, THE (BRITISH)	1952	83	3*	3.5	3.0	PACEMAKER	
HOLLYWOOD CANTEEN	1944	124		2.5	2.5	WARNER BROTHERS	
HOLLYWOOD CAVALCADE	1939	96		3.0	3.0	20th CENTURY FOX	
HOLLYWOOD HOTEL	1937	109		2.5	2.5	WARNER BROTHERS	
HOLLYWOOD OR BUST	1956	95	4	3.0	2.5	PARAMOUNT	
HOLLYWOOD REVUE (OF 1929), THE	1929	116		2.0		M-G-M	NOMINATED BEST PICTURE 1928/29
HOLLYWOOD STORY	1951	77		2.0	2.5	UNIVERSAL	
HOLY MATRIMONY	1943	87		3.5	3.0	20th CENTURY FOX	
HOMBRE	1967	111	6*	3.5	3.0	20th CENTURY FOX	
HOME AT SEVEN (BRITISH)	a1952	85	5	3.0	3.0	MAYER-KINGSLEY	
HOME BEFORE DARK	1958	137		2.5	3.0	WARNER BROTHERS	
HOME FROM THE HILL	1960	150	6*	4.0	3.0	M-G-M	
HOME IN INDIANA	1944	103		3.0	3.0	20th CENTURY FOX	
HOME IS THE HERO (IRISH)	1959	83		3.0	2.5	SHOWCORPORATION	
HOME OF THE BRAVE	1949	85	6	3.5	3.0	UNITED ARTISTS	
HOME, SWEET HOMICIDE	1946	90		1.5	2.0	20th CENTURY FOX	
HOMECOMING (CLARK GABLE, LANA TURNER)	1948	113	4	2.0	2.0	M-G-M	
HOMECOMING, THE (T.V. - PATRICIA NEAL)	1971	100	3*				
HOMER	1970	90	3			NATIONAL GENERAL	
HOMESTEADERS, THE	1953	62	2	2.0		ALLIED ARTISTS	
HOMESTRETCH, THE	1947	96		2.0	2.0	20th CENTURY FOX	
HOMICIDAL	1961	87		2.0	2.5	COLUMBIA	
HONDO	1953	84	6*	3.5	3.0	WARNER BROTHERS	
HONEY POT, THE	a1967	131	5-6*	3.0	3.0	UNITED ARTISTS	SLOW BUILDUP
HONEYCHILE	1951	90		2.0	1.5	REPUBLIC	
HONEYMOON (SHIRLEY TEMPLE, FRANCHOT TONE)	1947	74		2.0	2.0	RKO	
HONEYMOON (SPANISH - ANTHONY STEEL)	1959	90		1.5	2.0	RKO	
HONEYMOON AHEAD	1945	60		2.0	2.0	UNIVERSAL	
HONEYMOON FOR THREE	1941	77		2.0	2.5	WARNER BROTHERS	

‡ An asterisk (*) in THE FILM BUFF'S BIBLE column indicates that the film has been rated by the editor and/or staff. All other ratings in this column are based on a consensus of reviews (see NOTES).

TITLE (LEADING ACTORS SHOWN WHERE TWO OR MORE FILMS HAVE THE SAME OR SIMILAR TITLE)	YEAR RELEASED	RUNNING TIME IN MINUTES	THE FILM BUFF'S BIBLE ‡	STEVEN SCHEUER	LEONARD MALTIN	DISTRIBUTOR	COMMENT
HONEYMOON HOTEL	1964	89		2.0	1.5	M-G-M	
HONEYMOON IN BALI	1939	95		3.0	3.0	PARAMOUNT	
HONEYMOON KILLERS, THE	1970	110	4			CINERAMA RELEASING	
HONEYMOON MACHINE, THE	1961	82		3.0	2.5	M-G-M	
HONEYMOON WITH A STRANGER (T.V.)	1969	90		2.5		20th CENTURY FOX	
HONEYMOONS WILL KILL YOU (ITALIAN)	1964	91		1.5		AMERICAN-INTERNAT'L	
HONG KONG	1951	92		2.0	2.0	PARAMOUNT	
HONG KONG AFFAIR	1958	79		1.0	1.5	ALLIED ARTISTS	
HONG KONG CONFIDENTIAL	1958	67	2	2.5	2.5	UNITED ARTISTS	
HONG KONG HOT HARBOR (GERMAN)	1962	102		1.0		UCC FILMS	
HONKERS, THE	1972	103	3			UNITED ARTISTS	
HONKY	1971	89	1			JACK H. HARRIS	
HONKY TONK	1941	105		2.5	2.5	M-G-M	
HONOLULU	1939	83		2.5	2.5	M-G-M	
HONOLULU LU	1941	72		1.5		COLUMBIA	
HONOURABLE MURDER, AN (BRITISH)	1959	70		2.0		WARNER BROTHERS	
HOODLUM, THE	1951	61	2		2.0	UNITED ARTISTS	
HOODLUM EMPIRE	1952	98		2.5	2.5	REPUBLIC	
HOODLUM PRIEST, THE	1961	101	6*	3.5	3.0	UNITED ARTISTS	
HOODLUM SAINT, THE	1946	91		2.5	2.5	M-G-M	
HOOK, THE	1963	98		3.0	2.5	M-G-M	
HOOK, LINE AND SINKER (JERRY LEWIS, PETER LAWFORD)	1969	92	2			COLUMBIA	
HOOTENANNY HOOT	1963	91	1			M-G-M	
HOPPITY GOES TO TOWN (CARTOON)	a1941	78	4*	3.0		PARAMOUNT	
HORIZONS WEST	1952	81	3	2.5	2.5	UNIVERSAL	
HORIZONTAL LIEUTENANT, THE	1962	90		2.5	2.5	M-G-M	
HORN BLOWS AT MIDNIGHT, THE	1945	78		2.0	2.5	WARNER BROTHERS	
HORNET'S NEST (ROCK HUDSON, SYLVA KOSCINA)	1970	110	3			UNITED ARTISTS	
HORRIBLE DR HICHCOCK, THE (ITALIAN)	a1962	76		1.5	2.5	SIGMA III	
HORROR CASTLE	a1965	82	3	1.5	2.5	ZODIAC FILMS	ENGLISH LANGUAGE
HORROR CHAMBER OF DR FAUSTUS (FRENCH)	1963	94		2.0	2.0	LOPERT	
HORROR HOTEL (BRITISH)	1963	76	3	2.5	2.5	TRANS-LUX DIST.	
HORROR HOUSE	1970	79	1			AMERICAN-INTERNAT'L	
HORROR ISLAND	1941	60		2.0		UNIVERSAL	
HORROR OF DRACULA (BRITISH)	1958	82	5	3.0	3.0	UNIVERSAL	
HORROR OF FRANKENSTEIN, THE (BRITISH)	1970	95	2			LEVITT-PICKMAN	
HORROR OF IT ALL, THE (BRITISH)	1964	75	2			20th CENTURY FOX	
HORROR OF PARTY BEACH, THE	1964	82	1			20th CENTURY FOX	
HORROR OF THE BLOOD MONSTERS	1970	85	1			INDEPENDENT INT'L	
HORROR ON SNAPE ISLAND (BRITISH)	1972	88	1			FANFARE	
HORRORS OF THE BLACK MUSEUM (BRITISH)	1959	81	2	2.0	2.5	AMERICAN-INTERNAT'L	
HORSE FEATHERS	1932	70		3.5	3.5	PARAMOUNT	
HORSE IN THE GRAY FLANNEL SUIT, THE	1968	110	3			BUENA VISTA	
HORSE SOLDIERS, THE	1959	119	6*	2.0	3.0	UNITED ARTISTS	
HORSE WITH THE FLYING TAIL, THE (DOCUMENTARY)	1961	48	6			BUENA VISTA	
HORSEMEN, THE (OMAR SHARIF, LEIGH TAYLOR-YOUNG)	1971	110	4*			COLUMBIA	
HORSE'S MOUTH, THE (BRITISH - ROBERT BEATTY)	a1952	84		3.0		MAYER-KINGSLEY	
HORSE'S MOUTH, THE (BRITISH - ALEC GUINESS)	1958	93	7*	4.0	3.5	UNITED ARTISTS	
HOSPITAL, THE	1971	104	6-7*			UNITED ARTISTS	
HOSTAGES	1943	88		2.0	2.0	PARAMOUNT	
HOSTILE GUNS	1967	91	2	2.0		PARAMOUNT	
HOT ANGEL, THE	1958	73	3	2.0		PARAMOUNT	
HOT BLOOD	1956	85	3	1.5	2.5	COLUMBIA	
HOT BOX, THE	1972	87	3			NEW WORLD	
HOT CAR GIRL	1958	71		1.5		ALLIED ARTISTS	
HOT CARS	1956	60	2			UNITED ARTISTS	
HOT HORSE	1963	82	3			UNIVERSAL	
HOT ICE (BRITISH)	1952	85		3.0		APEX	
HOT MILLIONS (BRITISH)	1968	105	6*	3.5		M-G-M	
HOT NEWS	1953	68		1.5	1.5	ALLIED ARTISTS	
HOT ROCK, THE	a1972	101	6			20th CENTURY FOX	
HOT ROD GANG	1958	72		1.0	1.5	AMERICAN-INTERNAT'L	
HOT ROD GIRL	1956	75			1.0	AMERICAN-INTERNAT'L	
HOT ROD RUMBLE	1957	79		1.5	1.5	ALLIED ARTISTS	
HOT RODS TO HELL	1967	92	2	2.0	2.5	M-G-M	
HOT SHOTS	1956	61			-	ALLIED ARTISTS	
HOT SPELL	1958	86	6	3.0	3.0	PARAMOUNT	
HOT SUMMER NIGHT	1957	86		2.0	2.5	M-G-M	
HOTEL	1967	124	6	3.0		WARNER BROTHERS	
HOTEL BERLIN	1945	98		3.0		WARNER BROTHERS	
HOTEL FOR WOMEN	1939	83		1.5	2.0	20th CENTURY FOX	
HOTEL IMPERIAL	1939	67		2.0	2.0	PARAMOUNT	
HOTEL PARADISO (BRITISH)	1966	100	4	2.5	2.5	M-G-M	
HOTEL RESERVE (BRITISH)	1944	79		2.5	3.0	RKO	
HOTEL SAHARA (BRITISH)	1951	96		2.5	2.0	UNITED ARTISTS	
HOUDINI	1953	106		3.0	2.5	PARAMOUNT	
HOUND-DOG MAN	1959	87	5	3.0		20th CENTURY FOX	
HOUND OF THE BASKERVILLES, THE (BASIL RATHBONE)	1939	80		3.0	-	20th CENTURY FOX	
HOUND OF THE BASKERVILLES, THE (BRIT.- P. CUSHING)	1959	84	5*	3.0	3.0	UNITED ARTISTS	
HOUR BEFORE THE DAWN, THE	1944	75		2.0	2.0	PARAMOUNT	
HOUR OF DECISION (BRITISH)	1955	74		2.0	2.0	ASTOR	
HOUR OF GLORY (BRITISH)	a1948	106		3.0	3.0	SNADER PRODS.	
HOUR OF THE GUN	1967	100	4	2.5		UNITED ARTISTS	
HOUR OF THE WOLF (SWEDISH)	1968	88	6			LOPERT	

‡ An asterisk (*) in THE FILM BUFF'S BIBLE column indicates that the film has been rated by the editor and/or staff. All other ratings in this column are based on a consensus of reviews (see NOTES).

TITLE (LEADING ACTORS SHOWN WHERE TWO OR MORE FILMS HAVE THE SAME OR SIMILAR TITLE)	YEAR RELEASED	RUNNING TIME IN MINUTES	CRITICAL RATINGS			DISTRIBUTOR	COMMENT
			THE FILM BUFF'S BIBLE ‡	STEVEN SCHEUER	LEONARD MALTIN		
HOUR OF 13, THE (BRITISH)	1952	78		2.5	2.5	M-G-M	
HOURS OF LOVE, THE (ITALIAN)	1965	89	4		2.5	CINEMA V	
HOUSE ACROSS THE BAY, THE	1940	72		2.5	2.5	UNITED ARTISTS	
HOUSE ACROSS THE STREET, THE	1949	69		2.0	2.0	WARNER BROTHERS	
HOUSE BY THE RIVER	1950	88		2.0	2.0	REPUBLIC	
HOUSE IS NOT A HOME, A	1964	90	3	1.0		AVCO-EMBASSY	
HOUSE OF BAMBOO	1955	102		2.5	2.5	20th CENTURY FOX	
HOUSE OF CARDS	1969	105	4	2.5		UNIVERSAL	
HOUSE OF DARK SHADOWS	1970	96	2			M-G-M	
HOUSE OF DRACULA	1945	67		1.5	2.0	UNIVERSAL	
HOUSE OF FEAR, THE	1945	69	5*			UNIVERSAL	
HOUSE OF FRANKENSTEIN	1945	71		·	2.5	UNIVERSAL	
HOUSE OF FRIGHT (BRITISH)	1960	89	3			AMERICAN-INTERNAT'L	
HOUSE OF HORRORS	1946	65		1.5	2.0	UNIVERSAL	
HOUSE OF INTRIGUE, THE (ITALIAN)	1957	94		2.0	2.5	ALLIED ARTISTS	
HOUSE OF MYSTERY (BRITISH)	1961	56			2.5	ANGLO AMALGAMATED	
HOUSE OF NUMBERS	1957	92		2.0	2.5	M-G-M	
HOUSE OF 1,000 DOLLS (GERMAN)	1967	78	1	1.5		AMERICAN-INTERNAT'L	
HOUSE OF RICORDI (ITALIAN)	a1956	117		2.0	2.0	MANSON	
HOUSE OF ROTHSCHILD, THE	1934	86	6*		3.0	UNITED ARTISTS	NOMINATED BEST PICTURE
HOUSE OF STRANGERS	1949	101	6*	3.5	3.0	20th CENTURY FOX	
HOUSE OF THE DAMNED	1963	62	3			20th CENTURY FOX	
HOUSE OF THE SEVEN GABLES, THE	1940	89	7*	3.5	3.0	UNIVERSAL	
HOUSE OF THE SEVEN HAWKS, THE (BRITISH)	1959	92	3	2.5	2.5	M-G-M	
HOUSE OF USHER	1960	85	4*			AMERICAN-INTERNAT'L	
HOUSE OF WAX	1953	88	4	2.5	3.0	WARNER BROTHERS	
HOUSE OF WOMEN	1962	85	2	2.0	2.5	WARNER BROTHERS	
HOUSE ON GREENAPPLE ROAD (T.V.)	1970	100	5*	2.5		QM PRODS.	
HOUSE ON HAUNTED HILL	1959	75		2.5	2.0	ALLIED ARTISTS	
HOUSE ON 92ND ST, THE	1945	88	4*	3.5	3.0	20th CENTURY FOX	
HOUSE ON TELEGRAPH HILL	1951	93		2.0	2.5	20th CENTURY FOX	
HOUSE ON THE WATERFRONT, THE (FRENCH)	1955	90	4			UNION FILMS	
HOUSE THAT DRIPPED BLOOD, THE (BRITISH)	1971	101	4			CINERAMA RELEASING	
HOUSE THAT SCREAMED, THE (SPANISH)	1971	94	3			AMERICAN-INTERNAT'L	
HOUSE THAT WOULDN'T DIE, THE (T.V.)	1970	90		2.5		ABC FILMS	
HOUSEBOAT	1958	110	6	3.5	3.0	PARAMOUNT	
HOUSEHOLDER, THE (INDIAN)	1963	100	5			ROYAL FILMS INT'L	ENGLISH LANGUAGE
HOUSEKEEPER'S DAUGHTER, THE	1939	79		2.5	2.0	UNITED ARTISTS	
HOUSEWIFE	1934	69		2.0	2.0	WARNER BROTHERS	
HOUSTON STORY, THE	1956	79	3	2.0	2.5	COLUMBIA	
HOW AWFUL ABOUT ALLEN (T.V.)	1970	90		2.5		ABC FILMS	
HOW DO I LOVE THEE?	1970	98	3			CINERAMA RELEASING	
HOW GREEN WAS MY VALLEY	1941	118	6*	4.0	4.0	20th CENTURY FOX	BEST PICTURE AWARD
HOW I SPENT MY SUMMER VACATION (T.V.)	1967	100		2.0	2.0	UNIVERSAL	
HOW I WON THE WAR (BRITISH)	1967	109	4	2.5		UNITED ARTISTS	
HOW NOT TO ROB A DEPARTMENT STORE (FRENCH)	1965	95	3			ARTIXO PRODS.	
HOW SWEET IT IS!	1968	99	5	2.5		NATIONAL GENERAL	
HOW THE WEST WAS WON	1963	165	4-5*			M-G-M	NOMINATED BEST PICTURE
HOW TO BE VERY, VERY POPULAR	1955	89		3.0	2.5	20th CENTURY FOX	
HOW TO COMMIT MARRIAGE	1969	98	3			CINERAMA RELEASING	
HOW TO FRAME A FIGG	1971	103	4			UNIVERSAL	
HOW TO MAKE A MONSTER	1958	74		1.5	1.0	AMERICAN-INTERNAT'L	
HOW TO MARRY A MILLIONAIRE	1953	95	5*	3.0	3.0	20th CENTURY FOX	
HOW TO MURDER A RICH UNCLE (BRITISH)	1957	79	4	2.5	2.0	COLUMBIA	
HOW TO MURDER YOUR WIFE	1965	118	5	3.0	3.0	UNITED ARTISTS	
HOW TO SAVE A MARRIAGE AND RUIN YOUR LIFE	1968	102	4	2.5		COLUMBIA	
HOW TO SEDUCE A PLAYBOY (AUSTRIAN)	1966	94	1	1.0		CHEVRON	
HOW TO STEAL A MILLION	1966	127	7-8*	3.5	3.0	20th CENTURY FOX	
HOW TO STUFF A WILD BIKINI	1965	90		1.5	2.0	AMERICAN-INTERNAT'L	
HOW TO SUCCEED IN BUSINESS WITHOUT REALLY TRYING	1967	119	7	4.0		UNITED ARTISTS	
HOW TO SUCCEED WITH SEX	1970	77	1			MEDFORD FILMS	
HOWARDS OF VIRGINIA, THE	1940	122		3.5	2.5	COLUMBIA	
HOW'S ABOUT IT	1943	61		1.5		UNIVERSAL	
HUCKLEBERRY FINN (JACKIE COOGAN, JUNIOR DURKIN)	1931	80		2.5		PARAMOUNT	
HUCKSTERS, THE	1947	115	5-6*	3.0	3.0	M-G-M	
HUD	1963	112	7*	4.0	4.0	PARAMOUNT	
HUDSON'S BAY	1940	95		2.5	2.5	20th CENTURY FOX	
HUE AND CRY (BRITISH)	1947	82		3.0	3.0	FINE ARTS	
HUGS AND KISSES (SWEDISH)	1967	93	3			AVCO-EMBASSY	
HUK	1956	84		3.0	1.5	UNITED ARTISTS	
HULLABALOO	1940	77		2.0		M-G-M	
HUMAN CARGO	1936	66		1.5		20th CENTURY FOX	
HUMAN COMEDY, THE	1943	118	4*	4.0	3.5	M-G-M	NOMINATED BEST PICTURE
HUMAN DESIRE	1954	90		2.0	3.0	COLUMBIA	
HUMAN DUPLICATORS, THE	1965	82		2.0	2.0	ALLIED ARTISTS	
HUMAN JUNGLE, THE	1954	82		2.5	2.5	ALLIED ARTISTS	
HUMAN MONSTER, THE (BRITISH)	1939	73			2.5	MONOGRAM	
HUMORESQUE (JOAN CRAWFORD, JOHN GARFIELD)	1947	125		3.0	3.0	WARNER BROTHERS	
HUNCHBACK OF NOTRE DAME, THE (SILENT - LON CHANEY)	1923	122	4*		3.0	UNIVERSAL	
HUNCHBACK OF NOTRE DAME, THE (CHARLES LAUGHTON)	1939	117	6*	3.5	3.0	RKO	
HUNCHBACK OF NOTRE DAME, THE (FR. - ANTHONY QUINN)	1957	104	4	3.0	2.5	RKO	
HUNDRED HOUR HUNT (BRITISH)	1953	88		3.0		ABNER J. GRESHLER	
HUNGER (DANISH)	1966	115	6			SIGMA III	
HUNGRY HILL (BRITISH)	1947	92		2.5	2.0	UNIVERSAL	

‡ An asterisk (*) in THE FILM BUFF'S BIBLE column indicates that the film has been rated by the editor and/or staff. All other ratings in this column are based on a consensus of reviews (see NOTES).

TITLE (LEADING ACTORS SHOWN WHERE TWO OR MORE FILMS HAVE THE SAME OR SIMILAR TITLE)	YEAR RELEASED	RUNNING TIME IN MINUTES	THE FILM BUFF'S BIBLE ‡	STEVEN SCHEUER	LEONARD MALTIN	DISTRIBUTOR	COMMENT
HUNS, THE (ITALIAN)	1960	85	1	1.5		PRODUCERS INTERNAT'L	
HUNT, THE (ITALIAN - MARINA VLADY, FAUSTO TOZZI)	1960	86		1.5		AMERICAN-INTERNAT'L	
HUNT, THE (SPANISH - ISMAEL MERLO, ALFREDO MAYO)	1966	93	6	4.0		TRANS-LUX DIST.	
HUNT THE MAN DOWN	1950	68		3.0	2.0	RKO	
HUNTED, THE (PRESTON FOSTER, BELITA)	1948	67		2.5	2.5	ALLIED ARTISTS	
HUNTED MEN	1938	65		2.0		PARAMOUNT	
HUNTERS, THE	1958	108		2.5	2.5	20th CENTURY FOX	
HUNTERS ARE FOR KILLING (T.V.)	1970	100		2.5		CBS-TV	
HUNTERS OF THE DEEP (DOCUMENTARY)	1955	64	6	3.0		DIST. CORP. OF AMER.	
HUNTING PARTY, THE (BRITISH)	1971	108	1			UNITED ARTISTS	
HURRICANE, THE	1937	110	5*	3.5	3.5	UNITED ARTISTS	
HURRICANE ISLAND	1951	70		2.0	1.5	COLUMBIA	
HURRICANE SMITH (RAY MIDDLETON, JANE WYATT)	a1941	69		2.0		REPUBLIC	
HURRICANE SMITH (JOHN IRELAND, YVONNE DE CARLO)	1952	90		2.0	2.0	PARAMOUNT	
HURRY, CHARLIE, HURRY	1941	65		2.5		RKO	
HURRY SUNDOWN	1967	146	3	1.0		PARAMOUNT	
HURRY UP OR I'LL BE 30	1972	92				CINEGROUP COMPANY	
HUSBANDS	1970	138	4			COLUMBIA	
HUSH . . . HUSH, SWEET CHARLOTTE	1965	133	4*	3.0	3.0	20th CENTURY FOX	
HUSTLER, THE	1961	135	8*	4.0	4.0	20th CENTURY FOX	NOMINATED BEST PICTURE
HYPNOTIC EYE, THE	1960	79		1.5	2.0	ALLIED ARTISTS	
HYSTERIA (BRITISH)	1965	86	3			M-G-M	
I, A LOVER (DANISH)	1966	90	3			CROWN INTERNATIONAL	
I, A WOMAN (DANISH)	1965	90	4			AUDUBON	
I, A WOMAN, PART II (DANISH)	a1968	81	1			CHEVRON	
I, A WOMAN, PART III (DANISH)	a1970	85	1			CHEVRON	
I ACCUSE	1958	99		2.5	2.5	M-G-M	
I AIM AT THE STARS (BRITISH)	1960	107		3.0	3.0	COLUMBIA	
I AM A CAMERA (BRITISH)	1955	98	6	3.0	3.5	DIST. CORP. OF AMER.	
I AM A FUGITIVE FROM A CHAIN GANG	1932	93	5*	3.5	3.5	WARNER BROTHERS	NOMINATED BEST PICTURE 1932/33
I AM A THIEF	1935	64		2.0	2.0	WARNER BROTHERS	
I AM CURIOUS (BLUE) (SWEDISH)	1969	103	1			GROVE PRESS	
I AM CURIOUS (YELLOW) (SWEDISH)	1967	120	2*			GROVE PRESS	
I AM THE LAW	1938	83		3.0	2.5	COLUMBIA	
I BECAME A CRIMINAL (BRITISH)	a1947	78		3.0	2.5	WARNER BROTHERS	
I BELIEVE IN YOU (BRITISH)	1952	95	6	3.0	2.5	UNIVERSAL	
I BOMBED PEARL HARBOR (JAPANESE)	1960	98	3	2.0		PARADE	
I BURY THE LIVING	1958	75		2.5	2.0	UNITED ARTISTS	
I CALL FIRST	a1968	90	3			JOSEPH BRENNER	
I CAN GET IT FOR YOU WHOLESALE	1951	91		2.5	3.0	20th CENTURY FOX	
I CAN'T GIVE YOU ANYTHING BUT LOVE, BABY	1940	60		2.5		UNIVERSAL	
I CONFESS	1953	95	4	2.5	2.0	WARNER BROTHERS	
I COULD GO ON SINGING (BRITISH)	1963	99		2.0	2.5	UNITED ARTISTS	
I COVER BIG TOWN	1947	63			2.0	PARAMOUNT	
I COVER THE UNDERWORLD (SEAN MCCLORY)	1955	70			1.5	REPUBLIC	
I COVER THE WAR	1937	68			2.0	UNIVERSAL	
I COVER THE WATERFRONT	1933	70			3.0	UNITED ARTISTS	
I DEAL IN DANGER	1966	89	3		2.5	20th CENTURY FOX	
I DIED A THOUSAND TIMES	1955	109	4	2.0	2.0	WARNER BROTHERS	
I DON'T CARE GIRL, THE	1953	78	3	2.5	2.5	20th CENTURY FOX	
I DOOD IT	1943	102		2.5	2.5	M-G-M	
I DREAM OF JEANIE	1952	90		2.0	2.0	REPUBLIC	
I DREAM TOO MUCH	1935	95		3.0	2.5	RKO	
I DRINK YOUR BLOOD	1971	83				CINEMATION INDUS.	
I EAT YOUR SKIN	1971	81				CINEMATION INDUS.	
I ESCAPED FROM THE GESTAPO	a1943	75			2.0	MONOGRAM	
I EVEN MET HAPPY GYPSIES (YUGOSLAVIAN)	1967	90	5	3.0		PROMINENT FILMS	
I FOUND STELLA PARISH	1935	84		2.0	2.0	FIRST NATIONAL	
I GIVE MY HEART	a1936	87			2.5	WARNER BROTHERS	
I, JANE DOE	1948	85		1.5	1.5	REPUBLIC	
I KILLED WILD BILL HICKOCK	1956	63		1.0		ASSOCIATED ARTISTS	
I KNOW WHERE I'M GOING (BRITISH)	1945	91	7	4.0	4.0	UNIVERSAL	
I LIKE MONEY (BRITISH)	1961	81		2.0	2.5	20th CENTURY FOX	
I LIVE IN FEAR (JAPANESE)	1955	105	6			BRANDON	
I LIVE MY LIFE	1935	81		2.5	2.0	M-G-M	
I LOVE A BANDLEADER	1945	70		2.0	2.0	COLUMBIA	
I LOVE A MYSTERY	1945	70			2.0	COLUMBIA	
I LOVE A SOLDIER	1944	106		2.0	2.0	PARAMOUNT	
I LOVE MELVIN	1953	76		2.5	2.5	M-G-M	
I LOVE MY WIFE	1970	95	4			UNIVERSAL	
I LOVE TROUBLE	1947	94	5	3.0	3.0	COLUMBIA	
I LOVE YOU AGAIN	1940	99		3.0	3.0	M-G-M	
I LOVE YOU, ALICE B. TOKLAS	1968	94	4*	3.0		WARNER BROTHERS	
I LOVE, YOU LOVE (ITALIAN)	1961	90			2.5	ROYAL FILMS INT'L	
I LOVED A WOMAN	1933	90		2.5		FIRST NATIONAL	
I MARRIED A COMMUNIST	a1949	73		2.0	2.5	RKO	
I MARRIED A DOCTOR	1936	83		3.0		WARNER BROTHERS	
I MARRIED A MONSTER FROM OUTER SPACE	1958	78	2	2.0	2.0	PARAMOUNT	
I MARRIED A WITCH	1942	76		3.0	2.5	UNITED ARTISTS	
I MARRIED A WOMAN	1958	84	4		2.0	UNIVERSAL	
I MARRIED AN ANGEL	1942	84		2.0	2.0	M-G-M	

‡ An asterisk (*) in THE FILM BUFF'S BIBLE column indicates that the film has been rated by the editor and/or staff. All other ratings in this column are based on a consensus of reviews (see NOTES).

TITLE (LEADING ACTORS SHOWN WHERE TWO OR MORE FILMS HAVE THE SAME OR SIMILAR TITLE)	YEAR RELEASED	RUNNING TIME IN MINUTES	THE FILM BUFF'S BIBLE ‡	STEVEN SCHEUER	LEONARD MALTIN	DISTRIBUTOR	COMMENT
I MET A MURDERER (BRITISH)	1939	70		3.0		YORK PICTURES	
I MET HIM IN PARIS	1937	86		3.0	3.0	PARAMOUNT	
I MET MY LOVE AGAIN	1938	77		3.0	2.5	UNITED ARTISTS	
I, MOBSTER	1959	80		2.5	2.5	20th CENTURY FOX	
I NEVER SANG FOR MY FATHER	1970	90	5*			COLUMBIA	
I PASSED FOR WHITE	1960	93		1.5	2.0	ALLIED ARTISTS	
I REMEMBER MAMA	1948	134		4.0	3.5	RKO	
I SAW WHAT YOU DID	1965	82		2.0	3.0	UNIVERSAL	
I SHOT JESSE JAMES	1949	81	4	3.0	2.5	LIPPERT PRODS.	
I SPIT ON YOUR GRAVE (FRENCH)	1959	100	1			AUDUBON	
I SPY, YOU SPY (BRITISH)	a1966	92	3	2.5	2.5	AMERICAN-INTERNAT'L	
I TAKE THIS WOMAN (GARY COOPER, CAROLE LOMBARD)	1931	74		2.5		PARAMOUNT	
I TAKE THIS WOMAN (SPENCER TRACY, HEDY LAMARR)	1940	97		1.5	2.0	M-G-M	
I THANK A FOOL (BRITISH)	1962	100	4			M-G-M	
I, THE JURY	1953	87		2.0	2.0	UNITED ARTISTS	
I WAKE UP SCREAMING	1941	81	4*	3.0	3.0	20th CENTURY FOX	
I WALK ALONE	1948	98		2.0	2.0	PARAMOUNT	
I WALK THE LINE	1970	95	3			COLUMBIA	
I WALKED WITH A ZOMBIE	1943	69		3.0	3.0	RKO	
I WANT A DIVORCE	1940	75		1.5	2.5	PARAMOUNT	
I WANT TO LIVE	1958	120	7	4.0	3.5	UNITED ARTISTS	
I WANT WHAT I WANT (BRITISH)	1972	91	3*			CINERAMA RELEASING	
I WANT YOU	1952	102		2.0	3.0	RKO	
I WANTED WINGS	1941	131		2.5	2.0	PARAMOUNT	
I WAS A COMMUNIST FOR THE F.B.I.	1951	83		2.0	2.5	WARNER BROTHERS	
I WAS A MALE WAR BRIDE	1949	105	3*	3.0	2.5	20th CENTURY FOX	
I WAS A PARISH PRIEST (SPANISH)	1957	87		3.0			
I WAS A PRISONER ON DEVIL'S ISLAND	1941	71		2.0		COLUMBIA	
I WAS A SHOPLIFTER	1950	82		2.0	2.5	UNIVERSAL	
I WAS A TEENAGE FRANKENSTEIN	1957	72		1.5	1.5	AMERICAN-INTERNAT'L	
I WAS A TEENAGE WEREWOLF	1957	70	3*	1.5	2.0	AMERICAN-INTERNAT'L	
I WAS AN ADVENTURESS	1940	81		2.0	2.5	20th CENTURY FOX	
I WAS AN AMERICAN SPY	1951	85	2	2.0	2.5	ALLIED ARTISTS	
I WAS MONTY'S DOUBLE (BRITISH)	a1958	101		3.5	2.0	NTA PICTURES	
I WONDER WHO'S KISSING HER NOW	1947	108		3.0	2.5	20th CENTURY FOX	
ICE-CAPADES	1941	88		2.0		REPUBLIC	
ICE FOLLIES OF 1939	1939	82		2.0		M-G-M	
ICE PALACE	1960	113		2.5	2.5	WARNER BROTHERS	
ICE STATION ZEBRA	1968	148	4*	2.5		M-G-M	
ICELAND	1942	79		2.5	2.0	20th CENTURY FOX	
ICHABOD AND MR TOAD	a1949	67	6			RKO	
I'D CLIMB THE HIGHEST MOUNTAIN	1951	88		2.5	3.0	20th CENTURY FOX	
I'D RATHER BE RICH	1964	96		2.5	2.5	UNIVERSAL	
IDEAL HUSBAND, AN (BRITISH)	1947	96		2.5	2.5	20th CENTURY FOX	
IDENTITY UNKNOWN (RICHARD ARLEN)	1945	71			2.0	REPUBLIC	
IDENTITY UNKNOWN (BRITISH - RICHARD WYLER)	1960	66		1.5		PARAMOUNT	
IDIOT, THE (RUSSIAN - YURI YAKOVLEV)	1958	122	5		2.5	ARTKINO	
IDIOT'S DELIGHT	1939	105		3.5	3.5	M-G-M	
IDOL, THE (BRITISH)	1966	107	4			AVCO-EMBASSY	
IF . . . (BRITISH)	1968	110	5*	4.0		PARAMOUNT	
IF A MAN ANSWERS	1962	102	4*	2.0	2.5	UNIVERSAL	
IF ALL THE GUYS IN THE WORLD . . . (FRENCH)	a1956	95		2.5		UNITED ARTISTS	
IF EVERY GUY IN THE WORLD . . . (FRENCH)	a1956	95		2.5		UNITED ARTISTS	
IF HE HOLLERS, LET HIM GO!	1968	106		1.5		CINERAMA RELEASING	
IF I HAD A MILLION	1932	88	6*	3.5	3.5	PARAMOUNT	
IF I HAD MY WAY	1940	94			2.5	UNIVERSAL	
IF I WERE KING	1938	100	6*	3.0	3.0	PARAMOUNT	
IF I'M LUCKY	1946	79		2.0	2.0	20th CENTURY FOX	
IF IT'S TUESDAY, THIS MUST BE BELGIUM	1969	99	4			UNITED ARTISTS	
IF THIS BE SIN (BRITISH)	1950	72		1.5	2.0	UNITED ARTISTS	
IF WINTER COMES	1948	97	3	1.0	2.0	M-G-M	
IF YOU COULD ONLY COOK	1935	70		2.5	3.0	COLUMBIA	
IF YOU KNEW SUSIE	1948	90		2.0	2.5	RKO	
IKIRU (JAPANESE)	1952	140	7			BRANDON	
IL BIDONE (ITALIAN)	a1955	92	4*	2.5	2.0	ASTOR	
IL GRIDO (ITALIAN)	a1957	115	4	2.0	2.5	ASTOR	
IL SUCCESSO (ITALIAN)	a1963	103	6	3.5	3.0	AVCO-EMBASSY	
I'LL BE SEEING YOU	1944	85		2.5	2.5	UNITED ARTISTS	
I'LL BE YOURS	1947	93		2.5	2.0	UNIVERSAL	
I'LL CRY TOMORROW	1955	117	5-6*	4.0	3.5	M-G-M	
I'LL GET BY	1950	83		2.5	2.5	20th CENTURY FOX	
I'LL GET YOU (BRITISH)	1953	79	2	2.0	2.0	LIPPERT PRODS.	
I'LL GIVE A MILLION	1938	72		2.5	2.0	20th CENTURY FOX	
I'LL NEVER FORGET WHAT'S 'IS NAME (BRITISH)	1967	99	5	3.5		REGIONAL	
I'LL NEVER FORGET YOU (BRITISH)	1951	90		2.5	2.5	20th CENTURY FOX	
I'LL REACH FOR A STAR	a1937	83		2.0		REPUBLIC	
I'LL REMEMBER APRIL	1945	63		2.0	1.5	UNIVERSAL	
I'LL SEE YOU IN HELL (ITALIAN)	1963	83		1.5		MEDALLION	
I'LL SEE YOU IN MY DREAMS	1952	110		3.0	2.5	WARNER BROTHERS	
I'LL TAKE ROMANCE	1937	85			2.5	COLUMBIA	
I'LL TAKE SWEDEN	1965	96		2.5	2.0	UNITED ARTISTS	
I'LL TELL THE WORLD	1945	61			2.0	UNIVERSAL	
I'LL WAIT FOR YOU	1941	75		1.5		M-G-M	
ILLEGAL	1955	88		2.0	2.5	WARNER BROTHERS	

‡ An asterisk (*) in THE FILM BUFF'S BIBLE column indicates that the film has been rated by the editor and/or staff. All other ratings in this column are based on a consensus of reviews (see NOTES).

TITLE (LEADING ACTORS SHOWN WHERE TWO OR MORE FILMS HAVE THE SAME OR SIMILAR TITLE)	YEAR RELEASED	RUNNING TIME IN MINUTES	THE FILM BUFF'S BIBLE ‡	STEVEN SCHEUER	LEONARD MALTIN	DISTRIBUTOR	COMMENT
ILLEGAL CARGO (FRENCH)	1958	90		1.5			
ILLEGAL ENTRY	1949	84	4	2.5	2.5	UNIVERSAL	
ILLICIT INTERLUDE (SWEDISH)	a1951	90	5		2.5	ROBERT HAKIM	
ILLUSTRATED MAN, THE	1969	103	4*			WARNER BROTHERS	
I'M ALL RIGHT, JACK (BRITISH)	1959	104	5-6*	4.0	3.0	COLUMBIA	
I'M FROM MISSOURI	1939	80		3.0		PARAMOUNT	
I'M NO ANGEL	1933	87		3.0	3.5	PARAMOUNT	
I'M NOBODY'S SWEETHEART NOW	1940	63		2.5		UNIVERSAL	
IMITATION GENERAL	1958	120	4*	3.0	2.5	M-G-M	
IMITATION OF LIFE (CLAUDETTE COLBERT)	1934	106	5-6*	4.0	2.5	UNIVERSAL	NOMINATED BEST PICTURE
IMITATION OF LIFE (LANA TURNER, JOHN GAVIN)	1959	124		2.5	3.0	UNIVERSAL	
IMMORTAL, THE (T.V.)	1969	75		2.5		PARAMOUNT	
IMMORTAL BATTALION, THE (BRITISH)	a1944	106		3.5	3.0	20th CENTURY FOX	
IMMORTAL MONSTER, THE (ITALIAN)	1959	76		2.0			
IMMORTAL SERGEANT, THE	1943	91		2.5	2.5	20th CENTURY FOX	
IMMORTAL STORY, THE (FRENCH)	1968	63	6	3.5		FLEETWOOD FILMS	ENGLISH LANGUAGE
IMPACT	1949	111		1.5	2.5	UNITED ARTISTS	
IMPASSE	1969	100	2			UNITED ARTISTS	
IMPATIENT YEARS, THE	1944	91		2.0	2.5	COLUMBIA	
IMPERFECT ANGEL (GERMAN)	1964	98		1.5		PARAMOUNT	
IMPERFECT LADY, THE	1947	97		2.5	2.0	PARAMOUNT	
IMPERSONATOR, THE (BRITISH)	1961	64	2	2.0	2.0	CONTINENTAL	
IMPORTANCE OF BEING EARNEST, THE (BRITISH)	1952	95	7*	3.0	3.0	UNIVERSAL	
IMPOSSIBLE ON SATURDAY (FRENCH)	1965	120	6			MAGNA PICTURES	
IMPOSSIBLE YEARS, THE	1968	92	3	1.5		M-G-M	
IMPOSTER, THE	a1944	95		2.5	2.5	UNIVERSAL	
IN A LONELY PLACE	1950	91	6*	3.5	3.0	COLUMBIA	
IN-BETWEEN AGE, THE (BRITISH)	1958	76		2.0		ALLIED ARTISTS	
IN BROAD DAYLIGHT (T.V.)	1971	75	4*			ABC FILMS	
IN CALIENTE	1935	84		2.5	2.5	FIRST NATIONAL	
IN COLD BLOOD	1967	134	7	4.0		COLUMBIA	
IN ENEMY COUNTRY	1968	107		2.5	2.0	UNIVERSAL	
IN FAST COMPANY	1946	61			-	MONOGRAM	
IN HARM'S WAY	1965	165	3*	2.5		PARAMOUNT	
IN LIKE FLINT	1967	114	4*	3.0		20th CENTURY FOX	
IN LOVE AND WAR	1958	111		2.5	2.5	20th CENTURY FOX	
IN NAME ONLY (CAROLE LOMBARD, CARY GRANT)	1939	102		3.0	3.0	RKO	
IN NAME ONLY (T.V. - MICHAEL CALLAN, ANN PRENTISS)	1969	75		1.0		SCREEN GEMS	
IN OLD ARIZONA	1929	97				20th CENTURY FOX	NOMINATED BEST PICTURE 1928/29
IN OLD CALIFORNIA	1942	88		2.0	2.0	REPUBLIC	
IN OLD CHICAGO	1937	110	4*	3.5	3.5	20th CENTURY FOX	NOMINATED BEST PICTURE
IN OLD KENTUCKY	1935	86			2.5	20th CENTURY FOX	
IN OLD SACRAMENTO	1946	89		2.5		REPUBLIC	
IN OLD VIENNA (AUSTRIAN)	1956	69		1.0		REPUBLIC	
IN OUR TIME	1944	110		2.0	2.5	WARNER BROTHERS	
IN PERSON	1935	87		2.5		RKO	
IN SEARCH OF AMERICA (T.V.)	1971	90	5*	2.5		FOUR STAR	
IN SEARCH OF GREGORY (BRITISH)	1970	90	3	2.0		UNIVERSAL	
IN SEARCH OF THE CASTAWAYS (BRITISH)	1962	100	6			BUENA VISTA	
IN SOCIETY	1944	75			2.0	UNIVERSAL	
IN THE COOL OF THE DAY	1963	89	3	2.5	2.5	M-G-M	
IN THE DOGHOUSE (BRITISH)	1964	93	5	2.5		CONTINENTAL	
IN THE FRENCH STYLE	1963	106		3.0	2.5	COLUMBIA	
IN THE GOOD OLD SUMMERTIME	1949	102	6	3.0	3.0	M-G-M	
IN THE HEAT OF THE NIGHT	1967	109	7*	4.0		UNITED ARTISTS	BEST PICTURE AWARD
IN THE MEANTIME, DARLING	1944	72		2.0	2.0	20th CENTURY FOX	
IN THE MONEY	1958	61			-	ALLIED ARTISTS	
IN THE NAVY (ABBOTT & COSTELLO)	a1941	85		2.5	2.5	UNIVERSAL	
IN THE WAKE OF A STRANGER (BRITISH)	1958	69		2.0	2.0	PARAMOUNT	
IN THE YEAR OF THE PIG (DOCUMENTARY)	1969	101	6			PATHE CONTEMPARARY	
IN THIS OUR LIFE	1942	97		2.5	3.0	WARNER BROTHERS	
IN WHICH WE SERVE (BRITISH)	1942	114	4*	4.0	4.0	UNIVERSAL	NOMINATED BEST PICTURE
INADMISSIBLE EVIDENCE (BRITISH)	1968	96	6	4.0		PARAMOUNT	
INCENDIARY BLONDE	1945	113		3.0	3.0	PARAMOUNT	
INCIDENT, THE	1967	107	5	2.5		20th CENTURY FOX	
INCIDENT AT MIDNIGHT (BRITISH)	1963	58		2.0	2.0	SCHOENFELD FILM DIST	
INCIDENT AT PHANTOM HILL	1966	88		2.0	2.5	UNIVERSAL	
INCIDENT IN AN ALLEY	1962	83	3			UNITED ARTISTS	
INCIDENT IN SAIGON (FRENCH)	1960	85		1.5		AMERICAN-INTERNAT'L	
INCIDENT IN SAN FRANCISCO (T.V.)	1971	100		2.0		ABC FILMS	
INCREDIBLE JOURNEY, THE	1963	80	6			BUENA VISTA	
INCREDIBLE MR LIMPET, THE	1964	99		2.0	2.0	WARNER BROTHERS	
INCREDIBLE PETRIFIED WORLD, THE (BRITISH)	1958	70		1.5	2.0	GOVERNOR	
INCREDIBLE SHRINKING MAN, THE	1957	81	5	3.0	3.0	UNIVERSAL	
INCREDIBLE 2-HEADED TRANSPLANT, THE	1971	88	1			AMERICAN-INTERNAT'L	
INCREDIBLY STRANGE CREATURES WHO STOPPED LIVING AND BECAME MIXED-UP ZOMBIES, THE	1962	82		1.0		FAIRWAY INTERNAT'L	
INDESTRUCTIBLE MAN, THE	1956	70		1.0	2.0	ALLIED ARTISTS	
INDIAN FIGHTER, THE	1955	88	4	2.5	3.0	UNITED ARTISTS	
INDIAN PAINT	1966	91		2.0		CROWN INTERNATIONAL	
INDIAN SCARF, THE (GERMAN)	1963	85		1.5	2.0	UCC FILMS	
INDIAN UPRISING	1952	75		2.0	2.0	COLUMBIA	
INDISCREET (BRITISH)	1958	100		3.5	3.0	WARNER BROTHERS	
INDISCRETION OF AN AMERICAN WIFE	1954	63		2.0	2.5	COLUMBIA	

‡ An asterisk (*) in THE FILM BUFF'S BIBLE column indicates that the film has been rated by the editor and/or staff. All other ratings in this column are based on a consensus of reviews (see NOTES).

TITLE (LEADING ACTORS SHOWN WHERE TWO OR MORE FILMS HAVE THE SAME OR SIMILAR TITLE)	YEAR RELEASED	RUNNING TIME IN MINUTES	THE FILM BUFF'S BIBLE ‡	STEVEN SCHEUER	LEONARD MALTIN	DISTRIBUTOR	COMMENT
INFERNO	1953	83		3.0	2.5	20th CENTURY FOX	
INFORMATION RECEIVED (BRITISH)	1961	77	3		2.0	UNIVERSAL	
INFORMER, THE (VICOTR MCLAGLEN)	1935	91	6*	4.0	4.0	RKO	NOMINATED BEST PICTURE
INFORMERS, THE (BRITISH - NIGEL PATRICK)	a1965	104	4	2.5	3.0	CONTINENTAL	
INGA (SWEDISH)	1968	81	1	1.0		CINEMATION INDUS.	
INHERIT THE WIND	1960	127	7*	4.0	3.5	UNITED ARTISTS	
INHERITANCE, THE (BRITISH - JEAN SIMMONS)	a1947	98	4*	3.0	3.0	J. ARTHUR RANK	
INHERITANCE, THE (JAPANESE, DOCUMENTARY)	1964	60	6			SHOCHIKU	
INN OF THE SIXTH HAPPINESS, THE (BRITISH)	1958	158		3.5	3.0	20th CENTURY FOX	
INN ON DARTMOOR, THE (GERMAN)	1964	90		1.5		UCC FILMS	
INN ON THE RIVER, THE (GERMAN)	1962	95		1.5	2.5	UCC FILMS	
INNER SANCTUM	1948	62			2.0	FILM CLASSICS	
INNOCENT AFFAIR, AN	a1948	90	4	2.0	2.0	UNITED ARTISTS	
INNOCENTS, THE (BRITISH)	1961	100	6-7*	4.0		20th CENTURY FOX	
INNOCENTS IN PARIS (BRITISH)	1953	103		2.5	3.0	TUDOR PICTURES	
INSIDE A GIRLS' DORMITORY (FRENCH)	1953	102		2.0		ELLIS FILMS	
INSIDE DAISY CLOVER	1965	128	3*	2.5	2.5	WARNER BROTHERS	
INSIDE DETROIT	1956	82		2.0	2.0	COLUMBIA	
INSIDE JOB	1946	65		2.0	2.0	UNIVERSAL	
INSIDE NORTH VIET NAM (DOCUMENTARY)	1967	85	6	3.0		IMPACT FILMS	
INSIDE STORY, THE	1948	87		2.0	2.0	REPUBLIC	
INSIDE STRAIGHT	1951	89		2.0	2.5	M-G-M	
INSIDE THE MAFIA	1959	72	2	2.0	2.5	UNITED ARTISTS	
INSIDE THE WALLS OF FOLSOM PRISON	1951	87		2.0	2.5	WARNER BROTHERS	
INSPECTOR CALLS, AN (BRITISH)	1954	79		3.0	3.0	ASSOCIATED ARTISTS	
INSPECTOR CLOUSEAU (BRITISH)	1968	105	3	1.0		UNITED ARTISTS	
INSPECTOR GENERAL, THE	1949	102	4*	4.0	3.0	WARNER BROTHERS	
INSPECTOR MAIGRET (FRENCH)	a1958	110		2.5	2.5	LOPERT	
INSPIRATION	1931	74		2.0	2.5	M-G-M	
INTENT TO KILL (BRITISH)	1958	89	3*	1.5	2.5	20th CENTURY FOX	
INTERLUDE (JUNE ALLYSON, ROSSANO BRAZZI)	1957	90		2.5	2.5	UNIVERSAL	
INTERLUDE (BRITISH - OSCAR WERNER, BARBARA FERRIS)	1968	113	4-5*	2.0		COLUMBIA	
INTERMEZZO	1939	66	5-6*	3.0	3.5	UNITED ARTISTS	
INTERNATIONAL COUNTERFEITERS (GERMAN)	1957	70		1.0		REPUBLIC	
INTERNATIONAL HOUSE	1933	70	3*	3.0	3.5	PARAMOUNT	
INTERNATIONAL LADY	1941	102		2.5	2.5	UNITED ARTISTS	
INTERNATIONAL SETTLEMENT	1938	75		2.5	2.5	20th CENTURY FOX	
INTERNATIONAL SQUADRON	1941	87		2.5	2.5	WARNER BROTHERS	
INTERNES CAN'T TAKE MONEY	1937	77		2.0	-	PARAMOUNT	
INTERNS, THE	1962	120		2.0	3.0	COLUMBIA	
INTERPLAY	1970	97	1			TIMES-FILM CORP.	
INTERPOL CODE 8 (JAPANESE)	1965	94		1.0		PARAMOUNT	
INTERRUPTED JOURNEY, THE (BRITISH)	1949	80		2.5	2.5	CONTINENTAL	
INTERRUPTED MELODY	1955	106	6	3.0	3.5	M-G-M	
INTIMATE LIGHTING (CZECH)	1965	71	3*			PROMENADE	
INTIMATE RELATIONS (BRITISH)	a1953	85		1.5		CARROLL PICTURES	
INTOLERANCE (SILENT)	1916	220	3*				STRICTLY FOR CINEMA SCHOLARS
INTRIGUE (GEORGE RAFT, JUNE HAVOC)	1947	90		2.0	2.0	UNITED ARTISTS	
INTRUDER, THE (BRITISH - JACK HAWKINS)	1953	84		3.0	2.5	ASSOCIATED ARTISTS	
INTRUDER, THE (WILLIAM SHATNER)	a1962	80	5			PATHE-AMERICA	
INTRUDER IN THE DUST	1949	89	6	4.0	3.0	M-G-M	
INTRUDERS, THE (T.V. - DON MURRAY, ANNE FRANCIS)	a1967	100		2.5		UNIVERSAL	
INVADERS, THE (BRITISH)	a1941	105	6*	3.5	3.5	COLUMBIA	NOMINATED BEST PICTURE 1942
INVADERS FROM MARS	1953	78		1.5	2.0	20th CENTURY FOX	
INVASION (BRITISH)	1966	82		2.0	2.5	AMERICAN-INTERNAT'L	
INVASION OF THE ANIMAL PEOPLE	1962	72		1.0		MEDALLION	
INVASION OF THE BODY SNATCHERS	1956	80	5	3.5	3.0	ALLIED ARTISTS	
INVASION OF THE NEPTUNE MEN (JAPANESE)	1963	82		1.0		TELEWORLD	
INVASION OF THE SAUCER MEN	1957	69		2.0	1.5	AMERICAN-INTERNAT'L	
INVASION OF THE STAR CREATURES	1962	70		1.5		AMERICAN-INTERNAT'L	
INVASION OF THE VAMPIRES, THE (MEXICAN)	1962	92		1.0		AZTECA	
INVASION QUARTET (BRITISH)	1961	87	3			M-G-M	
INVASION 1700	1965	112	3			MEDALLION	
INVASION, U.S.A.	1953	74		1.5	1.5	COLUMBIA	
INVESTIGATION OF A CITIZEN ABOVE SUSPICION (ITAL.)	1970	112	7*			COLUMBIA	
INVINCIBLE BROTHERS MACISTE, THE (ITALIAN)	1964	92		1.0		ABC FILMS	
INVINCIBLE GLADIATOR, THE (ITALIAN)	1961	92	2	2.0	2.5	WARNER BROTHERS	
INVINCIBLE SIX	1970	94	2			CONTINENTAL	
INVISIBLE AGENT	1942	81			2.0	UNIVERSAL	
INVISIBLE BOY, THE	1957	85		2.5	2.5	M-G-M	
INVISIBLE CREATURE, THE (BRITISH)	a1959	70		2.0	2.0	AMERICAN-INTERNAT'L	
INVISIBLE DR MABUSE, THE (GERMAN)	1961	89		1.5	2.5	TELEWIDE SYSTEMS	
INVISIBLE GHOST, THE	1941	64			2.0	MONOGRAM	
INVISIBLE INVADERS	1959	67		1.0	1.5	UNITED ARTISTS	
INVISIBLE MAN, THE	1933	71	6*	3.5	3.5	UNIVERSAL	
INVISIBLE MAN RETURNS, THE	1940	81	5*	3.0	3.0	UNIVERSAL	
INVISIBLE MAN'S REVENGE, THE	1944	77			2.5	UNIVERSAL	
INVISIBLE MENACE	1938	55		2.5		WARNER BROTHERS	
INVISIBLE RAY, THE	1936	81		2.0	2.5	UNIVERSAL	
INVISIBLE STRIPES	1940	82		2.5	3.0	WARNER BROTHERS	
INVISIBLE TERROR, THE (GERMAN)	1963	102		1.5		UCC FILMS	
INVISIBLE WOMAN, THE	1941	72			2.5	UNIVERSAL	
INVITATION	1952	84	3*	3.0	2.5	M-G-M	
INVITATION TO A GUNFIGHTER	1964	92		2.0	2.5	UNITED ARTISTS	

‡ An asterisk (*) in THE FILM BUFF'S BIBLE column indicates that the film has been rated by the editor and/or staff. All other ratings in this column are based on a consensus of reviews (see NOTES).

TITLE (LEADING ACTORS SHOWN WHERE TWO OR MORE FILMS HAVE THE SAME OR SIMILAR TITLE)	YEAR RELEASED	RUNNING TIME IN MINUTES	THE FILM BUFF'S BIBLE ‡	STEVEN SCHEUER	LEONARD MALTIN	DISTRIBUTOR	COMMENT
INVITATION TO HAPPINESS	1939	95		2.5	2.5	PARAMOUNT	
INVITATION TO MURDER (BRITISH)	1962	55		2.0		ATLANTIC PICTURES	
IPCRESS FILE, THE (BRITISH)	1965	109	5*	4.0	3.5	UNIVERSAL	
IRENE	1940	104		2.5	3.0	RKO	
IRISH EYES ARE SMILING	1944	90		2.5	2.5	20th CENTURY FOX	
IRISH IN US, THE	1935	84		2.0	2.0	WARNER BROTHERS	
IRMA LA DOUCE	1963	142	5		2.5	UNITED ARTISTS	
IRON CURTAIN, THE	a1948	87		2.5	3.0	20th CENTURY FOX	
IRON DUKE, THE (BRITISH)	a1934	90	4*			GAUMONT-BRITISH	
IRON GLOVE, THE	1954	77	3	2.0	2.5	COLUMBIA	
IRON MAJOR, THE	1943	85		3.0	2.5	RKO	
IRON MAN (LEW AYRES, JEAN HARLOW)	1931	73			2.0	UNIVERSAL	
IRON MAN (JEFF CHANDLER, EVELYN KEYES)	1951	82		2.5	2.0	UNIVERSAL	
IRON MISTRESS, THE	1952	110		2.5	2.5	WARNER BROTHERS	
IRON PETTICOAT, THE (BRITISH)	1956	90	3	1.5		M-G-M	
IRON SHERIFF, THE	1957	73		2.0	1.5	UNITED ARTISTS	
IRONSIDE (T.V.)	1967	98			3.0	UNIVERSAL	
IROQUOIS TRAIL	1950	85		2.5	2.0	UNITED ARTISTS	
IS EVERYBODY HAPPY?	1943	73		2.5		COLUMBIA	
IS PARIS BURNING? (FRENCH)	1966	135	4*	2.0	2.0	PARAMOUNT	
IS THERE SEX AFTER DEATH?	1971	97	3			ABEL-CHILD	
IS YOUR HONEYMOON REALLY NECESSARY? (BRITISH)	1953	80		2.0		ASSOCIATED ARTISTS	
ISABEL (CANADIAN)	1968	108	6	3.5		PARAMOUNT	
ISADORA (BRITISH)	a1968	131	5*			UNIVERSAL	
ISLAND, THE (JAPANESE)	1961	96		3.5	3.0	ZENITH INTERNATIONAL	
ISLAND IN THE SKY (JOHN WAYNE, LLOYD NOLAN)	1953	109		3.0	2.5	WARNER BROTHERS	
ISLAND IN THE SUN	1957	119	4*	2.5	2.5	20th CENTURY FOX	
ISLAND OF DESIRE	1952	103		2.0	2.5	UNITED ARTISTS	
ISLAND OF DOOMED MEN	1940	67			2.0	COLUMBIA	
ISLAND OF LOST MEN	1939	63		1.5	1.5	PARAMOUNT	
ISLAND OF LOST SOULS	1933	70		3.0	3.0	PARAMOUNT	
ISLAND OF LOST WOMEN	1959	71	2	1.5	2.0	WARNER BROTHERS	
ISLAND OF LOVE	1963	101	4*	3.0	2.5	WARNER BROTHERS	
ISLAND OF TERROR (BRITISH)	1966	87	4	3.0		UNIVERSAL	
ISLAND OF THE BLUE DOLPHINS	1964	93	5	2.5		UNIVERSAL	
ISLAND PRINCESS, THE (ITALIAN)	1955	98		1.5	2.0	TRANS-AMERICA	
ISLAND RESCUE (BRITISH)	a1952	87	4	2.5	2.0	UNIVERSAL	
ISLE OF FURY	1936	60		1.5	2.0	WARNER BROTHERS	
ISLE OF LEVANT (DANISH, TRAVELOGUE)	1957	71	3			FILMS AROUND THE WLD.	
ISLE OF SIN (GERMAN)	1960	63			1.5	E.J. FANCEY	
ISLE OF THE DEAD	1945	72	4*	3.0	3.0	RKO	
ISN'T IT ROMANTIC?	1948	87	2	2.0	2.0	PARAMOUNT	
ISTANBUL	1957	84		2.0	2.0	UNIVERSAL	
ISTANBUL EXPRESS (T.V.)	1968	100		2.5		UNIVERSAL	
IT (BRITISH)	1967	95	2			WARNER BROTHERS	
IT AIN'T HAY	1943	80			2.5	UNIVERSAL	
IT ALL CAME TRUE	1940	97		2.5	2.5	WARNER BROTHERS	
IT ALWAYS RAINS ON SUNDAY (BRITISH)	1947	92		3.0	2.5	EAGLE LION	
IT CAME FROM BENEATH THE SEA	1955	80		2.0	2.0	COLUMBIA	
IT CAME FROM OUTER SPACE	1953	81		2.5	2.5	UNIVERSAL	
IT COMES UP MURDER	a1967	131	5-6*	3.0		UNITED ARTISTS	SLOW BUILDUP
IT CONQUERED THE WORLD	1956	68		2.0	2.0	AMERICAN-INTERNAT'L	
IT GROWS ON TREES	1952	84		2.5	2.0	UNIVERSAL	
IT HAD TO BE YOU	1947	98	4	2.5	2.5	COLUMBIA	
IT HAD TO HAPPEN	1936	79		2.5	2.0	20th CENTURY FOX	
IT HAPPENED AT THE WORLD'S FAIR	1963	105	3	2.0	3.0	M-G-M	
IT HAPPENED HERE (BRITISH)	1963	95	6			LOPERT	
IT HAPPENED IN ATHENS	1962	105	1			20th CENTURY FOX	
IT HAPPENED IN BROAD DAYLIGHT (SWISS)	1958	97	5	2.5		CONTINENTAL	
IT HAPPENED IN BROOKLYN	1947	105		2.5	2.0	M-G-M	
IT HAPPENED IN FLATBUSH	1942	80		2.5		20th CENTURY FOX	
IT HAPPENED IN PARIS (FRENCH - EVELYN KEYES)	1952	78		1.5		FILMS DE FRANCE	
IT HAPPENED IN ROME (ITALIAN)	1957	105	3	2.0		J. ARTHUR RANK	
IT HAPPENED IN THE PARK (FRENCH)	1957	81	6			ELLIS FILMS	
IT HAPPENED ON FIFTH AVENUE	1947	115		2.0	2.0	ALLIED ARTISTS	
IT HAPPENED ONE NIGHT	1934	105	6*	4.0	4.0	COLUMBIA	BEST PICTURE AWARD
IT HAPPENED ONE SUMMER	a1945	100	4*	3.0	3.0	20th CENTURY FOX	
IT HAPPENED TO JANE	a1959	98	5	2.5	2.5	COLUMBIA	
IT HAPPENED TOMORROW	1944	84		3.5	3.5	UNITED ARTISTS	
IT HAPPENS EVERY SPRING	1949	80	6	3.0	3.5	20th CENTURY FOX	
IT HAPPENS EVERY THURSDAY	1953	80		2.5	3.0	UNIVERSAL	
IT HAPPENS IN ROMA (ITALIAN)	1956	92		3.0			
IT MEANS THAT TO ME (FRENCH)	1962	88		1.5		ABC FILMS	
IT ONLY HAPPENS TO OTHERS	1971	88	4			GSF PRODUCTIONS	
IT SHOULD HAPPEN TO YOU	1954	81	5*	3.5	3.0	COLUMBIA	
IT SHOULDN'T HAPPEN TO A DOG	1946	70		2.0	2.5	20th CENTURY FOX	
IT STARTED IN NAPLES	1960	100	5*	3.0	2.5	PARAMOUNT	
IT STARTED IN PARADISE (BRITISH)	1953	88		3.0		ASTOR	
IT STARTED WITH A KISS	1959	104		2.5	2.5	M-G-M	
IT STARTED WITH EVE	1941	90		3.5	3.0	UNIVERSAL	
IT TAKES A THIEF (BRITISH)	a1960	89		1.5	2.0	VALIANT	
IT TAKES ALL KINDS	1969	98	3			GOLDSWORTHY	
IT! THE TERROR FROM BEYOND SPACE	1958	69		2.0	1.5	UNITED ARTISTS	
ITALIAN JOB, THE (BRITISH)	1969	101	4			PARAMOUNT	

‡ An asterisk (*) in THE FILM BUFF'S BIBLE column indicates that the film has been rated by the editor and/or staff. All other ratings in this column are based on a consensus of reviews (see NOTES).

TITLE (LEADING ACTORS SHOWN WHERE TWO OR MORE FILMS HAVE THE SAME OR SIMILAR TITLE)	YEAR RELEASED	RUNNING TIME IN MINUTES	THE FILM BUFF'S BIBLE ‡	STEVEN SCHEUER	LEONARD MALTIN	DISTRIBUTOR	COMMENT
ITALIAN STRAW HAT, THE (FRENCH, SILENT)	1927	76	3*			ALBATROSS	
ITALIANO BRAVE GENTE (ITALIAN)	a1963	156		2.5	3.0	AVCO-EMBASSY	
IT'S A BIG COUNTRY	1952	89		2.5	3.0	M-G-M	
IT'S A BIKINI WORLD	1967	86		2.0		TRANS-AMERICA	
IT'S A DOG'S LIFE	a1955	88		3.5	2.5	M-G-M	
IT'S A GIFT	1934	73	4*	3.0	4.0	PARAMOUNT	
IT'S A GREAT FEELING	1949	85	5	3.0	3.0	WARNER BROTHERS	
IT'S A GREAT LIFE (PENNY SINGLETON, ARTHUR LAKE)	1943	75		2.5	.	COLUMBIA	
IT'S A JOKE, SON	1947	63			2.0	EAGLE LION	
IT'S A MAD, MAD, MAD, MAD WORLD	1963	153	7			UNITED ARTISTS	
IT'S A PLEASURE	1945	90		2.0	2.0	RKO	
IT'S A WONDERFUL LIFE	1946	129	7	3.5	3.5	RKO	NOMINATED BEST PICTURE
IT'S A WONDERFUL WORLD (CLAUDETTE COLBERT)	1939	86		3.0	3.0	M-G-M	
IT'S ALWAYS FAIR WEATHER	1955	102	6	3.0	3.0	M-G-M	
IT'S GREAT TO BE YOUNG (LESLIE BROOKS, JIM LLOYD)	1946	68		1.0		COLUMBIA	
IT'S GREAT TO BE YOUNG (BRITISH - JOHN MILLS)	1956	92	5			FINE ARTS	
IT'S IN THE AIR	1935	80		2.5	2.0	M-G-M	
IT'S IN THE BAG (FRED ALLEN, JACK BENNY)	1945	87		3.0	3.0	UNITED ARTISTS	
IT'S LOVE I'M AFTER	1937	90	7*		3.0	FIRST NATIONAL	
IT'S NEVER TOO LATE (BRITISH)	1956	96		2.0	2.5	SEVEN ARTS	
IT'S NOT CRICKET (BRITISH)	1949	78		2.0		J. ARTHUR RANK	
IT'S ONLY MONEY	1962	84	4	2.5	3.0	PARAMOUNT	
IT'S TOUGH TO BE FAMOUS	1932	79		3.0		FIRST NATIONAL	
IT'S YOUR THING	1970	120	4			MEDFORD FILMS	
IVALLO THE GREAT (BULGARIAN)	1963	89		1.5		FOUR STAR	
IVAN (SON OF THE WHITE DEVIL)	1954	75		2.0		DIST. CORP. OF AMER.	
IVAN THE TERRIBLE, PART I (RUSSIAN)	1943	95	3*			ARTKINO	
IVAN THE TERRIBLE, PART II (RUSSIAN)	1958	87	6			ARTKINO	COMPLETED IN 1946
IVANHOE	1952	106	6	3.0	3.0	M-G-M	NOMINATED BEST PICTURE
I'VE ALWAYS LOVED YOU	1946	117	6		3.0	REPUBLIC	
I'VE LIVED BEFORE	1956	82		2.0	2.5	UNIVERSAL	
IVORY HUNTER (BRITISH)	a1951	97		3.5	2.5	UNIVERSAL	
IVY	1947	99		3.0	2.5	UNIVERSAL	
IVY LEAGUE KILLERS (CANADIAN)	1962	70		1.5		PARAMOUNT	
J. W. COOP	1972	112	5			COLUMBIA	
JACK AND THE BEANSTALK	1952	87		1.5	2.5	WARNER BROTHERS	
JACK FROST (RUSSIAN)	a1965	79	3*			AVCO-EMBASSY	
JACK LONDON	a1943	94		3.0	3.0	UNITED ARTISTS	
JACK MCCALL, DESPERADO	1953	76		2.0	2.0	COLUMBIA	
JACK OF DIAMONDS (GEORGE HAMILTON, JOSEPH COTTON)	1967	108	3	2.0		M-G-M	
JACK SLADE	1953	90	2		2.0	ALLIED ARTISTS	
JACK THE GIANT KILLER	1962	94	5		3.0	UNITED ARTISTS	
JACK THE RIPPER (BRITISH)	1959	88	2	2.0	2.0	PARAMOUNT	
JACKASS MAIL	1942	80		2.5	2.0	M-G-M	
JACKIE ROBINSON STORY, THE	1950	76		3.0	3.0	EAGLE LION	
JACKPOT (BRITISH - WILLIAM HARTNELL)	1960	71		1.5		GRAND NATIONAL	
JACKPOT, THE (JAMES STEWART, BARBARA HALE)	1950	85	4*	3.5	2.5	20th CENTURY FOX	
JACQUELINE (BRITISH)	1956	92		3.0	2.0	J. ARTHUR RANK	
JADE MASK, THE	1945	66		.		MONOGRAM	
JAGUAR	1956	66		1.5	1.5	REPUBLIC	
JAIL BUSTERS	1955	61				ALLIED ARTISTS	
JAIL HOUSE BLUES	1941	62		2.5		UNIVERSAL	
JAILBREAK (BRITISH - PETER REYNOLDS)	1960			2.0			
JAILBREAKERS, THE	1960	64	2	1.0		AMERICAN-INTERNAT'L	
JAILHOUSE ROCK	1957	96	3	2.0	3.0	M-G-M	
JALOPY	1953	62	1	.	.	ALLIED ARTISTS	
JAM SESSION	1944	77		2.0	2.0	COLUMBIA	
JAMAICA INN (BRITISH)	1939	98		3.5	2.0	PARAMOUNT	
JAMAICA RUN	1953	92		2.0	2.0	PARAMOUNT	
JAMBOREE (KAY MEDFORD, ROBERT PASTINE)	1957	86		1.5		WARNER BROTHERS	
JAMES DEAN STORY, THE (DOCUMENTARY)	1957	82		2.0	2.0	WARNER BROTHERS	
JAN HUS (CZECH)	1955	120		2.5		CONTEMPORARY	
JANE EYRE (JOAN FONTAINE, ORSON WELLES)	1944	96	5*	3.0	3.0	20th CENTURY FOX	
JANE EYRE (BRIT. - GEORGE C. SCOTT, SUSANNAH YORK)	1971	100	6*			BRITISH-LION	
JANIE	1944	106		2.5	2.5	WARNER BROTHERS	
JANIE GETS MARRIED	1946	89		2.5	2.5	WARNER BROTHERS	
JAPANESE WAR BRIDE	1952	91		2.0	2.5	20th CENTURY FOX	
JASON AND THE ARGONAUTS (BRITISH)	1963	104	4	2.5	2.5	COLUMBIA	
JASSY (BRITISH)	1944	96		1.5	2.5	UNIVERSAL	
JAVA HEAD (BRITISH - RALPH RICHARDSON)	1934	70			2.0	FIRST DIVISION	
JAYHAWKERS, THE	1959	100		2.5	2.5	PARAMOUNT	
JAZZ BALL	1956	60		2.0		HAL ROACH	
JAZZ BOAT (BRITISH)	1960	96		2.0	2.5	COLUMBIA	
JAZZ ON A SUMMER'S DAY (DOCUMENTARY)	1960	85	6			GALAXY ATTRACTIONS	
JAZZ SINGER, THE (AL JOLSON, MAY MCAVOY)	1927	88	3*	3.0	2.5	WARNER BROTHERS	
JAZZ SINGER, THE (DANNY THOMAS, PEGGY LEE)	1953	107	6	3.0	2.5	WARNER BROTHERS	
JEALOUSY	1945	71			2.0	REPUBLIC	
JEANNE EAGELS	1957	109		2.5	2.5	COLUMBIA	
JENNIE GERHARDT	1933	85		2.5	3.0	PARAMOUNT	
JENNIFER	1953	73	2		2.5	ALLIED ARTISTS	
JENNIFER ON MY MIND	1971	90	1			UNITED ARTISTS	

‡ An asterisk (*) in THE FILM BUFF'S BIBLE column indicates that the film has been rated by the editor and/or staff. All other ratings in this column are based on a consensus of reviews (see NOTES).

TITLE (LEADING ACTORS SHOWN WHERE TWO OR MORE FILMS HAVE THE SAME OR SIMILAR TITLE)	YEAR RELEASED	RUNNING TIME IN MINUTES	THE FILM BUFF'S BIBLE ‡	STEVEN SCHEUER	LEONARD MALTIN	DISTRIBUTOR	COMMENT
JENNY	1970	88	4			CINERAMA RELEASING	
JEOPARDY	1953	69		2.5	2.5	M-G-M	
JERUSALEM FILE, THE	1972	96	2			M-G-M	
JESSE JAMES	1939	105	4*	3.5	3.0	20th CENTURY FOX	
JESSE JAMES MEETS FRANKENSTEIN'S DAUGHTER	1966	82		1.0	1.5	AVCO-EMBASSY	
JESSE JAMES VS THE DALTONS	1954	65	2	2.0	2.0	COLUMBIA	
JESSE JAMES' WOMEN	1954	83		1.5	1.5	UNITED ARTISTS	
JESSICA	1962	112		2.0	2.5	UNITED ARTISTS	
JESUS TRIP, THE	1971	84				EMCO FILMS	
JET ATTACK	1958	68	2	1.5	1.0	AMERICAN-INTERNAT'L	
JET JOB	1952	63	2	1.5		MONOGRAM	
JET OVER THE ATLANTIC	1959	95		2.5	2.0	INTERCONTINENTAL	
JET PILOT (BRITISH)	1957	112	3			UNIVERSAL	
JET STORM	1959	88	6			UNITED PRODUCERS ORG.	
JEWEL ROBERY	1932	70		2.0	2.5	WARNER BROTHERS	
JEZEBEL	1938	104		3.0	3.5	WARNER BROTHERS	NOMINATED BEST PICTURE
JIGSAW (FRANCHOT TONE, JEAN WALLACE)	a1949	70	4		2.0	UNITED ARTISTS	
JIGSAW (BRITISH - JACK WARNER, RONALD LEWIS)	1962	107	3	2.5		BEVERLY	
JIGSAW (HARRY GUARDINO, BRADFORD DILLMAN)	1968	97	3	2.5	2.5	UNIVERSAL	
JIM THORPE - ALL AMERICAN	1951	107	4*	3.0	3.0	WARNER BROTHERS	
JIMMY THE GENT	1934	67		3.0	2.5	WARNER BROTHERS	
JINX MONEY	1948	68			-	MONOGRAM	
JITTERBUGS	1943	74			2.0	20th CENTURY FOX	
JIVARO	1954	91		2.5	2.0	PARAMOUNT	
JOAN OF ARC	1948	145	4*	2.5	2.5	RKO	CUT TO 100 MINUTES FOR T.V.
JOAN OF OZARK	1942	80		1.0	2.0	REPUBLIC	
JOAN OF PARIS	1942	95	5*	3.5	3.5	RKO	
JOAN OF THE ANGELS? (POLISH)	1961	101				TELEPIX CORP.	
JOANNA (BRITISH)	1968	107	4			20th CENTURY FOX	
JOE	1970	107	8*			CANNON RELEASING	
JOE AND ETHEL TURP CALL ON THE PRESIDENT	1939	70		2.5		M-G-M	
JOE BUTTERFLY	1957	90	4	2.0	2.5	UNIVERSAL	
JOE COCKER/MAD DOGS AND ENGLISHMEN (DOCUMENTARY)	a1971	114	5			M-G-M	
JOE DAKOTA	1957	79	5*	2.5	2.5	UNIVERSAL	
JOE HILL (SWEDISH)	a1971	113	5			PARAMOUNT	ENGLISH LANGUAGE
JOE KIDD	1972	88	3			UNIVERSAL	
JOE LOUIS STORY, THE	1953	88	4		2.0	UNITED ARTISTS	
JOE MACBETH (BRITISH)	1955	90		2.5	2.5	COLUMBIA	
JOE PALOOKA IN TRIPLE CROSS	a1951	60	1			MONOGRAM	
JOE SMITH, AMERICAN	1942	63		2.5	2.0	M-G-M	
JOHN AND JULIE (BRITISH)	1955	82		2.5		DIST. CORP. OF AMER.	
JOHN AND MARY	1969	92	5*			20th CENTURY FOX	
JOHN F. KENNEDY: YEARS OF LIGHTNING, DAY OF DRUMS	1966	87	7*			AVCO-EMBASSY	(DOCUMENTARY)
JOHN GOLDFARB, PLEASE COME HOME	1965	96	2*	1.5	1.5	20th CENTURY FOX	
JOHN LOVES MARY	1949	96	5	2.5	2.5	WARNER BROTHERS	
JOHN MEADE'S WOMAN	1937	87		1.5	2.0	AMERICAN RELEASING	
JOHN PAUL JONES	1959	126		2.5	2.5	WARNER BROTHERS	
JOHNNY ALLEGRO	1949	81		2.5	2.5	COLUMBIA	
JOHNNY ANGEL	1945	79		3.0	3.0	RKO	
JOHNNY APOLLO	1940	93		3.0	3.0	20th CENTURY FOX	
JOHNNY BANCO	1972	90				H.K. FILM DIST.	
JOHNNY BELINDA	1948	102	7	3.5	3.5	WARNER BROTHERS	NOMINATED BEST PICTURE
JOHNNY CASH! (DOCUMENTARY)	1969	94	5			CONTINENTAL	
JOHNNY COME LATELY	1943	97		2.5	2.5	UNITED ARTISTS	
JOHNNY CONCHO	1956	84	5*	2.0	2.5	UNITED ARTISTS	
JOHNNY COOL	1963	101		2.0	3.0	UNITED ARTISTS	
JOHNNY DARK	1954	85		2.0	2.5	UNIVERSAL	
JOHNNY DOESN'T LIVE HERE ANYMORE	a1944	79		3.0	2.5	MONOGRAM	
JOHNNY DOUGHBOY	1942	63		2.0		REPUBLIC	
JOHNNY EAGER	1941	107	6*	3.5	2.5	M-G-M	
JOHNNY GOT HIS GUN	1971	112	6			CINEMATION INDUS.	
JOHNNY GUITAR	1954	110	6*	3.0	3.0	REPUBLIC	
JOHNNY GUNMAN	1957	70		1.0		TUDOR PICTURES	
JOHNNY HAMLET	1972	91				TRANSVUE PICS.	
JOHNNY HOLIDAY	1950	92	4*	3.5	3.0	UNITED ARTISTS	
JOHNNY IN THE CLOUDS (BRITISH)	a1945	109		3.5	3.5	UNITED ARTISTS	
JOHNNY MINOTAUR	1971	80	2			IMPACT FILMS	
JOHNNY NOBODY (BRITISH)	1960	88	4	3.0	2.5	MEDALLION	
JOHNNY O'CLOCK	1947	95		2.5	2.5	COLUMBIA	
JOHNNY ONE-EYE	1950	78		2.0	2.0	UNITED ARTISTS	
JOHNNY RENO	1966	83	2			PARAMOUNT	
JOHNNY ROCCO	1958	84		2.0	2.0	ALLIED ARTISTS	
JOHNNY STOOL PIGEON	1949	76		2.5	2.5	UNIVERSAL	
JOHNNY TIGER	1966	102	3	2.5	2.5	UNIVERSAL	
JOHNNY TREMAINE	1957	80	4*			BUENA VISTA	
JOHNNY TROUBLE	1957	80	4	2.0	2.5	WARNER BROTHERS	
JOHNNY, YOU'RE WANTED (BRITISH)	1956	72		1.5		EROS FILMS	
JOHNNY YUMA (ITALIAN)	1966	99	1			ATLANTIC PICTURES	
JOKER, THE (FR. - ANOUK AIMEE, JEAN-PIERRE CASSEL)	1960	86	4			LOPERT	
JOKER IS WILD, THE	1958	126	5	3.0	3.0	PARAMOUNT	
JOKERS, THE (BRIT.- MICHAEL CRAWFORD, OLIVER REED)	1967	94	7*	3.5	3.0	UNIVERSAL	
JOLLY BAD FELLOW, A (BRITISH)	a1964	96	6*	3.5	2.0	CONTINENTAL	
JOLSON SINGS AGAIN	1950	96	4*	4.0	3.5	COLUMBIA	
JOLSON STORY, THE	1946	128	6*	4.0	3.5	COLUMBIA	

‡ An asterisk (*) in THE FILM BUFF'S BIBLE column indicates that the film has been rated by the editor and/or staff. All other ratings in this column are based on a consensus of reviews (see NOTES).

TITLE (LEADING ACTORS SHOWN WHERE TWO OR MORE FILMS HAVE THE SAME OR SIMILAR TITLE)	YEAR RELEASED	RUNNING TIME IN MINUTES	THE FILM BUFF'S BIBLE ‡	STEVEN SCHEUER	LEONARD MALTIN	DISTRIBUTOR	COMMENT
JONES FAMILY IN HOLLYWOOD	1939	60		2.0		20th CENTURY FOX	
JOSEPH AND HIS BRETHREN	a1960	103		1.5	2.0	COLORAMA FEATURES	
JOSEPH KILIAN (CZECH)	1966	40	6			CONTEMPORARY	
JOSEPHINE AND MEN (BRITISH)	1955	97		2.0		CONTINENTAL	
JOSETTE	1938	73		2.5	2.5	20th CENTURY FOX	
JOUR DE FETE (FRENCH)	a1949	75	4			MAYER-KINGSLEY	
JOURNEY, THE	1959	125	4*	2.5	3.0	M-G-M	
JOURNEY BENEATH THE DESERT	1963	105		1.5		AVCO-EMBASSY	
JOURNEY FOR MARGARET	1942	81		3.5	3.0	M-G-M	
JOURNEY INTO FEAR	1942	69		3.5	3.0	RKO	
JOURNEY INTO LIGHT	1951	87	3	2.5	2.5	20th CENTURY FOX	
JOURNEY INTO NOWHERE (BRITISH)	1963	67	5*	2.5		PRESIDENT FILMS	
JOURNEY OF ROBERT F. KENNEDY, THE (DOCUMENTARY)	1970	75		3.5		WOLPER PRODS.	
JOURNEY THROUGH ROSEBUD	1972	93	4			GSF	
JOURNEY TO FREEDOM (BRITISH)	1957	60		1.0	1.5	REPUBLIC	
JOURNEY TO JERUSALEM, A (DOCUMENTARY)	1968	84	6	3.0		SIGMA III	
JOURNEY TO SHILOH	1968	101		2.0	1.5	UNIVERSAL	
JOURNEY TO THE CENTER OF THE EARTH	1959	132	6*	3.0	3.0	20th CENTURY FOX	
JOURNEY TO THE FAR SIDE OF THE SUN	1969	99	3			UNIVERSAL	
JOURNEY TO THE LOST CITY (GERMAN)	1959	94		1.5	2.5	AMERICAN-INTERNAT'L	
JOURNEY TO THE SEVENTH PLANET (DANISH)	1961	80	2	2.0	2.0	AMERICAN-INTERNAT'L	
JOURNEY TOGETHER (BRITISH)	1945	95			2.0	ENGLISH FILMS	
JOURNEY'S END	1930	130				TIFFANY PRODS.	
JOY HOUSE (FRENCH)	a1964	95		2.5	2.5	M-G-M	
JOY IN THE MORNING	1965	103		2.5	2.0	M-G-M	
JOY OF LIVING	1938	90		3.5	3.0	RKO	
JOY RIDE	1958	60	3	3.0	1.5	ALLIED ARTISTS	
JUAREZ	1939	132	6-7*	4.0	3.0	WARNER BROTHERS	SLOW BUILDUP
JUBAL	1956	101	5*	3.5	2.5	COLUMBIA	
JUBILEE TRAIL	1954	103	4	2.5	2.5	REPUBLIC	
JUDGE, THE	1949	69			1.5	EAST COAST	
JUDGE HARDY AND SON	1939	87		2.0	-	M-G-M	
JUDGE HARDY'S CHILDREN	1938	78		2.5	-	M-G-M	
JUDGE STEPS OUT, THE	1949	91	4	2.5	2.5	RKO	
JUDGMENT AT NUREMBERG	1961	189	9*	4.0	4.0	UNITED ARTISTS	NOMINATED BEST PICTURE
JUDITH	1966	109	4	1.0		PARAMOUNT	
JUGGLER, THE	1953	86		3.0	2.5	COLUMBIA	
JUKE BOX RHYTHM	1959	81		1.0	1.5	COLUMBIA	
JUKE GIRL	1942	90		2.5	2.5	WARNER BROTHERS	
JULES AND JIM (FRENCH)	1962	105	6*			JANUS FILMS	
JULIA MISBEHAVES	1948	99	6	2.5	3.0	M-G-M	
JULIE	1956	99	4	2.0	2.5	M-G-M	
JULIE THE REDHEAD (FRENCH)	1959	96	4	2.5		SHAWN INTERNATIONAL	
JULIET OF THE SPIRITS (ITALIAN)	1965	145	2*		3.0	RIZZOLI FILM	
JULIETTA (FRENCH)	1957	96		2.0	2.5	KINGSLEY INTERNAT'L	
JULIETTE DE SADE (ITALIAN)	1970	83	1			HAVEN INTERNATIONAL	
JULIUS CAESAR (MARLIN BRANDO, JAMES MASON)	1953	120	7	4.0	3.5	M-G-M	NOMINATED BEST PICTURE
JULIUS CAESAR (BRITISH - CHARLTON HESTON)	1970	117	3			AMERICAN-INTERNAT'L	
JUMP INTO HELL	1955	93	3	2.0	2.5	WARNER BROTHERS	
JUMPING JACKS	1952	96		2.5	2.5	PARAMOUNT	
JUNE BRIDE	1948	97	6*	3.0	3.0	WARNER BROTHERS	
JUNGLE, THE	1952	74	2		1.5	LIPPERT PRODS.	
JUNGLE BOOK, THE (SABU)	1942	109		2.0	3.0	UNITED ARTISTS	
JUNGLE BOOK, THE (CARTOON)	1967	78	6			BUENA VISTA	
JUNGLE CAPTIVE	1945	63		1.0	1.0	UNIVERSAL	
JUNGLE CAT (DOCUMENTARY)	1960	70	6			BUENA VISTA	
JUNGLE FIGHTERS (BRITISH)	a1961	105	3*	3.5	3.0	CONTINENTAL	
JUNGLE GENTS	1954	64				ALLIED ARTISTS	
JUNGLE GIRL AND THE SLAVER (GERMAN)	1959	70		1.0		MEDALLION	
JUNGLE GODDESS	1948	65			1.5	SCREEN GUILD	
JUNGLE GOLD	1944	100		2.5	2.0	REPUBLIC	RE-EDITED SERIAL
JUNGLE HEADHUNTERS (DOCUMENTARY)	1951	66		2.5		RKO	
JUNGLE HELL	1956	78		1.0		MEDALLION	
JUNGLE IS A WOMAN, THE	1955			1.0			
JUNGLE JIM	1948	73		1.5	-	COLUMBIA	
JUNGLE JIM IN THE FORBIDDEN LAND	1952	65		1.5	-	COLUMBIA	
JUNGLE MAN-EATERS	1954	68		1.5	-	COLUMBIA	
JUNGLE MANHUNT	1951	66		1.5	-	COLUMBIA	
JUNGLE MOON MEN	1955	70		1.5	-	COLUMBIA	
JUNGLE PATROL	1948	70		3.5		20th CENTURY FOX	
JUNGLE PRINCESS, THE	1936	85		1.5	3.0	AMERICAN RELEASING	
JUNGLE STAMPEDE	1950	60		1.5		REPUBLIC	
JUNGLE WOMAN	1944	54			1.5	UNIVERSAL	
JUNIOR ARMY	1942	71		1.5		COLUMBIA	
JUNIOR BONNER	1972	100	4			CINERAMA RELEASING	
JUNIOR MISS	1945	94		3.0	2.5	20th CENTURY FOX	
JUPITER'S DARLING	1955	96		2.0	2.5	M-G-M	
JUST ACROSS THE STREET	1952	78		2.5	2.0	UNIVERSAL	
JUST AROUND THE CORNER	1938	70		2.0	2.0	20th CENTURY FOX	
JUST BEFORE DAWN	1946	65			-	COLUMBIA	
JUST FOR FUN	1963	72	2			COLUMBIA	
JUST FOR YOU	1952	104		2.5	3.0	PARAMOUNT	
JUST OFF BROADWAY	1942	66		2.0	2.0	20th CENTURY FOX	
JUST THIS ONCE	1952	90		2.5	2.5	M-G-M	

‡ An asterisk (*) in THE FILM BUFF'S BIBLE column indicates that the film has been rated by the editor and/or staff. All other ratings in this column are based on a consensus of reviews (see NOTES).

"a" TO LEFT OF YEAR INDICATES THAT FILM HAS AN ALTERNATE TITLE

TITLE (LEADING ACTORS SHOWN WHERE TWO OR MORE FILMS HAVE THE SAME OR SIMILAR TITLE)	YEAR RELEASED	RUNNING TIME IN MINUTES	THE FILM BUFF'S BIBLE ‡	STEVEN SCHEUER	LEONARD MALTIN	DISTRIBUTOR	COMMENT
JUSTICE IS DONE (FRENCH)	1950	95	6			JOSEPH BURSTYN	
JUSTINE (ANOUK AIMEE, MICHAEL YORK)	1969	115	3			20th CENTURY FOX	
JUVENILE JUNGLE	1958	69		1.5		REPUBLIC	
KALEIDOSCOPE (BRITISH)	1966	103	4	2.0		WARNER BROTHERS	
KANAL (POLISH)	a1956	96		4.0	3.0	KINGSLEY INTERNAT'L	
KANGAROO	1952	84		2.0	2.0	20th CENTURY FOX	
KANSAN, THE	1943	79			2.5	UNITED ARTISTS	
KANSAS CITY BOMBER	1972	99	2			M-G-M	
KANSAS CITY CONFIDENTIAL	1953	98		3.0	2.0	UNITED ARTISTS	
KANSAS CITY KITTY	1944	63		2.5	2.0	COLUMBIA	
KANSAS PACIFIC	1953	73		2.5	2.0	ALLIED ARTISTS	
KANSAS RAIDERS	1950	80		2.5	1.5	UNIVERSAL	
KANSAS TERRITORY	1952	73		2.5		MONOGRAM	
KARAMOJA (DOCUMENTARY)	1954	60	4			HALLMARK PRODS.	
KARATE	1961	80		1.0		JOSEPH BRENNER	
KATHLEEN	1941	88		1.5	2.0	M-G-M	
KATHY O'	1958	99		3.5	2.5	UNIVERSAL	
KATIE DID IT	1951	81	4	2.5	2.5	UNIVERSAL	
KAZAN	1949	65		2.0		COLUMBIA	
KEEP 'EM FLYING	1941	86		2.5	3.0	UNIVERSAL	
KEEP 'EM SLUGGING	1943	60		-		UNIVERSAL	
KEEP IT CLEAN (BRITISH)	1955	74		1.5		UCC FILMS	
KEEP OFF MY GRASS	1972	90				CAPITOL PRODS.	
KEEP TALKING, BABY (FRENCH)	1961	95		1.0		PARAMOUNT	
KEEP YOUR POWDER DRY	1945	93		1.5	2.0	M-G-M	
KEEPER OF THE BEES (HARRY DAVENPORT, MIKE DUANE)	1947	68	3			COLUMBIA	
KEEPER OF THE FLAME	1942	100		3.0	3.0	M-G-M	
KEEPING COMPANY	1940	80		2.5		M-G-M	
KELLY AND ME	1957	86		2.5	2.0	UNIVERSAL	
KELLY'S HEROES	1970	145	4			M-G-M	
KENNEL MURDER CASE	1933	73		2.5	-	WARNER BROTHERS	
KENNER	1969	92	2			M-G-M	
KENTUCKIAN, THE	1955	104	4*	2.5	2.5	UNITED ARTISTS	
KENTUCKY	1938	95	4*	3.0	3.0	20th CENTURY FOX	
KENTUCKY MOONSHINE	1938	85		3.0	2.0	20th CENTURY FOX	
KES (BRITISH)	1970	113	6			UNITED ARTISTS	
KETTLES IN THE OZARKS, THE	1956	81		2.0	-	UNIVERSAL	
KETTLES ON OLD MACDONALD'S FARM, THE	1957	80		2.0	-	UNIVERSAL	
KEY, THE (WILLIAM POWELL, EDNA BEST)	1934	71		3.0		WARNER BROTHERS	
KEY, THE (BRITISH - WILLIAM HOLDEN, SOPHIA LOREN)	1958	125	4*	3.0	2.5	COLUMBIA	
KEY LARGO	1948	101	6*	3.0	3.5	WARNER BROTHERS	
KEY MAN (BRITISH - ANGELA LANSBURY, KIETH ANDES)	a1954	78		2.0	2.5	CASINO FILMS	
KEY MAN, THE (BRITISH - LEE PATTERSON)	1957	63		1.5		UNITED ARTISTS	
KEY TO MURDER, THE	1956	71		1.0		ALEXANDER WILSON	
KEY TO THE CITY	1950	99	4*	2.5	2.5	M-G-M	
KEY WITNESS (JEFFREY HUNTER, PAT CROWLEY)	1960	82		2.5	2.5	M-G-M	
KEYS OF THE KINGDOM, THE	1944	137		3.0	3.0	20th CENTURY FOX	
KHARTOUM (BRITISH)	1966	134	5*	3.5		UNITED ARTISTS	
KHYBER PATROL	1954	71	3	2.5	2.0	UNITED ARTISTS	
KID, THE (SILENT)	1920	59				FIRST NATIONAL	
KID COMES BACK, THE	1938	61		2.5		WARNER BROTHERS	
KID DYNAMITE	a1943	73				MONOGRAM	
KID FOR TWO FARTHINGS, A (BRITISH)	1955	96		4.0	3.0	LOPERT	
KID FROM BROOKLYN, THE	1946	114		3.0	3.0	RKO	
KID FROM CLEVELAND, THE	1949	89		2.0	2.0	REPUBLIC	
KID FROM KANSAS, THE	1941	66		2.5	1.5	UNIVERSAL	
KID FROM KOKOMO, THE	1939	92		2.0		WARNER BROTHERS	
KID FROM LEFT FIELD, THE	1953	80		2.5	2.0	20th CENTURY FOX	
KID FROM SPAIN, THE	1932	90		3.0	3.0	UNITED ARTISTS	
KID FROM TEXAS, THE (AUDIE MURPHY, GALE STORM)	1950	78		2.0	2.0	UNIVERSAL	
KID GALAHAD (EDWARD G. ROBINSON, WAYNE MORRIS)	a1937	101		3.5	3.0	WARNER BROTHERS	
KID GALAHAD (ELVIS PRESLEY, GIG YOUNG)	1962	78		2.5	2.5	UNITED ARTISTS	
KID GLOVE KILLER	1942	74		3.0		M-G-M	
KID MILLIONS	1934	90		3.0	3.0	UNITED ARTISTS	
KID NIGHTENGALE	1939	57		2.5		WARNER BROTHERS	
KID RODELO	1966	91	2	2.0		PARAMOUNT	
KIDNAPPED (FREDDIE BARTHOLOMEW, WARNER BAXTER)	1938	90	4*	2.5	2.5	20th CENTURY FOX	
KIDNAPPED (RODDY MCDOWALL, DAN O'HERLIHY)	1948	80			2.0	MONOGRAM	
KIDNAPPED (PETER FINCH, JAMES MACARTHUR)	1960	97	4			BUENA VISTA	
KIDNAPPED (BRIT.- MICHAEL CAINE, LAWRENCE DOUGLAS)	1972	100	4			AMERICAN-INTERNAT'L	
KILL A DRAGON	1967	91	1			UNITED ARTISTS	
KILL BABY KILL (ITALIAN)	1966	83	3			EUROPIX-CONSOLIDATED	
KILL HER GENTLY (BRITISH)	1958	63		2.0	2.0	COLUMBIA	
KILL ME TOMORROW (BRITISH)	1958	80		2.0	2.0	TUDOR PICTURES	
KILL OR BE KILLED (LAWRENCE TIERNEY)	1950	67			1.5	EAGLE LION	
KILL OR CURE (BRITISH)	1962	88	3	2.0		M-G-M	
KILL THE UMPIRE	1950	78		2.5	3.0	COLUMBIA	
KILL THEM ALL AND COME BACK ALONE (ITALIAN)	1969	98	1			FANFARE	
KILLER APE	1953	68		1.5	-	COLUMBIA	
KILLER IS LOOSE, THE	1956	73	4	3.0	2.5	UNITED ARTISTS	
KILLER LEOPARD	1954	70			-	ALLIED ARTISTS	

‡ An asterisk (*) in THE FILM BUFF'S BIBLE column indicates that the film has been rated by the editor and/or staff. All other ratings in this column are based on a consensus of reviews (see NOTES).

TITLE (LEADING ACTORS SHOWN WHERE TWO OR MORE FILMS HAVE THE SAME OR SIMILAR TITLE)	YEAR RELEASED	RUNNING TIME IN MINUTES	THE FILM BUFF'S BIBLE ‡	STEVEN SCHEUER	LEONARD MALTIN	DISTRIBUTOR	COMMENT
KILLER MCCOY	1947	104		2.0	3.0	M·G·M	
KILLER SHARK	1950	76			1.5	MONOGRAM	
KILLER SHREWS, THE	1959	72	3	1.0		MCLENDON	
KILLER SPY (FRENCH)	1958	82		2.0	2.0	AMERICAN-INTERNAT'L	
KILLER THAT STALKED NEW YORK, THE	1950	79		2.5	2.5	COLUMBIA	
KILLERS, THE (BURT LANCASTER, AVA GARDNER)	1946	105	6*	4.0	4.0	UNIVERSAL	
KILLERS, THE (LEE MARVIN, ANGIE DICKINSON)	1964	95		2.5	2.5	UNIVERSAL	
KILLERS ARE CHALLANGED (ITALIAN)	a1965	93		2.0	2.0	AMERICAN-INTERNAT'L	
KILLERS' CAGE (BRITISH)	a1958	78	3	1.5			
KILLERS FROM SPACE	1954	71	2		2.0	RKO	
KILLER'S KISS	1955	67		2.0	2.0	UNITED ARTISTS	
KILLERS OF KILIMANJARO (BRITISH)	1959	91		2.0	2.0	COLUMBIA	
KILLERS OF THE EAST (ITALIAN)	1958	75		1.0		TELEDYNAMICS	
KILLERS THREE	1968	88	1			AMERICAN-INTERNAT'L	
KILLING, THE	1956	83	6	3.0	3.5	UNITED ARTISTS	
KILLING GAME, THE (FRENCH)	1967	94	4	2.5		REGIONAL	
KILLING OF SISTER GEORGE, THE (BRITISH)	1968	137	5			CINERAMA RELEASING	
KILROY WAS HERE	1947	68	2		1.5	MONOGRAM	
KIM	1951	113	6	3.0	3.5	M·G·M	
KIMBERLY JIM (SOUTH AFRICAN)	1965	82		2.0	2.0	AVCO-EMBASSY	
KIND HEARTS AND CORONETS (BRITISH)	1949	104	7*	4.0	3.5	EAGLE LION	
KIND LADY (ALINE MACMAHON, BASIL RATHBONE)	a1935	78		3.0		M·G·M	
KIND LADY (ETHEL BARRYMORE, MAURICE EVANS)	1951	78		2.5	3.0	M·G·M	
KIND OF LOVING, A (BRITISH)	1962	112	6		3.0	GOVERNOR	
KINDAR THE INVULNERABLE (ITALIAN)	1964	98		1.0		ABC FILMS	
KING AND COUNTRY (BRITISH)	1964	86	7*	3.5	3.0	LANDAU/UNGER COM. UN.	
KING AND FOUR QUEENS, THE	1956	86		2.0	2.5	UNITED ARTISTS	
KING AND I, THE	1956	133	7*	4.0	3.5	20th CENTURY FOX	NOMINATED BEST PICTURE
KING AND THE CHORUS GIRL, THE	1937	94		3.5	3.5	WARNER BROTHERS	
KING CREOLE	1958	116		2.5	2.5	PARAMOUNT	
KING IN NEW YORK, A (BRITISH)	1957	105	4			ARCHWAY	
KING IN SHADOW (GERMAN)	1956	78		2.5	2.0	EXCLUSIVE INTERNAT'L	
KING KONG	1933	100	6*	4.0	4.0	RKO	
KING KONG ESCAPES (JAPANESE)	1967	96	1			UNIVERSAL	
KING KONG VS GODZILLA (JAPANESE)	1962	90			2.5	UNIVERSAL	
KING LEAR (BRITISH)	1971	134	6			ALTURA FILMS	
KING, MURRAY	1969	86	4			EYER PRODUCTIONS	
KING OF ALCATRAZ	1938	56		2.5	2.5	PARAMOUNT	
KING OF BURLESQUE	1935	83		3.0	3.0	20th CENTURY FOX	
KING OF CHINATOWN	1939	60		2.0	2.5	PARAMOUNT	
KING OF HEARTS (FRENCH)	1966	102	6			LOPERT	
KING OF KINGS (SILENT - H. B. WARNER)	1927	115	4*			PATHE	
KING OF KINGS (JEFFREY HUNTER)	1961	168	5	3.5	3.0	M·G·M	
KING OF THE CORAL SEA (AUSTRALIAN)	1954	86		2.0	2.5	ALLIED ARTISTS	
KING OF THE GRIZZLIES	1970	93	3			BUENA VISTA	
KING OF THE JUNGLE	1933	65		2.0	2.5	PARAMOUNT	
KING OF THE KHYBER RIFLES	1954	100		2.0	2.5	20th CENTURY FOX	
KING OF THE LUMBERJACKS	1940	58		2.0		WARNER BROTHERS	
KING OF THE MONGOLS (JAPANESE)	1960	88		2.0		AMERICAN-INTERNAT'L	
KING OF THE ROARING TWENTIES	1961	106	5*	2.5	2.5	ALLIED ARTISTS	
KING OF THE UNDERWORLD	1939	69		2.5	2.5	WARNER BROTHERS	
KING OF THE VIKINGS (SPANISH)	1964	81		1.0		AMERICAN-INTERNAT'L	
KING OF THE WILD HORSES	1947	79			1.5	COLUMBIA	
KING OF THE WILD STALLIONS	1959	75	3*	1.5	2.0	ALLIED ARTISTS	
KING OF THE ZOMBIES	1941	67			1.5	MONOGRAM	
KING ON HORSEBACK (FRENCH)	1958	88		2.0		UN. MOTION PIC. ORG.	
KING RAT	1965	133	7*	4.0	3.0	COLUMBIA	
KING RICHARD AND THE CRUSADERS	1954	114	5*	2.5	2.5	WARNER BROTHERS	
KING SOLOMON'S MINES	1950	102	5-6*	4.0	3.5	M·G·M	NOMINATED BEST PICTURE
KING STEPS OUT, THE	1936	85			3.0	COLUMBIA	
KINGDOM IN THE CLOUDS	1971	88				XEROX FILMS	
KINGS GO FORTH	1958	109		2.5	3.0	UNITED ARTISTS	
KINGS OF THE SUN	1963	108		2.5	2.5	UNITED ARTISTS	
KING'S PIRATE, THE	1967	100		2.0	2.5	UNIVERSAL	
KING'S RHAPSODY (BRITISH)	a1954	93		1.5	2.0	UNITED ARTISTS	
KING'S ROW	1942	127		4.0	3.5	WARNER BROTHERS	NOMINATED BEST PICTURE
KING'S STORY, A (BRITISH, DOCUMENTARY)	1965	100	6*			CONTINENTAL	
KING'S THIEF, THE	1955	78		2.0	3.0	M·G·M	
KING'S VACATION, THE	1933	60		3.0	2.5	WARNER BROTHERS	
KIPPS (BRITISH)	a1941	82		3.0		20th CENTURY FOX	
KISMET (LORETTA YOUNG, OTIS SKINNER)	1931	92		2.0		FIRST NATIONAL	
KISMET (RONALD COLMAN, MARLENE DIETRICH)	a1944	100		3.0	3.0	M·G·M	
KISMET (HOWARD KEEL, ANN BLYTH)	1955	113	5*	2.0	2.5	M·G·M	
KISS AND TELL	1945	90		3.0	2.5	COLUMBIA	
KISS BEFORE DYING, A	1956	94	4	3.5	3.0	UNITED ARTISTS	
KISS FOR CORLISS, A	a1949	88		1.0	2.0	UNITED ARTISTS	
KISS IN THE DARK, A	1949	87	4	2.0	2.0	WARNER BROTHERS	
KISS KISS - BANG BANG (SPANISH)	1966	90			2.5	RIZZOLI FILM	
KISS ME AGAIN	1931	74		3.0		FIRST NATIONAL	
KISS ME DEADLY	1955	105	2	2.0	2.0	UNITED ARTISTS	
KISS ME KATE	1953	109	6	4.0	3.0	M·G·M	
KISS ME, KISS ME, KISS ME!	1967	80	2			WILLIAM MISHKIN	
KISS ME, STUPID	1964	126	1			LOPERT	
KISS OF DEATH	1947	98	5*	3.5	3.5	20th CENTURY FOX	

‡ An asterisk (*) in THE FILM BUFF'S BIBLE column indicates that the film has been rated by the editor and/or staff. All other ratings in this column are based on a consensus of reviews (see NOTES).

TITLE (LEADING ACTORS SHOWN WHERE TWO OR MORE FILMS HAVE THE SAME OR SIMILAR TITLE)	YEAR RELEASED	RUNNING TIME IN MINUTES	THE FILM BUFF'S BIBLE ‡	STEVEN SCHEUER	LEONARD MALTIN	DISTRIBUTOR	COMMENT
KISS OF EVIL (BRITISH)	a1963	88		2.5	2.5	UNIVERSAL	
KISS OF FIRE (JACK PALANCE, BARBARA RUSH)	1955	87	3	2.5	2.5	UNIVERSAL	
KISS OF THE VAMPIRE (BRITISH)	a1963	88		2.5	2.5	UNIVERSAL	
KISS THE BLOOD OFF MY HANDS	1948	79		2.0	2.0	UNIVERSAL	
KISS THE BOYS GOODBYE	1941	85		3.0	2.5	PARAMOUNT	
KISS THE GIRLS AND MAKE THEM DIE (ITALIAN)	1967	106	3			COLUMBIA	ENGLISH VERSION
KISS THE OTHER SHEIK (ITALIAN)	1968	85	1			M-G-M	
KISS THEM FOR ME	1957	105		2.0	2.5	20th CENTURY FOX	
KISS TOMORROW GOODBYE	1950	102		2.5	3.0	WARNER BROTHERS	
KISSES FOR BREAKFAST	1941	85		2.0		WARNER BROTHERS	
KISSES FOR MY PRESIDENT	1964	113		2.0	2.5	WARNER BROTHERS	
KISSIN' COUSINS	1964	96	3	2.0	2.5	M-G-M	
KISSING BANDIT, THE	1949	102		2.0	2.0	M-G-M	
KIT CARSON	1940	97		2.5	3.0	UNITED ARTISTS	
KITCHEN, THE (BRITISH)	1961	74	6			KINGSLEY INTERNAT'L	
KITTEN WITH A WHIP	1964	83		2.0	2.0	UNIVERSAL	
KITTY	1945	103	5*	2.5	3.0	PARAMOUNT	
KITTY FOYLE	1940	108		4.0	3.5	RKO	NOMINATED BEST PICTURE
KLONDIKE ANNIE	1936	80		2.0	3.0	PARAMOUNT	
KLONDIKE KATE	1943	64			1.5	COLUMBIA	
KLUTE	1971	114	4*			WARNER BROTHERS	
KNACK . . . AND HOW TO GET IT, THE (BRITISH)	1965	84	6			UNITED ARTISTS	
KNICKERBOCKER HOLIDAY	1944	85		2.0	2.0	UNITED ARTISTS	
KNIFE IN THE WATER (POLISH)	1962	94	4*	4.0	3.5	KANAWHA FILMS LTD.	
KNIGHT WITHOUT ARMOR (BRITISH)	1937	107		3.0	3.0	UNITED ARTISTS	
KNIGHTS OF THE BLACK CROSS	1958	105	3			TELEWIDE SYSTEMS	
KNIGHTS OF THE ROUND TABLE	1954	115	5*		2.5	M-G-M	
KNOCK ON ANY DOOR	1949	100		2.5	3.0	COLUMBIA	
KNOCK ON WOOD	1954	103	6	3.0	3.0	PARAMOUNT	
KNOCKOUT (ARTHUR KENNEDY, ANTHONY QUINN)	1941	73		2.0	2.5	WARNER BROTHERS	
KNUTE ROCKNE - ALL AMERICAN	1940	98	4*	3.5	3.0	WARNER BROTHERS	
KON-TIKI (DOCUMENTARY)	1951	73	6*	3.5	3.0	RKO	
KONA COAST	1968	93	3	2.5		WARNER BROTHERS	
KONGA (BRITISH)	1961	90		2.0	2.0	AMERICAN-INTERNAT'L	
KONGO	1932	85		2.0	2.5	M-G-M	
KOROSHI (T.V.)	1966	93		2.0		INDEP. TV CORP (ITC)	
KOTCH	1971	118	5*			CINERAMA RELEASING	
KRAKATOA, EAST OF JAVA	1969	128	3			CINERAMA RELEASING	
KREMLIN LETTER, THE	1970	113	3			20th CENTURY FOX	
KRONOS	1957	78		1.5	2.0	20th CENTURY FOX	
KWAIDAN (JAPANESE)	1965	125	6			CONTINENTAL	THREE STORIES
L-SHAPED ROOM, THE (BRITISH)	1962	124	7*	4.0	3.0	COLUMBIA	
LA BELLE AMERICAINE (FRENCH)	1961	100	5	3.0		CONTINENTAL	
LA BOHEME (ITALIAN)	1965	107	7			WARNER BROTHERS	
LA BONNE SOUP (FRENCH)	1964	97	5			INTERNAT'L CLASSICS	
LA CHAMADE (FRENCH)	1968	102	3			LOPERT	
LA CHINOISE (FRENCH)	a1967	95	6	4.0		LEACOCK-PENNEBAKER	
LA COLLECTIONEUSE (FRENCH)	a1967	88	5			PATHE CONTEMPARARY	
LA DOLCE VITA (ITALIAN)	1960	180	6-8*	4.0	3.5	ASTOR	
LA FAVORITA (ITALIAN)	1952	79		1.5		CONTINENTAL	
LA FEMME INFIDELE (FRENCH)	1969	97	6			ALLIED ARTISTS	
LA FUGA (ITALIAN)	a1965	92	3			INTERNAT'L CLASSICS	
LA GUERRE EST FINIE (FRENCH)	a1966	121	3*			BRANDON	
LA LUPA (ITALIAN)	a1954	95	4			REPUBLIC	
LA MATERNELLE (FRENCH)	1932	86		3.0		TAPERNOUX-METROPOLIS	
LA NOTTE (ITALIAN)	a1961	120	6			LOPERT	
LA NOTTE BRAVA (ITALIAN)	a1959	96	1			MILLER PRODUCING CO.	
LA PARISIENNE (FRENCH)	1957	87		3.5	2.5	UNITED ARTISTS	
LA PRISONNIERE (FRENCH)	1968	104	6			AVCO-EMBASSY	
LA RONDE (FRENCH - ANTON WALBROOK, SIMONE SIMON)	1950	100	7			COMMERCIAL PICS.	
LA SONNAMBULA (ITALIAN)	a1952	79		1.5		CONTINENTAL	
LA SORCIERE (FRENCH)	1956	97	6			ELLIS FILMS	
LA STRADA (ITALIAN)	1954	115	6*	4.0	4.0	TRANS-LUX DIST.	
LA TIA TULA (SPANISH)	a1965	98	6			UNITED INTERNATIONAL	
LA TRAVIATA (ITAL. - ANNA MOFFO, GINO BECHI)	1966	110		2.5		ROYAL FILMS INT'L	
LA VIACCIA (ITALIAN)	a1960	102		3.0	2.5	AVCO-EMBASSY	
LA VIE DE CHATEAU (FRENCH)	a1966	92	4			ROYAL FILMS INT'L	
LA VISITA (ITALIAN)	1966	115	6			PROMENADE	
LAD: A DOG	1962	98		2.0	2.5	WARNER BROTHERS	
LADDIE	1940	70		2.5		RKO	
LADIES COURAGEOUS	1944	88		2.0	2.0	UNIVERSAL	
LADIES' DAY	1943	62		1.5		RKO	
LADIES FIRST (FRENCH)	a1963	90		1.5	2.0	PARAMOUNT	
LADIES IN LOVE	1936	97		2.5	2.5	CHESTERFIELD	
LADIES IN RETIREMENT	1941	92		3.5	3.5	COLUMBIA	
LADIES' MAN (WILLIAM POWELL, KAY FRANCIS)	1931	70		2.0	2.0	PARAMOUNT	
LADIES' MAN (EDDIE BRACKEN, CASS DALEY)	1947	91		2.0	2.0	PARAMOUNT	
LADIES' MAN (FRENCH - EDDIE CONSTANTINE)	1962	95		2.0		PARAMOUNT	
LADIES' MAN, THE (JERRY LEWIS, HELEN TRAUBEL)	1961	106		2.5	3.0	PARAMOUNT	
LADIES MUST LIVE	1940	58		1.5		WARNER BROTHERS	
LADIES OF THE BIG HOUSE	1932	76		2.0	2.5	PARAMOUNT	

‡ An asterisk (*) in THE FILM BUFF'S BIBLE column indicates that the film has been rated by the editor and/or staff. All other ratings in this column are based on a consensus of reviews (see NOTES).

TITLE (LEADING ACTORS SHOWN WHERE TWO OR MORE FILMS HAVE THE SAME OR SIMILAR TITLE)	YEAR RELEASED	RUNNING TIME IN MINUTES	THE FILM BUFF'S BIBLE ‡	STEVEN SCHEUER	LEONARD MALTIN	DISTRIBUTOR	COMMENT
LADIES OF THE CHORUS	1948	61			2.0	COLUMBIA	
LADIES SHOULD LISTEN	1934	62		1.5	2.0	PARAMOUNT	
LADIES WHO DO (BRITISH)	1963	85		2.0	2.5	CONTINENTAL	
LADY AND THE BANDIT, THE	1951	79		2.5	2.0	COLUMBIA	
LADY AND THE MOB, THE	1939	66		3.0	2.5	COLUMBIA	
LADY AND THE MONSTER, THE	1944	86		2.0	2.0	REPUBLIC	
LADY AND THE TRAMP (CARTOON)	1955	75	5*			BUENA VISTA	
LADY BE GOOD	1941	111		3.0	3.0	M-G-M	
LADY BODYGUARD	1943	70		2.0		PARAMOUNT	
LADY BY CHOICE	1934	78			2.5	COLUMBIA	
LADY CHATTERLEY'S LOVER (FRENCH)	1955	102	4			KINGSLEY INTERNAT'L	
LADY CONFESSES, THE	1945	66			1.5	PRODUCERS RELEASING	
LADY CONSENTS, THE	1936	75		2.0	2.5	RKO	
LADY DANCES, THE	a1934	99		3.5	3.0	M-G-M	
LADY DOCTOR (ITALIAN)	1956	90		2.0	2.5		
LADY EVE, THE	1941	97	6*	4.0	4.0	PARAMOUNT	
LADY FOR A DAY	1933	95			3.0	COLUMBIA	NOMINATED BEST PICTURE 1932/33
LADY FOR A NIGHT	1941	87		2.0	2.0	REPUBLIC	
LADY FROM CHEYENNE	1941	87			2.5	UNIVERSAL	
LADY FROM CHUNGKING	1942	66			2.0	PRODUCERS RELEASING	
LADY FROM KENTUCKY, THE	1939	75		2.0		PARAMOUNT	
LADY FROM LOUISIANA	1941	82		2.5	2.5	REPUBLIC	
LADY FROM SHANGHAI, THE	1948	87	4*	3.0	3.0	COLUMBIA	
LADY FROM TEXAS, THE	1951	77		2.5	2.0	UNIVERSAL	
LADY GAMBLES, THE	1949	99		2.5	3.0	UNIVERSAL	
LADY GANGSTER	1942	62		2.0		WARNER BROTHERS	
LADY GODIVA (OF COVENTRY)	1955	89		2.0	2.5	UNIVERSAL	
LADY HAS PLANS, THE	1942	77		2.0	2.0	PARAMOUNT	
LADY IN A CAGE	1964	93	3		2.5	PARAMOUNT	
LADY IN A JAM	1942	78		2.0	2.5	UNIVERSAL	
LADY IN CEMENT	1968	93	3	1.5		20th CENTURY FOX	
LADY IN DISTRESS (BRITISH)	1942	76		3.0	2.5	TIMES FILM CORP.	
LADY IN QUESTION, THE	1940	81			2.5	COLUMBIA	
LADY IN THE CAR WITH GLASSES AND A GUN, THE (FR.)	1970	100	3			COLUMBIA	ENGLISH VERSION
LADY IN THE DARK	1944	100		3.5	2.5	PARAMOUNT	
LADY IN THE IRON MASK	1952	78		2.0	2.0	20th CENTURY FOX	
LADY IN THE LAKE	1946	103	6*	3.5	3.0	M-G-M	
LADY IN THE MORGUE	1938	67		3.0	3.0	UNIVERSAL	
LADY IS WILLING, THE	1942	92	4*	3.0	3.0	COLUMBIA	
LADY KILLER (JAMES CAGNEY, MAE CLARKE)	1933	76		3.0	3.0	WARNER BROTHERS	
LADY L	1965	124		3.0	2.5	M-G-M	
LADY LIBERTY	1972	95	2			UNITED ARTISTS	
LADY LUCK	1946	97		3.0	3.0	CHESTERFIELD	
LADY OF BURLESQUE	1943	91		3.0	3.0	UNITED ARTISTS	
LADY OF MONZA, THE	1970	98	1			TOWER	
LADY OF SECRETS	1936	73			2.5	COLUMBIA	
LADY OF THE TROPICS	1939	92		2.5	2.0	M-G-M	
LADY OF VENGEANCE (BRITISH)	1957	73		1.5	2.0	UNITED ARTISTS	
LADY ON A TRAIN	1945	93		3.0	3.0	UNIVERSAL	
LADY ON THE TRACKS, THE (CZECH)	1968	83	4			ROYAL FILMS INT'L	
LADY PAYS OFF, THE	1951	80		2.0	2.5	UNIVERSAL	
LADY POSSESSED, A	1952	87		1.5	2.0	REPUBLIC	
LADY SAYS NO, THE	1951	80		2.0	2.0	UNITED ARTISTS	
LADY SCARFACE	1941	69		2.0	2.0	RKO	
LADY TAKES A CHANCE, A	1943	86		4.0	3.0	RKO	
LADY TAKES A FLYER, THE	1958	84		2.0	2.5	UNIVERSAL	
LADY TAKES A SAILOR, THE	1949	99		3.0	2.0	WARNER BROTHERS	
LADY VANISHES, THE (BRITISH)	1938	97	6*	4.0	3.5	GAUMONT-BRITISH	
LADY WANTS MINK, THE	1953	92	5	3.0	3.0	REPUBLIC	
LADY WINDERMERE'S FAN (SILENT)	1925	87		3.0		WARNER BROTHERS	
LADY WITH A LAMP, THE (BRITISH)	1951	110		3.0	3.0	CONTINENTAL	
LADY WITH RED HAIR	1940	81		2.5	2.0	WARNER BROTHERS	
LADY WITH THE DOG, THE (RUSSIAN)	1960	86			2.5	ARTKINO	
LADY WITHOUT PASSPORT, A	1950	72		2.5	2.5	M-G-M	
LADYBUG, LADYBUG	1963	81	6			UNITED ARTISTS	
LADYKILLERS, THE (BRITISH - ALEC GUINNESS)	1955	97	7	4.0	3.0	CONTINENTAL	
LADY'S FROM KENTUCKY, THE	1939	67			2.5	PARAMOUNT	
LADY'S MORALS, A	1930	75			2.0	M-G-M	
LAFAYETTE (FRENCH)	1962	112		2.0	2.5	MACO FILM	
LAFAYETTE ESCADRILLE	1958	93		1.5	2.5	WILLIAM A. WELLMAN	
LAKE PLACID SERENADE	1944	85		2.0	2.0	REPUBLIC	
LANCELOT AND GUINEVERE (BRITISH)	a1963	116	3	3.0	2.5	UNIVERSAL	
LANCER SPY	1937	84		2.5	3.0	20th CENTURY FOX	
LAND OF FURY (BRITISH)	1955	82	4			UNIVERSAL	
LAND OF THE PHARAOHS	1955	106	6*	3.0	2.0	WARNER BROTHERS	
LAND RAIDERS	1970	101	2			COLUMBIA	
LAND UNKNOWN, THE	1957	78		2.0	2.0	UNIVERSAL	
LANDLORD, THE	1970	113	4			UNITED ARTISTS	
LANDRU (FRENCH)	a1963	114		2.5	2.5	AVCO-EMBASSY	
LARCENY	1948	89	4	2.5	2.5	UNIVERSAL	
LARCENY, INC.	1942	95	3*	3.0	3.5	WARNER BROTHERS	
LAS VEGAS HILLBILLYS	1966	90	2	1.0		WOOLNER BROTHERS	
LAS VEGAS NIGHTS	1941	89		1.5		PARAMOUNT	
LAS VEGAS SHAKEDOWN	1955	79		2.0	2.0	ALLIED ARTISTS	

‡ An asterisk (*) in THE FILM BUFF'S BIBLE column indicates that the film has been rated by the editor and/or staff. All other ratings in this column are based on a consensus of reviews (see NOTES).

TITLE (LEADING ACTORS SHOWN WHERE TWO OR MORE FILMS HAVE THE SAME OR SIMILAR TITLE)	YEAR RELEASED	RUNNING TIME IN MINUTES	THE FILM BUFF'S BIBLE ‡	STEVEN SCHEUER	LEONARD MALTIN	DISTRIBUTOR	COMMENT
LAS VEGAS STORY, THE	1952	52		2.0	2.0	RKO	
LASSIE COME HOME	1943	88		3.5	3.0	M-G-M	
LASSIE'S GREAT ADVENTURE	1963	103	4			20th CENTURY FOX	
LAST ADVENTURE, THE (FRENCH)	1967	102	3			UNIVERSAL	
LAST ANGRY MAN, THE	1959	100	6*	3.0	3.0	COLUMBIA	
LAST BANDIT, THE	1949	80		2.5		REPUBLIC	
LAST BLITZKRIEG, THE	1959	84		2.0	2.0	COLUMBIA	
LAST BRIDGE, THE (AUSTRIAN)	1953	95		4.0	3.5	UNION FILMS	
LAST CHALLENGE, THE	1967	96	3	2.5		M-G-M	
LAST CHANCE, THE (SWISS)	1945	105		4.0		M-G-M	
LAST CHAPTER, THE (DOCUMENTARY)	1966	90	6			BEN-LAR PRODS.	
LAST CHARGE, THE (ITALIAN)	1964	88		1.0			
LAST COMMAND, THE (SILENT - EMIL JANNINGS)	1928	91				PARAMOUNT	NOMINATED BEST PICTURE 1927/28
LAST COMMAND, THE (STERLING HAYDEN)	1955	110		3.5	2.5	REPUBLIC	
LAST DAYS OF POMPEII, THE (PRESTON FOSTER)	1935	96	5*	3.5	3.0	RKO	
LAST DAYS OF POMPEII, THE (ITALIAN - STEVE REEVES)	1959	105	3	2.5	2.5	RKO	
LAST ESCAPE	1970	90	3			UNITED ARTISTS	
LAST FRONTIER, THE	a1956	98		2.0	2.5	COLUMBIA	
LAST GANGSTER, THE	1937	81		3.0	3.0	M-G-M	
LAST GLORY OF TROY, THE (ITALIAN)	a1961	108		1.5		MEDALLION	
LAST GRENADE, THE (BRITISH)	1970	94	1			CINERAMA RELEASING	
LAST GUN, THE (SPANISH)	1964	88		1.0		PARKSIDE PRODS.	
LAST GUNFIGHT, THE (JAPANESE)	1964	95		3.0		COM. UNITED T.V.	
LAST HOLIDAY (BRITISH)	1950	88		4.0	3.0	STRATFORD PICS.	
LAST HUNT, THE	1956	108		3.0	2.5	M-G-M	
LAST HURRAH, THE	1958	121	6*	4.0	3.0	COLUMBIA	
LAST LAUGH, THE (GERMAN, SILENT)	1924	71	1*			UNIVERSAL	NO TITLES
LAST MAN ON EARTH, THE (ITALIAN)	1964	86	2	2.0	2.0	AMERICAN-INTERNAT'L	
LAST MAN TO HANG, THE (BRITISH)	1956	75		1.5	2.0	COLUMBIA	
LAST MILE, THE (MICKEY ROONEY, CLIFFORD DAVID)	1959	81	4	2.5	2.5	UNITED ARTISTS	
LAST MOVIE, THE	1971	108	2			UNIVERSAL	
LAST MUSKETEER, THE (REX ALLEN, MARY ELLEN KAY)	1952	67		2.5		REPUBLIC	
LAST MUSKETEER, THE (FRENCH - GEORGES MARCHAL)	1954	95		1.5	2.0		
LAST OF MRS CHENEY	1929	94				M-G-M	
LAST OF THE BADMEN	1957	79		2.0	2.0	ALLIED ARTISTS	
LAST OF THE BUCCANEERS	1950	79		2.0	1.5	COLUMBIA	
LAST OF THE COMMANCHES	1953	85		2.5	2.0	COLUMBIA	
LAST OF THE DESPERADOES	1955	71		1.5		ASSOC'D FILM DISTS.	
LAST OF THE FAST GUNS	1958	82		2.5	2.0	UNIVERSAL	
LAST OF THE MOBILE HOT-SHOTS	1970	108	2			WARNER BROTHERS	
LAST OF THE MOHICANS, THE	1936	91	5*	3.0	3.0	UNITED ARTISTS	
LAST OF THE PAGANS	1935	84		2.5		M-G-M	
LAST OF THE RED HOT LOVERS	1972	98	4*			PARAMOUNT	
LAST OF THE REDMEN	1947	77			2.5	COLUMBIA	
LAST OF THE SECRET AGENTS?, THE	1966	92	2		2.0	PARAMOUNT	
LAST OF THE SKI BUMS, THE	1969	86	4	3.0		U-M PRODS.	
LAST OF THE VIKINGS, THE (ITALIAN)	1960	102		1.5	2.0	MEDALLION	
LAST OUTPOST, THE (CARY GRANT, CLAUDE RAINS)	1935	70		2.5	3.0	PARAMOUNT	
LAST OUTPOST, THE (RONALD REAGAN, RHONDA FLEMING)	1951	88		2.0	2.5	PARAMOUNT	
LAST PARADISE, THE (DOCUMENTARY)	1958	83	4			UNITED ARTISTS	
LAST PICTURE SHOW, THE	1971	118	6-7*			COLUMBIA	NOMINATED BEST PICTURE
LAST POSSE, THE	1953	73		3.0	2.0	COLUMBIA	
LAST REBEL, THE (MEXICAN - CARLOS THOMPSON)	1961	83	3			STERLING WORLD DISTS.	
LAST REBEL, THE (JOE NAMATH, JACK ELAM)	1971	90	2			COLUMBIA	
LAST RIDE, THE	1944	56		2.0	2.0	WARNER BROTHERS	
LAST RIDE TO SANTA CRUZ, THE (GERMAN)	1964	99		1.5		CASINO FILMS	
LAST RUN, THE	1971	100	4*			M-G-M	
LAST SAFARI, THE (BRITISH)	1967	115	4	2.5		PARAMOUNT	
LAST SHOT YOU HEAR, THE (BRITISH)	1969	91	2			20th CENTURY FOX	
LAST STAGECOACH WEST	1957	67		1.5	1.5	REPUBLIC	
LAST SUMMER	1969	97	6			ALLIED ARTISTS	
LAST SUNSET, THE	1961	112	4	2.0	2.5	UNIVERSAL	
LAST TEN DAYS, THE (GERMAN)	a1955	108	6	3.5	3.0	COLUMBIA	SEMI-DOCUMENTARY
LAST TIME I SAW ARCHIE, THE	1961	98	4*	2.0	1.5	UNITED ARTISTS	
LAST TIME I SAW PARIS, THE	1954	116		2.5	3.0	M-G-M	
LAST TRAIN FROM BOMBAY	1952	72		2.0	1.5	COLUMBIA	
LAST TRAIN FROM GUN HILL, THE	1959	94		2.5	3.0	PARAMOUNT	
LAST TRAIN FROM MADRID, THE	1937	77		2.0	2.0	PARAMOUNT	
LAST VALLEY, THE (BRITISH)	1971	126	3			CINERAMA RELEASING	
LAST VOYAGE, THE	1960	91	6-7*	2.5	3.0	M-G-M	
LAST WAGON, THE	1956	99	4	2.5	3.0	20th CENTURY FOX	
LAST WARNING, THE	1939	63		3.0		UNIVERSAL	
LAST WOMAN ON EARTH, THE	1960	71		2.0	1.0	FILMGROUP	
LAST YEAR AT MARIENBAD (FRENCH)	1961	93	4-6*	3.5	3.0	ASTOR	
LATE GEORGE APLEY, THE	1947	98	6*	3.0	3.0	20th CENTURY FOX	
LATE LIZ, THE	1971	120	4			DICK ROSS & ASSOC.	
LATIN LOVERS (LANA TURNER, RICARDO MONTALBAN)	1953	104		2.0	2.5	M-G-M	
LATIN LOVERS (ITALIAN)	1961	80			2.0	GALA	EIGHT STORIES
LATITUDE ZERO	1970	99	1			NATIONAL GENERAL	
LAUGH YOUR BLUES AWAY	1942	70		2.0		COLUMBIA	
LAUGHING ANNE (BRITISH)	a1953	90	3		2.0	REPUBLIC	
LAUGHING WOMAN, THE	1970	90	2			AUDUBON	
LAUGHTER	1930	81			2.5	PARAMOUNT	
LAUGHTER IN PARADISE (BRITISH)	1951	93	5	4.0	2.5	STRATFORD PICS.	

‡ An asterisk (*) in THE FILM BUFF'S BIBLE column indicates that the film has been rated by the editor and/or staff. All other ratings in this column are based on a consensus of reviews (see NOTES).

TITLE (LEADING ACTORS SHOWN WHERE TWO OR MORE FILMS HAVE THE SAME OR SIMILAR TITLE)	YEAR RELEASED	RUNNING TIME IN MINUTES	THE FILM BUFF'S BIBLE ‡	STEVEN SCHEUER	LEONARD MALTIN	DISTRIBUTOR	COMMENT
LAUGHTER IN THE DARK (BRITISH)	1969	101	4			LOPERT	
LAURA	1944	88	7*	3.5	4.0	20th CENTURY FOX	
LAUREL AND HARDY'S LAUGHING 20'S	1965	90	6		3.5	M-G-M	
LAVENDER HILL MOB, THE (BRITISH)	1951	78	7*	4.0	3.5	UNIVERSAL	
L'AVVENTURA (ITALIAN)	a1960	145	4*	4.0		JANUS FILMS	
LAW, THE (ITALIAN)	a1958	120	3	2.0	2.0	AVCO-EMBASSY	
LAW AND DISORDER (BRITISH - MICHAEL REDGRAVE)	1958	76	4	3.0	2.5	CONTINENTAL	
LAW AND JAKE WADE, THE	1958	86		2.5	3.0	M-G-M	
LAW AND ORDER (WALTER HUSTON, HARRY CAREY)	1932	70			3.0	UNIVERSAL	
LAW AND ORDER (RONALD REAGAN, DOROTHY MALONE)	1953	80	4	2.0		UNIVERSAL	
LAW AND THE LADY, THE	1951	105	4			M-G-M	
LAW IS THE LAW, THE (FRENCH)	1957	103		2.5	2.5	CONTINENTAL	
LAW OF THE LAWLESS	1964	87	3		2.5	PARAMOUNT	
LAW OF THE STREETS (FRENCH)	1956	100		1.5		COLUMBIA	
LAW OF THE TROPICS	1941	76		2.0	2.0	WARNER BROTHERS	
LAW OF THE UNDERWORLD	1938	61		2.0		RKO	
LAW VS BILLY THE KID, THE	1954	73	2	2.0	2.0	COLUMBIA	
LAW WEST OF TOMBSTONE, THE	1938	73		3.0		RKO	
LAWLESS, THE	1950	83		3.5	2.0	PARAMOUNT	
LAWLESS BREED, THE	1953	83	4	2.0	2.5	UNIVERSAL	
LAWLESS EIGHTIES, THE	1957	70		2.0	2.0	REPUBLIC	
LAWLESS RIDER, THE	1954	62		1.0		UNITED ARTISTS	
LAWLESS STREET, A	1955	78	4	3.0	2.5	COLUMBIA	
LAWMAN, THE	1971	98	3			UNITED ARTISTS	
LAWRENCE OF ARABIA (BRITISH)	1962	221	7*	4.0		COLUMBIA	BEST PICTURE AWARD
LAWYER, THE	1970	120	5			PARAMOUNT	
LAWYER MAN	1932	72		3.0	2.5	WARNER BROTHERS	
LAY THAT RIFLE DOWN	1955	71		1.5	1.5	REPUBLIC	
LE BONHEUR (FRENCH)	1965	87	6			CLOVER FILMS	
LE BOUCHER (FRENCH)	a1969	93	5			CINERAMA RELEASING	
LE DEPART (BELGIAN)	a1967	90	4			PATHE CONTEMPARARY	
LE MANS	1971	106	4			NATIONAL GENERAL	
LE MILLION (FRENCH)	1931	80	3*			TOBIS	
LE PETIT SOLDAT (FRENCH)	a1962	88	6			WEST END FILMS	COMPLETED IN 1960
LE PLAISIR (FRENCH)	1952	96	6			KINGSLEY INTERNAT'L	
LE VIOL (SWEDISH)	a1967	90	4			FREENA FILMS	
LEAGUE OF GENTLEMEN, THE (BRITISH)	1960	114	5*	4.0	3.0	KINGSLEY INTERNAT'L	
LEARNING TREE, THE	1969	107	3*			WARNER BROTHERS	
LEASE OF LIFE (BRITISH)	1954	94	5*	3.5	2.5	ITALIAN FILMS EXPORT	
LEATHER BOYS, THE (BRITISH)	1964	108	5	2.0	3.0	ALLIED ARTISTS	
LEATHER GLOVES	1948	75			2.0	COLUMBIA	
LEATHER SAINT, THE	1956	86	3	2.0	2.5	PARAMOUNT	
LEATHERNECKS HAVE LANDED, THE	1936	67		2.0		REPUBLIC	
LEAVE HER TO HEAVEN	1945	111		2.5	3.0	20th CENTURY FOX	
LEAVE IT TO BLONDIE	1945	75		2.5	.	COLUMBIA	
LEAVE IT TO HENRY	1949	57			1.5	MONOGRAM	
LEBANESE MISSION, THE (FRENCH)	1956	90		2.5			
LEDA (FRENCH)	a1959	110		2.0	2.5	TIMES FILM CORP.	
LEECH WOMAN, THE	1960	77	2	2.0	1.5	UNIVERSAL	
LEFT HAND OF GOD, THE	1955	87	4*	2.5	3.0	20th CENTURY FOX	
LEFT-HANDED GUN, THE	1958	102	4	3.0	2.5	WARNER BROTHERS	
LEFT, RIGHT AND CENTRE (BRITISH)	1959	95		2.5	2.0	BCG FILMS	
LEGEND OF LOBO, THE	1962	67	4*			BUENA VISTA	
LEGEND OF LYLAH CLARE, THE	1968	130	3	2.5		M-G-M	
LEGEND OF NIGGER CHARLEY, THE	1972	99	3			PARAMOUNT	
LEGEND OF THE LOST	1957	109		2.5	2.0	UNITED ARTISTS	
LEGEND OF TOM DOOLEY, THE	1959	79		1.5	2.0	COLUMBIA	
LEGENDARY CHAMPIONS, THE (DOCUMENTARY)	1968	77	6	3.5		TURN OF CENT. FIGHTS	
LEGION OF THE DOOMED	1958	75		1.0	1.5	ALLIED ARTISTS	
LEGIONS OF THE NILE (ITALIAN)	1959	91	1			20th CENTURY FOX	
LEMON DROP KID, THE (BOB HOPE, MARILYN MAXWELL)	1951	91	4	3.0	2.5	PARAMOUNT	
LEMONADE JOE (CZECH)	1964	90		3.0		ALLIED ARTISTS	
LEO THE LAST (BRITISH)	1970	103	4			UNITED ARTISTS	
LEONARDO DA VINCI (ITALIAN, DOCUMENTARY)	1952	70	6			PICTURA FILMS	
LEOPARD, THE (ITALIAN)	1963	165	3*	2.5	3.0	20th CENTURY FOX	
LEOPARD MAN, THE	1943	66		3.5	3.5	RKO	
LES BICHES (FRENCH)	a1968	104	3			JACK H. HARRIS	
LES BONNES FEMMES (FRENCH)	1960	95	6			ROBERT HAKIM	
LES CARABINIERS (FRENCH)	a1963	80	6			WEST END FILMS	
LES ENFANTS DU PARADIS (FRENCH)	a1945	188	5*	4.0	3.5	TRICOLORE	
LES GAULOISES BLEUES (FRENCH)	1968	93	3			LOPERT	
LES GIRLS	1957	114	4*	4.0	3.5	M-G-M	
LES LIAISONS DANGEREUSES (FRENCH)	1959	106	6			ASTOR	
LES MISERABLES (FREDRIC MARCH, CHARLES LAUGHTON)	1935	108	6*	4.0	3.5	UNITED ARTISTS	NOMINATED BEST PICTURE
LES MISERABLES (MICHAEL RENNIE, ROBERT NEWTON)	1952	104	5*	2.5	3.0	20th CENTURY FOX	
LES MISERABLES (FRENCH - JEAN GABIN)	1957	210		3.0		CONTINENTAL	USUALLY SHOWN IN TWO PARTS
LESSON IN LOVE, A (SWEDISH)	1953	95	5			JANUS FILMS	
LET FREEDOM RING	1939	100		3.0	2.5	M-G-M	
LET IT ALL HANG OUT	1971	75				ATCO GIBRALTER	
LET IT BE (BRITISH, DOCUMENTARY)	1970	80	4			UNITED ARTISTS	
LET NO MAN WRITE MY EPITAPH	1960	106		2.0	3.0	COLUMBIA	
LET US LIVE	1939	68		2.5	2.5	COLUMBIA	
LET'S BE HAPPY (BRITISH)	1957	106	3	2.5	2.5	ALLIED ARTISTS	
LET'S DANCE	1950	112	4	2.0	2.5	PARAMOUNT	

‡ An asterisk (*) in THE FILM BUFF'S BIBLE column indicates that the film has been rated by the editor and/or staff. All other ratings in this column are based on a consensus of reviews (see NOTES).

TITLE (LEADING ACTORS SHOWN WHERE TWO OR MORE FILMS HAVE THE SAME OR SIMILAR TITLE)	YEAR RELEASED	RUNNING TIME IN MINUTES	CRITICAL RATINGS			DISTRIBUTOR	COMMENT
			THE FILM BUFF'S BIBLE ‡	STEVEN SCHEUER	LEONARD MALTIN		
LET'S DO IT AGAIN	1953	95	4	2.5	3.0	COLUMBIA	
LET'S FACE IT	1943	76		2.0	2.0	PARAMOUNT	
LET'S GET MARRIED (RALPH BELLAMY, IDA LUPINO)	1937	69		2.5		COLUMBIA	
LET'S GET TOUGH!	1942	62			-	MONOGRAM	
LET'S GO NAVY	1951	68	2		-	MONOGRAM	
LET'S GO STEADY	1945	60		1.5		COLUMBIA	
LET'S HAVE FUN	1943	65		2.0		COLUMBIA	
LET'S KILL UNCLE	1966	92	3			UNIVERSAL	
LET'S LIVE A LITTLE	1948	85		2.5	2.5	20th CENTURY FOX	
LET'S LIVE AGAIN	1948	67	2			20th CENTURY FOX	
LET'S MAKE IT LEGAL	1951	77	4	2.5	2.5	20th CENTURY FOX	
LET'S MAKE LOVE	1960	118		2.5	3.0	20th CENTURY FOX	
LET'S MAKE MUSIC	1941	85		2.0		RKO	
LET'S MAKE UP (BRITISH)	a1954	93		1.5	2.0	UNITED ARTISTS	
LET'S ROCK	1958	79		2.0		COLUMBIA	
LET'S SCARE JESSICA TO DEATH	1971	89	3			PARAMOUNT	
LET'S TALK ABOUT WOMEN (ITALIAN)	1964	108	6			AVCO-EMBASSY	NINE EPISODES
LETTER, THE (JEANNE EAGELS)	1929	72				PARAMOUNT	
LETTER, THE (BETTE DAVIS)	1940	97	6*	3.5	3.5	WARNER BROTHERS	NOMINATED BEST PICTURE
LETTER FOR EVIE, A	1945	89		2.5	2.0	M-G-M	
LETTER FROM AN UNKNOWN WOMAN	1948	90	3*	3.5	3.5	UNIVERSAL	
LETTER OF INTRODUCTION	1938	104			2.5	UNIVERSAL	
LETTER TO THREE WIVES, A	1949	103	6*	4.0	4.0	20th CENTURY FOX	NOMINATED BEST PICTURE
LETTERS FROM MY WINDMILL (FRENCH)	1954	114	6			TOHAN	
LIANE, JUNGLE GODDESS (GERMAN)	1956	85	1			DIST. CORP. OF AMER.	
LIBEL (BRITISH)	1959	100	5*	2.5	2.5	M-G-M	
LIBELED LADY	1936	98		3.5	3.0	M-G-M	NOMINATED BEST PICTURE
LIBERATION OF L. B. JONES, THE	1970	101	4			COLUMBIA	
LIBERTINE, THE (ITALIAN)	1968	90	2			AUDUBON	
LICENSE TO KILL (FRENCH)	1964	95		1.5	2.0	FOUR STAR	
LICKERISH QUARTET, THE	1970	90	3			AUDUBON	
LT. ROBIN CRUSOE, U.S.N.	1966	110	3			BUENA VISTA	
LIEUTENANT WORE SKIRTS, THE	1956	99		2.5	2.5	20th CENTURY FOX	
LIFE AND DEATH OF COLONEL BLIMP, THE (BRITISH)	a1943	148		4.0	3.0	ARCHERS-GENERAL	
LIFE AND LOVES OF MOZART, THE (GERMAN)	1956	87		2.5		BAKROS INTERNATIONAL	
LIFE AT STAKE, A	a1954	78		2.0	2.5	CASINO FILMS	
LIFE AT THE TOP (BRITISH)	1965	117		2.5	2.5	ROYAL FILMS INT'L	
LIFE BEGINS	1932	71		2.5	3.0	FIRST NATIONAL	
LIFE BEGINS AT COLLEGE	a1937	94		3.0	2.5	20th CENTURY FOX	
LIFE BEGINS AT EIGHT-THIRTY	1942	85		2.5	2.5	20th CENTURY FOX	
LIFE BEGINS AT FORTY	1935	85		3.0	3.0	20th CENTURY FOX	
LIFE BEGINS AT 17	1958	75	2	1.0		COLUMBIA	
LIFE BEGINS FOR ANDY HARDY	1941	100		2.5	-	M-G-M	
LIFE BEGINS IN COLLEGE	a1937	94		3.0	2.5	20th CENTURY FOX	
LIFE IN EMERGENCY WARD 10 (BRITISH)	1958	86		2.0		EROS FILMS	
LIFE IN THE BALANCE, A	1955	74		2.0	2.0	20th CENTURY FOX	
LIFE, LOVE, DEATH (FRENCH)	1969	115	6			LOPERT	
LIFE OF DONIZETTI (ITALIAN)	1951	98		2.0		LUPA FILM	
LIFE OF EMILE ZOLA, THE	1937	116	7*	4.0	4.0	WARNER BROTHERS	BEST PICTURE AWARD
LIFE OF HER OWN, A	1950	108		2.0	2.5	M-G-M	
LIFE OF JIMMY DOLAN	1933	70		2.5		WARNER BROTHERS	
LIFE OF RILEY, THE	1949	87	4			UNIVERSAL	
LIFE OF VERGIE WINTERS, THE	1934	82		2.5	2.5	RKO	
LIFE UPSIDE DOWN (FRENCH)	1965	93		3.0	2.5	LANDAU/UNGER COM. UN.	
LIFE WITH BLONDIE	1946	64		2.5	-	COLUMBIA	
LIFE WITH FATHER	1947	118	6*	4.0	3.0	WARNER BROTHERS	
LIFE WITH HENRY	1941	81		2.5		PARAMOUNT	
LIFEBOAT	1944	96	6*	3.0	3.5	20th CENTURY FOX	
LIGHT ACROSS THE STREET, THE (FRENCH)	a1955	99	4	2.0	2.5	UN. MOTION PIC. ORG.	
LIGHT AT THE EDGE OF THE WORLD	1971	122	3			NATIONAL GENERAL	
LIGHT FANTASTIC, THE	1963	85		1.5		AVCO-EMBASSY	
LIGHT FINGERS (BRITISH)	1957	86		2.0	2.0	CANFIELD PRODS.	
LIGHT IN THE FOREST, THE	1958	93	5			BUENA VISTA	
LIGHT IN THE PIAZZA (BRITISH)	1962	101	5	3.0	3.5	M-G-M	
LIGHT THAT FAILED, THE	1939	97		3.5	3.0	PARAMOUNT	
LIGHT TOUCH, THE (STEWART GRANGER, PIER ANGELI)	1951	110		2.5	2.5	M-G-M	
LIGHTNING BOLT (ITALIAN)	1966	96	1			WOOLNER BROTHERS	
LIGHTNING STRIKES TWICE (RICHARD TODD, RUTH ROMAN)	1951	91		2.5	2.5	WARNER BROTHERS	
LIGHTS OF NEW YORK, THE	1928	57				WARNER BROTHERS	
LIKELY STORY, A	1947	88		3.5	2.5	RKO	
LI'L ABNER (GRANVILLE OWEN, MARTHA O'DRISCOLL)	1940	78		2.0		RKO	
LI'L ABNER (PETER PALMER, LESLIE PARRISH)	1959	114	5	2.5	2.5	PARAMOUNT	
LILACS IN THE SPRING (BRITISH)	a1954	93		1.5	2.0	UNITED ARTISTS	
LILI	1953	81	7	4.0	4.0	M-G-M	
LILI MARLENE (BRITISH)	1950	75		2.0		RKO	
LILIES OF THE FIELD	1963	94	6*	4.0	3.0	UNITED ARTISTS	NOMINATED BEST PICTURE
LILITH	1964	114	4		2.5	COLUMBIA	
LILLIAN RUSSELL	1940	127		2.5	2.0	20th CENTURY FOX	
LIMEHOUSE BLUES	a1934	65		1.5	2.0	PARAMOUNT	
LIMELIGHT (CHARLIE CHAPLIN, CLAIRE BLOOM)	1952	143	8			UNITED ARTISTS	
LIMPING MAN, THE (BRITISH)	1953	76		2.0	2.0	LIPPERT PRODS.	
LINEUP, THE	1958	86		2.5	2.5	COLUMBIA	
LINKS OF JUSTICE (BRITISH)	1958	68		1.5		J. ARTHUR RANK	
LION, THE (BRITISH)	1962	96	4	2.0	2.5	20th CENTURY FOX	

‡ An asterisk (*) in THE FILM BUFF'S BIBLE column indicates that the film has been rated by the editor and/or staff. All other ratings in this column are based on a consensus of reviews (see NOTES).

TITLE (LEADING ACTORS SHOWN WHERE TWO OR MORE FILMS HAVE THE SAME OR SIMILAR TITLE)	YEAR RELEASED	RUNNING TIME IN MINUTES	THE FILM BUFF'S BIBLE ‡	STEVEN SCHEUER	LEONARD MALTIN	DISTRIBUTOR	COMMENT
LION AND THE HORSE, THE	1952	83	4	2.0	2.0	WARNER BROTHERS	
LION HUNTERS, THE	1951	75		·		MONOGRAM	
LION IN WINTER, THE (BRITISH)	1968	132	6*	4.0		AVCO-EMBASSY	NOMINATED BEST PICTURE
LION IS IN THE STREET, A	1953	88	4			WARNER BROTHERS	
LION OF ST MARK, THE (ITALIAN)	1963	87			2.0	AVCO-EMBASSY	
LION OF THEBES, THE (ITALIAN)	1964	89		1.0		AVCO-EMBASSY	
LIONS ARE LOOSE, THE (FRENCH)	1961	96		2.5		FRANCO-LONDON	
LIONS LOVE	1969	110	4			MAX L. RABB	
LIQUIDATOR, THE (BRITISH)	1966	104	4		2.5	M-G-M	
LISA	1962	112		2.5	2.0	20th CENTURY FOX	
LISBON	1956	90	4	3.0	2.5	REPUBLIC	
LISETTE	1961	83		1.5			
LIST OF ADRIAN MESSENGER, THE	1963	98	6*	3.0	3.0	UNIVERSAL	
LISTEN DARLING	1938	70		2.5	2.5	M-G-M	
LISTEN, LET'S MAKE LOVE (ITALIAN)	1968	91	1			LOPERT	
LITTLE AMERICA (DOCUMENTARY)	1935	52		3.0		PARAMOUNT	
LITTLE ARK, THE	1972	101	6			NATIONAL GENERAL	
LITTLE BIG HORN	1951	86	4	3.0	2.5	LIPPERT PRODS.	
LITTLE BIG MAN	1970	139	7*			NATIONAL GENERAL	
LITTLE BIT OF HEAVEN, A	1940	87			2.0	UNIVERSAL	
LITTLE BOY LOST	1953	95	5*	3.5	3.0	PARAMOUNT	
LITTLE CAESAR	1930	77	5*	3.5	3.5	FIRST NATIONAL	
LITTLE COLONEL, THE	1935	80			3.0	20th CENTURY FOX	
LITTLE EGYPT	1951	82	2	2.0	2.5	UNIVERSAL	
LITTLE FAUSS AND BIG HALSY	1970	99	3			PARAMOUNT	
LITTLE FOXES, THE	1941	116	6*	4.0	3.5	RKO	NOMINATED BEST PICTURE
LITTLE FUGITIVE, THE	1953	75	4*	3.5	3.0	JOSEPH BURSTYN	
LITTLE GIANT (ABBOTT & COSTELLO)	1946	91		2.0	2.0	UNIVERSAL	
LITTLE GIANT, THE (EDWARD G. ROBINSON, MARY ASTOR)	1933	75	4*	3.5		FIRST NATIONAL	
LITTLE HUT, THE	1957	78	4	3.0	2.5	M-G-M	
LITTLE KIDNAPPERS, THE (BRITISH)	1954	93		4.0	3.0	UNITED ARTISTS	
LITTLE LORD FAUNTLEROY	1936	98		3.0	3.0	NEW TRENDS ASSOC.	
LITTLE MEN	1940	84			2.0	RKO	
LITTLE MINISTER, THE	1934	110	6*	3.5	3.5	RKO	
LITTLE MISS BIG	1946	57		2.0		UNIVERSAL	
LITTLE MISS BROADWAY (SHIRLEY TEMPLE)	1938	70		2.0	2.0	20th CENTURY FOX	
LITTLE MISS BROADWAY (JEAN PORTER, JOHN SHELTON)	1947	69		1.5		COLUMBIA	
LITTLE MISS MARKER	1934	80		3.0	3.0	PARAMOUNT	
LITTLE MISS THOROUGHBRED	1938	63		2.0		WARNER BROTHERS	
LITTLE MISTER JIM	1947	61		3.0		M-G-M	
LITTLE MURDERS	1971	110	6*			20th CENTURY FOX	
LITTLE NELLIE KELLY	1940	100		2.5	2.5	M-G-M	
LITTLE NUNS, THE (ITALIAN)	1963	100	4	3.0	2.5	AVCO-EMBASSY	
LITTLE OLD NEW YORK	1940	100		2.5	2.5	20th CENTURY FOX	
LITTLE ONES, THE (BRITISH)	1965	81	6			COLUMBIA	
LITTLE ORVIE	1940	68		2.0		RKO	
LITTLE PRINCESS, THE	1939	91	4*	3.5	3.0	20th CENTURY FOX	
LITTLE REBELS, THE (FRENCH)	1955	93		2.5			
LITTLE SAVAGE, THE	1959	73	2	2.0		20th CENTURY FOX	
LITTLE SHEPHERD OF KINGDOM COME, THE	1961	108	4	2.0	2.5	20th CENTURY FOX	
LITTLE SHOP OF HORRORS, THE	1960	70	4	3.0		FILMGROUP	
LITTLE SOLDIER, THE (FRENCH)	a1962	88	6		·	WEST END FILMS	COMPLETED IN 1960
LITTLE TOKYO, U.S.A.	1942	64		1.5		20th CENTURY FOX	
LITTLE WOMEN (KATHARINE HEPBURN, JOAN BENNETT)	1933	107		4.0	4.0	RKO	NOMINATED BEST PICTURE 1932/33
LITTLE WOMEN (JUNE ALLYSON, PETER LAWFORD)	1949	121		2.5	2.5	M-G-M	
LITTLE WORLD OF DON CAMILLO (FRENCH)	1951	96	6	3.0	2.5	ITALIAN FILMS EXPORT	
LITTLEST HOBO, THE	1958	77	5*	2.5	2.5	ALLIED ARTISTS	
LITTLEST OUTLAW, THE	1955	73	5*			BUENA VISTA	
LITTLEST REBEL, THE	1935	70			3.0	20th CENTURY FOX	
LIVE A LITTLE, LOVE A LITTLE	1968	90	2			M-G-M	
LIVE FAST, DIE YOUNG	1958	82	2	2.0	2.0	UNIVERSAL	
LIVE FOR LIFE (FRENCH)	1967	130	6			UNITED ARTISTS	
LIVE, LOVE AND LEARN	1937	78		2.5	2.5	M-G-M	
LIVE WIRES	1946	64			·	MONOGRAM	
LIVELY SET, THE	1964	95		2.0	2.5	UNIVERSAL	
LIVES OF A BENGAL LANCER	1935	109	5*	3.5	4.0	PARAMOUNT	NOMINATED BEST PICTURE
LIVING COFFIN, THE (MEXICAN)	1965	72		1.0		TRANS-INTERNATIONAL	
LIVING FREE (BRITISH)	1972	92	4			COLUMBIA	
LIVING HEAD, THE (MEXICAN)	1959	75		1.0		AZTECA	
LIVING IN A BIG WAY	1947	103		2.0	2.0	M-G-M	
LIVING IT UP	1954	95		2.0	3.0	PARAMOUNT	
LIVING ON VELVET	1935	80		2.0	2.0	FIRST NATIONAL	
LIZZIE	1957	81		2.0	2.5	M-G-M	
LLOYDS OF LONDON	1936	115	4*	3.5	3.5	20th CENTURY FOX	
LOAN SHARK	1952	74		2.5	2.0	LIPPERT PRODS.	
LOCAL BOY MAKES GOOD	1931	67		2.5	2.5	FIRST NATIONAL	
LOCK UP YOUR DAUGHTERS	1969	102	3			COLUMBIA	
LOCKER SIXTY-NINE (BRITISH)	1962	56		2.0	2.0	ANGLO AMALGAMATED	
LOCKET, THE	1946	86		2.0	2.0	RKO	
LODGER, THE (GEORGE SANDERS, MERLE OBERON)	1944	84		2.5	3.0	20th CENTURY FOX	
LOLA (CHARLES BRONSON, SUSAN GEORGE)	1970	88	4			AMERICAN-INTERNAT'L	
LOLA MONTES (FRENCH)	a1955	110	4	1.5		BRANDON	
LOLITA (BRITISH)	1962	152	5*	3.0	3.0	M-G-M	
LONDON TOWN (BRITISH)	1946	100		2.0		CONTINENTAL	

‡ An asterisk (*) in THE FILM BUFF'S BIBLE column indicates that the film has been rated by the editor and/or staff. All other ratings in this column are based on a consensus of reviews (see NOTES).

Top header notes:

"a" TO LEFT OF YEAR INDICATES THAT FILM HAS AN ALTERNATE TITLE

CRITICAL RATINGS

TITLE (LEADING ACTORS SHOWN WHERE TWO OR MORE FILMS HAVE THE SAME OR SIMILAR TITLE)	YEAR RELEASED	RUNNING TIME IN MINUTES	THE FILM BUFF'S BIBLE ‡	STEVEN SCHEUER	LEONARD MALTIN	DISTRIBUTOR	COMMENT
LONE COWBOY	1933	68		3.0		PARAMOUNT	
LONE GUN, THE	1954	78	2	2.0	2.0	UNITED ARTISTS	
LONE HAND, THE	1953	80		2.0	2.5	UNIVERSAL	
LONE RANGER, THE	1956	86		2.0	2.5	WARNER BROTHERS	
LONE RANGER AND LOST CITY OF GOLD, THE	1958	80		1.5	2.0	UNITED ARTISTS	
LONE STAR	1952	94		2.5	2.5	M-G-M	
LONE TEXAN, THE	1959	70		1.5	1.5	20th CENTURY FOX	
LONE WOLF AND HIS LADY, THE	1949	60			-	COLUMBIA	
LONE WOLF IN LONDON, THE	1947	68			-	COLUMBIA	
LONE WOLF IN MEXICO, THE	1947	69			-	COLUMBIA	
LONE WOLF IN PARIS, THE	1938	66		2.5		COLUMBIA	
LONE WOLF KEEPS A DATE, THE	1941	65			-	COLUMBIA	
LONE WOLF MEETS A LADY, THE	1940	71			-	COLUMBIA	
LONE WOLF RETURNS, THE	1936	69			-	COLUMBIA	
LONE WOLF SPY HUNT, THE	1939	67		2.5		COLUMBIA	
LONE WOLF STRIKES, THE	1940	57		2.5	-	COLUMBIA	
LONE WOLF TAKES A CHANCE, THE	1941	76			-	COLUMBIA	
LONELINESS OF LONG DISTANCE RUNNER, THE (BRITISH)	1962	103	6*	4.0	4.0	CONTINENTAL	
LONELY ARE THE BRAVE	1962	107	6*	3.0	3.0	UNIVERSAL	
LONELY HEARTS BANDITS	1950	60		1.5		REPUBLIC	
LONELY MAN, THE	1957	87	4	2.5	3.0	PARAMOUNT	
LONELY NIGHT (DOCUMENTARY)	1952	65	6			MAYER-KINGSLEY	
LONELY PROFESSION, THE (T.V.)	1969	100		3.0		UNIVERSAL	
LONELYHEARTS	1958	102		2.5	2.5	UNITED ARTISTS	
LONESOME TRAIL, THE	1955	73	2	2.5	2.0	LIPPERT PRODS.	
LONG ABSENCE, THE (FRENCH)	1961	85	6			COMMERCIAL PICS.	
LONG AGO TOMORROW	1971	111	7			CINEMA V	
LONG DARK HALL, THE (BRITISH)	1951	86		2.5	2.5	EAGLE LION	
LONG DAY'S DYING, THE (BRITISH)	1968	93	4	2.0		PARAMOUNT	
LONG DAY'S JOURNEY INTO NIGHT	1962	136	7*	4.0	4.0	AVCO-EMBASSY	
LONG DUEL, THE (BRITISH)	1967	115	4			PARAMOUNT	
LONG GRAY LINE, THE	1955	138	6	3.0	3.0	COLUMBIA	
LONG HAUL, THE (BRITISH)	1957	88		1.5	2.0	COLUMBIA	
LONG, HOT SUMMER, THE	1958	115	5*	3.5	3.0	20th CENTURY FOX	
LONG JOHN SILVER (AUSTRALIAN)	1955	109		2.5	2.5	NEW TRENDS ASSOC.	
LONG, LONG TRAILER, THE	1954	96		3.0	2.5	M-G-M	
LONG LOST FATHER	1934	63		2.0		RKO	
LONG MEMORY, THE (BRITISH)	1953	96		2.0	2.0	ASTOR	
LONG NIGHT, THE (HENRY FONDA, BARBARA BEL GEDDES)	1947	101	4	2.0	2.0	RKO	
LONG RIDE FROM HELL	1969	94	1			CINERAMA RELEASING	
LONG RIDE HOME, THE	a1967	88	4*	2.5		COLUMBIA	
LONG RIFLE AND THE TOMAHAWK, THE	1956	88		1.5		INDEP. TV CORP (ITC)	
LONG ROPE, THE (BRIT.- DONALD HOUSTON, SUSAN SHAW)	a1953	72		3.0		ASSOCIATED ARTISTS	
LONG ROPE, THE (HUGH MARLOWE, ALAN HALE)	1961	61		2.5	2.0	20th CENTURY FOX	
LONG SEARCH, THE (SWEDISH)	1949	82		2.0			
LONG SHADOW, THE (BRITISH)	1961	64			1.5	SCREEN GEMS	
LONG SHIPS, THE (BRITISH)	1964	124		2.0	2.5	COLUMBIA	
LONG, SWIFT SWORD OF SIEGFRIED, THE	1971	92				ENTERTAINM'T VENTURES	
LONG, THE SHORT AND THE TALL, THE (BRITISH)	a1961	105	3*	3.5	3.0	CONTINENTAL	
LONG VOYAGE HOME, THE	1940	104		4.0	4.0	UNITED ARTISTS	NOMINATED BEST PICTURE
LONG WAIT, THE	1954	93		2.0	2.0	UNITED ARTISTS	
LONGEST DAY, THE	1962	180	6*	4.0		20th CENTURY FOX	NOMINATED BEST PICTURE
LONGEST HUNDRED MILES, THE (T.V.)	1966	100		2.5	2.0	UNIVERSAL	
LONGSTREET (T.V.)	1971	90	6*	3.0		PARAMOUNT	
LOOK BACK IN ANGER (BRITISH)	1959	99	4*	4.0	3.5	WARNER BROTHERS	
LOOK FOR THE SILVER LINING	1949	100		2.5	2.5	WARNER BROTHERS	
LOOK IN ANY WINDOW	1961	87		2.0	2.0	ALLIED ARTISTS	
LOOK WHO'S LAUGHING	1941	79		2.5		RKO	
LOOKING FOR DANGER	1957	62			-	ALLIED ARTISTS	
LOOKING FOR LOVE	1964	83	2		1.0	M-G-M	
LOOKING GLASS WAR, THE (BRITISH)	1970	108	2			COLUMBIA	
LOOPHOLE	1954	80		2.5	2.5	ALLIED ARTISTS	
LOOSE IN LONDON	1953	62	4		-	ALLIED ARTISTS	
LOOT (BRITISH)	1972	90	3			BRITISH-LION	
LOOTERS, THE	1955	87		2.0	2.5	UNIVERSAL	
LORD JEFF	1938	78		2.5	2.0	M-G-M	
LORD JIM (BRITISH)	1965	154	3*	3.0	2.5	COLUMBIA	
LORD LOVE A DUCK	1966	95	5	3.0		UNITED ARTISTS	
LORD OF THE FLIES (BRITISH)	1963	91	6*	3.0	3.0	CONTINENTAL	
LORD OF THE JUNGLE	1955	69			-	ALLIED ARTISTS	
LORNA	1964	78	1			EVE RELEASING CORP.	
LORNA DOONE	1951	88		2.5	2.5	COLUMBIA	
LOS OLVIDADOS (MEXICAN)	a1951	80	4*			MAYER-KINGSLEY	
LOS TARANTOS (SPANISH)	1963	81		3.0	3.0	SIGMA III	
LOSER TAKES ALL (BRITISH)	1956	88		2.5	2.0	DIST. CORP. OF AMER.	
LOSERS, THE	1970	95	2			FANFARE	
LOSS OF INNOCENCE (BRITISH)	1961	99	6*	4.0	2.5	COLUMBIA	
LOST (BRITISH)	1955	89		3.0	2.5	J. ARTHUR RANK	
LOST ANGEL	1943	91		2.0	2.5	M-G-M	
LOST BATTALION, THE	1962	83		2.0		AMERICAN-INTERNAT'L	
LOST BOUNDARIES	1949	99	7	3.5	3.0	FOUR CONTINENTS	
LOST COMMAND	1966	127		2.5	3.0	COLUMBIA	
LOST CONTINENT (ITALIAN, DOCUMENTARY)	1954	64	6			LOPERT	
LOST CONTINENT, THE (CESAR ROMERO)	1951	86	2		2.5	LIPPERT PRODS.	

‡ An asterisk (*) in THE FILM BUFF'S BIBLE column indicates that the film has been rated by the editor and/or staff. All other ratings in this column are based on a consensus of reviews (see NOTES).

TITLE (LEADING ACTORS SHOWN WHERE TWO OR MORE FILMS HAVE THE SAME OR SIMILAR TITLE)	YEAR RELEASED	RUNNING TIME IN MINUTES	THE FILM BUFF'S BIBLE ‡	STEVEN SCHEUER	LEONARD MALTIN	DISTRIBUTOR	COMMENT
LOST CONTINENT, THE (BRITISH - ERIC PORTER)	1968	98	2	2.0		20th CENTURY FOX	
LOST FLIGHT, THE	1970	104	4*			UNIVERSAL	
LOST HONEYMOON	1947	71	3		2.0	EAGLE LION	
LOST HORIZON (RONALD COLEMAN)	1937	118	8*	3.5	4.0	COLUMBIA	NOMINATED BEST PICTURE
LOST IN A HAREM	1944	89		2.0	2.5	M-G-M	
LOST IN ALASKA	a1952	76	2	2.5	2.0	UNIVERSAL	
LOST ISLAND OF KIOGA	1938	100		2.0	2.0	REPUBLIC	RE-EDITED SERIAL
LOST LAGOON	1958	79		2.0	1.5	UNITED ARTISTS	
LOST MAN, THE	1969	113	3*	2.5		UNIVERSAL	
LOST MISSILE, THE	1958	70		2.0	2.0	UNITED ARTISTS	
LOST MOMENT, THE	1947	88	5	3.5	3.0	UNIVERSAL	
LOST ONE, THE (ITALIAN)	a1948	82		3.0		COLUMBIA	
LOST PATROL, THE	1934	74		3.5	4.0	RKO	
LOST PEOPLE, THE (BRITISH)	1949	89		3.0		J. ARTHUR RANK	
LOST PLANET AIRMEN	1949	65		1.5	1.5	REPUBLIC	RE-EDITED SERIAL
LOST SEX (JAPANESE)	1966	97	5			CHEVRON	
LOST SQUADRON, THE	1932	72		3.0	2.5	RKO	
LOST TREASURE OF THE AZTECS (ITALIAN)	1959	85		1.0		AMERICAN-INTERNAT'L	
LOST TRIBE, THE	1949	72		1.5		COLUMBIA	
LOST VOLCANO, THE	1950	75	2			MONOGRAM	
LOST WEEKEND, THE	1945	101	7*	4.0	4.0	PARAMOUNT	BEST PICTURE AWARD
LOST WORLD, THE (SILENT - BESSIE LOVE)	1925	108			2.5	FIRST NATIONAL	
LOST WORLD, THE (MICHAEL RENNIE, JILL ST JOHN)	1960	98		2.5	2.0	20th CENTURY FOX	
LOST WORLD OF SINBAD, THE (JAPANESE)	1965	95	3	1.5		AMERICAN-INTERNAT'L	
LOUISA	1950	90	6	2.5	3.0	UNIVERSAL	
LOUISIANA HAYRIDE	1944	67		1.5	2.0	COLUMBIA	
LOUISIANA PURCHASE	1941	98		3.5	2.5	PARAMOUNT	
LOUISIANA STORY	1948	77	4*			LOPERT	
LOVE AFFAIR (CHARLES BOYER, IRENE DUNNE)	1939	87		4.0		RKO	NOMINATED BEST PICTURE
LOVE AFFAIR (YUGOSLAVIAN - EVA RAS, RUZICA SOKIC)	a1967	70	6			BRANDON	
LOVE AND KISSES	1965	87		2.0	2.5	UNIVERSAL	
LOVE AND LARCENY (ITALIAN)	1959	94	5		2.5	MAJOR FILM	
LOVE AND LEARN	1947	83		1.5	2.0	WARNER BROTHERS	
LOVE AND MARRIAGE (ITALIAN)	1964	106	3			AVCO-EMBASSY	
LOVE AND THE FRENCHWOMAN (FRENCH)	1960	143	6	3.0	3.0	KINGSLEY INTERNAT'L	
LOVE AT TWENTY (FRENCH-ITAL.-JAP.-GERMAN-POLISH)	1962	110		3.5	2.5	AVCO-EMBASSY	FIVE STORIES
LOVE BEFORE BREAKFAST	1936	70			2.5	UNIVERSAL	
LOVE BUG, THE	1969	110	6	3.0		BUENA VISTA	
LOVE CRAZY	1941	100		3.0	3.0	M-G-M	
LOVE CYCLES	1972	87				H.K. FILM DIST.	
LOVE DOCTORS, THE	1969	90	1			SIGMA III	
LOVE FINDS ANDY HARDY	1938	90		3.0	·	M-G-M	
LOVE FROM A STRANGER	1947	81		2.5	2.5	EAGLE LION	
LOVE FROM PARIS (GERMAN)	1961	87		3.0		MEDALLION	
LOVE GOD?, THE	1969	101	3	1.0		UNIVERSAL	
LOVE GODDESSES, THE	1965	87	5		2.5	CONTINENTAL	FILM CLIPS
LOVE HAPPY	1950	91		2.5	2.5	UNITED ARTISTS	
LOVE HAS MANY FACES	1965	105	3	2.0	2.5	COLUMBIA	
LOVE HATE LOVE (T.V.)	1971	90		3.0		ABC FILMS	
LOVE, HONOR AND BEHAVE	1938	71		3.0		WARNER BROTHERS	
LOVE, HONOR AND GOODBYE	1945	87		1.5	2.0	REPUBLIC	
LOVE IN A GOLDFISH BOWL	1961	88		3.0	1.0	PARAMOUNT	
LOVE IN A HOT CLIMATE (FRENCH)	1959	70		1.5		HOFFBERG	
LOVE IN BLOOM	1935	75		2.5	2.0	PARAMOUNT	
LOVE IN 4 DIMENSIONS (ITALIAN)	1965	108	6			ELDORADO PICS. INT'L	
LOVE IN JAMAICA (FRENCH)	1957	90		1.5			
LOVE-IN '72	1971	86				WILLIAM MISHKIN	
LOVE IN THE AFTERNOON	1957	130	7*	3.0	3.5	ALLIED ARTISTS	
LOVE IN THE CITY (ITALIAN)	1953	90		2.5	2.0	ITALIAN FILMS EXPORT	
LOVE-INS, THE	1967	86	1			COLUMBIA	
LOVE IS A BALL	1963	111		2.0	2.5	UNITED ARTISTS	
LOVE IS A FOUR LETTER WORD (CANADIAN)	1971	93				ALLIED ARTISTS	
LOVE IS A FUNNY THING (FRENCH)	1970	110	6			UNITED ARTISTS	
LOVE IS A MANY-SPLENDORED THING	1955	102	4*	2.5	3.0	20th CENTURY FOX	NOMINATED BEST PICTURE
LOVE IS BETTER THAN EVER	1952	81		2.5	2.5	M-G-M	
LOVE IS MY PROFESSION (FRENCH)	1958	111	3			KINGSLEY INTERNAT'L	
LOVE IS NEWS	1937	78		2.0	2.0	20th CENTURY FOX	
LOVE LAUGHS AT ANDY HARDY	1946	93		2.0	·	M-G-M	
LOVE LETTERS	1945	101		2.0	2.0	PARAMOUNT	
LOVE LOTTERY, THE (BRITISH)	1953	89		2.0	2.0	CONTINENTAL	
LOVE MACHINE, THE	1971	108	3*			COLUMBIA	
LOVE MAKERS, THE (ITALIAN - JEAN-PAUL BELMONDO)	a1960	102		3.0	2.5	AVCO-EMBASSY	
LOVE MATCH, THE (BRITISH)	1955	85		2.0		BRITISH-LION	
LOVE MATES (SWEDISH)	1961	90	3			ALTURA FILMS	
LOVE ME FOREVER	1935	90			2.5	COLUMBIA	
LOVE ME - LOVE ME NOT (BRITISH)	1962	86		2.0		TRANSCONTINENTAL	
LOVE ME OR LEAVE ME	1955	122	6	3.5	3.5	M-G-M	
LOVE ME TENDER	1956	89		2.0	2.5	20th CENTURY FOX	
LOVE ME TONIGHT	1932	104	4.5*	3.0	3.5	PARAMOUNT	
LOVE NEST	1951	84		2.0	2.0	20th CENTURY FOX	
LOVE OF THREE QUEENS (ITALIAN)	1953	90		1.5		FOUR STAR	
LOVE ON A BUDGET	1938	64		2.0		20th CENTURY FOX	
LOVE ON A PILLOW (FRENCH)	1962	102	2		2.0	ROYAL FILMS INT'L	
LOVE ON THE DOLE (BRITISH)	1941	100		3.0	3.0	UNITED ARTISTS	

‡ An asterisk (*) in THE FILM BUFF'S BIBLE column indicates that the film has been rated by the editor and/or staff. All other ratings in this column are based on a consensus of reviews (see NOTES).

TITLE (LEADING ACTORS SHOWN WHERE TWO OR MORE FILMS HAVE THE SAME OR SIMILAR TITLE) "a" TO LEFT OF YEAR INDICATES THAT FILM HAS AN ALTERNATE TITLE	YEAR RELEASED	RUNNING TIME IN MINUTES	THE FILM BUFF'S BIBLE ‡	STEVEN SCHEUER	LEONARD MALTIN	DISTRIBUTOR	COMMENT
LOVE ON THE RIVIERA (ITALIAN)	1963	88	3			ULTRA PICTURES CORP.	
LOVE ON THE RUN	1936	80		2.5	2.5	M-G-M	
LOVE PARADE, THE	1929	110			2.5	PARAMOUNT	NOMINATED BEST PICTURE 1929/30
LOVE SLAVES OF THE AMAZON	1957	81	2	1.5	2.0	UNIVERSAL	
LOVE SPECIALIST, THE (ITALIAN)	1958	99	3			MEDALLION	
LOVE STORY (BRITISH - STEWART GRANGER)	1944	113		2.5	3.0	J. ARTHUR RANK	
LOVE STORY (RYAN O'NEAL, ALI MACGRAW)	1970	100	8*			PARAMOUNT	NOMINATED BEST PICTURE
LOVE THAT BRUTE	1950	85		2.5	2.5	20th CENTURY FOX	
LOVE - THE ITALIAN WAY (ITALIAN)	1964	90	3			TRANS-LUX DIST.	
LOVE THY NEIGHBOR	1940	82		3.0	2.5	PARAMOUNT	
LOVE UNDER FIRE	1937	75		2.5	2.5	20th CENTURY FOX	
LOVE WITH THE PROPER STRANGER	1963	100	6*	3.0	3.0	PARAMOUNT	
LOVED ONE, THE	1965	116	4			M-G-M	
LOVELY TO LOOK AT	1952	105	5	2.5		M-G-M	
LOVELY WAY TO DIE, A	1968	104	2	2.0		UNIVERSAL	
LOVEMAKER, THE (SPANISH - BETSY BLAIR, J. SUAREZ)	1958	98	5	2.5		TRANS-LUX DIST.	
LOVER BOY (BRITISH)	a1954	99		2.5	2.5	20th CENTURY FOX	
LOVER COME BACK (LUCILLE BALL, GEORGE BRENT)	1946	90		2.5	2.5	UNIVERSAL	
LOVER COME BACK (ROCK HUDSON, DORIS DAY)	1962	107	7*	3.0	3.5	UNIVERSAL	
LOVERS, THE (FRENCH)	1958	90	5		3.0	ZENITH INTERNATIONAL	
LOVERS AND LOLLIPOPS	1956	80		2.5	2.5	TRANS-LUX DIST.	
LOVERS AND OTHER STRANGERS	1970	106	4*			CINERAMA RELEASING	
LOVERS, HAPPY LOVERS!	a1954	99		2.5	2.5	20th CENTURY FOX	
LOVERS OF MONTPARNASSE, THE (FRENCH)	a1958	110	5		2.5	CONTINENTAL	
LOVERS OF PARIS (FRENCH)	a1957	115		2.5	2.5	CONTINENTAL	
LOVERS OF TERUEL, THE (FRENCH)	1962	90	5			CONTINENTAL	
LOVERS ON A TIGHTROPE (FRENCH)	1960	90		1.5		INTERWORLD FILM	
LOVES OF A BLONDE, THE (CZECH)	1965	88			3.0	PROMINENT FILMS	
LOVES OF CARMEN, THE	1948	99		2.5	2.5	COLUMBIA	
LOVES OF EDGAR ALLEN POE, THE	1942	67		2.5	2.0	20th CENTURY FOX	
LOVES OF ISADORA, THE (BRITISH)	a1968	131	5*			UNIVERSAL	
LOVES OF JOANNA GODDEN, THE (BRITISH)	1947	89		2.5		ASSOC. BRITISH-PATHE	
LOVES OF SALAMMBO, THE (ITALIAN)	1959	72	2		2.0	20th CENTURY FOX	
LOVES OF THREE QUEENS (ITALIAN)	a1953	90			2.0	FOUR STAR	
LOVING	1970	90	4			COLUMBIA	
LOVING COUPLES (SWEDISH)	1965	113	6			PROMINENT FILMS	
LOVING YOU	1957	101	4*	2.0	2.5	PARAMOUNT	
LUCK OF GINGER COFFEY, THE (CANADIAN)	1964	100	5*	4.0	3.5	CONTINENTAL	
LUCK OF THE IRISH, THE	1948	99		2.5	2.5	20th CENTURY FOX	
LUCKY CISCO KID	1940	68		2.0		20th CENTURY FOX	
LUCKY JIM (BRITISH)	1957	95	4			KINGSLEY INTERNAT'L	
LUCKY JORDAN	1942	84		2.5	2.5	PARAMOUNT	
LUCKY ME	1954	100		2.0	2.0	WARNER BROTHERS	
LUCKY NICK CAIN	1951	87		3.0	2.5	20th CENTURY FOX	
LUCKY NIGHT	1939	90		1.5	1.5	M-G-M	
LUCKY PARTNERS	1940	102	4*	2.5	2.5	RKO	
LUCKY STIFF, THE	1949	99		2.0	2.0	UNITED ARTISTS	
LUCKY TO BE A WOMAN (ITALIAN)	1955	90		2.5	2.5	FILMS AROUND THE WLD.	
LUCY GALLANT	1955	104		2.5	2.5	PARAMOUNT	
LULLABY OF BROADWAY, THE	1951	92		2.0	2.5	WARNER BROTHERS	
LULU BELLE	1948	87		1.5	2.0	COLUMBIA	
LUPO!	1971	100	5			CANNON RELEASING	
LURE OF THE SILA (ITALIAN)	1953	74	3			ITALIAN FILMS EXPORT	
LURE OF THE SWAMP	1957	74	2		1.5	20th CENTURY FOX	
LURE OF THE WILDERNESS	1952	92		2.5	2.5	20th CENTURY FOX	
LURED	a1947	102		2.5	2.5	UNIVERSAL	
LUST FOR A VAMPIRE (BRITISH)	1971	95	1			LEVITT-PICKMAN	
LUST FOR GOLD (IDA LUPINO, GLENN FORD)	1949	90	4*	4.0	2.5	COLUMBIA	
LUST FOR LIFE	1956	122	8	4.0	4.0	M-G-M	
LUST TO KILL	1957	69		1.0		BARJUL INTERNATIONAL	
LUSTY MEN, THE	1952	113	4*	3.5	3.0	RKO	
LUV	1967	95	4	2.5		COLUMBIA	
LUXURY LINER (GEORGE BRENT, JANE POWELL)	1948	98		2.0	2.0	M-G-M	
LYDIA	1941	100		3.5	3.0	UNITED ARTISTS	
LYDIA BAILEY	1952	89		2.5	2.5	20th CENTURY FOX	
'M' (GERMAN - PETER LORRE)	1930	92	6*			PARAMOUNT	
'M' (DAVID WAYNE, HOWARD DA SILVA)	1951	88	5		2.5	COLUMBIA	
M.M.M. 83 (ITALIAN)	1965	78		1.5		AMERICAN-INTERNAT'L	
MA & PA KETTLE	1949	75		3.0	-	UNIVERSAL	
MA & PA KETTLE AT HOME	1954	81		2.5	-	UNIVERSAL	
MA & PA KETTLE AT THE FAIR	1952	78		2.5	-	UNIVERSAL	
MA & PA KETTLE AT WAIKIKI	1955	79		2.5	-	UNIVERSAL	
MA & PA KETTLE BACK ON THE FARM	1951	80		2.5	-	UNIVERSAL	
MA & PA KETTLE GO TO TOWN	1950	79	4	2.0	-	UNIVERSAL	
MA & PA KETTLE ON VACATION	1953	75	4	2.5	-	UNIVERSAL	
MA BARKER'S KILLER BROOD	1960	82	2		2.0	FILMSERVICE	
MACABRE	1958	73	2	2.0	2.0	ALLIED ARTISTS	
MACAO	1952	80		2.0	2.0	RKO	
MACARIO (MEXICAN)	1960	91	6			AZTECA	
MACBETH (ORSON WELLES, JEANETTE NOLAN)	1948	105	5*	3.0	3.0	REPUBLIC	
MACBETH (BRITISH - MAURICE EVANS, JUDITH ANDERSON)	1961	108				BRITISH-LION	

‡ An asterisk (*) in THE FILM BUFF'S BIBLE column indicates that the film has been rated by the editor and/or staff. All other ratings in this column are based on a consensus of reviews (see NOTES).

TITLE (LEADING ACTORS SHOWN WHERE TWO OR MORE FILMS HAVE THE SAME OR SIMILAR TITLE)	YEAR RELEASED	RUNNING TIME IN MINUTES	THE FILM BUFF'S BIBLE ‡	STEVEN SCHEUER	LEONARD MALTIN	DISTRIBUTOR	COMMENT
MACBETH (BRITISH - JON FINCH, FRANCESCA ANNIS)	1971	140	6			COLUMBIA	
MACHETE	1958	75	1			UNITED ARTISTS	
MACHINE GUN KELLY	1958	80		2.0	2.5	AMERICAN-INTERNAT'L	
MACHINE GUN MCCAIN (ITALIAN)	1970	94	2			COLUMBIA	ENGLISH LANGUAGE
MACHISTE IN KING SOLOMON'S MINES (ITALIAN)	1963	92		1.0		AVCO-EMBASSY	
MACHISTE AGAINST HERCULES IN THE VALE OF WOE	a1964	95		1.5		AVCO-EMBASSY	
MACHISTE, STRONGEST MAN IN THE WORLD (ITALIAN)	1962	97		1.0		GOLDEN ERA	
MACHO CALLAHAN	1970	99	3			AVCO-EMBASSY	
MACISTE - THE MIGHTY (ITALIAN)	1960	87			2.0	PANTON	
MACKENNA'S GOLD	1969	128	4	1.5		COLUMBIA	
MACOMBER AFFAIR, THE	1947	89	4*	3.5	3.5	UNITED ARTISTS	
MACUMBA LOVE	1960	86		1.5	1.5	UNITED ARTISTS	
MAD ABOUT MEN (BRITISH)	1955	90		2.0			
MAD ABOUT MUSIC	1938	98		3.0	3.0	UNIVERSAL	
MAD AT THE WORLD	1955	72		2.5	1.5	FILMMAKERS	
MAD DOCTOR, THE	1941	90		2.0	2.0	PARAMOUNT	
MAD DOCTOR OF MARKET STREET, THE	1942	61		1.5	1.5	UNIVERSAL	
MAD DOG COLL	1961	86		1.5	1.5	COLUMBIA	
MAD DOGS AND ENGLISHMEN (DOCUMENTARY)	a1971	114	5			M-G-M	
MAD EXECUTIONERS, THE (GERMAN)	1965	92		1.5	2.0	PARAMOUNT	
MAD GENIUS, THE	1931	81	3*	3.0	2.5	WARNER BROTHERS	
MAD GHOUL, THE	1943	65		2.5	2.5	UNIVERSAL	
MAD LITTLE ISLAND (BRITISH)	1958	94	4	2.5	2.0	J. ARTHUR RANK	
MAD LOVE	1935	83		2.5	3.0	M-G-M	
MAD MAGICIAN, THE	1954	72		2.0	2.5	COLUMBIA	
MAD MARTINDALES, THE	1942	65		1.5		20th CENTURY FOX	
MAD MISS MANTON, THE	1938	65		3.5	2.5	RKO	
MAD ROOM, THE	1969	92	5	3.0		COLUMBIA	
MAD WEDNESDAY	a1947	89	5		2.5	UNITED ARTISTS	
MADAM SATAN	1930	80		1.0	2.5	M-G-M	
MADAME (FRENCH)	1962	100		2.0	2.5	AVCO-EMBASSY	
MADAME BOVARY (JENNIFER JONES, JAMES MASON)	1949	115	6	3.0	2.5	M-G-M	
MADAME BUTTERFLY (SYLVIA SIDNEY, CARY GRANT)	1932	86		2.5	2.5	PARAMOUNT	
MADAME BUTTERFLY (ITALIAN - KAORU YACHIGUSA)	1955	114	6			ITALIAN FILMS EXPORT	
MADAME CURIE	1943	124		3.5	3.0	M-G-M	NOMINATED BEST PICTURE
MADAME DU BARRY	1934	77		3.0		WARNER BROTHERS	
MADAME SIN (BRITISH)	1972	90	4*			SCOTIA-BARBER	
MADAME X (LEWIS STONE, RUTH CHATTERTON)	1929	95		1.0		M-G-M	
MADAME X.(LANA TURNER, JOHN FORSYTHE)	1966	99		2.0	2.5	UNIVERSAL	
MADDALENA (ITALIAN - LISA GASTONI, ERIC WOOFE)	1971	105				INT'L CO-PRODUCTIONS	
MADE FOR EACH OTHER (JAMES STEWART, C. LOMBARD)	1939	85	4*	4.0	3.0	UNITED ARTISTS	
MADE FOR EACH OTHER (RENEE TAYLOR, JOSEPH BOLOGNA)	1971	104	4			20th CENTURY FOX	
MADE IN HEAVEN (BRITISH)	1952	80		2.5		J. ARTHUR RANK	
MADE IN ITALY (ITALIAN)	1966	101	6			ROYAL FILMS INT'L	
MADE IN PARIS (ANN-MARGRET, LOUIS JOURDAN)	1966	103		1.5	2.5	M-G-M	
MADELEINE (BRITISH - ANN TODD)	a1949	101		4.0	2.5	UNIVERSAL	
MADELEINE (GERMAN - EVA BARTOK)	1958	86			1.5		
MADEMOISELLE (BRITISH-FRENCH)	1966	103	3			LOPERT	FRENCH LANGUAGE
MADEMOISELLE FIFI	1944	69		2.0	2.0	RKO	
MADEMOISELLE FROM PARIS (FRENCH)	a1955	92		1.5		REGENT	
MADIGAN	1968	101	4*	2.5	3.5	UNIVERSAL	
MADIGAN'S MILLIONS	1969	77	2			AMERICAN-INTERNAT'L	
MADISON AVENUE	1962	94		2.0	2.5	20th CENTURY FOX	
MADMEN OF MANDORAS	1964	74			2.0	CROWN INTERNATIONAL	
MADNESS OF THE HEART (BRITISH)	1949	74		2.5		UNIVERSAL	
MADONNA OF THE DESERT	1948	60		2.0		REPUBLIC	
MADONNA OF THE SEVEN MOONS (BRITISH)	1944	88		3.0	3.0	UNIVERSAL	
MADONNA'S SECRET, THE	1946	79		3.0	2.0	REPUBLIC	
MADRON	1970	93	1			FOUR STAR-EXCELSIOR	
MADWOMAN OF CHAILLOT, THE (BRITISH)	1969	145	4			WARNER BROTHERS	
MAEDCHEN IN UNIFORM (GERMAN)	1965	91		2.0	2.5	SEVEN ARTS	
MAFIOSO (ITALIAN)	1962	100	6			ZENITH INTERNATIONAL	
MAGGIE, THE (BRITISH)	a1954	93		3.0	2.5	UNIVERSAL	
MAGIC BOW, THE (BRITISH)	1946	105		2.5	2.5	UNIVERSAL	
MAGIC BOX, THE (BRITISH)	1951	103	7	3.0	4.0	J. ARTHUR RANK	
MAGIC CARPET, THE	1951	84	2	2.0	2.0	COLUMBIA	
MAGIC CHRISTIAN, THE (BRITISH)	1970	93	4			AMERICAN-INTERNAT'L	
MAGIC FACE, THE	1951	89	4	3.0	2.0	COLUMBIA	
MAGIC FIRE	1956	95		2.0	2.0	REPUBLIC	
MAGIC FOUNTAIN, THE	1964	90		2.0		WARNER BROTHERS	
MAGIC GARDEN, THE (BRITISH)	a1951	63	6	3.5		MAYER-KINGSLEY	
MAGIC GARDEN OF STANLEY SWEETHEART, THE	1970	113	4			M-G-M	
MAGIC SWORD, THE	1962	80		1.5	2.5	UNITED ARTISTS	
MAGIC TOWN	1947	103		2.5	2.5	RKO	
MAGIC VOYAGE OF SINBAD, THE	1961	77		1.0		FILMGROUP	
MAGIC WEAVER, THE (RUSSIAN)	1965	90		3.0		ALLIED ARTISTS	
MAGIC WORLD OF TOPO GIGIO, THE (ITALIAN)	1965	75			1.5	COLUMBIA	
MAGICIAN, THE (SWEDISH)	1958	102	6		3.0	JANUS FILMS	
MAGNET, THE (BRITISH)	1951	78	7	4.0	3.0	UNIVERSAL	
MAGNETIC MONSTER, THE	1953	76		2.0	2.5	UNITED ARTISTS	
MAGNIFICENT AMBERSONS, THE	1942	88	4*	4.0	4.0	RKO	NOMINATED BEST PICTURE
MAGNIFICENT BRUTE, THE	1936	80		2.5	2.0	UNIVERSAL	
MAGNIFICENT CUCKOLD, THE (ITALIAN)	1964	117	4		2.5	CONTINENTAL	
MAGNIFICENT DOLL, THE	1946	95	3*	2.0	2.0	UNIVERSAL	

‡ An asterisk (*) in THE FILM BUFF'S BIBLE column indicates that the film has been rated by the editor and/or staff. All other ratings in this column are based on a consensus of reviews (see NOTES).

At top of header: "a" TO LEFT OF YEAR INDICATES THAT FILM HAS AN ALTERNATE TITLE — CRITICAL RATINGS

TITLE (LEADING ACTORS SHOWN WHERE TWO OR MORE FILMS HAVE THE SAME OR SIMILAR TITLE)	YEAR RELEASED	RUNNING TIME IN MINUTES	THE FILM BUFF'S BIBLE ‡	STEVEN SCHEUER	LEONARD MALTIN	DISTRIBUTOR	COMMENT
MAGNIFICENT DOPE, THE	1942	83	5*	3.0	3.0	20th CENTURY FOX	
MAGNIFICENT FRAUD, THE	1939	78		2.0	2.0	PARAMOUNT	
MAGNIFICENT MATADOR, THE	1955	94		2.5	2.5	20th CENTURY FOX	
MAGNIFICENT OBSESSION	1954	108	5	2.5	2.5	UNIVERSAL	
MAGNIFICENT ROGUE, THE	1946	74		3.0		REPUBLIC	
MAGNIFICENT ROUGHNECKS	1956	73		2.0	1.0	ALLIED ARTISTS	
MAGNIFICENT SEVEN, THE (JAPANESE - TOSHIRO MIFUNE)	a1954	160	5*	4.0	3.0	TOHO	ORIGINALLY 200 MINUTES
MAGNIFICENT SEVEN, THE (YUL BRYNNER, ELI WALLACH)	1960	126	6*	3.0	3.0	UNITED ARTISTS	
MAGNIFICENT SINNER, THE (FRENCH)	1959	95		2.5	2.0	FILM-MART	
MAGNIFICENT YANKEE, THE	1950	80	6	3.5	3.0	M-G-M	
MAGUS, THE (BRITISH)	1968	116	6	3.0		20th CENTURY FOX	
MAID IN PARIS (FRENCH - DANY ROBIN, DANIEL GELIN)	1957	84		2.5	2.0	CONTINENTAL	
MAID IN SWEDEN	1971	90				CANNON RELEASING	
MAID OF SALEM	1937	86		3.0	3.0	PARAMOUNT	
MAIDEN FOR A PRINCE, A (ITALIAN)	1966	92	2			ROYAL FILMS INT'L	
MAID'S NIGHT OUT	1938	64		2.0	2.0	RKO	
MAIDSTONE	1970	110	3			SUPREME MIX	
MAIL ORDER BRIDE	a1964	83	4			M-G-M	
MAILBAG ROBBERY (BRITISH)	1958	70		2.0	2.0	TUDOR PICTURES	
MAIN ATTRACTION, THE (BRITISH)	1962	90	3			M-G-M	
MAIN CHANCE, THE (BRITISH)	1965	61		2.0	2.5	AVCO-EMBASSY	
MAIN STREET AFTER DARK	1944	57		1.5	2.5	M-G-M	
MAIN STREET KID, THE	1948	64		2.0		REPUBLIC	
MAIN STREET TO BROADWAY	1953	102		2.0	2.5	M-G-M	
MAISIE	1939	74		2.5	-	M-G-M	
MAISIE GETS HER MAN	1942	85		2.0	-	M-G-M	
MAISIE GOES TO RENO	1944	90		2.0	-	M-G-M	
MAISIE WAS A LADY	1941	79		2.0	-	M-G-M	
MAJIN, THE MONSTER OF TERROR (JAPANESE)	1966	82		1.0		AMERICAN-INTERNAT'L	
MAJOR AND THE MINOR, THE	1942	100	5-6*	3.5	3.5	PARAMOUNT	
MAJOR BARBARA (BRITISH)	1941	115		4.0	4.0	UNITED ARTISTS	
MAJOR DUNDEE	1965	134		2.5	2.5	COLUMBIA	
MAJORITY OF ONE, A	1962	153	5*	2.5	2.5	WARNER BROTHERS	
MAKE A FACE	1971	90	3			KAREN SPERLING	
MAKE BELIEVE BALLROOM	1949	79	3	1.5		COLUMBIA	
MAKE HASTE TO LIVE	1954	90	4	3.0	2.5	REPUBLIC	
MAKE ME AN OFFER (BRITISH)	1954	88		2.5	2.5	DOMINANT PICTURES	
MAKE MINE LAUGHS	1949	64		2.0	1.5	RKO	
MAKE MINE MINK (BRITISH)	1960	101	6*	3.5		CONTINENTAL	
MAKE WAY FOR A LADY	1936	65		2.5	2.0	RKO	
MAKE WAY FOR LILA (SWEDISH)	1958	90	4	2.5		PARAMOUNT	
MAKE WAY FOR TOMORROW	1937	92		3.5	3.5	PARAMOUNT	
MAKE YOUR OWN BED	1944	82		1.5	1.5	WARNER BROTHERS	
MAKING IT	1971	97	4			20th CENTURY FOX	
MALAGA (BRIT. - TREVOR HOWARD, DOROTHY DANDRIDGE)	1960	97		2.0	2.5	WARNER BROTHERS	
MALAMONDO (DOCUMENTARY)	1964	79	3			MAGNA PICTURES	
MALAYA	1950	98		2.5	2.5	M-G-M	
MALCOLM X (DOCUMENTARY)	1972	92	5			WARNER BROTHERS	
MALE ANIMAL, THE	1942	101	5*	3.5	3.5	WARNER BROTHERS	
MALE COMPANION (FRENCH)	1964	92	4			INTERNAT'L CLASSICS	
MALE HUNT (FRENCH)	1964	89		3.0	3.0	PATHE CONTEMPARARY	
MALPAS MYSTERY, THE (BRITISH)	1960	60	4	2.0		SCHOENFELD FILM DIST	
MALTA STORY, THE (BRITISH)	1953	103		2.5		UNIVERSAL	
MALTESE BIPPY, THE	1969	92	3			M-G-M	
MALTESE FALCON, THE (HUMPHREY BOGART, MARY ASTOR)	1941	100	8*	4.0	4.0	WARNER BROTHERS	NOMINATED BEST PICTURE
MAMBO (ITALIAN)	1955	94	3	2.0	2.5	PARAMOUNT	
MAMMY	1930	84			2.0	WARNER BROTHERS	
MAM'ZELLE PIGALLE (FRENCH)	a1955	86	3	2.0	2.5	FILMS AROUND THE WLD	
MAN, THE	1972	93	5			PARAMOUNT	
MAN ABOUT THE HOUSE, A (BRITISH)	1947	96		3.0	2.5	20th CENTURY FOX	
MAN ABOUT TOWN (JACK BENNY, DOROTHY LAMOUR)	1939	85		3.0	3.0	PARAMOUNT	
MAN ABOUT TOWN (FRENCH - MAURICE CHEVALIER)	1947	89		2.5	3.0	RKO	
MAN AFRAID	1957	84		2.0	2.5	UNIVERSAL	
MAN ALIVE	1945	70		2.5	2.5	RKO	
MAN ALONE, A	1955	96		3.5	2.5	REPUBLIC	
MAN AND A WOMAN, A (FRENCH)	1966	102	7*	4.0	3.5	ALLIED ARTISTS	
MAN AND BOY	1971	98	4			LEVITT-PICKMAN	
MAN AND CHILD (FRENCH)	1957	90		2.0		PARAMOUNT	
MAN AND THE MONSTER, THE (MEXICAN)	1962	78		1.0		TRANS-INTERNATIONAL	
MAN AT THE CARLTON TOWER (BRITISH)	1961	57		2.0	2.0	ANGLO AMALGAMATED	
MAN BAIT (BRITISH)	1951	77	3	3.0	2.0	LIPPERT PRODS.	
MAN BEAST, THE	1957	69		1.5		MEDALLION	
MAN BEHIND THE GUN, THE	1953	82		2.0	2.0	WARNER BROTHERS	
MAN BETRAYED, A (JOHN WAYNE, FRANCES DEE)	a1941	83		2.0	2.0	REPUBLIC	
MAN BETWEEN, THE (BRITISH)	1953	101	5*	3.5	3.0	UNITED ARTISTS	
MAN CALLED ADAM, A	1966	102	4	2.5	2.5	AVCO-EMBASSY	
MAN CALLED DAGGER, A	1968	82	2	1.0		M-G-M	
MAN CALLED FLINTSTONE, THE (CARTOON)	1966	87	4		2.5	COLUMBIA	
MAN CALLED GANNON, A	1969	105	4	3.0		UNIVERSAL	
MAN CALLED HORSE, A	1970	114	4*			NATIONAL GENERAL	
MAN CALLED PETER, A	1955	119	6	3.5	3.0	20th CENTURY FOX	
MAN CALLED SLEDGE, A	1971	90	2			COLUMBIA	
MAN COULD GET KILLED, A	1966	99		2.5	2.5	UNIVERSAL	
MAN CRAZY	1953	79	2	1.5		20th CENTURY FOX	

‡ An asterisk (*) in THE FILM BUFF'S BIBLE column indicates that the film has been rated by the editor and/or staff. All other ratings in this column are based on a consensus of reviews (see NOTES).

TITLE (LEADING ACTORS SHOWN WHERE TWO OR MORE FILMS HAVE THE SAME OR SIMILAR TITLE)	YEAR RELEASED	RUNNING TIME IN MINUTES	THE FILM BUFF'S BIBLE ‡	STEVEN SCHEUER	LEONARD MALTIN	DISTRIBUTOR	COMMENT
MAN DETAINED (BRITISH)	1961	59		2.0	2.5	ANGLO AMALGAMATED	
MAN-EATER OF KUMAON	1948	79		2.5	2.5	UNIVERSAL	
MAN ESCAPED, A (FRENCH)	1956	102	7	3.5		CONTINENTAL	
MAN FOR ALL SEASONS, A (BRITISH)	1966	120	9*			COLUMBIA	BEST PICTURE AWARD
MAN FROM BITTER RIDGE, THE	1955	80		2.0	2.5	UNIVERSAL	
MAN FROM CAIRO (ITALIAN)	1953	82		2.0	2.0	LIPPERT PRODS.	
MAN FROM COCODY (FRENCH)	1965	90		2.0		AMERICAN-INTERNAT'L	
MAN FROM COLORADO, THE	1948	99		3.0	3.0	COLUMBIA	
MAN FROM DAKOTA, THE	1940	75		2.0	2.5	M-G-M	
MAN FROM DEL RIO	1956	82		2.0	2.0	UNITED ARTISTS	
MAN FROM DOWN UNDER, THE	1943	103		2.0	2.5	M-G-M	
MAN FROM FRISCO	1944	91		2.5		REPUBLIC	
MAN FROM GALVESTON, THE	1964	57	2			WARNER BROTHERS	
MAN FROM GOD'S COUNTRY	1958	72		2.0	2.0	ALLIED ARTISTS	
MAN FROM LARAMIE, THE	1955	104		3.0	3.0	COLUMBIA	
MAN FROM NOWHERE, THE	1970	107	1			G. G. PRODUCTIONS	
MAN FROM O.R.G.Y., THE	1970	72	1			CINEMATION INDUS.	
MAN FROM OKLAHOMA, THE (GERMAN - RICH HORN)	1964	85		1.0		PARKSIDE PRODS.	
MAN FROM PLANET X, THE	1951	70	2		1.5	UNITED ARTISTS	
MAN FROM THE ALAMO, THE	1953	79	3	2.5	2.5	UNIVERSAL	
MAN FROM THE DINERS' CLUB, THE	1963	96	4	2.5	2.5	COLUMBIA	
MAN FROM YESTERDAY, THE (CLAUDETTE COLBERT)	1932	71		1.5	2.0	PARAMOUNT	
MAN HUNT (WALTER PIDGEON, GEORGE SANDERS)	1941	105	6*	3.0	3.5	20th CENTURY FOX	
MAN I KILLED, THE	a1932	94		3.0	3.0	PARAMOUNT	
MAN I LOVE, THE	1947	96	4	2.5	2.5	WARNER BROTHERS	
MAN I MARRIED, THE	1940	77		3.0	3.0	20th CENTURY FOX	
MAN IN A COCKED HAT (BRITISH)	1959	88		2.5	2.5	SHOWCORPORATION	
MAN IN GREY, THE (BRITISH)	1943	116	4*	3.0	3.0	UNIVERSAL	
MAN IN HALF MOON STREET, THE	1944	92		2.0	2.0	PARAMOUNT	
MAN IN HIDING (BRITISH)	1953	79		2.0	1.5	UNITED ARTISTS	
MAN IN OUTER SPACE (CZECH)	1964	85		2.0		AMERICAN-INTERNAT'L	
MAN IN THE ATTIC	1953	82		2.0	2.5	20th CENTURY FOX	
MAN IN THE BACK SEAT, THE (BRITISH)	1961	57		2.5		ANGLO AMALGAMATED	
MAN IN THE DARK (EDMOND O'BRIEN, AUDREY TOTTER)	1953	70	3	2.5	2.5	COLUMBIA	
MAN IN THE DARK (WILLIAM SYLVESTER)	1965	80	3			UNIVERSAL	
MAN IN THE GRAY FLANNEL SUIT, THE	1956	153	6	2.5	3.5	20th CENTURY FOX	
MAN IN THE IRON MASK, THE	1939	110		3.0	3.0	UNITED ARTISTS	
MAN IN THE MIDDLE, THE (BRITISH - ROBERT MITCHUM)	1964	94	4*	2.5	2.0	20th CENTURY FOX	
MAN IN THE MOON (BRITISH)	1960	98	5	3.0	3.0	TRANS-LUX DIST.	
MAN IN THE NET, THE	1959	97	3	2.5	2.5	UNITED ARTISTS	
MAN IN THE RAINCOAT, THE (FRENCH)	1956	87	6	3.0		KINGSLEY INTERNAT'L	
MAN IN THE ROAD, THE (BRITISH)	1956	84		2.0	1.5	REPUBLIC	
MAN IN THE SADDLE	1951	87		2.5	2.0	COLUMBIA	
MAN IN THE SHADOW	1958	80		2.5	2.5	UNIVERSAL	
MAN IN THE TRUNK, THE	1942	71		1.0		20th CENTURY FOX	
MAN IN THE VAULT	1956	73		1.5	1.5	RKO	
MAN IN THE WHITE SUIT, THE (BRITISH)	1951	84	7*	4.0	3.5	UNIVERSAL	
MAN IN THE WILDERNESS	1971	105	5*			WARNER BROTHERS	
MAN INSIDE, THE (BRITISH)	1958	90		2.5	1.5	COLUMBIA	
MAN IS ARMED, THE	1956	70		2.0	1.5	REPUBLIC	
MAN-MADE MONSTER	1941	59		2.0	2.0	UNIVERSAL	
MAN NAMED ROCCA, A (FRENCH)	1961	106		2.0		TELEWIDE SYSTEMS	
MAN OF A THOUSAND FACES	1957	122	6*	3.5	3.5	UNIVERSAL	
MAN OF ARAN (DOCUMENTARY)	1934	74	4*			GAUMONT-BRITISH	
MAN OF CONFLICT	1954	72	2		2.0	ATLAS	
MAN OF CONQUEST	1939	105		2.5	2.5	REPUBLIC	
MAN OF EVIL (BRITISH)	a1944	107		1.5	2.0	UNITED ARTISTS	
MAN OF IRON (ITALIAN - PIETRO GERMI)	a1956	105	6		3.0	CONTINENTAL	
MAN OF THE WEST	1958	100		2.5	2.5	UNITED ARTISTS	
MAN OF THE WORLD	1931	71		2.0	2.0	PARAMOUNT	
MAN OF TWO WORLDS	1934	97		3.0		RKO	
MAN ON A STRING	1960	92		2.5	3.0	COLUMBIA	
MAN ON A TIGHTROPE	1953	105	4*	3.0	3.0	20th CENTURY FOX	
MAN ON FIRE	1957	95	5	2.5	2.5	M-G-M	
MAN ON THE EIFFEL TOWER, THE	1948	82	6	3.5	3.0	RKO	
MAN ON THE FLYING TRAPEZE, THE	1935	65	6*	3.5	3.5	PARAMOUNT	
MAN ON THE RUN (BRITISH - BURGESS MEREDITH)	1948	74				STRATFORD PICS.	
MAN OR GUN	1958	79		1.5	2.0	REPUBLIC	
MAN OUTSIDE, THE (BRITISH)	1968	97	2			ALLIED ARTISTS	
MAN-PROOF	1938	74		2.5	2.0	M-G-M	
MAN THEY COULD NOT HANG, THE	1939	72			2.5	COLUMBIA	
MAN TO MAN TALK (FRENCH)	a1958	89	4	2.5	2.0	CONTINENTAL	
MAN-TRAP (JEFFREY HUNTER, DAVID JANSSEN)	1961	93	3		2.5	PARAMOUNT	
MAN UPSTAIRS, THE (BRITISH)	1958	88	5	3.0	3.0	KINGSLEY INTERNAT'L	
MAN WHO BROKE THE BANK AT MONTE CARLO, THE	1935	70			2.5	20th CENTURY FOX	
MAN WHO CAME TO DINNER, THE	1941	112		4.0	3.5	WARNER BROTHERS	
MAN WHO CHANGED HIS MIND, THE (BRITISH)	a1936	61		1.5	2.0	GAUMONT-BRITISH	
MAN WHO CHEATED HIMSELF, THE	1951	81		2.5	2.5	20th CENTURY FOX	
MAN WHO COULD CHEAT DEATH, THE (BRITISH)	1959	83		2.5	2.0	PARAMOUNT	
MAN WHO COULD WORK MIRACLES, THE (BRITISH)	1937	82	6*	3.0	3.5	UNITED ARTISTS	
MAN WHO DARED, THE (PRESTON FOSTER, ZITA JOHANN)	1933	75		3.0		20th CENTURY FOX	
MAN WHO DARED, THE (JANE BRYAN, CHARLIE GRAPEWIN)	1939	60		2.0		WARNER BROTHERS	
MAN WHO DARED, THE (LESLIE BROOKS, GEO. MACREADY)	1946	65		2.5		COLUMBIA	
MAN WHO DIED TWICE, THE	1958	70		1.5	2.0	REPUBLIC	

‡ An asterisk (*) in THE FILM BUFF'S BIBLE column indicates that the film has been rated by the editor and/or staff. All other ratings in this column are based on a consensus of reviews (see NOTES).

TITLE (LEADING ACTORS SHOWN WHERE TWO OR MORE FILMS HAVE THE SAME OR SIMILAR TITLE)	YEAR RELEASED	RUNNING TIME IN MINUTES	THE FILM BUFF'S BIBLE ‡	STEVEN SCHEUER	LEONARD MALTIN	DISTRIBUTOR	COMMENT
MAN WHO FOUND HIMSELF	1937	67		1.5		RKO	
MAN WHO HAD POWER OVER WOMEN, THE (BRITISH)	1970	90	2			WARNER BROTHERS	
MAN WHO HAUNTED HIMSELF, THE (BRITISH)	1970	94	1			LEVITT-PICKMAN	
MAN WHO KNEW TOO MUCH, THE	1956	120	6*	3.5	2.5	PARAMOUNT	
MAN WHO LIKED FUNERALS, THE (BRITISH)	1959	60		2.0		J. ARTHUR RANK	
MAN WHO LIVED AGAIN, THE (BRITISH)	a1936	61		1.5	2.0	GAUMONT-BRITISH	
MAN WHO LIVED TWICE, THE	1936	73			2.0	COLUMBIA	
MAN WHO LOVED REDHEADS, THE (BRITISH)	1955	89	6	3.5		UNITED ARTISTS	
MAN WHO NEVER WAS, THE	1956	103	5*	2.5	3.0	20th CENTURY FOX	
MAN WHO PLAYED GOD, THE	1932	81	5*	4.0	2.5	WARNER BROTHERS	
MAN WHO RETURNED TO LIFE	1942	60		2.5		COLUMBIA	
MAN WHO SHOT LIBERTY VALANCE, THE	1962	122	5*	3.0	2.5	PARAMOUNT	
MAN WHO TALKED TOO MUCH, THE	1940	75		2.0	2.5	WARNER BROTHERS	
MAN WHO TURNED TO STONE, THE	1957	80		1.0	1.0	COLUMBIA	
MAN WHO UNDERSTOOD WOMEN, THE	1959	105	4	3.0	2.5	20th CENTURY FOX	
MAN WHO WAGGED HIS TAIL, THE (SPANISH)	1957	91	6	2.5		CONTINENTAL	
MAN WHO WANTED TO LIVE FOREVER, THE (T.V.)	1970	90	5*	2.5		ABC FILMS	
MAN WHO WAS NOBODY, THE (BRITISH)	1960	58		2.0		ANGLO AMALGAMATED	
MAN WHO WOULDN'T DIE, THE	1942	65		1.5	2.0	20th CENTURY FOX	
MAN WHO WOULDN'T TALK, THE (LLOYD NOLAN)	1940	72		2.0	2.0	20th CENTURY FOX	
MAN WHO WOULDN'T TALK, THE (BR. - ANTHONY QUAYLE)	1958	85	4	2.5		SHOWCORPORATION	
MAN WITH A CLOAK, THE	1951	81		2.5	2.5	M-G-M	
MAN WITH A MILLION (BRITISH)	a1954	90	5-6*	3.0	2.5	UNITED ARTISTS	
MAN WITH CONNECTIONS (FRENCH)	1971	95	5			COLUMBIA	
MAN WITH MY FACE, THE	1951	86	4		2.0	UNITED ARTISTS	
MAN WITH NINE LIVES, THE	1940	73			2.5	COLUMBIA	
MAN WITH THE BALLOONS, THE (ITALIAN)	1964	85	4	1.5		SIGMA III	
MAN WITH THE GOLDEN ARM, THE	1955	119	6*	3.0	3.0	UNITED ARTISTS	
MAN WITH THE GOLDEN KEYS (FRENCH)	1956	90		2.0			
MAN WITH THE GUN	1955	83		2.5	2.5	UNITED ARTISTS	
MAN WITH TWO FACES (TAB HUNTER)	1964	80		1.5		COM. UNITED T.V.	
MAN WITH TWO FACES, THE (EDWARD G. ROBINSON)	1934	72		3.0	2.0	FIRST NATIONAL	
MAN WITH TWO HEADS, THE	1972	80				WILLIAM MISHKIN	
MAN WITHOUT A STAR	1955	89		3.0	2.5	UNIVERSAL	
MANCHURIAN CANDIDATE, THE	1962	126	8*	4.0	3.5	UNITED ARTISTS	
MANDALAY	1934	65		2.0	2.5	FIRST NATIONAL	
MANDRAGOLA (ITALIAN)	a1965	98	4			EUROPIX-CONSOLIDATED	
MANDY (BRITISH)	a1952	93	6	4.0	3.0	UNIVERSAL	
MANFISH	1956	76		1.5	2.0	UNITED ARTISTS	
MANHANDLED	1949	97		2.0	2.0	PARAMOUNT	
MANHATTAN ANGEL	1948	68		1.5		COLUMBIA	
MANHATTAN HEARTBEAT	1940	71		2.0		20th CENTURY FOX	
MANHATTAN MELODRAMA	1934	93		3.5	3.0	M-G-M	
MANHUNT IN SPACE	1954	78		1.0		OFFICIAL INDUSTRIES	
MANHUNT IN THE JUNGLE	1958	79		2.0	1.0	WARNER BROTHERS	
MANIA (BRITISH)	a1960	97	3	3.0		VALIANT	
MANIAC, THE (BRITISH)	1963	86	3	2.5	2.5	COLUMBIA	
MANILA CALLING	1942	81		2.0	2.0	20th CENTURY FOX	
MANNEQUIN	1937	95		2.0	2.5	M-G-M	
MANON (FRENCH)	1949	91	6			DISCINA INTERNAT'L	
MANPOWER	1941	105	3*	3.0	3.0	WARNER BROTHERS	
MAN'S CASTLE, A	1933	75			3.5	COLUMBIA	
MAN'S FAVORITE SPORT?	1964	120		2.5	2.5	UNIVERSAL	
MAN'S WORLD, A	1942	60		2.0		COLUMBIA	
MANSTER, THE	1962	72	1	1.0		LOPERT	
MANY HAPPY RETURNS	1934	60		2.0		PARAMOUNT	
MANY RIVERS TO CROSS	1955	92		3.0	2.5	M-G-M	
MARA MARU	1952	98		2.0	2.5	WARNER BROTHERS	
MARA OF THE WILDERNESS	1965	90	3		2.5	ALLIED ARTISTS	
MARACAIBO	1958	88	3	2.5	2.5	PARAMOUNT	
MARAT/SADE (BRITISH)	a1967	115	6			UNITED ARTISTS	
MARAUDERS, THE (DAN DURYEA, KEENAN WYNN)	1955	81		2.0	2.0	M-G-M	
MARAUDERS OF THE SEA (BRITISH)	1962	85					
MARCO POLO (ITALIAN)	1961	95	2*	2.0	2.5	AMERICAN-INTERNAT'L	ENGLISH VERSION
MARCO THE MAGNIFICENT (FRENCH)	1966	100	2	1.0	2.5	M-G-M	
MARCUS WELBY, M.D. (T.V.)	1969	100		2.5		UNIVERSAL	
MARDI GRAS	1958	107		2.5	2.5	20th CENTURY FOX	
MARGIE	1946	94		3.0	3.0	20th CENTURY FOX	
MARGIN FOR ERROR	1943	74		2.5	2.0	20th CENTURY FOX	
MARGO (ISRAELI)	1971	96	5			CANNON RELEASING	
MARIANNE OF MY YOUTH (FRENCH)	1955	105		2.0		UN. MOTION PIC. ORG.	
MARIE ANTOINETTE (NORMA SHEARER, TYRONE POWER)	1938	160		3.0	2.5	M-G-M	
MARIE ANTOINETTE (FRENCH - MICHELE MORGAN)	1956	102		2.0	2.5	RIZZOLI FILM	
MARIE DU PORT (FRENCH)	a1949	95	6			BELLON-FOULKE	
MARIE-OCTOBRE (FRENCH)	a1959	98	6			LOPERT	
MARIE OF THE ISLES (ITALIAN)	1961	111		1.5		TELEWIDE SYSTEMS	
MARILYN	1963	88	5	2.5		20th CENTURY FOX	
MARINE RAIDERS	1944	91		2.0	2.0	RKO	
MARINERS OF THE SKY	a1936	72		2.0		REPUBLIC	
MARINES FLY HIGH	1940	68		3.0		RKO	
MARINES, LET'S GO	1961	104	2		1.5	20th CENTURY FOX	
MARJOE (DOCUMENTARY)	1972	88				CINEMA V	
MARJORIE MORNINGSTAR	1958	123		3.0	2.5	WARNER BROTHERS	
MARK, THE (BRITISH)	1961	127	7*	4.0	4.0	CONTINENTAL	

‡ An asterisk (*) in THE FILM BUFF'S BIBLE column indicates that the film has been rated by the editor and/or staff. All other ratings in this column are based on a consensus of reviews (see NOTES).

TITLE (LEADING ACTORS SHOWN WHERE TWO OR MORE FILMS HAVE THE SAME OR SIMILAR TITLE)	YEAR RELEASED	RUNNING TIME IN MINUTES	THE FILM BUFF'S BIBLE ‡	STEVEN SCHEUER	LEONARD MALTIN	DISTRIBUTOR	COMMENT
MARK OF CAIN (BRITISH)	1948	88		2.5		J. ARTHUR RANK	
MARK OF THE DEVIL	1972	90	1			HALLMARK	
MARK OF THE GORILLA	1950	68		1.5	-	COLUMBIA	
MARK OF THE HAWK, THE	1958	83	4*	2.0	3.0	UNIVERSAL	
MARK OF THE PHOENIX (BRITISH)	1957	63		1.5		UNITED ARTISTS	
MARK OF THE RENEGADE	1951	81		2.5	2.5	UNIVERSAL	
MARK OF THE VAMPIRE (LIONEL BARRYMORE, B. LUGOSI)	1935	85		3.0	3.0	M-G-M	
MARK OF THE WHISTLER, THE	1944	61		3.0	-	COLUMBIA	
MARK OF ZORRO, THE (SILENT - DOUGLAS FAIRBANKS)	1920	80	5*		3.5	UNITED ARTISTS	
MARK OF ZORRO, THE (TYRONE POWER, BASIL RATHBONE)	1940	93	5*	3.5	3.5	20th CENTURY FOX	
MARKED WOMAN	1937	96		3.5	3.0	WARNER BROTHERS	
MARKSMAN, THE	1953	62		2.0	1.5	ALLIED ARTISTS	
MARLOWE	1969	100	3			M-G-M	
MARNIE	1964	129	5*	2.0	2.5	UNIVERSAL	
MAROC 7 (BRITISH)	1967	91	3	2.0		PARAMOUNT	
MAROONED	1969	134	4*			COLUMBIA	
MARRIAGE CAME TUMBLING DOWN, THE (FRENCH)	1968	88	6			ROYAL FILMS INT'L	
MARRIAGE-GO-ROUND, THE	1961	98	4	2.0	2.5	20th CENTURY FOX	
MARRIAGE IS A PRIVATE AFFAIR	1944	116		2.0	2.0	M-G-M	
MARRIAGE ITALIAN STYLE (ITALIAN)	1964	102	6	3.5	3.0	AVCO-EMBASSY	
MARRIAGE OF A YOUNG STOCKBROKER, THE	1971	95	4			20th CENTURY FOX	
MARRIAGE OF FIGARO, THE (FRENCH)	1959	105	6			PATHE CONTEMPARARY	
MARRIAGE ON THE ROCKS	1965	109	4	2.5		WARNER BROTHERS	
MARRIED BACHELOR	1941	81		2.5		M-G-M	
MARRIED BEFORE BREAKFAST	1937	70		2.5		M-G-M	
MARRIED COUPLE, A (CANADIAN)	1969	97	4			AQUARIUS	
MARRIED WOMAN, THE (FRENCH)	1965	95	4		2.5	ROYAL FILMS INT'L	
MARRY ME (BRITISH)	1949	97		2.5		J. ARTHUR RANK	
MARRY ME AGAIN	1954	73	4	3.0	2.0	RKO	
MARRY ME! MARRY ME! (FRENCH)	1968	87	4*			ALLIED ARTISTS	
MARRY THE BOSS' DAUGHTER	1941	60		1.0		20th CENTURY FOX	
MARRYING KIND, THE	1952	93	3*	3.5	3.0	COLUMBIA	
MARS, GOD OF WAR (ITALIAN)	1960	92		1.0		AVCO-EMBASSY	
MARSHALL'S DAUGHTER, THE	1953	71		1.0	1.5	UNITED ARTISTS	
MARTIN LUTHER	1953	103	6			DE ROCHEMONT	
MARTY	1955	99	6*	4.0	3.5	UNITED ARTISTS	BEST PICTURE AWARD
MARY BURNS, FUGITIVE	1935	84		2.5	3.0	PARAMOUNT	
MARY LOU	1948	66		1.0		COLUMBIA	
MARY, MARY	1963	126		2.5	2.5	WARNER BROTHERS	
MARY OF SCOTLAND	1936	123	5*	3.5	3.5	RKO	
MARY POPPINS	1964	140	7			BUENA VISTA	NOMINATED BEST PICTURE
MARY, QUEEN OF SCOTS (BRITISH)	1971	128	7*			UNIVERSAL	
MARYJANE	1968	95	1			AMERICAN-INTERNAT'L	
MARYLAND	1940	92		2.5	2.5	20th CENTURY FOX	
MASCULINE FEMININE (FRENCH)	1966	103	6			ROYAL FILMS INT'L	
M*A*S*H	1970	116	5*			20th CENTURY FOX	NOMINATED BEST PICTURE
MASK, THE (CANADIAN)	1961	83	2			WARNER BROTHERS	
MASK OF DIIJON, THE	1946	73			2.0	PRODUCERS RELEASING	
MASK OF DIMITRIOS, THE	1944	95		2.5	3.0	WARNER BROTHERS	
MASK OF FU MANCHU, THE	1932	72		1.5	2.5	M-G-M	
MASK OF THE AVENGER	1951	83		2.0	2.5	COLUMBIA	
MASK OF THE MUSKETEERS (ITALIAN)	1960	101		1.5		AMERICAN-INTERNAT'L	
MASKED CONQUERER, THE (ITALIAN)	1960	94		1.0		AMERICAN-INTERNAT'L	
MASKED MAN AGAINST THE PIRATES, THE (SPANISH)	1962	105		1.0		ABC FILMS	
MASQUE OF THE RED DEATH, THE (BRITISH)	1964	84	4			AMERICAN-INTERNAT'L	
MASQUERADE (BRITISH)	1965	102	4*	3.5	2.5	UNITED ARTISTS	
MASQUERADE IN MEXICO	1945	96		1.5	2.0	PARAMOUNT	
MASQUERADER, THE	1933	78		2.0	2.5	UNITED ARTISTS	
MASSACRE (DANE CLARK, JAMES CRAIG)	1956	76	3*	2.0	2.0	20th CENTURY FOX	
MASSACRE AT FORT PERDITION (SPANISH)	1965	95		2.0		AVCO-EMBASSY	
MASSACRE CANYON	1954	66		2.0		COLUMBIA	
MASSACRE RIVER	1949	75		2.0	1.5	ALLIED ARTISTS	
MASTER MINDS	1949	64			-	MONOGRAM	
MASTER OF BALLANTRAE, THE (BRITISH)	1953	89		2.5	2.5	WARNER BROTHERS	
MASTER OF THE WORLD	1961	104	5*	3.0	3.0	AMERICAN-INTERNAT'L	
MASTER PLAN (BRITISH)	1954	77		1.5		ASTOR	
MASTER RACE, THE	1944	96		3.0	3.0	RKO	
MASTER SPY (BRITISH)	1963	71	3	2.5	2.5	ALLIED ARTISTS	
MASTERS OF THE CONGO JUNGLE (BELGIAN, DOCUMENTARY)	1959	88	6			20th CENTURY FOX	
MASTERSON OF KANSAS	1955	73		2.0	2.0	COLUMBIA	
MATA HARI	1932	91		3.5	3.0	M-G-M	
MATA HARI'S DAUGHTER (ITALIAN)	a1962	102		2.0	2.0	TRANS-AMERICA	
MATCH KING, THE	1932	79		3.0		FIRST NATIONAL	
MATCHLESS (ITAL.- PATRICK O'NEAL, IRA FURSTENBERG)	1966	104	3			UNITED ARTISTS	
MATCHMAKER, THE	1958	101	6*	3.0	3.0	PARAMOUNT	
MATING GAME, THE	1959	96	6	3.0	3.0	M-G-M	
MATING OF MILLIE, THE	1948	87	5	2.5	2.5	COLUMBIA	
MATING SEASON, THE	1951	101	5	2.5	2.5	PARAMOUNT	
MATING URGE, THE (DOCUMENTARY)	1958	116	6			CITATION	
MATTER OF DAYS, A (FRENCH)	1969	96	4			ROYAL FILMS INT'L	
MATTER OF INNOCENCE, A (BRITISH)	1967	102		2.0	2.5	UNIVERSAL	
MATTER OF LIFE AND DEATH, A (BRITISH)	a1946	104	7*	3.5	3.5	UNIVERSAL	
MATTER OF MORALS, A	1960	90	4			UNITED ARTISTS	
MATTER OF RESISTANCE, A (FRENCH)	a1966	92	4			ROYAL FILMS INT'L	

‡ An asterisk (*) in THE FILM BUFF'S BIBLE column indicates that the film has been rated by the editor and/or staff. All other ratings in this column are based on a consensus of reviews (see NOTES).

SEND THIS CARD TODAY FOR ADDITIONAL FREE INFORMATION

To **HOLLYWOOD FILM ARCHIVE**
8344 MELROSE AVENUE
HOLLYWOOD, CALIF. 90069

☐ New FILM BULLETIN with News and Reviews
☐ CINEMA BOOK BULLETIN with Information and Reviews
☐ An ALL NEW Illustrated Edition of FILM BUFF'S BIBLE

PLEASE PRINT

Name _____ Position _____

Organization _____

Address _____

City _____ State _____ Zip _____

Comments: _____

FIRST CLASS
PERMIT NO. 55687
Hollywood, Calif.

BUSINESS REPLY MAIL

NO POSTAGE STAMP NECESSARY IF MAILED IN THE UNITED STATES

POSTAGE WILL BE PAID BY

HOLLYWOOD FILM ARCHIVE

8344 MELROSE AVENUE

HOLLYWOOD, CALIFORNIA 90069

TITLE (LEADING ACTORS SHOWN WHERE TWO OR MORE FILMS HAVE THE SAME OR SIMILAR TITLE)	YEAR RELEASED	RUNNING TIME IN MINUTES	THE FILM BUFF'S BIBLE ‡	STEVEN SCHEUER	LEONARD MALTIN	DISTRIBUTOR	COMMENT
MATTER OF WHO, A (BRITISH)	1961	90		2.5	3.0	HERTS-LION INT'L	
MAURIZIUS CASE, THE (FRENCH)	1953	110		2.5			
MAVERICK, THE	1952	71		2.5		ALLIED ARTISTS	
MAVERICK QUEEN, THE	1956	92	3	2.5	2.5	REPUBLIC	
MAXIME (FRENCH)	1958	93		2.0	2.5	ELLIS FILMS	
MAYA	1966	91	4			M-G-M	
MAYBE I'LL COME HOME IN THE SPRING (T.V.)	1971	75	3*	3.0		ABC FILMS	
MAYERLING (FRENCH)	1968	140	4			M-G-M	
MAYOR OF 44TH STREET	1942	86		2.5		RKO	
MAYOR OF HELL, THE	1933	80	3*	3.0		WARNER BROTHERS	
MAYTIME	1937	132		3.0	3.0	M-G-M	
MAYTIME IN MAYFAIR (BRITISH)	1949	94		2.0	2.5	REALART	
MAZE, THE	1953	81		3.0	2.0	ALLIED ARTISTS	
MCCABE AND MRS MILLER	1971	115	5*			WARNER BROTHERS	
MCCLOUD: WHO KILLED MISS U.S.A.?	1970	100		2.0		UNIVERSAL	
MCCONNELL STORY, THE	1955	107	4*	2.5	3.0	WARNER BROTHERS	
MCGUIRE, GO HOME (BRITISH)	1966	101		2.5	2.5	CONTINENTAL	
MCHALE'S NAVY	1964	93		2.0	2.0	UNIVERSAL	
MCHALE'S NAVY JOINS THE AIR FORCE	1965	90		2.0	2.0	UNIVERSAL	
MCKENZIE BREAK, THE (BRITISH)	1970	106	6			UNITED ARTISTS	
MCLINTOCK!	1963	127	3*	2.5	3.0	UNITED ARTISTS	
MCMASTERS, THE	1970	89	4			CHEVRON	
ME (FRENCH)	a1968	81	7			ALTURA FILMS	
ME AND THE COLONEL	1958	105	5*	3.5	2.5	COLUMBIA	
ME, NATALIE	1969	111	5			NATIONAL GENERAL	
MEANEST MAN IN THE WORLD, THE	1943	57		2.5	2.0	20th CENTURY FOX	
MEDAL FOR BENNY, A	1945	77	5*	3.5	3.5	PARAMOUNT	
MEDEA (ITALIAN)	1971	110	5			NEW LINE CINEMA	
MEDICINE BALL CARAVAN (DOCUMENTARY)	1971	89	2			WARNER BROTHERS	
MEDITERRANEAN HOLIDAY (TRAVELOGUE)	1964	130	6			CONTINENTAL	
MEDIUM, THE	1951	84	6	3.5	2.5	TRANSFILM	
MEDIUM COOL	1969	110	6			PARAMOUNT	
MEDUSA AGAINST THE SON OF HERCULES (ITALIAN)	1963	93		1.0		AVCO-EMBASSY	
MEET BOSTON BLACKIE	1941	61		3.0	-	COLUMBIA	
MEET DANNY WILSON	1952	86		2.5	2.5	UNIVERSAL	
MEET DR CHRISTIAN	1939	63			2.0	RKO	
MEET JOHN DOE	1941	135		3.0	3.0	WARNER BROTHERS	
MEET ME AFTER THE SHOW	1951	86		2.0	2.5	20th CENTURY FOX	
MEET ME AT THE FAIR	1953	87	4	3.0	2.5	UNIVERSAL	
MEET ME IN LAS VEGAS	1956	112		2.5	2.5	M-G-M	
MEET ME IN ST LOUIS	1944	113	5-6*	3.5	4.0	M-G-M	
MEET ME TONIGHT (BRITISH)	a1952	81		4.0	2.5	CONTINENTAL	THREE STORIES
MEET MR LUCIFER (BRITISH)	1953	83		3.0	2.0	J. ARTHUR RANK	
MEET PETER FOSS (GERMAN)	1961			2.5			
MEET THE NELSONS	a1952	76	4		2.0	UNIVERSAL	
MEET THE PEOPLE	1944	100		2.0	2.5	M-G-M	
MEET THE STEWARTS	1942	73		3.0		COLUMBIA	
MEIN KAMPF (SWEDISH, DOCUMENTARY)	1960	118		3.5	3.0	COLUMBIA	
MELBA (BRITISH)	1953	113		3.0	2.5	UNITED ARTISTS	
MELINDA	1972	109	3			M-G-M	
MELODY (BRITISH)	1971	103	6			LEVITT-PICKMAN	
MELODY FOR THREE	1941	67			2.0	RKO	
MEMBER OF THE WEDDING, THE	1952	91	5*	4.0	3.0	COLUMBIA	
MEN, THE	a1950	86	3*	4.0	3.5	UNITED ARTISTS	
MEN AGAINST THE SKY	1940	75		2.0	1.5	RKO	
MEN AGAINST THE SUN (BRITISH)	1953	64		2.5		MONARCH	
MEN AND WOLVES (ITALIAN)	1957	98		2.0		COLUMBIA	
MEN ARE NOT GODS (BRITISH)	1937	82		2.0	2.5	UNITED ARTISTS	
MEN ARE SUCH FOOLS	1938	70		2.5		WARNER BROTHERS	
MEN IN HER DIARY	1945	73		2.5	2.5	UNIVERSAL	
MEN IN HER LIFE, THE	1941	90			2.5	COLUMBIA	
MEN IN WAR	1957	104		3.0	2.5	UNITED ARTISTS	
MEN IN WHITE	1934	80		3.0	2.5	M-G-M	
MEN OF BOYS TOWN	1941	106		2.0	2.5	M-G-M	
MEN OF BRAZIL (BRAZILIAN)	1960	68			2.0		
MEN OF SHERWOOD FOREST (BRITISH)	1954	77		2.0	2.0	ASTOR	
MEN OF THE FIGHTING LADY	1954	80		2.5	3.0	M-G-M	
MEN OF TWO WORLDS (BRITISH)	a1946	109		2.5	2.0	UNIVERSAL	
MEN WHO TREAD ON THE TIGER'S TAIL (JAPANESE)	1953	60	5*			BRANDON	COMPLETED IN 1945
MEN WITH WINGS	1938	105		3.0	2.5	PARAMOUNT	
MEN WITHOUT NAMES	1935	66		2.5		PARAMOUNT	
MEN WITHOUT SOULS	1940	62			2.0	COLUMBIA	
MENACE (GERTRUDE MICHAEL, PAUL CAVANAGH)	1934	58		2.5		PARAMOUNT	
MENACE, THE (FRENCH - ROBERT HOSSEIN)	1960	90		1.5		WARNER BROTHERS	
MENANCE IN THE NIGHT (BRITISH)	1958	78		2.0	1.5	UNITED ARTISTS	
MEPHISTO WALTZ, THE	1971	115	3			20th CENTURY FOX	
MERCENARY, THE	1970	105	3			UNITED ARTISTS	
MERCILESS TRAP, THE (JAPANESE)	1964	82		1.5		COM. UNITED T.V.	
MERMAIDS OF TIBURON, THE	1962	77	2	1.0		FILMGROUP	
MERRILL'S MARAUDERS	1962	98	5	4.0	2.5	WARNER BROTHERS	
MERRILY WE GO TO HELL	1932	78		2.5	2.5	PARAMOUNT	
MERRILY WE LIVE	1938	90			3.0	M-G-M	
MERRY ANDREW	1958	103	4*	2.5	2.5	M-G-M	
MERRY MONAHANS, THE	1944	91		3.0	3.0	UNIVERSAL	

‡ An asterisk (*) in THE FILM BUFF'S BIBLE column indicates that the film has been rated by the editor and/or staff. All other ratings in this column are based on a consensus of reviews (see NOTES).

TITLE (LEADING ACTORS SHOWN WHERE TWO OR MORE FILMS HAVE THE SAME OR SIMILAR TITLE)	YEAR RELEASED	RUNNING TIME IN MINUTES	THE FILM BUFF'S BIBLE ‡	STEVEN SCHEUER	LEONARD MALTIN	DISTRIBUTOR	COMMENT
MERRY WIDOW, THE (SILENT - MAE MURRAY, J. GILBERT)	1925	111				M-G-M	
MERRY WIDOW, THE (MAURICE CHEVALIER)	a1934	99		3.5	3.0	M-G-M	
MERRY WIDOW, THE (LANA TURNER)	1952	105		2.5	2.5	M-G-M	
MERRY WIVES OF RENO	1934	64		2.5		WARNER BROTHERS	
MERRY WIVES OF WINDSOR, THE (AUSTRIAN)	1965	97	6			SIGMA III	ENGLISH LANGUAGE
MERTON OF THE MOVIES (SILENT - GLENN HUNTER)	1924	85				PARAMOUNT	BELIEVED LOST
MERTON OF THE MOVIES (RED SKELTON, V. O'BRIEN)	1947	82	4			M-G-M	
MESSAGE TO GARCIA, A	1936	77	4*		3.0	20th CENTURY FOX	
MESSILINA (ITALIAN - BELINDA LEE, SPYROS FOKAS)	1960	84		1.5		AMERICAN-INTERNAT'L	
MESSILINA AGAINST THE SON OF HERCULES (ITALIAN)	1963	98		1.5		AVCO-EMBASSY	
METEOR MONSTER (BRITISH)	1958	73		1.0		UCC FILMS	
METROPOLIS (GERMAN, SILENT)	1926	139	4*			PARAMOUNT	
MEXICAN HAYRIDE	1948	77		2.5	2.0	UNIVERSAL	
MEXICAN MANHUNT	1953	71		1.5	1.5	ALLIED ARTISTS	
MEXICAN SPITFIRE	1940	67		2.5		RKO	
MEXICAN SPITFIRE AT SEA	1942	72		2.0		RKO	
MEXICAN SPITFIRE OUT WEST	1942	76		2.0		RKO	
MEXICAN SPITFIRE SEES A GHOST	1942	69		1.5		RKO	
MEXICAN SPITFIRE'S BABY	1941	70		2.0		RKO	
MEXICAN SPITFIRE'S BLESSED EVENT	1943	63		2.0		RKO	
MEXICAN SPITFIRE'S ELEPHANT	1942	64		2.0		RKO	
MEXICANA	1945	83		1.0		REPUBLIC	
MGM'S BIG PARADE OF COMEDY	a1964	91	4*	3.5	2.5	M-G-M	
MIAMI EXPOSE	1956	73		2.0	1.5	COLUMBIA	
MIAMI STORY, THE	1954	75		2.0	2.0	COLUMBIA	
MICHAEL AND HELGA (GERMAN)	a1968	87	2			AMERICAN-INTERNAT'L	
MICHAEL SHAYNE, PRIVATE DETECTIVE	1940	77		2.5	2.5	20th CENTURY FOX	
MICHAEL STROGOFF (CURT JURGENS, GENEVIEVE PAGE)	a1956	115	4	2.0		CONTINENTAL	(ITALIAN)
MICHIGAN KID, THE	1947	69		1.0	2.0	UNIVERSAL	
MICKEY	1948	87			2.0	EAGLE LION	
MICKEY ONE	1965	93	3*	3.5	3.0	COLUMBIA	
MIDAS RUN	a1969	106	4			CINERAMA RELEASING	
MIDDLE OF THE NIGHT	1959	118		2.5	2.5	COLUMBIA	
MIDNIGHT	1939	94		2.5	3.0	PARAMOUNT	
MIDNIGHT COWBOY, THE	1969	111	9*			UNITED ARTISTS	BEST PICTURE AWARD
MIDNIGHT INTRUDER	1938	68		2.5		UNIVERSAL	
MIDNIGHT LACE	1960	108	5*	2.5	3.0	UNIVERSAL	
MIDNIGHT STORY, THE	1957	89		2.0	2.5	UNIVERSAL	
MIDSUMMER NIGHT'S DREAM, A (JAMES CAGNEY)	1935	132		3.5	3.0	WARNER BROTHERS	NOMINATED BEST PICTURE
MIDSUMMER NIGHT'S DREAM, A (CZECH - PUPPETS)	1959	74	6	3.0		SHOWCORPORATION	
MIGHTY BARNUM, THE	1934	87			3.0	UNITED ARTISTS	
MIGHTY CRUSADERS, THE (ITALIAN)	1957	87		1.5	2.0	FALCON	
MIGHTY JOE YOUNG	1949	94	5	3.0	3.0	RKO	
MIGHTY JUNGLE, THE	1964	88		1.5		PARAMOUNT	
MIGHTY MCGURK, THE	1946	85		2.0	1.5	M-G-M	
MIGHTY URSUS, THE (ITALIAN)	1961	78	2	1.5	2.0	UNITED ARTISTS	
MIKADO, THE (KENNY BAKER, JEAN COLIN)	1939	90		3.5	3.0	UNIVERSAL	
MIKADO, THE (BRIT. - DONALD ADAMS, PHILIP POTTER)	1967	125	6			WARNER BROTHERS	
MILDRED PIERCE	1945	113	6*	3.0	3.5	WARNER BROTHERS	NOMINATED BEST PICTURE
MILKMAID, THE (FINNISH)	1955	70	1			VINOD INTERNATIONAL	
MILKMAN, THE	1950	87	4	2.0	2.0	UNIVERSAL	
MILKY WAY, THE (HAROLD LLOYD, ADOLPHE MENJOU)	1936	88		3.0		PARAMOUNT	
MILKY WAY, THE (FRENCH - PAUL FRANKEUR)	1969	105	6			UNITED ARTISTS	
MILL OF THE STONE WOMEN (ITALIAN)	1960	94	3	1.5		PARADE	
MILL ON THE PO (ITALIAN)	1949	96	6			LUX FILM AMERICA	
MILLER'S BEAUTIFUL WIFE, THE (ITALIAN)	a1955	95	6			DIST. CORP. OF AMER.	
MILLERSON CASE, THE	1947	72	2		-	COLUMBIA	
MILLHOUSE: A WHITE COMEDY	1971	92	5			NEW YORKER FILMS	
MILLIE'S DAUGHTER	1947	72		1.0		COLUMBIA	
MILLION DOLLAR BABY	1941	100		2.0	2.0	WARNER BROTHERS	
MILLION DOLLAR DUCK, THE	1971	92	4			BUENA VISTA	
MILLION DOLLAR KID	1944	65				MONOGRAM	
MILLION DOLLAR LEGS (W. C. FIELDS)	1932	64	3*	3.5	3.5	PARAMOUNT	
MILLION DOLLAR LEGS (BETTY GRABLE)	1939	59		1.5	2.5	PARAMOUNT	
MILLION DOLLAR MANHUNT (BRITISH)	1957	65		1.0		PARAMOUNT	
MILLION DOLLAR MERMAID	1952	115		2.5	2.5	M-G-M	
MILLION DOLLAR PURSUIT	1951	60		2.0		REPUBLIC	
MILLION DOLLAR WEEKEND	1948	72			2.0	EAGLE LION	
MILLION EYES OF SU-MURU, THE (BRITISH)	1967	95	1			AMERICAN-INTERNAT'L	
MILLIONAIRE, THE	1931	81		3.0		WARNER BROTHERS	
MILLIONAIRE FOR CHRISTY, A	1951	91		2.0	2.5	20th CENTURY FOX	
MILLIONAIRE PLAYBOY	1940	64		2.0		RKO	
MILLIONAIRES IN PRISON	1940	64		2.5		RKO	
MILLIONAIRESS, THE (BRITISH)	1960	90		2.0	2.5	20th CENTURY FOX	
MIN AND BILL	1930	69			2.5	M-G-M	
MIND BENDERS, THE (BRITISH)	1963	99	4	2.5	3.0	AMERICAN-INTERNAT'L	
MIND OF MR SOAMES, THE (BRITISH)	1970	95	6			COLUMBIA	
MIND YOUR OWN BUSINESS	1937	75		2.5		PARAMOUNT	
MINE OWN EXECUTIONER (BRITISH)	1947	105	5	3.5	3.0	20th CENTURY FOX	
MINI-SKIRT MOB, THE	1968	82	1	1.0		AMERICAN-INTERNAT'L	
MINISTRY OF FEAR	1944	85	6*	3.5	3.5	PARAMOUNT	
MINIVER STORY, THE	1950	104		2.0	2.5	M-G-M	
MINNESOTA CLAY (ITALIAN)	1964	95	2			HARLEQUIN INTERNAT'L	
MINNIE AND MOSKOWITZ	1972	114	5			UNIVERSAL	

‡ An asterisk (*) in THE FILM BUFF'S BIBLE column indicates that the film has been rated by the
editor and/or staff. All other ratings in this column are based on a consensus of reviews (see NOTES).

TITLE (LEADING ACTORS SHOWN WHERE TWO OR MORE FILMS HAVE THE SAME OR SIMILAR TITLE)	YEAR RELEASED	RUNNING TIME IN MINUTES	THE FILM BUFF'S BIBLE ‡	STEVEN SCHEUER	LEONARD MALTIN	DISTRIBUTOR	COMMENT
MINOTAUR, THE (ITALIAN)	1960	95		2.0	1.5	UNITED ARTISTS	
MINUTE TO PRAY, A SECOND TO DIE, A (ITALIAN)	1967	97	2	1.5		CINERAMA RELEASING	
MINX, THE	1970	84	1			CAMBIST	
MIRACLE, THE (CARROLL BAKER, ROGER MOORE)	1959	121		2.5	2.5	WARNER BROTHERS	
MIRACLE CAN HAPPEN, A	a1948	107		2.0	2.5	UNITED ARTISTS	
MIRACLE IN MILAN (ITALIAN)	1951	96	6			JOSEPH BURSTYN	
MIRACLE IN THE RAIN	1956	107		2.5	2.5	WARNER BROTHERS	
MIRACLE OF LOVE, THE (GERMAN)	1968	83	3			TIMES FILM CORP.	
MIRACLE OF MARCELINO, THE (FRENCH)	a1955	90		4.0		UN. MOTION PIC. ORG.	
MIRACLE OF MORGAN'S CREEK, THE	1944	99	5*	3.0	4.0	PARAMOUNT	
MIRACLE OF OUR LADY OF FATIMA, THE	a1952	102	5	3.0	3.0	WARNER BROTHERS	
MIRACLE OF THE BELLS, THE	1948	120	3	1.5	1.5	RKO	
MIRACLE OF THE HILLS, THE	1959	73		2.0	1.5	20th CENTURY FOX	
MIRACLE OF THE WHITE STALLIONS, THE	1963	118	4			BUENA VISTA	
MIRACLE ON 34TH STREET	1947	96	6*	4.0	3.5	20th CENTURY FOX	NOMINATED BEST PICTURE
MIRACLE WORKER, THE	1962	106	7*	4.0	3.5	UNITED ARTISTS	
MIRACLES FOR SALE	1939	71		2.0		M-G-M	
MIRACULOUS JOURNEY	1948	83			1.5	FILM CLASSICS	
MIRAGE	1965	109		3.0	3.0	UNIVERSAL	
MIRANDA (BRITISH)	1948	79		2.5	2.5	EAGLE LION	
MIRROR HAS TWO FACES, THE (FRENCH)	1958	98		2.0	2.5	CONTINENTAL	
MISADVENTURES OF MERLIN JONES, THE	1964	88	4			BUENA VISTA	
MISFITS, THE	1961	124	3*	3.0	3.0	UNITED ARTISTS	
MISS ANNIE ROONEY	1942	84			2.0	UNITED ARTISTS	
MISS GRANT TAKES RICHMOND	1949	87		3.0	2.5	COLUMBIA	
MISS JULIE (SWEDISH)	1950	91	7			TRANS-GLOBAL PICS.	
MISS PINKERTON	1932	66		2.0	2.0	FINE ARTS	
MISS ROBIN CRUSOE	1954	75		1.0	1.5	20th CENTURY FOX	
MISS ROBIN HOOD (BRITISH)	1952	78		2.5	2.0	EROS FILMS	
MISS SADIE THOMPSON	1954	91	4	2.5	3.0	COLUMBIA	
MISS SUSIE SLAGLE'S	1945	88		-	2.5	PARAMOUNT	
MISS TATLOCK'S MILLIONS	1948	101	6*	3.5	3.0	PARAMOUNT	
MISSILE BASE AT TANIAK	1953	100		1.5	1.5	REPUBLIC	RE-EDITED SERIAL
MISSILE MONSTERS	1958	75		1.0	1.5	REPUBLIC	
MISSILE TO THE MOON	1958	78		1.0	1.0	ASTOR	
MISSILES FROM HELL (BRITISH)	1958	82		1.5	2.0	NTA PICTURES	
MISSING CORPSE, THE	1945	62			1.5	PRODUCERS RELEASING	
MISSING JUROR, THE	1944	65	4*	2.5	3.0	COLUMBIA	
MISSION BATANGAS	1968	100		2.0		MANSON	
MISSION OF THE SEA HAWK (BRITISH)	1962	83		2.0			
MISSION OVER KOREA	1953	85		2.0	1.5	COLUMBIA	
MISSION TO HELL (GERMAN)	1964	95		1.0		UCC FILMS	
MISSION TO MOROCCO	1959	79		1.5			
MISSION TO MOSCOW	1943	123		3.5	3.5	WARNER BROTHERS	
MISSION TO VENICE (FRENCH)	1963	88		1.5		SCREEN GEMS	
MISSISSIPPI	1935	73	5*	3.0	3.5	PARAMOUNT	
MISSISSIPPI GAMBLER, THE (TYRONE POWER)	1953	98	4	3.0	2.5	UNIVERSAL	
MISSISSIPPI MERMAID, THE (FRENCH)	1969	110	3			UNITED ARTISTS	
MISSOURI TRAVELER, THE	1958	104		3.0	2.5	BUENA VISTA	
MR ACE	1946	84			2.5	UNITED ARTISTS	
MR AND MRS NORTH	1941	67		3.0	2.5	M-G-M	
MR AND MRS SMITH	1941	95		3.0	3.0	RKO	
MR ARKADIN (BRITISH)	a1955	99		3.0	2.5	CARI	
MR BELVEDERE GOES TO COLLEGE	1949	83	4	2.0	2.0	20th CENTURY FOX	
MR BELVEDERE RINGS THE BELL	1951	87	4*	3.0	2.5	20th CENTURY FOX	
MR BLANDINGS BUILDS HIS DREAM HOUSE	1948	94	6	3.5	3.0	RKO	
MR BUDDWING	1966	100		2.0	2.5	M-G-M	
MR BUG GOES TO TOWN (CARTOON)	a1941	78	4*	3.0		PARAMOUNT	
MR CORY	1957	92	4	3.5	2.5	UNIVERSAL	
MR DEEDS GOES TO TOWN	1936	115	7*	4.0	3.5	COLUMBIA	NOMINATED BEST PICTURE
MR DENNING DRIVES NORTH (BRITISH)	1951	93		3.0	2.5	CARROLL PICTURES	
MR DISTRICT ATTORNEY	1947	81	3			COLUMBIA	
MR DRAKE'S DUCK (BRITISH)	1951	76	4	3.0	3.0	UNITED ARTISTS	
MR DYNAMITE	1941	63		2.5		UNIVERSAL	
MR 880	1950	90	5*	3.5	3.0	20th CENTURY FOX	
MR EMMANUEL (BRITISH)	1944	93		3.0		UNITED ARTISTS	
MR HEX	1946	63				MONOGRAM	
MR HOBBS TAKES A VACATION	1962	116		2.5	2.5	20th CENTURY FOX	
MR HULOT'S HOLIDAY (FRENCH)	1953	91	4-6*	4.0	3.0	G-B-D INTERNATIONAL	
MR IMPERIUM	1951	87	3	2.0	2.5	M-G-M	
MR JERICHO (BRITISH, T.V.)	1970	75		2.5		INDEP. TV CORP (ITC)	
MR LORD SAYS NO (BRITISH)	1952	76	5	3.0		LONDON FILMS	
MR LUCKY	1943	98	6*	3.5	3.0	RKO	
MR MOSES	1965	113		2.0	2.5	UNITED ARTISTS	
MR MOTO IN DANGER ISLAND	1939	63				20th CENTURY FOX	
MR MOTO TAKES A CHANCE	1938	63		2.0	-	20th CENTURY FOX	
MR MOTO TAKES A VACATION	1939	61		1.5	-	20th CENTURY FOX	
MR MOTO'S GAMBLE	1938	71			-	20th CENTURY FOX	
MR MOTO'S LAST WARNING	1939	71			-	20th CENTURY FOX	
MR MUGGS RIDES AGAIN	1945	63			-	MONOGRAM	
MR MUSIC	1950	113		2.5	2.5	PARAMOUNT	
MR PEABODY AND THE MERMAID	1948	89		2.5	2.5	UNIVERSAL	
MR PEEK-A-BOO (FRENCH)	1951	74		3.0		UNITED ARTISTS	
MR PERRIN AND MR TRAILL (BRITISH)	1948	90		3.5	2.0	EAGLE LION	

‡ An asterisk (*) in THE FILM BUFF'S BIBLE column indicates that the film has been rated by the editor and/or staff. All other ratings in this column are based on a consensus of reviews (see NOTES).

TITLE (LEADING ACTORS SHOWN WHERE TWO OR MORE FILMS HAVE THE SAME OR SIMILAR TITLE)	YEAR RELEASED	RUNNING TIME IN MINUTES	THE FILM BUFF'S BIBLE ‡	STEVEN SCHEUER	LEONARD MALTIN	DISTRIBUTOR	COMMENT
MR POTTS GOES TO MOSCOW (BRITISH)	a1953	93	6	3.0		STRATFORD PICS.	
MR RECKLESS	1948	66	2	1.5		PARAMOUNT	
MR ROBERTS	1955	123	5*	4.0	3.0	WARNER BROTHERS	NOMINATED BEST PICTURE
MR ROBINSON CRUSOE	1932	72		3.0		UNITED ARTISTS	
MR ROCK AND ROLL	1957	86	1	1.0		PARAMOUNT	
MR SARDONICUS	1961	89		2.5	2.0	COLUMBIA	
MR SCOUTMASTER	1953	87		2.0	3.0	20th CENTURY FOX	
MR SKEFFINGTON	1944	146		2.0	3.0	WARNER BROTHERS	
MR SMITH GOES TO WASHINGTON	1939	125	7*	4.0	4.0	COLUMBIA	NOMINATED BEST PICTURE
MR SOFT TOUCH	1949	93		2.5	2.0	COLUMBIA	
MR STEVE (FRENCH)	1957	100		2.5		PARAMOUNT	
MR UNIVERSE	1951	79	3		1.5	EAGLE LION	
MR WINKLE GOES TO WAR	1944	80		3.0	2.5	COLUMBIA	
MR WISE GUY	1942	70		-		MONOGRAM	
MRS BROWN, YOU'VE GOT A LOVELY DAUGHTER (BRITISH)	1968	95	3	2.0		M-G-M	
MRS MIKE	1949	99	4	3.0	2.5	UNITED ARTISTS	
MRS MINIVER	1942	134	6*	4.0	3.5	M-G-M	BEST PICTURE AWARD
MRS O'MALLEY AND MR MALONE	1950	69		2.5	2.0	M-G-M	
MRS PARKINGTON	1944	124		3.0	3.0	M-G-M	
MRS POLLIFAX - SPY	1971	110	3			UNITED ARTISTS	
MRS WIGGS OF THE CABBAGE PATCH (W. C. FIELDS)	1934	80	3*	2.5	3.0	PARAMOUNT	
MRS WIGGS OF THE CABBAGE PATCH (FAY BAINTER)	1942	80		1.5	2.5	PARAMOUNT	
MISTRESS, THE (JAPANESE)	1953	106		2.5		HARRISON PICTURES	
MISTRESS OF THE WORLD (GERMAN)	1959	98		2.0		MEDALLION	
MISTY	1961	92	6			20th CENTURY FOX	
MITSOU (FRENCH)	1956	92	5			ZENITH INTERNATIONAL	
MIX ME A PERSON (BRITISH)	1962	116		2.5		BRITISH-LION	
MOB, THE	1951	87		3.0	2.0	COLUMBIA	
MOB TOWN	1941	70		2.0	-	UNIVERSAL	
MOBY DICK (JOHN BARRYMORE, JOAN BENNETT)	1930	116			3.0	WARNER BROTHERS	
MOBY DICK (GREGORY PECK, RICHARD BASEHART)	1956	116	6*	3.0	3.0	WARNER BROTHERS	
MODEL AND THE MARRIAGE BROKER, THE	1952	103	6	3.0	3.0	20th CENTURY FOX	
MODEL FOR MURDER (BRITISH)	1959	75		2.0	2.0	CINEMA ASSOCIATES	
MODEL SHOP	1969	95	3			COLUMBIA	
MODEL WIFE	1941	78			2.5	UNIVERSAL	
MODELS, INC	1952	73	1			MUTUAL	
MODERATO CANTABILE (FRENCH)	1960	92	6			ROYAL FILMS INT'L	
MODERN TIMES (SILENT)	1936	85	7			UNITED ARTISTS	
MODESTY BLAISE (BRITISH)	1966	119		-	2.0	20th CENTURY FOX	
MODIGLIANI OF MONTPARNASSE (FRENCH)	a1958	110	5		2.5	CONTINENTAL	
MOGAMBO	1953	115	5*	3.0	3.5	M-G-M	
MOHAWK	1956	79			2.5	20th CENTURY FOX	
MOKEY	1942	88		2.0	2.0	M-G-M	
MOLE MEN AGAINST THE SON OF HERCULES (ITALIAN)	1963	98		1.0		AVCO-EMBASSY	
MOLE PEOPLE, THE	1956	78		2.0	2.0	UNIVERSAL	
MOLLY	a1950	83		2.5	2.5	PARAMOUNT	
MOLLY AND ME	1945	76		3.0	3.0	20th CENTURY FOX	
MOLLY MAGUIRES, THE	1970	123	6			PARAMOUNT	
MOMENT OF TRUTH (ITALIAN - MIGUEL MATEO MIGUELIN)	1965	110	6			RIZZOLI FILM	
MOMENT OF TRUTH, THE (FRENCH - MICHELE MORGAN)	1952	89		2.0	2.0	ARLAN PICTURES	
MOMENT TO MOMENT	1966	108		2.5	2.5	UNIVERSAL	
MOMENT'S CARESS, A	1971	90				KONOVER FILM DIST.	
MONA KENT	1961	75		1.0		ASTOR	
MONDO CANE (ITALIAN, DOCUMENTARY)	a1961	105	6*	2.5	2.5	TIMES FILM CORP.	
MONDO PAZZO (ITALIAN, DOCUMENTARY)	a1964	96	2			RIZZOLI FILM	
MONEY AND THE WOMAN	1940	65		2.0		WARNER BROTHERS	
MONEY FROM HOME	1953	100		2.0	3.0	PARAMOUNT	
MONEY TRAP, THE	1966	91		2.0	2.5	M-G-M	
MONEY, WOMEN AND GUNS	1959	80		2.5	2.0	UNIVERSAL	
MONGOLS, THE (ITALIAN)	1960	105	2	2.5	2.0	COLORAMA FEATURES	
MONIQUE (BRITISH)	1970	86	2			AVCO-EMBASSY	
MONITORS, THE	1969	92	2			CUE	
MONK, THE (T.V.)	1969	90		3.0		ABC FILMS	
MONKEY BUSINESS (MARX BROTHERS)	1931	77	4*	4.0	3.5	PARAMOUNT	
MONKEY BUSINESS (GINGER ROGERS, CARY GRANT)	1952	97	5	3.0	3.0	20th CENTURY FOX	
MONKEY IN WINTER (FRENCH)	1962	104	6			M-G-M	
MONKEY ON MY BACK	1957	93		3.0	2.5	UNITED ARTISTS	
MONKEYS, GO HOME	1967	101	4			BUENA VISTA	
MONKEY'S UNCLE, THE	1965	87	5			BUENA VISTA	
MONOCLE, THE (FRENCH)	1964	97		1.0		FOUR STAR	
MONOLITH MONSTERS, THE	1957	77		2.0	2.0	UNIVERSAL	
MONPTI (GERMAN)	1957	97	5	2.5		BAKROS INTERNATIONAL	
MONSIEUR BEAUCAIRE (BOB HOPE, JOAN CAULFIELD)	1946	93	5*	3.5	3.0	PARAMOUNT	
MONSIEUR GANGSTER (FRENCH)	1960	98		2.5		AMERICAN-INTERNAT'L	
MONSIEUR ROBINSON CRUSOE (FRENCH)	1959	88		2.0		LES FILMS DU CYCLOPE	
MONSIEUR VERDOUX	1947	123	7			UNITED ARTISTS	
MONSOON	1952	79		1.5	1.5	UNITED ARTISTS	
MONSTER AND THE GIRL, THE	1941	63		1.0		PARAMOUNT	
MONSTER DEMOLISHER (MEXICAN)	1960	74		1.0		TRANS-INTERNATIONAL	
MONSTER FROM A PREHISTORIC PLANET (JAPANESE)	1963	85		1.0		AMERICAN-INTERNAT'L	
MONSTER FROM GREEN HELL	1957	71		2.0		DIST. CORP. OF AMER.	
MONSTER FROM THE SURF	1965	85		1.0		AMERICAN-INTERNAT'L	
MONSTER MAKER, THE	1944	62			2.0	PRODUCERS RELEASING	
MONSTER OF PIEDRAS BLANCAS, THE	1958	71		1.5	2.0	VANWICK	

‡ An asterisk (*) in THE FILM BUFF'S BIBLE column indicates that the film has been rated by the editor and/or staff. All other ratings in this column are based on a consensus of reviews (see NOTES).

TITLE (LEADING ACTORS SHOWN WHERE TWO OR MORE FILMS HAVE THE SAME OR SIMILAR TITLE)	YEAR RELEASED	RUNNING TIME IN MINUTES	THE FILM BUFF'S BIBLE ‡	STEVEN SCHEUER	LEONARD MALTIN	DISTRIBUTOR	COMMENT
MONSTER ON THE CAMPUS	1958	76	2	2.5	2.5	UNIVERSAL	
MONSTER THAT CHALLENGED THE WORLD, THE	1957	83		2.0	2.5	UNITED ARTISTS	
MONSTER ZERO (JAPANESE)	1970	92	1			MARON FILMS, LTD.	
MONSTROSITY	a1964	70			1.5	EMERSON FILMS	
MONTANA	1950	76		2.0	2.5	WARNER BROTHERS	
MONTANA BELLE	1952	81		2.0	2.0	RKO	
MONTANA MIKE	a1947	95		2.5	2.5	UNITED ARTISTS	
MONTANA TERRITORY	1952	64	2	2.0	2.0	COLUMBIA	
MONTE CARLO	1930	90			2.5	PARAMOUNT	
MONTE CARLO BABY (FRENCH)	1951	79	2	1.5		MONOGRAM	ENGLISH LANGUAGE
MONTE CARLO STORY, THE	1957	99		2.0	2.0	UNITED ARTISTS	
MONTE WALSH	1970	98	4			NATIONAL GENERAL	
MONTERY POP (DOCUMENTARY)	1967	80	6	3.5		LEACOCK-PENNEBAKER	
MONTPARNASSE 19 (FRENCH)	a1958	110	5		2.5	CONTINENTAL	
MOON AND SIXPENCE, THE	1942	89		3.5	3.0	UNITED ARTISTS	
MOON AND THE SLEDGEHAMMER (BRITISH, DOCUMENTARY)	1971	65	4			IMPACT FILMS	
MOON IS BLUE, THE	1953	99	5	2.0	2.5	UNITED ARTISTS	
MOON IS DOWN, THE	1943	90	4*	3.5	3.0	20th CENTURY FOX	
MOON OVER BURMA	1940	76		1.0	2.0	PARAMOUNT	
MOON OVER HER SHOULDER	1942	68		2.5		20th CENTURY FOX	
MOON OVER MIAMI	1941	91		3.0	2.5	20th CENTURY FOX	
MOON PILOT	1962	98	4			BUENA VISTA	
MOON SPINNERS, THE	1964	118	6			BUENA VISTA	
MOON ZERO TWO (BRITISH)	1969	100	3			WARNER BROTHERS	
MOONFLEET	1955	89		2.0	2.5	M-G-M	
MOONLIGHT AND CACTUS	1944	60			1.5	UNIVERSAL	
MOONLIGHT MURDER	1936	68		1.5		M-G-M	
MOONLIGHTER, THE	1953	75	3		2.0	WARNER BROTHERS	
MOONLIGHTING MISTRESS	1971	88				DALIA PRODS.	
MOONLIGHTING WIVES	1966	86	1			CRADDOCK FILMS	
MOONRAKER, THE (BRITISH)	1958	82		2.0	3.0	ASSOC. BRITISH-PATHE	
MOONRISE	1948	90		2.5	2.5	REPUBLIC	
MOON'S OUR HOME, THE	1936	80		2.5	2.0	PARAMOUNT	
MOONSHINE WAR, THE	1970	101	2			M-G-M	
MOONTIDE	1942	94		2.5	2.5	20th CENTURY FOX	
MOONWOLF (GERMAN)	1964	74		2.0		ALLIED ARTISTS	
MORALIST, THE (ITALIAN)	1957	86		2.0		AVERS FILM	
MORE (LUXEMBOURG)	1969	110	5			CINEMA V	ENGLISH LANGUAGE
MORE THAN A MIRACLE (ITALIAN)	1966	105	3	2.5		M-G-M	
MORE THAN A SECRETARY	1936	77		3.0	2.0	COLUMBIA	
MORE THE MERRIER, THE	1943	104		4.0	3.0	COLUMBIA	NOMINATED BEST PICTURE
MORGAN! (BRITISH)	1966	97	8*	4.0	3.5	CINEMA V	
MORGAN THE PIRATE (ITALIAN)	1960	93		2.0	2.0	M-G-M	
MORITURI	a1965	123	5		2.5	20th CENTURY FOX	
MORNING GLORY	1933	74		3.5	3.5	RKO	
MORO WITCH DOCTOR	1964	61	1			20th CENTURY FOX	
MOROCCO	1930	90		2.0	3.0	PARAMOUNT	
MOROZHKO (RUSSIAN)	a1965	79	3*			AVCO-EMBASSY	
MORTAL STORM, THE	1940	100	6*	3.0	3.5	M-G-M	
MOSQUITO SQUADRON (BRITISH)	1970	90	3			UNITED ARTISTS	
MOSS ROSE	1947	82		3.0	2.5	20th CENTURY FOX	
MOST DANGEROUS MAN ALIVE	1961	82		1.0	2.0	COLUMBIA	
MOST WANTED MAN (IN THE WORLD), THE (FRENCH)	1962	85	1	1.5	2.0	ASTOR	
MOST WONDERFUL MOMENT, THE (ITALIAN)	1957	94		2.5	2.0	ELLIS FILMS	
MOTHER CAREY'S CHICKENS	1938	82		2.5	2.0	RKO	
MOTHER DIDN'T TELL ME	1950	88		2.5	2.5	20th CENTURY FOX	
MOTHER IS A FRESHMAN	1949	81	4	2.0	2.5	20th CENTURY FOX	
MOTHER WORE TIGHTS	1947	107		3.0	3.0	20th CENTURY FOX	
MOTHRA (JAPANESE)	1961	100		2.0	2.0	COLUMBIA	
MOTORCYCLE GANG	1957	78		1.5	1.5	AMERICAN-INTERNAT'L	
MOULIN ROUGE	1952	123	8*	3.5	3.5	UNITED ARTISTS	NOMINATED BEST PICTURE
MOUNTAIN, THE	1956	105	4*	2.5	2.5	PARAMOUNT	
MOUNTAIN MUSIC	1937	77		2.0		PARAMOUNT	
MOUNTAIN ROAD, THE	1960	102	4*	2.0	2.0	COLUMBIA	
MOURNING BECOMES ELECTRA	1947	173	4*	3.0	3.0	RKO	
MOUSE ON THE MOON, THE (BRITISH)	1963	85	7*		3.5	LOPERT	
MOUSE THAT ROARED, THE (BRITISH)	1959	83	6*	3.5	3.5	COLUMBIA	
MOUTHPIECE, THE	1932	90		3.5	2.5	WARNER BROTHERS	
MOVE	1970	90	3			20th CENTURY FOX	
MOVE OVER, DARLING	1963	103	4	2.0	2.5	20th CENTURY FOX	
MOVIE CRAZY	1932	96		3.0		PARAMOUNT	
MOVIE MURDERER, THE (T.V.)	1970	100		2.5		UNIVERSAL	
MOZAMBIQUE (BRITISH)	1965	98	2			SEVEN ARTS	
MUDLARK, THE	1950	99	6*	3.0	2.5	20th CENTURY FOX	
MUG TOWN	1943	60				UNIVERSAL	
MUGGER, THE	1958	74	2			UNITED ARTISTS	
MUHAIR (SPANISH)	1969	84	1			HAVEN INTERNATIONAL	
MUMMY, THE (BORIS KARLOFF, ZITA JOHANN)	1932	72		3.0	3.5	UNIVERSAL	
MUMMY, THE (BR. - PETER CUSHING, CHRISTOPHER LEE)	1959	88	4			UNIVERSAL	
MUMMY'S CURSE, THE	1944	62			2.0	UNIVERSAL	
MUMMY'S GHOST, THE	1944	60		2.0	2.0	UNIVERSAL	
MUMMY'S HAND, THE	1940	67		2.0	2.0	UNIVERSAL	
MUMMY'S SHROUD, THE (BRITISH)	1967	84	1			20th CENTURY FOX	
MUMMY'S TOMB, THE	1942	61		1.5	1.5	UNIVERSAL	

‡ An asterisk (*) in THE FILM BUFF'S BIBLE column indicates that the film has been rated by the editor and/or staff. All other ratings in this column are based on a consensus of reviews (see NOTES).

TITLE (LEADING ACTORS SHOWN WHERE TWO OR MORE FILMS HAVE THE SAME OR SIMILAR TITLE)	"a" TO LEFT OF YEAR INDICATES THAT FILM HAS AN ALTERNATE TITLE ↓ YEAR RELEASED	RUNNING TIME IN MINUTES	THE FILM BUFF'S BIBLE ‡	STEVEN SCHEUER	LEONARD MALTIN	DISTRIBUTOR	COMMENT
MUMSY, NANNY, SONNY AND GIRLY (BRITISH)	a1970	101	3			CINERAMA RELEASING	
MUNSTER, GO HOME	1966	96		2.0	2.5	UNIVERSAL	
MURDER A LA MOD	1968	80		2.5		ARIES DOCUMENTARIES	
MURDER AHOY (BRITISH)	1964	93	4			M-G-M	
MURDER AMONG FRIENDS	1941	67		2.0		20th CENTURY FOX	
MURDER AT 45 R.P.M. (FRENCH)	1960	98		2.0	2.5	GALA	
MURDER AT THE GALLOP (BRITISH)	1963	81	3*			M-G-M	
MURDER AT THE VANITIES	1934	70		2.0	2.5	PARAMOUNT	
MURDER BY CONTRACT	1958	81		2.5	2.0	COLUMBIA	
MURDER CLINIC, THE (ITALIAN)	1966	86	1			EUROPIX-CONSOLIDATED	
MURDER CZECH STYLE (CZECH)	1967	90	6			ROYAL FILMS INT'L	
MURDER, HE SAYS	1945	91	3*	3.0	3.0	PARAMOUNT	
MURDER IN GREENWICH VILLAGE	1937	68		2.0		COLUMBIA	
MURDER IN MISSISSIPPI	1965	85	1			TIGER PRODS.	
MURDER IN REVERSE (BRITISH)	1945	88	6	3.0		FOUR CONTINENTS	
MURDER IN THE AIR	1940	55		2.0	1.5	WARNER BROTHERS	
MURDER IN THE BIG HOUSE	1942	59		2.0		WARNER BROTHERS	
MURDER IN THE MUSIC HALL	1946	84		2.5	2.0	REPUBLIC	
MURDER IN TIMES SQUARE	1943	65		2.0		COLUMBIA	
MURDER, INC.	1960	103	5	3.0	3.0	20th CENTURY FOX	
MURDER IS MY BEAT	1955	77		1.5	2.0	ALLIED ARTISTS	
MURDER IS MY BUSINESS	1946	64			2.0	PRODUCERS RELEASING	
MURDER MAN, THE	1935	70		2.5	2.5	M-G-M	
MURDER MOST FOUL (BRITISH)	1964	90	4*			M-G-M	
MURDER, MY SWEET	a1944	95		3.5	2.5	RKO	
MURDER ON APPROVAL (BRITISH)	a1956	90		2.0	2.0	RKO	
MURDER ON DIAMOND ROW (BRITISH)	1937	77		2.5		UNITED ARTISTS	
MURDER ON MONDAY (BRITISH)	a1952	85	5	3.0	3.0	MAYER-KINGSLEY	
MURDER ON THE BRIDLE PATH	1936	66		2.5		RKO	
MURDER OVER NEW YORK	1940	65		.		20th CENTURY FOX	
MURDER PARTY (GERMAN)	1961	79		2.5		SCREEN GEMS	
MURDER, SHE SAID (BRITISH)	1961	86	6			M-G-M	
MURDER WILL OUT (BRITISH - VALERIE HOBSON)	a1952	83		3.5	3.0	KRAMER HYAMS	
MURDER WITHOUT TEARS	1953	64	3	2.0		ALLIED ARTISTS	
MURDERER'S ROW	1966	108		2.5		COLUMBIA	
MURDERS IN THE RUE MORGUE (BELA LUGOSI)	1932	75		1.5	2.0	UNIVERSAL	
MURDERS IN THE RUE MORGUE (JASON ROBARDS)	1971	86	2			AMERICAN-INTERNAT'L	
MURIEL (FRENCH)	1963	115			2.5	LOPERT	
MURIETA	1965	108	3			WARNER BROTHERS	
MURMUR OF THE HEART (FRENCH)	1971	118	6			PALOMAR PICTURES	
MURPHY'S WAR (BRITISH)	1971	106	4			PARAMOUNT	
MUSCLE BEACH PARTY	1964	94		2.0	2.0	AMERICAN-INTERNAT'L	
MUSIC BOX KID, THE	1960	74	1			UNITED ARTISTS	
MUSIC FOR MILLIONS	1944	120		2.5	2.5	M-G-M	
MUSIC IN MANHATTAN	1944	80		2.5		RKO	
MUSIC IN MY HEART	1940	70		3.0	2.0	COLUMBIA	
MUSIC IS MAGIC	1935	65			2.0	20th CENTURY FOX	
MUSIC LOVERS, THE (BRITISH)	1971	122	4			UNITED ARTISTS	
MUSIC MAN, THE (JIMMY DORSEY, JUNE PREISSER)	1948	68				MONOGRAM	
MUSIC MAN, THE (ROBERT PRESTON, SHIRLEY JONES)	1962	151	8*	4.0	3.5	WARNER BROTHERS	NOMINATED BEST PICTURE
MUSKETEERS OF THE SEA (ITALIAN)	1960	116		1.5	2.0	AMERICAN-INTERNAT'L	
MUSS 'EM UP	1936	68		2.5		RKO	
MUTINEERS, THE	a1949	60		1.5	1.5	COLUMBIA	
MUTINY	1952	77	3	3.0	1.5	UNITED ARTISTS	
MUTINY IN OUTER SPACE	1965	81	2	2.5		ALLIED ARTISTS	
MUTINY ON THE BLACKHAWK	1939	66		1.5		UNIVERSAL	
MUTINY ON THE BOUNTY (CLARK GABLE, C. LAUGHTON)	1935	132	8*	4.0	4.0	M-G-M	BEST PICTURE AWARD
MUTINY ON THE BOUNTY (MARLIN BRANDO, T. HOWARD)	1962	179	4*	3.0	2.5	M-G-M	NOMINATED BEST PICTURE
MY BABY IS BLACK	1965	75	2			U.S. FILMS	
MY BILL	1938	64		2.0	2.5	WARNER BROTHERS	
MY BLOOD RUNS COLD	1965	104	2	1.5		WARNER BROTHERS	
MY BLUE HEAVEN	1950	96		2.5	2.5	20th CENTURY FOX	
MY BROTHER TALKS TO HORSES	1947	93	3*	2.5	2.0	M-G-M	
MY BROTHER, THE OUTLAW	a1951	82		2.0	2.0	EAGLE LION	
MY BROTHER'S KEEPER (BRITISH)	1948	96		3.0	2.0	EAGLE LION	
MY BUDDY	1944	69		2.5		REPUBLIC	
MY COUSIN RACHEL	1952	98	6-7*	3.5	3.0	20th CENTURY FOX	
MY DARLING CLEMENTINE	1946	97	4*	3.5	3.5	20th CENTURY FOX	
MY DEAR SECRETARY	1948	94		3.0	2.5	UNITED ARTISTS	
MY DOG, BUDDY	1960	77	4			COLUMBIA	
MY DREAM IS YOURS	1949	101		2.5	2.5	WARNER BROTHERS	
MY FAIR LADY	1964	170	10*			WARNER BROTHERS	BEST PICTURE AWARD
MY FATHER'S HOUSE (PALESTINIAN)	1947	85	5			KLINE LEVIN	ENGLISH LANGUAGE
MY FAVORITE BLONDE	1942	78		3.5	3.0	PARAMOUNT	
MY FAVORITE BRUNETTE	1947	87	6	3.0	3.0	PARAMOUNT	
MY FAVORITE SPY (KAY KYSER, ELLEN DREW)	1942	86		2.5	2.0	RKO	
MY FAVORITE SPY (BOB HOPE, HEDY LAMARR)	1951	93	6	3.0	3.0	PARAMOUNT	
MY FAVORITE WIFE	1940	88	5*	4.0	3.0	RKO	
MY FOOLISH HEART	1949	98	3*	3.0	3.0	RKO	
MY FORBIDDEN PAST	1951	81		2.0	2.5	RKO	
MY FRIEND FLICKA	1943	89	4*	3.0	3.0	20th CENTURY FOX	
MY FRIEND IRMA	1949	103		2.0	2.0	PARAMOUNT	
MY FRIEND IRMA GOES WEST	1950	90		2.0	2.5	PARAMOUNT	
MY GAL SAL	1942	103	3*	3.0	3.0	20th CENTURY FOX	

‡ An asterisk (*) in THE FILM BUFF'S BIBLE column indicates that the film has been rated by the editor and/or staff. All other ratings in this column are based on a consensus of reviews (see NOTES).

TITLE (LEADING ACTORS SHOWN WHERE TWO OR MORE FILMS HAVE THE SAME OR SIMILAR TITLE)	YEAR RELEASED	RUNNING TIME IN MINUTES	THE FILM BUFF'S BIBLE ‡	STEVEN SCHEUER	LEONARD MALTIN	DISTRIBUTOR	COMMENT
MY GEISHA	1962	120	4	2.0	2.5	PARAMOUNT	
MY GIRL TISA	1948	95		2.5	2.5	UNITED ARTISTS	
MY GUN IS QUICK	1957	88		1.5	1.5	UNITED ARTISTS	
MY HEART BELONGS TO DADDY	1943	75		1.5		PARAMOUNT	
MY LIFE TO LIVE (FRENCH)	1962	82	4			PATHE CONTEMPARARY	
MY LIFE WITH CAROLINE	1941	81		2.5	2.5	RKO	
MY LITTLE CHICKADEE	1940	83	4*	4.0	2.5	UNIVERSAL	
MY LOVE CAME BACK	1940	81		3.0	2.5	WARNER BROTHERS	
MY LOVER, MY SON (BRITISH)	1970	95	2			M-G-M	
MY LUCKY STAR	1938	84		3.0	2.5	20th CENTURY FOX	
MY MAN AND I	1952	99		2.5	2.5	M-G-M	
MY MAN GODFREY (WILLIAM POWELL, CAROLE LOMBARD)	1936	95	6-7*	4.0	3.5	UNIVERSAL	
MY MAN GODFREY (JUNE ALLYSON, DAVID NIVEN)	1957	92		2.5	2.5	UNIVERSAL	
MY NAME IS IVAN (RUSSIAN)	a1962	84	6*	3.0	3.0	SHORE INTERNATIONAL	
MY NAME IS JULIA ROSS	1945	65		3.5	3.5	COLUMBIA	
MY NIGHT AT MAUD'S (FRENCH)	1969	105	6			PATHE CONTEMPARARY	
MY OUTLAW BROTHER	a1951	82		2.0	2.0	EAGLE LION	
MY OWN TRUE LOVE	1949	84		2.0	2.0	PARAMOUNT	
MY PAL GUS	1952	83		3.0	2.5	20th CENTURY FOX	
MY PAL WOLF	1944	76		2.5		RKO	
MY REPUTATION	1946	96		2.5	3.0	WARNER BROTHERS	
MY SECRET LIFE	1971	92	2			JACK H. HARRIS	
MY SEVEN LITTLE SINS (FRENCH)	a1956	98		2.0	2.0	KINGSLEY INTERNAT'L	
MY SIDE OF THE MOUNTAIN (CANADIAN)	1969	100	6			PARAMOUNT	
MY SISTER EILEEN (ROSALIND RUSSELL, JANET BLAIR)	1942	96		3.5	2.5	COLUMBIA	
MY SISTER EILEEN (JANET LEIGH, BETTY GARRETT)	1955	108	4*	3.0	3.5	COLUMBIA	
MY SISTER, MY LOVE (SWEDISH)	1966	97	5			SIGMA III	
MY SIX CONVICTS	1952	104	6	3.5	3.0	COLUMBIA	
MY SIX LOVES	1963	101		1.5	2.5	PARAMOUNT	
MY SON JOHN	1952	122	4	1.0	2.5	PARAMOUNT	
MY SON, MY SON	1940	115		3.0	3.0	UNITED ARTISTS	
MY SON, THE HERO (ITALIAN)	1961	111			2.0	UNITED ARTISTS	
MY SWEET CHARLIE (T.V.)	1970	97	6	3.5		UNIVERSAL	
MY UNCLE ANTOINE (CANADIAN)	1971	110	6			NAT'L FILM BOARD CAN	FRENCH LANGUAGE
MY UNCLE, MR HULOT (FRENCH)	1956	116		4.0	4.0	CONTINENTAL	
MY WIFE IS A PANTHER (FRENCH)	1960	90		2.0			
MY WIFE'S BEST FRIEND	1952	87		2.5	2.0	20th CENTURY FOX	
MY WILD IRISH ROSE	1947	101	4	2.0	2.0	WARNER BROTHERS	
MYRA BRECKINRIDGE	1970	94	2			20th CENTURY FOX	
MYSTERIANS, THE (JAPANESE)	1957	87		2.0	2.5	M-G-M	
MYSTERIES OF THE DEEP (DOCUMENTARY)	1960	24	6			BUENA VISTA	
MYSTERIOUS DOCTOR, THE	1943	57		1.5	2.5	WARNER BROTHERS	
MYSTERIOUS INTRUDER, THE	1946	61			.	COLUMBIA	
MYSTERIOUS ISLAND (BRITISH)	1961	101	2*	3.0	3.0	COLUMBIA	
MYSTERIOUS MAGICIAN, THE (GERMAN)	1965	95		1.5	2.5	UCC FILMS	
MYSTERIOUS MR MOTO	1938	62			.	20th CENTURY FOX	
MYSTERY BROADCAST	1943	63		2.5		REPUBLIC	
MYSTERY IN MEXICO	1948	66		2.5		RKO	
MYSTERY OF EDWIN DROOD, THE	1935	86		3.0	3.0	UNIVERSAL	
MYSTERY OF MARIE ROGET, THE	1942	91		2.5	2.5	UNIVERSAL	
MYSTERY OF MR X	1934	85		2.5		M-G-M	
MYSTERY OF THE BLACK JUNGLE	a1955	72		1.0	1.5	REPUBLIC	
MYSTERY OF THE WHITE ROOM	1939	57		2.0		UNIVERSAL	
MYSTERY OF THUG ISLAND, THE (ITALIAN)	1966	88	1			COLUMBIA	
MYSTERY SEA RAIDER	1940	78		2.0		PARAMOUNT	
MYSTERY SHIP	1941	65		2.5		COLUMBIA	
MYSTERY STREET	1950	93		3.0	2.5	M-G-M	
MYSTERY SUBMARINE (MACDONALD CAREY)	1950	78		2.0	2.5	UNIVERSAL	
MYSTERY SUBMARINE (BRITISH - JAMES R. JUSTICE)	a1962	92	3		1.5	UNIVERSAL	
NABONGA	a1944	75			1.5	PRODUCERS RELEASING	
NAKED AFRICA (DOCUMENTARY)	1957	69		2.5		AMERICAN-INTERNAT'L	
NAKED ALIBI	1954	86		2.0	2.5	UNIVERSAL	
NAKED AMONG THE WOLVES (EAST GERMAN)	1963	100	6			LOPERT	
NAKED AND THE DEAD, THE	1958	131		2.0	3.0	WARNER BROTHERS	
NAKED ANGELS	1969	83	1			FAVORITE FILMS	
NAKED AUTUMN (FRENCH)	1961	96	6			UN. MOTION PIC. ORG.	
NAKED BRIGADE, THE	1965	99		1.5	2.0	UNIVERSAL	
NAKED CITY, THE	1948	96	5*	3.5	3.5	UNIVERSAL	
NAKED DAWN, THE	1955	82	4	2.5	2.5	UNIVERSAL	
NAKED EARTH (BRITISH)	1958	96	4	2.0	1.5	20th CENTURY FOX	
NAKED EDGE, THE	1961	99		2.5	2.5	UNITED ARTISTS	
NAKED EYE, THE (DOCUMENTARY)	1957	71	6			FILM REPRESENTATIONS	
NAKED GENERAL, THE (JAPANESE)	1958	93	6			TOHO	
NAKED GUN	1956	69		1.5		ASSOC'D FILM DISTS.	
NAKED HEART, THE (BRITISH - MICHELE MORGAN)	1950	96		1.0	2.0	ASSOCIATED ARTISTS	
NAKED HILLS, THE	1956	73		2.0	1.5	ALLIED ARTISTS	
NAKED IN THE SUN	1957	79		2.5	2.0	ALLIED ARTISTS	
NAKED JUNGLE, THE	1954	95		2.5	3.0	PARAMOUNT	
NAKED KISS, THE	1964	93		1.0	2.5	ALLIED ARTISTS	
NAKED MAJA, THE	1959	111		2.0	2.0	UNITED ARTISTS	
NAKED NIGHT, THE (SWEDISH)	a1953	82	3*			TIMES FILM CORP.	

‡ An asterisk (*) in THE FILM BUFF'S BIBLE column indicates that the film has been rated by the editor and/or staff. All other ratings in this column are based on a consensus of reviews (see NOTES).

TITLE (LEADING ACTORS SHOWN WHERE TWO OR MORE FILMS HAVE THE SAME OR SIMILAR TITLE)	YEAR RELEASED	RUNNING TIME IN MINUTES	THE FILM BUFF'S BIBLE ‡	STEVEN SCHEUER	LEONARD MALTIN	DISTRIBUTOR	COMMENT
NAKED PARADISE	1957	68			1.0	AMERICAN-INTERNAT'L	
NAKED PREY, THE	1966	95	4	3.0	3.0	PARAMOUNT	
NAKED RUNNER, THE (BRITISH)	1967	103	3	1.0		WARNER BROTHERS	
NAKED SPUR, THE	1953	91		3.0	2.5	M-G-M	
NAKED STREET, THE	1954	84		2.5	2.0	UNITED ARTISTS	
NAKED ZOO	1970		1			HAVEN FILMS	
NAME OF THE GAME IS KILL!, THE	1968	88	1			FANFARE	
NAMU, THE KILLER WHALE	1966	88	4*	2.0	2.5	UNITED ARTISTS	
NANA (ANNA STEN, PHILLIPS HOLMES)	1934	89		2.5	2.5	UNITED ARTISTS	
NANA (FRENCH - CHARLES BOYER, MARTINE CAROL)	1955	118	6			TIMES FILM CORP.	
NANA (ANNA GAEL, GILLIAN HILLS)	1971	105	1			DISTINCTION FILMS	
NANCY DREW AND THE HIDDEN STAIRCASE	1939	60		2.5	1.5	WARNER BROTHERS	
NANCY DREW, DETECTIVE	1938	60		2.5	1.5	WARNER BROTHERS	
NANCY DREW, REPORTER	1939	68		2.5	1.5	WARNER BROTHERS	
NANCY DREW, TROUBLE SHOOTER	1939	69		2.5	1.5	WARNER BROTHERS	
NANCY GOES TO RIO	1950	99		2.5	2.5	M-G-M	
NANCY STEELE IS MISSING	1937	85		2.5	2.5	20th CENTURY FOX	
NANNY, THE (BRITISH)	1965	93	3*	2.5	3.0	20th CENTURY FOX	
NANOOK OF THE NORTH (SILENT, DOCUMENTARY)	1922	55		4.0		PATHE	
NAPOLEON AND SAMANTHA	1972	92	4			BUENA VISTA	
NAPOLEON II - L'AIGLON (FRENCH)	1964	105		2.0		MAJESTIC PICS.	
NARROW CORNER, THE	1933	71		2.5	2.0	WARNER BROTHERS	
NARROW MARGIN, THE	1952	70		3.0	2.5	RKO	
NASHVILLE REBEL	1966	91	5			AMERICAN-INTERNAT'L	
NASTY RABBIT, THE	a1964	85		1.0	2.0	FAIRWAY INTERNAT'L	
NATIONAL BARN DANCE	1944	76		2.0		PARAMOUNT	
NATIONAL VELVET	1944	125	7*	3.5	3.5	M-G-M	
NATIVE DRUMS (ITALIAN)	1955	100		1.0		WALTER READE	
NATIVE SON (ARGENTINE)	1951	95	3			CLASSIC PICTURES	ENGLISH LANGUAGE
NATURE'S HALF ACRE (DOCUMENTARY)	1952	33	6			BUENA VISTA	
NAUGHTY ARLETTE (BRITISH)	a1950	86		2.0		EAGLE LION	
NAUGHTY BUT NICE	1939	90		2.5	2.5	WARNER BROTHERS	
NAUGHTY GIRL (FRENCH)	a1955	86	3	2.0	2.5	FILMS AROUND THE WLD	
NAUGHTY MARIETTA	1935	106		3.5	2.5	M-G-M	NOMINATED BEST PICTURE
NAUGHTY MARTINE (FRENCH)	1953	90		2.0		PRESIDENT FILMS	
NAUGHTY NINETIES, THE	1945	76		2.0	2.0	UNIVERSAL	
NAVAJO	1952	70	4*	3.0		LIPPERT PRODS.	
NAVAJO JOE (ITALIAN)	1966	89	1			UNITED ARTISTS	
NAVAJO RUN	1964	79	3			AMERICAN-INTERNAT'L	
NAVY BLUE AND GOLD	1937	94		3.0	2.5	M-G-M	
NAVY BLUES	1941	108		3.0	3.0	WARNER BROTHERS	
NAVY COMES THROUGH, THE	1942	82		3.0	2.0	RKO	
NAVY HEROES (BRITISH)	a1955	93		2.5		DIST. CORP. OF AMER.	
NAVY VS THE NIGHT MONSTERS, THE	a1966	87	2			REALART	
NAVY WIFE (JOAN BENNETT, GARY MERRILL)	1956	83	2	2.0	1.5	ALLIED ARTISTS	
NAZARIN, THE (MEXICAN)	1959	92	6			ALTURA FILMS	
NAZI AGENT	1942	82		2.5		M-G-M	
NEANDERTHAL MAN, THE	1953	78			1.5	UNITED ARTISTS	
NEAPOLITAN CAROUSEL (ITALIAN)	1954	116	5			LUX FILM AMERICA	
NEARLY A NASTY ACCIDENT (BRITISH)	1961	86	3		2.0	UNIVERSAL	
'NEATH BROOKLYN BRIDGE	1942	61			-	MONOGRAM	
NEBRASKAN, THE	1953	68		2.0	2.0	COLUMBIA	
NED KELLY (BRITISH)	1970	100	3			UNITED ARTISTS	
NEGATIVES (BRITISH)	1968	90	5	3.0		CONTINENTAL	
NEON CEILING, THE (T.V.)	1971	100	5-6*	2.5		UNIVERSAL	
NEPTUNE'S DAUGHTER	1949	93		2.5	3.0	M-G-M	
NERO AND THE BURNING OF ROME (ITALIAN)	1955	97		2.0		FOUR STAR	
NERO'S MISTRESS (ITALIAN)	1956	104	1			MANHATTAN FILMS	
NEST OF SPIES (FRENCH)	1957	85		1.5		AMERICAN-INTERNAT'L	
NEVADA (ROBERT MITCHUM, ANNE JEFFREYS)	1944	62		2.5	2.0	RKO	
NEVADA SMITH	1966	130	4	2.5		PARAMOUNT	
NEVADAN, THE	1950	81		2.0	2.0	COLUMBIA	
NEVER A DULL MOMENT (IRENE DUNNE, FRED MACMURRAY)	1950	89		2.5	2.5	RKO	
NEVER A DULL MOMENT (DICK VAN DYKE)	1968	100	4			BUENA VISTA	
NEVER BACK LOSERS (BRITISH)	1961	61		2.0		ANGLO AMALGAMATED	
NEVER FEAR	1950	82	4		2.0	EAGLE LION	
NEVER GIVE A SUCKER AN EVEN BREAK	1941	71	4*	3.5	2.5	UNIVERSAL	
NEVER LET GO (BRITISH)	1960	90		2.0	2.5	CONTINENTAL	
NEVER LET ME GO	1953	94		2.5	2.5	M-G-M	
NEVER LOVE A STRANGER	1958	91		2.0	2.5	ALLIED ARTISTS	
NEVER MENTION MURDER (BRITISH)	1965	56		2.0		AVCO-EMBASSY	
NEVER ON SUNDAY (GREEK)	1960	91	6*	4.0	3.5	LOPERT	ENGLISH LANGUAGE
NEVER PUT IT IN WRITING (BRITISH)	1964	93	3			ALLIED ARTISTS	
NEVER SAY DIE (MARTHA RAYE, BOB HOPE)	1939	80		2.5	2.5	PARAMOUNT	
NEVER SAY GOODBYE (ERROL FLYNN)	1946	97	4	2.5	2.5	WARNER BROTHERS	
NEVER SAY GOODBYE (ROCK HUDSON)	1956	96		2.5	2.5	UNIVERSAL	
NEVER SO FEW	1959	124		2.5	2.5	M-G-M	
NEVER STEAL ANYTHING SMALL	1959	94		2.5	2.5	UNIVERSAL	
NEVER TAKE NO FOR AN ANSWER (ITALIAN)	1951	82	6	3.0		SOUVAINE SELECTIVE	
NEVER TOO LATE	1965	105	5	3.0		WARNER BROTHERS	
NEVER TRUST A GAMBLER	1951	79		2.0	1.5	COLUMBIA	
NEVER WAVE AT A WAC	1953	87		2.5	2.5	RKO	
NEW ADVENTURES OF TARZAN	1935	75			-	BURROUGHS-TARZAN	
NEW CENTURIONS, THE	1972	103	5			COLUMBIA	

‡ An asterisk (*) in THE FILM BUFF'S BIBLE column indicates that the film has been rated by the editor and/or staff. All other ratings in this column are based on a consensus of reviews (see NOTES).

TITLE (LEADING ACTORS SHOWN WHERE TWO OR MORE FILMS HAVE THE SAME OR SIMILAR TITLE)	YEAR RELEASED	RUNNING TIME IN MINUTES	THE FILM BUFF'S BIBLE ‡	STEVEN SCHEUER	LEONARD MALTIN	DISTRIBUTOR	COMMENT
NEW FACES	1954	99	5		2.5	20th CENTURY FOX	
NEW FACES OF 1937	1937	100		3.0		RKO	
NEW INTERNS, THE	1964	123		2.5	2.5	COLUMBIA	
NEW KIND OF LOVE, A	1963	110		2.5	2.5	PARAMOUNT	
NEW LEAF, A	1971	102	6*			PARAMOUNT	
NEW LIFE STYLE	1970	91	1			DOT DISTRIBUTING	
NEW MEXICO	1951	76		2.0	2.5	UNITED ARTISTS	
NEW MOON	1940	105		2.5	2.5	M-G-M	
NEW ORLEANS	1947	89	4	2.0		UNITED ARTISTS	
NEW ORLEANS AFTER DARK	1958	69		1.0	1.5	ALLIED ARTISTS	
NEW ORLEANS UNCENSORED	1955	76		2.0	1.5	COLUMBIA	
NEW WORLD, A (MEXICAN)	1958	72		1.5		AZTECA	
NEW YORK CONFIDENTIAL	1955	87		2.5	2.5	WARNER BROTHERS	
NEW YORK TOWN	1941	94		2.5	2.5	PARAMOUNT	
NEWS HOUNDS	1947	68		.		MONOGRAM	
NEWS IS MADE AT NIGHT	1939	73		2.0		20th CENTURY FOX	
NEXT!	1971	81	1			MARON FILMS, LTD.	
NEXT OF KIN (BRITISH)	1942	90		3.5		UNIVERSAL	
NEXT TIME I MARRY	1938	75		3.0		RKO	
NEXT TIME WE LOVE	1936	87		2.5	3.0	UNIVERSAL	
NEXT TO NO TIME (BRITISH)	1958	93		2.0	2.0	SHOWCORPORATION	
NEXT VOICE YOU HEAR, THE	1950	82		3.0	2.5	M-G-M	
NIAGARA	1953	89	4	2.5	3.0	20th CENTURY FOX	
NICE GIRL?	1941	95			3.0	UNIVERSAL	
NICE GIRL LIKE ME, A (BRITISH)	1969	90	3			AVCO-EMBASSY	
NICE LITTLE BANK THAT SHOULD BE ROBBED, A	1958	87		2.0	2.0	20th CENTURY FOX	
NICHOLAS AND ALEXANDRA (BRITISH)	1971	183	7*			COLUMBIA	NOMINATED BEST PICTURE
NICHOLAS NICKLEBY (BRITISH)	1947	108		3.0	3.0	UNIVERSAL	
NICK CARTER - MASTER DETECTIVE	1939	60		2.0	2.5	M-G-M	
NIGHT AFFAIR (FRENCH)	1958	92	3			PRESIDENT FILMS	
NIGHT AFTER NIGHT	1932	70	3*	2.5	2.5	PARAMOUNT	
NIGHT AMBUSH (BRITISH)	a1957	93	6	3.0	3.0	J. ARTHUR RANK	
NIGHT AND DAY	1946	128	5*	3.5	2.0	WARNER BROTHERS	
NIGHT AND THE CITY (BRITISH)	1950	101		2.0	2.5	20th CENTURY FOX	
NIGHT AT EARL CARROLL'S, A	1940	63		1.5		PARAMOUNT	
NIGHT AT THE OPERA, A	1935	96	3*	4.0	4.0	M-G-M	
NIGHT BEFORE THE DIVORCE, THE	1942	67		1.0		20th CENTURY FOX	
NIGHT CHASE (T.V.)	1970	100		2.5		CINEMA CENTER 100	
NIGHT CLUB SCANDAL	1937	70		2.5	2.5	PARAMOUNT	
NIGHT CREATURES (BRITISH)	1962	81	3	2.5	2.0	UNIVERSAL	
NIGHT DIGGER, THE	1971	100	4			M-G-M	
NIGHT EDITOR	1946	68		3.0	2.0	COLUMBIA	
NIGHT FIGHTERS, THE (BRITISH)	1960	88	3	2.5	2.5	UNITED ARTISTS	
NIGHT FREIGHT	1955	79		2.5	2.5	ALLIED ARTISTS	
NIGHT GALLERY (T.V.)	1969	100		2.5		UNIVERSAL	
NIGHT GAMES (SWEDISH)	1966	104	5			MONDIAL FILMS	
NIGHT HAS A THOUSAND EYES	1948	80		2.0	2.5	PARAMOUNT	
NIGHT HEAVEN FELL, THE (FRENCH)	a1958	90		1.5	2.5	KINGSLEY INTERNAT'L	
NIGHT HOLDS TERROR, THE	1955	86	4	2.5	2.0	COLUMBIA	
NIGHT IN CASABLANCA, A	1946	85		2.5	2.5	UNITED ARTISTS	
NIGHT IN NEW ORLEANS, A	1942	75		1.5	1.5	PARAMOUNT	
NIGHT IN PARADISE, A	1946	84		2.5	2.5	UNIVERSAL	
NIGHT INTO MORNING	1951	86	4*	2.5	3.0	M-G-M	
NIGHT IS MY FUTURE (SWEDISH)	1947	87		2.5	2.5	AVCO-EMBASSY	
NIGHT IS YOUNG, THE	1935	82		3.0		M-G-M	
NIGHT KEY, THE	1937	67		2.0	1.5	UNIVERSAL	
NIGHT MONSTER, THE	1942	73		2.0	2.0	UNIVERSAL	
NIGHT MUST FALL (ROBERT MONTGOMERY)	1937	117		3.5	3.5	M-G-M	
NIGHT MUST FALL (BRITISH - ALBERT FINNEY)	1964	101	4	2.5	2.5	M-G-M	
NIGHT MY NUMBER CAME UP, THE (BRITISH)	1955	94	6	3.5	3.0	CONTINENTAL	
NIGHT NURSE	1931	72			2.5	WARNER BROTHERS	
NIGHT OF ADVENTURE, A	1944	65		2.5		RKO	
NIGHT OF DARK SHADOWS	1971	97	3			M-G-M	
NIGHT OF JANUARY 16TH, THE	1941	79		2.0	1.5	PARAMOUNT	
NIGHT OF NIGHTS, THE	1939	85		2.0		PARAMOUNT	
NIGHT OF THE BLOOD BEAST	1958	65		2.0		AMERICAN-INTERNAT'L	
NIGHT OF THE FOLLOWING DAY, THE	1969	93	4	2.5		UNIVERSAL	
NIGHT OF THE GENERALS, THE (BRITISH)	1967	147		2.5	2.0	COLUMBIA	
NIGHT OF THE GREAT ATTACK, THE (ITALIAN)	1964	91		1.5		FOUR STAR	
NIGHT OF THE GRIZZLY, THE	1966	102		2.5	2.5	PARAMOUNT	
NIGHT OF THE HUNTER, THE	1955	90	5*	4.0	3.0	UNITED ARTISTS	
NIGHT OF THE IGUANA, THE	1964	125	8*	4.0	3.0	M-G-M	
NIGHT OF THE LIVING DEAD	1968	90	2	1.0		CONTINENTAL	
NIGHT OF THE QUARTER MOON	a1959	96	2	1.0	1.5	M-G-M	
NIGHT PASSAGE	1957	90	4	2.5	3.0	UNIVERSAL	
NIGHT PEOPLE	1954	93		2.5	3.0	20th CENTURY FOX	
NIGHT PLANE FROM CHUNGKING	1943	68		2.5		PARAMOUNT	
NIGHT RIDERS (MEXICAN - GASTON SANTOS)	1963	77		1.5		COM. UNITED T.V.	
NIGHT RUNNER, THE	1957	79		2.0	2.0	UNIVERSAL	
NIGHT SLAVES (T.V.)	1970	90		2.0		ABC FILMS	
NIGHT SONG	1947	102		2.0	2.0	RKO	
NIGHT THE WORLD EXPLODED, THE	1957	94		2.0	2.0	COLUMBIA	
NIGHT THEY KILLED RASPUTIN, THE (ITALIAN)	a1960	95		2.0	2.0	RKO	
NIGHT THEY RAIDED MINSKY'S, THE	1968	100	5	3.5		UNITED ARTISTS	

‡ An asterisk (*) in THE FILM BUFF'S BIBLE column indicates that the film has been rated by the editor and/or staff. All other ratings in this column are based on a consensus of reviews (see NOTES).

TITLE (LEADING ACTORS SHOWN WHERE TWO OR MORE FILMS HAVE THE SAME OR SIMILAR TITLE)	YEAR RELEASED	RUNNING TIME IN MINUTES	THE FILM BUFF'S BIBLE ‡	STEVEN SCHEUER	LEONARD MALTIN	DISTRIBUTOR	COMMENT
NIGHT TIDE	1963	84	3	2.5		AMERICAN-INTERNAT'L	
NIGHT TO REMEMBER, A (BRIAN AHERNE, LORETTA YOUNG)	1942	91	5*	3.5	3.5	LOPERT	
NIGHT TO REMEMBER, A (BRITISH - KENNETH MORE)	1958	123	8*	4.0	4.0	LOPERT	
NIGHT TRAIN (BRITISH - REX HARRISON, M. LOCKWOOD)	1940	93		3.5		20th CENTURY FOX	
NIGHT TRAIN (POLISH - LUCYNA WINNICKA)	1959	90			2.0	CURZON	
NIGHT TRAIN FOR INVERNESS (BRITISH)	1959	68		2.0		PARAMOUNT	
NIGHT TRAIN TO MILAN (ITALIAN)	1965	90		2.5		AVCO-EMBASSY	
NIGHT TRAIN TO PARIS (BRITISH)	1964	64	2			20th CENTURY FOX	
NIGHT UNTO NIGHT	1949	92		1.0	2.5	WARNER BROTHERS	
NIGHT VISITOR	1971	102	4			UMC PICTURES	
NIGHT WALKER, THE	1965	86	4	2.5	3.0	UNIVERSAL	
NIGHT WATCH, THE (FRENCH)	1960	118	6			CONSORT/ORION	
NIGHT WITHOUT SLEEP	1952	77		2.5	2.0	20th CENTURY FOX	
NIGHT WITHOUT STARS (BRITISH)	1953	75		2.5		RKO	
NIGHTCOMERS, THE (BRITISH)	1972	95	3			AVCO-EMBASSY	
NIGHTFALL	1957	78		2.5	2.5	COLUMBIA	
NIGHTMARE (BRIAN DONLEVY, DIANA BARRYMORE)	1942	81		2.5		UNIVERSAL	
NIGHTMARE (EDWARD G. ROBINSON)	1956	89			2.5	UNITED ARTISTS	
NIGHTMARE (BRITISH - DAVID KNIGHT, MOIRA REDMOND)	1964	83	4		3.0	UNIVERSAL	
NIGHTMARE ALLEY	1947	111	4-5*	3.5	3.5	20th CENTURY FOX	
NIGHTMARE CASTLE (ITALIAN)	1965	90		1.5	2.0	ALLIED ARTISTS	
NIGHTMARE IN THE SUN	1965	80		1.5	1.5	SCREEN GEMS	
NIGHTMARE IN WAX	1969	95	1			CROWN INTERNATIONAL	
NIGHTS OF CABIRIA (ITALIAN)	a1957	110	3*	3.5	3.5	LOPERT	
NIGHTS OF LUCRETIA BORGIA, THE (ITALIAN)	1959	108	2			COLUMBIA	
NIGHTS OF RASPUTIN (ITALIAN)	a1960	95		2.0	2.0	RKO	
NIKKI, WILD DOG OF THE NORTH	1961	74	6			BUENA VISTA	
NINA B. AFFAIR, THE (FRENCH)	1959	105		2.0		ABC FILMS	
NINE GIRLS	1944	78		3.0	2.5	COLUMBIA	
NINE HOURS TO RAMA (BRITISH)	1963	125		3.5	2.5	20th CENTURY FOX	
NINE LIVES (NORWEGIAN)	1958	90	6	2.5		DE ROCHEMONT	
NINE LIVES ARE NOT ENOUGH	1941	63		2.0		WARNER BROTHERS	
1984 (BRITISH)	1956	90	5*	3.5	3.0	COLUMBIA	
NINETY DEGREES IN THE SHADE (CZECH)	1965	90	6*	3.5	2.5	LANDAU/UNGER COM. UN.	
99 RIVER STREET	1953	83	5	3.5	3.0	UNITED ARTISTS	
99 WOMEN (SPANISH)	1968	90	1			LANDAU/UNGER COM. UN.	
NINOTCHKA	1939	110	5*	3.5	3.5	M-G-M	NOMINATED BEST PICTURE
NINTH CIRCLE, THE (YUGOSLAVIAN)	1960	90	6			INTERPROGRESS TRADING	
NITWITS, THE	1935	81		3.0	3.0	RKO	
NO BLADE OF GRASS (BRITISH)	1970	80	3			M-G-M	
NO DOWN PAYMENT	1957	105		2.5	3.0	20th CENTURY FOX	
NO DRUMS, NO BUGLES	1971	85	4			CINERAMA RELEASING	
NO ESCAPE (DEAN JAGGER)	a1943	75			2.0	MONOGRAM	
NO ESCAPE (LEW AYRES, MARJORIE STEELE)	a1953	76		2.0	1.5	UNITED ARTISTS	
NO ESCAPE (FRENCH - RAF VALLONE)	1958	101		2.0		ELLIS FILMS	
NO EXIT	1962	85	5			ZENITH INTERNATIONAL	
NO FUNNY BUSINESS	1934	60		1.0		PRINCIPAL	
NO HANDS ON THE CLOCK	1941	76		3.0		PARAMOUNT	
NO HIGHWAY IN THE SKY (BRITISH)	a1951	98	5*	3.5	3.0	20th CENTURY FOX	
NO HOLDS BARRED	1952	65			-	MONOGRAM	
NO LEAVE, NO LOVE	1946	119	4	2.0	2.0	M-G-M	
NO LOVE FOR JOHNNIE (BRITISH)	1961	110	6	4.0	3.0	AVCO-EMBASSY	
NO MAN IS AN ISLAND	a1962	114	4*	2.5	2.5	UNIVERSAL	
NO MAN OF HER OWN (CLARK GABLE, CAROLE LOMBARD)	1932	85		2.5	2.5	PARAMOUNT	
NO MAN OF HER OWN (BARBARA STANWYCK, JOHN LUND)	1950	98	4	2.5	2.5	PARAMOUNT	
NO MAN'S LAND (RUSS HARVEY, KIM LEE)	1962	72		1.5		CINEMA VIDEO INT'L	
NO MAN'S WOMAN	1955	96		2.0	2.0	REPUBLIC	
NO MINOR VICES	1948	96	3	1.5	2.0	M-G-M	
NO MORE EXCUSES	1968	55	5	3.5		IMPACT FILMS	
NO MORE LADIES	1935	81		2.5	2.5	M-G-M	
NO, MY DARLING DAUGHTER (BRITISH)	1961	85	3	2.5	2.5	ZENITH INTERNATIONAL	
NO NAME ON THE BULLET	1959	77	4	2.5	2.5	UNIVERSAL	
NO ONE MAN	1932	73		1.5	2.0	PARAMOUNT	
NO ORCHIDS FOR MISS BLANDISH (BRITISH)	1948	78		3.0		RKO	
NO PLACE FOR A LADY	1943	67		2.0		COLUMBIA	
NO PLACE FOR JENNIFER (BRITISH)	1949	90			2.0	STRATFORD PICS.	
NO PLACE LIKE HOMICIDE (BRITISH)	a1961	87		2.0	2.5	AVCO-EMBASSY	
NO PLACE TO HIDE	1956	71		1.5	2.5	ALLIED ARTISTS	
NO PLACE TO LAND	1958	78	1	1.5	1.5	REPUBLIC	
NO QUESTIONS ASKED	1951	81		2.0	2.5	M-G-M	
NO RESTING PLACE (BRITISH)	1951	79		2.5		CLASSIC PICTURES	
NO RETURN ADDRESS	1961	76		1.5		TELEDYNAMICS	
NO ROAD BACK (BRITISH)	1957	83		2.0		RKO	
NO ROOM FOR THE GROOM	1952	82		2.0	2.5	UNIVERSAL	
NO SAD SONGS FOR ME	1950	89	5	2.0	3.0	COLUMBIA	
NO SAFETY AHEAD (BRITISH)	1958	68		1.5		PARAMOUNT	
NO SUN IN VENICE (FRENCH)	1957	97	4			KINGSLEY INTERNAT'L	
NO SURVIVORS PLEASE (GERMAN)	1963	92		1.5		UCC FILMS	
NO TIME FOR COMEDY	1940	93		3.0	3.0	WARNER BROTHERS	
NO TIME FOR FLOWERS	1953	83		2.5	2.0	RKO	
NO TIME FOR LOVE	1943	83		3.0	3.0	PARAMOUNT	
NO TIME FOR SERGEANTS	1958	111	4*	3.0	3.5	WARNER BROTHERS	
NO TIME FOR TEARS (BRITISH)	1957	86		3.0		ASSOC. BRITISH-PATHE	
NO TIME TO BE YOUNG	1957	82		2.0	2.0	COLUMBIA	

‡ An asterisk (*) in THE FILM BUFF'S BIBLE column indicates that the film has been rated by the editor and/or staff. All other ratings in this column are based on a consensus of reviews (see NOTES).

TITLE (LEADING ACTORS SHOWN WHERE TWO OR MORE FILMS HAVE THE SAME OR SIMILAR TITLE)	YEAR RELEASED	RUNNING TIME IN MINUTES	THE FILM BUFF'S BIBLE ‡	STEVEN SCHEUER	LEONARD MALTIN	DISTRIBUTOR	COMMENT
NO TIME TO KILL	1962	72		1.0		MEDALLION	
NO TREES IN THE STREET (BRITISH)	1958	96		2.5	2.0	ASSOC. BRITISH-PATHE	
NO WAY BACK (GERMAN - IVAN DESNY, RUTH NIEHAUS)	1955	71		2.0		FINE ARTS	
NO WAY OUT	1950	106	6	3.5	2.5	20th CENTURY FOX	
NO WAY TO TREAT A LADY	1968	108	6	3.5		PARAMOUNT	
NOAH'S ARK	1929	75		2.0	2.5	WARNER BROTHERS	
NOB HILL	1945	95		2.0	1.5	20th CENTURY FOX	
NOBODY LIVES FOREVER	1946	100	4	2.5	3.0	WARNER BROTHERS	
NOBODY RUNS FOREVER (BRITISH)	a1968	93	4	2.5		CINERAMA RELEASING	
NOBODY WAVED GOODBYE (CANADIAN)	1964	80	5*		3.0	CINEMA V	
NOBODY'S PERFECT	1968	103	3	2.0	2.5	UNIVERSAL	
NOCTURNE	1946	88	4	3.0	3.0	RKO	
NONE BUT THE BRAVE (FRANK SINATRA, CLINT WALKER)	1965	110	4	2.0		WARNER BROTHERS	
NONE BUT THE LONELY HEART	1944	113		3.5	3.5	RKO	
NONE BUT THE LONELY SPY (ITALIAN)	1964	90		1.0		FOUR STAR	
NONE SHALL ESCAPE	1944	85		3.5	3.0	COLUMBIA	
NOOSE HANGS HIGH, THE	1948	77		2.0	2.0	EAGLE LION	
NORA PRENTISS	1947	111	2*	1.0	2.5	WARNER BROTHERS	
NORTH BY NORTHWEST	1959	136	6*	3.5	3.5	M-G-M	
NORTH STAR, THE	a1943	105		2.5	2.5	RKO	
NORTH TO ALASKA	1960	122	5	3.5	3.0	20th CENTURY FOX	
NORTH WEST MOUNTED POLICE	1940	125		3.0	2.5	PARAMOUNT	
NORTHERN PATROL	1953	63	1	1.5		ALLIED ARTISTS	
NORTHERN PURSUIT	1943	94		2.5	2.5	WARNER BROTHERS	
NORTHWEST OUTPOST	1947	91		1.5	1.5	REPUBLIC	
NORTHWEST PASSAGE	1940	126	5-6*	3.5	3.5	M-G-M	
NORTHWEST RANGERS	1942	64		1.5		M-G-M	
NORTHWEST STAMPEDE	1948	79			2.5	EAGLE LION	
NORWOOD	1970	96	3			PARAMOUNT	
NOT A LADIES' MAN	1942	60		2.0		COLUMBIA	
NOT AS A STRANGER	1955	135	5*	3.0	3.0	UNITED ARTISTS	
NOT MINE TO LOVE (ISRAELI)	1967	90	4			NOEL MEADOW	
NOT OF THIS EARTH	1957	67		2.0	2.0	ALLIED ARTISTS	
NOT ON YOUR LIFE (SPANISH)	1963	90	6			PATHE CONTEMPARARY	
NOT SO DUSTY (BRITISH)	1956	74		1.5		EROS FILMS	
NOT WANTED	1949	94	5		2.5	FOUR CONTINENTS	
NOT WITH MY WIFE, YOU DON'T!	1966	118		2.5	2.5	WARNER BROTHERS	
NOTHING BUT A MAN	1965	92	4*	4.0	3.0	CINEMA V	
NOTHING BUT BLONDES (BRITISH)	1957	92		2.0		HAL ROACH	
NOTHING BUT THE BEST (BRITISH)	1964	99	4*		3.5	ROYAL FILMS INT'L	
NOTHING BUT THE TRUTH	1941	90		3.0		PARAMOUNT	
NOTHING BUT TROUBLE	1944	69		1.5	2.0	M-G-M	
NOTORIOUS	1946	103	5-6*	3.5	3.5	RKO	SLOW BUILDUP
NOTORIOUS GENTLEMAN (BRITISH - REX HARRISON)	a1945	109	6	3.5	3.0	UNIVERSAL	
NOTORIOUS LANDLADY, THE	1962	123	4*	3.0	2.5	COLUMBIA	
NOTORIOUS LONE WOLF, THE	1946	64			.	COLUMBIA	
NOTORIOUS MR MONKS, THE	1958	70		1.5	2.0	REPUBLIC	
NOTORIOUS SOPHIE LANG	1934	64			2.5	PARAMOUNT	
NOVEL AFFAIR, A (BRITISH)	a1957	83	6	3.0	3.0	CONTINENTAL	
NOW AND FOREVER (GARY COOPER, CAROLE LOMBARD)	1934	81		2.5	2.5	PARAMOUNT	
NOW, VOYAGER	1942	117	6*	2.5	3.5	WARNER BROTHERS	
NOW YOU SEE HIM, NOW YOU DON'T	1972	88	4			BUENA VISTA	
NOW YOU SEE IT, NOW YOU DON'T (T.V.)	1968	100		1.5		UNIVERSAL	
NOWHERE TO GO (BRITISH)	1958	87	1			M-G-M	
NUDE IN A WHITE CAR (FRENCH)	a1958	87		2.5	2.5	TRANS-LUX DIST.	
NUMBER ONE	1969	105	3	1.0		UNITED ARTISTS	
NUMBER SIX (BRITISH)	1962	59		2.0	2.0	ANGLO AMALGAMATED	
NUN, THE (FRENCH)	1971	130	5			ALTURA FILMS	
NUN AND THE SERGEANT, THE	1962	73		1.0	2.0	UNITED ARTISTS	
NUN'S STORY, THE	1959	149	9*	4.0	3.5	WARNER BROTHERS	NOMINATED BEST PICTURE
NURSE EDITH CAVELL	1939	95		2.5	3.0	RKO	
NURSE ON WHEELS (BRITISH)	1963	86	2			JANUS FILMS	
NURSE'S SECRET, THE	1941	65		2.5		WARNER BROTHERS	
NUTTY, NAUGHTY CHATEAU (FRENCH)	1964	100			2.5	LOPERT	
NUTTY PROFESSOR, THE	1963	107		2.0	3.0	PARAMOUNT	
NYLON NOOSE, THE (GERMAN)	1963	74		1.5		MEDALLION	
NYOKA AND THE LOST SECRETS OF HIPPOCRATES	1942	100		2.0	2.5	REPUBLIC	RE-EDITED SERIAL
08/15 (GERMAN)	1954	110	4			TIMES FILM CORP.	
O. HENRY'S FULL HOUSE	1952	117	5*	3.0	2.5	20th CENTURY FOX	FIVE STORIES
O.S.S.	1946	107		3.0	3.0	PARAMOUNT	
O.S.S. 117 - MISSION FOR A KILLER (FRENCH)	a1965	84	3		2.5	AVCO-EMBASSY	
OASIS (FRENCH)	1954	84				20th CENTURY FOX	
OBJECTIVE, BURMA!	1945	142		3.5	3.5	WARNER BROTHERS	
OBLIGING YOUNG LADY	1941	80		3.5	2.5	RKO	
OBLONG BOX, THE (BRITISH)	1969	91	3	2.0		AMERICAN-INTERNAT'L	
OBSESSED, THE (BRITISH)	1951	77		2.0	2.0	UNITED ARTISTS	
OBSESSION (FRENCH - MICHELLE MORGAN)	1954	103		2.5		GIBE FILMS	
OBSESSION (SWEDISH - MATTHIAS HENRICKSON)	1965	104	4			O.R.P. COMPANY	
OCEAN'S 11	1960	127	6*		2.5	WARNER BROTHERS	SLOW BUILDUP
OCTOBER MAN, THE (BRITISH)	a1947	86		3.0	3.0	EAGLE LION	
OCTOBER MOTH (BRITISH)	1959	54			1.5	J. ARTHUR RANK	

‡ An asterisk (*) in THE FILM BUFF'S BIBLE column indicates that the film has been rated by the editor and/or staff. All other ratings in this column are based on a consensus of reviews (see NOTES).

TITLE (LEADING ACTORS SHOWN WHERE TWO OR MORE FILMS HAVE THE SAME OR SIMILAR TITLE)	YEAR RELEASED	RUNNING TIME IN MINUTES	THE FILM BUFF'S BIBLE ‡	STEVEN SCHEUER	LEONARD MALTIN	DISTRIBUTOR	COMMENT
ODD COUPLE, THE	1968	105	6*	4.0		PARAMOUNT	
ODD MAN OUT (BRITISH)	1947	115	6*	4.0	4.0	UNIVERSAL	
ODD OBSESSION (JAPANESE)	1960	96	4			HARRISON PICTURES	
ODDS AGAINST TOMORROW	1959	95	4*	3.0	3.0	UNITED ARTISTS	
ODETTE (BRITISH)	1950	106		3.5	2.5	LOPERT	
ODONGO (BRITISH)	1956	85		2.0	1.0	COLUMBIA	
OEDIPUS REX (CANADIAN - DOUGLAS CAMPBELL)	1957	87	5		2.5	MOTION PICTURE DISTS.	
OEDIPUS THE KING (BRITISH)	1968	97	5	3.0		UNIVERSAL	
OF FLESH AND BLOOD (FRENCH)	1962	92			2.5	TIMES FILM CORP.	
OF HUMAN BONDAGE (LESLIE HOWARD, BETTE DAVIS)	1934	83				RKO	
OF HUMAN BONDAGE (PAUL HENRIED, ELEANOR PARKER)	1946	105		2.5		WARNER BROTHERS	
OF HUMAN BONDAGE (BRITISH - KIM NOVAK, L. HARVEY)	1964	99		2.0	2.5	M-G-M	
OF HUMAN HEARTS	1938	100		3.5	3.5	M-G-M	
OF LIFE AND LOVE (ITALIAN)	1957	103		3.0	2.5	DIST. CORP. OF AMER.	
OF LOVE AND DESIRE	1963	97	1			20th CENTURY FOX	
OF LOVE AND LUST (SWEDISH)	1955	103	6			FILMS AROUND THE WLD.	
OF MEN AND MUSIC	1951	85	6			20th CENTURY FOX	
OF MICE AND MEN	1939	107	6*	4.0	4.0	UNITED ARTISTS	NOMINATED BEST PICTURE
OF STARS AND MEN (CARTOON)	1961	63	6			BRANDON	
OFF LIMITS	1953	89		2.5	3.0	PARAMOUNT	
OFFICER AND THE LADY	1941	59		2.5		COLUMBIA	
OH DAD, POOR DAD, MAMMA'S HUNG YOU IN THE CLOSET AND I'M FEELIN' SO SAD	1967	86	3	1.0		PARAMOUNT	
OH MEN, OH WOMEN	1957	90		3.0	2.5	20th CENTURY FOX	
OH, SUSANNA (ROD CAMERON, ADRIAN BOOTH)	1951	90		2.0	2.0	REPUBLIC	
OH! THOSE MOST SECRET AGENTS (ITALIAN)	1964	83			1.5	ALLIED ARTISTS	
OH! WHAT A LOVELY WAR (BRITISH)	1969	132	6	4.0		PARAMOUNT	
OH, YOU BEAUTIFUL DOLL	1949	93	4		2.5	20th CENTURY FOX	
O'HARA, UNITED STATES TREASURY (T.V.)	1971	100		2.0		UNIVERSAL	
OIL FOR THE LAMPS OF CHINA	1935	110	4*	3.0	3.0	WARNER BROTHERS	
OKINAWA	1952	67	2	2.0	2.0	COLUMBIA	
OKLAHOMA!	1955	145	7*	4.0	3.0	MAGNA PICTURES	
OKLAHOMA ANNIE	1952	90			1.5	REPUBLIC	
OKLAHOMA KID, THE	1939	85		3.0	3.0	WARNER BROTHERS	
OKLAHOMA TERRITORY	1960	67	2		2.0	UNITED ARTISTS	
OKLAHOMA WOMAN, THE	1956	72			1.0	AMERICAN-INTERNAT'L	
OKLAHOMAN, THE	1957	80	4	2.0	2.0	ALLIED ARTISTS	
OLD ACQUAINTANCE	1943	110		3.0	3.0	WARNER BROTHERS	
OLD DARK HOUSE, THE (BRITISH)	1963	86	4	2.5	2.5	COLUMBIA	
OLD ENGLISH	1930	88		3.0		WARNER BROTHERS	
OLD-FASHIONED WAY, THE	1934	66	4*	3.5	3.5	PARAMOUNT	
OLD HUTCH	1936	80		2.5	2.0	M-G-M	
OLD LOS ANGELES	1948	88		3.0		REPUBLIC	
OLD MAID, THE	1939	95		3.5	3.5	WARNER BROTHERS	
OLD MAN AND THE SEA, THE	1958	86	5*	3.0	3.0	WARNER BROTHERS	
OLD MAN WHO CRIED WOLF, THE (T.V.)	1970	75	4*	3.0		ABC FILMS	
OLD TESTAMENT, THE (ITALIAN)	1963	100		1.5		FOUR STAR	
OLD YELLER	1958	83	6			BUENA VISTA	
OLDEST PROFESSION, THE (FRENCH)	1967	97	1			VIP FILMS	SIX STORIES
OLIVER! (BRITISH)	1968	146	7	4.0		COLUMBIA	BEST PICTURE AWARD
OLIVER TWIST (BR. - ALEC GUINNESS, ROBERT NEWTON)	1948	105	6*	4.0	4.0	UNITED ARTISTS	
OLYMPIA (GERMAN, DOCUMENTARY)	1938	220	8			CONTEMPORARY	TWO PARTS
OLYMPIC ELK (DOCUMENTARY)	1952	27	5*			BUENA VISTA	
OMAR KHAYYAM	1957	101		2.0	2.5	PARAMOUNT	
OMEGA MAN, THE	1971	98	3			WARNER BROTHERS	
ON A CLEAR DAY YOU CAN SEE FOREVER	1970	130	4-5*			PARAMOUNT	
ON AN ISLAND WITH YOU	1948	107		2.5	2.5	M-G-M	
ON ANY STREET (ITALIAN)	a1959	96	1			MILLER PRODUCING CO.	
ON ANY SUNDAY (DOCUMENTARY)	1971	91	6*			CINEMA V	
ON APPROVAL (BRITISH)	1944	80		3.0	3.0	ENGLISH FILMS	
ON BORROWED TIME	1939	99		3.5	3.0	M-G-M	
ON DANGEROUS GROUND	1952	82	4	3.5	2.5	BRADY-WORLD	
ON DRESS PARADE	1939	62		2.0	.	WARNER BROTHERS	
ON FOOT, ON HORSE, AND ON WHEELS (FRENCH)	1957	90		2.0		UN. MOTION PIC. ORG.	
ON HER MAJESTY'S SECRET SERVICE (BRITISH)	1969	140	5	3.0		UNITED ARTISTS	
ON MOONLIGHT BAY	1951	98		2.5	2.5	WARNER BROTHERS	
ON MY WAY TO THE CRUSADES, I MET A GIRL WHO	1969	93	2			WARNER BROTHERS	
ON OUR MERRY WAY	a1948	107		2.0	2.5	UNITED ARTISTS	
ON STAGE EVERYBODY	1945	65		2.0	2.0	UNIVERSAL	
ON THE AVENUE	1937	89		2.5	3.0	20th CENTURY FOX	
ON THE BEACH	1959	133	6*	4.0	4.0	UNITED ARTISTS	
ON THE BEAT (BRITISH)	1962	105		3.0	2.5	UNITED ARTISTS	
ON THE DOUBLE	1961	92	4	2.5	3.0	PARAMOUNT	
ON THE ISLE OF SAMOA	1950	65		1.0	1.5	COLUMBIA	
ON THE LOOSE	1951	78	3		1.5	RKO	
ON THE RIVIERA	1951	89	6	3.0	3.0	20th CENTURY FOX	
ON THE RUN (BRITISH - EMRYS JONES, SARAH LAWSON)	1962	60		2.0		ANGLO AMALGAMATED	
ON THE THRESHOLD OF SPACE	1956	98	4	2.0	2.5	20th CENTURY FOX	
ON THE TOWN	1949	98	4*	4.0	4.0	M-G-M	
ON THE WATERFRONT	1954	108	8*	4.0	4.0	COLUMBIA	BEST PICTURE AWARD
ON THEIR OWN	1940	63		1.5		20th CENTURY FOX	
ON THIN ICE (GERMAN)	1961	90		1.5		COMET FILM	
ON TRIAL (FRENCH - DANIEL GELIN)	1953	70			2.0	NEW REALM	
ON WITH THE SHOW	1959	98		2.0		WARNER BROTHERS	

‡ An asterisk (*) in THE FILM BUFF'S BIBLE column indicates that the film has been rated by the editor and/or staff. All other ratings in this column are based on a consensus of reviews (see NOTES).

TITLE (LEADING ACTORS SHOWN WHERE TWO OR MORE FILMS HAVE THE SAME OR SIMILAR TITLE)	YEAR RELEASED	RUNNING TIME IN MINUTES	CRITICAL RATINGS			DISTRIBUTOR	COMMENT
			THE FILM BUFF'S BIBLE ‡	STEVEN SCHEUER	LEONARD MALTIN		
ON YOUR TOES	1939	94		2.0	2.5	WARNER BROTHERS	
ONCE A THIEF	1965	107		3.0	2.0	M-G-M	
ONCE BEFORE I DIE	1965	97	4		2.5	GOLDSTONE FILM ENT.	
ONCE BITTEN (FRENCH)	1960	90		1.5		UNIVERSAL	
ONCE MORE, MY DARLING	1949	94		2.5	2.5	UNIVERSAL	
ONCE MORE, WITH FEELING	1960	92	5*	3.0	2.5	COLUMBIA	
ONCE UPON A HONEYMOON	1942	117		3.0	2.5	RKO	
ONCE UPON A HORSE (DAN ROWAN, DICK MARTIN)	1958	85		2.0	1.5	UNIVERSAL	
ONCE UPON A THURSDAY	a1942	66		2.5		M-G-M	
ONCE UPON A TIME (CARY GRANT, JANET BLAIR)	1944	89		2.5	2.5	COLUMBIA	
ONCE UPON A TIME IN THE WEST (ITALIAN)	1969	144	4			PARAMOUNT	ENGLISH LANGUAGE
ONCE YOU KISS A STRANGER	1969	106	2			WARNER BROTHERS	
ONE AND ONLY, GENUINE, ORIGINAL FAMILY BAND, THE	1968	110	3	1.0		BUENA VISTA	
ONE BIG AFFAIR	1952	80	2	2.5	2.0	UNITED ARTISTS	
ONE BODY TOO MANY	1944	75		2.0	2.0	PARAMOUNT	
ONE CROWDED NIGHT	1940	68		2.0		RKO	
ONE DANGEROUS NIGHT	1943	77			-	COLUMBIA	
ONE DAY IN THE LIFE OF IVAN DENISOVICH (BRITISH)	1971	100	6			CINERAMA RELEASING	
ONE DESIRE	1955	94		2.5	2.5	UNIVERSAL	
ONE-EYED JACKS	1961	141	6*	3.0	2.5	PARAMOUNT	
ONE FATAL HOUR	a1936	64		2.0	2.0	FIRST NATIONAL	
ONE FOOT IN HEAVEN	1941	108	6*	4.0	3.5	WARNER BROTHERS	NOMINATED BEST PICTURE
ONE FOOT IN HELL	1960	90		2.5	2.5	20th CENTURY FOX	
ONE GIRL'S CONFESSION	1953	74		2.0	1.0	COLUMBIA	
ONE GOOD TURN (BRITISH)	1954	90		2.5	2.0	J. ARTHUR RANK	
ONE HEAVENLY NIGHT	1931	82		2.0		UNITED ARTISTS	
ONE HOUR WITH YOU	1932	80		3.0	3.5	PARAMOUNT	NOMINATED BEST PICTURE 1931/32
ONE HUNDRED AND ONE DALMATIANS (CARTOON)	1961	80	4*			BUENA VISTA	
100 CRIES OF TERROR (MEXICAN)	1965	96		1.5		K. GORDEN MURRAY	TWO STORIES
100 MEN AND A GIRL	1937	84		3.0	3.0	UNIVERSAL	NOMINATED BEST PICTURE
100 RIFLES	1969	110	3			20th CENTURY FOX	
ONE IN A MILLION	1936	95		3.0	3.0	20th CENTURY FOX	
ONE IS A LONELY NUMBER	1972	97	5			M-G-M	
ONE JUMP AHEAD (BRITISH)	1955	66		2.0		J. ARTHUR RANK	
ONE LAST FLING	1949	74	2	2.0	2.0	WARNER BROTHERS	
ONE MAN'S WAY	1964	105		2.5	3.0	UNITED ARTISTS	
ONE MILLION B.C.	1940	80		2.0	2.5	UNITED ARTISTS	
ONE MILLION YEARS B.C. (BRITISH)	1966	100	3*	1.5	2.0	20th CENTURY FOX	
ONE MINUTE TO ZERO	1952	105		2.0	2.5	RKO	
ONE MORE TIME (BRITISH)	1970	93	3			UNITED ARTISTS	
ONE MORE TOMORROW	1946	88		2.0	2.0	WARNER BROTHERS	
ONE MORE TRAIN TO ROB	1971	108	4			UNIVERSAL	
ONE MYSTERIOUS NIGHT	1944	61			-	COLUMBIA	
ONE NIGHT AT DINNER (ITALIAN)	1969	110	3			INT'L CO-PRODUCTIONS	
ONE NIGHT IN LISBON	1941	97		2.5	2.5	PARAMOUNT	
ONE NIGHT OF LOVE	1934	82			3.5	COLUMBIA	NOMINATED BEST PICTURE
ONE NIGHT WITH YOU (BRITISH)	1948	90		2.0		UNIVERSAL	
ONE OF OUR AIRCRAFT IS MISSING (BRITISH)	1942	106	5*	3.5	3.5	UNITED ARTISTS	
ONE ON TOP OF THE OTHER (ITALIAN)	1970	103	3			GGP RELEASING	
ONE POTATO, TWO POTATO	1964	92	6*	4.0	3.5	CINEMA V	
ONE SPY TOO MANY	1966	102	4		-	M-G-M	
ONE STEP TO ETERNITY (FRENCH)	1954	94		2.5	2.0	ELLIS FILMS	
ONE SUMMER OF HAPPINESS (SWEDISH)	1952	95	6			TIMES FILM CORP.	
ONE SUNDAY AFTERNOON (DENNIS MORGAN, JANIS PAIGE)	1948	90		2.5	2.5	WARNER BROTHERS	
ONE THAT GOT AWAY, THE (BRITISH)	1957	111		4.0	3.5	J. ARTHUR RANK	
ONE THIRD OF A NATION	1939	79			2.5	PARAMOUNT	
1001 ARABIAN NIGHTS (CARTOON)	1959	75	4*	2.5	2.5	COLUMBIA	
1,000 CONVICTS AND A WOMAN!	1971	94	3			AMERICAN-INTERNAT'L	
1,000 PLANE RAID, THE	a1969	94	3			UNITED ARTISTS	
ONE TOUCH OF VENUS	1948	81		2.5	2.5	UNIVERSAL	
ONE, TWO, THREE	1961	108	8*	3.5	4.0	UNITED ARTISTS	
ONE WAY PASSAGE	1932	69		3.0	3.5	WARNER BROTHERS	
ONE WAY STREET	1950	79		2.5	2.5	UNIVERSAL	
ONE WAY TO LOVE	1946	83		2.5	2.5	COLUMBIA	
ONE WOMAN'S STORY (BRITISH)	a1949	86		3.5	3.5	UNIVERSAL	
ONIBABA (JAPANESE)	a1965	99	6			TOHO	
ONIONHEAD	1958	110	4	2.5	2.5	WARNER BROTHERS	
ONLY A WOMAN (GERMAN)	1962	80		2.0		WARNER BROTHERS	
ONLY ANGELS HAVE WINGS	1939	121		3.0	3.5	COLUMBIA	
ONLY GAME IN TOWN, THE	1970	113	4			20th CENTURY FOX	
ONLY ONE NEW YORK (DOCUMENTARY)	1964	75	4*	2.5		AVCO-EMBASSY	
ONLY THE FRENCH CAN (FRENCH)	a1954	93		3.5	2.5	UN. MOTION PIC. ORG.	
ONLY THE VALIANT	1951	105	4	2.0	2.0	WARNER BROTHERS	
ONLY TWO CAN PLAY (BRITISH)	1961	106	6*	4.0	3.0	COLUMBIA	
ONLY WHEN I LARF (BRITISH)	1968	104	5	2.0		PARAMOUNT	
OPEN CITY (ITALIAN)	1945	105	7	4.0	4.0	MAYER-BURSTYN	
OPEN THE DOOR AND SEE ALL THE PEOPLE	1964	82		2.0	2.5	NOEL PRODUCTIONS	
OPENED BY MISTAKE	1940	67		2.0		PARAMOUNT	
OPERATION ABDUCTION (FRENCH)	1957	85		1.5		AMERICAN-INTERNAT'L	
OPERATION AMSTERDAM (BRITISH)	1959	105	4	2.0		20th CENTURY FOX	
OPERATION ATLANTIS (ITALIAN)	1965	83		1.5		AMERICAN-INTERNAT'L	
OPERATION BIKINI	1963	83	2	2.0	2.0	AMERICAN-INTERNAT'L	
OPERATION BOTTLENECK	1961	78		1.5	1.5	UNITED ARTISTS	
OPERATION BULLSHINE (BRITISH)	1959	83		2.0		ASSOC. BRITISH-PATHE	

‡ An asterisk (*) in THE FILM BUFF'S BIBLE column indicates that the film has been rated by the editor and/or staff. All other ratings in this column are based on a consensus of reviews (see NOTES).

TITLE (LEADING ACTORS SHOWN WHERE TWO OR MORE FILMS HAVE THE SAME OR SIMILAR TITLE)	YEAR RELEASED	RUNNING TIME IN MINUTES	THE FILM BUFF'S BIBLE ‡	STEVEN SCHEUER	LEONARD MALTIN	DISTRIBUTOR	COMMENT
OPERATION C.I.A.	1965	90	2	1.5	2.5	ALLIED ARTISTS	
OPERATION CAMEL (DANISH)	1961	70		1.0		AMERICAN-INTERNAT'L	
OPERATION CAVIAR (FRENCH)	1959	85		2.0		AMERICAN-INTERNAT'L	
OPERATION CONSPIRACY (BRITISH)	a1957	69		2.0	1.5	REPUBLIC	
OPERATION CROSSBOW	a1965	116	6	3.0		M-G-M	
OPERATION DAMES	1959	74		2.0		AMERICAN-INTERNAT'L	
OPERATION DELILAH	1964	86		1.5		NTA PICTURES	
OPERATION DIPLOMAT (BRITISH)	1953	70		2.5		BUTCHER'S	
OPERATION DIPLOMATIC PASSPORT (FRENCH)	1962	85		1.5		AMERICAN-INTERNAT'L	
OPERATION DISASTER (BRITISH)	a1950	102	4*	3.5	3.0	UNIVERSAL	
OPERATION EICHMANN	1961	93		2.0	2.5	ALLIED ARTISTS	
OPERATION GOLD INGOT (FRENCH)	1963	85		2.0		AMERICAN-INTERNAT'L	
OPERATION HAYLIFT	1950	75	4		2.0	LIPPERT PRODS.	
OPERATION HONG KONG (GERMAN)	1964	95	1	-		CASINO FILMS	
OPERATION KID BROTHER (ITALIAN)	1967	104	1			UNITED ARTISTS	
OPERATION MAD BALL	1957	105	3*	3.5	2.0	COLUMBIA	
OPERATION MANHUNT	1954	77	3	2.5		UNITED ARTISTS	
OPERATION MERMAID (BRITISH)	a1963	73		3.0	2.0	J. ARTHUR RANK	
OPERATION PACIFIC	1951	111		1.5	3.0	WARNER BROTHERS	
OPERATION PETTICOAT	1959	124		3.5	2.5	UNIVERSAL	
OPERATION SECRET	1952	108		3.0	2.0	WARNER BROTHERS	
OPERATION SNAFU (BRITISH)	a1962	89	3	2.0	2.5	AMERICAN-INTERNAT'L	
OPERATION SNATCH (BRITISH)	1962	83		2.5	2.0	CONTINENTAL	
OPERATION STOGIE (BRITISH)	1960	75		1.5		WARNER BROTHERS	
OPERATION WARHEAD (BRITISH)	a1962	89	3	2.0	2.5	AMERICAN-INTERNAT'L	
OPERATION X (BRITISH)	1951	79	2		2.0	COLUMBIA	
OPPOSITE SEX, THE	1956	117	6	3.0	3.0	M-G-M	
ORCHESTRA WIVES	1942	98		3.0	3.0	20th CENTURY FOX	
ORDERED TO LOVE (GERMAN)	1961	88			2.5	TRANSOCEAN FILMS	
ORDERS ARE ORDERS (BRITISH)	1954	78		2.5	2.0	DIST. CORP. OF AMER.	
ORDERS TO KILL (BRITISH)	1958	93	5*	3.5	2.5	UN. MOTION PIC. ORG.	
OREGON PASSAGE	1958	82		2.0	1.5	ALLIED ARTISTS	
OREGON TRAIL, THE (FRED MACMURRAY, WILLIAM BISHOP)	1959	86		1.5	2.0	20th CENTURY FOX	
ORGANIZATION, THE	1971	107	5-6*			UNITED ARTISTS	
ORGANIZER, THE (ITALIAN)	1963	126	7*	4.0	3.0	CONTINENTAL	
ORIENTALS, THE (ITALIAN)	1960	110		1.0		GALATEA PRODS.	
ORPHANS OF THE STORM (SILENT)	1921	133	5*			UNITED ARTISTS	
ORPHEUS (FRENCH)	1950	94	3*			DISCINA INTERNAT'L	
OSCAR, THE	1966	119		2.0	2.5	AVCO-EMBASSY	
OSCAR WILDE (BRITISH)	1960	98	5		2.5	FILMS AROUND THE WLD.	
O'SHAUGHNESSY'S BOY	1935	88		2.5	2.5	M-G-M	
OTHELLO (ITALIAN - ORSON WELLES)	1951	91		3.0	2.5	UNITED ARTISTS	
OTHELLO (RUSSIAN - SERGEI BONDARCHUK)	1955	108				UNIVERSAL	
OTHELLO (BRITISH - LAURENCE OLIVIER, MAGGIE SMITH)	1965	166	7			WARNER BROTHERS	
OTHER, THE	1972	100	2*			20th CENTURY FOX	
OTHER LOVE, THE	1947	95		2.5	2.5	UNITED ARTISTS	
OTHER MAN, THE (T.V.)	1970	100		2.0		UNIVERSAL	
OTHER SIDE OF MADNESS, THE	1971	85				AURIC LTD.	
OTHER VOICES (DOCUMENTARY)	1969	103	6	3.0		DHS FILMS	
OTHER WOMAN, THE	1954	81		2.0	1.0	20th CENTURY FOX	
OTLEY (BRITISH)	1969	90	5	3.0		COLUMBIA	
OUR BETTERS	1933	78		2.0	2.5	RKO	
OUR BLUSHING BRIDES	1930	79			2.0	M-G-M	
OUR DAILY BREAD	1934	74	4*		3.0	UNITED ARTISTS	
OUR HEARTS WERE GROWING UP	1946	83		2.5	2.5	PARAMOUNT	
OUR HEARTS WERE YOUNG AND GAY	1944	81		3.0	3.0	PARAMOUNT	
OUR LEADING CITIZEN	1939	88		2.5		PARAMOUNT	
OUR LITTLE GIRL	1935	63			2.5	20th CENTURY FOX	
OUR MAN FLINT	1966	107	5*	3.5	2.5	20th CENTURY FOX	
OUR MAN IN HAVANA (BRITISH)	1959	111	6*	3.0	2.5	COLUMBIA	
OUR MAN IN JAMAICA	1965	96		1.5		PARAMOUNT	
OUR MAN IN THE CARIBBEAN (BRITISH)	1962	85		2.0		TRANSCONTINENTAL	
OUR MISS BROOKS	1956	85	4	2.5	2.5	WARNER BROTHERS	
OUR MOTHER'S HOUSE (BRITISH)	1967	105	4*			M-G-M	
OUR RELATIONS	1936	65			2.5	M-G-M	
OUR TOWN	1940	90	3*	4.0	3.5	UNITED ARTISTS	NOMINATED BEST PICTURE
OUR VERY OWN	1950	93	3*	2.0	2.5	RKO	
OUR VINES HAVE TENDER GRAPES	1945	105		3.0	3.5	M-G-M	
OUR WIFE	1941	95		2.5	2.5	COLUMBIA	
OUT OF IT	1970	97	1			UNITED ARTISTS	
OUT OF SIGHT	1966	87	1	1.5	1.5	UNIVERSAL	
OUT OF THE BLUE	1947	84		2.5	2.5	EAGLE LION	
OUT OF THE CLOUDS (BRITISH)	1954	88			2.0	J. ARTHUR RANK	
OUT OF THE DEPTHS	1945	61		2.0		COLUMBIA	
OUT OF THE FOG (IDA LUPINO, JOHN GARFIELD)	1941	93		3.0	3.0	WARNER BROTHERS	
OUT OF THE PAST	1947	97	4*	3.0	3.0	RKO	
OUT OF THIS WORLD (EDDIE BRACKEN, V. LAKE)	1945	96		2.5	2.5	PARAMOUNT	
OUT OF THIS WORLD (TRAVELOGUE)	1954	75	4			CARROLL PICTURES	
OUT-OF-TOWNERS, THE	1970	98	6*	3.0		PARAMOUNT	
OUT WEST WITH THE HARDYS	1938	90		2.5	-	M-G-M	
OUTBACK (AUSTRALIAN)	1971	109	4			UNITED ARTISTS	
OUTCAST, THE (JOHN DEREK, JOAN EVANS)	1954	90	3	3.0	2.5	REPUBLIC	
OUTCAST OF THE ISLANDS (BRITISH)	1951	102	7	4.0	3.0	UNITED ARTISTS	
OUTCASTS OF POKER FLAT, THE (ANNE BAXTER)	1952	81		2.5	2.5	20th CENTURY FOX	

‡ An asterisk (*) in THE FILM BUFF'S BIBLE column indicates that the film has been rated by the editor and/or staff. All other ratings in this column are based on a consensus of reviews (see NOTES).

TITLE (LEADING ACTORS SHOWN WHERE TWO OR MORE FILMS HAVE THE SAME OR SIMILAR TITLE)	YEAR RELEASED	RUNNING TIME IN MINUTES	THE FILM BUFF'S BIBLE ‡	STEVEN SCHEUER	LEONARD MALTIN	DISTRIBUTOR	COMMENT
OUTCASTS OF THE CITY	1958	61		1.5	1.5	REPUBLIC	
OUTCRY, THE (ITALIAN)	a1957	115	4	2.0	2.5	ASTOR	
OUTLAW, THE	1943	123		1.5	2.0	RKO	
OUTLAW RIDERS	1971	86				ACE INTERNATIONAL	
OUTLAW STALLION, THE	a1954	64		1.0	1.5	COLUMBIA	
OUTLAW TERRITORY	a1953	74	4	2.5		REALART	
OUTLAW WOMEN	1952	75	3			LIPPERT PRODS.	
OUTLAW'S DAUGHTER, THE	1954	75		2.0	1.5	20th CENTURY FOX	
OUTLAWS IS COMING, THE	1965	89	3		2.0	COLUMBIA	
OUTLAW'S SON	1957	89		2.0	2.0	UNITED ARTISTS	
OUTPOST IN INDO-CHINA (FRENCH)	1964	85		2.0		AMERICAN-INTERNAT'L	
OUTPOST IN MALAYA (BRITISH)	a1952	88		2.0	2.5	UNITED ARTISTS	
OUTPOST IN MOROCCO	1949	92		1.5	2.0	UNITED ARTISTS	
OUTRAGE (MALA POWERS, TOD ANDREWS)	1950	75	3			RKO	
OUTRAGE, THE (PAUL NEWMAN, CLAIRE BLOOM)	1964	97	4	3.5	2.5	M-G-M	
OUTRIDERS, THE	1950	93		3.0	2.0	M-G-M	
OUTSIDE THE LAW	1956	81		1.0	1.5	UNIVERSAL	
OUTSIDE THE WALL	1950	80		2.0	2.5	UNIVERSAL	
OUTSIDER, THE (BRITISH - RICHARD ATTENBOROUGH)	1948	98		3.0		KORDA	
OUTSIDER, THE (TONY CURTIS, JAMES FRANCISCUS)	1962	108	5	3.5	2.5	UNIVERSAL	
OUTSIDER, THE (T.V. - DARREN MCGAVIN)	1967	100			2.5	UNIVERSAL	
OUTWARD BOUND	1930	84		3.0		WARNER BROTHERS	
OVER-EXPOSED	1956	80		1.5	1.5	COLUMBIA	
OVER MY DEAD BODY	1942	68		2.0	2.5	20th CENTURY FOX	
OVER THE HILL GANG, THE (T.V.)	1969	90				ABC FILMS	
OVER THE HILL GANG RIDES AGAIN, THE (T.V.)	1970	90		2.0		ABC FILMS	
OVER THE MOON (BRITISH)	1940	78		1.5	1.5	UNITED ARTISTS	
OVER THE WAVES	a1942	71		2.0		M-G-M	
OVER THERE 1914-1918 (FRENCH, DOCUMENTARY)	1963	90	6	3.0		PATHE CONTEMPARARY	
OVER 21	1945	102		2.5	3.0	COLUMBIA	
OVERCOAT, THE (RUSSIAN)	1965	78	4*			TIMES FILM CORP.	
OVERLAND PACIFIC	1954	73		2.5	2.0	UNITED ARTISTS	
OVERLANDERS, THE (AUSTRALIAN)	1946	91		3.5		UNIVERSAL	
OWL AND THE PUSSYCAT, THE	1970	95	5			COLUMBIA	
OX-BOW INCIDENT, THE	1943	75	7*	4.0	4.0	20th CENTURY FOX	NOMINATED BEST PICTURE
P. J.	1968	109	4	2.5		UNIVERSAL	
PACE THAT THRILLS, THE	1952	63	3	2.0		RKO	
PACIFIC ADVENTURE (AUSTRALIAN)	1947	95		3.0		COLUMBIA	
PACIFIC BLACKOUT	1942	76		1.5		PARAMOUNT	
PACIFIC LINER	1939	75		3.0	2.0	RKO	
PACK UP YOUR TROUBLES (LAUREL & HARDY)	1932	68			2.5	M-G-M	
PACK UP YOUR TROUBLES (RITZ BROTHERS)	1939	75		2.0	2.0	20th CENTURY FOX	
PAD (AND HOW TO USE IT), THE	1966	86		2.5	2.5	UNIVERSAL	
PADDY (IRISH)	1970	97	5			ALLIED ARTISTS	
PAGAN LOVE SONG	1950	76	4	2.0	2.0	M-G-M	
PAGANS, THE (ITALIAN)	1958	80			1.5	ALLIED ARTISTS	
PAGE MISS GLORY	1935	90		2.0	2.5	WARNER BROTHERS	
PAID	1931	80			2.5	M-G-M	
PAID IN FULL	1950	105		1.5	2.5	PARAMOUNT	
PAID TO KILL (BRITISH)	1954	70		1.5	2.0	LIPPERT PRODS.	
PAINT YOUR WAGON	1969	106	4	1.5		PARAMOUNT	
PAINTED HILLS, THE	1951	65	3	2.5	2.5	M-G-M	
PAINTED VEIL, THE	1934	83		3.0	2.5	M-G-M	
PAINTING THE CLOUDS WITH SUNSHINE	1951	87		2.0	2.0	WARNER BROTHERS	
PAIR OF BRIEFS, A (BRITISH)	1962	90	3			J. ARTHUR RANK	
PAISAN (ITALIAN)	1946	90	7	3.5	3.5	MAYER-BURSTYN	SIX EPISODES
PAJAMA GAME, THE	1957	101	5*	3.0	3.0	WARNER BROTHERS	
PAJAMA PARTY	1964	85		2.0	2.5	AMERICAN-INTERNAT'L	
PAL JOEY	1957	111		2.5	3.0	COLUMBIA	
PALACES OF A QUEEN (BRITISH, DOCUMENTARY)	1966	80	4			UNIVERSAL	
PALEFACE, THE	1948	91	6	3.0	3.0	PARAMOUNT	
PALM BEACH STORY, THE	1942	90	5-6*	4.0	3.5	PARAMOUNT	
PALM SPRINGS WEEKEND	1963	100		2.0	2.5	WARNER BROTHERS	
PALMY DAYS	1931	77		2.5	2.5	UNITED ARTISTS	
PALOMINO, THE	1950	75	4	2.0		COLUMBIA	
PAMELA, PAMELA YOU ARE . . .	1969	90	1			DISTRIBPIX	
PAN-AMERICANA	1945	84			2.0	RKO	
PANAMA HATTIE	1942	79		2.5	2.5	M-G-M	
PANAMA LADY	1939	65		2.0		RKO	
PANAMA SAL	1957	70		2.0	1.0	REPUBLIC	
PANDORA AND THE FLYING DUTCHMAN (BRITISH)	1951	121	5*	3.0	2.5	M-G-M	
PANHANDLE	1948	84		3.0		MONOPOL	
PANIC (FRENCH - VIVIANE ROMANCE)	1947	83	7			TRICOLORE	
PANIC (BRITISH - DYSON LOVELL, JANINE GRAY)	1963	69		2.0		SCREEN GEMS	
PANIC BUTTON	1964	90		2.0	2.5	GORTON ASSOCIATES	
PANIC IN NEEDLE PARK, THE	1971	110	5			20th CENTURY FOX	
PANIC IN THE CITY	1968	96	2			LANDAU/UNGER COM. UN.	
PANIC IN THE PARLOR (BRITISH)	1957	81	4	2.0	2.5	DIST. CORP. OF AMER.	
PANIC IN THE STREETS	1950	83	5*	3.5	3.0	20th CENTURY FOX	
PANIC IN YEAR ZERO	1962	95	5*	3.0	2.5	AMERICAN-INTERNAT'L	
PANTALOONS (FRENCH)	1956	93		3.0	2.5	UN. MOTION PIC. ORG.	

‡ An asterisk (*) in THE FILM BUFF'S BIBLE column indicates that the film has been rated by the editor and/or staff. All other ratings in this column are based on a consensus of reviews (see NOTES).

TITLE (LEADING ACTORS SHOWN WHERE TWO OR MORE FILMS HAVE THE SAME OR SIMILAR TITLE)	YEAR RELEASED	RUNNING TIME IN MINUTES	THE FILM BUFF'S BIBLE ‡	STEVEN SCHEUER	LEONARD MALTIN	DISTRIBUTOR	COMMENT
PAPA, MAMA, THE MAID AND I (FRENCH)	1954	96	5		2.5	COLUMBIA	
PAPA'S DELICATE CONDITION	1963	98		2.0	2.5	PARAMOUNT	
PAPER LION	1968	105	6	3.5		UNITED ARTISTS	
PAPER MAN (T.V.)	1971	75	4-5*			20th CENTURY FOX	
PARACHUTE BATALLION	1941	75		2.5	2.0	RKO	
PARACHUTE NURSE	1942	63		2.0		COLUMBIA	
PARADES	1972	95	5			CINERAMA RELEASING	
PARADINE CASE, THE	1947	131	5	2.5	2.5	SELZNICK RELEASING	
PARADISE ALLEY	1961	85		2.0	1.5	ASTOR	
PARADISE FOR THREE	1938	75		2.0	2.0	M-G-M	
PARADISE, HAWAIIAN STYLE	1966	91		2.0	2.5	PARAMOUNT	
PARADISE LAGOON (BRITISH)	a1957	93	5	3.0	2.0	COLUMBIA	
PARADISIO	1963	82	1			VIP DISTRIBUTORS	
PARAMOUNT ON PARADE	1930	102			2.5	PARAMOUNT	
PARANOIA (ITALIAN - MARCELLO MASTROIANNI)	1965	120		2.0		CARLO PONTI	THREE STORIES
PARANOIA (ITALIAN - CARROLL BAKER, LOU CASTEL)	1968	91	1			LANDAU/UNGER COM. UN	ENGLISH LANGUAGE
PARANOIAC (BRITISH)	1963	80	4		2.5	UNIVERSAL	
PARATROOP COMMAND	1959	83	4	2.5		AMERICAN-INTERNAT'L	
PARATROOPER, THE (BRITISH)	1954	87		2.0	2.0	COLUMBIA	
PARDNERS	1956	90		2.0	2.5	PARAMOUNT	
PARDON MY FRENCH	1951	81		2.0	2.5	UNITED ARTISTS	
PARDON MY PAST	1945	88		3.5	3.0	COLUMBIA	
PARDON MY RHYTHM	1944	62		1.5	2.0	UNIVERSAL	
PARDON MY SARONG	1942	84		3.0	3.0	UNIVERSAL	
PARDON MY TRUNK (ITALIAN)	a1952	83		2.0	1.5	ARLAN PICTURES	
PARDON US	1931	55			2.5	M-G-M	
PARENT TRAP, THE	1961	124	6			BUENA VISTA	
PARIAHS OF GLORY (FRENCH)	1964	95		2.5		ABC FILMS	
PARIS AFTER DARK	1943	85		2.0	2.0	20th CENTURY FOX	
PARIS BLUES	1961	98	3*	3.5	3.0	UNITED ARTISTS	
PARIS CALLING	1941	95			3.0	UNIVERSAL	
PARIS DOES STRANGE THINGS	1957	86		2.0	2.0	WARNER BROTHERS	
PARIS EXPRESS, THE	1953	83		2.5	2.5	GEORGE SCHAEFER	
PARIS HOLIDAY	1958	100		2.5	2.5	UNITED ARTISTS	
PARIS HONEYMOON	1939	92		2.5	2.5	PARAMOUNT	
PARIS IN SPRING	1935	83		2.5	.	PARAMOUNT	
PARIS IN THE MONTH OF AUGUST (FRENCH)	1966	97	4	2.5		TRANS-LUX DIST.	
PARIS MODEL	1953	81	2	2.0	1.5	COLUMBIA	
PARIS PICK-UP (FRENCH)	1962	85	3			PARAMOUNT	
PARIS PLAYBOYS	1954	62	3		.	ALLIED ARTISTS	
PARIS SECRET (DOCUMENTARY)	1965	84	3			CINEMA V	
PARIS UNDERGROUND	1945	97		3.0	2.5	UNITED ARTISTS	
PARIS WHEN IT SIZZLES	1964	110	4		2.0	PARAMOUNT	
PARK ROW	1952	83	4	3.0	2.5	UNITED ARTISTS	
PARNELL	1937	119		2.0		M-G-M	
PAROLE, INC.	1948	71			2.0	EAGLE LION	
PARRISH	1961	137	4	2.5	1.5	WARNER BROTHERS	
PARSON AND THE OUTLAW, THE	1957	71		1.0	1.5	COLUMBIA	
PARSON OF PANAMINT, THE	1941	84		3.0	2.5	PARAMOUNT	
PART-TIME WIFE (BRITISH)	1961	70		1.5	1.5	WARNER BROTHERS	
PARTNER, THE (BRITISH)	1963	58		2.0		ANGLO AMALGAMATED	
PARTNERS IN CRIME (BRITISH - BERNARD LEE)	1961	54		2.0		ANGLO AMALGAMATED	
PARTY, THE	1968	99	4	2.5		UNITED ARTISTS	
PARTY CRASHERS, THE	1958	78	2	2.0	1.5	PARAMOUNT	
PARTY GIRL, THE	1958	99		2.0	2.5	M-G-M	
PARTY GIRLS FOR THE CANDIDATE	a1964	84	1			ATLANTIC PICTURES	
PARTY'S OVER, THE (BRITISH)	1965	94			2.0	ALLIED ARTISTS	
PASSAGE FROM HONG KONG	1941	61		2.0		WARNER BROTHERS	
PASSAGE TO MARSEILLE	1944	110		3.0	2.5	WARNER BROTHERS	
PASSAGE WEST	1951	80		2.0	1.5	PARAMOUNT	
PASSING STRANGER, THE (BRITISH)	1954	67		3.0		WALTER READE	
PASSION	1954	84	3	2.0	2.5	RKO	
PASSION OF ANNA, THE (SWEDISH)	1970	99	6*			UNITED ARTISTS	
PASSION OF SLOW FIRE, THE (FRENCH)	a1961	91	6	3.0		TRANS-LUX DIST.	
PASSIONATE SENTRY, THE (BRITISH)	a1952	84		3.0	2.0	FINE ARTS	
PASSIONATE SUMMER (FRENCH - RAF VALLONE)	1957	97	5	2.0		KINGSLEY INTERNAT'L	
PASSIONATE SUMMER (BRITISH - VIRGINIA MCKENNA)	1958	104				J. ARTHUR RANK	
PASSIONATE THIEF, THE (ITALIAN)	1960	105		2.5	2.5	AVCO-EMBASSY	
PASSPORT FOR A CORPSE (ITALIAN)	1962	84		1.5		MEDALLION	
PASSPORT TO ADVENTURE	a1943	64		2.0	2.0	RKO	
PASSPORT TO ALCATRAZ	1940	60		1.5		COLUMBIA	
PASSPORT TO CHINA (BRITISH)	1961	75	2	2.0	2.0	COLUMBIA	
PASSPORT TO DESTINY	a1943	64		2.0	2.0	RKO	
PASSPORT TO HELL (FRENCH)	1964	101		1.0		FOUR STAR	
PASSPORT TO PIMLICO (BRITISH)	1948	72	4*	4.0	3.5	EAGLE LION	
PASSPORT TO TREASON (BRITISH)	1956	80		2.0	1.5	ASTOR	
PASSWORD IS COURAGE, THE (BRITISH)	1962	116	5*	2.5	3.0	M-G-M	
PASTOR HALL (BRITISH)	1940	90		2.5		UNITED ARTISTS	
PAT AND MIKE	1952	94	4*	3.5	3.0	M-G-M	
PATCH OF BLUE, A	1965	105	7*	3.5	3.0	M-G-M	
PATH OF HOPE, THE (ITALIAN)	1950	101		2.5		LUX FILM AMERICA	
PATHER PANCHALI (INDIAN)	1956	112	7	4.0	3.0	HARRISON PICTURES	
PATHFINDER, THE	1953	78		2.0	1.5	COLUMBIA	
PATHFINDER AND THE MOHICAN, THE	1956	90		1.5		INDEP. TV CORP (ITC)	

‡ An asterisk (*) in THE FILM BUFF'S BIBLE column indicates that the film has been rated by the editor and/or staff. All other ratings in this column are based on a consensus of reviews (see NOTES).

TITLE (LEADING ACTORS SHOWN WHERE TWO OR MORE FILMS HAVE THE SAME OR SIMILAR TITLE)	YEAR RELEASED	RUNNING TIME IN MINUTES	THE FILM BUFF'S BIBLE ‡	STEVEN SCHEUER	LEONARD MALTIN	DISTRIBUTOR	COMMENT
PATHS OF GLORY	1957	86	8*	4.0	4.0	UNITED ARTISTS	
PATRIOT, THE (SILENT)	1928	113				PARAMOUNT	NOM. BEST PIC., BELIEVED LOST
PATSY, THE	1964	101		2.0	2.0	PARAMOUNT	
PATTERN FOR MURDER (GERMAN)	1964	80		1.0		COM. UNITED T.V.	
PATTERNS	1956	83	5*	3.5	3.5	UNITED ARTISTS	
PATTERNS FOR PLUNDER	1964	81	4				
PATTON	1970	173	7*			20th CENTURY FOX	BEST PICTURE AWARD
PAULA	1952	80		3.0	2.5	COLUMBIA	
PAWNBROKER, THE	1965	110	10*	4.0	4.0	LANDAU/UNGER COM. UN	
PAWNEE	1957	80		1.5	2.0	REPUBLIC	
PAY OR DIE	1960	110		3.0	2.5	ALLIED ARTISTS	
PAYMENT DEFERRED	1932	75		2.5	3.0	M-G-M	
PAYMENT IN BLOOD (ITALIAN)	1967	90	1			COLUMBIA	
PAYMENT ON DEMAND	1951	90	6	2.5	3.0	RKO	
PAYROLL (BRITISH)	1961	80	2	2.5	2.5	ALLIED ARTISTS	
PEACE KILLERS, THE	1971	88	1			TRANSVUE PICTURES	
PEACEMAKER, THE	1956	82	4		2.0	UNITED ARTISTS	
PEACH THIEF, THE (BULGARIAN)	1964	84	5			BRANDON	
PEARL, THE	1948	77	6*	4.0	3.5	RKO	
PEARL OF DEATH, THE	1944	69			-	UNIVERSAL	
PEARL OF THE SOUTH PACIFIC	1955	86	2*		1.5	RKO	
PECK'S BAD BOY	1934	70			2.5	20th CENTURY FOX	
PECK'S BAD BOY WITH THE CIRCUS	1938	78			2.0	RKO	
PEEPING TOM (BRITISH)	1960	86		1.0		ASTOR	
PEGGY	1950	77	4	2.0	2.5	UNIVERSAL	
PEKING EXPRESS	1951	95		2.0	2.5	PARAMOUNT	
PENALTY, THE (EDWARD ARNOLD, LIONEL BARRYMORE)	1941	81		2.0	2.0	M-G-M	
PENDULUM	1969	104	5	3.0		COLUMBIA	
PENELOPE	1966	97	3	2.0		M-G-M	
PENGUIN POOL MURDER, THE	1932	70		2.5	2.5	RKO	
PENNIES FROM HEAVEN	1936	90		3.0	2.0	COLUMBIA	
PENNY PRINCESS (BRITISH)	1952	94	4		3.0	UNIVERSAL	
PENNY SERENADE	1941	125		3.5	3.5	COLUMBIA	
PENNYWHISTLE BLUES (BRITISH)	a1951	63	6	3.5		MAYER-KINGSLEY	
PENROD AND HIS TWIN BROTHER	1938	63		2.5	2.0	WARNER BROTHERS	
PENROD AND SAM (BILLY MAUCH, FRANK CRAVEN)	1937	64		2.5	2.5	WARNER BROTHERS	
PENROD'S DOUBLE TROUBLE	1938	61		2.5	2.0	WARNER BROTHERS	
PENTHOUSE, THE (BR.- SUZY KENDALL, TERENCE MORGAN)	1967	96	3			PARAMOUNT	
PEOPLE AGAINST O'HARA, THE	1951	102	4*	3.0	2.5	M-G-M	
PEOPLE ARE FUNNY	1946	93		1.5		PARAMOUNT	
PEOPLE MEET AND SWEET MUSIC FILLS THE HEART	1967	94	2			TRANS-LUX DIST.	(SWEDISH)
PEOPLE NEXT DOOR, THE	1970	93	4			AVCO-EMBASSY	
PEOPLE VS DR KILDARE, THE	1941	78		2.0	-	M-G-M	
PEOPLE WILL TALK (MARY BOLAND, CHARLES RUGGLES)	1935	67		2.5	2.5	PARAMOUNT	
PEOPLE WILL TALK (JEANNE CRAIN, CARY GRANT)	1951	110	4*	3.5	3.5	20th CENTURY FOX	
PEPE	1960	195	4	2.5	1.0	COLUMBIA	
PEPOTE (SPANISH)	1956	88		3.0		UN. MOTION PIC. ORG.	
PERCY (BRITISH)	1971	100	1			M-G-M	
PERFECT FRIDAY (BRITISH)	1970	94	6			CHEVRON	
PERFECT FURLOUGH, THE	1959	93		3.0	2.5	UNIVERSAL	
PERFECT MARRIAGE, THE	1947	87		2.0	2.0	PARAMOUNT	
PERFECT SPECIMEN, THE	1937	97		3.0		FIRST NATIONAL	
PERFECT STRANGERS (BRITISH - ROBERT DONAT)	a1945	102		3.0	3.0	M-G-M	
PERFECT STRANGERS (GINGER ROGERS, DENNIS MORGAN)	1950	88		1.5	2.5	WARNER BROTHERS	
PERFECT WOMAN, THE (BRITISH)	1949	87		2.0	2.5	EAGLE LION	
PERFORMANCE (BRITISH)	1970	106	2			WARNER BROTHERS	
PERILOUS HOLIDAY	1946	89		3.0	3.0	COLUMBIA	
PERILOUS JOURNEY, A	1953	90		2.0	2.0	REPUBLIC	
PERILS OF PAULINE (BETTY HUTTON)	1947	90	5*	3.0		PARAMOUNT	
PERILS OF PAULINE, THE (PAMELA AUSTIN)	1967	99		1.5	2.0	UNIVERSAL	
PERIOD OF ADJUSTMENT	1962	112		3.0	2.5	M-G-M	
PERRI (DOCUMENTARY)	1957	74	6			BUENA VISTA	TRUE LIFE FANTASY
PERSONA (SWEDISH)	1966	81	6			LOPERT	
PERSONAL AFFAIR (BRITISH)	1953	83	4	2.5	2.0	UNITED ARTISTS	
PERSONAL PROPERTY	1937	84		2.0	2.5	M-G-M	
PERSONALITY KID (ANITA LOUISE, MICHAEL DUANE)	1946	68		2.0		COLUMBIA	
PERSUADER, THE	1957	72		2.0	2.0	ALLIED ARTISTS	
PETE KELLY'S BLUES	1955	95		2.5	2.5	WARNER BROTHERS	
PETE SEEGER . . . A SONG AND A STONE (DOCUMENTARY)	1972	85	5			THEATRE EXCH. ACTIV.	
PETER IBBETSON	1935	85		2.0	2.5	PARAMOUNT	
PETER PAN (CARTOON)	1953	77	6			RKO	
PETER RABBIT AND TALES OF BEATRIX POTTER (BRITISH)	a1971	90	6			M-G-M	FIVE STORIES
PETRIFIED FOREST, THE	1936	83	5*	4.0	3.5	WARNER BROTHERS	
PETTICOAT FEVER	1936	81		2.5	2.5	M-G-M	
PETTY GIRL, THE	1950	87		3.0	2.5	COLUMBIA	
PETULIA (BRITISH)	1968	105	3*	3.0		WARNER BROTHERS	
PEYTON PLACE	1957	162	6*	3.0	3.5	20th CENTURY FOX	NOMINATED BEST PICTURE
PHAEDRA (GREEK)	1962	115	6			LOPERT	ENGLISH LANGUAGE
PHANTOM FROM SPACE	1953	72	2		1.5	UNITED ARTISTS	
PHANTOM HORSE, THE (JAPANESE)	1956	90		2.5		HARRISON PICTURES	
PHANTOM LADY	1944	87		3.5	3.5	UNIVERSAL	
PHANTOM OF SOHO, THE (GERMAN)	1963	92	1			PRODUCERS RELEASING	
PHANTOM OF THE OPERA, THE (SILENT - LON CHANEY)	1925	94				UNIVERSAL	
PHANTOM OF THE OPERA, THE (NELSON EDDY, C. RAINS)	1943	92		3.0	3.0	UNIVERSAL	

‡ An asterisk (*) in THE FILM BUFF'S BIBLE column indicates that the film has been rated by the editor and/or staff. All other ratings in this column are based on a consensus of reviews (see NOTES).

TITLE (LEADING ACTORS SHOWN WHERE TWO OR MORE FILMS HAVE THE SAME OR SIMILAR TITLE) "a" TO LEFT OF YEAR INDICATES THAT FILM HAS AN ALTERNATE TITLE	YEAR RELEASED	RUNNING TIME IN MINUTES	THE FILM BUFF'S BIBLE ‡	STEVEN SCHEUER	LEONARD MALTIN	DISTRIBUTOR	COMMENT
PHANTOM OF THE OPERA, THE (BRITISH - HERBERT LOM)	1962	84		3.0	2.0	UNIVERSAL	
PHANTOM OF THE RUE MORGUE	1954	84		2.5	2.0	WARNER BROTHERS	
PHANTOM PLANET, THE	1962	82	2	2.0	1.5	AMERICAN-INTERNAT'L	
PHANTOM PRESIDENT, THE	1932	80		3.0	2.0	PARAMOUNT	
PHANTOM RAIDERS	1940	70		2.0		M-G-M	
PHANTOM STAGECOACH, THE	1957	69		1.5	1.5	COLUMBIA	
PHANTOM SUBMARINE, THE	1940	71		2.0		COLUMBIA	
PHANTOM THIEF, THE	1946	65		2.0		COLUMBIA	
PHARAOH'S CURSE, THE	1957	66		2.0	2.0	UNITED ARTISTS	
PHARAOH'S WOMAN, THE (ITALIAN)	1960	87	2		2.0	UNIVERSAL	
PHENIX CITY STORY, THE	a1955	100		3.0	2.5	ALLIED ARTISTS	
PHFFFT	1954	91	4*	3.5	3.0	COLUMBIA	
PHILADELPHIA STORY, THE	1940	112	7*	3.5	4.0	M-G-M	NOMINATED BEST PICTURE
PHILO VANCE RETURNS	1947	64			-	PRODUCERS RELEASING	
PHILO VANCE'S GAMBLE	1947	62			-	PRODUCERS RELEASING	
PHILO VANCE'S SECRET MISSION	1947	58			-	PRODUCERS RELEASING	
PHOENIX CITY STORY, THE	a1955	100		3.0	2.5	ALLIED ARTISTS	
PHONE CALL FROM A STRANGER	1952	96	6*	3.0	3.0	20th CENTURY FOX	
PHONE RINGS EVERY NIGHT, THE (GERMAN)	1962	82		1.5		EMERY PICTURES	
PHONY AMERICAN, THE (GERMAN)	1961	72		2.0	2.5	SIGNAL INT'L	
PHOTO FINISH (FRENCH)	1957	110		1.5	2.0		
PICCADILLY INCIDENT (BRITISH)	a1946	88		3.0	3.0	M-G-M	
PICCADILLY JIM	1936	100		3.0	3.0	M-G-M	
PICK A STAR	1937	70			2.5	M-G-M	
PICKPOCKET (FRENCH)	1959	75	6			NEW YORKER FILMS	
PICKUP (BEVERLY MICHAELS, HUGO HAAS)	1951	78	4	2.5	1.5	COLUMBIA	
PICKUP ALLEY (BRITISH)	1957	92		2.0	1.5	COLUMBIA	
PICKUP ON 101	1972	93	3			AMERICAN-INTERNAT'L	
PICKUP ON SOUTH STREET	1953	80		2.5	2.5	20th CENTURY FOX	
PICKWICK PAPERS (BRITISH)	1952	115	7	3.5	3.0	MAYER-KINGSLEY	
PICNIC	1956	113	6*	3.0	3.5	COLUMBIA	NOMINATED BEST PICTURE
PICNIC ON THE GRASS (FRENCH)	1959	91	4			KINGSLEY-UNION	
PICTURA (DOCUMENTARY)	1951	82	6			PICTURA FILMS	
PICTURE MOMMY DEAD	1966	88	3	2.5	2.5	AVCO-EMBASSY	
PICTURE OF DORIAN GRAY, THE	1945	110	7*	3.0	3.5	M-G-M	
PIECES OF DREAMS	1970	100	4			UNITED ARTISTS	
PIED PIPER, THE (MONTY WOLLEY, ANNE BAXTER)	1942	87	5*	3.5	3.0	20th CENTURY FOX	NOMINATED BEST PICTURE
PIED PIPER, THE (BR.- JACK WILD, DONALD PLEASENCE)	1972	90	4			PARAMOUNT	
PIED PIPER OF HAMELIN, THE	1957	87		2.0	2.5	NTA PICTURES	
PIER 5 - HAVANA	1959	67	2			UNITED ARTISTS	
PIER 13	1940	66		2.0	1.5	20th CENTURY FOX	
PIER 23	1951	58	2			LIPPERT PRODS.	
PIERRE OF THE PLAINS	1942	66		2.0		M-G-M	
PIERROT LE FOU (FRENCH)	1965	110	3*			PATHE CONTEMPARARY	
PIGEON, THE (T.V.)	1969	90		2.0		ABC FILMS	
PIGEON THAT TOOK ROME, THE	1962	101	5*	2.5	2.5	PARAMOUNT	
PIGEONS	a1971	87	4			PLAZA PICTURES	
PIGSKIN PARADE	1936	93		3.0	3.0	20th CENTURY FOX	
PILGRIMAGE	1933	90	3*			20th CENTURY FOX	
PILLAR OF FIRE, THE	1963	76		3.0		HOFFBERG	
PILLARS OF THE SKY	1956	95		2.5	2.5	UNIVERSAL	
PILLOW OF DEATH	1945	55		2.0	2.0	UNIVERSAL	
PILLOW TALK	1959	110	8*	4.0	3.5	UNIVERSAL	
PILLOW TO POST	1945	92		2.0	2.0	UNITED ARTISTS	
PILOT NO. 5	1943	70		1.5	2.0	M-G-M	
PIMPERNEL SMITH (BRITISH)	a1941	118	6*	3.5	3.0	ANGLO-AMERICAN	
PIN-UP GIRL	1944	83		2.0	2.5	20th CENTURY FOX	
PINK ANGELS, THE	1971	81				CROWN INTERNATIONAL	
PINK JUNGLE, THE	1968	104		2.0	2.5	UNIVERSAL	
PINK PANTHER, THE	1964	113	6*	4.0	2.5	UNITED ARTISTS	
PINK STRING AND SEALING WAX (BRITISH)	1946	95		2.5		EAGLE LION	
PINKY	1949	102	6*	3.0	3.0	20th CENTURY FOX	
PIRATE, THE	1948	102	5	3.5	3.0	M-G-M	
PIRATE AND THE SLAVE GIRL (ITALIAN)	1959	87		1.5	2.0	CREST	
PIRATE OF THE BLACK HAWK (ITALIAN)	1958	75	1	1.5		FILMGROUP	
PIRATES OF BLOOD RIVER, THE (BRITISH)	1962	84	3		2.0	COLUMBIA	
PIRATES OF CAPRI, THE	a1949	94	4		2.0	FOUR CONTINENTS	
PIRATES OF MONTERY	1947	77		2.0	2.0	UNIVERSAL	
PIRATES OF THE COAST (ITALIAN)	1961	102		1.5		WARNER BROTHERS	
PIRATES OF THE MISSISSIPPI, THE (GERMAN)	1964	95		1.5		RAPIDFILM	
PIRATES OF TORTUGA	1961	97		1.5	2.0	20th CENTURY FOX	
PIRATES OF TRIPOLI	1955	72		2.0	2.0	COLUMBIA	
PISTOL FOR RINGO, A (ITALIAN)	1965	97	3		2.5	AVCO-EMBASSY	
PIT AND THE PENDULUM, THE	1961	95	5*	2.5		AMERICAN-INTERNAT'L	
PIT OF LONELINESS (FRENCH)	a1951	95	4			DAVIS DIST.	
PIT STOP	1969	92	1			DISTRIBUTORS INT'L	
PITFALL, THE	1948	84	4*	3.5	3.5	UNITED ARTISTS	
PITTSBURGH	1942	98		2.0	2.0	UNIVERSAL	
PIZZA TRIANGLE, THE (ITALIAN)	a1970	95	6			WARNER BROTHERS	
PLACE CALLED GLORY, A (GERMAN)	1965	92	2		2.0	AVCO-EMBASSY	
PLACE CALLED TODAY, A	1972	103	1			AVCO-EMBASSY	
PLACE FOR LOVERS, A (ITALIAN)	a1968	88	2			M-G-M	ENGLISH LANGUAGE
PLACE IN THE SUN, A	1951	122	7*	4.0	4.0	PARAMOUNT	NOMINATED BEST PICTURE
PLACE OF ONE'S OWN, A (BRITISH)	1945	92		3.0	2.5	EAGLE LION	

‡ An asterisk (*) in THE FILM BUFF'S BIBLE column indicates that the film has been rated by the editor and/or staff. All other ratings in this column are based on a consensus of reviews (see NOTES).

TITLE (LEADING ACTORS SHOWN WHERE TWO OR MORE FILMS HAVE THE SAME OR SIMILAR TITLE)	YEAR RELEASED	RUNNING TIME IN MINUTES	THE FILM BUFF'S BIBLE ‡	STEVEN SCHEUER	LEONARD MALTIN	DISTRIBUTOR	COMMENT
PLACE TO GO, A (BRITISH)	1964	87		2.0		WALTER READE	
PLAGUE OF THE ZOMBIES, THE (BRITISH)	1966	91	3		2.5	20th CENTURY FOX	
PLAINSMAN, THE (GARY COOPER, JEAN ARTHUR)	1936	113	5*	3.5	3.0	PARAMOUNT	
PLAINSMAN, THE (DON MURRAY, GUY STOCKWELL)	1966	92		2.0	1.5	UNIVERSAL	
PLAINSMAN AND THE LADY, THE	1946	87		2.0	2.0	REPUBLIC	
PLAN 9 FROM OUTER SPACE (BRITISH)	a1956	79		1.0	1.0	DIST. CORP. OF AMER.	
PLANET OF BLOOD	a1966	83		2.0		AMERICAN-INTERNAT'L	
PLANET OF THE APES	1968	112	8*	4.0		20th CENTURY FOX	
PLANET OF THE VAMPIRES (ITALIAN)	a1965	86	2	1.5	2.5	AMERICAN-INTERNAT'L	
PLANETS AGINST US (FRENCH)	1960	83		1.0		TELEWORLD	
PLATINUM HIGH SCHOOL	a1960	93		1.0	2.0	M-G-M	
PLAY DIRTY (BRITISH)	1969	117	3			UNITED ARTISTS	
PLAY GIRL	1941	75		2.0	2.5	RKO	
PLAY IT AGAIN, SAM	1972	86	6*			PARAMOUNT	
PLAY IT COOL (BRITISH)	1962	74		1.5	1.5	ALLIED ARTISTS	
PLAY MISTY FOR ME	1971	102	4			UNIVERSAL	
PLAYBACK (BRITISH)	1962	63		2.0		ANGLO AMALGAMATED	
PLAYBOY OF THE WESTERN WORLD, THE (IRISH)	1962	100	7	4.0		JANUS FILMS	
PLAYGIRL (SHELLEY WINTERS, BARRY SULLIVAN)	1954	85		2.5	2.5	UNIVERSAL	
PLAYGIRL AFTER DARK (BRITISH)	1960	92	3			TOPAZ FILMS	
PLAYGIRL AND THE WAR MINISTER	1963	90	2			UNION FILMS	
PLAYGROUND, THE	a1965	95	6			JERAND PICS.	
PLAYMATES	1941	94		2.0	1.5	RKO	
PLAZA SUITE	1971	115	6			PARAMOUNT	
PLEASE BELIEVE ME	1950	87		2.5	2.5	M-G-M	
PLEASE DON'T EAT MY MOTHER!	1972	98				BOXOFFICE INTERNAT'L	
PLEASE DON'T EAT THE DAISIES	1960	111	5*	3.0	3.0	M-G-M	
PLEASE, MR BALZAC (FRENCH)	1957	99		2.0	3.0	DIST. CORP. OF AMER.	
PLEASE MURDER ME	1956	78		2.0	2.5	DIST. CORP. OF AMER.	
PLEASE TURN OVER (BRITISH)	1960	86		2.0	2.5	COLUMBIA	
PLEASURE OF HIS COMPANY, THE	1961	115	6*	2.5	3.5	PARAMOUNT	
PLEASURE SEEKERS, THE	1965	107	3	2.5	2.5	20th CENTURY FOX	
PLOT THICKENS, THE	1936	69		2.0	2.0	RKO	
PLOT TO ASSASSINATE HITLER, THE (GERMAN)	1961	90		2.5		PARAMOUNT	
PLUNDER OF THE SUN	1953	81		2.0	2.5	WARNER BROTHERS	
PLUNDER ROAD	1957	71	4	3.5	2.5	20th CENTURY FOX	
PLUNDERERS, THE (ROD CAMERON, FORREST TUCKER)	1948	87		2.5	2.0	REPUBLIC	
PLUNDERERS, THE (JEFF CHANDLER, JOHN SAXON)	1960	93		2.5	2.5	ALLIED ARTISTS	
PLUNDERERS OF PAINTED FLATS, THE	1959	77		1.5	1.5	REPUBLIC	
PLYMOUTH ADVENTURE	1952	105	4*	3.0	3.0	M-G-M	
POACHER'S DAUGHTER, THE (IRISH)	1958	74		2.5	2.5	SHOWCORPORATION	
POCKET MONEY	1972	98	3			NATIONAL GENERAL	
POCKETFUL OF MIRACLES	1961	136		3.0	2.5	UNITED ARTISTS	
POINT, THE (CARTOON, T.V.)	1971	90		3.5		ABC FILMS	
POINT BLANK	1967	92	4	2.5		M-G-M	
POINT OF ORDER (DOCUMENTARY)	1964	97	6*			CONTINENTAL	
POINT OF TERROR	1971	88	4			CROWN INTERNATIONAL	
POISON (FRENCH)	1957	83		2.5			
POISON IVY (FRENCH)	1953	90		2.0	2.0	PARAMOUNT	
POLICE DOG STORY, THE	1961	62	3			UNITED ARTISTS	
POLICE NURSE	1963	64	2			20th CENTURY FOX	
POLICEMAN, THE (ISRAELI)	1971	86	4*			EPHI LTD.	
POLLY OF THE CIRCUS	1932	72		1.5	2.0	M-G-M	
POLLYANNA	1960	134	6			BUENA VISTA	
POLO JOE	1936	62		2.0	2.0	WARNER BROTHERS	
PONY EXPRESS	1953	101	4	2.5	3.0	PARAMOUNT	
PONY SOLDIER	1952	82		2.5	2.5	20th CENTURY FOX	
POOL OF LONDON (BRITISH)	1951	85	6	3.0		UNIVERSAL	
POOR BUT BEAUTIFUL (ITALIAN)	1958	103	4	2.5		TRANS-LUX DIST.	
POOR COW (BRITISH)	1967	101	4	2.5		NATIONAL GENERAL	
POOR LITTLE RICH GIRL, THE	1936	72		3.0	3.0	20th CENTURY FOX	
POOR WHITE TRASH	a1957	85	1			UNITED ARTISTS	
POP ALWAYS PAYS	1940	67		2.0		RKO	
POPCORN	1969	85	1			SHERPIX	
POPE JOAN	1972	132	3			COLUMBIA	
POPI	1969	115	7	4.0		UNITED ARTISTS	
POPPY	1936	75	5*	3.0	2.5	PARAMOUNT	
POPPY IS ALSO A FLOWER, THE (T.V.)	a1966	100	4*		1.0	COMET FILM	
PORGY AND BESS	1959	138	6*	3.5	2.5	COLUMBIA	
PORK CHOP HILL	1959	97	5	3.0	3.0	UNITED ARTISTS	
PORT AFRIQUE	1956	92		2.0	2.0	COLUMBIA	
PORT OF FORTY THIEVES	1944	58		3.0		REPUBLIC	
PORT OF HELL	1954	80		2.0	2.0	ALLIED ARTISTS	
PORT OF NEW YORK	1949	96		3.0	2.0	EAGLE LION	
PORT OF REVENGE (BRITISH)	1961	90		1.5			
PORT OF SEVEN SEAS	1938	81		2.0	2.0	M-G-M	
PORT SINISTER	1953	65		1.5		RKO	
PORTLAND EXPOSE	1957	72	4			ALLIED ARTISTS	
PORTNOY'S COMPLAINT	1972	101	3			WARNER BROTHERS	
PORTRAIT IN BLACK	1960	112	4*	2.5	2.5	UNIVERSAL	
PORTRAIT OF A MOBSTER	1961	108	2	2.5	2.5	WARNER BROTHERS	
PORTRAIT OF A SINNER (BRITISH)	a1959	96		2.0	2.5	AMERICAN-INTERNAT'L	
PORTRAIT OF CLARE (BRITISH)	1951	94			2.0	STRATFORD PICS.	
PORTRAIT OF JENNIE	1948	86	6*	3.5	3.5	SELZNICK RELEASING	

‡ An asterisk (*) in THE FILM BUFF'S BIBLE column indicates that the film has been rated by the editor and/or staff. All other ratings in this column are based on a consensus of reviews (see NOTES).

TITLE (LEADING ACTORS SHOWN WHERE TWO OR MORE FILMS HAVE THE SAME OR SIMILAR TITLE)	YEAR RELEASED	RUNNING TIME IN MINUTES	THE FILM BUFF'S BIBLE ‡	STEVEN SCHEUER	LEONARD MALTIN	DISTRIBUTOR	COMMENT
POSSE FROM HELL	1961	89		2.0	2.0	UNIVERSAL	
POSSESSED (JOAN CRAWFORD, CLARK GABLE)	1931	72			2.5	M-G-M	
POSSESSED (JOAN CRAWFORD, VAN HEFLIN)	1947	108		2.5	2.5	WARNER BROTHERS	
POSSESSION OF JOEL DELANEY, THE	1972	105	3			PARAMOUNT	
POSSESSORS, THE (FRENCH)	1959	94	5	2.5	2.5	LOPERT	
POST OFFICE INVESTIGATOR	1949	59	3	2.0		REPUBLIC	
POSTMAN ALWAYS RINGS TWICE, THE	1946	113	4*	3.5	4.0	M-G-M	
POSTMARK FOR DANGER (BRITISH)	1956	84			2.0	RKO	
POT O' GOLD	1941	86		2.0	2.0	UNITED ARTISTS	
POTBOUILLE (FRENCH)	a1957	115		2.5	2.5	CONTINENTAL	
POTEMKIN (RUSSIAN, SILENT)	1925	70	5-6*			AMKINO	
POUND	1970	92	4			UNITED ARTISTS	
POVERTY AND NOBILITY (ITALIAN)	1954	83		2.0			
POWDER KEG (T.V.)	1971	100		2.0		FILMWAYS	
POWDER RIVER	1953	78		2.0	2.0	20th CENTURY FOX	
POWDER TOWN	1942	79		2.0		RKO	
POWER, THE	1968	109	3	2.0		M-G-M	
POWER AND THE GLORY, THE (SPENCER TRACY)	1933	76		2.5		20th CENTURY FOX	
POWER AND THE PRIZE, THE	1956	98	4*	2.5	2.5	M-G-M	
POWER DIVE	1941	65		2.0		PARAMOUNT	
POWER OF THE PRESS	1943	64		1.5		COLUMBIA	
POWER OF THE WHISTLER, THE	1945	66		2.5	-	COLUMBIA	
POWERS GIRL, THE	1942	93		2.0	2.0	UNITED ARTISTS	
PRACTICALLY YOURS	1944	90		2.0	2.0	PARAMOUNT	
PREACHERMAN	1971	87	4			PREACHERMAN CORP.	
PREHISTORIC WOMEN (LAURETTE LUEZ, ALLAN NIXON)	1950	74		1.0	1.0	UNITED ARTISTS	
PREHISTORIC WOMEN (BRITISH - MARTINE BESWICK)	1967	91	1			20th CENTURY FOX	
PRELUDE TO FAME (BRITISH)	1950	88		3.5		UNIVERSAL	
PREMATURE BURIAL, THE	1962	81	5*			AMERICAN-INTERNAT'L	
PREMEDITATED (FRENCH)	1960	90		2.0			
PREMIER MAY (FRENCH)	a1958	89	4	2.5	2.0	CONTINENTAL	
PRESCRIPTION MURDER (T.V.)	1968	100		2.5	2.5	UNIVERSAL	
PRESENTING LILY MARS	1943	104		2.0	2.0	M-G-M	
PRESIDENT'S ANALYST, THE	1967	104	4*	3.5		PARAMOUNT	
PRESIDENT'S LADY, THE	1953	96	5*	2.5	3.0	20th CENTURY FOX	
PRESSURE POINT	1962	91	6*	3.0	3.0	UNITED ARTISTS	
PRETENDER, THE	1947	69		3.0	2.5	REPUBLIC	
PRETTY BABY	1950	92		2.5	2.0	WARNER BROTHERS	
PRETTY BOY FLOYD	1960	96		2.0	2.0	CONTINENTAL	
PRETTY MAIDS ALL IN A ROW	1971	92	3			M-G-M	
PRETTY POISON	1968	89	5	4.0		20th CENTURY FOX	
PRICE OF FEAR, THE	1956	79	2	2.0	2.5	UNIVERSAL	
PRICE OF SILENCE, THE (BRITISH)	1960	75		2.0		ALLIED ARTISTS	
PRIDE AND PREJUDICE	1940	118	4*	3.0	3.0	M-G-M	
PRIDE AND THE PASSION, THE	1957	132	5*	2.5	2.5	UNITED ARTISTS	
PRIDE OF MARYLAND	1951	60		2.0		REPUBLIC	
PRIDE OF ST LOUIS, THE	1952	92		2.5	2.5	20th CENTURY FOX	
PRIDE OF THE BLUE GRASS (STANLEY CLEMENTS)	1954	71		2.0	2.0	ALLIED ARTISTS	
PRIDE OF THE BOWERY	1940	63			-	MONOGRAM	
PRIDE OF THE MARINES	1945	119		3.5	3.5	WARNER BROTHERS	
PRIDE OF THE YANKEES	1942	128	4*	4.0	4.0	RKO	NOMINATED BEST PICTURE
PRIEST'S WIFE, THE (ITALIAN)	1971	106	3			WARNER BROTHERS	
PRIME CUT	1972	91	5*			NATIONAL GENERAL	
PRIME OF MISS JEAN BRODIE, THE (BRITISH)	1969	116	9*			20th CENTURY FOX	
PRIMROSE PATH, THE	1940	93		2.0	2.5	RKO	
PRINCE AND THE PAUPER, THE	1937	120		3.5	3.5	WARNER BROTHERS	
PRINCE AND THE SHOWGIRL, THE (BRITISH)	1957	115	6*	3.0	2.5	WARNER BROTHERS	
PRINCE OF FOXES	1949	107	4	2.0	2.5	20th CENTURY FOX	
PRINCE OF PIRATES	1953	80	3	2.0	2.5	COLUMBIA	
PRINCE OF PLAYERS	1955	102		3.0	2.5	20th CENTURY FOX	
PRINCE OF THIEVES, THE	1948	72			2.0	COLUMBIA	
PRINCE VALIANT	1954	100		2.5	2.5	20th CENTURY FOX	
PRINCE WHO WAS A THIEF, THE	1951	88		2.0	2.5	UNIVERSAL	
PRINCESS AND THE PIRATE, THE	1944	94		3.0	3.0	RKO	
PRINCESS COMES ACROSS, THE	1936	76		3.0	3.0	PARAMOUNT	
PRINCESS OF THE NILE	1954	71		2.0	2.5	20th CENTURY FOX	
PRINCESS O'ROURKE	1943	94		3.5	3.5	WARNER BROTHERS	
PRIORITIES ON PARADE	1942	79		1.0		PARAMOUNT	
PRISON SHIP	1945	60		2.0		COLUMBIA	
PRISON WARDEN	1949	62	2			COLUMBIA	
PRISONER, THE (BRITISH)	1955	94	6	4.0	3.0	COLUMBIA	
PRISONER OF SHARK ISLAND, THE	1936	95		3.0	3.0	20th CENTURY FOX	
PRISONER OF THE IRON MASK, THE (ITALIAN)	1961	78		1.5	2.5	AMERICAN-INTERNAT'L	
PRISONER OF THE JUNGLE (FRENCH)	1958	82		1.5		AMERICAN-INTERNAT'L	
PRISONER OF THE VOLGA (ITALIAN)	1958	102	3	1.5	2.5	PARAMOUNT	
PRISONER OF WAR	1954	80		2.0	2.0	M-G-M	
PRISONER OF ZENDA, THE (RONALD COLEMAN)	1937	101	7*	3.5	3.5	UNITED ARTISTS	
PRISONER OF ZENDA, THE (STEWART GRANGER)	1952	101		2.5	3.0	M-G-M	
PRISONERS IN PETTICOATS	1950	90		1.0		REPUBLIC	
PRISONERS OF THE CASBAH	1953	78	3*	1.5	1.5	COLUMBIA	
PRIVATE AFFAIRS OF BEL AMI, THE	1947	112		2.5	2.5	UNITED ARTISTS	
PRIVATE ANGELO (BRITISH)	1949	106		3.0		ASSOC. BRITISH-PATHE	
PRIVATE BUCKAROO	1942	68		1.5	2.0	UNIVERSAL	
PRIVATE DETECTIVE (JANE WYMAN, DICK FORAN)	1939	55		2.0		FIRST NATIONAL	

‡ An asterisk (*) in THE FILM BUFF'S BIBLE column indicates that the film has been rated by the editor and/or staff. All other ratings in this column are based on a consensus of reviews (see NOTES).

TITLE (LEADING ACTORS SHOWN WHERE TWO OR MORE FILMS HAVE THE SAME OR SIMILAR TITLE)	YEAR RELEASED	RUNNING TIME IN MINUTES	THE FILM BUFF'S BIBLE ‡	STEVEN SCHEUER	LEONARD MALTIN	DISTRIBUTOR	COMMENT
PRIVATE DETECTIVE 62	1933	67		3.0		WARNER BROTHERS	
PRIVATE DUTY NURSES	1971	80				NEW WORLD	
PRIVATE EYES	1953	64				ALLIED ARTISTS	
PRIVATE HELL 36	1954	81	4	3.0	2.5	FILMMAKERS	
PRIVATE LIFE OF DON JUAN, THE (BRITISH)	1934	80		2.0	2.0	UNITED ARTISTS	
PRIVATE LIFE OF HENRY VIII, THE (BRITISH)	1933	97	6-7*	3.5	4.0	UNITED ARTISTS	NOMINATED BEST PICTURE 1932/33
PRIVATE LIFE OF SHERLOCK HOLMES, THE (BRITISH)	1970	125	4			UNITED ARTISTS	
PRIVATE LIVES	1931	85		3.0		M-G-M	
PRIVATE LIVES OF ADAM AND EVE, THE	1960	86		1.0	1.5	UNIVERSAL	
PRIVATE LIVES OF ELIZABETH AND ESSEX	a1939	106	5-6*	3.5	3.5	WARNER BROTHERS	
PRIVATE NAVY OF SERGEANT O'FARRELL, THE	1968	92	3	1.0		UNITED ARTISTS	
PRIVATE NUMBER	1936	80		2.5	2.0	20th CENTURY FOX	
PRIVATE NURSE	1941	61		1.5		20th CENTURY FOX	
PRIVATE PROPERTY	1960	79	3			CITATION	
PRIVATE WAR OF MAJOR BENSON, THE	1955	100	5*	3.0	2.5	UNIVERSAL	
PRIVATE WORLDS	1935	84		2.5	2.5	PARAMOUNT	
PRIVATE'S AFFAIR, A	1959	92		2.0	2.5	20th CENTURY FOX	
PRIVATE'S PROGRESS (BRITISH)	1956	102	6	3.5	3.0	DIST. CORP. OF AMER.	
PRIVILEGE (BRITISH)	1967	103	6		3.0	UNIVERSAL	
PRIZE, THE	1963	136	6*	2.5	3.0	M-G-M	
PRIZE OF ARMS, A (BRITISH)	1961	105		3.0	2.5	BRITISH-LION	
PRIZE OF GOLD, A (BRITISH)	1954	100	5	3.0	3.0	COLUMBIA	
PRIZEFIGHTER AND THE LADY, THE	1933	102		2.5		M-G-M	
PROBLEM GIRLS	1953	70		1.5		COLUMBIA	
PRODIGAL, THE (LANA TURNER, EDMUND PURDOM)	1955	114		1.5	2.5	M-G-M	
PRODUCERS, THE	1968	88	6-7*	3.5		AVCO-EMBASSY	
PROFESSIONAL SOLDIER	1935	75		2.5	2.5	20th CENTURY FOX	
PROFESSIONAL SWEETHEART	1933	68		2.0	2.0	RKO	
PROFESSIONALS, THE (BRITISH - WILLIAM LUCAS)	1960	61		2.0		AMERICAN-INTERNAT'L	
PROFESSIONALS, THE (BURT LANCASTER, LEE MARVIN)	1966	116	6*	4.0	3.0	COLUMBIA	
PROFESSOR BEWARE	1938	87		2.5	2.5	PARAMOUNT	
PROJECT M-7 (BRITISH)	a1953	79	5	3.0		UNIVERSAL	
PROJECT X (CHRISTOPHER GEORGE, GRETA BALDWIN)	1968	97	2	1.0		PARAMOUNT	
PROJECTED MAN, THE (BRITISH)	1966	77	2			UNIVERSAL	
PROJECTIONIST, THE	1971	88	5			MARON FILMS, LTD.	
PROMISE AT DAWN (FRENCH)	1971	101	6			AVCO-EMBASSY	
PROMISE HER ANYTHING (BRITISH)	1966	97		2.5	2.5	PARAMOUNT	
PROMISES, PROMISES	1964	75	1			NTD, INC.	
PROMOTER, THE (BRITISH)	1952	88	7*	4.0	3.0	UNIVERSAL	
PROUD AND THE BEAUTIFUL, THE (FRENCH)	1954	94	6	3.5	3.0	KINGSLEY INTERNAT'L	
PROUD AND THE PROFANE, THE	1956	111		3.0	2.5	PARAMOUNT	
PROUD, DAMNED AND DEAD	1969	119	2			FERDE GROFE JR.	
PROUD ONES, THE (ROBERT RYAN, VIRGINIA MAYO)	1956	94	4*	3.0	2.5	20th CENTURY FOX	
PROUD REBEL, THE	1958	103	5*	3.5	3.0	BUENA VISTA	
PROUD STALLION, THE (CZECH)	1964	84		2.5		TELEWORLD	
PROWLER, THE	1951	92	6	3.5	3.0	UNIVERSAL	
PRUDENCE AND THE PILL (BRITISH)	1968	92	3	1.0		20th CENTURY FOX	
PSYCH-OUT	1968	101	4	3.0		AMERICAN-INTERNAT'L	
PSYCHE 59 (BRITISH)	1964	94		2.0	2.5	COLUMBIA	
PSYCHIATRIST: GOD BLESS THE CHILDREN, THE (T.V.)	1970	100		2.5		UNIVERSAL	
PSYCHO	1960	109	6*	3.0	3.5	PARAMOUNT	
PSYCHO-CIRCUS (BRITISH)	a1967	83	3	2.0		AMERICAN-INTERNAT'L	
PSYCHOMANIA	1964	90	2	1.5	2.5	VICTORIA	
PSYCHOPATH, THE (BRITISH)	1966	83	5		3.0	PARAMOUNT	
PSYCHOUT FOR MURDER (ITALIAN)	1969	88	1			TIMES FILM CORP.	
PSYCOSISSIMO (ITALIAN)	1961	88	3			ELLIS FILMS	
PT 109	1963	140		2.5	2.0	WARNER BROTHERS	
PUBLIC AFFAIR, A	1962	75		3.0		PARADE	
PUBLIC DEB NO. 1	1940	80		2.0		20th CENTURY FOX	
PUBLIC ENEMY (JAMES CAGNEY, JEAN HARLOW)	1931	83	3-4*	3.0	3.5	WARNER BROTHERS	
PUBLIC EYE, THE	1972	90	4			UNIVERSAL	
PUBLIC HERO NUMBER ONE	1935	81		3.0	3.0	M-G-M	
PUBLIC PIGEON NO. 1	1957	79		2.0	2.0	UNIVERSAL	
PUFNSTUF	1970	94	3			UNIVERSAL	
PUMPKIN EATER, THE (BRITISH)	1964	110	4*	3.5	3.0	ROYAL FILMS INT'L	
PUNISHMENT BATTALION (GERMAN)	1964	90		2.5		PARAMOUNT	
PUNISHMENT PARK	1971	88	2			SHERPIX	
PUPPET ON A CHAIN (BRITISH)	1971	98	4			CINERAMA RELEASING	
PURE HELL OF ST TRINIANS, THE (BRITISH)	1960	94		2.5	2.0	CONTINENTAL	
PURPLE GANG, THE	1960	85		2.0	2.0	ALLIED ARTISTS	
PURPLE HEART, THE	1944	99		3.0	3.0	20th CENTURY FOX	
PURPLE HEART DIARY	1951	73	3	1.0		COLUMBIA	
PURPLE HILLS, THE	1961	60		2.0	1.5	20th CENTURY FOX	
PURPLE MASK, THE	1955	82	3	2.5	2.5	UNIVERSAL	
PURPLE NOON (FRENCH)	1960	115	6	3.5	3.0	TIMES FILM CORP.	
PURPLE PLAIN, THE (BRITISH)	1954	100	6	3.0	3.0	UNITED ARTISTS	
PURSUED	1947	101	4*	3.0	3.0	WARNER BROTHERS	
PURSUERS, THE (BRITISH)	1961	63		1.5	2.0	WARNER BROTHERS	
PURSUIT	1935	62		2.5		M-G-M	
PURSUIT ACROSS THE DESERT (SPANISH)	1961	79		1.5		COM. UNITED T.V.	
PURSUIT AND LOVES OF QUEEN VICTORIA (GERMAN)	a1958	108	2*			BUENA VISTA	
PURSUIT OF HAPPINESS, THE (FRANCIS LEDERER)	1934	72		3.5		PARAMOUNT	
PURSUIT OF HAPPINESS, THE (MICHAEL SARRAZIN)	1971	93	4			COLUMBIA	
PURSUIT OF THE GRAF SPEE (BRITISH)	1957	106		3.0	2.5	J. ARTHUR RANK	

‡ An asterisk (*) in THE FILM BUFF'S BIBLE column indicates that the film has been rated by the editor and/or staff. All other ratings in this column are based on a consensus of reviews (see NOTES).

TITLE (LEADING ACTORS SHOWN WHERE TWO OR MORE FILMS HAVE THE SAME OR SIMILAR TITLE)	YEAR RELEASED	RUNNING TIME IN MINUTES	THE FILM BUFF'S BIBLE ‡	STEVEN SCHEUER	LEONARD MALTIN	DISTRIBUTOR	COMMENT
PURSUIT TO ALGIERS	1945	65		.		UNIVERSAL	
PUSHER, THE	1960	81	2			UNITED ARTISTS	
PUSHOVER, THE	1954	88	4	3.5	2.5	COLUMBIA	
PUSSYCAT, PUSSYCAT, I LOVE YOU	1970	99	1			UNITED ARTISTS	
PUTNEY SWOPE	1969	84	3*			CINEMA V	
PUZZLE OF A DOWNFALL CHILD	1970	104	3			UNIVERSAL	
PUZZLE OF THE RED ORCHID, THE (GERMAN)	a1962	94		2.0	2.0	UCC FILMS	
PYGMALION (BRITISH)	1938	85		4.0	4.0	M-G-M	NOMINATED BEST PICTURE
PYGMY ISLAND	1950	69		1.5	.	COLUMBIA	
PYRO (SPANISH)	a1964	99	2	2.0	2.5	AMERICAN-INTERNAT'L	
Q PLANES (BRITISH)	a1939	82	4*	3.5	3.0	COLUMBIA	
QUACKSER FORTUNE HAS A COUSIN IN THE BRONX	1970	90	6			UMC PICTURES	
QUALITY STREET	1937	84		3.0	3.0	RKO	
QUANTEZ	1957	80	3	2.0	2.5	UNIVERSAL	
QUANTRILL'S RAIDERS	1958	68		2.0	2.0	ALLIED ARTISTS	
QUARANTINED (T.V.)	1970	90		2.5		PARAMOUNT	
QUARE FELLOW, THE (IRISH)	1962	85	7		3.5	ASTOR	
QUARTERBACK, THE	1940	69		2.0		PARAMOUNT	
QUARTET (BRITISH)	1948	120	7*	4.0	4.0	EAGLE LION	FOUR STORIES
QUEBEC	1951	85		2.0	2.0	PARAMOUNT	
QUEEN, THE (DOCUMENTARY)	1968	68	6	4.0		GROVE PRESS	
QUEEN BEE	1955	95		3.0	3.0	COLUMBIA	
QUEEN CHRISTINA	1933	97		3.5	4.0	M-G-M	
QUEEN FOR A DAY	1951	107	5	3.0		UNITED ARTISTS	
QUEEN FOR CAESAR, A (FRENCH)	1962	91		2.5		COM. UNITED T.V.	
QUEEN IS CROWNED, A (DOCUMENTARY)	1953	89	7*			J. ARTHUR RANK	
QUEEN OF BABYLON, THE (ITALIAN)	1956	98		1.0	1.5	20th CENTURY FOX	
QUEEN OF BROADWAY	a1943	73			.	MONOGRAM	
QUEEN OF BURLESQUE	1946	70			1.5	PRODUCERS RELEASING	
QUEEN OF OUTER SPACE	1958	80		1.5	1.5	ALLIED ARTISTS	
QUEEN OF SHEBA, THE (SILENT - BETTY BLYTHE)	1921	92				20th CENTURY FOX	BELIEVED LOST
QUEEN OF SHEBA, THE (ITALIAN - GINO CERVI)	1952	103		1.5		LIPPERT PRODS.	
QUEEN OF SPADES (BRITISH - ANTON WALBROOK)	1949	95	6	3.0		STRATFORD PICS.	
QUEEN OF SPADES (RUSSIAN - OLEG STRIZHENOV)	1960	100			2.5	ARTKINO	
QUEEN OF THE MOB	1940	61		2.0		PARAMOUNT	
QUEEN OF THE NILE (ITALIAN)	1961	85		2.0	2.0	WARNER BROTHERS	
QUEEN OF THE PIRATES (ITALIAN)	1960	79	2		2.0	COLUMBIA	
QUEEN OF THE SEAS (ITALIAN)	1960	87		1.5		AMERICAN-INTERNAT'L	
QUEENS, THE (ITALIAN - CLAUDIA CARDINALE)	1966	122	5			ROYAL FILMS INT'L	FOUR STORIES
QUEEN'S GUARDS, THE (BRITISH)	1960	110		2.0	2.0	20th CENTURY FOX	
QUENTIN DURWARD (BRITISH)	1955	101	5	3.0		M-G-M	
QUESTION OF ADULTERY, A (BRITISH)	a1958	86		2.0	2.5	NTA PICTURES	
QUESTION 7	1961	107	4			DE ROCHEMONT	
QUICK AND THE DEAD, THE	1963	92		2.0		BECKMAN FILMS	
QUICK, BEFORE IT MELTS	1965	98		2.0	2.5	M-G-M	
QUICK GUN, THE	1964	87	3		2.0	COLUMBIA	
QUICK MILLIONS	1931	69				20th CENTURY FOX	
QUICKSAND	1950	79	4	2.5	2.5	UNITED ARTISTS	
QUIET AMERICAN, THE	1958	120		3.0	2.5	UNITED ARTISTS	
QUIET DAYS IN CLICHY (DANISH)	1970	90	2			GROVE PRESS	ENGLISH LANGUAGE
QUIET MAN, THE	1952	129	8*	4.0	4.0	REPUBLIC	NOMINATED BEST PICTURE
QUIET ONE, THE (DOCUMENTARY)	1948	67	8	3.5		MAYER-BURSTYN	
QUIET PLACE IN THE COUNTRY, A (ITALIAN)	1970	106	3			UNITED ARTISTS	
QUIET PLEASE, MURDER	1942	70		2.5	2.5	20th CENTURY FOX	
QUIET WEDDING (BRITISH)	1941	80		2.0		UNIVERSAL	
QUIET WOMAN, THE (BRITISH)	1949	69		3.0		EROS FILMS	
QUILLER MEMORANDUM, THE (BRITISH)	1966	105	3*	2.5		20th CENTURY FOX	
QUINCANNON, FRONTIER SCOUT	1956	83		2.0	1.5	UNITED ARTISTS	
QUO VADIS (ROBERT TAYLOR, DEBORAH KERR)	1951	171	6-7*	3.5	3.0	M-G-M	NOMINATED BEST PICTURE
R.C.M.P. AND THE TREASURE OF GHENGHIS KHAN	1948	100		1.5	1.5	REPUBLIC	RE-EDITED SERIAL
R.P.M.	1970	92	4			COLUMBIA	
RA EXPEDITIONS, THE (DOCUMENTARY)	1971	105	6*			INTERWEST FILM CORP.	
RABBIT, RUN	1970	94	4			WARNER BROTHERS	
RABBIT TRAP, THE	1959	72	4	2.0	2.5	UNITED ARTISTS	
RACE STREET	1948	79		2.0	2.0	RKO	
RACERS, THE	1955	112		2.0	2.5	20th CENTURY FOX	
RACHEL AND THE STRANGER	1948	93		3.0	3.0	RKO	
RACHEL, RACHEL	1968	101	5*	4.0		WARNER BROTHERS	NOMINATED BEST PICTURE
RACING BLOOD	1954	78		2.0		20th CENTURY FOX	
RACING FEVER	1965	80		1.0	1.0	ALLIED ARTISTS	
RACK, THE	1956	100	4*	3.0	3.0	M-G-M	
RACKET, THE (SILENT - THOMAS MEIGHAN)	1928	85				PARAMOUNT	NOMINATED BEST PICTURE 1927/28
RACKET, THE (ROBERT MITCHUM, LIZABETH SCOTT)	1951	88		3.0	2.5	RKO	
RACKET BUSTERS	1938	71		3.0	2.0	WARNER BROTHERS	
RACKET MAN, THE	1944	65		2.5		COLUMBIA	
RADIO STARS ON PARADE	1945	69		1.5		RKO	
RAFFLES (DAVID NIVEN, OLIVIA DE HAVILLAND)	1939	72		2.0	2.5	UNITED ARTISTS	
RAGE	1966	103	3	1.0		COLUMBIA	

‡ An asterisk (*) in THE FILM BUFF'S BIBLE column indicates that the film has been rated by the editor and/or staff. All other ratings in this column are based on a consensus of reviews (see NOTES).

TITLE (LEADING ACTORS SHOWN WHERE TWO OR MORE FILMS HAVE THE SAME OR SIMILAR TITLE)	YEAR RELEASED	RUNNING TIME IN MINUTES	THE FILM BUFF'S BIBLE ‡	STEVEN SCHEUER	LEONARD MALTIN	DISTRIBUTOR	COMMENT
RAGE AT DAWN	1955	87	4		2.0	RKO	
RAGE IN HEAVEN	1941	83		2.0	2.0	M-G-M	
RAGE OF PARIS, THE	1938	75		2.5	2.5	UNIVERSAL	
RAGE OF THE BUCCANEERS, THE (ITALIAN)	1961	90			2.0	COLORAMA FEATURES	
RAGE TO LIVE, A	1965	101	3*	1.5		UNITED ARTISTS	
RAGING TIDE, THE	1951	93		2.0	2.5	UNIVERSAL	
RAID, THE	1954	83		2.5	3.0	20th CENTURY FOX	
RAID ON ROMMEL	1971	99	3			UNIVERSAL	
RAIDERS, THE (RICHARD CONTE, VIVECA LINDFORS)	a1952	80		2.0	2.5	UNIVERSAL	
RAIDERS, THE (ROBERT CULP, BRIAN KEITH)	1964	75	3		2.5	UNIVERSAL	
RAIDERS FROM BENEATH THE SEA	1965	73	1			20th CENTURY FOX	
RAIDERS OF LEYTE GULF, THE	1963	80	3	2.5	2.5	HEMISPHERE	
RAIDERS OF OLD CALIFORNIA	1957	72		2.0	1.0	REPUBLIC	
RAIDERS OF THE SEVEN SEAS	1953	88	3	2.5	2.5	UNITED ARTISTS	
RAIDERS OF THE SPANISH MAIN (BRITISH)	1962	88		2.0			
RAILROAD MAN, THE (ITALIAN)	a1956	105	6		3.0	CONTINENTAL	
RAILROADED	1947	71		3.0		EAGLE LION	
RAILS INTO LARAMIE	1954	81		2.0	2.0	UNIVERSAL	
RAILWAY CHILDREN, THE (BRITISH)	1971	109	5			UNIVERSAL	
RAIN (JOAN CRAWFORD, WALTER HUSTON)	1932	85		3.0		UNITED ARTISTS	
RAIN FOR A DUSTY SUMMER	1972	91				DO/BAR	
RAIN PEOPLE, THE	1969	101	5	3.0		WARNER BROTHERS	
RAINBOW ISLAND	1944	97		2.5	2.5	PARAMOUNT	
RAINBOW JACKET, THE (BRITISH)	1954	99		3.0	2.0	J. ARTHUR RANK	
RAINBOW ON THE RIVER	1936	87				RKO	
RAINBOW 'ROUND MY SHOULDER	1952	78		2.5	1.5	COLUMBIA	
RAINMAKER, THE (BURT LANCASTER, KATHARINE HEPBURN)	1956	121	6*	3.5	3.0	PARAMOUNT	
RAINS CAME, THE	1939	103		2.5	2.5	20th CENTURY FOX	
RAINS OF RANCHIPUR, THE	1955	104		2.5	2.5	20th CENTURY FOX	
RAINTREE COUNTY	1957	168	5*	3.0	3.0	M-G-M	
RAISIN IN THE SUN, A	1961	128	7*	4.0	4.0	COLUMBIA	
RAISING A RIOT (BRITISH)	1955	92		3.0		CONTINENTAL	
RAISING THE WIND (BRITISH)	a1961	91	5		2.5	HERTS-LION INT'L	
RALLY 'ROUND THE FLAG, BOYS!	1958	106	4*	2.0	2.5	20th CENTURY FOX	
RAMONA	1936	90		2.0	2.0	20th CENTURY FOX	
RAMPAGE	1963	98		2.0	2.5	WARNER BROTHERS	
RAMPAGE AT APACHE WELLS (GERMAN)	1966	90			2.0	COLUMBIA	
RAMPARTS OF CLAY (ALGERIAN)	1971	87	7			CINEMA V	
RAMROD	1947	94		2.5	2.5	UNITED ARTISTS	
RAMSBOTTOM RIDES AGAIN (BRITISH)	1956	93		1.0		BRITISH-LION	
RANCHO NOTORIOUS	1952	89	5	3.5	3.5	RKO	
RANDOM HARVEST	1942	124	5*	3.0	3.0	M-G-M	NOMINATED BEST PICTURE
RANGERS OF FORTUNE	1940	80		2.5	2.5	PARAMOUNT	
RANSOM	1956	109		2.5	2.5	M-G-M	
RANSOM FOR A DEAD MAN (T.V.)	1971	100	4*	2.5		UNIVERSAL	
RAPE, THE (SWEDISH)	a1967	90	4			FREENA FILMS	
RAPTURE (FRENCH - DEAN STOCKWELL, PATRICIA GOZZI)	1965	104	4*		3.0	INTERNAT'L CLASSICS	ENGLISH LANGUAGE
RARE BREED, THE	1966	97	5		2.5	UNIVERSAL	
RASCAL (STEVE FORREST, BILL MUMY)	1969	85	4			BUENA VISTA	
RASCALS (JANE WITHERS, ROCHELLE HUDSON)	1938	77		1.5		20th CENTURY FOX	
RASHOMON (JAPANESE)	1950	86	6*	4.0	3.5	RKO	
RASPUTIN AND THE EMPRESS	1932	133		3.5	3.5	M-G-M	
RASPUTIN - THE MAD MONK (BRITISH)	1966	91	3		2.0	20th CENTURY FOX	
RAT RACE, THE	1960	105	6	3.0	3.0	PARAMOUNT	
RATIONING	1944	93		1.5	2.5	M-G-M	
RATON PASS	1951	84	3	2.5	2.5	WARNER BROTHERS	
RATTLE OF A SIMPLE MAN (BRITISH)	1964	95	5*	3.5	3.0	CONTINENTAL	
RAVAGERS, THE	1965	79			1.5	HEMISPHERE	
RAVEN, THE (BORIS KARLOFF, BELA LUGOSI)	1935	62		2.0	3.0	UNIVERSAL	
RAVEN, THE (VINCENT PRICE, BORIS KARLOFF)	1963	86	2			AMERICAN-INTERNAT'L	
RAW DEAL	1948	79		3.5	3.0	EAGLE LION	
RAW EDGE	1956	76		2.0	2.5	UNIVERSAL	
RAW WEEKEND (DOCUMENTARY)	1969	62	1			BOXOFFICE INTERNAT'L	
RAW WIND IN EDEN	1958	89	3	2.5	2.5	UNIVERSAL	
RAWHIDE	a1951	86		2.5	2.5	20th CENTURY FOX	
RAWHIDE TRAIL, THE	1958	67		1.5	1.5	ALLIED ARTISTS	
RAWHIDE YEARS, THE	1956	85		3.0		UNIVERSAL	
RAYMIE	1960	72		2.5	2.0	ALLIED ARTISTS	
RAZOR'S EDGE, THE	1946	146	4*	2.5	3.5	20th CENTURY FOX	NOMINATED BEST PICTURE
RAZZIA (FRENCH)	1958	105	6			KASSLER FILMS	
REACH FOR GLORY (BRITISH)	1962	89	5		2.5	ROYAL FILMS INT'L	
REACH FOR THE SKY (BRITISH)	1956	123	5	3.5	1.5	J. ARTHUR RANK	
REACHING FOR THE MOON	1931	90			2.5	UNITED ARTISTS	
REACHING FOR THE SUN	1941	90		2.5	2.5	PARAMOUNT	
READY FOR THE PEOPLE	1964	54	2			WARNER BROTHERS	
REAL GLORY, THE	1939	95		3.0	3.0	UNITED ARTISTS	
REAP THE WILD WIND	1942	124		3.0	3.0	PARAMOUNT	
REAR WINDOW	1954	112	7*	4.0	4.0	PARAMOUNT	
REBECCA	1940	130		4.0	4.0	UNITED ARTISTS	BEST PICTURE AWARD
REBECCA OF SUNNYBROOK FARM	1938	80		2.5	2.5	20th CENTURY FOX	
REBEL CITY	1953	63		2.0		ALLIED ARTISTS	
REBEL FLIGHT TO CUBA (GERMAN)	1962	92		1.5		TELEWIDE SYSTEMS	
REBEL GIRLS (PHILIPPINE)	1955	65		1.5		TRANS-WORLD	
REBEL GLADIATORS, THE (ITALIAN)	1962	98		1.5		TELEWIDE SYSTEMS	

‡ An asterisk (*) in THE FILM BUFF'S BIBLE column indicates that the film has been rated by the editor and/or staff. All other ratings in this column are based on a consensus of reviews (see NOTES).

TITLE (LEADING ACTORS SHOWN WHERE TWO OR MORE FILMS HAVE THE SAME OR SIMILAR TITLE)	YEAR RELEASED	RUNNING TIME IN MINUTES	THE FILM BUFF'S BIBLE ‡	STEVEN SCHEUER	LEONARD MALTIN	DISTRIBUTOR	COMMENT
REBEL IN TOWN	1956	78		2.0	2.0	UNITED ARTISTS	
REBEL ROUSERS	1970		1			FOUR STAR-EXCELSIOR	
REBEL SET, THE	1959	52		1.5	1.5	ALLIED ARTISTS	
REBEL WITHOUT A CAUSE	1955	111	6	3.5	3.5	WARNER BROTHERS	
RECKLESS	1935	96		2.0	2.5	M-G-M	
RECKLESS AGE	1944	63		2.0		UNIVERSAL	
RECKLESS MOMENT, THE	1949	82	5	3.5	3.5	COLUMBIA	
RECKONING, THE (BRITISH)	1969	108	4			COLUMBIA	
RED AND THE WHITE, THE (HUNGARIAN)	1967	92	6			BRANDON	
RED BADGE OF COURAGE, THE	1951	69	7	4.0	3.5	M-G-M	
RED BALL EXPRESS	1952	83		2.0	3.0	UNIVERSAL	
RED BALLOON (FRENCH)	1956	35	7			LOPERT	
RED CANYON	1949	82	4	2.0	2.0	UNIVERSAL	
RED CIRCLE, THE (GERMAN - KARL SAEBISCH)	1960	94		1.5	2.5	UCC FILMS	
RED CLOAK, THE (ITALIAN)	1955	95		1.5		SEFO FILMS INT'L	
RED CULOTTES, THE (FRENCH)	1963	105		2.0		ABC FILMS	
RED DANUBE, THE	1949	119		2.5	2.5	M-G-M	
RED DESERT (DON BARRY, TOM NEAL)	1949	60				LIPPERT PRODS.	
RED DESERT (ITAL. - MONICA VITTI, RICHARD HARRIS)	1965	116	6			RIZZOLI FILM	
RED DRAGON (GERMAN - STEWART GRANGER)	1965	90	3		2.5	WOOLNER BROTHERS	
RED DRAGON, THE (SIDNEY TOLER)	1945	64			·	MONOGRAM	
RED DUST	1932	83		2.0	3.5	M-G-M	
RED GARTERS	1954	91		2.5	2.5	PARAMOUNT	
RED HAND, THE (GERMAN)	1960	98		1.5		UCC FILMS	
RED HEADED WOMAN	1932	74			3.0	M-G-M	
RED, HOT AND BLUE	1949	84	4	2.5	2.5	PARAMOUNT	
RED HOUSE, THE	1947	100	6	3.5	3.0	UNITED ARTISTS	
RED INN, THE (FRENCH)	1951	100		2.0	2.5	DAVIS DIST.	
RED LIGHT	1949	83		2.0	2.0	UNITED ARTISTS	
RED LINE 7000	1965	110	3	3.0		PARAMOUNT	
RED LION (JAPANESE)	1971	116				TOHO	
RED MANTLE, THE (DANISH)	a1967	92	6	3.5		PRENTOULIS FILMS	
RED MENACE, THE	1949	87		2.0		REPUBLIC	
RED MOUNTAIN	1952	84	4	2.5	2.5	PARAMOUNT	
RED PLANET MARS	1952	87	2	2.5	2.5	UNITED ARTISTS	
RED PONY, THE	1949	89		3.0	3.0	REPUBLIC	
RED RIVER	1948	125	8*	4.0	4.0	UNITED ARTISTS	
RED SHEIK, THE (ITALIAN)	1961	90		1.0		TELEWIDE SYSTEMS	
RED SHOES, THE (BRITISH)	1948	133	6*	3.0	3.0	EAGLE LION	NOMINATED BEST PICTURE
RED SKIES OF MONTANA	1952	89		2.0	2.5	20th CENTURY FOX	
RED SKY AT MORNING (RICHARD THOMAS, C. BURNS)	1971	113	5			UNIVERSAL	
RED SNOW	1952	75	3	2.0		COLUMBIA	
RED STALLION, THE	1947	82	3		1.5	EAGLE LION	
RED STALLION IN THE ROCKIES	1949	85			2.0	EAGLE LION	
RED SUN (FRENCH)	1972	112	3			NATIONAL GENERAL	ENGLISH VERSION
RED SUNDOWN	1956	81		2.0	2.5	UNIVERSAL	
RED TENT, THE (ITALIAN-RUSSIAN)	1971	121	3			PARAMOUNT	ENGLISH VERSION
RED TOMAHAWK	1967	82	2			PARAMOUNT	
RED, WHITE, AND BLACK, THE	1971	97				HIRSCHMAN-NORTHERN	
REDHEAD AND THE COWBOY, THE	1951	82		2.0	2.5	PARAMOUNT	
REDHEAD FROM MANHATTAN	1943	59		2.0		COLUMBIA	
REDHEAD FROM WYOMING, THE	1953	80		1.5	2.5	UNIVERSAL	
REDMEN AND THE RENEGADES, THE	1956	89		1.5		INDEP. TV CORP (ITC)	
REFLECTIONS IN A GOLDEN EYE	1967	108	4	2.5		WARNER BROTHERS	
REFORM SCHOOL GIRL	1957	71		1.5	1.0	AMERICAN-INTERNAT'L	
REFORMER AND THE REDHEAD, THE	1950	90	4	2.0	2.5	M-G-M	
REFUGEE, THE	a1940	79		3.0	2.5	REPUBLIC	
REIGN OF TERROR	a1949	89	4	3.0	3.0	EAGLE LION	
REIVERS, THE	1969	107	5-6*	4.0		NATIONAL GENERAL	
RELENTLESS	1948	93	5		2.5	COLUMBIA	
RELUCTANT ASTRONAUT, THE	1967	102		1.5	2.0	UNIVERSAL	
RELUCTANT DEBUTANTE, THE	1958	94		2.5	2.5	M-G-M	
RELUCTANT HEROES (BRITISH)	1951	81		1.5		EROS FILMS	
RELUCTANT SAINT, THE (ITALIAN)	1962	105	6			ROYAL FILMS INT'L	
RELUCTANT SPY, THE (FRENCH)	1963	93		2.0	2.5	AVCO-EMBASSY	
RELUCTANT WIDOW, THE (BRITISH)	1950	91		1.5	1.5	FINE ARTS	
REMAINS TO BE SEEN	1953	89	4	2.5	3.0	M-G-M	
REMARKABLE ANDREW, THE	1942	80		2.5	2.5	PARAMOUNT	
REMARKABLE MR PENNYPACKER, THE	1959	87		2.0	2.5	20th CENTURY FOX	
REMBRANDT (BRITISH)	1936	84	6*	3.5	3.5	UNITED ARTISTS	
REMEDY FOR RICHES	1940	60			2.0	RKO	
REMEMBER?	1939	83		2.0	2.0	M-G-M	
REMEMBER PEARL HARBOR	1942	76		1.5		REPUBLIC	
REMEMBER THE DAY	1941	85		3.0	3.0	20th CENTURY FOX	
REMEMBER THE NIGHT	1940	86	6*	3.0	3.0	PARAMOUNT	
RENDEZVOUS	1935	91		3.0	2.5	M-G-M	
RENDEZVOUS WITH ANNIE	1946	89		2.5		REPUBLIC	
REPEAT PERFORMANCE	1947	93	4	2.0	2.5	EAGLE LION	
REPENT AT LEISURE	1941	66		2.0		RKO	
REPORT ON THE PARTY AND GUESTS, A (CZECH)	1966	71	4			SIGMA III	
REPRIEVE	a1962	105		2.5	3.0	ALLIED ARTISTS	
REPRISAL	1956	74		2.5	2.5	COLUMBIA	
REPTILE, THE (BRITISH)	1966	90	4		3.0	20th CENTURY FOX	
REPTILICUS (DANISH)	1961	81	1	1.5		AMERICAN-INTERNAT'L	

‡ An asterisk (*) in THE FILM BUFF'S BIBLE column indicates that the film has been rated by the editor and/or staff. All other ratings in this column are based on a consensus of reviews (see NOTES).

"a" TO LEFT OF YEAR INDICATES THAT FILM HAS AN ALTERNATE TITLE

TITLE (LEADING ACTORS SHOWN WHERE TWO OR MORE FILMS HAVE THE SAME OR SIMILAR TITLE)	YEAR RELEASED	RUNNING TIME IN MINUTES	THE FILM BUFF'S BIBLE ‡	STEVEN SCHEUER	LEONARD MALTIN	DISTRIBUTOR	COMMENT
REPULSION (BRITISH)	1965	104	2*		4.0	ROYAL FILMS INT'L	
REQUIEM FOR A GUNFIGHTER	1965	91	3	1.5	1.5	AVCO-EMBASSY	
REQUIEM FOR A HEAVYWEIGHT	a1962	87	7*	3.5	3.0	COLUMBIA	
REST IS SILENCE, THE (GERMAN)	1959	106		2.5	3.0	FILMS AROUND THE WLD.	
RESTLESS BREED, THE	1957	81		2.0	2.0	20th CENTURY FOX	
RESTLESS YEARS, THE	1958	86		2.0	2.5	UNIVERSAL	
RETIK, THE MOON MENACE	1952	100		1.0	1.5	REPUBLIC	RE-EDITED SERIAL
RETREAT, HELL!	1952	95	5		2.5	WARNER BROTHERS	
RETURN FROM THE ASHES (BRITISH)	1965	104	5	3.0	3.0	WARNER BROTHERS	
RETURN FROM THE SEA	1954	80	3	2.5	2.0	ALLIED ARTISTS	
RETURN OF A STRANGER (BRITISH)	1961	63		2.5	2.5	WARNER BROTHERS	
RETURN OF COUNT YORGA	1971	97	2			AMERICAN-INTERNAT'L	
RETURN OF DR X, THE	1939	62		2.0	2.0	WARNER BROTHERS	
RETURN OF DON CAMILLO, THE (FRENCH)	1953	115	4	3.5	2.5	ITALIAN FILMS EXPORT	
RETURN OF DRACULA, THE	a1958	77		2.0	2.0	UNITED ARTISTS	
RETURN OF FRANK JAMES, THE	1940	92		3.0	3.0	20th CENTURY FOX	
RETURN OF JACK SLADE, THE	1955	79	3		2.0	ALLIED ARTISTS	
RETURN OF JESSE JAMES, THE	1950	75		2.5	2.5	LIPPERT PRODS.	
RETURN OF MAJIN (JAPANESE)	1965	86	1	-		AMERICAN-INTERNAT'L	
RETURN OF MONTE CRISTO, THE	1946	91	4	2.5	2.0	COLUMBIA	
RETURN OF MR MOTO, THE (BRITISH)	1965	71	2		-	20th CENTURY FOX	
RETURN OF OCTOBER, THE	1948	98	4	2.5	2.0	COLUMBIA	
RETURN OF PETER GRIMM, THE	1935	83		3.0	3.0	RKO	
RETURN OF SABATA	1972	106				UNITED ARTISTS	
RETURN OF SOPHIE LANG, THE	1936	65		2.5	2.5	PARAMOUNT	
RETURN OF THE APE MAN	1944	60			2.0	MONOGRAM	
RETURN OF THE BAD MEN	1948	90		2.5	2.5	RKO	
RETURN OF THE CISCO KID, THE	1939	70		2.5		20th CENTURY FOX	
RETURN OF THE FLY, THE	1959	80	4*	2.0	2.5	20th CENTURY FOX	
RETURN OF THE FRONTIERSMAN	1950	74		2.0	2.0	WARNER BROTHERS	
RETURN OF THE GUNFIGHTER (T.V.)	1967	98		2.5	2.5	M-G-M	
RETURN OF THE SCARLET PIMPERNEL, THE (BRITISH)	1938	80		1.5	2.0	UNITED ARTISTS	
RETURN OF THE SEVEN	1966	95	2	1.0		UNITED ARTISTS	
RETURN OF THE TEXAN	1952	88		2.0	2.0	20th CENTURY FOX	
RETURN OF THE VAMPIRE, THE	1943	69		2.0	2.0	COLUMBIA	
RETURN OF THE WHISTLER, THE	1948	63			-	COLUMBIA	
RETURN TO PARADISE	1953	100	4	2.5	2.0	UNITED ARTISTS	
RETURN TO PEYTON PLACE	1961	122	3	1.0	2.0	20th CENTURY FOX	
RETURN TO SENDER (BRITISH)	1963	63		2.0	2.0	ANGLO AMALGAMATED	
RETURN TO TREASURE ISLAND	1954	75		1.0	1.5	UNITED ARTISTS	
RETURN TO WARBOW	1958	67		2.0	1.5	COLUMBIA	
REUNION IN FRANCE	1942	104		1.5	2.0	M-G-M	
REUNION IN RENO	1951	79		2.5	2.5	UNIVERSAL	
REUNION IN VIENNA	1933	100		3.0	3.0	M-G-M	
REVEILLE WITH BEVERLY	1943	78		2.0	2.0	COLUMBIA	
REVENGE AGENT	1951			1.0			
REVENGE AT DAYBREAK	1958	84		2.0			
REVENGE OF BLACK EAGLE (ITALIAN)	1964	97		1.5		SCREEN GEMS	
REVENGE OF FRANKENSTEIN, THE (BRITISH)	1958	91	5*	2.5	3.0	COLUMBIA	
REVENGE OF IVANHOE, THE (ITALIAN)	1964	100		1.0		TRANS-AMERICA	
REVENGE OF THE BARBARIANS (ITALIAN)	1963	104		1.5		AMERICAN-INTERNAT'L	
REVENGE OF THE CONQUERED (ITALIAN)	1964	84		1.0		AMERICAN-INTERNAT'L	
REVENGE OF THE CREATURE	1955	82		2.0	2.0	UNIVERSAL	
REVENGE OF THE GLADIATORS (ITALIAN)	1965	100		1.0	1.5	PARAMOUNT	
REVENGE OF THE MUSKETEERS (ITALIAN)	1962	97		1.0		AMERICAN-INTERNAT'L	
REVENGE OF THE PIRATES (ITALIAN)	1951	95		1.5	2.0	ALLIED ARTISTS	
REVENGE OF THE ZOMBIES	1943	61			1.5	MONOGRAM	
REVENGE OF URSUS (ITALIAN)	1960	99		1.0		TELEWIDE SYSTEMS	
REVENGERS, THE	1972	106	3			NATIONAL GENERAL	
REVOLT AT FORT LARAMIE	1957	73		2.5	2.0	UNITED ARTISTS	
REVOLT IN THE BIG HOUSE	1958	79	4	2.5	2.5	ALLIED ARTISTS	
REVOLT OF MAMIE STOVER, THE	1956	92		2.5	2.5	20th CENTURY FOX	
REVOLT OF THE BARBARIANS (ITALIAN)	1964	99		1.0		TRANS-AMERICA	
REVOLT OF THE MAMALUKES (EGYPTIAN)	1960	90		1.5		FOUR STAR	
REVOLT OF THE MERCENARIES (ITALIAN)	1961	102		1.5		WARNER BROTHERS	
REVOLT OF THE PRAETORIANS (ITALIAN)	1963	95		1.0		ABC FILMS	
REVOLT OF THE SLAVES, THE (ITALIAN)	1961	90	2			UNITED ARTISTS	
REVOLT OF THE TARTARS (ITALIAN)	a1956	115	4	2.0		CONTINENTAL	
REVOLT OF THE ZOMBIES	1936	65			2.0	ACADEMY PICTURES	
REVOLUTION (DOCUMENTARY)	1968	86	4			LOPERT	
REVOLUTIONARY, THE	1970	100	5			UNITED ARTISTS	
REWARD, THE	1965	92	3		2.5	20th CENTURY FOX	
RHAPSODY	1954	115	6*	2.5	2.5	M-G-M	
RHAPSODY IN BLUE	1945	139	6*	3.5	2.5	WARNER BROTHERS	
RHINO!	1964	91		2.5	2.5	M-G-M	
RHUBARB	1951	95		3.5	2.5	PARAMOUNT	
RHYTHM HITS THE ICE	a1942	79		1.5		REPUBLIC	
RHYTHM ON THE RANGE	1936	87		2.0	2.5	PARAMOUNT	
RHYTHM ON THE RIVER	1940	92		3.0	3.0	PARAMOUNT	
RIBALD TALES OF ROBIN HOOD	1969	83	1			ENTERTAINMENT VENTURES	
RICE GIRL (ITALIAN)	1955	81		2.0	2.5	ULTRA PICTURES CORP.	
RICH ARE ALWAYS WITH US, THE	1932	73		2.5	2.0	FIRST NATIONAL	
RICH MAN, POOR GIRL	1938	65		2.5	2.0	M-G-M	
RICH, YOUNG AND PRETTY	1951	95		2.5	2.5	M-G-M	

‡ An asterisk (*) in THE FILM BUFF'S BIBLE column indicates that the film has been rated by the editor and/or staff. All other ratings in this column are based on a consensus of reviews (see NOTES).

TITLE (LEADING ACTORS SHOWN WHERE TWO OR MORE FILMS HAVE THE SAME OR SIMILAR TITLE) "a" TO LEFT OF YEAR INDICATES THAT FILM HAS AN ALTERNATE TITLE	YEAR RELEASED	RUNNING TIME IN MINUTES	CRITICAL RATINGS			DISTRIBUTOR	COMMENT
			THE FILM BUFF'S BIBLE ‡	STEVEN SCHEUER	LEONARD MALTIN		
RICHARD III (BRITISH)	1955	158	7	4.0	3.5	LOPERT	
RICHEST GIRL IN THE WORLD, THE (NINA, FREDERIK)	1960	78			1.5	UNIFILMS	(DANISH)
RICOCHET ROMANCE	1954	80		2.0	2.5	UNIVERSAL	
RIDE A CROOKED MILE	1938	78		2.0		PARAMOUNT	
RIDE A CROOKED TRAIL	1958	87	4		2.5	UNIVERSAL	
RIDE A VIOLENT MILE	1957	80			1.5	20th CENTURY FOX	
RIDE BACK, THE	1957	79	5	3.0	3.0	UNITED ARTISTS	
RIDE BEYOND VENGEANCE	1966	100	2	2.0	2.5	COLUMBIA	
RIDE CLEAR OF DIABLO	1954	80		2.0	2.5	UNIVERSAL	
RIDE 'EM COWBOY	1942	86		2.5	2.5	UNIVERSAL	
RIDE IN THE WHIRLWIND	1967	82		3.0		WALTER READE	
RIDE LONESOME	1959	73		2.5	2.0	COLUMBIA	
RIDE OUT FOR REVENGE	1957	79	2	2.5	1.5	UNITED ARTISTS	
RIDE THE HIGH COUNTRY	a1962	94	5*	4.0	3.5	M-G-M	
RIDE THE HIGH IRON	1956	74		1.5	1.5	COLUMBIA	
RIDE THE HIGH WIND (SOUTH AFRICAN)	1966	77		2.0		FEATURE FILM CORP.	
RIDE THE MAN DOWN	1953	90		3.0	2.0	REPUBLIC	
RIDE THE PINK HORSE	1947	101	5*	4.0	3.5	UNIVERSAL	
RIDE THE WILD SURF	1964	101		2.0	2.5	COLUMBIA	
RIDE TO HANGMAN'S TREE, THE	1967	90		2.0	2.5	UNIVERSAL	
RIDE, VAQUERO	1953	90		2.0	2.5	M-G-M	
RIDER ON A DEAD HORSE	1962	72	1	2.0	1.5	ALLIED ARTISTS	
RIDER ON THE RAIN (FRENCH)	1970	115	6-7*			AVCO-EMBASSY	ENGLISH VERSION
RIDERS OF VENGEANCE	a1952	80		2.0	2.5	UNIVERSAL	
RIDERS TO THE STARS	1954	81	3*	2.5	2.5	UNITED ARTISTS	
RIDING HIGH (DOROTHY LAMOUR, DICK POWELL)	1943	112		3.0	2.5	PARAMOUNT	
RIDING HIGH (BING CROSBY, NANCY OLSON)	1950	112	5	2.5	2.5	PARAMOUNT	
RIDING SHOTGUN	1954	74		2.0	2.0	WARNER BROTHERS	
RIFF-RAFF (FRENCH - ROBERT HOSSEIN, MARINA VLADY)	1961	109		2.0		ELLIS FILMS	
RIFF RAFF GIRLS (FRENCH)	1959	97			2.5	CONTINENTAL	
RIFFRAFF (JEAN HARLOW, SPENCER TRACY)	1935	89		2.0	2.5	M-G-M	
RIFFRAFF (PAT O'BRIEN, ANN JEFFREYS)	1947	80		3.0	3.0	RKO	
RIFIFI (FRENCH)	1954	113	7	4.0	4.0	UN. MOTION PIC. ORG.	
RIFIFI IN TOKYO (FRENCH)	1961	89	2		2.0	M-G-M	
RIGHT APPROACH, THE	1961	92	3		2.0	20th CENTURY FOX	
RIGHT CROSS	1950	90		2.5	2.5	M-G-M	
RIGHT HAND OF THE DEVIL	1963	72		1.5		CINEMA VIDEO INT'L	
RIGHT ON	1970	78		3.5		LEACOCK-PENNEBAKER	
RIGHT TO THE HEART	1942	74		2.0		20th CENTURY FOX	
RIKISHA MAN, THE (JAPANESE)	1958	105	6			CORY FILM CORP.	
RING, THE	1952	79		2.5	2.0	UNITED ARTISTS	
RING-A-DING RHYTHM	1962	78	2			COLUMBIA	
RING OF BRIGHT WATER (BRITISH)	1969	107	6			CINERAMA RELEASING	
RING OF FEAR	1954	93		2.0	2.0	WARNER BROTHERS	
RING OF FIRE	1961	91		2.0	2.5	M-G-M	
RING OF TERROR (GERMAN)	1962	72		1.5		MEDALLION	
RING OF TREASON (BRITISH)	1964	89	4			PARAMOUNT	
RINGS AROUND THE WORLD (DOCUMENTARY)	1966	98	6			COLUMBIA	
RINGS ON HER FINGERS	1942	85		2.5	2.5	20th CENTURY FOX	
RINGSIDE	1949	63	2			LIPPERT PRODS.	
RINGSIDE MAISIE	1941	96		2.0	-	M-G-M	
RIO	1939	75			2.5	UNIVERSAL	
RIO BRAVO	1959	141		2.5	3.0	WARNER BROTHERS	
RIO CONCHOS	1964	107		2.0	3.0	20th CENTURY FOX	
RIO GRANDE	1950	105	5	3.5	3.0	REPUBLIC	
RIO LOBO	1970	114	4			NATIONAL GENERAL	
RIO RITA (BEBE DANIELS, JOHN BOLES)	1929	135				RKO	
RIO RITA (KATHRYN GRAYSON, ABBOTT & COSTELLO)	1942	91		3.0	2.5	M-G-M	
RIOT	1969	97	4			PARAMOUNT	
RIOT IN CELL BLOCK 11	1954	80	5*	3.0	3.0	ALLIED ARTISTS	
RIOT IN JUVENILE PRISON	1959	71		2.0	1.0	UNITED ARTISTS	
RIOT ON SUNSET STRIP	1967	82	2			AMERICAN-INTERNAT'L	
RIPTIDE	1934	90		2.0	3.0	M-G-M	
RISE AND FALL OF LEGS DIAMOND, THE	1960	101	4	3.0	2.5	WARNER BROTHERS	
RISE AND SHINE	1941	93		3.0	2.5	20th CENTURY FOX	
RISE OF LOUIS XIV, THE (FRENCH)	1970	100	3*			BRANDON	
RISING OF THE MOON, THE (IRISH)	1957	81	6	3.0	2.5	WARNER BROTHERS	THREE STORIES
RISK, THE (BRITISH)	1960	81	4	3.0	3.0	KINGSLEY INTERNAT'L	
RITUAL OF EVIL (T.V.)	1970	100		2.5		UNIVERSAL	
RIVALS, THE (BRITISH)	1961	82		2.0		BBC	
RIVER, THE (DOCUMENTARY)	1937	30	4*			U. S. GOV'T.	
RIVER, THE (NORA SWINBURNE, ESMOND KNIGHT)	1951	99	6	4.0	2.5	UNITED ARTISTS	
RIVER BEAT (BRITISH)	1954	70	3			LIPPERT PRODS.	
RIVER CHANGES, THE (GERMAN)	1956	91		2.0		WARNER BROTHERS	
RIVER GANG	1945	64		2.5		UNIVERSAL	
RIVER LADY	1948	78	3		2.0	UNIVERSAL	
RIVER OF EVIL (GERMAN)	1964	86		1.5			
RIVER OF GOLD (T.V.)	1971	90	1*	1.5		ABC FILMS	
RIVER OF NO RETURN	1954	91	4*	2.5	2.5	20th CENTURY FOX	
RIVER OF THREE JUNKS, THE (FRENCH)	1957	90		1.5		TRANS-AMERICA	
RIVERRUN	1970	87	6			COLUMBIA	
RIVER'S EDGE, THE	1957	87	5	3.0	3.0	20th CENTURY FOX	
RIVER'S END (DENNIS MORGAN, VICTOR JORY)	a1940	69		2.0		WARNER BROTHERS	
ROAD HOUSE	1948	95		3.0	3.0	20th CENTURY FOX	

‡ An asterisk (*) in THE FILM BUFF'S BIBLE column indicates that the film has been rated by the editor and/or staff. All other ratings in this column are based on a consensus of reviews (see NOTES).

TITLE (LEADING ACTORS SHOWN WHERE TWO OR MORE FILMS HAVE THE SAME OR SIMILAR TITLE)	YEAR RELEASED	RUNNING TIME IN MINUTES	THE FILM BUFF'S BIBLE ‡	STEVEN SCHEUER	LEONARD MALTIN	DISTRIBUTOR	COMMENT
ROAD HUSTLERS, THE	1968	94	3			AMERICAN-INTERNAT'L	
ROAD RACERS	1959	73		1.5		AMERICAN-INTERNAT'L	
ROAD SHOW	1941	87		2.5	2.5	UNITED ARTISTS	
ROAD TO BALI, THE	1953	91		3.0	3.0	PARAMOUNT	
ROAD TO DENVER, THE	1955	90		2.5	2.5	REPUBLIC	
ROAD TO GLORY, THE	1936	95		3.0	3.0	20th CENTURY FOX	
ROAD TO HONG KONG, THE	1962	91		3.0	2.5	UNITED ARTISTS	
ROAD TO MOROCCO, THE	1942	83		3.0	3.0	PARAMOUNT	
ROAD TO RIO, THE	1947	100		3.0	3.0	PARAMOUNT	
ROAD TO SALINA	1971	96	3			AVCO-EMBASSY	
ROAD TO SINGAPORE, THE (BOB HOPE, BING CROSBY)	1940	84		3.0	2.5	PARAMOUNT	
ROAD TO UTOPIA, THE	1946	89		3.5	3.0	PARAMOUNT	
ROAD TO ZANZIBAR, THE	1941	92		3.5	2.5	PARAMOUNT	
ROADBLOCK	1951	73	3	2.5		RKO	
ROAR OF THE CROWD	1953	71		2.0	1.5	ALLIED ARTISTS	
ROARING TWENTIES, THE	1939	104	5-6*	3.0	3.5	WARNER BROTHERS	
ROB ROY, THE HIGHLAND ROGUE	1953	84	6			RKO	
ROBBER'S ROOST	1955	82		1.5	2.0	UNITED ARTISTS	
ROBBERY (BRITISH)	1967	114	5*	2.5	3.0	AVCO-EMBASSY	
ROBBERY, ROMAN STYLE (ITALIAN)	1964	93		2.0		PARAMOUNT	
ROBBERY UNDER ARMS (BRITISH)	1957	99		2.5	2.0	J. ARTHUR RANK	
ROBBY	1968	90	3			BLUEWOOD FILMS	
ROBE, THE	1953	135	5*	3.0	3.0	20th CENTURY FOX	NOMINATED BEST PICTURE
ROBERTA	1935	105	5*			RKO	
ROBIN AND THE SEVEN HOODS	1964	103		3.0	2.5	WARNER BROTHERS	
ROBIN HOOD AND THE PIRATES (ITALIAN)	1964	88		1.5		AVCO-EMBASSY	
ROBIN HOOD OF EL DORADO	1936	86		2.5	2.5	M-G-M	
ROBINSON CRUSOE	a1954	90	6*	3.5	3.0	UNITED ARTISTS	
ROBINSON CRUSOE OF MYSTERY ISLAND	1936	100		1.5	2.0	REPUBLIC	RE-EDITED SERIAL
ROBINSON CRUSOE ON MARS	1964	110	4		2.5	PARAMOUNT	
ROBOT VS THE AZTEC MUMMY, THE (MEXICAN)	1960	65		1.0		AZTECA	
ROCAMBOLE (FRENCH)	1962	106			2.5	INDEP. TV CORP (ITC)	
ROCCO AND HIS BROTHERS (ITALIAN)	1960	95	7	3.5	3.5	ASTOR	ORIGINALLY 175 MINUTES
ROCK-A-BYE BABY	1958	103		2.5	3.0	PARAMOUNT	
ROCK ALL NIGHT	1957	65		1.5		AMERICAN-INTERNAT'L	
ROCK AROUND THE CLOCK	1956	77		2.0	2.0	COLUMBIA	
ROCK AROUND THE WORLD (BRITISH)	1957	71		2.0	1.5	AMERICAN-INTERNAT'L	
ROCK ISLAND TRAIL	1950	90		2.0		REPUBLIC	
ROCK 'N ROLL REVUE	1956	65		2.0		CINEMA-VUE	
ROCK, PRETTY BABY	1957	89		2.0	2.0	UNIVERSAL	
ROCK, ROCK, ROCK	1956	83		1.5		DIST. CORP. OF AMER.	
ROCKET FROM CALBUCH, THE (SPANISH)	1958	90		2.5		TRANS-LUX DIST.	
ROCKET MAN, THE	1954	79		1.5	2.0	20th CENTURY FOX	
ROCKETSHIP X-M	1950	77		3.0	3.0	LIPPERT PRODS.	
ROCKINGHORSE WINNER, THE (BRITISH)	1950	91	6	3.5	3.5	UNIVERSAL	
ROCKY MOUNTAIN	1950	83		2.0	2.5	WARNER BROTHERS	
RODAN (JAPANESE)	1956	70	4	2.0	2.0	DIST. CORP. OF AMER.	
RODEO	1952	70		2.5	1.5	MONOGRAM	
ROGER TOUHY, GANGSTER	1944	65		2.5	2.5	20th CENTURY FOX	
ROGUE COP	1954	92	5	3.0	3.0	M-G-M	
ROGUE RIVER	1950	81	4	3.5	2.0	EAGLE LION	
ROGUE'S MARCH	1953	84		2.0	2.0	M-G-M	
ROGUES OF SHERWOOD FOREST	1950	80	4	2.0	2.0	COLUMBIA	
ROGUE'S REGIMENT	1948	86		2.5	2.0	UNIVERSAL	
ROLAND THE MIGHTY (ITALIAN)	1961	86		1.5		ABC FILMS	
ROMAN HOLIDAY	1953	119	8*	4.0	3.5	PARAMOUNT	NOMINATED BEST PICTURE
ROMAN SCANDALS	1933	93		2.5	3.0	UNITED ARTISTS	
ROMAN SPRING OF MRS STONE, THE	1961	104	5	3.0	3.0	WARNER BROTHERS	
ROMANCE	1930	78		2.0		M-G-M	
ROMANCE AND RHYTHM	1940	86		2.5		REPUBLIC	
ROMANCE OF A HORSE THIEF	1971	101	4			ALLIED ARTISTS	
ROMANCE OF ROSY RIDGE, THE	1947	105	6	3.0	3.0	M-G-M	
ROMANCE OF THE RIO GRANDE	1941	73		2.0		20th CENTURY FOX	
ROMANCE ON THE HIGH SEAS	1948	99	5	3.0	3.0	WARNER BROTHERS	
ROMANOFF AND JULIET	1961	103	4*	3.5	2.5	UNIVERSAL	
ROME ADVENTURE	1962	119		2.0	3.0	WARNER BROTHERS	
ROME 11 O'CLOCK (ITALIAN)	1952	107	7			TIMES FILM CORP.	
ROME, 1585	1963	85		1.0		AMERICAN-INTERNAT'L	
ROMEO AND JULIET (LESLIE HOWARD, NORMA SHEARER)	1936	127	7*	4.0	4.0	M-G-M	NOMINATED BEST PICTURE
ROMEO AND JULIET (LAURENCE HARVEY, SUSAN SHENTALL)	1954	140	6*	3.5	3.0	UNITED ARTISTS	(BRITISH)
ROMEO AND JULIET (RUDOLPH NUREYEV, MARGOT FONTEYN)	1966	124				AVCO-EMBASSY	(BRITISH)
ROMEO AND JULIET (LEONARD WHITING, OLIVIA HUSSEY)	1968	138	8			PARAMOUNT	NOMINATED BEST PICTURE (BRIT.)
ROMMEL'S TREASURE (ITALIAN)	1955	85	4	2.0		MEDALLION	
ROMULUS AND THE SABINES (ITALIAN)	1961	101		2.0		AVCO-EMBASSY	
ROOF, THE (ITALIAN)	1956	91	6	3.0	2.5	TRANS-LUX DIST.	
ROOKIE, THE	1960	86		1.5	1.0	20th CENTURY FOX	
ROOKIE FIREMAN	1950	63	3			COLUMBIA	
ROOKIES IN BURMA	1943	62		1.5		RKO	
ROOM AT THE TOP (BRITISH)	1958	115	9*	4.0	4.0	CONTINENTAL	NOMINATED BEST PICTURE 1959
ROOM FOR ONE MORE	a1952	98	6	3.5	3.0	WARNER BROTHERS	
ROOM 43 (BRITISH)	1958	93	3			CORY FILM CORP.	
ROOM SERVICE	1938	78		2.5	3.0	RKO	
ROOM 13 (GERMAN)	1964	82		1.5		UCC FILMS	
ROOMMATES (BR.- JAMES R. JUSTICE, LESLIE PHILLIPS)	a1961	91	5		2.5	HERTS-LION INT'L	

‡ An asterisk (*) in THE FILM BUFF'S BIBLE column indicates that the film has been rated by the editor and/or staff. All other ratings in this column are based on a consensus of reviews (see NOTES).

TITLE (LEADING ACTORS SHOWN WHERE TWO OR MORE FILMS HAVE THE SAME OR SIMILAR TITLE)	YEAR RELEASED	RUNNING TIME IN MINUTES	THE FILM BUFF'S BIBLE ‡	STEVEN SCHEUER	LEONARD MALTIN	DISTRIBUTOR	COMMENT
ROOMMATES (DAN MASON, HARVEY MARKS)	1971	90	1			CLAYTON G. PANTAGES	
ROONEY (BRITISH)	1958	88	5*	3.0	2.0	J. ARTHUR RANK	
ROOSEVELT STORY, THE (DOCUMENTARY)	1947	80	6			UNITED ARTISTS	
ROOTS, THE (MEXICAN)	1954	96		2.5		HARRISON PICTURES	FOUR STORIES
ROOTS OF HEAVEN, THE	1958	131	5*	3.0	2.5	20th CENTURY FOX	
ROPE	1948	80	6	3.5	3.0	WARNER BROTHERS	
ROPE AROUND THE NECK (FRENCH)	1964	85		2.0		COM. UNITED T.V.	
ROPE OF SAND	1949	104	4	2.5	3.0	PARAMOUNT	
ROSE BOWL STORY, THE	1952	73		2.0	2.0	MONOGRAM	
ROSE FOR EVERYONE, A (ITALIAN)	a1966	107	2			ROYAL FILMS INT'L	
ROSE MARIE (JEANETTE MACDONALD, NELSON EDDY)	a1936	113		3.0	3.0	M-G-M	
ROSE MARIE (ANN BLYTH, HOWARD KEEL)	1954	115		2.5	2.5	M-G-M	
ROSE OF CIMARRON	1952	72	3	2.0		20th CENTURY FOX	
ROSE OF THE RANCHO	1936	82		2.0		PARAMOUNT	
ROSE OF WASHINGTON SQUARE	1939	86		3.0	2.5	20th CENTURY FOX	
ROSE TATTOO, THE	1955	117	7	4.0	3.5	PARAMOUNT	NOMINATED BEST PICTURE
ROSEANNA MCCOY	1949	89	3*	2.0	2.0	GOLDWYN	
ROSELAND	1971	90				BOXOFFICE INTERNAT'L	
ROSEMARY (GERMAN)	a1958	105		3.5	2.5	FILMS AROUND THE WLD	
ROSEMARY'S BABY	1968	136	7*	4.0		PARAMOUNT	
ROSES FOR THE PROSECUTOR (GERMAN)	1960	92	6			AMER. METROPOLITAN	
ROSIE!	1967	98		1.5	3.0	UNIVERSAL	
ROTTEN TO THE CORE (BRITISH)	1965	88	5*		3.0	CINEMA V	
ROUGE ET NOIR (FRENCH)	1958	145	6		3.0	DIST. CORP. OF AMER.	
ROUGH NIGHT IN JERICHO	1967	104	3	1.0		UNIVERSAL	
ROUGH, TOUGH AND READY	1945	66		1.5		COLUMBIA	
ROUGHLY SPEAKING	1945	117	4*	3.0	3.0	WARNER BROTHERS	
ROUGHSHOD	1949	88		2.5	2.5	RKO	
ROUND-UP, THE (RICHARD DIX, PATRICIA MORISON)	1941	90		1.5		PARAMOUNT	
ROUND UP, THE (HUNGARIAN - JANOS GORBE, T. MOLNAR)	1966	94	6			ALTURA FILMS	
ROUNDERS, THE	1965	85	4*	3.0		M-G-M	
ROUSTABOUT	1964	101	4	3.5	2.5	PARAMOUNT	
ROXIE HART	1942	75	6*	2.5	2.5	20th CENTURY FOX	
ROYAL AFFAIRS IN VERSAILLES (FRENCH)	a1954	152		2.5	2.5	TIMES FILM CORP.	
ROYAL AFRICAN RIFLES, THE	1953	75	2	1.5	2.0	ALLIED ARTISTS	
ROYAL BALLET, THE (BRITISH)	1960	131	7			LOPERT	
ROYAL FAMILY OF BROADWAY	1931	82		3.0		PARAMOUNT	
ROYAL JOURNEY (CANADIAN, DOCUMENTARY)	1952	47	6			NAT'L FILM BOARD CAN	
ROYAL SCANDAL, A	1945	94	6*	2.5	2.5	20th CENTURY FOX	
ROYAL WEDDING	1951	93	6	3.0	3.0	M-G-M	
RUBY GENTRY	1953	82	4	3.0	2.5	20th CENTURY FOX	
RUE DE PARIS (FRENCH)	a1959	90	4*			LOPERT	
RUFFIANS, THE (FRENCH)	1959	92		2.0		ELLIS FILMS	
RUGGED O'RIORDANS (AUSTRALIAN)	1950	76	5			UNIVERSAL	
RUGGLES OF RED GAP (CHARLES LAUGHTON, C. RUGGLES)	1935	90	6*	4.0	4.0	PARAMOUNT	NOMINATED BEST PICTURE
RULERS OF THE SEA	1939	96		3.0	2.5	PARAMOUNT	
RULES OF THE GAME (FRENCH)	1938	110	5*			JANUS FILMS	
RUMBA	1935	77		1.5	2.0	PARAMOUNT	
RUMBLE ON THE DOCKS	1956	82		2.0	2.0	COLUMBIA	
RUN A CROOKED MILE (T.V.)	1969	100		2.5		UNIVERSAL	
RUN, ANGEL, RUN!	1969	94	1			FANFARE	
RUN, APPALOOSA, RUN!	1966	48	5			BUENA VISTA	
RUN FOR COVER	1955	93		3.0	2.5	PARAMOUNT	
RUN FOR THE SUN	1956	99	6		3.0	UNITED ARTISTS	
RUN FOR YOUR MONEY, A (BRITISH)	1949	83		3.5	3.0	UNIVERSAL	
RUN FOR YOUR WIFE (ITALIAN)	1965	97	3			ALLIED ARTISTS	
RUN LIKE A THIEF	1967	92	1			FEATURE FILM CORP.	
RUN OF THE ARROW	1957	86		2.5	2.5	UNIVERSAL	
RUN SILENT, RUN DEEP	1958	93	4*	3.0	3.0	UNITED ARTISTS	
RUN, SIMON RUN (T.V.)	1970	90		3.0		ABC FILMS	
RUN THE WILD RIVER (DOCUMENTARY)	1971	95	5			JACK CURREY	
RUN WILD, RUN FREE (BRITISH)	1969	98	6			COLUMBIA	
RUNAROUND, THE	1946	86		3.0	2.0	UNIVERSAL	
RUNAWAY, THE (FR. - PIERRE BRASSEUR, JOEL FLATEAU)	1958	100		2.0			
RUNAWAY BUS, THE (BRITISH)	1954	78		2.0		EROS FILMS	
RUNAWAY DAUGHTERS	1956	90		1.5		AMERICAN-INTERNAT'L	
RUNNING MAN, THE (BRITISH)	1963	103	5*	3.0	3.0	COLUMBIA	
RUNNING TARGET	1956	83		3.0	1.5	UNITED ARTISTS	
RUNNING WILD	1955	81		1.5	2.5	UNIVERSAL	
RUSS MEYER'S VIXEN	a1969	71	2			EVE RELEASING CORP.	
RUSSIA (DOCUMENTARY)	1972	108	4			THEODORE HOLCOMB	
RUSSIAN ADVENTURE (DOCUMENTARY)	a1966	140	4			UNITED ROADSHOW	
RUSSIANS ARE COMING THE RUSSIANS ARE COMING, THE	1966	120	6*	3.5		UNITED ARTISTS	NOMINATED BEST PICTURE
RUTHLESS	1948	104		2.0	2.0	EAGLE LION	
RUTHLESS FOUR, THE	1969	96	3			GOLDSTONE FILM ENT.	
RX MURDER (BRITISH)	1958	85		2.0	2.0	20th CENTURY FOX	
RYAN'S DAUGHTER (BRITISH)	1970	175	6*			M-G-M	
$ (DOLLARS)	a1971	120	5			COLUMBIA	
S.O.S. PACIFIC (BRITISH)	1959	92	4		2.5	UNIVERSAL	
SAADIA	1954	82		1.5	1.5	M-G-M	
SABAKA	1955	81			2.0	UNITED ARTISTS	

‡ An asterisk (*) in THE FILM BUFF'S BIBLE column indicates that the film has been rated by the editor and/or staff. All other ratings in this column are based on a consensus of reviews (see NOTES).

TITLE (LEADING ACTORS SHOWN WHERE TWO OR MORE FILMS HAVE THE SAME OR SIMILAR TITLE)	YEAR RELEASED	RUNNING TIME IN MINUTES	THE FILM BUFF'S BIBLE ‡	STEVEN SCHEUER	LEONARD MALTIN	DISTRIBUTOR	COMMENT
SABATA (ITALIAN)	1970	106	2			UNITED ARTISTS	
SABOTAGE SQUAD	1942	64		2.0		COLUMBIA	
SABOTEUR	1942	108	5*	3.5	2.5	UNIVERSAL	
SABOTEUR, CODE NAME - MORITURI, THE	a1965	123	5		2.5	20th CENTURY FOX	
SABRE JET	1953	96	4	2.5	2.5	UNITED ARTISTS	
SABRINA	1954	113	7*	3.5	3.5	PARAMOUNT	
SABU AND THE MAGIC RING	1957	61		2.0	1.5	ALLIED ARTISTS	
SACCO AND VANZETTI	1971	120	4*			UMC PICTURES	
SAD HORSE, THE	1959	78		2.0	2.0	20th CENTURY FOX	
SAD SACK, THE	1957	98		3.0	2.5	PARAMOUNT	
SADDLE THE WIND	1958	84		2.5	3.0	M-G-M	
SADDLE TRAMP	1950	77	4	3.0	2.5	UNIVERSAL	
SADIE MCKEE	1934	90		2.5	2.5	M-G-M	
SAFARI (DOUGLAS FAIRBANKS JR)	1940	80		2.0	2.0	PARAMOUNT	
SAFARI (VICTOR MATURE)	1956	91		2.5	2.5	COLUMBIA	
SAFARI DRUMS	1953	71			-	ALLIED ARTISTS	
SAFE AT HOME!	1962	83		2.0	2.0	COLUMBIA	
SAFE PLACE, A	1971	94	2			COLUMBIA	
SAFECRACKER, THE (BRITISH)	1958	96	4*	2.0	2.0	M-G-M	
SAGA OF HEMP BROWN, THE	1958	80		2.0	2.0	UNIVERSAL	
SAHARA	1943	97		3.0	3.5	COLUMBIA	
SAIGON	1948	94		2.0	2.0	PARAMOUNT	
SAIL A CROOKED SHIP	1962	88		2.0	2.5	COLUMBIA	
SAIL INTO DANGER (BRITISH)	1957	72		2.0	2.0	J. ARTHUR RANK	
SAILOR BEWARE (DEAN MARTIN, JERRY LEWIS)	1952	108		2.5	2.5	PARAMOUNT	
SAILOR FROM GIBRALTAR, THE (BRITISH)	1967	89	3			LOPERT	
SAILOR OF THE KING (BRITISH)	1953	83		2.5	2.5	20th CENTURY FOX	
SAILOR TAKES A WIFE, THE	1945	91		2.0	2.0	M-G-M	
SAILOR'S HOLIDAY	1944	80		1.5		COLUMBIA	
SAILOR'S LADY	1940	66			2.0	20th CENTURY FOX	
ST BENNY THE DIP	1951	80	3	3.0	2.5	UNITED ARTISTS	
SAINT IN LONDON, THE (BRITISH)	1939	72		2.5	-	RKO	
SAINT IN NEW YORK, THE	1938	72		3.0	-	RKO	
SAINT IN PALM SPRINGS, THE	1941	66		2.5	-	RKO	
SAINT JOAN	1957	110	4*	2.5	2.0	UNITED ARTISTS	
ST LOUIS BLUES	1958	93		2.5	2.5	PARAMOUNT	
ST LOUIS KID	1934	67		3.0	2.5	WARNER BROTHERS	
SAINT MEETS THE TIGER, THE (BRITISH)	1941	70		2.5	-	RKO	
SAINT STRIKES BACK, THE	1939	64		3.0	-	RKO	
SAINT TAKES OVER, THE	1940	69		3.0	-	RKO	
ST VALENTINE'S DAY MASSACRE, THE	1967	100		2.0	2.5	20th CENTURY FOX	
SAINTED SISTERS, THE	1948	89		2.5	2.5	PARAMOUNT	
SAINTLY SINNERS	1962	78	2			UNITED ARTISTS	
SAINTS AND SINNERS (BRITISH)	1949	85	6	3.0		LOPERT	
SAINT'S DOUBLE TROUBLE, THE	1940	68		2.0	-	RKO	
SAINT'S GIRL FRIDAY, THE (BRITISH)	1954	70		2.0	-	RKO	
SAINT'S VACATION, THE (BRITISH)	1941	78		2.5	-	RKO	
SAKIMA AND THE MASKED MARVEL	1943	100		2.5	2.5	REPUBLIC	RE-EDITED SERIAL
SALADIN AND THE GREAT CRUSADES (EGYPTIAN)	1963	90		1.5		FOUR STAR	
SALESMAN (DOCUMENTARY)	1969	90	7	4.0		MAYSLES FILM	
SALLAH (ISRAELI)	1964	110	6			PALISADES INTERNAT'L	
SALLY AND ST ANNE	1952	90		2.5	2.5	UNIVERSAL	
SALLY, IRENE AND MARY	1938	72		2.5	3.0	20th CENTURY FOX	
SALLY OF THE SAWDUST (SILENT)	1925	104	4*			UNITED ARTISTS	
SALOME	1953	103		2.5	2.5	COLUMBIA	
SALOME, WHERE SHE DANCED	1945	90		1.0	1.0	UNIVERSAL	
SALT AND PEPPER (BRITISH)	1968	101	3	2.0		UNITED ARTISTS	
SALT OF THE EARTH (WILL GEER, MERVIN WILLIAMS)	1954	94		3.0		INDEPENDENT PRODS.	
SALT TO THE DEVIL (BRITISH)	1950	120	7			EAGLE LION	
SALTO (POLISH)	1965	104	6			KANAWHA FILMS LTD.	
SALTY O'ROURKE	1945	97	3*	3.0	3.0	PARAMOUNT	
SALUTE FOR THREE	1943	75		2.0		PARAMOUNT	
SALUTE TO THE MARINES	1943	101		2.0	2.5	M-G-M	
SALZBURG CONNECTION, THE	1972	93	3			20th CENTURY FOX	
SAM HILL - WHO KILLED THE MYSTERIOUS MR FOSTER?	1971	100		2.5		UNIVERSAL	
SAM WHISKEY	1969	96	3			UNITED ARTISTS	
SAMAR	1962	89	3	3.0	2.0	WARNER BROTHERS	
SAMSON (ITALIAN)	1961	95		1.0		TELEWIDE SYSTEMS	
SAMSON AGAINST THE SHEIK (ITALIAN)	1960	95		1.0		TELEWIDE SYSTEMS	
SAMSON AND DELILAH	1949	128	6*	3.5	2.5	PARAMOUNT	
SAMSON AND THE SEA BEASTS (ITALIAN)	1963	84		1.0		AMERICAN-INTERNAT'L	
SAMSON AND THE SEVEN CHALLANGES (ITALIAN)	1964	91		1.0			
SAMSON AND THE SEVEN MIRACLES OF THE WORLD (ITAL.)	1961	80	2	1.5		AMERICAN-INTERNAT'L	
SAMSON AND THE SLAVE QUEEN (ITALIAN)	1963	86	1	1.5	1.5	AMERICAN-INTERNAT'L	
SAMSON AND THE VAMPIRE WOMAN (MEXICAN)	1963	89		1.0		AZTECA	
SAMSON IN THE WAX MUSEUM (MEXICAN)	1963	90		1.0		AZTECA	
SAMURAI (JAPANESE)	1955	92	6			FINE ARTS	
SAN ANTONE	1953	90	2	2.5		REPUBLIC	
SAN ANTONIO	1945	111		2.5	3.0	WARNER BROTHERS	
SAN DEMETRIO, LONDON (BRITISH)	1943	76		3.0		20th CENTURY FOX	
SAN DIEGO, I LOVE YOU	1944	83			3.0	UNIVERSAL	
SAN FRANCISCO	1936	115		3.5	3.5	M-G-M	NOMINATED BEST PICTURE
SAN FRANCISCO INTERNATIONAL AIRPORT (T.V.)	1970	100		2.5		UNIVERSAL	
SAN FRANCISCO STORY, THE	1952	80		2.0	2.0	WARNER BROTHERS	

‡ An asterisk (*) in THE FILM BUFF'S BIBLE column indicates that the film has been rated by the editor and/or staff. All other ratings in this column are based on a consensus of reviews (see NOTES).

TITLE (LEADING ACTORS SHOWN WHERE TWO OR MORE FILMS HAVE THE SAME OR SIMILAR TITLE)	YEAR RELEASED	RUNNING TIME IN MINUTES	THE FILM BUFF'S BIBLE ‡	STEVEN SCHEUER	LEONARD MALTIN	DISTRIBUTOR	COMMENT
SAN QUENTIN (PAT O'BRIEN, HUMPHREY BOGART)	1937	70		3.0	2.5	FIRST NATIONAL	
SAN QUENTIN (LAWRENCE TIERNEY)	1946	66		2.0	2.5	RKO	
SANCTUARY	1961	100		2.0	2.0	20th CENTURY FOX	
SAND	a1949	78		2.0	2.0	20th CENTURY FOX	
SAND CASTLE, THE	1961	67		3.5	2.5	DE ROCHEMONT	
SAND, LOVE, AND SALT (ITALIAN)	1956	89		2.0			
SAND PEBBLES, THE	1966	191	4*			20th CENTURY FOX	NOMINATED BEST PICTURE
SANDERS (BRITISH)	1964	84		2.5		20th CENTURY FOX	
SANDOKAN AGAINST THE LEOPARD OF SARAWAK (ITALIAN)	a1964	88		1.5	2.0	SCREEN GEMS	
SANDOKAN FIGHTS BACK (ITALIAN)	1964	96		1.5	2.0	SCREEN GEMS	
SANDOKAN THE GREAT (ITALIAN)	1965	105	3		2.0	M-G-M	
SANDPIPER, THE	1965	116	5-6*	2.0	2.5	M-G-M	
SANDS OF BEERSHEBA (ISRAELI)	1964	90		2.5	2.5	LANDAU/UNGER COM. UN.	
SANDS OF IWO JIMA	1949	110	4*	3.5	3.5	REPUBLIC	
SANDS OF THE DESERT (BRITISH)	1960	92				WARNER BROTHERS	
SANDS OF THE KALAHARI (BRITISH)	1965	119	5	3.0	3.0	PARAMOUNT	
SANDY GETS HER MAN	1940	74		2.5	1.5	UNIVERSAL	
SANDY IS A LADY	1940	65			1.5	UNIVERSAL	
SANGAREE	1953	94		2.0	2.5	PARAMOUNT	
SANJURO (JAPANESE)	1961	96	6			TOHO	
SANTA CLAUS CONQUERS THE MARTIANS	1964	80			2.0	AVCO-EMBASSY	
SANTA FE	1951	89		2.0	2.0	COLUMBIA	
SANTA FE PASSAGE	1955	70		3.0	2.0	REPUBLIC	
SANTA FE TRAIL	1940	110		3.0	3.0	WARNER BROTHERS	
SANTIAGO	1956	93		2.0	2.5	WARNER BROTHERS	
SAPPHIRE (BRITISH)	1959	92	5*	4.0	3.0	UNIVERSAL	
SAPPHO, DARLING	1969	100	1			CAMBIST	
SAPS AT SEA	1940	57			2.5	UNITED ARTISTS	
SARABAND (BRITISH)	a1948	95		3.0	3.0	EAGLE LION	
SARACEN BLADE, THE	1954	76		2.0	1.5	COLUMBIA	
SARACENS, THE (ITALIAN)	1960	89		1.5		AMERICAN-INTERNAT'L	
SARAH AND SON	1930	76			2.0	PARAMOUNT	
SARATOGA	1937	94		2.5	2.5	M-G-M	
SARATOGA TRUNK	1945	135		2.5	1.5	WARNER BROTHERS	
SARGE - THE BADGE OR THE CROSS (T.V.)	1971	100		3.0		UNIVERSAL	
SASKATCHEWAN	1954	87	4	2.5	2.5	UNIVERSAL	
SATAN BUG, THE	1965	114	4*	2.5	3.0	UNITED ARTISTS	
SATAN MET A LADY	1936	75		2.0	2.0	WARNER BROTHERS	
SATAN NEVER SLEEPS	a1962	126	3	1.5	2.0	20th CENTURY FOX	
SATAN'S SADISTS	1970	86	1			INDEPENDENT INT'L	
SATAN'S SATELLITES	1958	70		1.0	1.5	REPUBLIC	
SATCHMO THE GREAT	1957	63	6			UNITED ARTISTS	
SATELLITE IN THE SKY (BRITISH)	1956	84		2.5	2.5	WARNER BROTHERS	
SATURDAY MORNING (DOCUMENTARY)	1971	88				COLUMBIA	
SATURDAY NIGHT AND SUNDAY MORNING (BRITISH)	1960	90	5*	4.0	3.5	CONTINENTAL	
SATURDAY'S CHILDREN	1940	101		3.0	2.5	WARNER BROTHERS	
SATURDAY'S HERO (JOHN DEREK, DONNA REED)	1951	111	5*	3.0	2.5	COLUMBIA	
SATURDAY'S MILLIONS	1933	72		1.5		UNIVERSAL	
SATYRICON (ITALIAN)	a1970	127	1*			UNITED ARTISTS	
SAVAGE, THE	1952	95	4	2.5	2.5	PARAMOUNT	
SAVAGE DRUMS	1951	73		2.0	2.0	LIPPERT PRODS.	
SAVAGE EYE, THE	1960	68	6	4.0	3.0	TRANS-LUX DIST.	
SAVAGE GRINGO (SPANISH)	1965	82		1.5		AMERICAN-INTERNAT'L	
SAVAGE GUNS, THE	1962	83	3			M-G-M	
SAVAGE HORDE (WILLIAM ELLIOTT, ADRIAN BOOTH)	1950	90		2.5		REPUBLIC	
SAVAGE HORDES, THE (ITALIAN - ETTORE MANNI)	1961	82			2.0	EAGLE	
SAVAGE INNOCENTS, THE (ITALIAN-FRENCH)	1960	89		3.0	2.5	PARAMOUNT	ENGLISH LANGUAGE
SAVAGE MUTINY	1953	73		1.5	.	COLUMBIA	
SAVAGE PAMPAS (SPANISH)	1966	97		1.0	2.0	COMET FILM	
SAVAGE SAM	1963	103	4			BUENA VISTA	
SAVAGE SEVEN, THE	1968	97	2	1.0		AMERICAN-INTERNAT'L	
SAVAGE SPLENDOR (DOCUMENTARY)	1949	60	6			RKO	
SAVAGE WILD, THE (DOCUMENTARY)	1969	103	3			AMERICAN-INTERNAT'L	
SAWDUST AND TINSEL (SWEDISH)	a1953	82	3*			TIMES FILM CORP.	
SAXON CHARM, THE	1948	88	3*	3.5	3.0	UNIVERSAL	
SAY HELLO TO YESTERDAY (BRITISH)	1970	92	3			CINERAMA RELEASING	
SAY IT IN FRENCH	1938	70		2.5	2.0	PARAMOUNT	
SAY ONE FOR ME	1959	119		2.0	1.5	20th CENTURY FOX	
SAYONARA	1957	147	6*	3.5	3.5	WARNER BROTHERS	NOMINATED BEST PICTURE
SCALPHUNTERS, THE	1968	102	5	3.0		UNITED ARTISTS	
SCALPLOCK	1966	100		1.5	2.5	COLUMBIA	
SCAMPOLO (GERMAN)	1958	104		2.0		BAKROS INTERNATIONAL	
SCANDAL AT SCOURIE	1953	90		2.5	2.5	M-G-M	
SCANDAL IN PARIS, A	a1946	100	4	3.0	3.0	UNITED ARTISTS	
SCANDAL IN SORRENTO (ITALIAN)	1957	92			1.5	DIST. CORP. OF AMER.	
SCANDAL, INC.	1956	79		1.5	1.5	REPUBLIC	
SCANDAL SHEET (BRODERICK CRAWFORD, DONNA REED)	1952	82		2.5		COLUMBIA	
SCANDAL STREET (GEORGE BANCROFT, KAY FRANCIS)	1931	77			2.5	PARAMOUNT	
SCANDLOUS JOHN	1971	112	4			BUENA VISTA	
SCAPEGOAT, THE (BRITISH - ALEC GUINNESS)	1959	92		2.5	2.5	M-G-M	
SCAPEGOAT, THE (FRENCH - MICHELE MORGAN)	1963	94		2.0		PARAMOUNT	
SCAR, THE	a1948	83	5	3.0	3.0	EAGLE LION	
SCARAMOUCHE (STEWART GRANGER, ELEANOR PARKER)	1952	118	6*	3.0	3.5	M-G-M	
SCARECROW IN A GARDEN OF CUCUMBERS	1972	82	2			MARON FILMS, LTD.	

‡ An asterisk (*) in THE FILM BUFF'S BIBLE column indicates that the film has been rated by the editor and/or staff. All other ratings in this column are based on a consensus of reviews (see NOTES).

"a" TO LEFT OF YEAR INDICATES THAT FILM HAS AN ALTERNATE TITLE

CRITICAL RATINGS

TITLE (LEADING ACTORS SHOWN WHERE TWO OR MORE FILMS HAVE THE SAME OR SIMILAR TITLE)	YEAR RELEASED	RUNNING TIME IN MINUTES	THE FILM BUFF'S BIBLE ‡	STEVEN SCHEUER	LEONARD MALTIN	DISTRIBUTOR	COMMENT
SCARED STIFF (JACK HALEY, ANN SAVAGE)	1952	115				M-G-M	
SCARED STIFF (DEAN MARTIN, JERRY LEWIS)	1953	108	4	3.0	2.5	PARAMOUNT	
SCARED TO DEATH	1947	70			1.5	SCREEN GUILD	
SCARF, THE	1951	93		2.5	2.5	UNITED ARTISTS	
SCARFACE	1932	99				UNITED ARTISTS	
SCARFACE MOB, THE	1962	90		2.5	2.5	CARI	
SCARLET ANGEL	1952	80	4	2.5	2.5	UNIVERSAL	
SCARLET BARONESS, THE (GERMAN)	1962	85		2.0		CASINO FILMS	
SCARLET CLAW, THE	1944	74			.	UNIVERSAL	
SCARLET CLUE, THE	1945	65			.	MONOGRAM	
SCARLET COAT, THE	1955	101		2.0	2.5	M-G-M	
SCARLET EMPRESS, THE	1934	110		2.0	2.5	PARAMOUNT	
SCARLET HOUR, THE	1956	95		2.0	2.0	PARAMOUNT	
SCARLET PIMPERNEL, THE (BRITISH)	1935	95	5*	2.5	3.5	UNITED ARTISTS	
SCARLET SPEAR, THE (BRITISH)	1954	78		1.5	1.0	UNITED ARTISTS	
SCARLET STREET	1945	103		3.0	3.0	UNIVERSAL	
SCARS OF DRACULA, THE (BRITISH)	1970	94	2			LEVITT-PICKMAN	
SCAVENGERS, THE	1959	79	2	2.5		PARAMOUNT	
SCENE OF THE CRIME	1949	94	4	2.0	2.0	M-G-M	
SCHEHERAZADE (FRENCH)	1962	104		1.5		FOUR STAR	
SCHEMER, THE (FRENCH)	1959	105		2.0			
SCHOOL FOR LOVE (FRENCH)	1955	76	1	1.5	2.0	NTA PICTURES	
SCHOOL FOR SCOUNDRELS (BRITISH)	1960	94	6	3.0	3.0	CONTINENTAL	
SCORCHING FURY	1952	68		1.0			
SCORPIO LETTERS, THE (T.V.)	1967	98		1.0	3.0	M-G-M	
SCOTCH ON THE ROCKS (BRITISH)	1954	83	6	3.0		KINGSLEY INTERNAT'L	
SCOTLAND YARD	1941	68		2.5		20th CENTURY FOX	
SCOTLAND YARD INSPECTOR (BRITISH)	1952	73		2.0	2.0	LIPPERT PRODS.	
SCOTLAND YARD INVESTIGATOR	1945	68		2.0	2.0	REPUBLIC	
SCOTT OF THE ANTARCTIC (BRITISH)	1948	111		3.0	2.5	EAGLE LION	
SCOUNDREL, THE	1935	68		3.0		PARAMOUNT	
SCREAM AND SCREAM AGAIN (BRITISH)	1970	95	4			AMERICAN-INTERNAT'L	
SCREAM OF FEAR (BRITISH)	1961	81		3.0	3.0	COLUMBIA	
SCREAM OF THE DEMON LOVER	1971	75	1			NEW WORLD	
SCREAMING EAGLES	1956	81	.	2.0	2.0	ALLIED ARTISTS	
SCREAMING MIMI	1958	79		1.5	2.0	COLUMBIA	
SCREAMING SKULL, THE	1958	70	3	1.5		AMERICAN-INTERNAT'L	
SCROOGE (BRITISH - ALBERT FINNEY, ALEC GUINNESS)	1970	118	5			NATIONAL GENERAL	
SCUDDA HOO! SCUDDA HAY!	1948	95	4	2.0	2.0	20th CENTURY FOX	
SEA AROUND US, THE (DOCUMENTARY)	1953	61	6		3.0	RKO	
SEA CHASE, THE	1955	117		2.5	2.5	WARNER BROTHERS	
SEA DEVILS (VICTOR MCLAGLEN, PRESTON FOSTER)	1937	88		2.5		RKO	
SEA DEVILS (ROCK HUDSON, YVONNE DE CARLO)	1953	91	3	2.5	2.5	RKO	
SEA GULL, THE (BRITISH)	1968	141	6			WARNER BROTHERS	
SEA HAWK, THE	1940	127	5*	3.0	3.5	WARNER BROTHERS	
SEA HORNET, THE	1951	84		2.5	1.5	REPUBLIC	
SEA OF GRASS, THE	1947	131		2.5	2.5	M-G-M	
SEA OF LOST SHIPS	1954	85		2.0	2.0	REPUBLIC	
SEA PIRATE, THE (FRENCH)	1967	83	1			PARAMOUNT	ENGLISH LANGUAGE
SEA SHALL NOT HAVE THEM, THE (BRITISH)	1954	93		3.0	2.0	UNITED ARTISTS	
SEA TIGER	1952	75	2	2.0	1.5	MONOGRAM	
SEA WIFE (BRITISH)	1957	82		1.5	3.0	20th CENTURY FOX	
SEA WOLF, THE	1941	100		3.0	3.5	WARNER BROTHERS	
SEALED CARGO	1951	90	4	3.0	2.5	RKO	
SEALED LIPS	1941	62		2.0		UNIVERSAL	
SEALED VERDICT	1948	83	4	1.5	2.0	PARAMOUNT	
SEANCE ON A WET AFTERNOON (BRITISH)	1964	116	7*	4.0	4.0	ARTIXO PRODS.	
SEARCH, THE	1948	105	6*	4.0	4.0	M-G-M	
SEARCH FOR BRIDEY MURPHY, THE	1956	84		2.0	2.5	PARAMOUNT	
SEARCH FOR DANGER	1949	62			.	FOUR CONTINENTS	
SEARCH FOR PARADISE (TRAVELOGUE)	1957	120	5*			STANLEY WARNER	
SEARCHERS, THE	1956	119	6*	3.0	3.0	WARNER BROTHERS	
SEARCHING WIND, THE	1946	108		3.0	2.5	PARAMOUNT	
SEASIDE SWINGERS (BRITISH)	1965	94		2.5		AVCO-EMBASSY	
SEASON OF PASSION (AUSTRALIAN)	1960	92	4	3.0	2.5	UNITED ARTISTS	
SEBASTIAN (BRITISH)	1968	100	4	2.5		PARAMOUNT	
SECOND BEST SECRET AGENT IN THE WHOLE WIDE WORLD	1965	96		1.0	2.5	AVCO-EMBASSY	(BRITISH)
SECOND CHANCE (KENT TAYLOR, LOUISE CURRIE)	1947	62				20th CENTURY FOX	
SECOND CHANCE (ROBERT MITCHUM, LINDA DARNELL)	1953	82		2.5	2.5	RKO	
SECOND CHORUS	1940	83		2.0	2.0	PARAMOUNT	
SECOND FACE, THE	1950	77		3.0	2.5	EAGLE LION	
SECOND FIDDLE (SONJA HENJE, TYRONE POWER)	1939	86		2.0	2.5	20th CENTURY FOX	
SECOND GREATEST SEX, THE	1955	87	3	2.0	1.5	UNIVERSAL	
SECOND HONEYMOON	1937	79		2.5	2.5	20th CENTURY FOX	
SECOND TIME AROUND, THE	1961	99		3.0	2.5	20th CENTURY FOX	
SECOND WOMAN, THE	1951	91	4	3.0	2.5	UNITED ARTISTS	
SECONDS	1966	106	5	3.0	3.0	PARAMOUNT	
SECRET, THE (BRITISH)	1955	81		2.0			
SECRET AGENT FIREBALL (ITALIAN)	a1965	93		2.0	2.0	AMERICAN-INTERNAT'L	
SECRET AGENT OF JAPAN, THE	1942	72		1.5	2.0	20th CENTURY FOX	
SECRET AGENT SUPER DRAGON (ITALIAN)	1966	95	2		1.5	UNITED SCREEN ARTS	
SECRET AGENTS, THE (FRENCH)	a1965	87	3	2.5	2.5	AMERICAN-INTERNAT'L	
SECRET BEYOND THE DOOR	1948	98		1.5	2.0	UNIVERSAL	
SECRET BRIDE	1935	76		3.0	2.5	WARNER BROTHERS	

‡ An asterisk (*) in THE FILM BUFF'S BIBLE column indicates that the film has been rated by the editor and/or staff. All other ratings in this column are based on a consensus of reviews (see NOTES).

TITLE (LEADING ACTORS SHOWN WHERE TWO OR MORE FILMS HAVE THE SAME OR SIMILAR TITLE)	YEAR RELEASED	RUNNING TIME IN MINUTES	THE FILM BUFF'S BIBLE ‡	STEVEN SCHEUER	LEONARD MALTIN	DISTRIBUTOR	COMMENT
SECRET CEREMONY, THE (BRITISH)	1968	109	3	2.5		UNIVERSAL	
SECRET COMMAND	1944	82		3.0	3.0	COLUMBIA	
SECRET CONCLAVE, THE (ITALIAN)	1953	80		2.5		ITALIAN FILMS EXPORT	
SECRET DOOR, THE (BRITISH)	1964	72		1.5	1.5	ALLIED ARTISTS	
SECRET FILE 1413 (FRENCH)	1959	85		1.5		AMERICAN-INTERNAT'L	
SECRET FILE - HOLLYWOOD	1961	85		1.0		CROWN INTERNATIONAL	
SECRET FURY, THE	1950	86		2.0	3.0	RKO	
SECRET GARDEN, THE	1949	92	5*	3.0	3.0	M-G-M	
SECRET HEART, THE	1946	97		2.5	2.5	M-G-M	
SECRET INVASION, THE	1964	95	4	2.5	3.0	UNITED ARTISTS	
SECRET LAND, THE (DOCUMENTARY)	1948	71	6		3.0	M-G-M	
SECRET LIFE OF AN AMERICAN WIFE, THE	1968	92	4	1.5		20th CENTURY FOX	
SECRET LIFE OF WALTER MITTY, THE	1947	105	6*	3.5	3.0	RKO	
SECRET MARK OF D'ARTAGNAN, THE (ITALIAN)	1962	100		1.5	2.5	COLUMBIA	
SECRET MISSION (BRITISH)	1942	82		2.5	2.5	ENGLISH FILMS	
SECRET OF BLOOD ISLAND, THE (BRITISH)	1965	84	3		2.5	UNIVERSAL	
SECRET OF CONVICT LAKE, THE	1951	83		2.5	2.5	20th CENTURY FOX	
SECRET OF DEEP HARBOR	1961	70	1			UNITED ARTISTS	
SECRET OF DR KILDARE, THE	1939	84		2.0	.	M-G-M	
SECRET OF DR MABUSE (GERMAN)	1961	90		1.5	2.5	TELEWIDE SYSTEMS	
SECRET OF MONTE CRISTO, THE	1961	83	3			M-G-M	
SECRET OF MY SUCCESS, THE (BRITISH)	1965	96		1.5	1.5	M-G-M	
SECRET OF ST IVES, THE	1949	75		1.5		COLUMBIA	
SECRET OF SANTA VITTORIA, THE	1969	139	5	2.5		UNITED ARTISTS	
SECRET OF THE BLACK TRUNK, THE (GERMAN)	1962	96		1.5	2.5	UCC FILMS	
SECRET OF THE BLACK WIDOW, THE (GERMAN)	1964	107		1.5		CASINO FILMS	
SECRET OF THE CHINESE CARNATION, THE (GERMAN)	1965	95		1.0		UCC FILMS	
SECRET OF THE INCAS	1954	101		2.5	2.5	PARAMOUNT	
SECRET OF THE PURPLE REEF, THE	1960	80		2.0	2.0	20th CENTURY FOX	
SECRET OF THE RED ORCHID, THE (GERMAN)	a1962	94		2.0	2.0	UCC FILMS	
SECRET OF THE SPHINX (FRENCH)	1964	95		1.5		INDEP. TV CORP (ITC)	
SECRET OF THE TELEGIAN, THE (JAPANESE)	1963	86		1.5		PARAMOUNT	
SECRET OF THE WHISTLER, THE	1946	65		2.0	.	COLUMBIA	
SECRET OF TREASURE MOUNTAIN	1956	68		2.0	1.5	COLUMBIA	
SECRET PARTNER, THE (BRITISH)	1961	91		2.0	3.0	M-G-M	
SECRET PEOPLE, THE (BRITISH)	1952	96		2.5	2.0	LIPPERT PRODS.	
SECRET SERVICE INVESTIGATOR	1948	60		3.0		REPUBLIC	
SECRET SEVEN, THE (ITALIAN)	1963	92			1.0	M-G-M	
SECRET SIX, THE	1931	83		2.5	3.0	M-G-M	
SECRET VENTURE (BRITISH)	1955	68		2.0		REPUBLIC	
SECRET WAR OF HARRY FRIGG, THE	1968	110	4	2.0		UNIVERSAL	
SECRET WAYS, THE	1961	112	3	2.5	2.5	UNIVERSAL	
SECRET WORLD (FRENCH)	1968	94	5			20th CENTURY FOX	ENGLISH LANGUAGE
SECRETARY, THE	1972	85	1			UNITED FILM ORG.	
SECRETS OF A SECRETARY	1931	71		2.0	2.0	PARAMOUNT	
SECRETS OF AN ACTRESS	1938	71		2.5	2.5	WARNER BROTHERS	
SECRETS OF LIFE (DOCUMENTARY)	1956	70	6			BUENA VISTA	
SECRETS OF MONTE CARLO	1951	60	3	2.0		REPUBLIC	
SECRETS OF THE REEF (DOCUMENTARY)	1956	72	6			CONTINENTAL	
SECRETS OF WOMEN (SWEDISH)	1952	114	5			JANUS FILMS	
SECURITY RISK	1954	69		2.0	2.0	ALLIED ARTISTS	
SEDUCED AND ABANDONED (ITALIAN)	1964	118	5*	4.0	3.5	CONTINENTAL	
SEE HERE, PRIVATE HARGROVE	1944	101		3.0	3.0	M-G-M	
SEE HOW THEY RUN (JOHN FORSYTHE, SENTA BERGER)	1964	84		2.0		BRITISH-LION	
SEE MY LAWYER	1945	67		2.5		UNIVERSAL	
SEE NO EVIL	1971	89	4			COLUMBIA	
SEEKERS, THE (BRITISH)	1954	90		2.5	2.5	J. ARTHUR RANK	
SELLOUT, THE	1952	83		2.5	2.5	M-G-M	
SEMINOLE	1953	87	3*	2.5	2.5	UNIVERSAL	
SEMINOLE UPRISING	1955	74		2.0	1.5	COLUMBIA	
SENATOR WAS INDISCREET, THE	1947	81	5*	3.5	3.5	UNIVERSAL	
SEND ME NO FLOWERS	1964	100		2.0	3.0	UNIVERSAL	
SENECHAL THE MAGNIFICENT (FRENCH)	a1957	80	4	2.0	2.5	DIST. CORP. OF AMER.	
SENIOR PROM	1959	82		2.0	1.5	COLUMBIA	
SENSATIONS (OF 1945), THE	1944	86		2.5	2.5	UNITED ARTISTS	
SENSO (ITALIAN)	a1954	125		2.0	2.5	FLEETWOOD FILMS	
SENSUALITA (ITALIAN)	a1954	72		2.0	2.0	ITALIAN FILMS EXPORT	
SENTIMENTAL JOURNEY	1946	94		1.5	2.0	20th CENTURY FOX	
SEPARATE TABLES	1958	98	7*	4.0	4.0	UNITED ARTISTS	NOMINATED BEST PICTURE
SEPARATION (BRITISH)	1967		3			CONTINENTAL	
SEPTEMBER AFFAIR	1951	104		3.0	2.5	PARAMOUNT	
SEPTEMBER STORM	1960	99		1.5	1.0	20th CENTURY FOX	
SERAFINO (ITALIAN)	1968	94	6			ROYAL FILMS INT'L	
SERENA (BRITISH)	1962	62			2.5	BUTCHER'S	
SERENADE	1956	121		2.5	2.5	WARNER BROTHERS	
SERENGETI SHALL NOT DIE (GERMAN, DOCUMENTARY)	a1959	84	6	3.5		ALLIED ARTISTS	
SERGEANT, THE	1968	108	6	3.0		WARNER BROTHERS	
SERGEANT DEADHEAD	1965	89		2.0	2.0	AMERICAN-INTERNAT'L	
SERGEANT MADDEN	1939	82		2.0	2.0	M-G-M	
SERGEANT MIKE	1944	60		2.5		COLUMBIA	
SERGEANT RUTLEDGE	1960	118		2.5	2.5	WARNER BROTHERS	
SERGEANT RYKER	1968	85		2.0	2.5	UNIVERSAL	
SERGEANT WAS A LADY, THE	1961	72	3	1.5		UNIVERSAL	
SERGEANT X OF THE FOREIGN LEGION (FRENCH)	1960	85		1.5		AMERICAN-INTERNAT'L	

‡ An asterisk (*) in THE FILM BUFF'S BIBLE column indicates that the film has been rated by the editor and/or staff. All other ratings in this column are based on a consensus of reviews (see NOTES).

TITLE (LEADING ACTORS SHOWN WHERE TWO OR MORE FILMS HAVE THE SAME OR SIMILAR TITLE)	YEAR RELEASED	RUNNING TIME IN MINUTES	THE FILM BUFF'S BIBLE ‡	STEVEN SCHEUER	LEONARD MALTIN	DISTRIBUTOR	COMMENT
SERGEANT YORK	1941	134		4.0	3.5	WARNER BROTHERS	NOMINATED BEST PICTURE
SERGEANTS THREE	1962	112		2.0	2.5	UNITED ARTISTS	
SERPENT OF THE NILE	1953	81	2	2.0	1.5	COLUMBIA	
SERVANT, THE (BRITISH)	1963	115	7*	3.5	3.5	LANDAU/UNGER COM. UN.	
SET-UP, THE (ROBERT RYAN, AUDREY TOTTER)	1949	72	6	4.0	3.5	RKO	
SET UP, THE (BRITISH - MAURICE DENHAM)	1962	58		2.0		ANGLO AMALGAMATED	
SEVEN ANGRY MEN	1955	90	5	3.0	3.0	ALLIED ARTISTS	
SEVEN BRIDES FOR SEVEN BROTHERS	1954	102	7	4.0	3.0	M-G-M	NOMINATED BEST PICTURE
SEVEN CAPITAL SINS (FRENCH)	1962	113		3.0	2.0	AVCO-EMBASSY	SEVEN STORIES
SEVEN CHANCES (SILENT)	1925	57	6-7*			METRO-GOLDWYN	
SEVEN CITIES OF GOLD	1955	103		2.0	2.5	20th CENTURY FOX	
SEVEN DARING GIRLS (GERMAN)	1960	76			1.5	MANSON	
SEVEN DAYS ASHORE	1944	74		2.5		RKO	
SEVEN DAYS IN MAY	1964	120	7*	4.0	3.0	PARAMOUNT	
SEVEN DAYS' LEAVE	1942	87		2.5	2.5	RKO	
SEVEN DAYS TO NOON (BRITISH)	1950	93	5*	4.0	4.0	MAYER-KINGSLEY	
SEVEN DEADLY SINS (FRENCH)	1952	140		4.0		ARLAN PICTURES	SEVEN EPISODES
711 OCEAN DRIVE	1950	102	4*	2.5	2.5	COLUMBIA	
SEVEN FACES OF DR LAO	1964	100	4*			M-G-M	
SEVEN GOLDEN MEN (ITALIAN)	1965	87	2			WARNER BROTHERS	ENGLISH LANGUAGE
SEVEN GUNS TO MESA	1958	69		2.0		ALLIED ARTISTS	
SEVEN HILLS OF ROME	1958	107	5	2.5		M-G-M	
SEVEN IN DARKNESS (T.V.)	1969	75	5*	2.5		PARAMOUNT	
SEVEN IN THE SUN (ITALIAN)	1964	88		1.5		AVCO-EMBASSY	
SEVEN KEYS TO BALDPATE (PHILIP TERRY)	1947	66		2.0	2.5	RKO	
SEVEN LITTLE FOYS, THE	1955	95	6	3.0	3.0	PARAMOUNT	
SEVEN MEN FROM NOW	1956	78		2.0	2.0	WARNER BROTHERS	
SEVEN MILES FROM ALCATRAZ	1943	62		2.0		RKO	
SEVEN MINUTES, THE	1971	116	2			20th CENTURY FOX	
SEVEN SAMURAI, THE (JAPANESE)	a1954	160	5*	4.0	3.0	TOHO	ORIGINALLY 200 MINUTES
SEVEN SEAS TO CALAIS (ITALIAN)	1961	102	3			M-G-M	
SEVEN SINNERS	1940	87		3.0	3.0	UNIVERSAL	
SEVEN SLAVES AGAINST THE WORLD (ITALIAN)	a1965	96	2		1.0	PARAMOUNT	
SEVEN SURPRIZES (CANADIAN)	1964	77		3.0	2.5	QUARTET INTERNAT'L	
SEVEN SWEETHEARTS	1942	98		3.0	2.5	M-G-M	
SEVEN TASKS OF ALI BABA, THE (ITALIAN)	a1960	95		1.5		TELEWIDE SYSTEMS	
SEVEN THIEVES	1960	102	5*	3.5	3.5	20th CENTURY FOX	
SEVEN WAYS FROM SUNDOWN	1960	87		2.5	2.5	UNIVERSAL	
SEVEN WERE SAVED	1947	73		2.0		PARAMOUNT	
SEVEN WOMEN	1966	93	3	1.0	2.0	M-G-M	
SEVEN WOMEN FROM HELL	1961	88	2		2.0	20th CENTURY FOX	
SEVEN WONDERS OF THE WORLD	1956	120	5			STANLEY WARNER	
SEVEN YEAR ITCH, THE	1955	105	6*	4.0	3.0	20th CENTURY FOX	
SEVENTEEN (JACKIE COOPER, BETTY FIELD)	1940	78		2.5	2.5	PARAMOUNT	
7TH CAVALRY, THE	1956	75	4	3.0	2.5	COLUMBIA	
SEVENTH COMMANDMENT, THE (JONATHAN KIDD)	1961	82		1.0		CROWN INTERNATIONAL	
SEVENTH CONTINENT, THE (YUGOSLAVIAN)	1967	84	6			U-M PRODS.	
SEVENTH CROSS, THE	1944	110		3.5	3.0	M-G-M	
SEVENTH DAWN, THE	1964	123		1.0	2.5	UNITED ARTISTS	
SEVENTH HEAVEN (SILENT - JANET GAYNOR)	1927	94				20th CENTURY FOX	NOMINATED BEST PICTURE 1927/28
SEVENTH HEAVEN (SIMONE SIMON, JAMES STEWART)	1937	102		1.5	2.0	20th CENTURY FOX	
SEVENTH SEAL, THE (SWEDISH)	1956	105	6*			JANUS FILMS	
SEVENTH SIN, THE	1957	94	4	2.0	2.5	M-G-M	
SEVENTH SWORD, THE (ITALIAN)	1962	96		2.0	2.0	TELEWIDE SYSTEMS	
SEVENTH VEIL, THE (BRITISH)	1945	94		3.5	3.5	UNIVERSAL	
SEVENTH VICTIM, THE	1943	71		2.5	3.0	RKO	
7TH VOYAGE OF SINBAD, THE	1958	89		3.0	2.5	COLUMBIA	
79 A.D. (ITALIAN)	1961	113		1.5		AMERICAN-INTERNAT'L	
SEVERED HEAD, A (BRITISH)	1971	98	3			COLUMBIA	
SEX AND THE SINGLE GIRL	1965	114		2.5	2.5	WARNER BROTHERS	
SEX KITTENS GO TO COLLEGE	1960	94		1.0	1.5	ALLIED ARTISTS	
SEX OF ANGELS, THE (ITALIAN-GERMAN)	1969	104	1			LOPERT	
SHACK OUT ON 101	1955	80		1.5	2.5	ALLIED ARTISTS	
SHADOW IN THE SKY	1952	78		2.5	2.5	M-G-M	
SHADOW MAN, THE (BRITISH)	1953	75		2.5	2.0	LIPPERT PRODS.	
SHADOW OF A DOUBT (JOSEPH COTTON, TERESA WRIGHT)	1943	108	5-6*	4.0	3.5	UNIVERSAL	
SHADOW OF A WOMAN	1946	78		2.0		WARNER BROTHERS	
SHADOW OF EVIL (FRENCH)	1964	92	2			SEVEN ARTS	
SHADOW OF FEAR (BRITISH - MONA FREEMAN, JEAN KENT)	1956	76		2.5	2.0	UNITED ARTISTS	
SHADOW OF THE CAT (BRITISH)	1961	79	3		2.0	UNIVERSAL	
SHADOW OF THE THIN MAN	1941	97		2.5	·	M-G-M	
SHADOW OF TREASON (BRITISH)	1964	77		1.0		PARAMOUNT	
SHADOW OF ZORRO, THE (ITALIAN)	1962	84			1.5	ALLIED ARTISTS	
SHADOW ON THE LAND (T.V.)	1968	100	5*	2.0		SCREEN GEMS	
SHADOW ON THE WALL	1950	84		2.0	2.0	M-G-M	
SHADOW ON THE WINDOW, THE	1957	73		2.5	2.0	COLUMBIA	
SHADOW OVER ELVERON (T.V.)	1968	100		2.0	2.5	UNIVERSAL	
SHADOWS	1961	87	6			LION INT'L FILMS	
SHADOWS IN THE NIGHT	1944	67		2.0	·	COLUMBIA	
SHADOWS OF OUR FORGOTTEN ANCESTORS (RUSSIAN)	1964	100	6			ARTKINO	
SHADOWS OVER CHINATOWN	1946	64			·	MONOGRAM	
SHADY LADY	1945	94			2.0	UNIVERSAL	
SHAFT	1971	100	3			M-G-M	
SHAFT'S BIG SCORE	1972	105	4			M-G-M	

‡ An asterisk (*) in THE FILM BUFF'S BIBLE column indicates that the film has been rated by the editor and/or staff. All other ratings in this column are based on a consensus of reviews (see NOTES).

			CRITICAL RATINGS				
TITLE (LEADING ACTORS SHOWN WHERE TWO OR MORE FILMS HAVE THE SAME OR SIMILAR TITLE) ("a" TO LEFT OF YEAR INDICATES THAT FILM HAS AN ALTERNATE TITLE)	YEAR RELEASED	RUNNING TIME IN MINUTES	THE FILM BUFF'S BIBLE ‡	STEVEN SCHEUER	LEONARD MALTIN	DISTRIBUTOR	COMMENT
SHAGGY DOG, THE	1959	104	5*			BUENA VISTA	
SHAKE HANDS WITH THE DEVIL	1959	100	6*	3.0	3.0	UNITED ARTISTS	
SHAKE, RATTLE AND ROCK	1956	77		1.5		AMERICAN-INTERNAT'L	
SHAKEDOWN (HOWARD DUFF, PEGGY DOW)	1950	80		2.0	2.5	UNIVERSAL	
SHAKEDOWN, THE (BRITISH - TERENCE MORGAN)	1959	92	3		1.5	UNIVERSAL	
SHAKESPEARE WALLAH (INDIAN)	1965	115	6			CONTINENTAL	ENGLISH LANGUAGE
SHAKIEST GUN IN THE WEST, THE	1968	101		1.5	2.5	UNIVERSAL	
SHALAKO (BRITISH)	1968	113	2			CINERAMA RELEASING	
SHALL WE DANCE	1937	116		4.0	3.5	RKO	
SHAME (SWEDISH)	1968	103	7	4.0		LOPERT	
SHAMELESS OLD LADY, THE (FRENCH)	1965	95	7	4.0		CONTINENTAL	
SHANE	1953	118	6*	4.0	4.0	PARAMOUNT	NOMINATED BEST PICTURE
SHANGHAI	1935	75		2.5	2.5	PARAMOUNT	
SHANGHAI CHEST, THE	1948	56				MONOGRAM	
SHANGHAI COBRA, THE	1945	64			·	MONOGRAM	
SHANGHAI EXPRESS	1932	80	5*	3.5	3.0	PARAMOUNT	NOMINATED BEST PICTURE 1931/32
SHANGHAI GESTURE, THE	1941	106		2.0	2.0	UNITED ARTISTS	
SHANGHAI STORY, THE	1954	90		2.5	2.0	REPUBLIC	
SHANTY TRAMP	1967	72	3			TRANS-INTERNATIONAL	
SHANTYTOWN HONEYMOON	1972	85				LION DOG ENTERPRISES	
SHARAD OF ATLANTIS, THE	1936	100		1.5	1.5	REPUBLIC	RE-EDITED SERIAL
SHARE OUT, THE (BRITISH)	1962	61		2.5	2.5	SCHOENFELD FILM DIST.	
SHARK!	1968	94	1			EXCELSIOR	
SHARK RIVER	1953	80		2.0		UNITED ARTISTS	
SHARKFIGHTERS, THE	1956	73		2.0	1.5	UNITED ARTISTS	
SHE (BRITISH)	1965	105	4		2.5	M-G-M	
SHE AND HE (JAPANESE)	1964	110	6			BRANDON	
SHE COULDN'T SAY NO (EVE ARDEN, ROGER PRYOR)	1940	64		2.0		WARNER BROTHERS	
SHE COULDN'T SAY NO (ROBERT MITCHUM, JEAN SIMMONS)	1954	89		3.0	2.5	RKO	
SHE-CREATURE	1956	77		1.5		AMERICAN-INTERNAT'L	
SHE DEMONS	1958	80		1.5	1.5	ASTOR	
SHE DEVIL	1957	77		1.0	1.0	20th CENTURY FOX	
SHE DONE HIM WRONG	1933	66		3.0	4.0	PARAMOUNT	NOMINATED BEST PICTURE 1932/33
SHE GETS HER MAN	1945	65			1.5	UNIVERSAL	
SHE-GODS OF SHARK REEF	1958	65	2	1.5		AMERICAN-INTERNAT'L	
SHE LOVES ME NOT	1934	83		3.0	3.0	PARAMOUNT	
SHE MARRIED HER BOSS	1935	85		2.5	2.5	COLUMBIA	
SHE PLAYED WITH FIRE (BRITISH)	1958	95		2.5	2.0	COLUMBIA	
SHE WENT TO THE RACES	1945	86		2.0	2.0	M-G-M	
SHE-WOLF, THE (ITALIAN)	a1954	95	4			REPUBLIC	
SHE-WOLF OF LONDON	1946	61		2.0	2.0	UNIVERSAL	
SHE WORE A YELLOW RIBBON	1949	103	6	3.5	3.5	RKO	
SHE WOULDN'T SAY YES	1945	87			2.5	COLUMBIA	
SHEEP HAS FIVE LEGS, THE (FRENCH)	1954	95	6	3.0	3.0	UN. MOTION PIC. ORG.	
SHEEPMAN, THE	1958	85		3.5	3.0	M-G-M	
SHEIK, THE (SILENT)	1921	73				PARAMOUNT	
SHELL SHOCK	1964	84		1.5		PARAMOUNT	
SHENANDOAH	1965	105		2.5	3.0	UNIVERSAL	
SHEPHERD OF THE HILLS	1941	98		2.0	2.5	PARAMOUNT	
SHERIFF, THE (T.V.)	1971	90	5*	2.5		SCREEN GEMS	
SHERIFF OF FRACTURED JAW, THE (BRITISH)	1958	110	5			20th CENTURY FOX	
SHERIFF WAS A LADY, THE (GERMAN)	1964	88		1.0		SCREEN GEMS	
SHERLOCK HOLMES AND THE DEADLY NECKLACE (GERMAN)	1964	84		2.5		SCREEN GEMS	
SHERLOCK HOLMES AND THE SECRET WEAPON	1942	68			·	UNIVERSAL	
SHERLOCK HOLMES AND THE SPIDER WOMAN	1944	62			·	UNIVERSAL	
SHERLOCK HOLMES AND THE VOICE OF TERROR	1942	65			·	UNIVERSAL	
SHERLOCK HOLMES FACES DEATH	1943	68			·	UNIVERSAL	
SHERLOCK HOLMES IN WASHINGTON	1943	71	4*		·	UNIVERSAL	
SHE'S A SOLDIER TOO	1944	67		1.5	2.0	COLUMBIA	
SHE'S A SWEETHEART	1944	69		2.0	1.5	COLUMBIA	
SHE'S BACK ON BROADWAY	1953	95		2.5	2.5	WARNER BROTHERS	
SHE'S WORKING HER WAY THRU COLLEGE	1952	101		2.0	2.5	WARNER BROTHERS	
SHIELD FOR MURDER	1954	80	4	3.0	2.5	UNITED ARTISTS	
SHINBONE ALLEY (CARTOON)	1971	84	4			ALLIED ARTISTS	
SHINE ON HARVEST MOON (ANN SHERIDAN, D. MORGAN)	1944	112		2.5	2.5	WARNER BROTHERS	
SHINING HOUR, THE	1938	80		2.0	2.5	M-G-M	
SHINING VICTORY	1941	80		3.5	3.5	WARNER BROTHERS	
SHIP AHOY	1942	95		2.5	2.5	M-G-M	
SHIP OF CONDEMNED WOMEN (ITALIAN)	1953	90		2.0		PRESIDENT FILMS	
SHIP OF FOOLS	1965	142	7*	4.0	4.0	COLUMBIA	NOMINATED BEST PICTURE
SHIP THAT DIED OF SHAME, THE (BRITISH)	a1955	91		3.0	2.0	CONTINENTAL	
SHIP WAS LOADED, THE (BRITISH)	a1957	82	4		2.0	GEORGE K. ARTHUR	
SHIPMATES FOREVER	1935	109		2.5	2.5	FIRST NATIONAL	
SHIPS WITH WINGS (BRITISH)	1941	102		3.0	3.0	UNITED ARTISTS	
SHIPWRECK ISLAND	1961	93		2.5		COM. UNITED T.V.	
SHOCK	1946	70		1.5	1.5	20th CENTURY FOX	
SHOCK CORRIDOR	1963	101	1	1.5	1.5	ALLIED ARTISTS	
SHOCK TREATMENT	1964	94		1.5	2.0	20th CENTURY FOX	
SHOCK TROOPS (FRENCH)	1967	110	3			UNITED ARTISTS	
SHOCKING MISS PILGRIM, THE	1947	85	3	1.5	2.0	20th CENTURY FOX	
SHOCKPROOF	1949	79	5	3.0	3.0	COLUMBIA	
SHOE SHINE (ITALIAN)	1946	93	7	4.0	4.0	LOPERT	
SHOES OF THE FISHERMAN, THE	1968	162	5	2.0		M-G-M	
SHOOT, THE (GERMAN)	1964	120		2.0		SCREEN GEMS	

‡ An asterisk (*) in THE FILM BUFF'S BIBLE column indicates that the film has been rated by the editor and/or staff. All other ratings in this column are based on a consensus of reviews (see NOTES).

TITLE (LEADING ACTORS SHOWN WHERE TWO OR MORE FILMS HAVE THE SAME OR SIMILAR TITLE)	YEAR RELEASED	RUNNING TIME IN MINUTES	THE FILM BUFF'S BIBLE ‡	STEVEN SCHEUER	LEONARD MALTIN	DISTRIBUTOR	COMMENT
SHOOT FIRST	1953	88	4	3.0	2.5	UNITED ARTISTS	
SHOOT LOUD, LOUDER . . . . I DON'T UNDERSTAND (ITAL)	1966	100	3	2.5		AVCO-EMBASSY	
SHOOT-OUT AT MEDICINE BEND	1957	87	3	2.0		WARNER BROTHERS	
SHOOT THE PIANO PLAYER (FRENCH)	1960	92	3*		3.5	ASTOR	
SHOOTING, THE	1966	82		2.5		WALTER READE	
SHOOTING HIGH	1940	65		1.5	1.5	20th CENTURY FOX	
SHOOTOUT	1971	94	3			UNIVERSAL	
SHOOTOUT AT BIG SAG	1962	64	2			PARALLEL FILM DISTS.	
SHOP AROUND THE CORNER, THE	1940	97		3.0	3.5	M-G-M	
SHOP ON MAIN STREET, THE (CZECH)	1965	128	7*			PROMINENT FILMS	
SHOP SPOILED (BRITISH)	1956	67		1.5		EROS FILMS	
SHOPWORN	1932	72			2.0	COLUMBIA	
SHOPWORN ANGEL, THE	1938	85		2.0	2.5	M-G-M	
SHORT CUT TO HELL	1957	87		2.5	2.5	PARAMOUNT	
SHORT GRASS	1950	82	3	2.0		ALLIED ARTISTS	
SHORTEST DAY, THE (ITALIAN)	1963	89		2.5		MEDALLION	
SHOT IN THE DARK, A (WILLIAM LUNDIGAN, NAN WYNN)	1941	57		1.5		WARNER BROTHERS	
SHOT IN THE DARK, A (PETER SELLERS, ELKE SOMMER)	1964	101	6*	4.0	3.0	UNITED ARTISTS	(BRITISH)
SHOTGUN	1955	81		2.5	2.0	ALLIED ARTISTS	
SHOW BOAT (LAURA LA PLANTE, JOSEPH SCHILDKRAUT)	1929	129				UNIVERSAL	
SHOW BOAT (IRENE DUNNE, ALLAN JONES)	1936	110	6*			UNIVERSAL	
SHOW BOAT (KATHRYN GRAYSON, HOWARD KEEL)	1951	108	5*	3.0	2.5	M-G-M	
SHOW BUSINESS	1944	92			2.5	RKO	
SHOW OF SHOWS	1929	127				WARNER BROTHERS	
SHOW-OFF, THE	1946	83	5			M-G-M	
SHOW THEM NO MERCY	1935	76		3.0		20th CENTURY FOX	
SHOWDOWN (AUDIE MURPHY, KATHLEEN CROWLEY)	1963	79		2.0	2.0	UNIVERSAL	
SHOWDOWN, THE (WILLIAM ELLIOTT, WALTER BRENNAN)	1950	86	4*	3.0		REPUBLIC	
SHOWDOWN AT ABILENE	1956	80		2.0	2.0	UNIVERSAL	
SHOWDOWN AT BOOT HILL	1958	72	4		2.0	20th CENTURY FOX	
SHRIKE, THE	1955	88	5*	3.5	2.5	UNIVERSAL	
SHUT MY BIG MOUTH	1942	71			2.0	COLUMBIA	
SHUTTERED ROOM, THE (BRITISH)	1967	100	2	1.5		WARNER BROTHERS	
SICILIAN CLAN, THE (FRENCH)	1970	121	6			20th CENTURY FOX	
SICILIANS, THE (BRITISH)	1964	90		1.5		BUTCHER'S	
SIDE STREET (FARLEY GRANGER, CATHY O'DONNELL)	1950	83	4	2.5	3.0	M-G-M	
SIDELONG GLANCES OF A PIGEON KICKER, THE	a1971	87	4			PLAZA PICTURES	
SIDEWALKS OF LONDON (BRITISH)	a1938	85		2.5	3.0	PARAMOUNT	
SIEGE AT RED RIVER, THE	1954	81		2.5	2.5	20th CENTURY FOX	
SIEGE OF FORT BISMARK, THE (JAPANESE)	1965	99		2.0		UNIVERSAL	
SIEGE OF SIDNEY STREET, THE (BRITISH)	1960	94	3*	3.0	2.0	SCREEN GEMS	
SIEGE OF SYRACUSE (ITALIAN)	1959	87		1.0	1.5	PARAMOUNT	
SIEGE OF THE SAXONS (BRITISH)	1963	85	2			COLUMBIA	
SIERRA	1950	83		2.0	2.5	UNIVERSAL	
SIERRA BARON	1958	80		2.0	2.0	20th CENTURY FOX	
SIERRA PASSAGE	1951	81			1.5	MONOGRAM	
SIERRA STRANGER	1957	74		1.5	1.5	COLUMBIA	
SIGN OF THE CROSS, THE	1932	124		3.5	3.0	PARAMOUNT	
SIGN OF THE GLADIATOR (ITALIAN)	1958	80	2*	1.5	1.5	AMERICAN-INTERNAT'L	
SIGN OF THE PAGAN	1954	92	4	2.0	2.0	UNIVERSAL	
SIGN OF THE RAM, THE	1948	84		2.5	2.5	COLUMBIA	
SIGN OF ZORRO, THE	1960	91	1			BUENA VISTA	
SIGNED, ARSENE LUPIN (FRENCH)	1959	90		2.0		M-G-M	
SIGNPOST TO MURDER	1965	74	3			M-G-M	
SILENCE, THE (SWEDISH - INGRID THULIN)	1963	95	6		3.5	JANUS FILMS	
SILENCERS, THE	1966	105	3	1.0		COLUMBIA	
SILENT CALL, THE	1961	63		2.5	1.0	20th CENTURY FOX	
SILENT ENEMY, THE (BRITISH)	1958	92	5*	3.0	2.5	UNIVERSAL	
SILENT GUN, THE (T.V.)	1971	75	4*	2.0		PARAMOUNT	
SILENT INVASION, THE (BRITISH)	1961	70		2.0		WARNER BROTHERS	
SILENT NIGHT, LONELY NIGHT (T.V.)	1969	100	6*	2.5		UNIVERSAL	
SILENT PARTNER	1944	55		3.0		REPUBLIC	
SILENT RUNNING	1972	90	5*			UNIVERSAL	
SILENT WORLD, THE (FRENCH, DOCUMENTARY)	1955	82	7	4.0	3.0	COLUMBIA	
SILK STOCKINGS	1957	117	6	3.0	3.0	M-G-M	
SILKEN AFFAIR, THE (BRITISH)	1956	96		2.5	2.5	DIST. CORP. OF AMER.	
SILVER CHALICE, THE	1955	144		2.5	2.0	WARNER BROTHERS	
SILVER CITY	1951	90		2.5	2.0	PARAMOUNT	
SILVER DOLLAR	1932	84		3.0	2.5	FIRST NATIONAL	
SILVER LODE	1954	80	3		2.5	RKO	
SILVER QUEEN	1942	80			2.0	UNITED ARTISTS	
SILVER RIVER	1948	110		2.5	1.5	WARNER BROTHERS	
SILVER WHIP, THE	1953	73		2.0	2.5	20th CENTURY FOX	
SIMBA (BRITISH)	1955	99	6	3.5	3.5	LIPPERT PRODS.	
SIMON AND LAURA (BRITISH)	1955	91		3.5	2.5	UNIVERSAL	
SIMON, KING OF THE WITCHES	1971	89	1			FANFARE	
SIMON OF THE DESERT (MEXICAN)	1965	45	6	3.5		ALTURA FILMS	
SIN OF HAROLD DIDDLEBOCK, THE	a1947	89	5		2.5	UNITED ARTISTS	
SIN OF MADELON CLAUDET	1931	74				M-G-M	
SIN TOWN (CONSTANCE BENNETT, BRODERICK CRAWFORD)	1942	75			2.5	UNIVERSAL	
SINBAD THE SAILOR	1947	117		3.0	3.0	RKO	
SINCE YOU WENT AWAY	1944	172		3.0	3.5	UNITED ARTISTS	NOMINATED BEST PICTURE
SINCERELY YOURS	1955	115		2.0	1.0	WARNER BROTHERS	
SINFUL DAVEY (BRITISH)	1969	95	4			UNITED ARTISTS	

‡ An asterisk (*) in THE FILM BUFF'S BIBLE column indicates that the film has been rated by the editor and/or staff. All other ratings in this column are based on a consensus of reviews (see NOTES).

TITLE (LEADING ACTORS SHOWN WHERE TWO OR MORE FILMS HAVE THE SAME OR SIMILAR TITLE)	YEAR RELEASED	RUNNING TIME IN MINUTES	THE FILM BUFF'S BIBLE ‡	STEVEN SCHEUER	LEONARD MALTIN	DISTRIBUTOR	COMMENT
SING AND SWING (BRITISH)	1964	77	2		2.0	UNIVERSAL	
SING, BABY, SING	1936	87		3.0	3.0	20th CENTURY FOX	
SING, BOY, SING	1958	90		2.0	2.0	20th CENTURY FOX	
SING, NEIGHBOR, SING	1944	70		2.0		REPUBLIC	
SING YOU SINNERS	1938	88	3*	3.5	3.0	PARAMOUNT	
SING YOUR WAY HOME	1945	72			1.5	RKO	
SING YOUR WORRIES AWAY	1942	71		2.5	2.0	RKO	
SINGAPORE	1947	79		2.0	2.0	UNIVERSAL	
SINGAPORE WOMAN	1941	64		2.0	2.0	WARNER BROTHERS	
SINGER NOT THE SONG, THE (BRITISH)	1961	129		2.0	2.5	WARNER BROTHERS	
SINGIN' IN THE RAIN	1952	103	5*	4.0	4.0	M-G-M	
SINGING FOOL	1928	110				WARNER BROTHERS	
SINGING GUNS	1950	91	4	2.0	1.5	REPUBLIC	
SINGING IN THE DARK	1956	84		1.0		BUDSAM DIST. CO.	
SINGING NUN, THE	1966	98	4*	2.0	2.0	M-G-M	
SINISTER MAN, THE (BRITISH)	1961	60		2.0		ANGLO AMALGAMATED	
SINK THE BISMARCK! (BRITISH)	1960	97	5-6*	3.0	3.0	20th CENTURY FOX	
SINNER, THE (ITALIAN - RUTH ROMAN)	a1959	81		1.5	1.0	RKO	
SINNER'S HOLIDAY	a1947	90		1.5	1.5	UNITED ARTISTS	
SINNERS IN THE SUN	1932	70		2.0	2.0	PARAMOUNT	
SINNERS OF PARIS (FRENCH)	1957	81		2.0		ELLIS FILMS	
SINS OF BABYLON (ITALIAN)	1963	80		1.0		AMERICAN-INTERNAT'L	
SINS OF CASANOVA (ITALIAN)	1958	104	6			TIMES FILM CORP.	
SINS OF JEZEBEL	1953	74	2	2.0	1.5	LIPPERT PRODS.	
SINS OF LOLA MONTES, THE (FRENCH)	a1955	110	4	1.5		BRANDON	
SINS OF MAN	1936	77		3.0		20th CENTURY FOX	
SINS OF RACHEL CADE, THE	1961	124		2.5	2.5	WARNER BROTHERS	
SINS OF ROME (ITALIAN)	1954	75		1.5	2.0	RKO	
SINS OF ROSE BERND, THE (GERMAN)	1957	85	6			PRESIDENT FILMS	
SIREN OF ATLANTIS	1948	75		1.0	1.0	UNITED ARTISTS	
SIREN OF BAGDAD	1953	77	3	2.5	2.5	COLUMBIA	
SIROCCO (HUMPHREY BOGART, MARTA TOREN)	1951	98		2.0	2.5	COLUMBIA	
SIS HOPKINS	1941	98		2.5	2.5	REPUBLIC	
SISTER ANGELE'S SECRET (FRENCH)	1956	90		2.0			
SISTER KENNY	1946	116	5-6*	3.5	3.5	RKO	
SISTERS, THE (ERROL FLYNN, BETTE DAVIS)	1938	98	4*	3.0	3.0	WARNER BROTHERS	
SITTING BULL	1954	105		2.5	2.0	UNITED ARTISTS	
SITTING PRETTY (GINGER ROGERS, JACK OAKIE)	1933	85		3.0	2.5	PARAMOUNT	
SITTING PRETTY (CLIFTON WEBB, ROBERT YOUNG)	1948	84	7*	3.5	3.5	PARAMOUNT	
SITTING TARGET (BRITISH)	1972	93	3			M-G-M	
SITUATION HOPELESS - BUT NOT SERIOUS	1965	97	3		2.0	PARAMOUNT	
SIX BLACK HORSES	1962	80		2.0	2.0	UNIVERSAL	
SIX BRIDGES TO CROSS	1955	96	4	3.0	2.5	UNIVERSAL	
SIX DAY BIKE RIDER	1934	69		2.5	2.5	FIRST NATIONAL	
SIX DAYS TO ETERNITY (ISRAELI, DOCUMENTARY)	1968	88	5			PEPPERCORN-WORMSER	
SIX OF A KIND	1934	62	4*	3.5	3.0	PARAMOUNT	
633 SQUADRON (BRITISH)	1964	95	4	3.0	2.5	UNITED ARTISTS	
16 FATHOMS DEEP	1948	82	5			MONOGRAM	
SIXTY GLORIOUS YEARS (BRITISH)	a1938	90		3.5	3.0	RKO	
SKEZAG (DOCUMENTARY)	1971	73	4			CINNAMON PRODS.	
SKI BUM, THE	1971	94	1			AVCO-EMBASSY	
SKI CHAMP, THE (GERMAN)	1962	90		2.0		COMET FILM	
SKI FEVER	1969	98	1			ALLIED ARTISTS	
SKI ON THE WILD SIDE (DOCUMENTARY)	1967	104	6			SIGMA III	
SKI PARTY	1965	90		2.0	2.0	AMERICAN-INTERNAT'L	
SKI TROOP ATTACK	1960	61		2.0		FILMGROUP	
SKIDOO	1968	98	1	1.0		PARAMOUNT	
SKIN GAME (JAMES GARNER, LOU GOSSETT)	1971	102	6*			WARNER BROTHERS	
SKIPPER SURPRISED HIS WIFE, THE	1950	85	3	2.0	1.5	M-G-M	
SKIPPY	1931	88		3.0		PARAMOUNT	NOMINATED BEST PICTURE 1930/31
SKIRTS AHOY!	1952	109		2.5	2.5	M-G-M	
SKULL, THE (BRITISH)	1965	83	2		2.5	PARAMOUNT	
SKULLDUGGERY	1970	105	1			UNIVERSAL	
SKY ABOVE HEAVEN (FRENCH)	1965	105		1.5		PARAMOUNT	
SKY ABOVE, THE MUD BELOW, THE (FR., DOCUMENTARY)	1961	90	6*	4.0	3.0	AVCO-EMBASSY	
SKY COMMANDO	1953	69		2.0	1.5	COLUMBIA	
SKY DRAGON	1949	64				MONOGRAM	
SKY FULL OF MOON	1952	73	3	3.0	2.0	M-G-M	
SKY GIANT	1938	80		3.0		RKO	
SKY MURDER	1940	72		1.5	2.0	M-G-M	
SKYDIVERS, THE	1963	75		1.5		CROWN INTERNATIONAL	
SKYJACKED	1972	101	5-6*			M-G-M	
SKYLARK	1941	94		3.0	3.5	PARAMOUNT	
SKY'S THE LIMIT, THE	1943	89		3.0	3.0	RKO	
SKYWATCH	1960	90		2.5		CONTINENTAL	
SLANDER	1957	81		2.0	2.5	M-G-M	
SLATTERY'S HURRICANE	1949	83	3*	2.5	2.5	20th CENTURY FOX	
SLAUGHTER	1972	92	3			AMERICAN-INTERNAT'L	
SLAUGHTER ON TENTH AVENUE	1957	103	6	3.0	3.0	UNIVERSAL	
SLAUGHTER TRAIL	1951	78	3		2.0	RKO	
SLAUGHTERHOUSE-FIVE	1972	104	5			UNIVERSAL	
SLAVE, THE (FRENCH - DANIEL GELIN)	1953	95		1.5		FILMS AROUND THE WLD	
SLAVE, THE (ITALIAN - STEVE REEVES)	a1962	102	2		1.5	M-G-M	
SLAVE GIRL (YVONNE DE CARLO, GEORGE BRENT)	1947	80		3.0	2.5	UNIVERSAL	

‡ An asterisk (*) in THE FILM BUFF'S BIBLE column indicates that the film has been rated by the editor and/or staff. All other ratings in this column are based on a consensus of reviews (see NOTES).

TITLE (LEADING ACTORS SHOWN WHERE TWO OR MORE FILMS HAVE THE SAME OR SIMILAR TITLE)	YEAR RELEASED	RUNNING TIME IN MINUTES	THE FILM BUFF'S BIBLE ‡	STEVEN SCHEUER	LEONARD MALTIN	DISTRIBUTOR	COMMENT
SLAVE GIRLS OF SHEBA (ITALIAN)	1961	92		1.0		AMERICAN-INTERNAT'L	
SLAVE QUEEN OF BABYLON (ITALIAN)	1962	101		1.5		AMERICAN-INTERNAT'L	
SLAVE SHIP	1937	92		3.0	3.0	20th CENTURY FOX	
SLAVE TRADE IN WORLD TODAY (DOCUMENTARY)	1964	86	3			CONTINENTAL	
SLAVES (STEPHEN BOYD, OSSIE DAVIS)	1969	110	2	1.0		CONTINENTAL	
SLAVES OF BABYLON	1953	82		2.0	2.0	COLUMBIA	
SLAVES OF THE INVISIBLE MONSTER	1950	100		1.0	1.0	REPUBLIC	RE-EDITED SERIAL
SLEEP MY LOVE	1948	97	4*	3.0	3.0	UNITED ARTISTS	
SLEEPERS WEST	1941	74		2.0		20th CENTURY FOX	
SLEEPING BEAUTY (CARTOON)	1959	75	6			BUENA VISTA	
SLEEPING CAR MURDER, THE (FRENCH)	1965	92	5-6*		3.0	SEVEN ARTS	
SLEEPING CAR TO TRIESTE (BRITISH)	1948	94		3.0		EAGLE LION	
SLEEPING CITY, THE	1950	85		2.5	2.5	UNIVERSAL	
SLEEPING TIGER, THE (BRITISH)	1954	89	5	3.5	3.0	ASTOR	
SLEEPYTIME GAL	1942	82		2.5		REPUBLIC	
SLENDER THREAD, THE	1965	98		3.0	2.5	PARAMOUNT	
SLIGHT CASE OF LARCENY, A	1953	71		3.0	2.0	M-G-M	
SLIGHT CASE OF MURDER, A	1938	85	4*		3.5	WARNER BROTHERS	
SLIGHTLY DANGEROUS	1943	94		1.5	2.0	M-G-M	
SLIGHTLY FRENCH	1949	81		3.0	2.5	COLUMBIA	
SLIGHTLY HONORABLE	1940	83		3.5	3.0	UNITED ARTISTS	
SLIGHTLY SCARLET	1956	99	4	3.0	2.5	RKO	
SLIM	1937	80		2.5	2.5	WARNER BROTHERS	
SLIM CARTER	1957	82		3.0	2.0	UNIVERSAL	
SLIME PEOPLE, THE	1962	60		1.0	2.0	MEDALLION	
SLOGAN (FRENCH)	1970	94	3			ROYAL FILMS INT'L	
SMALL BACK ROOM, THE (BRITISH)	a1948	106		3.0	3.0	SNADER PRODS.	
SMALL TOWN DEB	1941	72		2.0		20th CENTURY FOX	
SMALL TOWN GIRL (JANET GAYNOR, ROBERT TAYLOR)	a1936	90		2.5	3.0	M-G-M	
SMALL TOWN GIRL (JANE POWELL, FARLEY GRANGER)	1953	93		2.5	2.0	M-G-M	
SMALL WORLD OF SAMMY LEE, THE (BRITISH)	1963	105	6			SEVEN ARTS	
SMALLEST SHOW ON EARTH, THE (BRITISH)	1957	80	4*	3.0	3.0	TIMES FILM CORP.	
SMART ALECKS	1942	88			-	MONOGRAM	
SMART GIRLS DON'T TALK	1948	81		2.0	2.0	WARNER BROTHERS	
SMART MONEY	1931	90			2.5	WARNER BROTHERS	
SMART WOMAN (CONSTANCE BENNETT, BRIAN AHERNE)	1948	93	5	3.0	3.0	ALLIED ARTISTS	
SMASH-UP - THE STORY OF A WOMAN	1947	103	6	3.0	3.0	UNIVERSAL	
SMASHING THE RACKETS	1938	60		3.0		RKO	
SMASHING TIME (BRITISH)	1967	96	5	3.0		PARAMOUNT	
SMIC, SMAC, SMOC (FRENCH)	1971	90	6			GSF PRODUCTIONS	
SMILES OF A SUMMER NIGHT (SWEDISH)	1956	108	5		3.0	JANUS FILMS	
SMILEY (AUSTRALIAN)	1956	97	4	2.0	2.5	20th CENTURY FOX	
SMILEY GETS A GUN (AUSTRALIAN)	1958	89		2.0	2.0	20th CENTURY FOX	
SMILIN' THROUGH (NORMA SHEARER, FREDRIC MARCH)	1932	97				M-G-M	NOMINATED BEST PICTURE 1932/33
SMILIN' THROUGH (JEANETTE MACDONALD, BRIAN AHERNE)	1941	100			2.5	M-G-M	
SMILING GHOST, THE	1941	71		2.0		WARNER BROTHERS	
SMILING LIEUTENANT, THE	1931	102		2.5		PARAMOUNT	NOMINATED BEST PICTURE 1931/32
SMITH!	1969	102	4			BUENA VISTA	
SMITH OF MINNESOTA	1942	66		2.0		COLUMBIA	
SMOKE SIGNAL	1955	88		2.0	2.5	UNIVERSAL	
SMOKY (FRED MACMURRAY, ANNE BAXTER)	1946	87		3.0	3.0	20th CENTURY FOX	
SMOKY (FESS PARKER, DIANA HYLAND)	1966	103	4*	2.5		20th CENTURY FOX	
SMOOTH AS SILK	1946	65		3.0		UNIVERSAL	
SMUGGLERS, THE (BRITISH - MICHAEL REDGRAVE)	1947	87		2.5		EAGLE LION	
SMUGGLERS, THE (T.V. - SHIRLEY BOOTH)	1968	100		2.0		UNIVERSAL	
SMUGGLER'S COVE	1948	66			- -	MONOGRAM	
SMUGGLER'S GOLD	1951	64		2.0	2.0	COLUMBIA	
SMUGGLER'S ISLAND	1951	75		2.0	2.0	UNIVERSAL	
SNAFU	1945	82		2.5	2.0	COLUMBIA	
SNAKE PIT, THE	1948	108	5*	3.5	3.5	20th CENTURY FOX	NOMINATED BEST PICTURE
SNAKE WOMAN, THE (BRITISH)	1961	68	1			UNITED ARTISTS	
SNIPER, THE	1952	87	3*	3.0	3.0	COLUMBIA	
SNIPER'S RIDGE	1961	61	3	2.5	2.0	20th CENTURY FOX	
SNOOPY COME HOME (CARTOON)	1972	90	5			NATIONAL GENERAL	
SNORKEL, THE (BRITISH)	1958	90	4	3.0	2.5	COLUMBIA	
SNOW CREATURE, THE	1954	70			1.5	UNITED ARTISTS	
SNOW JOB	a1972	90	3			WARNER BROTHERS	
SNOW QUEEN, THE (RUSSIAN, CARTOON)	1958	70	4		2.0	UNIVERSAL	
SNOW WAS BLACK (FRENCH)	1954	104	6			CONTINENTAL	
SNOW WHITE AND THE SEVEN DWARFS (CARTOON)	1937	82				RKO	
SNOW WHITE AND THE THREE STOOGES	1961	107	4*	2.5	1.0	20th CENTURY FOX	
SNOWBALL (BRITISH)	1960	69			2.0	J. ARTHUR RANK	
SNOWBOUND (BRITISH)	1948	85		3.0		UNIVERSAL	
SNOWFIRE	1958	78		2.5		ALLIED ARTISTS	
SNOWS OF KILIMANJARO, THE	1953	117	6	3.0	3.0	20th CENTURY FOX	
SO BIG (BARBARA STANWYCK, GEORGE BRENT)	1932	82		2.5		WARNER BROTHERS	
SO BIG (JANE WYMAN, STERLING HAYDEN)	1953	101	6	3.0	3.0	WARNER BROTHERS	
SO DARK THE NIGHT	1946	71		3.0		COLUMBIA	
SO DEAR TO MY HEART	1948	84	6			RKO	
SO ENDS OUR NIGHT	1941	117		4.0	3.5	UNITED ARTISTS	
SO EVIL MY LOVE	1948	109		2.5	3.0	PARAMOUNT	
SO EVIL, SO YOUNG (BRITISH)	1960	77		2.0		UNITED ARTISTS	
SO GOES MY LOVE	1946	88			2.5	UNIVERSAL	
SO LITTLE TIME (BRITISH)	1952	88	3*			MACDONALD	

‡ An asterisk (*) in THE FILM BUFF'S BIBLE column indicates that the film has been rated by the editor and/or staff. All other ratings in this column are based on a consensus of reviews (see NOTES).

TITLE (LEADING ACTORS SHOWN WHERE TWO OR MORE FILMS HAVE THE SAME OR SIMILAR TITLE)	YEAR RELEASED	RUNNING TIME IN MINUTES	THE FILM BUFF'S BIBLE ‡	CRITICAL RATINGS STEVEN SCHEUER	LEONARD MALTIN	DISTRIBUTOR	COMMENT
SO LONG AT THE FAIR (BRITISH)	1950	85	6	3.0	3.0	EAGLE LION	
SO LOVELY, SO DEADLY	1957	67		1.0		UNITED ARTISTS	
SO PROUDLY WE HAIL!	1943	126		2.5	3.0	PARAMOUNT	
SO RED THE ROSE	1935	82		2.5	2.5	PARAMOUNT	
SO THIS IS LOVE	1953	101	4	2.0	2.0	WARNER BROTHERS	
SO THIS IS NEW YORK	1948	79		3.0	2.0	UNITED ARTISTS	
SO THIS IS PARIS (TONY CURTIS, GLORIA DE HAVEN)	1955	96	4	3.0	2.5	UNIVERSAL	
SO WELL REMEMBERED (BRITISH)	1947	114	4*		3.0	RKO	
SO YOU WON'T TALK	1940	69			2.0	COLUMBIA	
SO YOUNG, SO BAD	1950	91	4	2.5	2.0	UNITED ARTISTS	
SOCRATES	1971	120				NEW YORKER FILMS	
SODOM AND GOMORRAH (ITALIAN)	1961	154		2.5	2.5	20th CENTURY FOX	ENGLISH LANGUAGE
SOFI	1968	92	4			GOLDEN BEAR	
SOFIA	1948	82			2.0	FILM CLASSICS	
SOFT SKIN, THE (FRENCH)	1964	120	5		3.0	CINEMA V	
SOFT SKIN ON BLACK SILK	1964	90	2			AUDUBON	
SOL MADRID	a1968		3	2.0		M-G-M	
SOLDIER, THE (YUGOSLAVIAN)	1965	100	5*			M-G-M	
SOLDIER AND THE LADY	a1937	85		3.0		RKO	
SOLDIER BLUE	1970	112	6			AVCO-EMBASSY	
SOLDIER IN THE RAIN	1963	88	4	3.0	3.0	ALLIED ARTISTS	
SOLDIER OF FORTUNE	1955	96		2.5	3.0	20th CENTURY FOX	
SOLDIERS OF PANCHO VILLA, THE (MEXICAN)	1959	84		2.0			
SOLDIERS THREE	1951	87	4*	2.0	3.0	M-G-M	
SOLE SURVIVOR (T.V.)	1970	100	4*	2.5		CINEMA CENTER 100	
SOLID GOLD CADILLAC, THE	1956	99	6*	3.5	3.0	COLUMBIA	
SOLITARE MAN	1933	65		3.0		M-G-M	
SOLO FOR SPARROW (BRITISH)	1962	58		2.0		SCHOENFELD FILM DIST	
SOLOMON AND SHEBA	1959	139		2.5	3.0	UNITED ARTISTS	
SOMBRA, THE SPIDER WOMAN	1947	100		1.5	2.0	REPUBLIC	RE-EDITED SERIAL
SOMBRERO	1953	103		2.0	1.5	M-G-M	
SOME CAME RUNNING	1958	127	5	2.5	2.5	M-G-M	
SOME GIRLS DO (BRITISH)	1969	91	1			UNITED ARTISTS	
SOME KIND OF A NUT	1969	89	2	1.0		UNITED ARTISTS	
SOME LIKE IT HOT (BOB HOPE, SHIRLEY ROSS)	a1939	64		2.0	2.5	PARAMOUNT	
SOME LIKE IT HOT (TONY CURTIS, JACK LEMMON)	1959	120	8*	4.0	4.0	UNITED ARTISTS	
SOME MAY LIVE (BRITISH)	1967	89			2.0	SHOWCORPORATION	
SOME OF MY BEST FRIENDS ARE . . .	1971	109	4			AMERICAN-INTERNAT'L	
SOMEBODY LOVES ME	1952	97	4	2.0	2.0	PARAMOUNT	
SOMEBODY UP THERE LIKES ME	1956	113	5*	3.5	3.5	M-G-M	
SOMEONE BEHIND THE DOOR	1971	97	3			GSF PRODUCTIONS	
SOMEONE TO REMEMBER	1943	80		3.0		REPUBLIC	
SOMETHING BIG	1971	108	3			NATIONAL GENERAL	
SOMETHING FOR A LONELY MAN (T.V.)	1968	100		3.0		UNIVERSAL	
SOMETHING FOR EVERYONE	a1970	112	6			NATIONAL GENERAL	
SOMETHING FOR THE BIRDS	1952	81	4	2.5	2.0	20th CENTURY FOX	
SOMETHING FOR THE BOYS	1944	85		3.0	2.5	20th CENTURY FOX	
SOMETHING IN THE WIND	1947	89		2.5	2.5	UNIVERSAL	
SOMETHING MONEY CAN'T BUY (BRITISH)	1952	82		2.5		UNIVERSAL	
SOMETHING OF VALUE	1957	113	4*	3.0	3.0	M-G-M	
SOMETHING TO LIVE FOR	1952	89	4	3.0	2.5	PARAMOUNT	
SOMETHING TO SHOUT ABOUT	1943	93		2.5	2.0	COLUMBIA	
SOMETHING WILD	1961	112		2.5	2.5	UNITED ARTISTS	
SOMETIMES A GREAT NOTION	a1971	114	5*			UNIVERSAL	
SOMEWHERE I'LL FIND YOU	1942	108		2.5	2.5	M-G-M	
SOMEWHERE IN THE NIGHT	1946	100		2.5	2.5	20th CENTURY FOX	
SON-DAUGHTER, THE	1932	79		2.5	2.5	M-G-M	
SON OF A GUNFIGHTER (SPANISH)	1965	92			1.5	M-G-M	
SON OF A SAILOR	1933	73		2.5	2.5	FIRST NATIONAL	
SON OF ALI BABA	1952	75		2.0	2.0	UNIVERSAL	
SON OF BELLE STARR	1953	70		2.0	2.0	ALLIED ARTISTS	
SON OF CAPTAIN BLOOD, THE (ITALIAN)	1962	88	3		2.5	PARAMOUNT	
SON OF DEAR CAROLINE, THE (FRENCH)	1955	90		2.0			
SON OF DR JEKYLL, THE	1951	77		2.0	1.5	COLUMBIA	
SON OF DRACULA	1943	78		2.5	2.5	UNIVERSAL	
SON OF FLUBBER	1963	100	4			BUENA VISTA	
SON OF FRANKENSTEIN	1939	95		3.0	3.0	UNIVERSAL	
SON OF FURY	1942	98		3.0	3.0	20th CENTURY FOX	
SON OF HERCULES IN THE LAND OF DARKNESS (ITALIAN)	1963	81		1.0		AVCO-EMBASSY	
SON OF HERCULES IN THE LAND OF FIRE (ITALIAN)	a1963	87		1.0	1.5	AVCO-EMBASSY	
SON OF KONG	1933	70		3.0	2.5	RKO	
SON OF LASSIE	1945	102		2.0	2.5	M-G-M	
SON OF MONTE CRISTO, THE	1940	102	5-6*	3.0	3.0	UNITED ARTISTS	
SON OF PALEFACE	1952	95		3.0	2.5	PARAMOUNT	
SON OF ROBIN HOOD, THE (BRITISH)	1958	77		1.5	2.0	20th CENTURY FOX	
SON OF SAMSON (ITALIAN)	1960	89	1	1.5		MEDALLION	
SON OF SINBAD	1955	88		1.5	1.5	RKO	
SON OF SPARTACUS (ITALIAN)	a1962	102	2		2.0	M-G-M	
SON OF THE GODS	1930	82			2.0	FIRST NATIONAL	
SON OF THE RED CORSAIR (ITALIAN)	1961	97		1.5		TELEWIDE SYSTEMS	
SON OF THE SHEIK (SILENT - RUDOLPH VALENTINO)	1926	74	4*		3.0	UNITED ARTISTS	
SONG AND THE SILENCE, THE	1969	80	4	3.0		CLOVERHOUSE	
SONG FOR MISS JULIE, A	1945	69			1.5	REPUBLIC	
SONG IS BORN, A	1948	113		2.0	2.5	RKO	

‡ An asterisk (*) in THE FILM BUFF'S BIBLE column indicates that the film has been rated by the editor and/or staff. All other ratings in this column are based on a consensus of reviews (see NOTES).

TITLE (LEADING ACTORS SHOWN WHERE TWO OR MORE FILMS HAVE THE SAME OR SIMILAR TITLE)	YEAR RELEASED	RUNNING TIME IN MINUTES	THE FILM BUFF'S BIBLE ‡	STEVEN SCHEUER	LEONARD MALTIN	DISTRIBUTOR	COMMENT
SONG OF BERNADETTE, THE	1943	156	5*	4.0	4.0	20th CENTURY FOX	NOMINATED BEST PICTURE
SONG OF INDIA	1949	77	3		2.0	COLUMBIA	
SONG OF LOVE	1947	119	6	2.5	2.5	M-G-M	
SONG OF MEXICO	1945	59		1.5		REPUBLIC	
SONG OF NORWAY	1970	150	5-6*			CINERAMA RELEASING	
SONG OF RUSSIA	1943	107		3.0	2.5	M-G-M	
SONG OF SCHEHERAZADE	1947	106		2.0	2.0	UNIVERSAL	
SONG OF SISTER MARIA, THE (SPANISH)	1953	81		3.0		CITATION	
SONG OF SONGS	1933	90		2.5	3.0	PARAMOUNT	
SONG OF SURRENDER	1949	93		2.0		PARAMOUNT	
SONG OF THE ISLANDS	1942	75		1.5	2.5	20th CENTURY FOX	
SONG OF THE LAND (DOCUMENTARY)	1953	71	4			UNITED ARTISTS	
SONG OF THE OPEN ROAD	1944	93		2.5	2.5	UNITED ARTISTS	
SONG OF THE SARONG	1945	65			2.0	UNIVERSAL	
SONG OF THE SOUTH (CARTOON)	1946	95	6			RKO	
SONG OF THE THIN MAN	1947	86		2.5	-	M-G-M	
SONG TO REMEMBER, A	1945	113		2.5	2.5	COLUMBIA	
SONG WITHOUT END	1960	141		2.5	2.5	COLUMBIA	
SONS AND LOVERS (BRITISH)	1960	100	6*	4.0	3.0	20th CENTURY FOX	NOMINATED BEST PICTURE
SONS O' GUNS	1936	82		2.5	2.0	WARNER BROTHERS	
SONS OF ADVENTURE	1948	60		2.5		REPUBLIC	
SONS OF KATIE ELDER, THE	1965	122		2.5	3.0	PARAMOUNT	
SONS OF THE DESERT	1933	68			3.0	M-G-M	
SOOKY	1931	85		2.0	2.5	PARAMOUNT	
SORCERESS, THE (FRENCH)	1955	97		3.0	2.5	METZGER & WOOG	
SORORITY GIRL	1957	60		1.5	1.5	AMERICAN-INTERNAT'L	
SORROW AND THE PITY, THE (FRENCH, DOCUMENTARY)	1971	260	4*			CINEMA V	ABOUT THREE HOURS TOO LONG
SORROWFUL JONES	1949	88	4*	2.5	2.5	PARAMOUNT	
SORRY, WRONG NUMBER	1948	89	7*	3.0	3.0	PARAMOUNT	
SOUL OF A MONSTER, THE	1944	61		1.0	1.0	COLUMBIA	
SOUL TO SOUL (DOCUMENTARY)	1971	96	6			CINERAMA RELEASING	
SOULS AT SEA	1937	92		3.0	3.0	PARAMOUNT	
SOUND AND THE FURY, THE	1959	115	5*	3.0	2.5	20th CENTURY FOX	
SOUND BARRIER, THE (BRITISH)	a1952	109	6*	4.0	3.5	UNITED ARTISTS	
SOUND OF ANGER, THE (T.V.)	1968	100		2.0		UNIVERSAL	
SOUND OF FURY, THE	a1951	92		3.0	2.5	UNITED ARTISTS	
SOUND OF MUSIC, THE	1965	171	8			20th CENTURY FOX	BEST PICTURE AWARD
SOUND OF TRUMPETS, THE (ITALIAN)	1961	90	4			JANUS FILMS	
SOUND OFF	1952	83		2.5	2.0	COLUMBIA	
SOUNDER	1972	105				20th CENTURY FOX	
SOUTH OF PAGO PAGO	1940	98		1.5	2.0	UNITED ARTISTS	
SOUTH OF ST LOUIS	1949	88		2.5	2.5	WARNER BROTHERS	
SOUTH OF SUEZ	1940	86		2.0		WARNER BROTHERS	
SOUTH OF TANA RIVER (DANISH)	1964	85		2.0		ASA FILMS	
SOUTH PACIFIC	1958	171	7*	3.5		MAGNA PICTURES	
SOUTH SEA SINNER	1950	88		2.0	2.0	UNIVERSAL	
SOUTH SEA WOMAN	1953	99	4	3.0	2.5	WARNER BROTHERS	
SOUTH SEAS ADVENTURE (DOCUMENTARY)	1958	120	4			STANLEY WARNER	
SOUTHERN COMFORTS	1971	80				BOXOFFICE INTERNAT'L	
SOUTHERN STAR, THE (FRENCH)	1969	104	4			COLUMBIA	ENGLISH VERSION
SOUTHERN YANKEE, A	1948	90	6	3.0	3.0	M-G-M	
SOUTHERNER, THE	1945	91		3.5	4.0	UNITED ARTISTS	
SOUTHSIDE 1-1000	1950	73	3	2.5	2.5	ALLIED ARTISTS	
SOUTHWEST PASSAGE	1954	82		2.5	2.0	UNITED ARTISTS	
SPACE CHILDREN, THE	1958	69	2*	2.0	1.5	PARAMOUNT	
SPACE MASTER X-7	1958	70		2.0	2.0	20th CENTURY FOX	
SPACEFLIGHT IC-1 (BRITISH)	1965	65			2.5	20th CENTURY FOX	
SPACEWAYS (BRITISH)	1953	76	2		1.5	LIPPERT PRODS.	
SPANISH AFFAIR (SPANISH)	1957	93		2.5	2.0	PARAMOUNT	
SPANISH GARDENER, THE (BRITISH)	1956	97	5	3.0	2.0	J. ARTHUR RANK	
SPANISH MAIN, THE	1945	100		2.5	2.5	RKO	
SPARE THE ROD (BRITISH)	1961	93		2.5	2.5	AVCO-EMBASSY	
SPARROWS CAN'T SING (BRITISH)	1963	93	6			JANUS FILMS	
SPARTACUS	1960	190	7*	4.0	3.5	UNIVERSAL	
SPARTACUS AND THE TEN GLADIATORS (ITALIAN)	1964	98		1.0		FOUR STAR	
SPAWN OF THE NORTH	1938	130	4*	3.0	3.0	PARAMOUNT	
SPEAKING OF MURDER (FRENCH)	1957	80		2.0	2.5	UN. MOTION PIC. ORG.	
SPECIAL AGENT	1935	78		3.0	2.5	WARNER BROTHERS	
SPECIAL DELIVERY	1955	86			2.0	COLUMBIA	
SPECTER OF THE ROSE	1946	90		3.0		REPUBLIC	
SPEED CRAZY	1959	75		1.5	1.0	ALLIED ARTISTS	
SPEEDWAY	1968	94	2	1.5		M-G-M	
SPELLBOUND (INGRID BERGMAN, GREGORY PECK)	1945	111		3.0	3.0	UNITED ARTISTS	NOMINATED BEST PICTURE
SPENCER'S MOUNTAIN	1963	119		2.0	2.0	WARNER BROTHERS	
SPIDER, THE (RICHARD CONTE, FAYE MARLOWE)	1945	62		2.0	2.0	20th CENTURY FOX	
SPIDER, THE (ED KEMMER, JUNE KENNY)	1958	72	2	2.0		AMERICAN-INTERNAT'L	
SPIDER AND THE FLY, THE (BRITISH)	1949	73		3.0	2.5	J. ARTHUR RANK	
SPIDER WOMAN STRIKES BACK, THE	1946	59		1.5	1.0	UNIVERSAL	
SPIDER'S WEB (BRITISH)	1960	89		1.5		UNITED ARTISTS	
SPIES A-GO-GO	a1964	85		1.0	2.0	FAIRWAY INTERNAT'L	
SPIN A DARK WEB (BRITISH)	1956	76		1.5	1.5	COLUMBIA	
SPINOUT	1966	93	3	1.0		M-G-M	
SPIRAL ROAD, THE	1962	145	5	3.0	3.0	UNIVERSAL	
SPIRAL STAIRCASE, THE	1946	83	5*	3.5	3.5	RKO	

‡ An asterisk (*) in THE FILM BUFF'S BIBLE column indicates that the film has been rated by the editor and/or staff. All other ratings in this column are based on a consensus of reviews (see NOTES).

TITLE (LEADING ACTORS SHOWN WHERE TWO OR MORE FILMS HAVE THE SAME OR SIMILAR TITLE)	YEAR RELEASED	RUNNING TIME IN MINUTES	THE FILM BUFF'S BIBLE ‡	STEVEN SCHEUER	LEONARD MALTIN	DISTRIBUTOR	COMMENT
SPIRIT IS WILLING, THE	1967	94	4	2.0		PARAMOUNT	
SPIRIT OF CULVER	1939	89		2.5	2.0	UNIVERSAL	
SPIRIT OF ST LOUIS, THE	1957	138	6	2.5	4.0	WARNER BROTHERS	
SPIRIT OF WEST POINT, THE	1947	77			2.5	FILM CLASSICS	
SPIRITISM (MEXICAN)	1965	85		1.0		TRANS-INTERNATIONAL	
SPIRITS OF THE DEAD	1969	117	2			AMERICAN-INTERNAT'L	
SPITFIRE (KATHARINE HEPBURN, ROBERT YOUNG)	1934	88		3.0	3.0	RKO	
SPITFIRE (BRITISH - LESLIE HOWARD, DAVID NIVEN)	a1943	90		3.5	3.0	RKO	
SPLENDOR	1935	77		2.5	2.5	UNITED ARTISTS	
SPLENDOR IN THE GRASS	1961	124	6*	3.5	3.0	WARNER BROTHERS	
SPLIT, THE (JIM BROWN, DIAHANN CARROLL)	1968	90	3	1.5		M-G-M	
SPLIT SECOND	1953	85		3.5	2.5	RKO	
SPOILERS, THE (MARLENE DIETRICH, JOHN WAYNE)	1942	87		3.0	2.5	UNIVERSAL	
SPOILERS, THE (ANNE BAXTER, JEFF CHANDLER)	1956	84		2.5	2.5	UNIVERSAL	
SPOILERS OF THE FOREST	1957	68		2.0	2.0	REPUBLIC	
SPOILERS OF THE NORTH	1947	66		1.0		REPUBLIC	
SPOILERS OF THE PLAINS	1951	68		2.5		REPUBLIC	
SPOILERS OF THE SEA	1957	91		2.0			
SPOOK BUSTERS	1946	68			-	MONOGRAM	
SPOOK CHASERS	1957	62			-	ALLIED ARTISTS	
SPOOKS RUN WILD	1941	69			-	MONOGRAM	
SPORTING CLUB, THE	1971	105	1			AVCO-EMBASSY	
SPREE (DOCUMENTARY)	1967	84	1			AMERICAN-INTERNAT'L	
SPRING IN PARK LANE (BRITISH)	1948	91		3.0	2.5	EAGLE LION	
SPRING MADNESS	1938	80		2.5	2.5	M-G-M	
SPRING PARADE	1940	89			3.0	UNIVERSAL	
SPRING REUNION	1957	79		2.0	2.0	UNITED ARTISTS	
SPRINGFIELD RIFLE	1952	93		2.5	2.5	WARNER BROTHERS	
SPRINGTIME IN THE ROCKIES (BETTY GRABLE)	1942	91		2.0	2.5	20th CENTURY FOX	
SPUTNIK (FRENCH)	a1958	85		2.0	2.0	FILMS AROUND THE WLD.	
SPY CHASERS	1955	61			-	ALLIED ARTISTS	
SPY HUNT	1950	75		2.5	2.5	UNIVERSAL	
SPY I LOVE, THE (FRENCH)	1964	90		2.0		FOUR STAR	
SPY IN BLACK (BRITISH)	a1939	82		3.0		COLUMBIA	
SPY IN THE SKY	1958	74	1	1.0		ALLIED ARTISTS	
SPY IN YOUR EYE (ITALIAN)	1965	88	3		2.0	AMERICAN-INTERNAT'L	
SPY KILLER, THE (T.V.)	1969	90		2.0		ABC FILMS	
SPY SHIP	1942	62		2.0		WARNER BROTHERS	
SPY SMASHER RETURNS	1942	100		2.5	2.5	REPUBLIC	RE-EDITED SERIAL
SPY SQUAD	1962	75		1.5		PARAMOUNT	
SPY WHO CAME IN FROM THE COLD, THE	1965	112	6*	4.0	3.5	PARAMOUNT	
SPY WITH A COLD NOSE, THE (BRITISH)	1966	93		3.0	2.0	AVCO-EMBASSY	
SPY WITH MY FACE, THE	1966	88	4		2.5	M-G-M	
SQUAD CAR	1960	60		1.0	1.0	20th CENTURY FOX	
SQUARE JUNGLE, THE	1956	86		2.0	2.5	UNIVERSAL	
SQUARE OF VIOLENCE (YUGOSLAVIAN)	1961	98	3			M-G-M	ENGLISH LANGUAGE
SQUARE RING, THE (BRITSH)	1953	83			2.0	REPUBLIC	
SQUARE SHOOTER, THE	1951	57		2.5		COLUMBIA	
SQUEAKER, THE (GERMAN)	1965	95		2.0	2.5	UCC FILMS	
STABLEMATES	1938	89		2.5	2.0	M-G-M	
STAGE DOOR	1937	93	6*	3.5	4.0	RKO	NOMINATED BEST PICTURE
STAGE DOOR CANTEEN	1943	132		2.0	2.5	UNITED ARTISTS	
STAGE FRIGHT	1950	111	5	2.5	2.5	WARNER BROTHERS	
STAGE STRUCK (DICK POWELL, JOAN BLONDELL)	1936	86		2.0	2.0	FIRST NATIONAL	
STAGE STRUCK (HENRY FONDA, SUSAN STRASBERG)	1958	95	4*	2.5	2.5	BUENA VISTA	
STAGE TO THUNDER ROCK	1964	82	4			PARAMOUNT	
STAGE TO TUCSON	1951	82	3	2.5		COLUMBIA	
STAGECOACH (JOHN WAYNE, CLAIRE TREVOR)	1939	96	4*	4.0	3.5	UNITED ARTISTS	NOMINATED BEST PICTURE
STAGECOACH (ANN-MARGRET, ALEX CORD)	1966	114		2.5	2.5	20th CENTURY FOX	
STAGECOACH TO DANCERS' ROCK	1962	72	2		2.0	UNIVERSAL	
STAGECOACH TO FURY	1956	114	3		1.5	20th CENTURY FOX	
STAIRCASE	1969	96	4	2.5		20th CENTURY FOX	
STAIRWAY TO HEAVEN (BRITISH)	a1946	104	7*	3.5	3.5	UNIVERSAL	
STAKEOUT	1962	81		1.5		CROWN INTERNATIONAL	
STAKEOUT ON DOPE STREET	1958	83		1.5	1.5	WARNER BROTHERS	
STALAG 17	1953	120	8*	4.0	3.5	PARAMOUNT	
STALKING MOON, THE	1969	109	6			NATIONAL GENERAL	
STALLION ROAD	1947	97	4	2.0		WARNER BROTHERS	
STAMBOUL QUEST	1934	88		2.5	2.5	M-G-M	
STAMPEDE	1949	78		2.5	2.5	ALLIED ARTISTS	
STAND AT APACHE RIVER, THE	1953	77		2.5	2.0	UNIVERSAL	
STAND BY FOR ACTION	1942	109		2.5	2.5	M-G-M	
STAND-IN	1937	91		3.0	2.5	UNITED ARTISTS	
STAND UP AND BE COUNTED	1972	99	4			COLUMBIA	
STAND UP AND CHEER	1934	80			3.0	20th CENTURY FOX	
STAND UP AND FIGHT	1939	105		2.0	2.0	M-G-M	
STANDING ROOM ONLY	1944	83		2.5	2.0	PARAMOUNT	
STANLEY	1972	106	1			CROWN INTERNATIONAL	
STANLEY AND LIVINGSTON	1939	101	6*	3.5	3.5	20th CENTURY FOX	
STAR! (JULIE ANDREWS, DANIEL MASSEY)	1968	175	5	2.0		20th CENTURY FOX	
STAR, THE (BETTE DAVIS, STERLING HAYDEN)	1952	89	6	3.0	3.5	20th CENTURY FOX	
STAR DUST	1940	85		2.5	2.0	20th CENTURY FOX	
STAR IN THE DUST	1956	80		2.0	2.0	UNIVERSAL	
STAR IS BORN, A (JANET GAYNOR, FREDRIC MARCH)	1937	111				UNITED ARTISTS	NOMINATED BEST PICTURE

‡ An asterisk (*) in THE FILM BUFF'S BIBLE column indicates that the film has been rated by the editor and/or staff. All other ratings in this column are based on a consensus of reviews (see NOTES).

TITLE (LEADING ACTORS SHOWN WHERE TWO OR MORE FILMS HAVE THE SAME OR SIMILAR TITLE)	YEAR RELEASED	RUNNING TIME IN MINUTES	THE FILM BUFF'S BIBLE ‡	STEVEN SCHEUER	LEONARD MALTIN	DISTRIBUTOR	COMMENT
STAR IS BORN, A (JUDY GARLAND, JAMES MASON)	1954	154	5*	4.0	3.5	WARNER BROTHERS	
STAR MAKER, THE	1939	94		2.5	2.5	PARAMOUNT	
STAR OF INDIA (BRITISH)	1953	97			2.5	UNITED ARTISTS	
STAR OF MIDNIGHT	1935	90		4.0		RKO	
STAR OF TEXAS, THE	1953	68	4	2.0		ALLIED ARTISTS	
STAR SPANGLED GIRL, THE	1971	93	3			PARAMOUNT	
STAR SPANGLED RHYTHM	1942	99		3.0	3.0	PARAMOUNT	
STAR WITNESS	1931	68		3.0		WARNER BROTHERS	
STARFIGHTERS, THE	1963	84	3	1.5		PARAMOUNT	
STARK FEAR	1962	86	3			ELLIS FILMS	
STARLIFT	1951	103		2.0	2.0	WARNER BROTHERS	
STARS AND STRIPES FOREVER	1952	89	6		2.5	20th CENTURY FOX	
STARS ARE SINGING, THE	1953	99		2.0	2.5	PARAMOUNT	
STARS IN MY CROWN	1950	89	5	2.5	2.5	M-G-M	
STARS LOOK DOWN (BRITISH)	1939	110		4.0	4.0	M-G-M	
STARS OVER BROADWAY	1935	89		3.0		WARNER BROTHERS	
START CHEERING	1938	78		2.5	3.0	COLUMBIA	
START THE REVOLUTION WITHOUT ME	1970	98	4			WARNER BROTHERS	
STATE DEPARTMENT FILE - 649	1948	87	3		2.0	FOUR CONTINENTS	
STATE FAIR (WILL ROGERS, JANET GAYNOR)	1933	80				20th CENTURY FOX	NOMINATED BEST PICTURE 1932/33
STATE FAIR (JEANNE CRAIN, DANA ANDREWS)	a1945	100	4*	3.0	3.0	20th CENTURY FOX	
STATE FAIR (PAT BOONE, BOBBY DARIN)	1962	118	3	2.0	1.0	20th CENTURY FOX	
STATE OF THE UNION	1948	124	7	3.0	3.5	M-G-M	
STATE PENITENTIARY	1950	66		1.5	2.0	COLUMBIA	
STATE SECRET (BRITISH)	a1950	97	4*	4.0	3.0	COLUMBIA	
STATE'S ATTORNEY	1932	73		2.5	2.5	RKO	
STATION SIX - SAHARA (BRITISH)	1963	97	3	3.0	1.5	ALLIED ARTISTS	
STATION WEST	1948	92	5	3.0	3.0	RKO	
STATUE, THE	1971	92	1			CINERAMA RELEASING	
STAY AWAY JOE	1968	102	1	1.0		M-G-M	
STEAGLE, THE	1971	90	3			AVCO-EMBASSY	
STEAMBOAT 'ROUND THE BEND	1935	96			2.5	20th CENTURY FOX	
STEEL AGAINST THE SKY	1941	68		2.0	2.0	WARNER BROTHERS	
STEEL BAYONET, THE (BRITISH)	1957	85		2.0	2.0	UNITED ARTISTS	
STEEL CAGE, THE	1954	80		1.5	2.0	UNITED ARTISTS	
STEEL CLAW, THE	1961	96	3	2.5	2.5	WARNER BROTHERS	
STEEL FIST, THE	1952	73		2.0	1.5	MONOGRAM	
STEEL HELMET, THE	1951	84	5	3.5	1.5	LIPPERT PRODS.	
STEEL JUNGLE, THE	1956	86		2.0	1.5	WARNER BROTHERS	
STEEL KEY, THE (BRITISH)	1953	69		3.0	2.5	EROS FILMS	
STEEL LADY, THE	1953	84	3	2.5	2.5	UNITED ARTISTS	
STEEL TOWN	1952	85		2.0	2.0	UNIVERSAL	
STEEL TRAP, THE	1952	85		3.5	2.5	20th CENTURY FOX	
STEFANIA (GREEK)	a1967	92	1			CHANCELLOR FILMS	
STELLA (ANN SHERIDAN, VICTOR MATURE)	1950	83		2.5	2.5	20th CENTURY FOX	
STELLA DALLAS (BARBARA STANWYCK, JOHN BOLES)	1937	111		2.5	3.0	UNITED ARTISTS	
STEP BY STEP	1946	62		2.0	2.0	RKO	
STEP DOWN TO TERROR	1959	75		2.0	2.0	UNIVERSAL	
STEP LIVELY	1944	88		3.0	3.0	RKO	
STEP OUT OF LINE, A (T.V.)	1971	100		3.0		CINEMA CENTER 100	
STEPMOTHER, THE	1972	94	1			CROWN INTERNATIONAL	
STEPPIN' IN SOCIETY	1945	72		2.0	1.5	REPUBLIC	
STERILE CUCKOO, THE	a1969	107	6-7*			PARAMOUNT	
STEWARDESSES, THE	1969	93	1			SHERPIX	
STILETTO	1969	100	2			AVCO-EMBASSY	
STOLEN FACE (BRITISH)	1952	71	3	3.0		LIPPERT PRODS.	
STOLEN HEAVEN	1938	88		3.0	1.5	PARAMOUNT	
STOLEN HOLIDAY	1937	80		2.0		WARNER BROTHERS	
STOLEN HOURS	1963	100		1.5	2.5	UNITED ARTISTS	
STOLEN KISSES (FRENCH)	1968	90	6			LOPERT	
STOLEN LIFE, A	1946	107		2.5	2.5	WARNER BROTHERS	
STOOGE, THE	1953	100		2.0	2.5	PARAMOUNT	
STOP! LOOK! AND LAUGH!	1960	78		2.0	2.5	COLUMBIA	
STOP ME BEFORE I KILL (BRITISH)	1961	93		2.5	2.0	COLUMBIA	
STOP THE WORLD - I WANT TO GET OFF (BRITISH)	1966	98	4	2.5		WARNER BROTHERS	
STOP TRAIN 349 (GERMAN)	1963	95		2.0	2.0	ALLIED ARTISTS	
STOP, YOU'RE KILLING ME	1953	86		2.0	2.0	WARNER BROTHERS	
STOPOVER TOKYO	1957	100		2.0	2.5	20th CENTURY FOX	
STORK CLUB, THE	1945	98		2.5	2.5	PARAMOUNT	
STORK TALK (BRITISH)	1962	85			2.0	PARADE	
STORM, THE	1938	85			2.5	UNIVERSAL	
STORM AT DAYBREAK	1933	80		2.0	2.5	M-G-M	
STORM CENTER	1956	85	3*	3.0	1.5	COLUMBIA	
STORM FEAR	1956	88	3	2.5	2.0	UNITED ARTISTS	
STORM IN A TEACUP (BRITISH)	1937	103		3.0	3.0	UNITED ARTISTS	
STORM OVER LISBON	1944	86		2.0	2.0	REPUBLIC	
STORM OVER THE NILE (BRITISH)	1956	113		2.5	2.5	COLUMBIA	
STORM OVER TIBET	1952	87	4	2.0		COLUMBIA	
STORM RIDER, THE	1957	70			1.5	20th CENTURY FOX	
STORM WARNING	1951	93	5	2.5	2.5	WARNER BROTHERS	
STORMY, THE THOROUGHBRED	1954	45	4*			BUENA VISTA	
STORMY WEATHER	1943	77		3.0	3.0	20th CENTURY FOX	
STORY OF A THREE-DAY PASS, THE (FRENCH)	1967	90	6	3.5		SIGMA III	
STORY OF A WOMAN	1969	90	2	2.0		UNIVERSAL	

‡ An asterisk (*) in THE FILM BUFF'S BIBLE column indicates that the film has been rated by the editor and/or staff. All other ratings in this column are based on a consensus of reviews (see NOTES).

TITLE (LEADING ACTORS SHOWN WHERE TWO OR MORE FILMS HAVE THE SAME OR SIMILAR TITLE)	YEAR RELEASED	RUNNING TIME IN MINUTES	THE FILM BUFF'S BIBLE ‡	STEVEN SCHEUER	LEONARD MALTIN	DISTRIBUTOR	COMMENT
STORY OF ALEXANDER GRAHAM BELL, THE	1939	97	5*	3.5	3.0	20th CENTURY FOX	
STORY OF DAVID, A (BRITISH)	1960	90		2.0		AMERICAN-INTERNAT'L	
STORY OF DR EHRLICH'S MAGIC BULLET, THE	a1940	103		4.0	4.0	WARNER BROTHERS	
STORY OF DR WASSELL, THE	1944	140		2.0	2.5	PARAMOUNT	
STORY OF ESTHER COSTELLO, THE (BRITISH)	1957	104		2.0	2.5	COLUMBIA	
STORY OF G. I. JOE, THE	a1945	109	3*	3.5	3.5	UNITED ARTISTS	
STORY OF LOUIS PASTEUR	1936	87		4.0	3.5	WARNER BROTHERS	NOMINATED BEST PICTURE
STORY OF MANKIND, THE	1957	100		1.5	2.0	WARNER BROTHERS	
STORY OF MOLLY X, THE	1949	82		2.0	2.5	UNIVERSAL	
STORY OF ROBIN HOOD, THE (BRITISH)	a1952	84	6			RKO	
STORY OF RUTH, THE	1960	132		2.5	2.5	20th CENTURY FOX	
STORY OF SEABISCUIT, THE	1949	93		2.5	2.5	WARNER BROTHERS	
STORY OF THE COUNT OF MONTE CRISTO, THE (FRENCH)	a1962	132	3		2.5	WARNER BROTHERS	
STORY OF THREE LOVES, THE	1953	122	6	3.0	3.0	M-G-M	
STORY OF VERNON AND IRENE CASTLE, THE	1939	93	3*	3.0	3.0	RKO	
STORY OF VICKIE, THE (GERMAN)	a1958	108	2*			BUENA VISTA	
STORY OF WILL ROGERS, THE	1952	109		2.5	3.0	WARNER BROTHERS	
STORY ON PAGE ONE, THE	1960	123	6	3.0	3.0	20th CENTURY FOX	
STOWAWAY (SHIRLEY TEMPLE, ROBERT YOUNG)	1936	86		3.0	2.5	20th CENTURY FOX	
STOWAWAY GIRL (BRITISH)	1957	87		2.0	2.5	PARAMOUNT	
STOWAWAY IN THE SKY (FRENCH)	1960	82	6			LOPERT	
STRAIT-JACKET	1964	89	4	2.5	2.5	COLUMBIA	
STRANDED	1935	76		2.5	2.0	WARNER BROTHERS	
STRANGE ADVENTURE, A	1956	70		2.0	1.5	REPUBLIC	
STRANGE AFFAIR, THE (BRITISH)	1968	106	3	1.0		PARAMOUNT	
STRANGE AFFAIR OF UNCLE HARRY, THE	a1945	80		3.0	3.0	UNIVERSAL	
STRANGE AFFECTION (BRITISH)	a1957	84		2.5	2.0	JOSEPH BRENNER	
STRANGE ALIBI (ARTHUR KENNEDY, JOAN PERRY)	1941	63		2.0		WARNER BROTHERS	
STRANGE ALIBI (SIGNE HASSO, JOHN SHEPPARD)	a1946	65		2.0	2.0	20th CENTURY FOX	
STRANGE AWAKENING (BRITISH)	1958	69		1.0	1.5	ANGLO AMALGAMATED	
STRANGE BARGAIN	1949	68		2.0	2.0	RKO	
STRANGE BEDFELLOWS	1965	98		2.5	2.5	UNIVERSAL	
STRANGE CARGO	1940	105		3.0	3.0	M-G-M	
STRANGE CONFESSION	a1944	95		2.5	2.5	UNIVERSAL	
STRANGE CONQUEST	1946	64		2.0	2.0	UNIVERSAL	
STRANGE COUNTESS, THE (GERMAN)	1961	96		1.5	2.0	CASINO FILMS	
STRANGE DEATH OF ADOLF HITLER, THE	1943	72		2.0	2.0	UNIVERSAL	
STRANGE DOOR, THE	1951	81		1.5	1.5	UNIVERSAL	
STRANGE FASCINATION	1952	80	2	1.5	1.0	COLUMBIA	
STRANGE HOLIDAY	1946	54		2.0	2.0	PRODUCERS RELEASING	
STRANGE INTERLUDE	1932	110	3*	3.0	3.0	M-G-M	
STRANGE INTRUDER	1956	82			2.0	ALLIED ARTISTS	
STRANGE INTRUSION (GERMAN)	a1953	80		1.5		TELEWIDE SYSTEMS	
STRANGE JOURNEY	1946	65			1.5	20th CENTURY FOX	
STRANGE LADY IN TOWN	1955	112		2.5	2.5	WARNER BROTHERS	
STRANGE LOVE OF MARTHA IVERS	1946	117		3.5	3.0	PARAMOUNT	
STRANGE MR GREGORY, THE	1946	63			2.0	MONOGRAM	
STRANGE ONE, THE (BEN GAZZARA, GEORGE PEPPARD)	a1957	100	3*	3.5	3.0	COLUMBIA	
STRANGE ONES, THE (FRENCH - NICOLE STEPHANE)	a1950	95	5			MAYER-KINGSLEY	
STRANGE TRIANGLE	a1946	65		2.0	2.0	20th CENTURY FOX	
STRANGE VENGEANCE OF ROSALIE, THE	1972	107	1			20th CENTURY FOX	
STRANGE WOMAN, THE	1946	100	4	2.0	2.0	UNITED ARTISTS	
STRANGE WORLD	1952	85	2	2.0		UNITED ARTISTS	
STRANGER, THE (ORSON WELLES, EDWARD G. ROBINSON)	1946	95		3.5	3.0	RKO	
STRANGER, THE (ITALIAN - MARCELLO MASTROIANNI)	1967	104	5			PARAMOUNT	FRENCH LANGUAGE
STRANGER AT MY DOOR (MACDONALD CAREY, P. MEDINA)	1956	85	4	3.0	2.5	REPUBLIC	
STRANGER FROM HONG KONG (FRENCH)	1964	85		1.0		AMERICAN-INTERNAT'L	
STRANGER IN BETWEEN, THE (BRITISH)	a1952	84	6	3.0	3.0	UNIVERSAL	
STRANGER IN HOLLYWOOD	1971	96				RODA PRODS., INC.	
STRANGER IN MY ARMS	1959	88	4	2.0	2.5	UNIVERSAL	
STRANGER IN TOWN (BRITISH - ALEX NICOL)	1957	74		2.0		ASTOR	
STRANGER IN TOWN, A (FRANK MORGAN, R. CARLSON)	1943	67		2.5		M-G-M	
STRANGER IN TOWN, A (ITALIAN - TONY ANTHONY)	1966	86	2	1.5		M-G-M	
STRANGER KNOCKS, A (DANISH)	1960	81	5	3.5		TRANS-LUX DIST.	
STRANGER ON HORSEBACK	1955	66		3.0	2.0	UNITED ARTISTS	
STRANGER ON THE PROWL (ITALIAN)	1952	73		2.5	2.5	UNITED ARTISTS	
STRANGER ON THE RUN (T.V.)	1967	100		2.5	2.5	UNIVERSAL	
STRANGER ON THE THIRD FLOOR	1940	64		3.0	3.0	RKO	
STRANGER RETURNS, THE (ITALIAN)	1967	90	2	1.5		M-G-M	
STRANGER WORE A GUN, THE	1953	83	2	2.0	2.0	COLUMBIA	
STRANGERS, THE (ITALIAN)	1954	97		2.5	1.5	FINE ARTS	
STRANGER'S HAND, THE (BRITISH)	1954	85	4*	3.5	3.0	DIST. CORP. OF AMER.	
STRANGERS IN AFRICA	1971	95				MANSON	
STRANGERS IN LOVE	1932	76		2.0	2.0	PARAMOUNT	
STRANGERS IN THE CITY	1962	83		2.5		AVCO-EMBASSY	
STRANGERS IN THE NIGHT	1944	56		3.0		REPUBLIC	
STRANGERS MAY KISS	1931	85		2.0	2.0	M-G-M	
STRANGERS' MEETING (BRITISH)	1957	64		2.0		J. ARTHUR RANK	
STRANGERS ON A TRAIN	1951	101	6*	3.5	4.0	WARNER BROTHERS	
STRANGER'S RETURN, THE	1933	89		3.0		M-G-M	
STRANGERS WHEN WE MEET	1960	117	4	2.5	2.5	COLUMBIA	
STRANGLEHOLD (BRITISH)	1962	73		2.5		J. ARTHUR RANK	
STRANGLER, THE	1964	89	3	2.5	3.0	ALLIED ARTISTS	
STRANGLER OF BLACKMOOR CASTLE (GERMAN)	1960	91		1.5		TELEWIDE SYSTEMS	

‡ An asterisk (*) in THE FILM BUFF'S BIBLE column indicates that the film has been rated by the editor and/or staff. All other ratings in this column are based on a consensus of reviews (see NOTES).

TITLE (LEADING ACTORS SHOWN WHERE TWO OR MORE FILMS HAVE THE SAME OR SIMILAR TITLE)	YEAR RELEASED	RUNNING TIME IN MINUTES	THE FILM BUFFS BIBLE ‡	STEVEN SCHEUER	LEONARD MALTIN	DISTRIBUTOR	COMMENT
STRANGLERS OF BOMBAY, THE (BRITISH)	1959	80	3	3.0	2.5	COLUMBIA	
STRANGLER'S WEB (BRITISH)	1960	61		2.0		AVCO-EMBASSY	
STRATEGIC AIR COMMAND	1955	114		2.5	2.5	PARAMOUNT	
STRATEGY OF TERROR	1969	90	2			UNIVERSAL	
STRATFORD ADVENTURE, THE (CANADIAN, DOCUMENTARY)	1954	40	5			CONTINENTAL	
STRATTON STORY, THE	1949	106	3*	3.0	3.5	M-G-M	
STRAW DOGS (BRITISH)	1971	113	6*			CINERAMA RELEASING	
STRAWBERRY BLONDE, THE	1941	97	4*	3.0	3.0	WARNER BROTHERS	
STRAWBERRY STATEMENT, THE	1970	103	5			M-G-M	
STRAY DOG (JAPANESE)	1949	122	4			TOHO	
STREET BANDITS	1951	54	1			REPUBLIC	
STREET OF CHANCE (WILLIAM POWELL, KAY FRANCIS)	1930	75		3.0		PARAMOUNT	
STREET OF CHANCE (BURGESS MEREDITH, CLAIRE TREVOR)	1942	74		3.0	2.5	PARAMOUNT	
STREET OF DARKNESS	1958	60		1.0		REPUBLIC	
STREET OF MEMORIES	1940	70		1.5		20th CENTURY FOX	
STREET OF SHAME (JAPANESE)	1956	96	4			HARRISON PICTURES	
STREET SCENE	1931	80		3.5	3.5	UNITED ARTISTS	
STREET WITH NO NAME, THE	1948	91	5*	3.5	3.0	20th CENTURY FOX	
STREETCAR NAMED DESIRE, A	1951	125	8*	4.0	4.0	WARNER BROTHERS	NOMINATED BEST PICTURE
STREETS OF LAREDO	1949	92	4	3.0	2.5	PARAMOUNT	
STREETS OF SAN FRANCISCO	1949	60		2.0		REPUBLIC	
STRICTLY DISHONORABLE	1951	86	4	2.0	2.0	M-G-M	
STRIKE IT RICH	1948	81		2.0		ALLIED ARTISTS	
STRIKE ME DEADLY	1963	81		1.5		MEDALLION	
STRIKE ME PINK	1936	104		3.5	3.0	UNITED ARTISTS	
STRIKE UP THE BAND	1940	120		2.5	2.5	M-G-M	
STRIP, THE	1951	85		2.5	2.0	M-G-M	
STRIP TEASE MURDER (BRITISH)	1963	66		1.5		PARAMOUNT	
STRIPPER, THE	1963	95	5	2.5		20th CENTURY FOX	
STROMBOLI (ITALIAN)	1950	81	2		1.5	RKO	
STRONGHOLD	1952	82	2		1.5	LIPPERT PRODS.	
STRONGROOM (BRITISH)	1962	80	3			BRITISH-LION	
STUDENT NURSES, THE	1970	85	1			NEW WORLD	
STUDENT PRINCE, THE (ANN BLYTH, EDMUND PURDOM)	1954	107	5*	2.0	2.0	M-G-M	
STUDS LONIGAN	1960	95	3			UNITED ARTISTS	
STUDY IN TERROR, A (BRITISH)	1965	95	3		-	COLUMBIA	
SUBJECT WAS ROSES, THE	1968	107	6*			M-G-M	
SUBMARINE COMMAND	1951	87		2.5	2.5	PARAMOUNT	
SUBMARINE D-1	1937	54	3*	3.0		FIRST NATIONAL	
SUBMARINE PATROL	1938	95		3.5		20th CENTURY FOX	
SUBMARINE RAIDER	1942	64		2.5		COLUMBIA	
SUBMARINE SEAHAWK	1959	83	3	1.5		AMERICAN-INTERNAT'L	
SUBMARINE X-1 (BRITISH)	1968	89	3			UNITED ARTISTS	
SUBTERFUGE (BRITISH)	1969	96	3			COM. UNITED T.V.	
SUBTERRANEANS, THE	1960	89		1.0	2.5	M-G-M	
SUBURBAN WIVES (BRITISH)	1972	87	1			SCOTIA INTERNATIONAL	
SUBWAY IN THE SKY (BRITISH)	1959	85		2.0	1.5	UNITED ARTISTS	
SUCCESS, THE (ITALIAN)	a1963	103	6	3.5	3.0	AVCO-EMBASSY	
SUCCESSFUL CALAMITY	1932	72		3.0		WARNER BROTHERS	
SUCCUBUS (GERMAN)	1968	83	1			AMERICAN-INTERNAT'L	
SUCH GOOD FRIENDS	1971	100	3			PARAMOUNT	
SUCKER, THE (FRENCH)	1965	112	6			ROYAL FILMS INT'L	
SUDAN	1945	76		2.0	2.0	UNIVERSAL	
SUDDEN DANGER	1955	85		3.0	1.5	ALLIED ARTISTS	
SUDDEN FEAR	1952	110	6	3.0	3.5	RKO	
SUDDEN TERROR	1971	95				NATIONAL GENERAL	
SUDDENLY	1954	77	6	3.5	3.5	UNITED ARTISTS	
SUDDENLY IT'S SPRING	1947	87	3	1.5	2.0	PARAMOUNT	
SUDDENLY, LAST SUMMER	1959	114	4*	3.0	3.5	COLUMBIA	
SUEZ	1938	104		3.0	3.0	20th CENTURY FOX	
SUGARFOOT	a1951	80	2	2.0	2.5	WARNER BROTHERS	
SUICIDE BATTALION	1958	79		1.5	1.0	AMERICAN-INTERNAT'L	
SUICIDE MISSION (BRITISH)	1954	69		1.5	2.0	COLUMBIA	
SUITOR, THE (FRENCH)	1963	83	6			ATLANTIC PICTURES	
SULEIMAN THE CONQUERER (ITALIAN)	1962	99		1.5		TELEWIDE SYSTEMS	
SULLIVANS, THE	a1944	111		4.0	3.0	20th CENTURY FOX	
SULLIVAN'S EMPIRE	1967	85	3		2.5	UNIVERSAL	
SULLIVAN'S TRAVELS	1941	91	6*	3.5	3.5	PARAMOUNT	
SUMMER AND SMOKE	1961	118	6*	3.5	3.5	PARAMOUNT	
SUMMER HOLIDAY (GLORIA DE HAVEN, MICKEY ROONEY)	1948	92		2.5	2.5	M-G-M	
SUMMER HOLIDAY (BR. - LAURI PETERS, CLIFF RICHARD)	1963	100	4	3.0		AMERICAN-INTERNAT'L	
SUMMER LOVE	1958	85		2.0	2.0	UNIVERSAL	
SUMMER MAGIC	1963	109	4			BUENA VISTA	
SUMMER OF '42	1971	102	6*			WARNER BROTHERS	
SUMMER PLACE, A	1959	130	5*	1.5	3.0	WARNER BROTHERS	
SUMMER STOCK	1950	109		2.5	3.0	M-G-M	
SUMMER STORM	1944	106		3.0	3.0	UNITED ARTISTS	
SUMMER TO REMEMBER, A (RUSSIAN)	1960	80	7			KINGSLEY INTERNAT'L	
SUMMERSKIN (ARGENTINIAN)	1961	100	4			ANGEL PRODUCTIONS	
SUMMERTIME	1955	99	7	3.5	3.5	UNITED ARTISTS	
SUMMERTREE	1971	88	4			COLUMBIA	
SUN ALSO RISES, THE	1957	129		2.5	3.0	20th CENTURY FOX	
SUN COMES UP, THE	1949	93		2.0	2.0	M-G-M	
SUN NEVER SETS, THE	1939	98			2.5	PARAMOUNT	

‡ An asterisk (*) in THE FILM BUFF'S BIBLE column indicates that the film has been rated by the editor and/or staff. All other ratings in this column are based on a consensus of reviews (see NOTES).

TITLE (LEADING ACTORS SHOWN WHERE TWO OR MORE FILMS HAVE THE SAME OR SIMILAR TITLE)	YEAR RELEASED	RUNNING TIME IN MINUTES	THE FILM BUFF'S BIBLE ‡	STEVEN SCHEUER	LEONARD MALTIN	DISTRIBUTOR	COMMENT
SUN SETS AT DAWN	1951	71		2.5		UNITED ARTISTS	
SUN SHINES BRIGHT, THE	1953	92		3.5	2.5	REPUBLIC	
SUN VALLEY SERANADE	1941	86		3.0	3.0	20th CENTURY FOX	
SUNBONNET SUE	1945	89			2.0	MONOGRAM	
SUNDAY, BLOODY SUNDAY (BRITISH)	1971	110	3*			UNITED ARTISTS	
SUNDAY DINNER FOR A SOLDIER	1944	86	3*		3.0	20th CENTURY FOX	
SUNDAY ENCOUNTER (FRENCH)	1959	90		2.0			
SUNDAY IN NEW YORK	1964	105	6*	3.0	3.0	M-G-M	
SUNDAY PUNCH	1942	75		1.5		M-G-M	
SUNDAYS AND CYBELE (FRENCH)	1962	110	7		3.5	COLUMBIA	
SUNDERIN (GERMAN)	a1951	83	4			CELLINI FILMS	
SUNDOWN	1941	90		2.5	2.5	UNITED ARTISTS	
SUNDOWNERS, THE (ROBERT PRESTON, CATHY DOWNS)	1950	83		3.5	2.5	EAGLE LION	
SUNDOWNERS, THE (ROBERT MITCHUM, DEBORAH KERR)	1960	133	6*	4.0	4.0	WARNER BROTHERS	NOMINATED BEST PICTURE
SUNFLOWER (ITALIAN)	1970	105	4			AVCO-EMBASSY	
SUNNY (MARILYN MILLER, LAWRENCE GRAY)	1930	81		2.0		FIRST NATIONAL	
SUNNY (ANNA NEAGLE, RAY BOLGER)	1941	98			2.5	RKO	
SUNNY SIDE OF THE STREET	1951	71		2.0	1.5	COLUMBIA	
SUNRISE AT CAMPOBELLO	1960	143	7	4.0	3.0	WARNER BROTHERS	
SUNSCORCHED (SPANISH)	1964	78		1.5		FEATURE FILM CORP.	ENGLISH LANGUAGE
SUNSET BOULEVARD	1950	110	8*	4.0	4.0	PARAMOUNT	NOMINATED BEST PICTURE
SUNSHINE PATRIOT, THE (T.V.)	1968	100		3.5		UNIVERSAL	
SUPER FLY	1972	97	4			WARNER BROTHERS	
SUPER SLEUTH	1937	70		3.0		RKO	
SUPERNATURAL	1933	60		2.0	2.5	PARAMOUNT	
SUPPORT YOUR LOCAL GUNFIGHTER	1971	92	3			UNITED ARTISTS	
SUPPORT YOUR LOCAL SHERIFF	1969	92	6			UNITED ARTISTS	
SUPPOSE THEY GAVE A WAR AND NOBODY CAME	1970	113	4			CINERAMA RELEASING	
SURF PARTY	1964	68	1	1.0		20th CENTURY FOX	
SURFARI (DOCUMENTARY)	1967	90	2			DON BROWN	
SURGEON'S KNIFE, THE (BRITISH)	1957	75		2.0	2.0	DIST. CORP. OF AMER.	
SURPRISE PACKAGE	1960	100		2.5	2.5	COLUMBIA	
SURRENDER	1950	90		2.0	2.5	REPUBLIC	
SURRENDER - HELL!	1959	85		1.5	2.0	ALLIED ARTISTS	
SUSAN AND GOD	1940	115		2.5	2.5	M-G-M	
SUSAN SLADE	1961	116		2.0	2.5	WARNER BROTHERS	
SUSAN SLEPT HERE	1954	98	4*	3.0	2.5	RKO	
SUSANNAH OF THE MOUNTIES	1939	78		2.0	2.5	20th CENTURY FOX	
SUSPECT, THE (CHARLES LAUGHTON)	1945	85		3.5	3.5	UNIVERSAL	
SUSPENDED ALIBI (BRITISH)	1956	64		1.0	1.5	J. ARTHUR RANK	
SUSPENSE	1946	101		3.0	2.0	MONOGRAM	
SUSPICION	1941	99	5*	3.5	3.5	RKO	NOMINATED BEST PICTURE
SUTTER'S GOLD	1936	94			3.0	UNIVERSAL	
SUZY	1936	99		2.0	2.0	M-G-M	
SVENGALI (JOHN BARRYMORE, MARIAN MARSH)	1931	76		3.5	3.0	WARNER BROTHERS	
SVENGALI (BRIT. - HILDEGARDE NEFF, DONALD WOLFIT)	1955	82	4	2.0	2.5	M-G-M	
SWAMP DIAMONDS	a1955	73		1.5	1.5	WOOLNER BROTHERS	
SWAMP FIRE	1946	69		1.5	2.0	PARAMOUNT	
SWAMP GIRL	1971	78				JACK VAUGHN PRODS.	
SWAMP OF THE LOST MONSTERS, THE (MEXICAN)	1965	80		1.0		TRANS-INTERNATIONAL	
SWAMP WATER	1941	90		2.5	2.5	20th CENTURY FOX	
SWAMP WOMEN	a1955	73		1.5	1.5	WOOLNER BROTHERS	
SWAN, THE	1956	112		2.5	3.0	M-G-M	
SWAN LAKE (RUSSIAN, DOCUMENTARY)	1957	81	6			COLUMBIA	
SWANEE RIVER	1939	84		2.5	2.5	20th CENTURY FOX	
SWAPPERS, THE (BRITISH)	a1970	86	1			TRANS-AMERICA	
SWEATER GIRL	1942	77		1.5		PARAMOUNT	
SWEDEN - HEAVEN AND HELL (ITALIAN, DOCUMENTARY)	1968	90	1			AVCO-EMBASSY	
SWEDISH WEDDING NIGHT (SWEDISH)	1965	96	3			ROYAL FILMS INT'L	
SWEET ADELINE	1935	87		3.0	2.5	WARNER BROTHERS	
SWEET AND LOWDOWN	1944	75		1.5	2.0	20th CENTURY FOX	
SWEET AND SOUR (FRENCH)	1963	93	3			PATHE CONTEMPARARY	
SWEET BIRD OF YOUTH	1962	120	7*	3.5	3.5	M-G-M	
SWEET BODY OF DEBORAH, THE (ITALIAN)	1968	95	2			WARNER BROTHERS	
SWEET CHARITY	1969	157	7			UNIVERSAL	
SWEET GEORGIA	1972	81				BOXOFFICE INTERNAT'L	
SWEET LIGHT IN A DARK ROOM (CZECH)	1960	93	6			PROMENADE	
SWEET LOVE, BITTER	1967	92	5			FILM 2 ASSOCIATES	
SWEET NOVEMBER	1968	114	5	3.0		WARNER BROTHERS	
SWEET RIDE, THE	1968	110		2.0		20th CENTURY FOX	
SWEET ROSIE O'GRADY	1943	74		3.0	2.5	20th CENTURY FOX	
SWEET SAVIOUR	1971	90	1			TRANS WORLD ATTRACS.	
SWEET SMELL OF SUCCESS	1957	96	6*	4.0	3.0	UNITED ARTISTS	
SWEET, SWEET RACHEL (T.V.)	1971	73	2*			ABC FILMS	
SWEET SWEETBACK'S BAADASSSSS SONG	1971	97	3			CINEMATION INDUS.	
SWEET TORONTO (DOCUMENTARY)	1972	135				PENNEBAKER PRODS.	
SWEETHEART OF SIGMA CHI	1946	75	2			MONOGRAM	
SWEETHEART OF THE GODS (GERMAN)	1959	107		2.5		TELEWIDE SYSTEMS	
SWEETHEARTS	1938	120		3.0	3.0	M-G-M	
SWEETHEARTS ON PARADE	1953	90	3	2.0		REPUBLIC	
SWELL GUY	1947	87	4			UNIVERSAL	
SWIMMER, THE	1968	94	5	3.5		COLUMBIA	
SWIMMING POOL, THE	1970	87	3			AVCO-EMBASSY	
SWINDLE, THE (ITALIAN)	a1955	92	4*	2.5	2.0	ASTOR	

‡ An asterisk (*) in THE FILM BUFF'S BIBLE column indicates that the film has been rated by the editor and/or staff. All other ratings in this column are based on a consensus of reviews (see NOTES).

TITLE (LEADING ACTORS SHOWN WHERE TWO OR MORE FILMS HAVE THE SAME OR SIMILAR TITLE)	YEAR RELEASED	RUNNING TIME IN MINUTES	THE FILM BUFF'S BIBLE ‡	STEVEN SCHEUER	LEONARD MALTIN	DISTRIBUTOR	COMMENT
SWING FEVER	1944	80		1.0	1.5	M-G-M	
SWING HIGH, SWING LOW	1937	97		2.5		PARAMOUNT	
SWING SHIFT MAISIE	1943	87		2.0	-	M-G-M	
SWING TIME	1936	103		3.5	4.0	RKO	
SWING YOUR LADY	1938	79	2*	2.5		WARNER BROTHERS	
SWING YOUR PARTNER	1943	72		1.5		REPUBLIC	
SWINGER, THE	1966	81		1.0	2.0	PARAMOUNT	
SWINGERS' PARADISE	1965	82	2			AMERICAN-INTERNAT'L	
SWINGIN' ALONG	1962	74	3			20th CENTURY FOX	
SWINGIN' MAIDEN, THE (BRITISH)	1962	98	3			COLUMBIA	
SWINGIN' ON A RAINBOW	1945	72		2.5		REPUBLIC	
SWINGIN' SUMMER, A	1965	80	2			UNITED SCREEN ARTS	
SWINGTIME JOHNNY	1944	61		2.5	1.5	UNIVERSAL	
SWIRL OF GLORY, A	1951	80	2	2.0	2.5	WARNER BROTHERS	
SWISS FAMILY ROBINSON (THOMAS MITCHELL, EDNA BEST)	1940	93		3.0	3.0	RKO	
SWISS FAMILY ROBINSON (JOHN MILLS, D. MCGUIRE)	1960	126	5*			BUENA VISTA	
SWISS MISS	1938	72			2.0	M-G-M	
SWITZERLAND (DOCUMENTARY)	1955	35	5*			BUENA VISTA	
SWORD AND THE CROSS, THE (ITALIAN)	1956	87	2	1.5		VALIANT	
SWORD AND THE DRAGON, THE (RUSSIAN)	1956	84	3	2.5		VALIANT	
SWORD AND THE ROSE, THE	1953	93	4			RKO	
SWORD IN THE DESERT	1949	100	5	2.5	2.5	UNIVERSAL	
SWORD IN THE STONE, THE (CARTOON)	1963	75	6			BUENA VISTA	
SWORD OF ALI BABA, THE	1965	81	2	1.5	2.0	UNIVERSAL	
SWORD OF DAMASCUS (ITALIAN)	1962	93		1.0		AMERICAN-INTERNAT'L	
SWORD OF EL CID, THE (SPANISH)	1963	85		1.0	2.0	TRANS-AMERICA	
SWORD OF GRANADA (SPANISH)	1960	80		1.5		AZTECA	
SWORD OF ISLAM (ITALIAN)	1962	90		1.0			
SWORD OF LANCELOT (BRITISH)	a1963	116	3	3.0	2.5	UNIVERSAL	
SWORD OF MONTE CRISTO, THE	1951	81	2	2.0	2.0	20th CENTURY FOX	
SWORD OF SHERWOOD FOREST (BRITISH)	1960	80	4	2.5	2.5	COLUMBIA	
SWORD OF THE CONQUEROR (ITALIAN)	1961	95		1.5	1.5	UNITED ARTISTS	
SWORD OF THE EMPIRE (ITALIAN)	1963	80		1.0		AMERICAN-INTERNAT'L	
SWORD OF VENUS	1953	73	1			RKO	
SWORD WITHOUT A COUNTRY (ITALIAN)	1965	100		1.5		AVCO-EMBASSY	
SWORDSMAN, THE	1948	81	4		2.0	COLUMBIA	
SWORDSMAN OF SIENA (ITALIAN)	1962	92	4			M-G-M	
SWORN ENEMY	1936	62		3.0		M-G-M	
SYLVIA	1965	115	4*	2.5	2.5	PARAMOUNT	
SYLVIA SCARLETT	1935	97		3.0	2.5	RKO	
SYMPATHY FOR THE DEVIL (BRITISH)	a1970	99	4			NEW LINE CINEMA	
SYMPHONIE PASTORALE (FRENCH)	1946	115	6			FILMS INTERNATIONAL	
SYMPHONY FOR A MASSACRE (FRENCH)	1965	110	4			SEVEN ARTS	
SYMPHONY OF SIX MILLION	1932	94		3.0		RKO	
SYNANON	a1965	106		2.5	2.5	COLUMBIA	
SYNCOPATION (ADOLPHE MENJOU, JACKIE COOPER)	1942	88		2.0	2.0	RKO	
SYSTEM, THE (FRANK LOVEJOY, JOAN WELDON)	1953	90		2.0	2.0	WARNER BROTHERS	
T.A.M.I. SHOW, THE	a1965	110	3			AMERICAN-INTERNAT'L	
T-BIRD GANG	1959	75	3	1.5		SPARTA	
T-MEN	1947	96		3.5	2.5	EAGLE LION	
T. R. BASKIN	a1971	90	4-5*			PARAMOUNT	
TABARIN (FRENCH)	1958	110		2.0		MAYFAIR	
TABOOS OF THE WORLD (DOCUMENTARY)	1965	97	1			AMERICAN-INTERNAT'L	
TABU (SILENT)	1931	81				PARAMOUNT	
TAFFY AND THE JUNGLE HUNTER	1965	87		1.5	2.0	ALLIED ARTISTS	
TAGGART	1965	85	3		2.5	UNIVERSAL	
TAHITI HONEY	1943	69		2.5		REPUBLIC	
TAIL SPIN	1939	84		2.0	2.0	20th CENTURY FOX	
TAILOR'S MAID, THE (ITALIAN)	1957	92	5		2.5	TRANS-LUX DIST.	
TAKE A GIANT STEP	1959	100	6	4.0		UNITED ARTISTS	
TAKE A GIRL LIKE YOU (BRITISH)	1970	96	3			COLUMBIA	
TAKE A LETTER, DARLING	1942	93		2.5	3.0	PARAMOUNT	
TAKE ALL YOU CAN GET	1972	81				H.K. FILM DIST.	
TAKE CARE OF MY LITTLE GIRL	1951	93	4	2.0	2.0	20th CENTURY FOX	
TAKE HER, SHE'S MINE	1963	98	4	2.0	2.0	20th CENTURY FOX	
TAKE IT BIG	1944	75		2.0		PARAMOUNT	
TAKE IT OR LEAVE IT	1944	70		1.5	1.5	20th CENTURY FOX	
TAKE ME OUT TO THE BALL GAME	1949	93		2.5	2.5	M-G-M	
TAKE ME TO TOWN	1953	81	4	3.0	2.5	UNIVERSAL	
TAKE MY LIFE (BRITISH)	1947	80		3.0		EAGLE LION	
TAKE ONE FALSE STEP	1949	94		2.5	2.5	UNIVERSAL	
TAKE THE HIGH GROUND	1953	101	4*	3.0	3.0	M-G-M	
TAKE THE MONEY AND RUN	1969	85	6*	4.0		CINERAMA RELEASING	
TAKERS, THE	1971	81				BOXOFFICE INTERNAT'L	
TAKING OFF	1971	92	5			UNIVERSAL	
TALE OF FIVE WOMEN, A (ITALIAN)	1952	86	5	3.0		UNITED ARTISTS	
TALE OF THE COCK	a1967	93	3			FILMWORLD	
TALE OF TWO CITIES, A (RONALD COLEMAN)	1936	121		4.0	4.0	M-G-M	NOMINATED BEST PICTURE
TALE OF TWO CITIES, A (BRITISH - DIRK BOGARDE)	1958	117	6	3.0		J. ARTHUR RANK	
TALES FROM THE CRYPT	1972	92	3			CINERAMA RELEASING	
TALES OF ADVENTURE	1954	90		1.5		PATHE	

‡ An asterisk (*) in THE FILM BUFF'S BIBLE column indicates that the film has been rated by the editor and/or staff. All other ratings in this column are based on a consensus of reviews (see NOTES).

TITLE (LEADING ACTORS SHOWN WHERE TWO OR MORE FILMS HAVE THE SAME OR SIMILAR TITLE)	YEAR RELEASED	RUNNING TIME IN MINUTES	THE FILM BUFF'S BIBLE ‡	STEVEN SCHEUER	LEONARD MALTIN	DISTRIBUTOR	COMMENT
TALES OF HOFFMANN, THE (BRITISH)	1951	127	6	3.0	2.5	LOPERT	
TALES OF MANHATTAN	1942	118		3.0	3.0	20th CENTURY FOX	
TALES OF PARIS (FRENCH)	1962	85	6			TIMES FILM CORP.	FOUR STORIES
TALES OF ROBIN HOOD	1951	60			1.5	LIPPERT PRODS.	
TALES OF TERROR	1962	120	4			AMERICAN-INTERNAT'L	THREE STORIES
TALK ABOUT A STRANGER	1952	65	1			M-G-M	
TALK OF THE TOWN, THE	1942	118		3.5	4.0	COLUMBIA	NOMINATED BEST PICTURE
TALL, DARK AND HANDSOME	1941	78		3.5	2.0	20th CENTURY FOX	
TALL IN THE SADDLE	1944	87		3.0	3.0	RKO	
TALL LIE, THE	a1952	93		3.5	2.0	LIPPERT PRODS.	
TALL MAN RIDING	1955	83		2.0	2.5	WARNER BROTHERS	
TALL MEN, THE	1955	122	2*	2.0	1.0	20th CENTURY FOX	
TALL STORY	1960	91		3.0	2.5	WARNER BROTHERS	
TALL STRANGER, THE	1957	81		3.0	2.0	ALLIED ARTISTS	
TALL T, THE	1957	78		2.5	2.0	COLUMBIA	
TALL TARGET, THE	1951	78	4	3.0	2.5	M-G-M	
TALL TEXAN, THE	1953	84	5	3.0		LIPPERT PRODS.	
TALL TIMBER (GEORGE O'BRIEN, BEATRICE ROBERTS)	a1937	65		3.0		RKO	
TALL WOMEN, THE (SPANISH)	1966	101	2		2.0	ALLIED ARTISTS	
TAM LIN	1971	107	1			AMERICAN-INTERNAT'L	
TAMAHINE (BRITISH)	1963	85	3			M-G-M	
TAMANGO (FRENCH)	1957	95	4	2.0	2.0	VALIANT	
TAMING, THE	1968	85	1			VICTORIA	
TAMING OF THE SHREW, THE	1966	122	6			COLUMBIA	
TAMING SUTTON'S GAL	1957	71		1.5	1.5	REPUBLIC	
TAMMY AND THE BACHELOR	a1957	89	4	2.5	3.0	UNIVERSAL	
TAMMY AND THE DOCTOR	1963	88		2.0	2.5	UNIVERSAL	
TAMMY AND THE MILLIONAIRE	1967	87	2		2.0	UNIVERSAL	
TAMMY TELL ME TRUE	1961	97		2.5	2.0	UNIVERSAL	
TAMPICO	1944	75		2.0	2.0	20th CENTURY FOX	
TANGANYIKA	1954	81		2.0	2.0	UNIVERSAL	
TANGIER	1946	76		2.0	2.0	UNIVERSAL	
TANGIER INCIDENT	1953	77	2		1.5	ALLIED ARTISTS	
TANK BATTALION	1958	80	1	1.0		AMERICAN-INTERNAT'L	
TANK COMMANDOS	1959	79		2.0		AMERICAN-INTERNAT'L	
TANK FORCE (BRITISH)	1958	81		2.0	1.5	COLUMBIA	
TANKS ARE COMING, THE	1951	90	4	2.0	2.0	WARNER BROTHERS	
TAP ROOTS	1948	109		2.5	2.5	UNIVERSAL	
TARANTULA	1955	80	4	2.5	2.5	UNIVERSAL	
TARAS BULBA	1962	122	4*	2.5	2.5	UNITED ARTISTS	
TARAWA BEACHHEAD	1958	77		2.0	2.5	COLUMBIA	
TARGET EARTH	1954	75		1.5	2.5	ALLIED ARTISTS	
TARGET - HONG KONG	1953	66	3	1.5		COLUMBIA	
TARGET, SEA OF CHINA	1954	100		1.0	1.5	REPUBLIC	RE-EDITED SERIAL
TARGET UNKNOWN	1951	90	4	2.5	2.5	UNIVERSAL	
TARGET ZERO	1955	92		1.5	2.0	WARNER BROTHERS	
TARGETS	1968	90	6	3.5		PARAMOUNT	
TARNISHED	1950	60		2.5		REPUBLIC	
TARNISHED ANGELS, THE (ROCK HUDSON, ROBERT STACK)	1958	91		2.5	2.5	UNIVERSAL	
TARNISHED HEROES (BRITISH)	1961	75		2.0		WARNER BROTHERS	
TARNISHED LADY	1931	83		1.5	2.5	PARAMOUNT	
TARS AND SPARS	1946	86		2.5		COLUMBIA	
TARTAR INVASION (ITALIAN)	1963	85		2.0		TELEWIDE SYSTEMS	
TARTARS, THE (ITALIAN)	1960	83	2		2.0	M-G-M	
TARTU (BRITISH)	a1943	103		2.5	2.5	M-G-M	
TARZAN AND HIS MATE	1934	105			-	M-G-M	
TARZAN AND THE AMAZONS	1945	76			-	RKO	
TARZAN AND THE GREAT RIVER	1967	88		1.0		PARAMOUNT	
TARZAN AND THE GREEN GODDESS	1938	72			-	PRINCIPAL	
TARZAN AND THE HUNTRESS	1947	72			-	RKO	
TARZAN AND THE JUNGLE BOY	1968	90		1.0		PARAMOUNT	
TARZAN AND THE LEOPARD WOMAN	1946	72			-	RKO	
TARZAN AND THE LOST SAFARI (BRITISH)	1957	84		2.0		M-G-M	
TARZAN AND THE MERMAIDS	1948	68			-	RKO	
TARZAN AND THE SHE-DEVIL	1953	76	1		-	RKO	
TARZAN AND THE SLAVE GIRL	1950	74	3		-	RKO	
TARZAN AND THE TRAPPERS	1958	74		1.5	-	RKO	
TARZAN AND THE VALLEY OF GOLD	1966	100	2			AMERICAN-INTERNAT'L	
TARZAN ESCAPES	1936	95			-	M-G-M	
TARZAN FINDS A SON	1939	90			-	M-G-M	
TARZAN GOES TO INDIA (BRITISH)	1962	86		2.5	-	M-G-M	
TARZAN, THE APE MAN (JOHNNY WEISSMULLER)	1932	99		2.5	-	M-G-M	
TARZAN, THE APE MAN (DENNIS MILLER)	1959	82		1.5	-	M-G-M	
TARZAN, THE MAGNIFICENT (BRITISH)	1960	88	4	3.0	-	PARAMOUNT	
TARZAN TRIUMPHS	1943	78			-	RKO	
TARZAN'S DEADLY SILENCE	1970	82	1			NATIONAL GENERAL	
TARZAN'S DESERT MYSTERY	1943	70			-	RKO	
TARZAN'S FIGHT FOR LIFE	1958	86		2.0	-	M-G-M	
TARZAN'S GREATEST ADVENTURE (BRITISH)	1959	88	4	3.0	-	PARAMOUNT	
TARZAN'S HIDDEN JUNGLE	1955	73	1		-	RKO	
TARZAN'S JUNGLE REBELLION	1970	92	2			NATIONAL GENERAL	
TARZAN'S MAGIC FOUNTAIN	1949	73			-	RKO	
TARZAN'S NEW YORK ADVENTURE	1942	71		3.0	-	M-G-M	
TARZAN'S PERIL	1951	79			-	RKO	

‡ An asterisk (*) in THE FILM BUFF'S BIBLE column indicates that the film has been rated by the editor and/or staff. All other ratings in this column are based on a consensus of reviews (see NOTES).

TITLE (LEADING ACTORS SHOWN WHERE TWO OR MORE FILMS HAVE THE SAME OR SIMILAR TITLE)	YEAR RELEASED	RUNNING TIME IN MINUTES	THE FILM BUFF'S BIBLE ‡	STEVEN SCHEUER	LEONARD MALTIN	DISTRIBUTOR	COMMENT
TARZAN'S REVENGE	1938	70			.	20th CENTURY FOX	
TARZAN'S SAVAGE FURY	1952	80			.	RKO	
TARZAN'S SECRET TREASURE	1941	81				M-G-M	
TARZAN'S THREE CHALLENGES	1963	92	3	1.5		M-G-M	
TASK FORCE	1949	116	6	3.0	2.5	WARNER BROTHERS	
TASTE OF HONEY, A (BRITISH)	1961	100	6-7*	4.0	3.5	CONTINENTAL	
TASTE THE BLOOD OF DRACULA (BRITISH)	1970	95	3			WARNER BROTHERS	
TATTERED DRESS, THE	1957	93		2.5	2.5	UNIVERSAL	
TATTOOED POLICE HORSE, THE	1964	48	5			BUENA VISTA	
TATTOOED STRANGER, THE	1950	64	5	2.5		RKO	
TAUR THE MIGHTY (ITALIAN)	1961	89		1.0		AMERICAN-INTERNAT'L	
TAWNY PIPIT, THE (BRITISH)	1944	81	6			UNIVERSAL	
TAXI (JAMES CAGNEY, LORETTA YOUNG)	1932	70		2.5	2.5	WARNER BROTHERS	
TAXI (DAN DAILEY, CONSTANCE SMITH)	1953	77	4	2.5	2.0	20th CENTURY FOX	
TAXI FOR TOBRUK (FRENCH)	1961	90		2.5	2.5	SEVEN ARTS	
TAZA, SON OF COCHISE	1954	79		2.0	2.0	UNIVERSAL	
TCHAIKOVSKY (RUSSIAN)	1971	105				WARNER BROTHERS	
TEA AND SYMPATHY	1956	122	6*	3.5	3.0	M-G-M	
TEA FOR TWO	1950	98	5	2.5	2.5	WARNER BROTHERS	
TEACHER AND THE MIRACLE, THE (ITALIAN)	1957	88		2.5	2.5	PRESIDENT FILMS	
TEACHER'S PET	1958	120	7*	3.5	3.0	PARAMOUNT	
TEAHOUSE OF THE AUGUST MOON, THE	1956	123	6	3.5	3.5	M-G-M	
TEAR GAS SQUAD	1940	55		2.0		WARNER BROTHERS	
TEARS FOR SIMON (BRITISH)	1956	91	5			REPUBLIC	
TECKMAN MYSTERY, THE (BRITISH)	1954	89		3.0	2.0	ASSOCIATED ARTISTS	
TEEN-AGE CRIME WAVE	1955	77	3	1.5		COLUMBIA	
TEEN-AGE REBEL	1956	94	4	1.5	2.5	20th CENTURY FOX	
TEENAGE BAD GIRL (BRITISH)	a1956	100		3.0	1.5	VALIANT	
TEENAGE CAVEMAN	1958	65	3	1.5		AMERICAN-INTERNAT'L	
TEENAGE DOLL	1957	68		1.0	1.0	ALLIED ARTISTS	
TEENAGE MILLIONAIRE	1961	84		1.5	1.0	UNITED ARTISTS	
TEENAGE MOTHER	1968	78	1			CINEMATION INDUS.	
TEENAGE REBELLION	a1967	81				TRANS AMERICAN	
TEENAGE WOLF PACK (GERMAN)	1956	89		2.5		DIST. CORP. OF AMER.	
TEENAGE ZOMBIES	1960	73		1.0		GOVERNOR	
TEENAGERS FROM OUTER SPACE	1959	87	2*	1.0	1.0	WARNER BROTHERS	
TEENIE TULIP	1969	80	1			CINEX	
TELEPHONE BOOK, THE	1971	89	1			ROSEBUD RELEASING	
TELL IT TO THE JUDGE	1949	87		2.5	2.5	COLUMBIA	
TELL ME LIES (BRITISH)	1968	116	5	3.5		CONTINENTAL	
TELL ME THAT YOU LOVE ME, JUNIE MOON	1970	113	4			PARAMOUNT	
TELL-TALE HEART, THE (BRITISH)	1961	78		2.5	2.0	BRIGADIER FILMS	
TELL THEM WILLIE BOY IS HERE	1970	96	3*	3.5		UNIVERSAL	
TEMBO (DOCUMENTARY)	1952	80	5	3.0		RKO	
TEMPEST (ITALIAN)	1958	125		3.0	2.5	PARAMOUNT	
TEMPEST IN THE FLESH (FRENCH)	1954	92	6			PACEMAKER PICS.	
TEMPLE OF THE WHITE ELEPHANTS (ITALIAN)	1964	85		1.0		AMERICAN-INTERNAT'L	
TEMPTATION (MERLE OBERON, PAUL LUKAS)	1946	92		2.0	2.0	UNIVERSAL	
TEN CENTS A DANCE	1945	60		1.5		COLUMBIA	
TEN COMMANDMENTS, THE (CHARLTON HESTON)	1956	219	6-7*			PARAMOUNT	NOMINATED BEST PICTURE
TEN DAYS THAT SHOOK THE WORLD (RUSSIAN, SILENT)	1928	105	2*			AMKINO	
TEN DAYS TO TULARA	1958	77		1.5	1.0	UNITED ARTISTS	
TEN DAYS' WONDER	1972	100	4			LEVITT-PICKMAN	
TEN GENTLEMEN FROM WEST POINT	1942	102		3.0	3.0	20th CENTURY FOX	
TEN GLADIATORS, THE (ITALIAN)	1961	104		1.0		AMERICAN-INTERNAT'L	
TEN LITTLE INDIANS (BRITISH)	1965	91		2.5	2.5	SEVEN ARTS	
TEN NORTH FREDERICK	1958	102	5*	3.0	3.0	20th CENTURY FOX	
10 RILLINGTON PLACE (BRITISH)	1971	111	5			COLUMBIA	
TEN SECONDS TO HELL	1959	93		2.0	2.5	UNITED ARTISTS	
TEN TALL MEN	1951	97	4	3.5	2.5	COLUMBIA	
10:30 PM SUMMER	1966	85	3			LOPERT	
TEN THOUSAND BEDROOMS	1957	114		2.5	2.0	M-G-M	
TEN WANTED MEN	1955	80		2.5	2.0	COLUMBIA	
TEN WHO DARED	1960	92	4			BUENA VISTA	
TENDER COMRADE	1943	102		2.5	2.0	RKO	
TENDER IS THE NIGHT	1962	146		2.5	2.5	20th CENTURY FOX	
TENDER MOMENT, THE (FRENCH)	1971	82	4			MARON FILMS, LTD.	
TENDER SCOUNDREL (FRENCH)	1966	94	3			AVCO-EMBASSY	
TENDER TRAP, THE	1955	111	6	3.0	3.5	M-G-M	
TENDER WARRIOR, THE	1971	75				WM. THOMPSON, INT'L	
TENDER YEARS, THE	1948	81	4		2.0	20th CENTURY FOX	
TENDERFOOT, THE	1932	70		2.5	2.5	FIRST NATIONAL	
TENNESSEE CHAMP	1954	73		2.5	2.5	M-G-M	
TENNESSEE JOHNSON	1942	103		3.5	2.5	M-G-M	
TENNESSEE'S PARTNER	1955	87	4	3.0	2.5	RKO	
TENSION	1949	95		2.5	2.5	M-G-M	
TENSION AT TABLE ROCK	1956	93		2.5	2.0	RKO	
TENTH AVENUE ANGEL	1948	74		1.0	1.0	M-G-M	
TENTH VICTIM, THE (ITALIAN)	1965	92	4-5*	3.5	3.0	AVCO-EMBASSY	ENGLISH LANGUAGE
TEOREMA (ITALIAN)	1968	93	5			CONTINENTAL	
TERESA	1951	102		3.5	2.0	M-G-M	
TERM OF TRIAL (BRITISH)	1962	113	5	3.5		WARNER BROTHERS	
TERRIBLE PEOPLE, THE (GERMAN)	a1960	95		2.0	2.0	UCC FILMS	
TERRIFIED	1963	81		1.0		CROWN INTERNATIONAL	

‡ An asterisk (*) in THE FILM BUFF'S BIBLE column indicates that the film has been rated by the editor and/or staff. All other ratings in this column are based on a consensus of reviews (see NOTES).

TITLE (LEADING ACTORS SHOWN WHERE TWO OR MORE FILMS HAVE THE SAME OR SIMILAR TITLE)	YEAR RELEASED	RUNNING TIME IN MINUTES	THE FILM BUFF'S BIBLE ‡	STEVEN SCHEUER	LEONARD MALTIN	DISTRIBUTOR	COMMENT
TERROR, THE (BORIS KARLOFF, JACK NICHOLSON)	1963	81	2	2.0	2.5	AMERICAN-INTERNAT'L	
TERROR AFTER MIDNIGHT (GERMAN)	1960	76		2.0		WOLPER TV	
TERROR AT BLACK FALLS	1962	76		1.0		PARAMOUNT	
TERROR AT MIDNIGHT	1956	70		2.0	2.0	REPUBLIC	
TERROR BY NIGHT	1946	60			-	UNIVERSAL	
TERROR FROM THE YEAR 5000	1958	68	2*	2.0		AMERICAN-INTERNAT'L	
TERROR IN A TEXAS TOWN	1958	80		2.0	1.5	UNITED ARTISTS	
TERROR IN THE CRYPT	1958	90		2.5		AMERICAN-INTERNAT'L	
TERROR IN THE HAUNTED HOUSE	a1958	80		2.0		HOWCO INTERNATIONAL	
TERROR IN THE JUNGLE	1969	85	1			CROWN INTERNATIONAL	
TERROR IN THE MIDNIGHT SUN (SWEDISH)	1958	73			2.0	HERTS-LION INT'L	
TERROR IS A MAN	1959	89		2.5	1.0	VALIANT	
TERROR OF ROME AGAINST THE SON OF HERCULES (ITAL.)	1963	100		1.0		AVCO-EMBASSY	
TERROR OF THE BLACK MASK (ITALIAN)	1960	96		1.5		AVCO-EMBASSY	
TERROR OF THE BLOODHUNTERS	1962	72		1.0		MEDALLION	
TERROR OF THE RED MASK (ITALIAN)	1960	90		1.5	2.0	FOUR STAR	
TERROR OF THE STEPPE (ITALIAN)	1963	97		1.0		AVCO-EMBASSY	
TERROR OF THE TONGS, THE (BRITISH)	1961	80		2.0	2.5	COLUMBIA	
TERROR ON A TRAIN	1953	72	5*	2.5	2.5	M-G-M	
TERRORNAUTS, THE (BRITISH)	1967	75	1			AVCO-EMBASSY	
TESS OF THE STORM COUNTRY	1960	84		2.0	2.5	20th CENTURY FOX	
TEST PILOT	1938	118		3.0	3.0	M-G-M	NOMINATED BEST PICTURE
TESTAMENT OF DR MABUSE, THE (GERMAN)	1961	87		2.0	2.5	TELEWIDE SYSTEMS	
TEXAN MEETS CALAMITY JANE, THE	1950	71		1.0	1.0	COLUMBIA	
TEXANS, THE	1938	92		2.0	2.0	PARAMOUNT	
TEXAS	1941	93	4*	3.5	3.0	COLUMBIA	
TEXAS ACROSS THE RIVER	1966	101		2.0	3.0	UNIVERSAL	
TEXAS, BROOKLYN AND HEAVEN	1948	76			2.0	UNITED ARTISTS	
TEXAS CARNIVAL	1951	77		3.0	2.0	M-G-M	
TEXAS LADY	1955	86		2.0	2.0	RKO	
TEXAS RANGERS, THE (FRED MACMURRAY, JACK OAKIE)	1936	95		2.0	3.0	PARAMOUNT	
TEXAS RANGERS, THE (GEORGE MONTGOMERY, GALE STORM)	1951	68		2.5	1.5	COLUMBIA	
TEXAS RANGERS RIDE AGAIN	1941	68		2.0	2.0	PARAMOUNT	
TEXICAN, THE	1966	86	2			COLUMBIA	
THANK YOU ALL VERY MUCH (BRITISH)	1969	106	5			COLUMBIA	
THANK YOU, JEEVES	1936	68		2.5	2.0	20th CENTURY FOX	
THANK YOU, MR MOTO	1937	67			-	20th CENTURY FOX	
THANK YOUR LUCKY STARS	1943	127		3.0	3.0	WARNER BROTHERS	
THANKS A MILLION	1935	87		3.0	3.0	20th CENTURY FOX	
THANKS FOR EVERYTHING	1938	73		3.0		20th CENTURY FOX	
THANKS FOR THE MEMORY	1938	75		3.0		PARAMOUNT	
THAT BRENNAN GIRL	1946	95		1.0		REPUBLIC	
THAT CERTAIN AGE	1938	95			3.0	UNIVERSAL	
THAT CERTAIN FEELING	1956	103	2*	3.5	1.0	PARAMOUNT	
THAT CERTAIN WOMAN	1937	93		2.0	2.5	WARNER BROTHERS	
THAT COLD DAY IN THE PARK (CANADIAN)	1969	110	3			LANDAU/UNGER COM. UN.	
THAT DARN CAT	1965	116	6			BUENA VISTA	
THAT FORSYTHE WOMAN	1949	114	4*	2.5	2.5	M-G-M	
THAT FUNNY FEELING	1965	93		2.5	2.5	UNIVERSAL	
THAT GANG OF MINE	1940	62			-	MONOGRAM	
THAT GIRL FROM PARIS	1936	110		3.0	2.5	RKO	
THAT HAGEN GIRL	1947	83	2	1.0	1.0	WARNER BROTHERS	
THAT HAMILTON WOMAN	a1941	128		3.0	3.0	UNITED ARTISTS	
THAT KIND OF WOMAN	1959	92		2.0	2.0	PARAMOUNT	
THAT LADY (BRITISH)	1955	100		2.0	2.5	20th CENTURY FOX	
THAT LADY IN ERMINE	1948	89	4	3.0	3.0	20th CENTURY FOX	
THAT MAN FROM RIO (FRENCH)	1964	114	6*		3.0	LOPERT	
THAT MAN FROM TANGIER	1953	80		1.5		UNITED ARTISTS	
THAT MAN GEORGE (FRENCH)	1966	90	3	1.5		ALLIED ARTISTS	ENGLISH LANGUAGE
THAT MAN IN ISTANBUL (FRENCH)	1965	117	4		2.5	COLUMBIA	
THAT MIDNIGHT KISS	1949	96	5	2.5	2.5	M-G-M	
THAT NIGHT	1957	88		3.0	2.5	UNIVERSAL	
THAT NIGHT IN RIO	1941	90		2.5	2.5	20th CENTURY FOX	
THAT NIGHT WITH YOU	1945	84		2.0	2.0	UNIVERSAL	
THAT OTHER WOMAN	1942	75		2.0		20th CENTURY FOX	
THAT SPLENDID NOVEMBER (ITALIAN)	1971	93	3			UNITED ARTISTS	
THAT TENNESSEE BEAT	1966	84	3			20th CENTURY FOX	
THAT TOUCH OF MINK	1962	99	6*	3.5	2.5	UNIVERSAL	
THAT UNCERTAIN FEELING	1941	84		3.0	3.0	UNITED ARTISTS	
THAT WAY WITH WOMEN	1947	84		2.0	2.0	WARNER BROTHERS	
THAT WOMAN (GERMAN)	1966	83	1			GLOBE	
THAT WOMAN OPPOSITE (BRITISH)	a1957	84		2.0	1.5	RKO	
THAT WONDERFUL URGE	1949	82		2.5	2.5	20th CENTURY FOX	
THAT'S MY BOY	1951	98	5	2.0	3.0	PARAMOUNT	
THAT'S MY MAN	1947	104	4	2.5		REPUBLIC	
THAT'S RIGHT, YOU'RE WRONG	1939	88		2.5		RKO	
THAT'S THE SPIRIT	1945	93			2.0	UNIVERSAL	
THEIR LAST NIGHT (FRENCH)	1953	90		2.0		COLUMBIA	
THELMA JORDAN	a1949	100	4		2.5	PARAMOUNT	
THEM	1954	94	3*	2.5	3.5	WARNER BROTHERS	
THEN CAME BRONSON (T.V.)	1969	100		2.0		M-G-M	
THEN THERE WERE THREE (ITALIAN)	a1961	74		2.5	2.0	PARADE	
THEODORA, SLAVE EMPRESS (ITALIAN)	1954	92		2.0	2.0	ITALIAN FILMS EXPORT	
THERE GOES BARDER (FRENCH)	a1955	90		1.5	2.5	PARAMOUNT	

‡ An asterisk (*) in THE FILM BUFF'S BIBLE column indicates that the film has been rated by the editor and/or staff. All other ratings in this column are based on a consensus of reviews (see NOTES).

TITLE (LEADING ACTORS SHOWN WHERE TWO OR MORE FILMS HAVE THE SAME OR SIMILAR TITLE)	YEAR RELEASED	RUNNING TIME IN MINUTES	THE FILM BUFF'S BIBLE ‡	STEVEN SCHEUER	LEONARD MALTIN	DISTRIBUTOR	COMMENT
THERE GOES MY GIRL	1937	74		3.0		RKO	
THERE GOES MY HEART	1938	81		2.5	3.0	UNITED ARTISTS	
THERE GOES THE GROOM	1937	65		2.5		RKO	
THERE WAS A CROOKED MAN (KIRK DOUGLAS, H. FONDA)	1970	126	6			WARNER BROTHERS	
THERE WAS A YOUNG LADY (BRITISH)	1952	85		2.0		ELLIS FILMS	
THERE WAS AN OLD COUPLE (RUSSIAN)	1965	110	6	4.0		ARTKINO	
THERE'S A GIRL IN MY SOUP (BRITISH)	1970	95	-			COLUMBIA	
THERE'S ALWAYS A PRICE TAG (FRENCH)	1957	102	4	2.0	2.5	J. ARTHUR RANK	
THERE'S ALWAYS A THURSDAY (BRITISH)	1957	62		2.0		J. ARTHUR RANK	
THERE'S ALWAYS A WOMAN	1938	82		3.0	3.0	COLUMBIA	
THERE'S ALWAYS TOMORROW	1956	84	4	2.5	2.5	UNIVERSAL	
THERE'S ALWAYS VANILLA	a1972	91	2			CAMBIST	
THERE'S MAGIC IN MUSIC	a1941	80		1.5		PARAMOUNT	
THERE'S NO BUSINESS LIKE SHOW BUSINESS	1954	117		3.0	1.5	20th CENTURY FOX	
THERESE AND ISABELLE (FRENCH)	1968	115	3			AUDUBON	
THERESE ETIENNE (FRENCH)	1957	95		2.0		WALTER READE	
THESE ARE THE DAMNED (BRITISH)	1963	77		2.0	3.0	COLUMBIA	
THESE GLAMOUR GIRLS	1939	80		3.0	2.5	M-G-M	
THESE THOUSAND HILLS	1959	96	4	2.5	3.0	20th CENTURY FOX	
THESE THREE	1936	93	6*	3.5	4.0	UNITED ARTISTS	
THESE WILDER YEARS	1956	91		2.5	2.5	M-G-M	
THEY ALL DIED LAUGHING (BRITISH)	a1964	96	6*	3.5	2.0	CONTINENTAL	
THEY ALL KISSED THE BRIDE	1942	85		2.5	2.5	COLUMBIA	
THEY CALL IT SIN	1932	75		2.0	2.0	FIRST NATIONAL	
THEY CALL ME MISTER TIBBS!	1970	108	4*	2.0		UNITED ARTISTS	
THEY CALL ME TRINITY	1971	110	3			AVCO-EMBASSY	
THEY CAME FROM BEYOND SPACE (BRITISH)	1967	85	1			AVCO-EMBASSY	
THEY CAME TO BLOW UP AMERICA	1943	73		2.0	2.0	20th CENTURY FOX	
THEY CAME TO CORDURA	1959	123	4	2.0	2.5	COLUMBIA	
THEY CAME TO ROB LAS VEGAS (SPANISH)	1968	129	3			WARNER BROTHERS	ENGLISH VERSION
THEY CAN'T HANG ME (BRITISH)	1955	75		2.5		LOPERT	
THEY DARE NOT LOVE	1941	76		1.5	1.5	COLUMBIA	
THEY DIED WITH THEIR BOOTS ON	1942	138		3.0	3.0	WARNER BROTHERS	
THEY DRIVE BY NIGHT	1940	93	4*	3.0	3.5	WARNER BROTHERS	
THEY GAVE HIM A GUN	1937	94		1.5	2.0	M-G-M	
THEY GOT ME COVERED	1943	95		2.5	2.0	RKO	
THEY KNEW WHAT THEY WANTED	1940	96		3.5	3.0	RKO	
THEY LIVE BY NIGHT	a1948	95	6			RKO	
THEY MADE ME A CRIMINAL (JOHN GARFIELD)	1939	92		3.0	2.5	WARNER BROTHERS	
THEY MADE ME A CRIMINAL (BRITISH - TREVOR HOWARD)	a1947	78		3.0	2.5	WARNER BROTHERS	
THEY MADE ME A KILLER	1946	64		2.5		PARAMOUNT	
THEY MET AT MIDNIGHT	a1946	88		3.0	3.0	M-G-M	
THEY MET IN ARGENTINA	1941	77		1.5	1.5	RKO	
THEY MET IN BOMBAY	1941	86		2.5	2.5	M-G-M	
THEY MIGHT BE GIANTS	1971	88	3*			UNIVERSAL	
THEY RODE WEST	1954	84		3.0	2.5	COLUMBIA	
THEY SHALL HAVE MUSIC	1939	101		2.5		UNITED ARTISTS	
THEY SHOOT HORSES, DON'T THEY?	1969	120	6*	4.0		CINERAMA RELEASING	
THEY WERE EXPENDABLE	1945	135		3.5	3.5	M-G-M	
THEY WERE SISTERS (BRITISH)	1945	114		3.0	2.5	UNIVERSAL	
THEY WERE SO YOUNG (GERMAN)	1955	80	4*	3.0	3.0	LIPPERT PRODS.	
THEY WERE TEN (ISRAELI)	1960	105	6			SCHWARTZ & SACHSON	
THEY WHO DARE (BRITISH)	1954	100		3.0	2.5	ALLIED ARTISTS	
THEY WON'T BELIEVE ME	1947	95	6	3.5	3.5	RKO	
THEY WON'T FORGET	1937	90		4.0	3.5	WARNER BROTHERS	
THIEF, THE	1952	85	3*	3.0	2.5	UNITED ARTISTS	NO DIALOGUE
THIEF OF BAGDAD, THE (SILENT - DOUGLAS FAIRBANKS)	1924	133	3*			UNITED ARTISTS	
THIEF OF BAGDAD, THE (BRIT. - SABU, CONRAD VEIDT)	1940	106	5*	2.0	4.0	UNITED ARTISTS	
THIEF OF BAGHDAD, THE (ITALIAN - STEVE REEVES)	1960	96		2.0	2.0	M-G-M	
THIEF OF DAMASCUS	1952	78		2.0	2.0	COLUMBIA	
THIEF OF PARIS (FRENCH)	1967	119	6			LOPERT	
THIEF OF VENICE	1953	91	4			20th CENTURY FOX	
THIEVES FALL OUT	1941	72		2.0	2.0	WARNER BROTHERS	
THIEVES' HIGHWAY	1949	94	5*	3.0	3.0	20th CENTURY FOX	
THIEVES' HOLIDAY	a1946	100	4	3.0	3.0	UNITED ARTISTS	
THIN ICE	1937	78		3.0	3.0	20th CENTURY FOX	
THIN MAN, THE	1934	93		3.5	-	M-G-M	NOMINATED BEST PICTURE
THIN MAN GOES HOME, THE	1944	100		2.5	-	M-G-M	
THIN RED LINE, THE	1964	99		2.5	2.5	ALLIED ARTISTS	
THING, THE	a1951	87	6	3.0	3.5	RKO	
THING FROM ANOTHER WORLD	a1951	87	6	3.0	3.5	RKO	
THING THAT COULDN'T DIE, THE	1958	69	2	1.5	2.0	UNIVERSAL	
THINGS OF LIFE, THE (FRENCH)	1970	89	6			COLUMBIA	
THINGS TO COME (BRITISH)	1936	113	7*	3.0	3.5	UNITED ARTISTS	
THINK FAST, MR MOTO	1937	66			-	20th CENTURY FOX	
THIRD ALIBI, THE (BRITISH)	1961	68		2.0		MODERN SOUND FILMS	
THIRD DAY, THE	1965	119	4*	2.5		WARNER BROTHERS	
THIRD FINGER, LEFT HAND	1940	96		2.0	2.0	M-G-M	
THIRD KEY, THE (BRITISH)	a1956	94	5	3.5	2.0	J. ARTHUR RANK	
THIRD MAN, THE (BRITISH)	1949	104	7*	4.0	4.0	SELZNICK RELEASING	
THIRD MAN ON THE MOUNTAIN, THE	1959	105	6*			BUENA VISTA	
THIRD SECRET, THE (BRITISH)	1964	103	3*	3.0		20th CENTURY FOX	
THIRD SEX, THE (GERMAN)	1957	80	4			D & F DISTRIBUTION	
THIRD VOICE, THE	1960	79	3*	4.0	3.0	20th CENTURY FOX	

‡ An asterisk (*) in THE FILM BUFF'S BIBLE column indicates that the film has been rated by the editor and/or staff. All other ratings in this column are based on a consensus of reviews (see NOTES).

			CRITICAL RATINGS				

"a" TO LEFT OF YEAR INDICATES THAT FILM HAS AN ALTERNATE TITLE

TITLE (LEADING ACTORS SHOWN WHERE TWO OR MORE FILMS HAVE THE SAME OR SIMILAR TITLE)	YEAR RELEASED	RUNNING TIME IN MINUTES	THE FILM BUFF'S BIBLE ‡	STEVEN SCHEUER	LEONARD MALTIN	DISTRIBUTOR	COMMENT
THIRTEEN FIGHTING MEN	1960	69		1.5	1.5	20th CENTURY FOX	
13 FRIGHTENED GIRLS	1963	89	3		2.0	COLUMBIA	
13 GHOSTS	1960	88		2.0	2.0	COLUMBIA	
13 HOURS BY AIR	1936	80		2.0	2.0	PARAMOUNT	
13 RUE MADELEINE	1947	95	4*	2.5	2.5	20th CENTURY FOX	
13 WEST STREET	1962	80	3	2.5	2.5	COLUMBIA	
13TH HOUR, THE	1947	65			-	COLUMBIA	
13TH LETTER, THE	1951	85		3.0	2.5	20th CENTURY FOX	
-30-	1959	96		2.5	2.5	WARNER BROTHERS	
THIRTY DAY PRINCESS	1934	75		2.5	2.5	PARAMOUNT	
30 FOOT BRIDE OF CANDY ROCK, THE	1959	75		1.5	2.0	COLUMBIA	
THIRTY IS A DANGEROUS AGE, CYNTHIA (BRITISH)	1968	85	5	3.5		COLUMBIA	
39 STEPS, THE (BRITISH - ROBERT DONAT, M. CARROLL)	1935	81	5-6*	4.0	4.0	GAUMONT-BRITISH	
39 STEPS, THE (BRITISH - KENNETH MORE, TANIA ELG)	1959	93	6*	2.5	2.5	20th CENTURY FOX	
THIRTY SECONDS OVER TOKYO	1944	138	4*	3.0	3.0	M-G-M	
36 HOURS (JAMES GARNER, EVA MARIE SAINT)	1965	115	6*	3.0	2.5	M-G-M	
THIRTY YEARS OF FUN	1963	85	6		4.0	20th CENTURY FOX	SILENT FILM CLIPS
THIS ABOVE ALL	1942	110		3.0	3.0	20th CENTURY FOX	
THIS ANGRY AGE	1958	111	3	1.5	2.0	COLUMBIA	
THIS COULD BE THE NIGHT	1957	103		3.0	2.5	M-G-M	
THIS EARTH IS MINE	1959	125	4	2.0	2.5	UNIVERSAL	
THIS GUN FOR HIRE	1942	80		3.5	3.0	PARAMOUNT	
THIS HAPPY BREED (BRITISH)	1944	110	7	4.0	3.5	UNIVERSAL	
THIS HAPPY FEELING	1958	92	5	3.0	3.0	UNIVERSAL	
THIS IS CINERAMA	1952	120	7			CINERAMA	
THIS IS KOREA (DOCUMENTARY)	1951	80	3			REPUBLIC	
THIS IS MY AFFAIR	1937	99		3.0	3.0	20th CENTURY FOX	
THIS IS MY LOVE	1954	91		2.0	2.0	RKO	
THIS IS NOT A TEST	1962	72		2.5		ALLIED ARTISTS	
THIS IS THE ARMY	1943	115	6			WARNER BROTHERS	
THIS IS THE LIFE	1944	87			2.0	UNIVERSAL	
THIS IS THE NIGHT	1932	78		2.5	2.5	PARAMOUNT	
THIS ISLAND EARTH	1955	87		2.5	2.5	UNIVERSAL	
THIS LAND IS MINE	1943	103		3.5	3.0	RKO	
THIS LOVE OF OURS	1945	90		2.5	2.5	UNIVERSAL	
THIS MAN MUST DIE (FRENCH)	1970	115	6			ALLIED ARTISTS	
THIS MAN'S NAVY	1945	100		3.0	3.0	M-G-M	
THIS MODERN AGE	1931	76		2.0		M-G-M	
THIS PROPERTY IS CONDEMNED	1966	110	3*	2.5		PARAMOUNT	
THIS REBEL BREED	a1960	90		2.0	2.0	WARNER BROTHERS	
THIS SAVAGE LAND	1969	97	3			UNIVERSAL	
THIS SIDE OF HEAVEN	1934	76		3.0		M-G-M	
THIS SIDE OF THE LAW	1950	74		2.0	2.0	WARNER BROTHERS	
THIS SPECIAL FRIENDSHIP (FRENCH)	1964	99	6			PATHE CONTEMPARARY	
THIS SPORTING LIFE (BRITISH)	1963	129	7*	4.0	3.5	CONTINENTAL	
THIS STUFF'LL KILL YA!	1971	100				ULTIMA	
THIS THING CALLED LOVE	1941	98		3.0	3.0	COLUMBIA	
THIS TIME FOR KEEPS (ANN RUTHERFORD, R. STERLING)	a1942	71		2.0		M-G-M	
THIS TIME FOR KEEPS (ESTHER WILLIAMS, L. MELCHIOR)	1947	105		2.5	2.5	M-G-M	
THIS WAS A WOMAN (BRITISH)	1948	102		2.0		20th CENTURY FOX	
THIS WOMAN IS DANGEROUS	1952	100		2.5	2.5	WARNER BROTHERS	
THIS WOMAN IS MINE	1941	91		2.0	2.0	UNIVERSAL	
THOMAS CROWN AFFAIR, THE	1968	102	5-6*	3.5		UNITED ARTISTS	
THOR AND THE AMAZON WOMAN (ITALIAN)	1963	95		1.0		WILCOX	
THOROUGHBREDS	1944	55		2.0		REPUBLIC	
THOROUGHBREDS DON'T CRY	1937	80		2.5	2.5	M-G-M	
THOROUGHLY MODERN MILLIE	1967	138	6*	3.5		UNIVERSAL	
THOSE CALLOWAYS	1964	131	6			BUENA VISTA	
THOSE DARING YOUNG MEN IN THEIR JAUNTY JALOPIES	1969	130	4	2.0		PARAMOUNT	(ITALIAN) ENGLISH LANGUAGE
THOSE ENDEARING YOUNG CHARMS	1945	81		2.0	2.0	RKO	
THOSE FANTASTIC FLYING FOOLS (BRITISH)	a1967	95	3		2.0	AMERICAN-INTERNAT'L	
THOSE MAGNIFICENT MEN IN THEIR FLYING MACHINES	1965	133	8*	4.0	3.0	20th CENTURY FOX	(BRITISH)
THOSE REDHEADS FROM SEATTLE	1953	90		2.0	2.0	PARAMOUNT	
THOSE WERE THE DAYS	1940	76		2.5	2.0	PARAMOUNT	
THOU SHALT NOT KILL (ITALIAN - LAURENT TERZIEFF)	1961	129			2.5	GALA	FRENCH LANGUAGE
THOUSAND AND ONE NIGHTS, A	1945	93			3.0	COLUMBIA	
THOUSAND CLOWNS, A	1965	118	7	4.0	3.5	UNITED ARTISTS	NOMINATED BEST PICTURE
THOUSAND EYES OF DR MABUSE, THE (GERMAN)	1960	103			2.5	GOLDEN ERA	
THOUSANDS CHEER	1943	126		3.0	3.0	M-G-M	
THREAT, THE (CHARLES MCGRAW, MICHAEL O'SHEA)	1949	66		3.0		RKO	
THREAT, THE (ROBERT KNAPP, LINDA LAWSON)	1960	66		1.0	2.0	WARNER BROTHERS	
THREE (YUGOSLAVIAN - VELIMIR-BATA ZIVOJINOVIC)	1965	79	6			IMPACT FILMS	
THREE (CHARLOTTE RAMPLING, ROBIE PORTER)	1969	104	5			UNITED ARTISTS	
THREE AND A HALF MUSKETEERS (ITALIAN)	1961	91		2.0		COM. UNITED T.V.	
THREE AVENGERS, THE (ITALIAN)	1964	98		1.0	1.5	ABC FILMS	
THREE BAD SISTERS	1956	76		2.0	1.5	UNITED ARTISTS	
THREE BITES OF THE APPLE	1967	98	3	2.0		M-G-M	
THREE BLIND MICE	1938	75		2.5	2.5	20th CENTURY FOX	
THREE BLONDES IN HIS LIFE	1960	86		1.0	2.0	PARAMOUNT	
THREE BRAVE MEN	1957	88	5	2.5	2.5	20th CENTURY FOX	
THREE CAME HOME	1950	106	5*	3.0	3.5	20th CENTURY FOX	
THREE CAME TO KILL	1960	70	2			UNITED ARTISTS	
THREE CASES OF MURDER (BRITISH)	1954	99		3.5	2.5	ASSOCIATED ARTISTS	THREE STORIES
THREE CHEERS FOR THE IRISH	1940	100		2.5	2.5	WARNER BROTHERS	

‡ An asterisk (*) in THE FILM BUFF'S BIBLE column indicates that the film has been rated by the editor and/or staff. All other ratings in this column are based on a consensus of reviews (see NOTES).

TITLE (LEADING ACTORS SHOWN WHERE TWO OR MORE FILMS HAVE THE SAME OR SIMILAR TITLE)	YEAR RELEASED	RUNNING TIME IN MINUTES	THE FILM BUFF'S BIBLE ‡	STEVEN SCHEUER	LEONARD MALTIN	DISTRIBUTOR	COMMENT
THREE COINS IN THE FOUNTAIN	1954	102	6	2.5	3.0	20th CENTURY FOX	NOMINATED BEST PICTURE
THREE COMRADES	1938	100	4*	3.5	3.5	M-G-M	
THREE-CORNERED MOON	1933	77		2.5	3.0	PARAMOUNT	
THREE DARING DAUGHTERS	1948	115		2.5	2.5	M-G-M	
THREE DESPARATE MEN	1951	71		2.5	1.5	LIPPERT PRODS.	
THREE ETC'S AND THE COLONEL (ITALIAN)	1962	99		1.5		EMERY PICTURES	
THREE FABLES OF LOVE (ITALIAN, FRENCH, SPANISH)	1963	76	6			JANUS FILMS	THREE STORIES, ORIGINALLY FOUR
THREE FACES OF EVE, THE	1957	91	4*	3.0	3.5	20th CENTURY FOX	
THREE FACES WEST	a1940	79		3.0	2.5	REPUBLIC	
THREE FOR BEDROOM C	1952	74	2	2.0	2.0	WARNER BROTHERS	
THREE FOR JAMIE DAWN	1956	81	3		2.0	ALLIED ARTISTS	
THREE FOR THE SHOW	1955	93		2.0	2.0	COLUMBIA	
THREE FORBIDDEN STORIES (ITALIAN)	1952	109	4			ELLIS FILMS	
THREE GIRLS ABOUT TOWN	1941	73		2.5	2.5	COLUMBIA	
THREE GODFATHERS (JOHN WAYNE, PEDRO ARMENDARIZ)	1949	106	5	3.0		M-G-M	
THREE GUNS FOR TEXAS	1968	99	2	2.5	2.0	UNIVERSAL	
THREE GUYS NAMED MIKE	1951	90		2.5	2.5	M-G-M	
THREE HEARTS FOR JULIA	1943	89		2.0	2.0	M-G-M	
THREE HOURS TO KILL	1954	77	5	3.0	3.0	COLUMBIA	
300 SPARTANS, THE	1962	114	3	2.0	1.5	20th CENTURY FOX	
THREE HUSBANDS	a1950	78		3.0	2.5	UNITED ARTISTS	
THREE IN THE ATTIC	1968	90	2	1.0		AMERICAN-INTERNAT'L	
THREE IN THE CELLAR	a1970	92	3			AMERICAN-INTERNAT'L	
THREE INTO TWO WON'T GO (BRITISH)	1969	93	6	3.0		UNIVERSAL	
THREE IS A FAMILY	1944	81		3.0	2.5	UNITED ARTISTS	
THREE LITTLE GIRLS IN BLUE	1946	90		2.5	3.0	20th CENTURY FOX	
THREE LITTLE SISTERS	1944	69		2.0		REPUBLIC	
THREE LITTLE WORDS	1950	102	6	3.0	3.0	M-G-M	
THREE LIVES OF THOMASINA, THE	1963	97	6			BUENA VISTA	
THREE LOVES HAS NANCY	1938	69		2.5	2.5	M-G-M	
THREE MEN IN A BOAT (BRITISH)	1956	95		3.0	2.0	VALIANT	
THREE MEN IN WHITE	1944	85		2.0	-	M-G-M	
THREE MEN ON A HORSE	1936	88		3.5	3.0	FIRST NATIONAL	
THREE MURDERESSES (FRENCH)	a1960	95		2.5	2.5	20th CENTURY FOX	
THREE MUSKETEERS, THE (WALTER ABLE, PAUL LUKAS)	1935	90	3*	3.0	2.0	RKO	
THREE MUSKETEERS, THE (DON AMECHE, RITZ BROTHERS)	1939	73		2.0	3.0	20th CENTURY FOX	
THREE MUSKETEERS, THE (LANA TURNER, GENE KELLY)	1948	125		3.0	2.5	M-G-M	
THREE NUTS IN SEARCH OF A BOLT	1964	80	1			HARLEQUIN INTERNAT'L	
THREE ON A COUCH	1966	109	3	1.0		COLUMBIA	
THREE ON A MATCH	1932	64		2.5	3.0	FIRST NATIONAL	
THREE ON A SPREE (BRITISH)	1961	83		1.5	1.5	UNITED ARTISTS	
THREE OUTLAWS, THE	1956	74		2.0		ASSOC'D FILM DISTS.	
THREE PENNY OPERA (CURT JURGENS, SAMMY DAVIS JR)	1963	83	3	2.0	2.5	AVCO-EMBASSY	(GERMAN) ENGLISH LANGUAGE
THREE RING CIRCUS	1955	103		2.0	2.0	PARAMOUNT	
THREE SAILORS AND A GIRL	1953	95		2.0	2.0	WARNER BROTHERS	
THREE SECRETS	1950	98	4*	3.0	3.0	WARNER BROTHERS	
THREE SISTERS, THE (RUSSIAN - LYUBOV SOKOLVA)	1964	112	6			BRANDON	
THREE SISTERS, THE (KIM STANLEY, GERALDINE PAGE)	1965	168		3.5	2.5	ELY LANDAU	
THREE SMART GIRLS	1937	86		3.5	3.5	UNIVERSAL	NOMINATED BEST PICTURE
THREE SMART GIRLS GROW UP	1939	87		3.0	3.0	UNIVERSAL	
THREE SONS O' GUNS	1941	64		2.0		WARNER BROTHERS	
THREE STEPS NORTH (ITALIAN)	1951	85	5	3.0		UNITED ARTISTS	
THREE STOOGES GO AROUND WORLD IN DAZE, THE	1963	94	3		2.5	COLUMBIA	
THREE STOOGES IN ORBIT, THE	1962	87		2.0	2.0	COLUMBIA	
THREE STOOGES MEET HERCULES, THE	1962	89	2	2.0	2.0	COLUMBIA	
THREE STOPS TO MURDER (BRITISH)	1954	.77		2.0		ASTOR	
THREE STRANGE LOVES (SWEDISH)	a1950	78	3			JANUS FILMS	
THREE STRANGERS	1946	92		3.0	3.5	WARNER BROTHERS	
THREE STRIPES IN THE SUN	1955	93		2.5	2.5	COLUMBIA	
THREE SWORDS OF ZORRO, THE (ITALIAN)	1964	88		1.5		NTA PICTURES	
3:10 TO YUMA	1957	92	6*	3.5	3.5	COLUMBIA	
THREE VIOLENT PEOPLE	1957	100		2.5	2.5	PARAMOUNT	
THREE WISE FOOLS	1946	90		2.0	2.0	M-G-M	
THREE WORLDS OF GULLIVER, THE	1960	100		3.0	3.0	COLUMBIA	
THREE YOUNG TEXANS	1954	78	2	2.0	2.0	20th CENTURY FOX	
THREEPENNY OPERA, THE (GERMAN - RUDOLPH FORSTER)	1931	112	6			BRANDON	
THREE'S A CROWD (T.V. - LARRY HAGMAN)	1969	75		2.5		SCREEN GEMS	
THRILL OF A ROMANCE	1945	105		2.0	2.0	M-G-M	
THRILL OF BRAZIL, THE	1946	91			2.5	COLUMBIA	
THRILL OF IT ALL, THE	1963	108	6	3.0	3.0	UNIVERSAL	
THRONE OF BLOOD (JAPANESE)	1957	105	5			BRANDON	
THROUGH A GLASS DARKLY (SWEDISH)	1960	91	5*			JANUS FILMS	
THUNDER AFLOAT	1939	94		2.5	2.5	M-G-M	
THUNDER ALLEY	1967	90	2			AMERICAN-INTERNAT'L	
THUNDER BAY	1953	102	4	2.5	3.0	UNIVERSAL	
THUNDER BELOW	1932	67		2.0	2.5	PARAMOUNT	
THUNDER BIRDS (GENE TIERNEY, PRESTON FOSTER)	1942	78		2.0	2.0	20th CENTURY FOX	
THUNDER IN CAROLINA	1960	92	3		2.0	HOWCO INTERNATIONAL	
THUNDER IN THE EAST (ALAN LADD, DEBORAH KERR)	1953	98	4	2.5	2.5	PARAMOUNT	
THUNDER IN THE SUN	1959	81		2.0	2.5	PARAMOUNT	
THUNDER IN THE VALLEY	1947	103		2.5	2.5	20th CENTURY FOX	
THUNDER ISLAND	1963	65	1			20th CENTURY FOX	
THUNDER OF DRUMS, A	1961	97		2.5	2.5	M-G-M	
THUNDER ON THE HILL	1951	84		3.0	3.0	UNIVERSAL	

‡ An asterisk (*) in THE FILM BUFF'S BIBLE column indicates that the film has been rated by the editor and/or staff. All other ratings in this column are based on a consensus of reviews (see NOTES).

TITLE (LEADING ACTORS SHOWN WHERE TWO OR MORE FILMS HAVE THE SAME OR SIMILAR TITLE)	YEAR RELEASED	RUNNING TIME IN MINUTES	THE FILM BUFF'S BIBLE ‡	STEVEN SCHEUER	LEONARD MALTIN	DISTRIBUTOR	COMMENT
THUNDER OVER ARIZONA	1956	75		2.0	2.0	REPUBLIC	
THUNDER OVER TANGIER (BRITISH)	1957	66		2.0	1.5	REPUBLIC	
THUNDER OVER THE PLAINS	1953	82		2.0	2.0	WARNER BROTHERS	
THUNDER PASS	1954	76		2.5	2.0	LIPPERT PRODS.	
THUNDER ROAD	1958	92		2.0	2.5	UNITED ARTISTS	
THUNDER ROCK (BRITISH)	1942	95		4.0	3.0	ENGLISH FILMS	
THUNDERBALL (BRITISH)	1965	125	6			UNITED ARTISTS	
THUNDERBIRDS (JOHN DEREK, JOHN BARRYMORE JR)	1952	98		2.0	2.5	REPUBLIC	
THUNDERCLOUD	a1950	74		2.5	2.5	WARNER BROTHERS	
THUNDERHEAD, SON OF FLICKA	1945	78		2.5	2.5	20th CENTURY FOX	
THUNDERING JETS	1958	73	2		1.5	20th CENTURY FOX	
THUNDERSTORM (SPANISH)	1956	88		1.5	1.0	ALLIED ARTISTS	
THX 1138	1971	88	5	3.0		WARNER BROTHERS	
THY NEIGHBOR'S WIFE	1953	77	2	1.5		20th CENTURY FOX	
TIARA TAHITI (BRITISH)	1962	100		2.5	2.0	ZENITH INTERNATIONAL	
. . . TICK . . . TICK . . . TICK . . .	1970	98	3*			M-G-M	
TICKET TO TOMAHAWK, A	1950	90		2.5	2.5	20th CENTURY FOX	
TICKLE ME	1965	90		2.0	2.5	ALLIED ARTISTS	
TICKLISH AFFAIR, A	1963	89	4	2.0	2.0	M-G-M	
TIGER AND THE PUSSYCAT, THE	1967	105		2.0	2.5	AVCO-EMBASSY	
TIGER BAY (BRITISH)	1959	105	7*	4.0	3.0	CONTINENTAL	
TIGER BY THE TAIL (BRITISH - LARRY PARKS)	a1955	83	3	2.0		UNITED ARTISTS	
TIGER MAKES OUT, THE	1967	95	3*	3.5		COLUMBIA	
TIGER OF THE SEA (JAPANESE)	1964	85		1.0		AMERICAN-INTERNAT'L	
TIGER OF THE SEVEN SEAS (ITALIAN)	1962	90			2.0	AVCO-EMBASSY	
TIGER SHARK	1932	80		3.0		FIRST NATIONAL	
TIGER WALKS, A	1964	91	4			BUENA VISTA	
TIGER WOMAN, THE	1945	57		3.0		REPUBLIC	
TIGHT LITTLE ISLAND (BRITISH)	1949	81	7	4.0	4.0	UNIVERSAL	
TIGHT SHOES	1941	68		3.5		UNIVERSAL	
TIGHT SPOT	1955	97	4*	3.5	3.5	COLUMBIA	
TIJUANA STORY, THE	1957	72	1	2.0	1.0	COLUMBIA	
TIKO AND THE SHARK (ITALIAN)	1962	88	3			M-G-M	
TILL THE CLOUDS ROLL BY	1947	137		3.0	2.5	M-G-M	
TILL THE END OF TIME	1946	105		3.5	3.0	RKO	
TILL WE MEET AGAIN (HERBERT MARSHALL, G. MICHAEL)	1936	72		2.0		PARAMOUNT	
'TIL WE MEET AGAIN (MERLE OBERON, GEORGE BRENT)	1940	99		3.0	2.5	WARNER BROTHERS	
TILL WE MEET AGAIN (RAY MILLAND, BARBARA BRITTON)	1944	88		2.0	2.0	PARAMOUNT	
TILLIE AND GUS	1933	58	5*	3.0	3.5	PARAMOUNT	
TIMBER	1942	60		2.5		UNIVERSAL	
TIMBER QUEEN	1943	66		2.0	1.5	PARAMOUNT	
TIMBERJACK	1955	94		2.0	2.0	REPUBLIC	
TIMBUKTU	1959	91		1.5	2.0	UNITED ARTISTS	
TIME BOMB (FRENCH - CURT JURGENS)	1959	92		2.5	2.0	ALLIED ARTISTS	
TIME FOR BURNING, A (DOCUMENTARY)	1966	60	6	4.0		LUTHERAN FILM ASSOC.	
TIME FOR KILLING, A	a1967	88	4*	2.5		COLUMBIA	
TIME, GENTLEMEN, PLEASE (BRITISH)	a1952	82		2.5		EROS FILMS	
TIME IN THE SUN, A (SWEDISH)	1969	105	3			UNIVERSAL	
TIME IS MY ENEMY (BRITISH)	1954	64		2.5		REPUBLIC	
TIME LIMIT	1957	96	5*	3.5	3.0	UNITED ARTISTS	
TIME LOST AND TIME REMEMBERED (BRITISH)	1966	91		2.5	3.0	CONTINENTAL	
TIME MACHINE, THE	1960	103	6*	3.5	3.5	M-G-M	
TIME OF DESIRE (SWEDISH)	1957	86	4			JANUS FILMS	
TIME OF INDIFFERENCE (ITALIAN)	1964	84		2.0	2.5	CONTINENTAL	
TIME OF THEIR LIVES, THE	1946	82		3.0	3.0	UNIVERSAL	
TIME OF YOUR LIFE, THE	1948	109	7	4.0	4.0	UNITED ARTISTS	
TIME OUT FOR LOVE (FRENCH)	1961	93		1.5	2.5	ZENITH INTERNATIONAL	
TIME OUT OF MIND	1947	88		2.0	2.0	UNIVERSAL	
TIME RUNNING OUT	1959	90		2.0		WARNER BROTHERS	
TIME, THE PLACE AND THE GIRL, THE	1946	105		2.5	2.5	WARNER BROTHERS	
TIME TO KILL (LLOYD NOLAN, HEATHER ANGEL)	1943	61		2.0		20th CENTURY FOX	
TIME TO LOVE AND A TIME TO DIE, A	1958	133		3.0	2.5	UNIVERSAL	
TIME TO REMEMBER (BRITISH)	1962	58		2.0		ANGLO AMALGAMATED	
TIME TO SING, A	1968	92	2			M-G-M	
TIME TRAVELERS, THE	1964	82		2.5	1.5	AMERICAN-INTERNAT'L	
TIME WITHOUT PITY (BRITISH)	1957	88		2.0	2.5	ASTOR	
TIMELOCK (BRITISH)	a1957	74		2.5		DIST. CORP. OF AMER.	
TIMES GONE BY (ITALIAN)	1953	110	6			ITALIAN FILMS EXPORT	
TIMETABLE	1956	79	4	3.0	2.0	UNITED ARTISTS	
TIN PAN ALLEY	1940	94		3.5	3.0	20th CENTURY FOX	
TIN STAR, THE	1957	93	5*	3.5	3.0	PARAMOUNT	
TINGLER, THE	1959	80	3	3.0	2.0	COLUMBIA	
TIP ON A DEAD JOCKEY	1957	129	5	3.0	3.0	M-G-M	
TITAN, THE (DOCUMENTARY)	1950	67	7			PANDORA FILMS	
TITANIC	1953	98	6	3.0	3.0	20th CENTURY FOX	
TITFIELD THUNDERBOLT, THE (BRITISH)	1953	84	6	4.0	3.0	UNIVERSAL	
TITICUT FOLLIES (DOCUMENTARY)	1967	85	7	4.0		GROVE PRESS	
TO BE A CROOK (FRENCH)	1965	93	4			COMET FILM	
TO BE OR NOT TO BE	1942	99		3.5	3.5	UNITED ARTISTS	
TO BED OR NOT TO BED (ITALIAN)	a1963	103	5		2.5	CONTINENTAL	
TO CATCH A SPY (FRENCH)	1957	85		2.0		AMERICAN-INTERNAT'L	
TO CATCH A THIEF	1955	97	6*	3.0	3.0	PARAMOUNT	
TO COMMIT A MURDER (FRENCH)	1970	91	3			CINERAMA RELEASING	
TO DIE IN MADRID (FRENCH, DOCUMENTARY)	1963	85	6*			ALTURA FILMS	

‡ An asterisk (*) in THE FILM BUFF'S BIBLE column indicates that the film has been rated by the editor and/or staff. All other ratings in this column are based on a consensus of reviews (see NOTES).

TITLE (LEADING ACTORS SHOWN WHERE TWO OR MORE FILMS HAVE THE SAME OR SIMILAR TITLE)	YEAR RELEASED	RUNNING TIME IN MINUTES	THE FILM BUFF'S BIBLE ‡	STEVEN SCHEUER	LEONARD MALTIN	DISTRIBUTOR	COMMENT
TO DIE OF LOVE (FRENCH)	1971	105	6			M-G-M	
TO EACH HIS OWN	1946	122	7*	4.0	3.0	PARAMOUNT	
TO FIND A MAN	1972	93	5			COLUMBIA	
TO HAVE AND HAVE NOT	1944	100	5-6*	3.5	3.5	WARNER BROTHERS	
TO HAVE AND TO HOLD (BRITISH - RAY BARRETT)	1961	71		2.0		ANGLO AMALGAMATED	
TO HELL AND BACK	1955	106	6	3.0	3.0	UNIVERSAL	
TO INGRID MY LOVE, LISA (SWEDISH)	1969	76	1			CANNON RELEASING	
TO KILL A MOCKINGBIRD	1963	129	6*	4.0	3.5	UNIVERSAL	NOMINATED BEST PICTURE
TO LIVE IN PEACE (ITALIAN)	1946	90	7			TIMES FILM CORP.	
TO LOVE (SWEDISH)	1964	88	4			PROMINENT FILMS	
TO MARY - WITH LOVE	1936	87		2.5	2.5	20th CENTURY FOX	
TO PARIS, WITH LOVE (BRITISH)	1955	78		2.5	2.5	CONTINENTAL	
TO PLEASE A LADY	1950	91		2.5	2.5	M-G-M	
TO SIR, WITH LOVE (BRITISH)	1967	105	7*	4.0	3.5	COLUMBIA	
TO THE ENDS OF THE EARTH	1948	109	5*	4.0	3.5	COLUMBIA	
TO THE SHORES OF HELL	1966	90	1			ROBERT PATRICK	
TO THE SHORES OF TRIPOLI	1942	86		2.5	2.5	20th CENTURY FOX	
TO THE VICTOR	1948	100	4	2.5	2.5	GAUMONT-BRITISH	
TO TRAP A SPY	1966	92	4		2.5	M-G-M	
TOAST OF NEW ORLEANS, THE	1950	97		2.5	2.5	M-G-M	
TOAST OF NEW YORK, THE	1937	109		3.0	3.0	RKO	
TOBACCO ROAD	1941	84		2.5	2.5	20th CENTURY FOX	
TOBOR THE GREAT	1954	77		1.5	1.5	REPUBLIC	
TOBRUK	1967	110		2.0	2.5	UNIVERSAL	
TOBY TYLER	1960	96	5*			BUENA VISTA	
TODAY WE LIVE	1933	113		2.0	2.0	M-G-M	
TODD KILLINGS, THE	1971	93	3			NATIONAL GENERAL	
TOGETHER (DOCUMENTARY)	1972	70	1			AMERICAN-INTERNAT'L	
TOGETHER AGAIN	1944	93	4*	3.0	3.0	COLUMBIA	
TOKLAT	1971	90	3			SUN INTERNATIONAL	
TOKOLOSHE (SOUTH AFRICAN)	1971	80	3			ARTISTS INTERNAT'L	
TOKYO AFTER DARK	1959	80		2.0	2.0	PARAMOUNT	
TOKYO FILE 212	1951	84		3.0		RKO	
TOKYO JOE	1949	88	4	2.0	2.5	COLUMBIA	
TOKYO OLYMPIAD (JAPANESE, DOCUMENTARY)	1965	93	5-6*			AMERICAN-INTERNAT'L	JAPANESE VERSION 135 MINUTES
TOKYO ROSE	1945	69		2.0	2.0	PARAMOUNT	
TOKYO STORY (JAPANESE)	1953	139				NEW YORKER FILMS	
TOM BROWN'S SCHOOL DAYS (CEDRIC HARDWICKE)	a1940	81		3.0	3.0	RKO	
TOM BROWN'S SCHOOLDAYS (BRITISH - ROBERT NEWTON)	1951	93	6*	3.5	3.0	UNITED ARTISTS	
TOM, DICK AND HARRY	1941	86	6-7*	4.0	3.5	RKO	
TOM JONES (BRITISH)	1963	128	10*	4.0	4.0	UNITED ARTISTS	BEST PICTURE AWARD
TOM THUMB (RUSS TAMBLYN, ALAN YOUNG)	1958	95	6			M-G-M	
TOMAHAWK	1951	82	4	2.0	2.5	UNIVERSAL	
TOMB OF LIGEIA, THE (BRITISH)	1964	81	2			AMERICAN-INTERNAT'L	
TOMB OF TORTURE (ITALIAN)	1966	88	2			TRANS-LUX DIST.	
TOMBOY AND THE CHAMP	1961	92	4		2.0	UNIVERSAL	
TOMBSTONE, THE TOWN TOO TOUGH TO DIE	1942	79		3.0		PARAMOUNT	
TOMORROW (ROBERT DUVALL, OLGA BELLIN)	1972	103	6			FILMGROUP	
TOMORROW AT TEN (BRITISH)	1963	80	3	2.5	2.5	GOVERNOR	
TOMORROW IS ANOTHER DAY	1951	90	4	3.0	2.5	WARNER BROTHERS	
TOMORROW IS FOREVER	1946	105		2.5	3.0	RKO	
TOMORROW IS MY TURN (FRENCH)	1960	117	5	2.5		SHOWCORPORATION	
TOMORROW IS TOO LATE (ITALIAN)	1952	103	6			JOSEPH BURSTYN	
TOMORROW THE WORLD	1944	86		4.0	3.5	UNITED ARTISTS	
TONIGHT AND EVERY NIGHT	1945	92	3*	3.5	3.0	COLUMBIA	
TONIGHT AT 8:30 (BRITISH)	a1952	81		4.0	2.5	CONTINENTAL	THREE STORIES
TONIGHT IS OURS	1933	76		2.5		PARAMOUNT	
TONIGHT WE RAID CALAIS	1943	70		2.5	2.5	20th CENTURY FOX	
TONIGHT WE SING	1953	109		3.0	2.5	20th CENTURY FOX	
TONIGHT'S THE NIGHT (BRITISH)	a1954	87	6	3.0	3.0	ALLIED ARTISTS	
TONIO KROGER (GERMAN)	1964	90	3	2.5		PATHE CONTEMPARARY	
TONKA	1958	97	5			BUENA VISTA	
TONY DRAWS A HORSE (BRITISH)	1950	91	5	2.5	2.5	FINE ARTS	
TONY ROME	1967	109	3	2.0		20th CENTURY FOX	
TOO BAD SHE'S BAD (ITALIAN)	1955	96		2.5	2.0	GETZ-KINGSLEY	
TOO HOT TO HANDLE (CLARK GABLE, MYRNA LOY)	1938	105	4*	3.5	3.0	M-G-M	
TOO HOT TO HANDLE (BRITISH - JAYNE MANSFIELD)	1959	92		1.5	2.0	ASSOC. BRITISH-PATHE	
TOO LATE BLUES	1962	100		2.0	2.0	PARAMOUNT	
TOO LATE FOR TEARS	1949	99		2.5	2.5	UNITED ARTISTS	
TOO LATE THE HERO	1970	133	4			CINERAMA RELEASING	
TOO LATE TO LOVE (FRENCH)	1959	90		2.5		CONTINENTAL	
TOO MANY CROOKS (BRIT. - TERRY-THOMAS, GEO. COLE)	1959	87	4	3.0	2.5	LOPERT	
TOO MANY GIRLS	1940	85		3.0		RKO	
TOO MANY HUSBANDS	1940	84		3.0	3.0	COLUMBIA	
TOO MANY LOVERS (FRENCH)	1957	105		2.0			
TOO MUCH HARMONY	1933	76		2.5	2.5	PARAMOUNT	
TOO MUCH, TOO SOON	1958	121		2.0	2.0	WARNER BROTHERS	
TOO SOON TO LOVE	1960	85	3			UNIVERSAL	
TOO YOUNG FOR LOVE (ITALIAN)	1955	88		2.0		ITALIAN FILMS EXPORT	
TOO YOUNG TO KISS	1951	91		3.0	2.5	M-G-M	
TOO YOUNG TO KNOW	1945	86		1.5	2.0	WARNER BROTHERS	
TOO YOUNG TO LOVE (BRITISH)	1959	88		1.5		J. ARTHUR RANK	
TOP BANANA	1954	100	6	3.5	3.0	UNITED ARTISTS	
TOP FLOOR GIRL (BRITISH)	1959	71		2.0		PARAMOUNT	

‡ An asterisk (*) in THE FILM BUFF'S BIBLE column indicates that the film has been rated by the editor and/or staff. All other ratings in this column are based on a consensus of reviews (see NOTES).

TITLE (LEADING ACTORS SHOWN WHERE TWO OR MORE FILMS HAVE THE SAME OR SIMILAR TITLE)	YEAR RELEASED	RUNNING TIME IN MINUTES	THE FILM BUFF'S BIBLE ‡	STEVEN SCHEUER	LEONARD MALTIN	DISTRIBUTOR	COMMENT
TOP GUN	1955	73	3		2.5	UNITED ARTISTS	
TOP HAT	1935	101	4*	4.0	4.0	RKO	NOMINATED BEST PICTURE
TOP MAN	1943	74		2.5	2.0	UNIVERSAL	
TOP O' THE MORNING	1949	100		2.5	2.5	PARAMOUNT	
TOP OF THE FORM (BRITISH)	1953	75		2.5		J. ARTHUR RANK	
TOP OF THE HEAP	1972	85	2			FANFARE	
TOP OF THE WORLD	1955	90	3	2.5	2.0	UNITED ARTISTS	
TOP SECRET (BRITISH)	a1952	93	6	3.0		STRATFORD PICS.	
TOP SECRET AFFAIR	1957	100	4*	2.0	2.5	WARNER BROTHERS	
TOPAZ	1969	125	3*			UNIVERSAL	
TOPAZE (JOHN BARRYMORE, MYRNA LOY)	1933	78		3.5	3.0	RKO	
TOPEKA	1953	60		2.5		ALLIED ARTISTS	
TOPKAPI	1964	120	7*	4.0	4.0	UNITED ARTISTS	
TOPPER	1937	97		3.5	3.5	M-G-M	
TOPPER RETURNS	1941	85		4.0	3.0	UNITED ARTISTS	
TOPPER TAKES A TRIP	1939	85		3.5	3.0	UNITED ARTISTS	
TORA! TORA! TORA!	1970	143	5			20th CENTURY FOX	
TORCH, THE (MEXICAN)	1950	90		2.0	2.0	EAGLE LION	ENGLISH LANGUAGE
TORCH SONG	1953	90	4	2.5	3.0	M-G-M	
TORMENT (SWEDISH - STIG JARREL, ALF KJELLIN)	1946	92	:			OXFORD FILMS	
TORMENTED	1960	75		1.5	1.0	ALLIED ARTISTS	
TORN CURTAIN	1966	128		2.0	2.5	UNIVERSAL	
TORPEDO ALLEY	1953	84	2		2.0	ALLIED ARTISTS	
TORPEDO BAY (ITALIAN)	1963	91		2.5	2.5	AMERICAN-INTERNAT'L	
TORPEDO OF DOOM, THE	1938	100		3.0	3.0	REPUBLIC	RE-EDITED SERIAL
TORPEDO RUN	1958	98		2.5	2.5	M-G-M	
TORRID ZONE	1940	88		3.0	3.5	WARNER BROTHERS	
TORTILLA FLAT	1942	105	4*	3.5	3.0	M-G-M	
TORTURE GARDEN (BRITISH)	1968	92	3	2.5		COLUMBIA	
TOSCA (ITALIAN)	1956	111	6			CASOLARO FILMS	
TOUCH, THE	1971	112	5			CINERAMA RELEASING	
TOUCH AND GO (BRITISH)	a1955	85		3.0	2.5	UNIVERSAL	
TOUCH OF DEATH (BRITISH)	1962	58		1.5		PLANET	
TOUCH OF EVIL	1958	95	4	3.5	3.0	UNIVERSAL	
TOUCH OF LARCENY, A (BRITISH)	1960	93	6	3.0	3.0	PARAMOUNT	
TOUCH OF THE SUN, A (BRITISH)	1956	80		1.5		UCC FILMS	
TOUCH OF TREASON, A (FRENCH)	1962	88		1.5		FOUR STAR	
TOUCHABLES, THE (BRITISH)	1968	97	1	1.0		20th CENTURY FOX	
TOUGH GUY	1936	77		2.5		M-G-M	
TOUGHER THEY COME, THE	1950	69		1.0	1.5	COLUMBIA	
TOUGHEST GUN IN TOMBSTONE	1958	72		2.0	1.5	UNITED ARTISTS	
TOUGHEST MAN ALIVE, THE	1955	72		2.5	2.0	ALLIED ARTISTS	
TOUGHEST MAN IN ARIZONA, THE	1952	90	3	2.5	2.5	REPUBLIC	
TOURNAMENT TEMPO	a1946	67		2.5		REPUBLIC	
TOVARICH	1937	98	6*	3.5	3.5	WARNER BROTHERS	
TOWARD THE UNKNOWN	1956	115		2.5	3.0	WARNER BROTHERS	
TOWER OF LONDON (BASIL RATHBONE, BORIS KARLOFF)	1939	92		2.5	3.0	UNIVERSAL	V. PRICE WAS IN BOTH VERSIONS
TOWER OF LONDON (VINCENT PRICE, MICHAEL PATE)	1962	79	4		2.5	UNITED ARTISTS	V. PRICE WAS IN BOTH VERSIONS
TOWER OF SCREAMING VIRGINS	1971	90				MARON FILMS, LTD.	
TOWN CALLED HELL, A	1971	95	1			SCOTIA INTERNATIONAL	
TOWN LIKE ALICE, A (BRITISH)	1956	117		3.5	2.5	LOPERT	
TOWN ON TRIAL (BRITISH)	1956	96		3.0	1.5	COLUMBIA	
TOWN TAMER	1965	89	2			PARAMOUNT	
TOWN WITHOUT PITY	1961	105	6*	2.0	2.0	UNITED ARTISTS	
TOY BOX, THE	1971	85				BOXOFFICE INTERNAT'L	
TOY TIGER	1956	88	5*	2.5	2.5	UNIVERSAL	
TOY WIFE, THE	1938	95		1.5	2.0	M-G-M	
TOYS ARE NOT FOR CHILDREN	1972	85	3			MARON FILMS, LTD.	
TOYS IN THE ATTIC	1963	90		2.5	2.5	UNITED ARTISTS	
TRACK OF THE CAT	1954	102	3*	2.0	2.0	WARNER BROTHERS	
TRACK OF THE VAMPIRE	1966	74		1.5		AMERICAN-INTERNAT'L	
TRACK OF THUNDER	1968	83	2	1.0		UNITED ARTISTS	
TRACK THE MAN DOWN (BRITISH)	1953	75			2.0	REPUBLIC	
TRADE WINDS	1938	90		3.0	3.0	UNITED ARTISTS	
TRADER HORN	1931	123		2.5	3.0	M-G-M	NOMINATED BEST PICTURE 1930/31
TRADER HORNEE	1970	90	1			ENTERTAINM'T VENTURES	
TRAIL OF THE LONESOME PINE (SYLVIA SIDNEY)	1936	102		2.0	3.0	PARAMOUNT	
TRAIL OF THE VIGILANTES	1940	78		4.0	2.5	UNIVERSAL	
TRAIL STREET	1947	84		2.0	2.0	RKO	
TRAIN, THE	1965	133	7-8*	3.5	4.0	UNITED ARTISTS	
TRAIN OF EVENTS (BRITISH)	1949	89		2.5		J. ARTHUR RANK	
TRAIN ROBBERY CONFIDENTIAL (BRAZILIAN)	a1962	102		2.0	2.5	TIMES FILM CORP.	
TRAIN TO ALCATRAZ	1948	66		2.5		REPUBLIC	
TRAITOR WITHIN, THE	1942	62		2.5		REPUBLIC	
TRAITORS, THE (BRITISH - PATRICK ALLEN)	1962	71	3		2.5	UNIVERSAL	
TRAITOR'S GATE (BRITISH)	1965	80			2.5	COLUMBIA	
TRAMP, TRAMP, TRAMP	1942	70		1.5	1.5	COLUMBIA	
TRAMPLERS, THE (ITALIAN)	1966	105	2	2.0	2.0	AVCO-EMBASSY	
TRANS-EUROP-EXPRESS (FRENCH)	1967	105	3			TRANS-AMERICA	
TRAP, THE (SIDNEY TOLER)	1946	68			.	MONOGRAM	
TRAP, THE (RICHARD WIDMARK, TINA LOUISE)	1959	84		2.5	2.5	PARAMOUNT	
TRAPEZE	1956	105	5*	2.5	3.0	UNITED ARTISTS	
TRAPP FAMILY, THE (GERMAN)	1958	105	3			20th CENTURY FOX	
TRAPPED	1949	78		3.5	2.5	EAGLE LION	

‡ An asterisk (*) in THE FILM BUFF'S BIBLE column indicates that the film has been rated by the editor and/or staff. All other ratings in this column are based on a consensus of reviews (see NOTES).

TITLE (LEADING ACTORS SHOWN WHERE TWO OR MORE FILMS HAVE THE SAME OR SIMILAR TITLE)	YEAR RELEASED	RUNNING TIME IN MINUTES	THE FILM BUFF'S BIBLE ‡	STEVEN SCHEUER	LEONARD MALTIN	DISTRIBUTOR	COMMENT
TRAPPED BY BOSTON BLACKIE	1948	67			-	COLUMBIA	
TRAPPED BY FEAR (FRENCH)	1960	85		2.0		AMERICAN-INTERNAT'L	
TRAPPED IN TANGIERS (ITALIAN)	1960	74		1.0	1.0	20th CENTURY FOX	
TRASH	1970	103	3	2.5		CINEMA V	
TRAUMA	1962	92		1.0	2.0	PARAMOUNT	
TRAVELING EXECUTIONER, THE	1970	95	3			M-G-M	
TRAVELING SALESWOMAN, THE	1950	75	2	2.0	2.0	COLUMBIA	
TRAVIS LOGAN, D.A. (T.V.)	1971	100		2.5		CBS-TV	
TREAD SOFTLY, STRANGER (BRITISH)	1958	91	2			SHOWCORPORATION	
TREASURE ISLAND (WALLACE BEERY, JACKIE COOPER)	1934	105		3.0	3.5	M-G-M	
TREASURE ISLAND (BOBBY DRISCOLL, ROBERT NEWTON)	1949	96	6			RKO	(BRITISH)
TREASURE OF LOST CANYON, THE	1952	82		1.5	2.0	UNIVERSAL	
TREASURE OF MONTE CRISTO, THE (BR. - RORY CALHOUN)	1960	95			2.0	REGAL INTERNATIONAL	
TREASURE OF PANCHO VILLA, THE	1955	96		2.0	1.5	RKO	
TREASURE OF RUBY HILLS	1955	71	2	2.0	1.5	ALLIED ARTISTS	
TREASURE OF SAN GENNARO (ITALIAN)	1966	102	3			PARAMOUNT	
TREASURE OF SAN TERESA, THE (BRITISH)	a1959	81		2.0		CONTINENTAL	
TREASURE OF SILVER LAKE (GERMAN)	1965	80	1			COLUMBIA	
TREASURE OF THE GOLDEN CONDOR	1953	93	5*	2.0	2.5	20th CENTURY FOX	
TREASURE OF THE SIERRA MADRE, THE	1948	126	8*	4.0	4.0	WARNER BROTHERS	NOMINATED BEST PICTURE
TREE, THE	1969	92	4			ROBERT GUENETTE	
TREE GROWS IN BROOKLYN, A	1945	128	6*	3.5	3.5	20th CENTURY FOX	
TRENT'S LAST CASE (BRITISH)	1952	90		2.0	2.5	REPUBLIC	
TRESPASSER, THE	1947	71		3.0		REPUBLIC	
TRIAL (GLENN FORD, ARTHUR KENNEDY)	1955	105	5*	3.5	3.0	M-G-M	
TRIAL, THE (ANTHONY PERKINS, JEANNE MOREAU)	1963	118	6	3.5	3.5	ASTOR	
TRIAL AND ERROR (BRITISH)	1962	88	4	2.5		M-G-M	
TRIAL AT KAMPILI (JAPANESE)	1963	91		2.0		PARAMOUNT	
TRIAL OF JOAN OF ARC (FRENCH)	1962	65	6			PATHE CONTEMPARARY	
TRIAL OF THE CANTONSVILLE NINE, THE	1972	85	4			CINEMA V	
TRIAL RUN (T.V.)	1968	100		2.5		UNIVERSAL	
TRIAL WITHOUT JURY	1950	60		2.0		REPUBLIC	
TRIALS OF OSCAR WILDE, THE (BRITISH)	a1960	123	6			KINGSLEY INTERNAT'L	
TRIALS OF PRIVATE SCHWEIK (GERMAN)	1964	83		1.5		SCREEN GEMS	
TRIBES (T.V.)	1970	90	6*	3.0		20th CENTURY FOX	
TRIBUTE TO A BAD MAN	1956	95	5	3.0	3.0	M-G-M	
TRILOGY	1969	100	7			ALLIED ARTISTS	THREE STORIES
TRIO (BRITISH)	1950	91	6*	3.5	3.5	PARAMOUNT	THREE STORIES, FIRST IS BEST
TRIP, THE	1967	85	2			AMERICAN-INTERNAT'L	
TRIPLE CROSS (CHRISTOPHER PLUMMER, TREVOR HOWARD)	1967	126	4	2.5		WARNER BROTHERS	(FR.-BRIT.) ENGLISH VERSION
TRIPLE DECEPTION (BRITISH)	1956	85		3.5	2.0	J. ARTHUR RANK	
TRIPLE PLAY (T.V.)	1971	100	5*	2.0		SCREEN GEMS	THREE STORIES
TRIPLE TROUBLE	1950	66				MONOGRAM	
TRIPOLI	1950	95		2.0	2.0	PARAMOUNT	
TRISTANA (SPANISH)	1970	99	6	4.0		MARON FILMS, LTD.	
TRIUMPH OF HERCULES, THE (ITALIAN)	1964	90		1.0	2.0	SCREEN GEMS	
TRIUMPH OF MICHAEL STROGOFF (FRENCH)	1964	118		1.5		SCREEN GEMS	
TRIUMPH OF ROBIN HOOD (ITALIAN)	1962	92		1.5		AVCO-EMBASSY	
TRIUMPH OF THE SON OF HERCULES (ITALIAN)	1963	87		1.0		AVCO-EMBASSY	
TRIUMPH OF THE TEN GLADIATORS (ITALIAN)	1964	94		1.0	2.0	FOUR STAR	
TRIUMPH OF THE WILL (GERMAN, DOCUMENTARY)	1935	140	8			CONTEMPORARY	
TROG (BRITISH)	1970	91	1*			WARNER BROTHERS	
TROIKA	1969	89	3			EMERSON	
TROJAN HORSE, THE (ITALIAN)	1961	105	3		2.5	COLORAMA FEATURES	
TROJAN WOMEN, THE	1971	105	5			CINERAMA RELEASING	
TROOPER HOOK	1957	81		2.5	2.5	UNITED ARTISTS	
TROPIC HOLIDAY	1938	78		2.0	2.5	PARAMOUNT	
TROPIC OF CANCER	1970	87	4	3.0		PARAMOUNT	
TROPIC ZONE	1953	94		2.0	1.5	PARAMOUNT	
TROPICAL HEAT WAVE	1952	74	2	2.0		REPUBLIC	
TROUBLE ALONG THE WAY	1953	110		1.5	2.5	WARNER BROTHERS	
TROUBLE AT 16	a1960	93		1.0	2.0	M-G-M	
TROUBLE FOR TWO	1936	75		3.0	3.0	M-G-M	
TROUBLE IN PARADISE	1932	83	6*		4.0	PARAMOUNT	
TROUBLE IN STORE (BRITISH)	1953	85			2.5	REPUBLIC	
TROUBLE IN THE GLEN (BRITISH)	a1953	90		2.0	2.0	REPUBLIC	
TROUBLE IN THE SKY (BRITISH)	a1960	92	4*	2.5		UNIVERSAL	
TROUBLE MAKERS	1948	69			-	MONOGRAM	
TROUBLE WITH ANGELS, THE	1966	112		2.0	2.5	COLUMBIA	
TROUBLE WITH GIRLS, THE	1969	101	2		-	M-G-M	
TROUBLE WITH HARRY, THE	1956	99		3.0	3.0	PARAMOUNT	
TROUBLE WITH WOMEN, THE	1947	80		2.0	2.0	PARAMOUNT	
TROUBLEMAKER, THE	1964	80	6		3.5	JANUS FILMS	
TRUCK BUSTERS	1943	58		2.0		WARNER BROTHERS	
TRUE CONFESSION	1937	84		3.5	3.0	PARAMOUNT	
TRUE GRIT	1969	128	7	4.0		PARAMOUNT	
TRUE STORY OF JESSE JAMES, THE	1957	92		2.5	2.5	20th CENTURY FOX	
TRUE STORY OF LYNN STUART, THE	1958	78		1.5	2.5	COLUMBIA	
TRUE TO LIFE	1943	94		2.5	3.0	PARAMOUNT	
TRUE TO THE ARMY	1942	76		2.0	2.0	PARAMOUNT	
TRUE TO THE NAVY	1930	71			2.5	PARAMOUNT	
TRUNK, THE (BRITISH)	1961	72	2		1.5	COLUMBIA	
TRUNK TO CAIRO (ISRAELI)	1965	80	1			AMERICAN-INTERNAT'L	ENGLISH LANGUAGE
TRUTH, THE (FRENCH)	1960	130	6			KINGSLEY INTERNAT'L	

‡ An asterisk (*) in THE FILM BUFF'S BIBLE column indicates that the film has been rated by the editor and/or staff. All other ratings in this column are based on a consensus of reviews (see NOTES).

TITLE (LEADING ACTORS SHOWN WHERE TWO OR MORE FILMS HAVE THE SAME OR SIMILAR TITLE)	YEAR RELEASED	RUNNING TIME IN MINUTES	THE FILM BUFF'S BIBLE ‡	STEVEN SCHEUER	LEONARD MALTIN	DISTRIBUTOR	COMMENT
TRUTH ABOUT MURDER, THE	1946	63		2.0		RKO	
TRUTH ABOUT SPRING, THE (BRITISH)	1965	102		2.5	3.0	UNIVERSAL	
TRUTH ABOUT WOMEN, THE (BRITISH)	1958	107	4	2.5	2.5	CONTINENTAL	
TRY AND GET ME	a1951	92		3.5	2.5	UNITED ARTISTS	
TRYGON FACTOR, THE (BRITISH)	1967	87	3			WARNER BROTHERS	
TUGBOAT ANNIE	1933	88		3.0	3.0	M-G-M	
TUGBOAT ANNIE SAILS AGAIN	1940	77		2.0	2.0	WARNER BROTHERS	
TULSA	1949	90		3.0	3.0	EAGLE LION	
TUMBLEWEED	1953	79	4	2.0	2.0	UNIVERSAL	
TUNA CLIPPER	1949	79			1.5	MONOGRAM	
TUNES OF GLORY (BRITISH)	1960	107	8*	4.0	4.0	LOPERT	
TUNNEL OF LOVE, THE	1958	98	5*	3.0	3.0	M-G-M	
TURN BACK THE CLOCK	1933	80		3.0		M-G-M	
TURN OFF THE MOON	1937	80		3.0		PARAMOUNT	
TURN ON TO LOVE	1969	79	2			HAVEN INTERNATIONAL	
TURN THE KEY SOFTLY (BRITISH)	1953	81		3.0	2.0	J. ARTHUR RANK	
TURNABOUT	1940	83		2.5		UNITED ARTISTS	
TURNING POINT, THE (WILLIAM HOLDEN, ALEXIS SMITH)	1952	85		2.5	2.5	PARAMOUNT	
TUTTLES OF TAHITI, THE	1942	91		3.0	3.0	RKO	
TUXEDO JUNCTION	1941	71		2.0		REPUBLIC	
TWELVE ANGRY MEN	1957	95	8*	4.0	4.0	UNITED ARTISTS	NOMINATED BEST PICTURE
TWELVE CHAIRS, THE	1970	94	6*	3.0		UMC PICTURES	
TWELVE HOURS TO KILL	1960	83		1.5	1.5	20th CENTURY FOX	
TWELVE O'CLOCK HIGH	1949	132	6*	4.0	4.0	20th CENTURY FOX	NOMINATED BEST PICTURE
TWELVE TO THE MOON	1960	74		1.5	1.0	COLUMBIA	
TWENTIETH CENTURY	1934	91		3.0	4.0	COLUMBIA	
TWENTY-FIFTH HOUR, THE (FRENCH)	1967	119	4-5*	3.0		M-G-M	ENGLISH LANGUAGE
TWENTY-FOUR HOURS TO KILL (BRITISH)	1965	83		1.0	2.5	SEVEN ARTS	
20 MILLION MILES TO EARTH	1957	82	3*	1.5	2.5	COLUMBIA	
20 MILLION SWEETHEARTS	1934	89		3.5	2.5	FIRST NATIONAL	
20 MULE TEAM	1940	84		2.0	2.0	M-G-M	
21 DAYS (BRITISH)	a1938	72		2.5	2.5	COLUMBIA	
21 DAYS TOGETHER (BRITISH)	a1938	72		2.5	2.5	COLUMBIA	
TWENTY PLUS TWO	a1961	102		1.5	2.0	ALLIED ARTISTS	
27TH DAY, THE	1957	75	4*	2.5	2.5	COLUMBIA	
20,000 EYES	1961	60		2.0	1.5	20th CENTURY FOX	
20,000 LEAGUES ACROSS THE LAND (FRENCH)	1959	90		2.5			
20,000 LEAGUES UNDER THE SEA	1954	122	6*			BUENA VISTA	
20,000 POUND KISS, THE (BRITISH)	1963	57		2.0	2.5	ANGLO AMALGAMATED	
20,000 YEARS IN SING SING	1933	81		2.5	3.0	FIRST NATIONAL	
23 PACES TO BAKER STREET (BRITISH)	1956	103	6	3.0	3.0	20th CENTURY FOX	
TWICE AROUND THE DAFFODILS (BRITISH)	1962	89			2.0	ANGLO AMALGAMATED	
TWICE BLESSED	1945	77		2.5		M-G-M	
TWICE TOLD TALES	1963	119	4		3.0	UNITED ARTISTS	
TWILIGHT FOR THE GODS	1958	120		2.0	2.5	UNIVERSAL	
TWILIGHT OF HONOR	a1963	115		2.0	2.5	M-G-M	
TWILIGHT PEOPLE, THE	1972	84	2			DIMENSION PICS.	
TWILIGHT WOMEN (BRITISH)	a1953	89		2.0		LIPPERT PRODS.	
TWIN BEDS	1942	85		2.0	2.0	UNITED ARTISTS	
TWINKLE IN GOD'S EYE	1955	73		2.0	2.0	REPUBLIC	
TWIST ALL NIGHT	a1962	85	2	1.5		AMERICAN-INTERNAT'L	
TWIST AROUND THE CLOCK	1961	82	2			COLUMBIA	
TWIST OF FATE (BRITISH)	1954	89		2.0	2.0	UNITED ARTISTS	
TWIST OF SAND, A (BRITISH)	1968	90	3			UNITED ARTISTS	
TWISTED NERVE (BRITISH)	1968	118	4			NATIONAL GENERAL	
TWISTED ROAD, THE	a1948	95	6			RKO	
'2' (I, A WOMAN, PART II) (DANISH)	a1968	81	1			CHEVRON	
TWO A PENNY (BRITISH)	1968	98	4*			WORLD WIDE PICS.	
TWO AGAINST THE WORLD (HUMPHREY BOGART)	a1936	64		2.0	2.0	FIRST NATIONAL	
TWO AND TWO MAKE SIX (BRITISH)	1962	89		2.0	2.0	UNION FILMS	
TWO ARE GUILTY (FRENCH)	1963	131	6			M-G-M	
TWO CENTS WORTH OF HOPE (ITALIAN)	1952	107	6			TIMES FILM CORP.	
TWO COLONELS, THE (ITALIAN)	1962	90		2.0		MEDALLION	
TWO DAUGHTERS (INDIAN)	1962	114	2*			JANUS FILMS	TWO STORIES
TWO DOLLAR BETTOR	1951	73			2.0	REALART	
TWO-FACED WOMAN	1941	94		3.0	2.5	M-G-M	
TWO FLAGS WEST	1950	92	4	2.0	2.0	20th CENTURY FOX	
TWO FOR THE ROAD (BRITISH)	1967	111	7-8*	4.0	3.0	20th CENTURY FOX	
TWO FOR THE SEESAW	1962	120	5*	3.0	3.0	UNITED ARTISTS	
TWO FOR TONIGHT	1935	61		2.5	2.5	PARAMOUNT	
TWO GALS AND A GUY	1951	71			2.0	UNITED ARTISTS	
TWO GENTLEMEN SHARING (BRITISH)	1969	112	4			AMERICAN-INTERNAT'L	
TWO GIRLS AND A SAILOR	1944	124		3.5	3.0	M-G-M	
TWO GIRLS ON BROADWAY	1940	71		2.5	2.0	M-G-M	
TWO GLADIATORS (ITALIAN)	1962	97		1.5		ABC FILMS	
TWO GUN LADY	1956	75		1.5	2.0	ASSOC'D FILM DISTS.	
TWO GUNS AND A BADGE	1954	69		1.5	1.5	ALLIED ARTISTS	
TWO GUYS FROM MILWAUKEE	1946	90			2.5	WARNER BROTHERS	
TWO GUYS FROM TEXAS	1948	86	4	2.5	2.5	WARNER BROTHERS	
TWO HEADED SPY, THE (BRITISH)	1958	93	5	3.0		COLUMBIA	
200 MOTELS (BRITISH)	1971	99	3			UNITED ARTISTS	
TWO IN A CROWD	1936	85		2.0		UNIVERSAL	
TWO IN A TAXI	1941	62		2.0		COLUMBIA	
TWO IN THE DARK	1936	74		3.0		RKO	

‡ An asterisk (*) in THE FILM BUFF'S BIBLE column indicates that the film has been rated by the editor and/or staff. All other ratings in this column are based on a consensus of reviews (see NOTES).

TITLE (LEADING ACTORS SHOWN WHERE TWO OR MORE FILMS HAVE THE SAME OR SIMILAR TITLE)	YEAR RELEASED	RUNNING TIME IN MINUTES	THE FILM BUFF'S BIBLE ‡	STEVEN SCHEUER	LEONARD MALTIN	DISTRIBUTOR	COMMENT
TWO-LANE BLACKTOP	1971	102	3			UNIVERSAL	
TWO LITTLE BEARS, THE	1961	81		2.0	2.0	20th CENTURY FOX	
TWO LIVING, ONE DEAD (BRITISH)	1965	92	4			EMERSON FILMS	
TWO LOST WORLDS	1950	61		2.0	2.0	EAGLE LION	
TWO LOVES	1961	100		2.0	2.0	M-G-M	
TWO-MAN SUBMARINE	1944	62		2.0		COLUMBIA	
TWO MRS CARROLLS, THE	1947	99		2.0	2.5	WARNER BROTHERS	
TWO MULES FOR SISTER SARA	1970	105	4			UNIVERSAL	
TWO NIGHTS WITH CLEOPATRA (ITALIAN)	1953	80		1.5		ULTRA PICTURES CORP.	
TWO OF A KIND	1951	75	4	2.5	2.5	COLUMBIA	
TWO OF US, THE (FRENCH)	1967	86	8*	4.0		CINEMA V	
TWO ON A GUILLOTINE	1965	107	3	1.0	2.5	WARNER BROTHERS	
TWO ORPHANS, THE (ITALIAN)	1966	97		1.5		PARKSIDE PRODS.	
TWO RODE TOGETHER	1961	109		2.5	2.5	COLUMBIA	
TWO SECONDS	1932	68		3.0	2.0	FIRST NATIONAL	
TWO SISTERS FROM BOSTON	1946	112		3.0	3.0	M-G-M	
TWO SMART PEOPLE	1946	93		1.5	2.0	M-G-M	
2001: A SPACE ODYSSEY	1968	141	7*			M-G-M	
TWO THOUSAND WOMEN (BRITISH)	a1944	97	5*	3.5		UNITED ARTISTS	
2000 YEARS LATER	1969	80	3			WARNER BROTHERS	
TWO TICKETS TO BROADWAY	1951	106		2.5	2.5	RKO	
TWO TICKETS TO LONDON	1943	79		2.0	2.0	UNIVERSAL	
TWO TICKETS TO PARIS	1962	78	1			COLUMBIA	
TWO-WAY STRETCH (BRITISH)	1960	87	6*	3.5	3.0	SHOWCORPORATION	
TWO WEEKS IN ANOTHER TOWN	1962	107	4	2.5	3.0	M-G-M	
TWO WEEKS IN SEPTEMBER (FRENCH)	1967	96	2			PARAMOUNT	ENGLISH VERSION
TWO WEEKS WITH LOVE	1950	92		2.5	2.5	M-G-M	
TWO WIVES AT ONE WEDDING (BRITISH)	1960	66		1.5	1.5	WARNER BROTHERS	
TWO WOMEN (ITALIAN)	1960	99	6*	4.0	4.0	AVCO-EMBASSY	
TWO WORLDS (GERMAN)	1959	85		2.0			
TWO YANKS IN TRINIDAD	1942	88		3.0	2.0	COLUMBIA	
TWO YEARS BEFORE THE MAST	1946	98	4	2.5	1.5	PARAMOUNT	
TWONKY, THE	1953	72		1.0	1.5	UNITED ARTISTS	
TYCOON	1947	128	4*	3.0	2.5	RKO	
TYPHOON	1940	70		1.5	2.5	PARAMOUNT	
TYPHOON OVER NAGASAKI (FRENCH)	1956	90		2.0		CURZON	
TYRANT OF CASTILE, THE (ITALIAN)	1964	104		1.0		FOUR STAR	
TYRANT OF LYDIA AGAINST THE SON OF HERCULES (ITAL)	1963	107		1.0		AVCO-EMBASSY	
TYRANT OF THE SEA	1950	70		1.5		COLUMBIA	
U-BOAT PRISONER	1944	65		2.0		COLUMBIA	
U-238 AND THE WITCH DOCTOR	1953	100		1.0	1.5	REPUBLIC	RE-EDITED SERIAL
UFO (UNIDENTIFID FLYING OBJECTS) (DOCUMENTARY)	a1956	92			2.0	UNITED ARTISTS	
UGETSU (JAPANESE)	1953	96	6	3.5	3.0	HARRISON PICTURES	
UGLY AMERICAN, THE	1963	120	5*	3.0	2.5	UNIVERSAL	
UGLY DACHSHUND, THE	1966	93	5			BUENA VISTA	
UGLY ONES, THE (ITALIAN)	1966	97	1			UNITED ARTISTS	
ULYSSES (ITALIAN - KIRK DOUGLAS, SILVANA MANGANO)	1955	104	4*	2.0	3.0	PARAMOUNT	ENGLISH LANGUAGE
ULYSSES (BRITISH - MILO O'SHEA, BARBARA JEFFORD)	1967	140	5*			CONTINENTAL	
ULYSSES AGAINST HERCULES (ITALIAN)	a1961	99		1.5	1.5	AVCO-EMBASSY	
UMBERTO D (ITALIAN)	1952	89	5*	4.0	3.5	HARRISON PICTURES	
UMBRELLAS OF CHERBOURG, THE (FRENCH)	1964	90	7*	3.0	3.5	LANDAU/UNGER COM. UN	
UNCERTAIN GLORY	1944	102		2.0	2.0	WARNER BROTHERS	
UNCHAINED	1955	75	3*	4.0	2.0	WARNER BROTHERS	
UNCLE, THE (BRITISH)	1964	87	6			LENART PRODUCTIONS	
UNCLE HARRY	a1945	80		3.0	3.0	UNIVERSAL	
UNCLE TOM'S CABIN (GERMAN - JOHN KITZMILLER)	1965	118	2			KROGER BABB	ENGLISH LANGUAGE
UNCLE VANYA (RUSSIAN)	1971	110	5			ARTKINO	
UNCLE WAS A VAMPIRE (ITALIAN)	1961	95		2.5		AVCO-EMBASSY	
UNCONQUERED, THE	1947	146		2.5	2.5	PARAMOUNT	
UNDEAD, THE	1957	75		1.5		AMERICAN-INTERNAT'L	
UNDEFEATED, THE (JOHN WAYNE, ROCK HUDSON)	1969	119	4*			20th CENTURY FOX	
UNDER CAPRICORN	1949	117		3.0	2.0	WARNER BROTHERS	
UNDER-COVER MAN (GEORGE RAFT)	1932	70	4*	2.0	2.0	PARAMOUNT	
UNDER FIRE	1957	78	4		2.0	20th CENTURY FOX	
UNDER MY SKIN	1950	86		2.0	2.5	20th CENTURY FOX	
UNDER TEN FLAGS	1960	92		2.0	2.5	PARAMOUNT	
UNDER THE GUN	1951	83	3	1.5	2.5	UNIVERSAL	
UNDER THE PARIS SKY (FRENCH)	1951	103	6			DISCINA INTERNAT'L	
UNDER THE RED ROBE (BRITISH)	1937	82			2.5	20th CENTURY FOX	
UNDER THE RED SEA (DOCUMENTARY)	1952	67	4			RKO	
UNDER THE YUM YUM TREE	1963	110		2.5	2.5	COLUMBIA	
UNDER TWO FLAGS	1936	105		2.5	3.0	20th CENTURY FOX	
UNDER WESTERN SKIES	1945	83		1.0	1.5	UNIVERSAL	
UNDERCOVER GIRL (ALEXIS SMITH, SCOTT BRADY)	1950	83		2.0	2.0	UNIVERSAL	
UNDERCOVER MAISIE	1947	90		2.0	-	M-G-M	
UNDERCOVER MAN, THE (GLENN FORD, NINA FOCH)	1949	83	6	3.0	3.0	COLUMBIA	
UNDERCOVER WOMAN	1946	56		2.0		REPUBLIC	
UNDERCURRENT	1946	116		2.5	2.5	M-G-M	
UNDERGROUND (JEFFREY LYNN, PHILIP DORN)	1941	95		3.0	3.0	WARNER BROTHERS	
UNDERGROUND (ROBERT GOULET, DANIELE GAUBERT)	1970	100	3			UNITED ARTISTS	
UNDERGROUND AGENT	1942	68		2.0		COLUMBIA	

‡ An asterisk (*) in THE FILM BUFF'S BIBLE column indicates that the film has been rated by the editor and/or staff. All other ratings in this column are based on a consensus of reviews (see NOTES).

TITLE (LEADING ACTORS SHOWN WHERE TWO OR MORE FILMS HAVE THE SAME OR SIMILAR TITLE)	YEAR RELEASED	RUNNING TIME IN MINUTES	CRITICAL RATINGS			DISTRIBUTOR	COMMENT
			THE FILM BUFF'S BIBLE ‡	STEVEN SCHEUER	LEONARD MALTIN		
UNDERSEA GIRL	1957	75		1.5	1.0	ALLIED ARTISTS	
UNDERTOW	1949	71		2.5	2.5	UNIVERSAL	
UNDERWATER	1955	99		2.5	2.0	RKO	
UNDERWATER CITY, THE	1962	78	1			COLUMBIA	
UNDERWATER WARRIOR	1958	90		2.0	2.5	M-G-M	
UNDERWORLD INFORMERS (BRITISH)	a1965	104	4	2.5	3.0	CONTINENTAL	
UNDERWORLD STORY, THE	a1950	90	4	3.0	3.0	UNITED ARTISTS	
UNDERWORLD U.S.A.	1961	99	3	3.0	3.0	COLUMBIA	
UNDYING MONSTER, THE	1942	60		2.5	2.0	20th CENTURY FOX	
UNEARTHLY, THE	1957	73		1.0	1.5	REPUBLIC	
UNEARTHLY STRANGER, THE (BRITISH)	1963	75	3	2.5		AMERICAN-INTERNAT'L	
UNEXPECTED UNCLE	1941	67		2.5		RKO	
UNFAITHFUL, THE (ANN SHERIDAN)	1947	109	4		2.5	WARNER BROTHERS	
UNFAITHFULLY YOURS	1948	105		3.0	3.0	20th CENTURY FOX	
UNFAITHFULS, THE (ITALIAN - GINA LOLLOBRIGIDA)	1952	89		1.5	2.5	ALLIED ARTISTS	
UNFINISHED BUSINESS	1941	96		2.0	2.0	UNIVERSAL	
UNFINISHED DANCE, THE	1947	100	5	2.5	2.5	M-G-M	
UNFORGIVEN, THE	1960	125	6	3.0	3.0	UNITED ARTISTS	
UNFORGOTTEN CRIME	a1942	72		3.5		REPUBLIC	
UNGUARDED HOUR, THE	1936	88		2.0		M-G-M	
UNGUARDED MOMENT, THE	1956	95	4	2.0	2.5	UNIVERSAL	
UNHOLY DESIRE (JAPANESE)	1964	150	6			TOHO	
UNHOLY FOUR, THE (BRITISH)	1954	80		2.0	1.5	LIPPERT PRODS.	
UNHOLY GARDEN, THE	1931	85		2.0	2.0	UNITED ARTISTS	
UNHOLY INTRUDERS, THE (GERMAN)	a1956	80		1.5		TELEWIDE SYSTEMS	
UNHOLY NIGHT, THE	1929	94			2.0	M-G-M	
UNHOLY PARTNERS	1941	94		2.5	3.0	M-G-M	
UNHOLY THREE	1930	75		2.0	2.0	M-G-M	
UNHOLY WIFE	1957	94		2.0	1.5	UNIVERSAL	
UNINHIBITED, THE (SPANISH)	1965	104	3			PEPPERCORN-WORMSER	
UNINVITED, THE	1944	98	6*	3.0	3.5	PARAMOUNT	
UNION DEPOT	1932	75		3.5	2.5	FIRST NATIONAL	
UNION PACIFIC	1939	133		3.0	3.0	PARAMOUNT	
UNION STATION	1950	80	5-6*	3.0	3.0	PARAMOUNT	
UNKNOWN GUEST, THE	1943	64		3.5	2.5	MONOGRAM	
UNKNOWN ISLAND	1948	76			1.5	FILM CLASSICS	
UNKNOWN MAN, THE	1951	86		2.5	2.5	M-G-M	
UNKNOWN TERROR, THE	1957	77			2.0	20th CENTURY FOX	
UNKNOWN WORLD	1951	63	1			LIPPERT PRODS.	
UNMAN, WITTERING AND ZIGO (BRITISH)	1971	100	5			PARAMOUNT	
UNMASKED	1950	60	2			REPUBLIC	
UNSEEN, THE	1945	81		3.5	2.0	PARAMOUNT	
UNSINKABLE MOLLY BROWN, THE	1964	128	5*	3.0		M-G-M	
UNSUSPECTED, THE	1947	103		2.5	2.5	WARNER BROTHERS	
UNTAMED (RAY MILLAND, AKIM TAMIROFF)	1940	83		2.5		PARAMOUNT	
UNTAMED (TYRONE POWER, SUSAN HAYWARD)	1955	111		2.0	3.0	20th CENTURY FOX	
UNTAMED BREED, THE	1948	79	3		2.0	COLUMBIA	
UNTAMED FRONTIER	1952	75		2.5	2.5	UNIVERSAL	
UNTAMED HEIRESS	1954	70		1.5	1.5	REPUBLIC	
UNTAMED YOUTH	1957	80		1.5	1.5	WARNER BROTHERS	
UNTIL HELL IS FROZEN (GERMAN)	1960	87			2.0	D.U.K.	
UNTIL THEY SAIL	1957	95		3.0	2.5	M-G-M	
UNTOUCHED (MEXICAN)	1956	85		2.5		EXCELSIOR	
UNWED MOTHER	1958	74		2.0	1.5	ALLIED ARTISTS	
UNWRITTEN CODE, THE	1944	61		1.5		COLUMBIA	
UP FROM THE BEACH	1965	99	4	3.0	2.5	20th CENTURY FOX	
UP FRONT	1951	92		3.0	2.5	UNIVERSAL	
UP GOES MAISIE	1946	89		2.0		M-G-M	
UP IN ARMS	1944	106		3.0	2.5	RKO	
UP IN CENTRAL PARK	1948	88		2.0	2.0	UNIVERSAL	
UP IN MABEL'S ROOM	1944	76		2.5	3.0	UNITED ARTISTS	
UP IN SMOKE	1957	64				ALLIED ARTISTS	
UP IN THE CELLAR	a1970	92	3			AMERICAN-INTERNAT'L	
UP PERISCOPE	1959	111	3*	2.5	2.5	WARNER BROTHERS	
UP THE CREEK (BRITISH)	1958	83		2.5	2.5	DOMINANT PICTURES	
UP THE DOWN STAIRCASE	1967	123	5*	4.0		WARNER BROTHERS	
UP THE MACGREGORS (ITALIAN)	1966	93	2			COLUMBIA	ENGLISH LANGUAGE
UP TO HIS EARS (FRENCH)	1965	94	4			LOPERT	
UP TO HIS NECK (BRITISH)	1954	89		2.0		J. ARTHUR RANK	
UPON THIS ROCK	1971	90				LEVITT-PICKMAN	
UPPER HAND, THE (FRENCH)	1966	86	3		2.5	PARAMOUNT	
UPSTAIRS AND DOWNSTAIRS (BRITISH)	1959	100	4	3.0	2.5	20th CENTURY FOX	
UPTIGHT	1968	104	5			PARAMOUNT	
UPTURNED GLASS, THE (BRITISH)	1947	87	3			UNIVERSAL	
URANIUM BOOM	1956	67		1.5	1.5	COLUMBIA	
URGE TO KILL (BRITISH)	1960	58		2.0		ANGLO AMALGAMATED	
URSUS IN THE LAND OF FIRE (ITALIAN)	a1963	87		1.0	1.5	AVCO-EMBASSY	
URSUS IN THE VALLEY OF THE LIONS (ITALIAN)	1961	82			2.0	GOLDEN ERA	
UTAH BLAINE	1957	75		2.0	1.5	COLUMBIA	
UTOPIA (FRENCH)	a1950	80		1.5	1.5	EXPLOITATION PICS.	

"a" TO LEFT OF YEAR INDICATES THAT FILM HAS AN ALTERNATE TITLE

‡ An asterisk (*) in THE FILM BUFF'S BIBLE column indicates that the film has been rated by the editor and/or staff. All other ratings in this column are based on a consensus of reviews (see NOTES).

TITLE (LEADING ACTORS SHOWN WHERE TWO OR MORE FILMS HAVE THE SAME OR SIMILAR TITLE)	YEAR RELEASED	RUNNING TIME IN MINUTES	THE FILM BUFF'S BIBLE ‡	STEVEN SCHEUER	LEONARD MALTIN	DISTRIBUTOR	COMMENT
V.I.P.'S, THE (BRITISH)	1963	119	5*	3.0	2.5	M-G-M	
VACATION FROM MARRIAGE (BRITISH)	a1945	111		3.0	3.0	M-G-M	
VACATION IN RENO	1946	60		1.5		RKO	
VAGABOND KING, THE (KATHRYN GRAYSON, ORESTE)	1956	88		2.0	2.5	PARAMOUNT	
VALDEZ IS COMING	1971	90	3			UNITED ARTISTS	
VALENTINO	1951	102	3	2.0	1.5	COLUMBIA	
VALERIE	1957	84		2.0	1.5	UNITED ARTISTS	
VALIANT, THE (BRITISH)	1962	89	4			UNITED ARTISTS	
VALIANT IS THE WORD FOR CARRIE	1936	110		2.5	2.5	PARAMOUNT	
VALLEY OF DECISION, THE	1945	111		3.0	3.0	M-G-M	
VALLEY OF GWANGI, THE	1969	95	1			WARNER BROTHERS	
VALLEY OF MYSTERY	1967	94	3		2.5	UNIVERSAL	
VALLEY OF THE DOLLS	1967	123	2	1.0		20th CENTURY FOX	
VALLEY OF THE DOOMED (GERMAN)	1962	83		1.5		AMERICAN-INTERNAT'L	
VALLEY OF THE DRAGONS	1961	79	3		1.5	COLUMBIA	
VALLEY OF THE EAGLES (BRITISH)	1951	85		2.5	2.5	LIPPERT PRODS.	
VALLEY OF THE GIANTS	1938	79		2.5	2.0	WARNER BROTHERS	
VALLEY OF THE HEADHUNTERS	1953	67		1.5	-	COLUMBIA	
VALLEY OF THE KINGS (ROBT. TAYLOR, ELEANOR PARKER)	1954	86		2.5	2.0	M-G-M	
VALLEY OF THE LIONS (ITALIAN)	1962	94		1.5		TELEWIDE SYSTEMS	
VALLEY OF THE REDWOODS	1960	63	3		1.5	20th CENTURY FOX	
VALLEY OF THE SUN	1942	84		3.0	3.0	RKO	
VALLEY OF THE ZOMBIES	1946	56		1.5	1.5	REPUBLIC	
VALUE FOR MONEY (BRITISH)	1955	93			3.0	J. ARTHUR RANK	
VAMPIRE, THE (JOHN BEAL, COLEEN GRAY)	a1957	74		2.0	1.5	UNITED ARTISTS	
VAMPIRE, THE (MEXICAN - ABEL SALAZAR)	1960	84		1.0		AZTECA	
VAMPIRE AND THE BALLERINA	1962	86	1			UNITED ARTISTS	
VAMPIRE BAT, THE	1933	63			2.5	MAJESTIC PICS.	
VAMPIRE-BEAST CRAVES BLOOD, THE	1970	81	1			PACEMAKER PICS.	
VAMPIRE LOVERS, THE (BRITISH)	1970	90	3			AMERICAN-INTERNAT'L	
VAMPIRE'S COFFIN, THE (MEXICAN)	1959	81		1.0		AZTECA	
VAMPIRE'S GHOST, THE	1945	53		1.5		REPUBLIC	
VANESSA, HER LOVE STORY	1935	74		2.0	2.0	M-G-M	
VANISHED (T.V.)	1971	200	3*	3.0		UNIVERSAL	
VANISHING AMERICAN, THE	1955	90		2.0	2.0	REPUBLIC	
VANISHING POINT	1971	99	4-5*			20th CENTURY FOX	
VANISHING PRAIRIE, THE (DOCUMENTARY)	1954	71	6*			BUENA VISTA	
VANISHING VIRGINIAN, THE	1942	97		2.0	1.5	M-G-M	
VANQUISHED, THE	1953	84		2.0	1.5	PARAMOUNT	
VARAN, THE UNBELIEVABLE (JAPANESE)	1962	70	1	1.0		CROWN INTERNATIONAL	
VARIETY (GERMAN, SILENT)	1925	92				PARAMOUNT	
VARIETY GIRL	1947	83		2.5	2.5	PARAMOUNT	
VARIETY TIME	1948	59		2.0		RKO	
VEILS OF BAGDAD	1953	82	2	2.0	2.5	UNIVERSAL	
VELVET TOUCH, THE	1948	97		2.5	2.5	RKO	
VELVET VAMPIRE, THE	1971	80	1			NEW WORLD	
VENDETTA (FAITH DOMERGUE, GEORGE DOLENZ)	1950	84	3			RKO	
VENETIAN AFFAIR, THE	1967	92		1.5	2.0	M-G-M	
VENGEANCE OF FU MANCHU, THE (BRITISH)	1967	89	1	1.0		WARNER BROTHERS	
VENGEANCE OF SHE, THE (BRITISH)	1968	101	2	1.5		20th CENTURY FOX	
VENGEANCE OF THE THREE MUSKETEERS (FRENCH)	1963	92		1.5		AVCO-EMBASSY	
VENGEANCE VALLEY	1951	83	4*	3.0	2.0	M-G-M	
VENICE, THE MOON, AND YOU (ITALIAN)	1958	100		1.5		GALA	
VENOM (DANISH)	1966	98	4			PEPPERCORN-WORMSER	
VENUS IN FURS (JAMES DARREN, BARBARA MCNAIR)	1970	86	1			AMERICAN-INTERNAT'L	
VERA CRUZ	1954	94	4	2.5	3.0	UNITED ARTISTS	
VERBOTEN	1959	93		2.0	1.5	COLUMBIA	
VERDICT, THE (SIDNEY GREENSTREET, PETER LORRE)	1946	86		2.5	2.5	WARNER BROTHERS	
VERDICT, THE (BRIT. - CEC LINDER, NIGEL DAVENPORT)	1964	55		2.0		AVCO-EMBASSY	
VERTIGO (JAMES STEWART, KIM NOVAK)	1958	120	5*	4.0	3.5	PARAMOUNT	
VERY CURIOUS GIRL, A (FRENCH)	a1969		4			REGIONAL	
VERY HAPPY ALEXANDER (FRENCH)	a1968	94	6			CINEMA V	
VERY HONORABLE GUY, A	1934	62		2.5	2.0	FIRST NATIONAL	
VERY PRIVATE AFFAIR, A (FRENCH)	1962	94	2			M-G-M	
VERY SPECIAL FAVOR, A	1965	104		2.5	2.5	UNIVERSAL	
VERY THOUGHT OF YOU, THE	1944	99		2.0	2.0	WARNER BROTHERS	
VERY YOUNG LADY, A	1941	79		2.0		20th CENTURY FOX	
VICE RAID	1960	71	1			UNITED ARTISTS	
VICE SQUAD, THE (PAUL LUKAS, KAY FRANCIS)	1931	80		2.0	2.5	PARAMOUNT	
VICE SQUAD (EDWARD G. ROBINSON, PAULETTE GODDARD)	1953	87	5	2.5	2.5	UNITED ARTISTS	
VICIOUS CIRCLE, THE (BRITISH - JOHN MILLS)	a1957	84		3.0	2.5	KASSLER FILMS	
VICKI	1953	85		2.0	2.5	20th CENTURY FOX	
VICTIM (BRITISH)	1961	100	6	3.5		PATHE-AMERICA	
VICTORIA THE GREAT (BRITISH)	1937	113		3.0		RKO	
VICTORS, THE	1963	175	5	3.5	3.0	COLUMBIA	
VICTORY	1940	78		3.0	3.0	PARAMOUNT	
VICTORY AT SEA (DOCUMENTARY)	1954	97	6*	4.0	3.0	UNITED ARTISTS	
VIEW FROM POMPEY'S HEAD, THE	1955	97	5	2.5	2.5	20th CENTURY FOX	
VIEW FROM THE BRIDGE, A	1962	110	5*	4.0	-	CONTINENTAL	
VIGIL IN THE NIGHT	1940	96	4*	3.5	3.0	RKO	
VIGILANTE TERROR	1953	70		2.0		ALLIED ARTISTS	
VIGILANTES RETURN, THE	1947	67			2.0	UNIVERSAL	
VIKING QUEEN, THE (BRITISH)	1967	91	2		2.0	20th CENTURY FOX	
VIKING WOMEN AND THE SEA SERPENT	1958	70		1.5		AMERICAN-INTERNAT'L	

‡ An asterisk (*) in THE FILM BUFF'S BIBLE column indicates that the film has been rated by the editor and/or staff. All other ratings in this column are based on a consensus of reviews (see NOTES).

TITLE (LEADING ACTORS SHOWN WHERE TWO OR MORE FILMS HAVE THE SAME OR SIMILAR TITLE)	YEAR RELEASED	RUNNING TIME IN MINUTES	THE FILM BUFF'S BIBLE ‡	STEVEN SCHEUER	LEONARD MALTIN	DISTRIBUTOR	COMMENT
VIKINGS, THE	1958	114	6*	2.5	2.5	UNITED ARTISTS	
VILLA!	1958	72		1.5	1.5	20th CENTURY FOX	
VILLA RIDES	1968	125	4			PARAMOUNT	
VILLAGE, THE (SWISS)	1953	83		3.0		UNITED ARTISTS	
VILLAGE OF THE DAMNED, THE (BRITISH)	1960	78	5	4.0	3.0	M-G-M	
VILLAGE OF THE GIANTS	1965	80		1.0	2.0	AVCO-EMBASSY	
VILLAIN (BRITISH)	1971	97	2			M-G-M	
VILLIAN STILL PURSUED HER, THE	1940	66		2.0	2.5	RKO	
VINTAGE, THE	1957	92		1.5	2.0	M-G-M	
VIOLENT AND THE DAMNED, THE (BRAZILIAN)	1959	92		1.5		MEDALLION	
VIOLENT FOUR, THE (ITALIAN)	1968	98	3			PARAMOUNT	
VIOLENT MEN, THE	1955	96		2.5	2.5	COLUMBIA	
VIOLENT MOMENT (BRITISH)	1958	61		2.0		SCHOENFELD FILM DIST.	
VIOLENT ONES (FRENCH - PAUL MEURISSE)	1958	100		3.0			
VIOLENT ONES, THE (FERNANDO LAMAS, ALDO RAY)	1967	84	1	1.0		FEATURE FILM CORP.	
VIOLENT PATRIOT, THE (ITALIAN)	1957	94		1.5		FOUR STAR	
VIOLENT PLAYGROUND (BRITISH)	1958	106		3.0		LOPERT	
VIOLENT ROAD	1958	86		2.0	2.5	WARNER BROTHERS	
VIOLENT SATURDAY	1955	91	5*	3.0	3.0	20th CENTURY FOX	
VIOLENT SUMMER (ITALIAN - ELEONORA ROSSI-DRAGO)	1959	99	6			FILMS AROUND THE WLD.	
VIOLENT SUMMER (FRENCH - MARTINE CAROL)	1961	85			2.0	S. F.	
VIRGIN AND THE GYPSY, THE (BRITISH)	1970	92	6			CHEVRON	
VIRGIN ISLAND (BRITISH)	1958	84		2.0	2.0	FILMS AROUND THE WLD.	
VIRGIN QUEEN, THE	1955	92	6	3.0	3.0	20th CENTURY FOX	
VIRGIN SOLDIERS, THE (BRITISH)	1969	96	6			COLUMBIA	
VIRGIN SPRING, THE (SWEDISH)	1960	88	6*		3.0	JANUS FILMS	
VIRGINIA	1941	110		2.0	2.0	PARAMOUNT	
VIRGINIA CITY	1940	121		3.0	2.5	WARNER BROTHERS	
VIRGINIAN, THE (GARY COOPER)	1929	90			2.5	PARAMOUNT	
VIRGINIAN, THE (JOEL MCCREA)	1946	90		3.0	2.5	PARAMOUNT	
VIRIDIANA (SPANISH)	1961	90	5*			KINGSLEY INTERNAT'L	
VIRTUOUS BIGAMIST, THE (FRENCH)	1957	90	4	2.5		KINGSLEY INTERNAT'L	
VIRTUOUS SIN, THE	1930	82			2.5	PARAMOUNT	
VISCOUNT, THE (FRENCH)	1967	98	1			WARNER BROTHERS	
VISIT, THE (INGRID BERGMAN, ANTHONY QUINN)	1964	100	5*	2.0	2.5	20th CENTURY FOX	
VISIT TO A SMALL PLANET	1960	85	3*	2.0	2.5	PARAMOUNT	
VISITORS, THE	1972	87	3			UNITED ARTISTS	
VITELLONI (ITALIAN)	a1953	103	6	4.0		API PRODUCTIONS	
VIVA CISCO KID	1940	70		1.5		20th CENTURY FOX	
VIVA LAS VEGAS	1964	86	4*	2.5	2.5	M-G-M	
VIVA MARIA (FRENCH)	1965	119	4			UNITED ARTISTS	
VIVA MAX!	1969	92	4			LANDAU/UNGER COM. UN.	
VIVA REVOLUTION (MEXICAN)	1956	106	5*	3.5		COLUMBIA	
VIVA VILLA!	1934	115		3.0	3.5	M-G-M	NOMINATED BEST PICTURE
VIVA ZAPATA	1952	113	6*	4.0	3.0	20th CENTURY FOX	
VIVACIOUS LADY	1938	90		3.5	3.0	RKO	
VIXEN (ERICA GAVIN, HARRISON PAGE)	a1969	71	2			EVE RELEASING CORP.	
VIXENS, THE (ANNE LINDEN, MARY KAHN)	a1969	82	3			STRATFORD PICS.	
VOGUES (OF 1938)	1937	108		2.0	2.0	UNITED ARTISTS	
VOICE IN THE MIRROR	1958	102	4	3.0	2.5	UNIVERSAL	
VOICE IN THE WIND	1944	85		3.0	3.0	UNITED ARTISTS	
VOICE OF BUGLE ANN, THE	1936	70		3.0	2.5	M-G-M	
VOICE OF SILENCE, THE (ITALIAN)	1952	85		2.0		RKO	
VOICE OF THE TURTLE	a1948	103		3.5	3.5	WARNER BROTHERS	
VOICE OF THE WHISTLER	1946	60				COLUMBIA	
VOLCANO (ITALIAN)	1953	106		2.0	2.0	UNITED ARTISTS	
VOLTAIRE	1933	72		3.5	3.0	WARNER BROTHERS	
VON RICHTHOFEN AND BROWN	a1971	97	3			UNITED ARTISTS	
VON RYAN'S EXPRESS	1965	117	5-6*		3.0	20th CENTURY FOX	
VOODOO HEARTBEAT	1972	88				TWI NATIONAL	
VOODOO ISLAND	1957	76		2.0	2.0	UNITED ARTISTS	
VOODOO MAN	1944	62			2.0	MONOGRAM	
VOODOO TIGER	1952	67		1.5	-	COLUMBIA	
VOODOO VILLAGE (DOCUMENTARY)	1963	70	6			CONTINENTAL	
VOODOO WOMAN	1957	77		1.5	1.5	AMERICAN-INTERNAT'L	
VOYAGE OF SILENCE (FRENCH)	1967	89	6			LOPERT	
VOYAGE TO DANGER (GERMAN)	1962	87		1.5			
VOYAGE TO THE BOTTOM OF THE SEA	1961	105	4*	2.5	3.0	20th CENTURY FOX	
VOYAGE TO THE END OF THE UNIVERSE (CZECH)	1964	75	2	1.5		AMERICAN-INTERNAT'L	
VULTURE, THE (BRITISH)	1967	91	1			PARAMOUNT	
WABASH AVENUE	1950	82	5	3.0	3.0	20th CENTURY FOX	
WAC FROM WALLA WALLA, THE	1952	83	3		1.5	REPUBLIC	
WACKIEST SHIP IN THE ARMY, THE	1960	99	4*	3.0	3.0	COLUMBIA	
WACO (HOWARD KEEL, JANE RUSSELL)	1966	85	2			PARAMOUNT	
WAGES OF FEAR, THE (FRENCH)	1953	140	5-6*	4.0	3.5	INT'L AFFILIATES	
WAGONMASTER	1950	86	5	3.0	3.0	RKO	
WAGONS ROLL AT NIGHT, THE	1941	84		2.5	2.5	WARNER BROTHERS	
WAGONS WEST	1952	70	4	2.0		MONOGRAM	
WAGONS WESTWARD	1940	69		2.0		REPUBLIC	
WAIKIKI WEDDING	1937	89		3.0	3.0	PARAMOUNT	
WAIT FOR THE DAWN (ITALIAN)	a1960	82	4	2.5		ALLIED ARTISTS	

‡ An asterisk (*) in THE FILM BUFF'S BIBLE column indicates that the film has been rated by the editor and/or staff. All other ratings in this column are based on a consensus of reviews (see NOTES).

TITLE (LEADING ACTORS SHOWN WHERE TWO OR MORE FILMS HAVE THE SAME OR SIMILAR TITLE)	YEAR RELEASED	RUNNING TIME IN MINUTES	THE FILM BUFF'S BIBLE ‡	STEVEN SCHEUER	LEONARD MALTIN	DISTRIBUTOR	COMMENT
WAIT 'TIL THE SUN SHINES, NELLIE	1952	108	6	4.0	3.0	20th CENTURY FOX	
WAIT UNTIL DARK	1967	108	6-7*		3.0	WARNER BROTHERS	
WAITING FOR CAROLINE	1969	83	4			LOPERT	
WAKE ISLAND	1942	78	3*	3.0	3.0	PARAMOUNT	NOMINATED BEST PICTURE
WAKE ME WHEN IT'S OVER	1960	126		2.0	3.0	20th CENTURY FOX	
WAKE ME WHEN THE WAR IS OVER (T.V.)	1969	90		1.5		ABC FILMS	
WAKE OF THE RED WITCH	1948	106		2.5	2.5	REPUBLIC	
WAKE UP AND DREAM	1946	92		2.0	2.0	20th CENTURY FOX	
WAKE UP AND LIVE	1937	91		2.5	3.0	20th CENTURY FOX	
WALK A CROOKED MILE	1948	91		2.5	2.5	COLUMBIA	
WALK A TIGHTROPE (BRITISH)	1964	78	2			PARAMOUNT	
WALK, DON'T RUN	1966	114	5*	2.5	3.0	COLUMBIA	
WALK EAST ON BEACON	1952	98	4	3.0	2.5	COLUMBIA	
WALK IN THE SHADOW (BRITISH)	1962	93	6		3.0	CONTINENTAL	
WALK IN THE SPRING RAIN, A	1970	100	2			COLUMBIA	
WALK IN THE SUN, A	1945	111	3*	3.5	3.5	20th CENTURY FOX	
WALK INTO HELL (AUSTRALIAN)	1956	93		3.0	1.5	PATRIC PICTURES	
WALK LIKE A DRAGON	1960	95		2.5	2.5	PARAMOUNT	
WALK ON THE WILD SIDE	1962	114		2.0	2.5	COLUMBIA	
WALK SOFTLY, STRANGER	1950	81	4	3.0	2.5	RKO	
WALK TALL	1960	60		1.5	1.5	20th CENTURY FOX	
WALK THE DARK STREETS	1956	74		1.5	1.5	DOMINANT PICTURES	
WALK THE PROUD LAND	1956	88		3.0	3.0	UNIVERSAL	
WALK WITH LOVE AND DEATH, A	1970	90	4			20th CENTURY FOX	
WALKABOUT (AUSTRALIAN)	1971	95	6			20th CENTURY FOX	
WALKING DEAD, THE	1936	66		2.0	3.0	WARNER BROTHERS	
WALKING HILLS, THE	1949	78	5	3.0	3.0	COLUMBIA	
WALKING MY BABY BACK HOME	1953	95	3	2.5	2.5	UNIVERSAL	
WALKING STICK, THE (BRITISH)	1970	101	3			M-G-M	
WALKING TARGET, THE	1960	74	3			UNITED ARTISTS	
WALL IN JERUSALEM, A (FRENCH, DOCUMENTARY)	1968	90	5			PARAMOUNT	
WALL OF DEATH (BRITISH)	1952	90		2.0		REALART	
WALL OF FURY (GERMAN)	1962	88		1.5		MEDALLION	
WALL OF NOISE	1963	112		2.5	2.5	WARNER BROTHERS	
WALLFLOWER	1948	77	5	3.0	3.0	WARNER BROTHERS	
WALLS CAME TUMBLING DOWN, THE	1946	82		3.0	3.0	COLUMBIA	
WALLS OF FEAR (FRENCH)	1962	85		2.0		AMERICAN-INTERNAT'L	
WALLS OF HELL, THE (PHILLIPINE)	1964	87			2.0	HEMISPHERE	
WALLS OF JERICHO, THE	1948	106		2.0	2.0	20th CENTURY FOX	
WALLS OF MALAPAGA, THE (FRENCH)	1949	89	7			FILMS INTERNATIONAL	
WALTZ OF THE TOREADORS (BRITISH)	1962	102	6	3.0	3.0	CONTINENTAL	
WANDA	1971	101	6			BARDENE INTERNAT'L	
WANDERER, THE (FRENCH)	1967	103	6			LEACOCK-PENNEBAKER	
WANTED FOR MURDER (BRITISH)	1946	95		2.5	2.5	20th CENTURY FOX	
WANTON CONTESSA, THE (ITALIAN)	a1954	125		2.0	2.5	FLEETWOOD FILMS	
WAR AGAINST MRS HADLEY, THE	1942	86		2.0	2.0	M-G-M	
WAR AND PEACE (HENRY FONDA, AUDREY HEPBURN)	1956	208	7	3.0	3.5	PARAMOUNT	
WAR AND PEACE (RUSSIAN - SERGEI BONDARCHUK)	1967	373	6*			CONTINENTAL	
WAR ARROW	1954	78		2.0	2.0	UNIVERSAL	
WAR BETWEEN MEN AND WOMEN, THE	1972	105	4			NATIONAL GENERAL	
WAR BETWEEN THE PLANETS	1971	80				FANFARE	
WAR DRUMS	1957	75		2.0	2.5	UNITED ARTISTS	
WAR GAME, THE (BRITISH, DOCUMENTARY)	1965	50	7			PATHE CONTEMPARARY	
WAR GODS OF BABYLON (ITALIAN)	1962	82		1.5		AMERICAN-INTERNAT'L	
WAR-GODS OF THE DEEP	a1965	85	1			AMERICAN-INTERNAT'L	
WAR HUNT	1962	81	4	3.5	2.5	UNITED ARTISTS	
WAR IS HELL	1964	82	3	2.5	2.0	ALLIED ARTISTS	
WAR ITALIAN STYLE (ITALIAN)	1965	74	2		2.0	AMERICAN-INTERNAT'L	
WAR LORD, THE	1965	123	4	3.0	3.0	UNIVERSAL	
WAR LOVER, THE (BRITISH)	1962	105	5*	2.5	2.5	COLUMBIA	
WAR OF THE BUTTONS, THE (FRENCH)	1962	92	4			BRONSTON DISTS.	
WAR OF THE COLOSSAL BEAST	1958	68	2	1.5		AMERICAN-INTERNAT'L	
WAR OF THE GARGANTUAS, THE	1970	93	1			MARON FILMS, LTD.	
WAR OF THE SATELLITES	1958	66		1.5	1.5	ALLIED ARTISTS	
WAR OF THE WILDCATS, THE	a1943	102		3.0	2.5	REPUBLIC	
WAR OF THE WORLDS, THE	1953	83	3*	3.0	3.0	PARAMOUNT	
WAR OF THE ZOMBIES, THE	1965	85	1			AMERICAN-INTERNAT'L	
WAR PAINT	1953	89	4	3.0	2.5	UNITED ARTISTS	
WAR PARTY	1965	72	1			20th CENTURY FOX	
WAR WAGON, THE	1967	101	6*	3.0		UNIVERSAL	
WARKILL	1967	100	3			UNIVERSAL	
WARLOCK	1959	121	6*	3.0	3.0	20th CENTURY FOX	
WARNING FROM SPACE (JAPANESE)	1963	87		1.5		AMERICAN-INTERNAT'L	
WARNING SHOT	1967	100	5	2.5		PARAMOUNT	
WARNING TO WANTONS (BRITISH)	1953	98		2.0		J. ARTHUR RANK	
WARPATH	1951	95		2.0	2.5	PARAMOUNT	
WARRENDALE (CANADIAN, DOCUMENTARY)	1966	100	6			GROVE PRESS	
WARRIOR AND THE SLAVE GIRL, THE (ITALIAN)	1958	89	2		2.0	COLUMBIA	
WARRIOR EMPRESS, THE (ITALIAN)	1960	89	2	1.5	2.0	COLUMBIA	
WARRIORS, THE	1955	85	3	2.5	2.5	ALLIED ARTISTS	
WARRIORS FIVE (ITALIAN)	1961	91	2	2.5	2.5	AMERICAN-INTERNAT'L	
WASHINGTON MELODRAMA	1941	80		2.0		M-G-M	
WASHINGTON STORY	1952	81	4	2.0	2.0	M-G-M	
WASP WOMAN, THE	1959	73		1.0		FILMGROUP	

‡ An asterisk (*) in THE FILM BUFF'S BIBLE column indicates that the film has been rated by the editor and/or staff. All other ratings in this column are based on a consensus of reviews (see NOTES).

TITLE (LEADING ACTORS SHOWN WHERE TWO OR MORE FILMS HAVE THE SAME OR SIMILAR TITLE)	YEAR RELEASED	RUNNING TIME IN MINUTES	THE FILM BUFF'S BIBLE ‡	STEVEN SCHEUER	LEONARD MALTIN	DISTRIBUTOR	COMMENT
WASTREL, THE (ITALIAN - VAN HEFLIN)	1960	84		1.5		MEDALLION	
WATCH IT SAILOR! (BRITISH)	1961	81			2.0	SCREEN GEMS	
WATCH ON THE RHINE	1943	114	7*	4.0	4.0	WARNER BROTHERS	NOMINATED BEST PICTURE
WATCH THE BIRDIE	1951	70		2.5	2.5	M-G-M	
WATCH YOUR STERN (BRITISH)	1960	88			2.0	MAGNA PICTURES	
WATER BIRDS (DOCUMENTARY)	1952	31	5*			BUENA VISTA	
WATERFRONT WOMEN (BRITISH)	a1950	80		1.5		J. ARTHUR RANK	
WATERHOLE #3	1967	95	4*	3.0		PARAMOUNT	
WATERLOO (ITALIAN-RUSSIAN)	1971	123	3*			PARAMOUNT	ENGLISH LANGUAGE
WATERLOO BRIDGE	1940	103	4*	3.0	3.5	M-G-M	
WATERLOO ROAD (BRITISH)	1944	77		3.0	2.0	EAGLE LION	
WATERMELON MAN	1970	97	3			COLUMBIA	
WATUSI	1959	85		2.0	2.5	M-G-M	
WAY AHEAD, THE (BRITISH)	a1944	106		3.5	3.0	20th CENTURY FOX	
WAY DOWN EAST (SILENT - LILLIAN GISH)	1920	107			2.5	UNITED ARTISTS	
WAY DOWN EAST (ROCHELLE HUDSON, HENRY FONDA)	1935	80			1.5	20th CENTURY FOX	
WAY FOR A SAILOR	1930	83			2.0	M-G-M	
WAY OF A GAUCHO	1952	91		2.0	2.0	20th CENTURY FOX	
WAY OF ALL FLESH, THE (SILENT - EMIL JANNINGS)	1927	94				PARAMOUNT	NOMINATED BEST PICTURE 1927/28
WAY OF ALL FLESH, THE (AKIM TAMIROFF, G. GEORGE)	1940	86		2.0	2.0	PARAMOUNT	
WAY OF YOUTH, THE (FRENCH)	1959	85		2.5	2.0		
WAY OUT (FRANK RODRIGUEZ, JAMES DUNLEAVY)	1967	102	4			PREMIER PRESENTATIONS	
WAY OUT, THE (BRITISH - GENE NELSON, MONA FREEMAN)	1956	90			2.0	RKO	
WAY OUT WEST	1936	65		3.0	3.0	M-G-M	
WAY TO LOVE, THE	1933	80		2.0	3.0	PARAMOUNT	
WAY TO THE GOLD, THE	1957	94		2.0	2.0	20th CENTURY FOX	
WAY . . . WAY OUT (JERRY LEWIS, CONNIE STEVENS)	1966	106	2	1.0		20th CENTURY FOX	
WAY WE LIVE NOW, THE	1970	110	3			UNITED ARTISTS	
WAY WEST, THE	1967	122	3	2.0		UNITED ARTISTS	
WAYS OF LOVE	1951	116	6			JOSEPH BURSTYN	
WAYWARD BUS, THE	1957	89		2.5	2.0	20th CENTURY FOX	
WAYWARD GIRL, THE (MARCIA HENDERSON, PETER WALKER)	1957	71		1.0	1.5	REPUBLIC	
WAYWARD GIRL, THE (NORWEGIAN - LIV ULLMANN)	1959	91			2.5	COMPTON-CAMEO	
WAYWARD WIFE, THE (ITALIAN)	a1953	92		1.5	2.0	ITALIAN FILMS EXPORT	
WE ARE ALL MURDERERS (FRENCH)	1952	108	7	4.0	3.0	KINGSLEY INTERNAT'L	
WE ARE IN THE NAVY NOW (BRITISH)	1962	102		3.0	2.0		
WE ARE NOT ALONE	1939	112		3.5	3.5	WARNER BROTHERS	
WE JOINED THE NAVY (BRITISH)	1962	105	4*			ASSOC. BRITISH-PATHE	
WE LIVE AGAIN	1934	82		2.5	2.0	UNITED ARTISTS	
WE SHALL RETURN	1963	92		1.0		CARI	
WE SHALL SEE (BRITISH)	1964	61		2.0		AVCO-EMBASSY	
WE STILL KILL THE OLD WAY (ITALIAN)	1967	92	6			LOPERT	
WE WERE DANCING	1942	94		2.0	2.0	M-G-M	
WE WERE STRANGERS	1949	106	3*	2.5	2.5	COLUMBIA	
WE WHO ARE ABOUT TO DIE	1937	82		3.0		RKO	
WE WHO ARE YOUNG	1940	79		1.5	2.0	M-G-M	
WEAK AND THE WICKED, THE (BRITISH)	1954	72	4		2.5	ALLIED ARTISTS	
WEAKER SEX, THE (BRITISH)	1948	84			2.0	EAGLE LION	
WEAPON, THE (BRITISH)	1956	81		2.5	2.5	REPUBLIC	
WEB, THE	1947	87	6	3.0	3.0	UNIVERSAL	
WEB OF EVIDENCE (BRITISH)	a1959	88	4	2.5	2.5	ALLIED ARTISTS	
WEB OF FEAR (FRENCH)	1964	92		2.0	2.5	COMET FILM	
WEB OF PASSION (FRENCH)	a1959	110		2.0	2.5	TIMES FILM CORP.	
WEB OF SUSPICION (BRITISH)	1959	70		2.0		PARAMOUNT	
WEDDING NIGHT (TESSA WYATT, DENNIS WATERMAN)	1970	99	3			AMERICAN-INTERNAT'L	(IRISH)
WEDDING NIGHT, THE (GARY COOPER, ANNA STEN)	1935	84	5-6*	3.0	2.5	UNITED ARTISTS	
WEDDING OF LILI MARLENE, THE (BRITISH)	1953	87		1.0		MONARCH	
WEDDING PARTY, THE	1969	90	4			AJAY FILMS	
WEE GEORDIE (BRITISH)	a1955	100	6	3.5	3.5	GEORGE K. ARTHUR	
WEE WILLIE WINKIE	1937	99		3.0	3.0	20th CENTURY FOX	
WEED OF CRIME, THE (JAPANESE)	1964	90		2.0		COM. UNITED T.V.	
WEEK-END IN HAVANA	1941	80		2.5	2.5	20th CENTURY FOX	
WEEK-END MARRIAGE	1932	66		2.0	2.0	FIRST NATIONAL	
WEEK END WITH FATHER	1951	83		2.5	2.5	UNIVERSAL	
WEEKEND (DANISH - JENS OSTERHOLM)	1963	84	3			CINEMA VIDEO INT'L	
WEEKEND (FRENCH - MIREILLE DARC, JEAN YANNE)	1968	103	5			GROVE PRESS	
WEEKEND AT DUNKIRK (FRENCH)	1966	101	3			20th CENTURY FOX	
WEEKEND AT THE WALDORF	1945	130		2.5	3.0	M-G-M	
WEEKEND FOR THREE	1941	61		3.0	2.0	RKO	
WEEKEND ITALIAN STYLE (ITALIAN)	1966	105	2			MARVIN FILMS	
WEEKEND MURDERS, THE	1972	98	3			M-G-M	
WEEKEND OF TERROR (T.V.)	1970	90		2.0		PARAMOUNT	
WEEKEND WITH LULU, A (BRITISH)	1961	89	4			COLUMBIA	
WEEKEND WITH THE BABYSITTER	1970	93	2			CROWN INTERNATIONAL	
WEIRD WOMAN	1944	64		2.5	2.5	UNIVERSAL	
WEIRD WORLD OF LSD	1967	72	1			AMERICANA ENT. ASSN.	
WELCOME HOME, SOLDIER BOYS	1972	91	3			20th CENTURY FOX	
WELCOME STRANGER	1947	107	4*	3.5	3.0	PARAMOUNT	
WELCOME TO HARD TIMES	1967	105	4*	2.5	3.0	M-G-M	
WELCOME TO THE CLUB (BRITISH)	1971	82	2			COLUMBIA	
WELL, THE	1951	84	6	4.0	3.0	UNITED ARTISTS	
WE'LL BURY YOU (DOCUMENTARY)	1962	75	4	2.5		COLUMBIA	
WELL-GROOMED BRIDE, THE	1946	75		2.0	2.0	PARAMOUNT	
WELLDIGGER'S DAUGHTER (FRENCH)	1941	123	7			SIRITZKY INTERNAT'L	

‡ An asterisk (*) in THE FILM BUFF'S BIBLE column indicates that the film has been rated by the editor and/or staff. All other ratings in this column are based on a consensus of reviews (see NOTES).

"a" TO LEFT OF YEAR INDICATES THAT FILM HAS AN ALTERNATE TITLE

CRITICAL RATINGS

TITLE (LEADING ACTORS SHOWN WHERE TWO OR MORE FILMS HAVE THE SAME OR SIMILAR TITLE)	YEAR RELEASED	RUNNING TIME IN MINUTES	THE FILM BUFF'S BIBLE ‡	STEVEN SCHEUER	LEONARD MALTIN	DISTRIBUTOR	COMMENT
WELLS FARGO	1937	115	4*	3.0	3.0	PARAMOUNT	
WE'RE NO ANGELS	1955	106		2.5	2.5	PARAMOUNT	
WE'RE NOT DRESSING	1934	63		3.0	3.0	PARAMOUNT	
WE'RE NOT MARRIED	1952	85	6	3.5	3.0	20th CENTURY FOX	
WEREWOLF, THE	1956	83		1.5	1.5	COLUMBIA	
WEREWOLF IN A GIRLS' DORMITORY (ITALIAN)	1961	82		1.0	1.0	M-G-M	
WEREWOLF OF LONDON, THE	1935	75		2.5	3.0	UNIVERSAL	
WEREWOLVES ON WHEELS	1971	84	1			FANFARE	
WEST 11 (BRITISH)	1963	93			1.5	WARNER BROTHERS	
WEST OF SHANGHAI	1937	65		2.0		WARNER BROTHERS	
WEST OF THE PECOS	1945	66		2.5		RKO	
WEST OF ZANZIBAR (BRITISH)	1954	94		2.0	2.0	UNIVERSAL	
WEST POINT OF THE AIR	1935	100		2.0	2.5	M-G-M	
WEST POINT STORY, THE	1950	107	4	2.0	2.5	WARNER BROTHERS	
WEST POINT WIDOW	1941	63		2.5		PARAMOUNT	
WEST SIDE KID, THE	1943	58		2.5		REPUBLIC	
WEST SIDE STORY	1961	155	9*			UNITED ARTISTS	BEST PICTURE AWARD
WESTBOUND	1959	72		2.0	2.5	WARNER BROTHERS	
WESTERN PACIFIC AGENT	1950	64		2.5		LIPPERT PRODS.	
WESTERN UNION	1941	94		3.0	3.0	20th CENTURY FOX	
WESTERNER, THE	1940	99	6*	3.0	3.5	UNITED ARTISTS	
WESTLAND CASE, THE	1937	63		3.0		UNIVERSAL	
WESTWARD HO THE WAGONS!	1957	90	6			BUENA VISTA	
WESTWARD PASSAGE	1932	75		2.0	2.0	RKO	
WESTWARD THE WOMEN	1952	118	4*	2.5	3.0	M-G-M	
WET ASPHALT (GERMAN)	1961	90		2.5		SCREEN GEMS	
WETBACKS	1956	89		1.5	1.5	BANNER	
WE'VE NEVER BEEN LICKED	1943	103		2.0	2.0	UNIVERSAL	
WHAT! (ITALIAN)	1963	92		2.0		TRANS-AMERICA	
WHAT A BLONDE	1945	71		2.0		RKO	
WHAT A CARVE UP (BRITISH)	a1961	87		2.0	2.0	AVCO-EMBASSY	
WHAT A LIFE	1939	75		3.0	3.0	PARAMOUNT	
WHAT A WAY TO GO!	1964	111	5*	2.0	2.5	20th CENTURY FOX	
WHAT A WOMAN!	1943	94		2.5	2.5	COLUMBIA	
WHAT AM I BID?	1967	92	1			EMERSON FILMS	
WHAT BECAME OF JACK AND JILL?	1972	93	3			20th CENTURY FOX	
WHAT DID YOU DO IN THE WAR, DADDY?	1966	119	3	1.0		UNITED ARTISTS	
WHAT DO YOU SAY TO A NAKED LADY?	1970	90	3			UNITED ARTISTS	
WHAT EVER HAPPENED TO AUNT ALICE?	1969	101	5			CINERAMA RELEASING	
WHAT EVER HAPPENED TO BABY JANE?	1962	132	6-7*	3.0	3.5	WARNER BROTHERS	
WHAT EVERY WOMAN KNOWS	1934	92		3.5	2.5	M-G-M	
WHAT EVERY WOMAN WANTS (BRITISH - WILLIAM FOX)	1962	69			1.5	UNITED ARTISTS	
WHAT NEXT, CORPORAL HARGROVE?	1945	95		2.5	2.5	M-G-M	
WHAT PRICE GLORY (SILENT - VICTOR MCLAGLEN)	1927	123				20th CENTURY FOX	
WHAT PRICE GLORY (JAMES CAGNEY, DAN DAILEY)	1952	111		2.5	2.5	20th CENTURY FOX	
WHAT PRICE MURDER (FRENCH)	1958	105		3.0	2.5	UN. MOTION PIC. ORG.	
WHAT'S GOOD FOR THE GOOSE (BRITISH)	1969	105	3			NAT'L SHOWMANSHIP	
WHAT'S NEW PUSSYCAT?	1965	108	3			UNITED ARTISTS	
WHAT'S SO BAD ABOUT FEELING GOOD?	1968	94	4	2.0		UNIVERSAL	
WHAT'S THE MATTER WITH HELEN?	1971	101	3*			UNITED ARTISTS	
WHAT'S UP DOC?	1972	94	6*			WARNER BROTHERS	
WHAT'S UP FRONT	a1964	87	3			FAIRWAY INTERNAT'L	
WHAT'S UP, TIGER LILY?	1966	80	4	3.0	2.5	AMERICAN-INTERNAT'L	
WHEEL, THE	1972	90				UPI-UNITED PICTURES	
WHEEL OF FATE (BRITISH - PATRIC DOONAN)	a1953	70		2.0		J. ARTHUR RANK	
WHEEL OF FORTUNE	a1941	83		2.0	2.0	REPUBLIC	
WHEELER DEALERS, THE	a1963	106	5*	3.0	3.0	M-G-M	
WHEELS OF FATE (FRENCH - JEAN SERVAIS)	a1956	105		2.0		CURZON	
WHEN A WOMAN LOVES (JAPANESE)	1959	97			2.5	SHOCHIKU	
WHEN A WOMAN MEDDLES (FRENCH)	1957	90		1.5			
WHEN COMEDY WAS KING	1960	81	5*	3.5	4.0	20th CENTURY FOX	SILENT FILM CLIPS
WHEN DINOSAURS RULED THE EARTH (BRITISH)	1970	100	1			WARNER BROTHERS	
WHEN EIGHT BELLS TOLL (BRITISH)	1971	94	5			CINERAMA RELEASING	
WHEN GANGLAND STRIKES	1956	70		2.0	2.0	REPUBLIC	
WHEN HELL BROKE LOOSE	1958	78		2.0	2.0	PARAMOUNT	
WHEN I GROW UP	1951	80		3.5	3.0	EAGLE LION	
WHEN IN ROME	1952	78	3	2.5	2.5	M-G-M	
WHEN LADIES MEET (JOAN CRAWFORD, ROBERT TAYLOR)	1941	108		2.0	2.0	M-G-M	
WHEN MY BABY SMILES AT ME	1948	98		2.5	2.5	20th CENTURY FOX	
WHEN STRANGERS MARRY	a1944	67		3.5	2.0	MONOGRAM	
WHEN THE BOUGH BREAKS (BRITISH)	1947	81		2.0		J. ARTHUR RANK	
WHEN THE BOYS MEET THE GIRLS	1965	110		2.0	2.0	M-G-M	
WHEN THE CLOCK STRIKES	1961	72	1			UNITED ARTISTS	
WHEN THE DALTONS RODE	1940	80		3.0	3.0	UNIVERSAL	
WHEN THE GIRLS TAKE OVER	1962	80		1.0		PARAMOUNT	
WHEN THE LEGENDS DIE	1972	106				20th CENTURY FOX	
WHEN THE REDSKINS RODE	1951	78		1.0	1.5	COLUMBIA	
WHEN TOMORROW COMES	1939	90		2.5	2.5	UNIVERSAL	
WHEN WILLIE COMES MARCHING HOME	1950	82		3.0	2.5	20th CENTURY FOX	
WHEN WORLDS COLLIDE	1951	81	4	2.0	2.5	PARAMOUNT	
WHEN YOU'RE IN LOVE	1937	104			2.5	COLUMBIA	
WHEN YOU'RE SMILING	1950	75	3	2.5		COLUMBIA	
WHEN'S YOUR BIRTHDAY?	1937	77			2.5	RKO	
WHERE ANGELS GO, TROUBLE FOLLOWS	1968	95		2.0	2.5	COLUMBIA	

‡ An asterisk (*) in THE FILM BUFF'S BIBLE column indicates that the film has been rated by the editor and/or staff. All other ratings in this column are based on a consensus of reviews (see NOTES).

TITLE (LEADING ACTORS SHOWN WHERE TWO OR MORE FILMS HAVE THE SAME OR SIMILAR TITLE)	YEAR RELEASED	RUNNING TIME IN MINUTES	THE FILM BUFF'S BIBLE ‡	STEVEN SCHEUER	LEONARD MALTIN	DISTRIBUTOR	COMMENT
WHERE ARE YOUR CHILDREN?	1944	73			1.5	MONOGRAM	
WHERE DANGER LIVES	1950	84		2.0	2.0	RKO	
WHERE DO WE GO FROM HERE?	1945	77		3.0	3.0	20th CENTURY FOX	
WHERE DOES IT HURT? (BRITISH)	1972	87				CINERAMA RELEASING	
WHERE EAGLES DARE (BRITISH)	1969	155	4			M-G-M	
WHERE IT'S AT	1969	104	2			UNITED ARTISTS	
WHERE LOVE HAS GONE	1964	114		1.5	2.5	PARAMOUNT	
WHERE THE BOYS ARE	1960	99		2.5	2.0	M-G-M	
WHERE THE BULLETS FLY (BRITISH)	1966	90	2	1.5	2.5	AVCO-EMBASSY	
WHERE THE HOT WIND BLOWS (ITALIAN)	a1958	120	3	2.0	2.0	AVCO-EMBASSY	
WHERE THE SIDEWALK ENDS	1950	95	4	2.0	2.5	20th CENTURY FOX	
WHERE THE SPIES ARE (BRITISH)	1966	113	5	3.0	3.0	M-G-M	
WHERE THE TRUTH LIES (FRENCH)	1962	83	1			PARAMOUNT	
WHERE THERE'S A WILL (BRITISH - WILL HAY)	1936	81				GAUMONT-BRITISH	
WHERE THERE'S A WILL (BRITISH - GEORGE COLE)	1955	77		2.0		EROS FILMS	
WHERE THERE'S LIFE	1947	75	5	3.0	3.0	PARAMOUNT	
WHERE WERE YOU WHEN THE LIGHTS WENT OUT?	1968	94	3*	1.0		M-G-M	
WHERE'S CHARLEY? (BRITISH)	1952	97	4*	4.0		WARNER BROTHERS	
WHERE'S JACK? (BRITISH)	1969	120	4			PARAMOUNT	
WHERE'S POPPA?	1970	84	5	3.5		UNITED ARTISTS	
WHEREVER SHE GOES (AUSTRALIAN)	1951	81	5	2.5		MAYER-KINGSLEY	
WHICH WAY TO THE FRONT?	1970	96	2			WARNER BROTHERS	
WHILE THE CITY SLEEPS	1956	100	5		3.0	RKO	
WHIP HAND	1951	82		2.0		RKO	
WHIPLASH	1949	91		2.0	2.0	WARNER BROTHERS	
WHIPPED, THE	a1950	90	4	3.0	3.0	UNITED ARTISTS	
WHIPSAW	1935	83		2.5	2.5	M-G-M	
WHIRLPOOL (GENE TIERNEY, RICHARD CONTE)	1950	97	5	3.0	3.0	20th CENTURY FOX	
WHIRLPOOL (BRITISH - JULIETTE GRECO)	1959	95		1.5		CONTINENTAL	
WHIRLPOOL (DANISH - KARL LANCHBURY)	1970	75	1			CINEMATION INDUS.	
WHISKEY AND SOFA (GERMAN)	1961	87		2.0		NTA PICTURES	
WHISPERERS, THE (BRITISH)	1967	105	6			LOPERT	
WHISPERING FOOTSTEPS	1943	55		3.5		REPUBLIC	
WHISPERING GHOSTS	1942	75		2.0	2.0	20th CENTURY FOX	
WHISPERING SMITH	1949	88	2*	3.0	3.0	PARAMOUNT	
WHISPERING SMITH VS SCOTLAND YARD (BRITISH)	1952	77	2		2.0	RKO	
WHISTLE AT EATON FALLS, THE	1951	96		2.5	2.5	COLUMBIA	
WHISTLE DOWN THE WIND (BRITISH)	1961	98	5*	4.0	3.0	PATHE-AMERICA	
WHISTLE STOP	1946	85		2.0	2.0	UNITED ARTISTS	
WHISTLER, THE	1944	59		2.0	-	COLUMBIA	
WHISTLING IN BROOKLYN	1943	87		2.5	2.5	M-G-M	
WHISTLING IN DIXIE	1942	74		2.5	3.0	M-G-M	
WHISTLING IN THE DARK (ERNEST TRUEX, UNA MERKEL)	1931	78		3.0		M-G-M	
WHISTLING IN THE DARK (RED SKELTON, CONRAD VEIDT)	1941	77		3.0	3.0	M-G-M	
WHITE ANGEL, THE	1936	75		3.0	2.0	FIRST NATIONAL	
WHITE BANNERS	1938	88		3.0	3.0	WARNER BROTHERS	
WHITE CARGO	1942	90		2.0	2.0	M-G-M	
WHITE CHRISTMAS	1954	120	5	3.0	2.0	PARAMOUNT	
WHITE CLIFFS OF DOVER, THE	1944	126		3.0	3.0	M-G-M	
WHITE CORRIDORS (BRITISH)	1951	85	6	3.0		J. ARTHUR RANK	
WHITE FEATHER	1955	102		2.0	2.5	20th CENTURY FOX	
WHITE FIRE (BRITISH)	1954	82		2.0		LIPPERT PRODS.	
WHITE HEAT	1949	114	6	3.5	3.5	WARNER BROTHERS	
WHITE HUNTRESS (BRITISH)	1957	69		2.0		AMERICAN-INTERNAT'L	
WHITE LIGHTNING	1953	61		1.5		ALLIED ARTISTS	
WHITE MANE (FRENCH)	1953	39	6			WILLIAM SNYDER	
WHITE NIGHTS, THE (ITALIAN)	1957	105		2.0	3.0	UN. MOTION PIC. ORG.	
WHITE ORCHID, THE	1955	81	3	1.5		UNITED ARTISTS	
WHITE PARADE, THE	1934	83				20th CENTURY FOX	NOMINATED BEST PICTURE
WHITE SAVAGE	1943	75			2.5	UNIVERSAL	
WHITE SEARCH, THE	1971	89				CINEMA HORIZONS	
WHITE SISTER, THE (SILENT - LILLIAN GISH)	1924	104				METRO	
WHITE SISTER, THE (HELEN HAYES, CLARK GABLE)	1933	101		2.5		M-G-M	
WHITE SLAVE SHIP (ITALIAN)	1961	92		2.0	1.5	AMERICAN-INTERNAT'L	
WHITE SPIDER, THE (GERMAN)	1963	105		1.5		UCC FILMS	
WHITE SQUAW, THE	1956	75		1.5	1.5	COLUMBIA	
WHITE TIE AND TAILS	1946	81	4	2.5	2.5	UNIVERSAL	
WHITE TOWER, THE	1950	98	5*	3.0	3.0	RKO	
WHITE TRAP, THE (BRITISH)	1959	58		2.0		ANGLO AMALGAMATED	
WHITE VOICES (ITALIAN)	1965	93	5		3.0	RIZZOLI FILM	
WHITE WARRIOR, THE (ITALIAN)	1959	86		1.5	1.5	WARNER BROTHERS	
WHITE WILDERNESS (DOCUMENTARY)	1958	72	6			BUENA VISTA	
WHITE WITCH DOCTOR	1953	96		2.5	2.5	20th CENTURY FOX	
WHITE ZOMBIE	1932	73			3.0	UNITED ARTISTS	
WHO ARE YOU MR SORGE? (FRENCH)	1960	135		3.5		ABC FILMS	
WHO DONE IT? (ABBOTT & COSTELLO)	1942	75		1.5	2.5	UNIVERSAL	
WHO IS HARRY KELLERMAN AND WHY IS HE SAYING THOSE TERRIBLE THINGS ABOUT ME?	1971	108	3*			NATIONAL GENERAL	
WHO IS HOPE SCHUYLER?	1942	57		1.0		20th CENTURY FOX	
WHO KILLED GAIL PRESTON?	1938	60			2.5	COLUMBIA	
WHO KILLED MARY WHATS'ERNAME?	1971	90	3			CANNON RELEASING	
WHO KILLED TEDDY BEAR?	1965	91	2			MAGNA PICTURES	
WHO SAYS I CAN'T RIDE A RAINDOW!	1971	85	3			TRANSVUE PICTURES	
WHO SLEW AUNTIE ROO? (BRITISH)	1971	91	3			AMERICAN-INTERNAT'L	

‡ An asterisk (*) in THE FILM BUFF'S BIBLE column indicates that the film has been rated by the editor and/or staff. All other ratings in this column are based on a consensus of reviews (see NOTES).

TITLE (LEADING ACTORS SHOWN WHERE TWO OR MORE FILMS HAVE THE SAME OR SIMILAR TITLE)	YEAR RELEASED	RUNNING TIME IN MINUTES	THE FILM BUFF'S BIBLE ‡	STEVEN SCHEUER	LEONARD MALTIN	DISTRIBUTOR	COMMENT
WHO STOLE THE BODY? (FRENCH)	a1962	95		1.5	2.0		
WHO WAS MADDOX? (BRITISH)	1964	62		2.0		AVCO-EMBASSY	
WHO WAS THAT LADY?	1960	115		2.5	3.0	COLUMBIA	
WHOLE TOWN'S TALKING, THE	1935	95		3.0	3.0	COLUMBIA	
WHOLE TRUTH, THE (BRITISH - STEWART GRANGER)	1958	84	4	2.0	2.5	COLUMBIA	
WHOLE TRUTH, THE (GERMAN - PETER VAN EYCK)	a1961	97		2.0		PARAMOUNT	
WHOLE WORLD IS WATCHING, THE (T.V.)	1969	100		2.0		UNIVERSAL	
WHOOPEE	1930	94				UNITED ARTISTS	
WHO'S AFRAID OF VIRGINIA WOOLF?	1966	131	9*	4.0		WARNER BROTHERS	NOMINATED BEST PICTURE
WHO'S BEEN SLEEPING IN MY BED?	1963	103		2.5	2.5	PARAMOUNT	
WHO'S GOT THE ACTION?	1962	93	4*	2.5	2.5	PARAMOUNT	
WHO'S MINDING THE MINT?	1967	97	5	3.0	3.5	COLUMBIA	
WHO'S MINDING THE STORE?	1963	90	3	1.5		PARAMOUNT	
WHO'S THAT KNOCKING AT MY DOOR?	a1968	90	3			JOSEPH BRENNER	
WHY BOTHER TO KNOCK (BRITISH)	a1964	88		2.0	1.5	SEVEN ARTS	
WHY MUST I DIE?	1960	86		1.5	2.0	AMERICAN-INTERNAT'L	
WICHITA	1955	81		2.5	2.5	ALLIED ARTISTS	
WICKED AS THEY COME (BRITISH)	1956	94			2.0	COLUMBIA	
WICKED CITY, THE (FRENCH)	1949	80		1.5	1.5	UNITED ARTISTS	
WICKED DREAMS OF PAULA SCHULTZ, THE	1968	113	2			UNITED ARTISTS	
WICKED GO TO HELL, THE (FRENCH)	1956	74		1.0		FANFARE	
WICKED LADY, THE (BRITISH)	1945	104	3	2.5	2.5	UNIVERSAL	
WICKED WOMAN	1954	77		3.0	1.5	UNITED ARTISTS	
WIDE BLUE ROAD, THE (ITALIAN)	1956	90		1.5	2.5		
WIDE BOY (BRITISH)	1952	67	3			REALART	
WIDE OPEN FACES	1938	67			2.5	COLUMBIA	
WIDOW, THE (ITALIAN)	1955	87			2.0	DIST. CORP. OF AMER.	ENGLISH LANGUAGE
WIDOW FROM MONTE CARLO, THE	1936	60		2.0		WARNER BROTHERS	
WIFE, DOCTOR AND NURSE	1937	85		2.5	2.5	20th CENTURY FOX	
WIFE, HUSBAND AND FRIEND	1939	80		2.5	3.0	20th CENTURY FOX	
WIFE OF MONTE CRISTO, THE	1946	80			2.0	PRODUCERS RELEASING	
WIFE SWAPPERS, THE (BRITISH)	a1970	86	1			TRANS-AMERICA	
WIFE TAKES A FLYER, THE	1942	86			2.0	COLUMBIA	
WIFE VERSUS SECRETARY	1936	88		2.0	3.0	M-G-M	
WIFE WANTED	1946	73			2.0	MONOGRAM	
WILD AFFAIR, THE (BRITISH)	1965	87	3			GOLDSTONE FILM ENT.	
WILD AND THE INNOCENT, THE	1959	84		2.5	2.5	UNIVERSAL	
WILD AND THE WILLING, THE (BRITISH)	a1962	113	3		2.0	UNIVERSAL	
WILD AND WONDERFUL	1964	88	4*	2.0	2.5	UNIVERSAL	
WILD ANGELS, THE	1966	93	2	1.0		AMERICAN-INTERNAT'L	
WILD BILL HICKOK RIDES	1942	82		2.0		WARNER BROTHERS	
WILD BLUE YONDER, THE	1951	98	4	2.5	2.5	REPUBLIC	
WILD BUNCH, THE	1969	140	3*			WARNER BROTHERS	
WILD CARGO (DOCUMENTARY)	1934	96		3.0		RKO	
WILD CATS ON THE BEACH (ITALIAN)	1959	96		2.0	2.5	AMERICAN-INTERNAT'L	
WILD CHILD, THE (FRENCH)	1970	85	6*			UNITED ARTISTS	
WILD COUNTRY	1971	100	5			BUENA VISTA	
WILD DAKOTAS, THE	1956	73		1.5		ASSOC'D FILM DISTS.	
WILD EYE, THE (ITALIAN)	1967	91	2			AMERICAN-INTERNAT'L	
WILD FOR KICKS (BRITISH)	a1960	86		1.0	2.0	VICTORIA	
WILD FRUIT (FRENCH)	1953	94		2.0		UN. MOTION PIC. ORG.	
WILD GEESE CALLING	1941	77		2.0	2.0	20th CENTURY FOX	
WILD GUITAR	1962	90		1.0		FAIRWAY INTERNAT'L	
WILD HARVEST (ALAN LADD, ROBERT PRESTON)	1947	92		1.5	1.5	PARAMOUNT	
WILD HEART, THE	1952	82		2.0	2.0	RKO	
WILD HERITAGE	1958	78		2.5	2.5	UNIVERSAL	
WILD IN THE COUNTRY	1961	114	3*	2.0	2.5	20th CENTURY FOX	
WILD IN THE SKY	1972	87				AMERICAN-INTERNAT'L	
WILD IN THE STREETS	1968	97	4	3.5		AMERICAN-INTERNAT'L	
WILD IS THE WIND	1957	114		3.0	2.5	PARAMOUNT	
WILD MAN OF BORNEO, THE	1941	78		1.5	2.0	M-G-M	
WILD 90	1968	90	1			SUPREME MIX INC.	
WILD NORTH, THE	1952	97	4	2.0	2.0	M-G-M	
WILD ON THE BEACH	1965	77	1			20th CENTURY FOX	
WILD ONE, THE	1954	79	7*	3.5	3.5	COLUMBIA	
WILD PACK, THE	1972	102				AMERICAN-INTERNAT'L	
WILD PARTY, THE	1956	81		2.0	1.5	UNITED ARTISTS	
WILD RACERS, THE	1968	81	1			AMERICAN-INTERNAT'L	
WILD REBELS, THE	1967	90	2			CROWN INTERNATIONAL	
WILD RIDE	1960	80		1.0		FILMGROUP	
WILD RIDERS	1971	91				CROWN INTERNATIONAL	
WILD RIVER	1960	107	5*	3.5	3.0	20th CENTURY FOX	
WILD ROVERS	1971	109	4			M-G-M	
WILD SEED, THE	1965	99		2.0	3.0	UNIVERSAL	
WILD STALLION	1952	72		2.5	1.5	MONOGRAM	
WILD STAMPEDE (MEXICAN)	1962	90		2.0		COM. UNITED T.V.	
WILD STRAWBERRIES (SWEDISH)	1958	90	6-7*			JANUS FILMS	
WILD WESTERNERS, THE	1963	70	2		1.5	COLUMBIA	
WILD WHEELS	1969	92	1			COLBY PRODUCTIONS	
WILD, WILD PLANET, THE (ITALIAN)	1965	93	1			M-G-M	
WILD, WILD WINTER	1966	80	2		2.0	UNIVERSAL	
WILD WOMEN (T.V.)	1970	90		1.5		ABC FILMS	
WILD YOUTH	1960	70		1.5		CINEMA ASSOC.	
WILDCAT BUS	1940	63		2.0		RKO	

‡ An asterisk (*) in THE FILM BUFF'S BIBLE column indicates that the film has been rated by the editor and/or staff. All other ratings in this column are based on a consensus of reviews (see NOTES).

TITLE (LEADING ACTORS SHOWN WHERE TWO OR MORE FILMS HAVE THE SAME OR SIMILAR TITLE)	YEAR RELEASED	RUNNING TIME IN MINUTES	THE FILM BUFF'S BIBLE ‡	STEVEN SCHEUER	LEONARD MALTIN	DISTRIBUTOR	COMMENT
WILL JAMES' SAND	a1949	78		2.0	2.0	20th CENTURY FOX	
WILL PENNY	1968	109	4*	3.5		PARAMOUNT	
WILL SUCCESS SPOIL ROCK HUNTER?	1957	94	5	2.5	2.5	20th CENTURY FOX	
WILLARD	1971	95	4			CINERAMA RELEASING	
WILLY WONKA AND THE CHOCOLATE FACTORY	1971	100	5			PARAMOUNT	
WILSON	1944	154	6*	4.0	3.5	20th CENTURY FOX	NOMINATED BEST PICTURE
WINCHESTER '73 (JAMES STEWART)	1950	92	6	3.0	3.0	UNIVERSAL	
WINCHESTER 73 (T.V. - TOM TRYON)	1967	100		2.0	2.5	UNIVERSAL	
WIND, THE (SILENT)	1928	75				M-G-M	
WIND ACROSS THE EVERGLADES	1958	93		2.5	2.5	WARNER BROTHERS	
WIND CANNOT READ, THE (BRITISH)	1958	115	4		2.5	20th CENTURY FOX	
WIND FROM THE EAST (FRENCH)	1969	95	1*			NEW LINE CINEMA	
WINDOM'S WAY (BRITISH)	1958	108		3.0	2.5	J. ARTHUR RANK	
WINDOW, THE	1949	73	7	3.5	3.5	RKO	
WING AND A PRAYER	1944	97	3*	3.0	3.0	20th CENTURY FOX	
WINGED VICTORY	1944	130		3.5	3.5	20th CENTURY FOX	
WINGS (SILENT)	1927	136				PARAMOUNT	BEST PICTURE AWARD 1927/28
WINGS AND THE WOMAN (BRITISH)	1942	94		3.0		RKO	
WINGS FOR THE EAGLE	1942	83		2.0	2.0	WARNER BROTHERS	
WINGS IN THE DARK	1935	75		2.5	2.5	PARAMOUNT	
WINGS OF CHANCE (CANADIAN)	1960	76	2		1.5	UNIVERSAL	
WINGS OF FIRE (T.V.)	1967	100		1.5	2.5	UNIVERSAL	
WINGS OF EAGLES, THE	1957	110		2.5	2.5	M-G-M	
WINGS OF THE HAWK	1953	80		2.0	2.0	UNIVERSAL	
WINGS OF THE MORNING (BRITISH)	1937	89		2.5	3.0	20th CENTURY FOX	
WINGS OF THE NAVY	1939	89		2.5		WARNER BROTHERS	
WINGS OVER HONOLULU	1937	78		2.0		UNIVERSAL	
WINK OF AN EYE	1958	72	1			UNITED ARTISTS	
WINNER TAKE ALL (JAMES CAGNEY, MARIAN NIXON)	1932	68		2.5	2.5	WARNER BROTHERS	
WINNIE THE POOH AND THE HONEY TREE (CARTOON)	1965	26	6			BUENA VISTA	
WINNING	1969	123	4*			UNIVERSAL	
WINNING OF THE WEST	1953	57	4			COLUMBIA	
WINNING TEAM, THE	1952	98		2.5	2.5	WARNER BROTHERS	
WINSLOW BOY, THE (BRITISH)	1948	97	7	4.0	3.5	EAGLE LION	
WINTER A GO-GO	1965	88	2		2.0	COLUMBIA	
WINTER CARNIVAL	1939	105		2.5	2.5	UNITED ARTISTS	
WINTER LIGHT (SWEDISH)	1962	80	6			JANUS FILMS	
WINTER MEETING	1948	104	3	2.5	2.5	WARNER BROTHERS	
WINTERSET	1936	78		4.0	4.0	RKO	
WINTERTIME	1943	82		2.5	2.0	20th CENTURY FOX	
WIRETAPPER	1955	80		1.5	1.0	CONTINENTAL	
WISE GIRL	1937	70		2.5	2.5	RKO	
WISHING WELL, THE (BRITISH)	1954	79		2.5		WELSH FILMS	
WISTFUL WIDOW OF WAGON GAP, THE	1947	78		2.0	2.0	UNIVERSAL	
WITCH WITHOUT A BROOM, A	1966	86	1			PRODUCERS RELEASING	
WITCHCRAFT (BRITISH)	1964	79	3		2.0	20th CENTURY FOX	
WITCHCRAFT '70	1970	75	1			TRANS-AMERICA	
WITCHES, THE (BRITISH - JOAN FONTAINE)	a1966	90	4	2.5		20th CENTURY FOX	
WITCHES, THE (ITALIAN - SILVANA MANGANO)	1969	100	1			LOPERT	
WITCHMAKER, THE	1969	97	2			EXCELSIOR	
WITCH'S CURSE, THE (ITALIAN)	1961	79	1	1.5		MEDALLION	
WITCH'S MIRROR, THE (MEXICAN)	1961	75	1*	1.0		AZTECA	
WITH A SONG IN MY HEART	1952	117	4*	3.5	3.0	20th CENTURY FOX	
WITH FIRE AND SWORD (ITALIAN)	a1961	96		2.0	1.5	TELEWIDE SYSTEMS	
WITH SIX YOU GET EGGROLL	1968	95	4	2.0		NATIONAL GENERAL	
WITH THESE HANDS	1950	50		3.0		CLASSIC PICTURES	DOCUMENTARY DRAMA
WITHIN THESE WALLS	1945	71		2.0	2.0	20th CENTURY FOX	
WITHOUT A STITCH (DANISH)	1970	96	1			VIP DISTRIBUTORS	
WITHOUT APPARENT MOTIVE	1972	102	6			20th CENTURY FOX	
WITHOUT HONOR	1949	69		1.5	2.0	UNITED ARTISTS	
WITHOUT LOVE	1945	111		3.0	3.0	M-G-M	
WITHOUT RESERVATIONS	1946	107		2.5	3.0	RKO	
WITHOUT WARNING	1952	75	5	3.5		UNITED ARTISTS	
WITNESS, THE (BRITISH)	1959	58		2.0		ANGLO AMALGAMATED	
WITNESS CHAIR, THE	1936	64		2.5	2.5	RKO	
WITNESS FOR THE PROSECUTION	1957	114	7*	4.0	4.0	UNITED ARTISTS	NOMINATED BEST PICTURE
WITNESS IN THE CITY (ITALIAN)	1959	90		2.5			
WITNESS IN THE DARK (BRITISH)	1959	62			1.5	J. ARTHUR RANK	
WITNESS TO MURDER	1954	83	5	3.0	3.0	UNITED ARTISTS	
WITNESS VANISHES, THE	1939	66		2.0		UNIVERSAL	
WITNESSES, THE (FRENCH, DOCUMENTARY)	1962	82	6			ALTURA FILMS	
WIVES AND LOVERS	1963	103		3.0	2.5	PARAMOUNT	
WIVES NEVER KNOW	1936	75		1.5	2.5	PARAMOUNT	
WIVES UNDER SUSPICION	1938	75		2.5	2.5	UNIVERSAL	
WIZARD OF BAGHDAD, THE	1960	92		1.5	2.0	20th CENTURY FOX	
WIZARD OF OZ, THE	1939	101	6*	4.0	4.0	M-G-M	NOMINATED BEST PICTURE
WOLF DOG (CANADIAN)	1958	61	1	1.5	1.5	20th CENTURY FOX	
WOLF LARSEN	1958	83		2.0	2.5	ALLIED ARTISTS	
WOLF MAN, THE	1941	71	4*	3.0	3.5	UNIVERSAL	
WOLVES OF THE DEEP (ITALIAN)	1959	93		2.5		AMERICAN-INTERNAT'L	
WOMAN AND TEMPTATION (ARGENTINE)	1966	85	1			PRENTOULIS FILMS	
WOMAN AND THE HUNTER, THE (BRITISH)	1957	79		1.5	1.5	NTA PICTURES	
WOMAN BAIT (FRENCH)	a1958	110		2.5	2.5	LOPERT	
WOMAN CHASES MAN	1937	71		3.0	2.5	UNITED ARTISTS	

‡ An asterisk (*) in THE FILM BUFF'S BIBLE column indicates that the film has been rated by the editor and/or staff. All other ratings in this column are based on a consensus of reviews (see NOTES).

TITLE (LEADING ACTORS SHOWN WHERE TWO OR MORE FILMS HAVE THE SAME OR SIMILAR TITLE)	YEAR RELEASED	RUNNING TIME IN MINUTES	THE FILM BUFF'S BIBLE ‡	STEVEN SCHEUER	LEONARD MALTIN	DISTRIBUTOR	COMMENT
WOMAN EATER, THE (BRITISH)	1957	70	1	1.5	1.5	COLUMBIA	
WOMAN FROM HEADQUARTERS	1950	60		2.0		REPUBLIC	
WOMAN FROM TANGIER, THE	1948	66		2.0		COLUMBIA	
WOMAN HATER (BRITISH)	1948	70		2.0	2.0	UNIVERSAL	
WOMAN HUNT (STEVEN PICCARO, LISA LU)	1962	60	1			20th CENTURY FOX	
WOMAN IN A DRESSING GOWN (BRITISH)	1957	93	4*	3.5	2.5	WARNER BROTHERS	
WOMAN IN GREEN	1945	68	4*	.		UNIVERSAL	
WOMAN IN HIDING	1950	92		2.0	2.0	UNIVERSAL	
WOMAN IN QUESTION, THE (BRITISH)	a1950	88		3.0	3.0	COLUMBIA	
WOMAN IN RED	1935	68		2.0	2.0	FIRST NATIONAL	
WOMAN IN THE DARK	1952	60		1.0		REPUBLIC	
WOMAN IN THE DUNES (JAPANESE)	1964	123	6			PATHE CONTEMPARARY	
WOMAN IN THE WINDOW	1944	99	6*	3.5	3.5	RKO	
WOMAN IN WHITE, THE	1948	109		2.0	2.0	WARNER BROTHERS	
WOMAN IS A WOMAN, A (FRENCH)	1964	80	4			PATHE CONTEMPARARY	
WOMAN LIKE SATAN, A (FRENCH)	a1958	100	2			LOPERT	
WOMAN OBSESSED	1959	102		2.0	2.5	20th CENTURY FOX	
WOMAN OF DISTINCTION, A	1950	85	3*	2.5	3.0	COLUMBIA	
WOMAN OF DOLWYN, THE (BRITISH)	a1949	95	4*	3.5	2.5	LOPERT	
WOMAN OF ROME (ITALIAN)	1954	92	4	2.0	2.0	DIST. CORP. OF AMER.	
WOMAN OF STRAW (BRITISH)	1964	117		2.5	2.5	UNITED ARTISTS	
WOMAN OF THE NORTH COUNTRY	1952	90		2.0	2.0	REPUBLIC	
WOMAN OF THE RIVER (ITALIAN)	1955	95	3		2.0	COLUMBIA	
WOMAN OF THE TOWN, THE	1943	90		3.5	3.0	UNITED ARTISTS	
WOMAN OF THE YEAR	1942	112		4.0	3.5	M-G-M	
WOMAN ON PIER 13, THE	a1949	73		2.0	2.5	RKO	
WOMAN ON THE BEACH, THE	1947	71	4	3.0	3.0	RKO	
WOMAN ON THE RUN	1950	77		3.0	3.0	UNIVERSAL	
WOMAN REBELS, A	1936	88		2.5	3.0	RKO	
WOMAN THEY ALMOST LYNCHED	1953	90	2	2.0	2.0	REPUBLIC	
WOMAN TIMES SEVEN	1967	100		2.5	3.0	AVCO-EMBASSY	SEVEN STORIES
WOMAN WANTED	1935	68		3.0		M-G-M	
WOMAN WHO CAME BACK, THE	1945	68			2.0	REPUBLIC	
WOMAN WHO WOULDN'T DIE	1965	84	3			WARNER BROTHERS	
WOMAN'S DEVOTION, A	a1956	88		2.0	2.0	REPUBLIC	
WOMAN'S FACE, A	1941	105		2.0	3.0	M-G-M	
WOMAN'S SECRET, A	1949	85	3	3.0	3.0	RKO	
WOMAN'S TEMPTATION, A (BRITISH)	1958	60		2.0		WARNER BROTHERS	
WOMAN'S VENGEANCE, A	1948	96	5	3.5	3.5	UNIVERSAL	
WOMAN'S WORLD, A	1954	94		2.5	3.0	20th CENTURY FOX	
WOMEN, THE	1939	132		3.5	4.0	M-G-M	
WOMEN AND WAR (FRENCH)	1962	100		2.0		PARAMOUNT	
WOMEN ARE LIKE THAT (KAY FRANCIS, PAT O'BRIEN)	1938	78			2.5	WARNER BROTHERS	
WOMEN ARE LIKE THAT (FRENCH - EDDIE CONSTANTINE)	1960	88		1.5		D.U.K.	
WOMEN ARE TALKATIVE (FRENCH)	1958	90		1.5			
WOMEN IN BONDAGE	1944	70			2.0	MONOGRAM	
WOMEN IN CAGES	1971	78	1			NEW WORLD	
WOMEN IN LOVE (BRITISH)	1969	130	3*			UNITED ARTISTS	
WOMEN IN PARADISE	1959	81		2.0		TELEWIDE SYSTEMS	
WOMEN IN THE WIND	1939	65		2.5		WARNER BROTHERS	
WOMEN MEN MARRY, THE	1937	61		2.0		M-G-M	
WOMEN OF DEVIL'S ISLAND (ITALIAN)	1962	86		1.0	1.5	AMERICAN-INTERNAT'L	
WOMEN OF PITCAIRN ISLAND, THE	1956	72	2*	1.5	1.5	20th CENTURY FOX	
WOMEN OF THE PREHISTORIC PLANET	1966	87	1			REALART	
WOMEN OF THE WORLD (ITALIAN, DOCUMENTARY)	1963	107	4			AVCO-EMBASSY	
WOMEN WITHOUT NAMES	1940	63		1.5		PARAMOUNT	
WOMEN'S PRISON	1955	80		2.0	2.0	COLUMBIA	
WONDER BAR	1934	84		2.5	2.5	FIRST NATIONAL	
WONDER MAN	1945	98	5*	3.5	3.5	RKO	
WONDERFUL COUNTRY, THE	1959	96		2.5	2.5	UNITED ARTISTS	
WONDERFUL TO BE YOUNG	1962	92	3			PARAMOUNT	
WONDERFUL WORLD OF THE BROTHERS GRIMM, THE	1962	135	6			M-G-M	
WONDERS OF ALADDIN, THE (ITALIAN)	1961	93		2.0	2.0	M-G-M	
WOODEN HORSE, THE (BRITISH)	1950	101	6			BRITISH-LION	
WOODSTOCK	1970	184	6			WARNER BROTHERS	
WORDS AND MUSIC	1948	119		2.5	2.5	M-G-M	
WORKING MAN, THE	1933	75			2.5	WARNER BROTHERS	
WORLD AND THE FLESH, THE	1932	75		2.5	2.0	PARAMOUNT	
WORLD BY NIGHT (ITALIAN, TRAVELOGUE)	1960	104	4			WARNER BROTHERS	
WORLD CHANGES, THE	1933	90		3.0	2.5	FIRST NATIONAL	
WORLD FOR RANSOM, THE	1954	82		2.5	2.0	ALLIED ARTISTS	
WORLD IN HIS ARMS, THE	1952	104		3.0	2.5	UNIVERSAL	
WORLD IN MY CORNER	1956	82		2.5	2.5	UNIVERSAL	
WORLD IN MY POCKET	1962	93	4	2.0		M-G-M	
WORLD OF ABBOTT AND COSTELLO, THE	1965	75	5		2.5	UNIVERSAL	FILM CLIPS
WORLD OF APU, THE (INDIAN)	1959	103	7	4.0		HARRISON PICTURES	
WORLD OF HANS CHRISTIAN ANDERSON, THE	1971	75				UNITED ARTISTS	
WORLD OF HENRY ORIENT, THE	1964	106	6-7*	4.0	3.5	UNITED ARTISTS	
WORLD OF SPORT FISHING, THE	1972	107				ALLIED ARTISTS	
WORLD OF SUZIE WONG, THE	1960	129	4	2.0	2.5	PARAMOUNT	
WORLD OF THE VAMPIRE, THE (MEXICAN)	1961	83		1.0		AZTECA	
WORLD PREMIERE	1941	70		3.0	2.5	PARAMOUNT	
WORLD, THE FLESH AND THE DEVIL, THE	1959	95	5*	3.0	2.0	M-G-M	
WORLD WAS HIS JURY, THE	1958	82		2.0	1.5	COLUMBIA	

‡ An asterisk (*) in THE FILM BUFF'S BIBLE column indicates that the film has been rated by the editor and/or staff. All other ratings in this column are based on a consensus of reviews (see NOTES).

TITLE (LEADING ACTORS SHOWN WHERE TWO OR MORE FILMS HAVE THE SAME OR SIMILAR TITLE)	YEAR RELEASED	RUNNING TIME IN MINUTES	THE FILM BUFF'S BIBLE ‡	STEVEN SCHEUER	LEONARD MALTIN	DISTRIBUTOR	COMMENT
WORLD WITHOUT END	1956	80		2.0	2.5	ALLIED ARTISTS	
WORLD WITHOUT SUN (FRENCH, DOCUMENTARY)	1964	93	7	4.0		COLUMBIA	
WORM'S EYE VIEW (BRITISH)	1951	78		2.5		EROS FILMS	
WOULD-BE GENTLEMAN, THE (FRENCH)	1960	95	6			KINGSLEY-UNION	
WR - MYSTERIES OF THE ORGANISM (YUGOSLAVIAN)	1971	80	2			CINEMA V	
WRATH OF GOD, THE	1972	111	3			M-G-M	
WRECK OF THE HESPERUS, THE	1948	70		2.0	2.0	COLUMBIA	
WRECK OF THE MARY DEARE, THE	1959	105	5*	2.5	2.5	M-G-M	
WRECKING CREW, THE (DEAN MARTIN, ELKE SOMMER)	1968	104	3			COLUMBIA	
WRESTLING WOMAN VS THE AZTEC MUMMY (MEXICAN)	1965	88		1.0		TRANS-INTERNATIONAL	
WRITTEN ON THE WIND	1956	99		3.0	3.0	UNIVERSAL	
WRONG ARM OF THE LAW, THE (BRITISH)	1963	91	5-6*	3.5	3.0	CONTINENTAL	
WRONG BOX, THE (BRITISH)	1966	105	6*			COLUMBIA	
WRONG KIND OF GIRL, THE	a1956	96	5*	3.0	3.5	20th CENTURY FOX	
WRONG MAN, THE	1957	105	3*	3.5	3.0	WARNER BROTHERS	
WRONG NUMBER (BRITISH)	1959	67		2.0		ANGLO AMALGAMATED	
WUSA	1970	116	5			PARAMOUNT	
WUTHERING HEIGHTS (LAURENCE OLIVIER, MERLE OBERON)	1939	103	6*	4.0	4.0	UNITED ARTISTS	NOMINATED BEST PICTURE
WUTHERING HEIGHTS (ANNA CALDER-MARSHALL, T DALTON)	1970	105	6			AMERICAN-INTERNAT'L	(BRITISH)
WYOMING (WALLACE BEERY)	1940	89		2.0	2.0	M-G-M	
WYOMING (WILLIAM ELLIOT)	1947	84		2.5	2.5	REPUBLIC	
WYOMING KID, THE	a1947	100		2.0	2.0	WARNER BROTHERS	
WYOMING MAIL	1950	87		2.0	2.5	UNIVERSAL	
WYOMING RENEGADES	1955	73		1.0	1.5	COLUMBIA	
X-15	1961	106		2.0	2.0	UNITED ARTISTS	
X-RAY OF A KILLER (FRENCH)	1963	85		2.0		AMERICAN-INTERNAT'L	
'X' - THE MAN WITH THE X-RAY EYES	a1963	80		2.5	2.5	AMERICAN-INTERNAT'L	
X THE UNKNOWN (BRITISH)	1956	78	2*	1.5	2.0	WARNER BROTHERS	
X Y & ZEE (BRITISH)	a1972	110	3			COLUMBIA	
YANCO (MEXICAN)	1961	85	4*			JERAND FILMS	
YANK AT ETON, A	1942	88		2.0	2.0	M-G-M	
YANK AT OXFORD, A	1938	100		3.0	3.0	M-G-M	
YANK IN ERMINE, A (BRITISH)	1955	84		2.0		M & A ALEXANDER	
YANK IN INDO-CHINA, A	1952	67		2.5	1.5	COLUMBIA	
YANK IN KOREA, A	1951	73	2	2.5	1.5	COLUMBIA	
YANK IN LONDON, A (BRITISH)	a1945	106		3.0		20th CENTURY FOX	
YANK IN THE R.A.F., A	1941	98		3.0	3.0	20th CENTURY FOX	
YANK IN VIET NAM, A	a1964	80		2.0	2.0	ALLIED ARTISTS	
YANK ON THE BURMA ROAD, A	1942	66		2.0		M-G-M	
YANKEE BUCCANEER	1952	86		2.0	2.5	UNIVERSAL	
YANKEE DOODLE DANDY	1942	126	6*	4.0	3.5	WARNER BROTHERS	NOMINATED BEST PICTURE
YANKEE PASHA	1954	84	3	2.5	2.5	UNIVERSAL	
YAQUI DRUMS	1956	71			1.5	ALLIED ARTISTS	
YEAR OF THE YAHOO	1971	90				LEWIS M. P. ENTERP'S	
YEARLING, THE	1946	134	6*	4.0	3.5	M-G-M	NOMINATED BEST PICTURE
YEARS BETWEEN, THE (BRITISH)	1946	88		2.5	2.5	UNIVERSAL	
YELLOW BALLOON, THE (BRITISH)	1952	80	4	3.0	2.5	ALLIED ARTISTS	
YELLOW CAB MAN, THE	1950	85		2.5	3.0	M-G-M	
YELLOW CANARY (BRITISH - ANNA NEAGLE, R. GREENE)	1943	98		2.5	2.5	RKO	
YELLOW CANARY, THE (BARBARA EDEN, PAT BOONE)	1963	93	3			20th CENTURY FOX	
YELLOW FIN	1951	74		3.0		MONOGRAM	
YELLOW JACK	1938	83		3.5	3.5	M-G-M	
YELLOW MOUNTAIN, THE	1954	78		1.5	1.5	UNIVERSAL	
YELLOW ROLLS-ROYCE, THE	1965	122	5*	4.0	3.0	M-G-M	THREE PART STORY
YELLOW SKY	1948	98	5*	3.0	3.0	20th CENTURY FOX	
YELLOW SQUADRON (GERMAN)	1955	80		2.0		ASSOCIATED ARTISTS	
YELLOW SUBMARINE (BRITISH, CARTOON)	1968	85	3*			UNITED ARTISTS	
YELLOW TOMAHAWK, THE	1954	82		2.0	2.0	UNITED ARTISTS	
YELLOWNECK	1955	83		3.0		REPUBLIC	
YELLOWSTONE KELLY	1959	91		2.5	2.5	WARNER BROTHERS	
YES, MY DARLING DAUGHTER	1939	86		3.0	2.5	WARNER BROTHERS	
YES, SIR, THAT'S MY BABY	1949	82		2.5	2.5	UNIVERSAL	
YESTERDAY AND TODAY (DOCUMENTARY)	1953	57	4	3.0		UNITED ARTISTS	FILM CLIPS
YESTERDAY, TODAY AND TOMORROW (ITALIAN)	1963	120	5*	3.5	4.0	AVCO-EMBASSY	THREE EPISODES
YESTERDAY'S ENEMY (BRITISH)	1959	95	4	2.5	1.5	COLUMBIA	
YO YO (FRENCH)	1964	92	4			MAGNA PICTURES	
YOG - MONSTER FROM SPACE (JAPANESE)	1970	84	1			AMERICAN-INTERNAT'L	
YOJIMBO (JAPANESE)	1961	110	6*		4.0	SENECA INTERNATIONAL	
YOKEL BOY	1942	69		3.0	1.5	REPUBLIC	
YOLANDA AND THE THIEF	1945	108		2.0	2.5	M-G-M	
YOU AND ME	1938	90		1.5	3.0	PARAMOUNT	
YOU ARE WHAT YOU EAT	1968	75	2			LANDAU/UNGER COM. UN	
YOU BELONG TO ME (HENRY FONDA, BARBARA STANWYCK)	1941	94		2.5	2.5	COLUMBIA	
YOU CAME ALONG	1945	103		2.0	2.5	PARAMOUNT	
YOU CAN'T BUY EVERYTHING	1934	85		3.0		M-G-M	
YOU CAN'T CHEAT AN HONEST MAN	1939	76	6*	3.0	3.5	UNIVERSAL	
YOU CAN'T GET AWAY WITH MURDER	1939	78		3.0	2.5	WARNER BROTHERS	
YOU CAN'T HAVE EVERYTHING	1937	99		3.0	3.0	20th CENTURY FOX	

‡ An asterisk (*) in THE FILM BUFF'S BIBLE column indicates that the film has been rated by the editor and/or staff. All other ratings in this column are based on a consensus of reviews (see NOTES).

TITLE (LEADING ACTORS SHOWN WHERE TWO OR MORE FILMS HAVE THE SAME OR SIMILAR TITLE)	YEAR RELEASED	RUNNING TIME IN MINUTES	THE FILM BUFF'S BIBLE ‡	STEVEN SCHEUER	LEONARD MALTIN	DISTRIBUTOR	COMMENT
YOU CAN'T RUN AWAY FROM IT	1956	95	4	2.0	2.0	COLUMBIA	
YOU CAN'T TAKE IT WITH YOU	1938	127	6*	3.0	3.5	COLUMBIA	BEST PICTURE AWARD
YOU CAN'T WIN 'EM ALL (BRITISH)	1970	97	1			COLUMBIA	
YOU FOR ME	1952	71		2.5	2.5	M-G-M	
YOU GOTTA STAY HAPPY	1948	100	5	2.5	2.5	UNIVERSAL	
YOU HAVE TO RUN FAST	1961	73	3			UNITED ARTISTS	
YOU KNOW WHAT SAILORS ARE (BRITISH)	1953	89		2.0	2.0	J. ARTHUR RANK	
YOU MUST BE JOKING (BRITISH)	1965	100	5			COLUMBIA	
YOU NEVER CAN TELL	1951	78	4	3.0	2.5	REALART	
YOU ONLY LIVE ONCE (HENRY FONDA, SYLVIA SIDNEY)	1937	86		3.5	3.0	UNITED ARTISTS	
YOU ONLY LIVE ONCE (FRENCH - KAREN BLANGUERNON)	1969	95	4			SIGMA III	
YOU ONLY LIVE TWICE (BRITISH)	1967	117	5			UNITED ARTISTS	
YOU SAID A MOUTHFUL	1932	75		3.0	3.0	FIRST NATIONAL	
YOU WERE MEANT FOR ME	1948	92	5	3.0	3.0	20th CENTURY FOX	
YOU WERE NEVER LOVLIER	1942	97	4*	3.0	3.5	COLUMBIA	
YOU'LL FIND OUT	1940	97		3.0		RKO	
YOU'LL NEVER GET RICH	1941	88		3.5	3.5	COLUMBIA	
YOUNG AMERICANS (DOCUMENTARY)	1967	104	4			COLUMBIA	
YOUNG AND DANGEROUS	1957	78			2.0	20th CENTURY FOX	
YOUNG AND THE BRAVE, THE	1963	84	3			M-G-M	
YOUNG AND THE DAMNED, THE (MEXICAN)	a1951	80	4*			MAYER-KINGSLEY	
YOUNG AND WILD	1958	69		2.0	1.5	REPUBLIC	
YOUNG AND WILLING (WILLIAM HOLDEN, EDDIE BRACKEN)	a1942	82		2.0	2.5	UNITED ARTISTS	
YOUNG AND WILLING (IAN MCSHANE, VIRGINIA MASKELL)	a1962	113	3		2.0	UNIVERSAL	(BRITISH)
YOUNG APHRODITES (GREEK)	1963	89	3			JANUS FILMS	
YOUNG AT HEART	1955	117		3.0	3.0	WARNER BROTHERS	
YOUNG BESS	1953	112	6	3.5	3.0	M-G-M	
YOUNG BILLY YOUNG	1969	88	2	1.0		UNITED ARTISTS	
YOUNG CAPTIVES, THE	1959	61		2.5	2.0	PARAMOUNT	
YOUNG CARUSO, THE	1953	77	4			ITALIAN FILMS EXPORT	
YOUNG CASSIDY	1965	110	5*	3.5	3.0	M-G-M	
YOUNG COUNTRY, THE	1970	90		2.5		UNIVERSAL	
YOUNG COUPLE, A (FRENCH)	1971	90	2			TRANS WORLD ATTRACS.	
YOUNG DANIEL BOONE	1950	71		1.0	1.5	MONOGRAM	
YOUNG DILLINGER	1965	102	3	1.5	2.5	ALLIED ARTISTS	
YOUNG DR KILDARE	1938	81		3.0	-	M-G-M	
YOUNG DOCTORS, THE	1961	100	5*	3.0	3.0	UNITED ARTISTS	
YOUNG DON'T CRY, THE	1957	89		2.0	2.0	COLUMBIA	
YOUNG GIRLS BEWARE (FRENCH)	1957	90		2.0		UN. MOTION PIC. ORG.	
YOUNG GIRLS OF GOOD FAMILIES (FRENCH)	1963	90		1.5		AVCO-EMBASSY	
YOUNG GIRLS OF ROCHEFORT, THE (FRENCH)	1967	126	4			WARNER BROTHERS	
YOUNG GUNS, THE	1956	84		2.5	2.0	ALLIED ARTISTS	
YOUNG GUNS OF TEXAS	1963	78	3	2.0	2.5	20th CENTURY FOX	
YOUNG HELLIONS	a1958	85		1.0	1.5	M-G-M	
YOUNG IDEAS	1943	77		1.5	1.5	M-G-M	
YOUNG IN HEART, THE	1938	90		3.5	3.5	UNITED ARTISTS	
YOUNG JESSE JAMES	1960	73		2.0	1.5	20th CENTURY FOX	
YOUNG LAND, THE	1959	89		2.0	2.5	COLUMBIA	
YOUNG LAWYERS, THE (T.V.)	1969	75		3.0		PARAMOUNT	
YOUNG LIONS, THE	1958	167	6*	3.5	3.5	20th CENTURY FOX	
YOUNG LOVERS, THE (KEEFE BRASSELLE, SALLY FORREST)	1949	85		3.5		FILMMAKERS	
YOUNG LOVERS, THE (BR. - ODILE VERSOIS, D. KNIGHT)	a1954	96	5	2.5		PACEMAKER PICS.	
YOUNG LOVERS, THE (PETER FONDA, SHARON HUGUNEY)	1964	105	3		2.0	M-G-M	
YOUNG MAN WITH A HORN	1950	112	5*	3.5	3.0	WARNER BROTHERS	
YOUNG MAN WITH IDEAS	1952	84		2.5	2.5	M-G-M	
YOUNG MR LINCOLN	1939	100	4*	3.0	3.5	20th CENTURY FOX	
YOUNG MR PITT (BRITISH)	1942	103		2.5	2.5	20th CENTURY FOX	
YOUNG ONE, THE (MEXICAN)	1960	96	3	2.0	1.5	VITALITE	
YOUNG PEOPLE	1940	78			2.0	20th CENTURY FOX	
YOUNG PHILADELPHIANS, THE	1959	136	6	3.0	3.0	WARNER BROTHERS	
YOUNG RACERS, THE	1963	87		2.0	2.0	AMERICAN-INTERNAT'L	
YOUNG RUNAWAYS, THE	1968	91	3			M-G-M	
YOUNG SAVAGES, THE	1961	110	6	3.0	3.0	UNITED ARTISTS	
YOUNG STRANGER, THE	1957	84	4*	3.0	3.0	UNIVERSAL	
YOUNG SWINGERS, THE	1963	71	3			20th CENTURY FOX	
YOUNG, THE EVIL AND THE SAVAGE, THE (ITALIAN)	1968	82	1			AMERICAN-INTERNAT'L	
YOUNG TOM EDISON	1940	82		3.0	3.0	M-G-M	
YOUNG TORLESS (GERMAN)	1966	87	6			KANAWHA FILMS LTD.	
YOUNG WARRIORS, THE	1967	93		2.0	2.0	UNIVERSAL	
YOUNG WIDOW	1946	100		2.0	2.0	UNITED ARTISTS	
YOUNG WIVES TALE (BRITISH)	1951	79			2.5	ALLIED ARTISTS	
YOUNGBLOOD HAWKE	1964	137		1.5	2.5	WARNER BROTHERS	
YOUNGER BROTHERS, THE	1949	77		2.0	2.5	WARNER BROTHERS	
YOUNGEST PROFESSION, THE	1943	82		3.0	2.5	M-G-M	
YOUNGEST SPY, THE (RUSSIAN)	a1962	84	6*	3.0	3.0	SHORE INTERNATIONAL	
YOUR CHEATIN' HEART	1965	99	5	3.0	3.0	M-G-M	
YOUR MONEY OR YOUR LIFE (FRENCH)	1966	91	4*			GALA	
YOUR PAST IS SHOWING (BRITISH)	1958	87	5*	3.5	2.5	J. ARTHUR RANK	
YOUR SHADOW IS MINE (FRENCH)	1962	91		1.5		CONTINENTAL	
YOUR TURN, DARLING (FRENCH)	a1963	90		1.5	2.0	PARAMOUNT	
YOU'RE A BIG BOY NOW	1967	96	6	3.0	3.5	WARNER BROTHERS	
YOU'RE A SWEETHEART	1937	96				UNIVERSAL	
YOU'RE IN THE ARMY NOW	1941	79		2.5	2.0	WARNER BROTHERS	
YOU'RE IN THE NAVY NOW	1951	93	4	2.0	2.0	20th CENTURY FOX	

‡ An asterisk (*) in THE FILM BUFF'S BIBLE column indicates that the film has been rated by the editor and/or staff. All other ratings in this column are based on a consensus of reviews (see NOTES).

TITLE (LEADING ACTORS SHOWN WHERE TWO OR MORE FILMS HAVE THE SAME OR SIMILAR TITLE)	YEAR RELEASED	RUNNING TIME IN MINUTES	CRITICAL RATINGS			DISTRIBUTOR	COMMENT
			THE FILM BUFF'S BIBLE ‡	STEVEN SCHEUER	LEONARD MALTIN		
YOU'RE MY EVERYTHING	1949	94	5	3.0	3.0	20th CENTURY FOX	
YOU'RE NEVER TOO YOUNG	1955	102		2.0	2.5	PARAMOUNT	
YOU'RE NOT SO TOUGH	1940	71			-	UNIVERSAL	
YOU'RE ONLY YOUNG ONCE	1938	78		2.5	-	M-G-M	
YOU'RE TELLING ME	1934	66	4*	4.0	3.0	PARAMOUNT	
YOUTH RUNS WILD	1944	67		3.0		RKO	
YOU'VE GOT TO WALK IT LIKE YOU TALK IT OR YOU'LL LOSE THAT BEAT	1971	85	2			J.E.R. PICTURES	
YOURS, MINE AND OURS	1968	111	4	2.0		UNITED ARTISTS	
YPOTRON - FINAL COUNTDOWN	1972	90				H.K. FILM DIST.	
YUMA (T.V.)	1971	90		1.5		ABC FILMS	
Z (FRENCH)	1969	127	10*			CINEMA V	NOMINATED BEST PICTURE
Z. P. G.	1972	95	2			PARAMOUNT	
ZABRISKIE POINT	1970	112	5			M-G-M	
ZACHARIAH	1971	91	4			CINERAMA RELEASING	
ZAMBA	1949	75			1.5	EAGLE LION	
ZANZABUKU (DOCUMENTARY)	1956	64		3.0		REPUBLIC	
ZAPATA	1971	102				AZTECA	
ZARAK (BRITISH)	1956	95		2.0	2.5	COLUMBIA	
ZATOICHI MEETS YOJIMBO (JAPANESE)	1972	116				BIOU OF JAPAN	
ZEBRA IN THE KITCHEN	1965	93	4	2.5	2.5	M-G-M	
ZEPPELIN (BRITISH)	1971	101	3			WARNER BROTHERS	
ZERO FOR CONDUCT (FRENCH)	1933	56	3*			BRANDON	
ZERO HOUR	1957	81		2.0	2.5	PARAMOUNT	
ZIEGFELD FOLLIES	1946	110		3.5	2.5	M-G-M	
ZIEGFELD GIRL	1941	131		2.5	3.0	M-G-M	
ZIGZAG (GEORGE KENNEDY, ANNE JACKSON)	1970	104	4			M-G-M	
ZITA (FRENCH)	1968	92	5			REGIONAL	
ZOMBIES OF MORA-TAU	1957	70		1.5	1.5	COLUMBIA	
ZOMBIES ON BROADWAY	1945	68		2.0	2.0	RKO	
ZORBA THE GREEK	1965	142	5*	4.0	3.5	INTERNAT'L CLASSICS	NOMINATED BEST PICTURE
ZORIKAN THE BARBARIAN (ITALIAN)	1960	92		1.0		FOUR STAR	
ZORRO RIDES AGAIN	1937	68		2.0	2.0	REPUBLIC	
ZORRO, THE AVENGER (SPANISH)	1961	90		1.5	2.5	WARNER BROTHERS	
ZOTZ	1962	87		2.0	2.0	COLUMBIA	
ZULU (BRITISH)	1964	138		3.0	3.0	AVCO-EMBASSY	

"a" TO LEFT OF YEAR INDICATES THAT FILM HAS AN ALTERNATE TITLE

‡ An asterisk (*) in THE FILM BUFF'S BIBLE column indicates that the film has been rated by the editor and/or staff. All other ratings in this column are based on a consensus of reviews (see NOTES).

APPENDIX. Index of Alternate Titles

Anyone who changes a movie title should be fined a minimum of $100,000 (except for translating from one language to another). The following pages are an index of several hundred films which have alternate titles. Not all titles in this index will be found in the previous portion of the book; in some cases only the more popular title was listed there.

A substantial number of these changes are due to the fact that many British films have different titles in the United States (e.g., the British picture **Seven Waves Away** is known in the U.S. as **Abandon Ship!**), and vice versa. Yes, Virginia, **The Sterile Cuckoo** and **The Fortune Cookie** are known in Great Britain as **Pookie** and **Meet Whiplash Willie**, respectively.

ABANDON SHIP!	SEVEN WAVES AWAY	
ABBOTT & COSTELLO IN THE NAVY	IN THE NAVY	
ABBOTT & COSTELLO LOST IN ALASKA	LOST IN ALASKA	
ABOMINABLE DR PHIBES, THE	DR PHIBES	
ABOMINABLE SNOWMAN	ABOMINABLE SNOWMAN OF THE HIMALAYAS, THE	
ABOMINABLE SNOWMAN OF THE HIMALAYAS, THE	ABOMINABLE SNOWMAN	
ACE IN THE HOLE	BIG CARNIVAL, THE	
ADMIRABLE CRICHTON, THE	PARADISE LAGOON	
ADVENTURE, THE (GABRIELE FERZETTI)	L'AVVENTURA	
ADVENTURERS, THE (JACK HAWKINS)	FORTUNE IN DIAMONDS	
ADVENTURES AT RUGBY	TOM BROWN'S SCHOOL DAYS (C. HARDWICKE)	
ADVENTURES OF A YOUNG MAN	HEMMINGWAY'S ADVENTURES OF A YOUNG MAN	
ADVENTURES OF HUCKLEBERRY FINN, THE	HUCKLEBERRY FINN (BOTH VERSIONS)	
ADVENTURES OF ICHABOD AND MR TOAD	ICHABOD AND MR TOAD	
ADVENTURES OF JACK LONDON	JACK LONDON	
ADVENTURES OF MANDERIN, THE	AFFAIR OF MADAME POMPADOUR, THE	
ADVENTURES OF MARTIN EDEN, THE	MARTIN EDEN	
ADVENTURES OF MICHAEL STROGOFF	MICHAEL STROGOFF (ANTON WALBROOK)	SOLDIER AND THE LADY
ADVENTURES OF ROBINSON CRUSOE	ROBINSON CRUSOE	
ADVENTURES OF TARTU, THE	TARTU	
AFFAIR, THE	THERE'S ALWAYS VANILLA	
AFFAIR OF MADAME POMPADOUR, THE	ADVENTURES OF MANDERIN, THE	
AFFAIRS IN VERSAILLES	ROYAL AFFAIRS IN VERSAILLES	
AFFAIRS OF DR HOLL, THE	DR HOLL	
AFFAIRS OF JIMMY VALENTINE	UNFORGOTTEN CRIME	
AFFAIRS OF MARTHA, THE	ONCE UPON A THURSDAY	
AFFAIRS OF MESSALINA, THE	MESSALINA (MARIA FELIX)	
AFRICAN ELEPHANT, THE	KING ELEPHANT	
AFRICAN FURY	CRY, THE BELOVED COUNTRY	
AGENT 38-24-36	RAVASHING IDIOT, A	
AGENT 36-24-36	COME SPY WITH ME	
AGENT Z55	DESPERATE MISSION (GERMAN COBBS)	
ALEXANDER	VERY HAPPY ALEXANDER	
ALI BABA AND THE SACRED CROWN	SEVEN TASKS OF ALI BABA, THE	
ALL THAT MONEY CAN BUY	DEVIL AND DANIEL WEBSTER, THE	
ALMOST A BRIDE	KISS FOR CORLISS, A	
AMAZING MR BEECHAM, THE	CHILTERN HUNDREDS, THE	
AMAZING MR X, THE	SPIRITUALIST, THE	
AMAZING MONSIEUR FABRE, THE	MONSIEUR FABRE	
AMERICA, AMERICA	ANATOLIAN SMILE, THE	
AMERICAN DREAM, AN	SEE YOU IN HELL, DARLING	
ANATOLIAN SMILE, THE	AMERICA, AMERICA	
ANATOMY OF A SYNDICATE	BIG OPERATOR, THE	
AND SO THEY WERE MARRIED (SIMONE SIMON)	JOHNNY DOESN'T LIVE HERE ANYMORE	
ANGEL, ANGEL, DOWN WE GO	CULT OF THE DAMNED	
ANOTHER CHANCE	TWILIGHT WOMEN	
ANY WEDNESDAY	BACHELOR GIRL APARTMENT	
ANYTHING GOES (BING CROSBY)	TOPS IS THE LIMIT	
ANZIO	BATTLE FOR ANZIO, THE	
APARAJITO	UNVANQUISHED, THE	
APPOINTMENT WITH VENUS	ISLAND RESCUE	
ARIZONA MISSION	GUN THE MAN DOWN	
ARMORED ATTACK	NORTH STAR, THE	
ARRIVEDERCI, BABY	DROP DEAD, DARLING	
ARTFUL PENETRATION, THE	BLACK ON WHITE	
AT THE CIRCUS	MARX BROTHERS AT THE CIRCUS	
ATOLL K	UTOPIA	
ATOMIC BRAIN, THE	MONSTROSITY	
ATTACK AND RETREAT	ITALIANO BRAVA GENTE	
ATTACK OF THE GIANT LEECHES	DEMONS OF THE SWAMP	
AUNT TULA	LA TIA TULA	
AUSTERLITZ	BATTLE OF AUSTERLITZ, THE	
AVENGER, THE (STEVE REEVES)	LAST GLORY OF TROY, THE	
BABES IN TOYLAND (LAUREL AND HARDY)	MARCH OF THE WOODEN SOLDIERS	
BACHELOR GIRL APARTMENT	ANY WEDNESDAY	
BACK AT THE FRONT	WILLIE AND JOE BACK AT THE FRONT	
BAD GIRL (ANNA NEAGLE)	MY TEENAGE DAUGHTER	TEENAGE BAD GIRL
BAD SISTER	WHITE UNICORN, THE	
BALLAD OF JOE HILL, THE	JOE HILL	
BAMBOLE!	FOUR KINDS OF LOVE	
BAMSE	TEDDY BEAR, THE	
BANG, BANG	BANG BANG KID, THE	
BANG BANG KID, THE	BANG, BANG	
BANG, BANG, YOU'RE DEAD!	OUR MAN IN MARRAKESH	I SPY, YOU SPY
BANG! YOU'RE DEAD	GAME OF DANGER	
BANYON	WALK UP AND DIE	
BAR SINISTER, THE	IT'S A DOG'S LIFE	
BARBADOS QUEST	MURDER ON APPROVAL	
BAREFOOT SAVAGE, THE	SENSUALITA	
BATTLE, THE	THUNDER IN THE EAST (CHARLES BOYER)	
BATTLE FOR ANZIO, THE	ANZIO	
BATTLE OF AUSTERLITZ, THE	AUSTERLITZ	
BATTLE OF THE SPARTANS	BRENNUS, EMEMY OF ROME	
BATTLE SHOCK	WOMAN'S DEVOTION, A	

CHILDISH THINGS	TALE OF THE COCK	
CHILDREN OF PARADISE	LES ENFANTS DU PARADIS	
CHILDREN'S HOUR, THE	LOUDEST WHISPER, THE	
CHILTERN HUNDREDS, THE	AMAZING MR BEECHAM, THE	
CHINESE GIRL, THE	LA CHINOISE	
CHRISTA	SWEDISH FLY GIRLS	
CHRISTMAS CAROL, A (ALASTAIR SIM)	SCROOGE (ALASTAIR SIM)	
CHRISTMAS EVE	SINNER'S HOLIDAY	
CINERAMA'S RUSSIAN ADVENTURE	RUSSIAN ADVENTURE	
CIRCLE, THE	VICIOUS CIRCLE, THE (JOHN MILLS)	
CIRCUS OF FEAR	PSYCHO-CIRCUS	
CITY AFTER MIDNIGHT	THAT WOMAN OPPOSITE	
CITY ON A HUNT	NO ESCAPE (LEW AYRES)	
CITY UNDER THE SEA	WAR-GODS OF THE DEEP	
CLAUDELLE INGLISH	YOUNG AND EAGER	
CLOAK WITHOUT DAGGER	OPERATION CONSPIRACY	
CLOUDS OVER EUROPE	Q PLANES	
CODE OF SILENCE	KILLER'S CAGE	
COLLECTOR, THE (PATRICK BAUCHAU)	LA COLLECTIONEUSE	
COLOSSUS, THE FORBIN PROJECT	FORBIN PROJECT, THE	
COLT .45	THUNDERCLOUD	
COME SPY WITH ME	AGENT 36-24-36	
CONE OF SILENCE	TROUBLE IN THE SKY	
CONFESSION (DENNIS O'KEEFE)	GRAFT AND CORRUPTION	
CONFESSIONS OF AN OPIUM EATER	EVILS OF CHINATOWN	
CONFIDENTIAL REPORT	MR ARKADIN	
CONVICTS FOUR	REPRIEVE	
CORRUPT ONES, THE	PEKING MEDALLION, THE	
COUNT OF MONTE CRISTO (LOUIS JOURDAN)	STORY OF THE COUNT OF MONTE CRISTO, THE	
COURAGEOUS MR PENN	PENN OF PENNSYLVANIA	
COURT MARTIAL (DAVID NIVEN)	CHARRINGTON, V.C.	
CRASH OF SILENCE	MANDY	
CRAZY WORLD	MONDO PAZZO	
CRIME AND PUNISHMENT (JEAN GABIN)	MOST DANGEROUS SIN, THE	
CRIME DOES NOT PAY	GENTLE ART OF MURDER, THE	
CROSS UP	TIGER BY THE TAIL (LARRY PARKS)	
CRUCIBLE, THE	WITCHES OF SALEM, THE	
CRUEL SWAMP	SWAMP DIAMONDS	SWAMP WOMEN
CRY, THE BELOVED COUNTRY	AFRICAN FURY	
CULT OF THE DAMNED	ANGEL, ANGEL, DOWN WE GO	
CURLEY	HAL ROACH COMEDY CARNIVAL, THE	
CURSE OF DRACULA, THE	RETURN OF DRACULA, THE	
CURSE OF THE DEMON	NIGHT OF THE DEMON	
DAFFODIL KILLER	DEVIL'S DAFFODIL, THE	
DAGGERS OF BLOOD	WITH FIRE AND SWORD	
DALEKS - INVASION EARTH 2150 A.D.	INVASION EARTH 2150 A.D.	
DAMN THE DEFIANT!	H.M.S. DEFIANT	
DAMNED, THE	TWILIGHT OF THE GODS	
DANGER GROWS WILD	POPPY IS ALSO A FLOWER	
DANGER ON THE RIVER	MISSISSIPPI GAMBLER (KENT TAYLOR)	
DANGER WITHIN	BREAKOUT (RICHARD TODD)	
DANGEROUS FEMALE	MALTESE FALCON, THE (BEBE DANIELS)	
DANGEROUS MOONLIGHT	SUICIDE SQUADRON	
DATE WITH A LONELY GIRL, A	T. R. BASKIN	
DAUGHTER, THE	I, A WOMAN, PART III	
DAWN PATROL (RICHARD BARTHELMESS)	FLIGHT COMMANDER (RICHARD BARTHELMESS)	
DEADLY DECISION	CANARIS (MASTER SPY)	
DEADLY IS THE FEMALE	GUN CRAZY	
DEATH DANCE AT MADELIA	INTRUDERS, THE (DON MURRAY)	
DEATH OF TARZAN, THE	DEATH OF THE APE-MAN	
DEATH OF THE APE-MAN	DEATH OF TARZAN, THE	
DECOY	MYSTERY SUBMARINE (JAMES R. JUSTICE)	
DEMENTIA 13	HAUNTED AND THE HUNTED, THE	
DEMON PLANET	PLANET OF BLOOD	PLANET OF THE VAMPIRES
DEMONS OF THE SWAMP	ATTACK OF THE GIANT LEECHES	
DEN OF DOOM	GLASS CAGE, THE (JOHN HOYT)	
DEPARTURE, THE	LE DEPART	
DERBY	ROLLER DERBY	
DERBY DAY	FOUR AGAINST FATE	
DESERT ATTACK	ICE COLD IN ALEX	
DESERT DESPERADOS	SINNER, THE (RUTH ROMAN)	
DESERT PATROL	SEA OF SAND	
DESPERATE MISSION (GERMAN COBBS)	AGENT Z55	
DESPERATE SIEGE	RAWHIDE	
DEVIL, THE	TO BED OR NOT TO BED	
DEVIL AND DANIEL WEBSTER, THE	ALL THAT MONEY CAN BUY	
DEVIL NEVER SLEEPS, THE	SATAN NEVER SLEEPS	
DEVIL'S BROTHER	FRA DIAVOLO	
DEVIL'S DAFFODIL, THE	DAFFODIL KILLER	
DEVIL'S OWN, THE	WITCHES, THE (JOAN FONTAINE)	
DIABOLIQUE	FIENDS, THE	LES DIABOLIQUES
DIAMOND EARRINGS, THE	EARRINGS OF MADAME DE, THE	MADAME DE . . .
DIAMOND HORSESHOE	BILLY ROSE'S DIAMOND HORSESHOE	
DIAMONDS AND CRIME	HI DIDDLE DIDDLE	

MONSTERS OF THE NIGHT	NAVY VS. THE NIGHT MONSTERS, THE	
MONSTROSITY	ATOMIC BRAIN, THE	
MONTANA MIKE	HEAVEN ONLY KNOWS	
MONTPARNASSE 19	LOVERS OF MONTPARNASSE, THE	MODIGLIANI OF MONTPARNASSE
MONTY'S DOUBLE	I WAS MONTY'S DOUBLE	
MORITURI	SABOTEUR, CODE NAME – MORITURI, THE	
MORNING DEPARTURE	OPERATION DISASTER	
MOROZHKO	JACK FROST	
MORT EN FRAUDE	FUGITIVE IN SAIGON	
MOST DANGEROUS SIN, THE	CRIME AND PUNISHMENT (JEAN GABIN)	
MUMSY, NANNY, SONNY AND GIRLY	GIRLY	
MURDER, MY SWEET	FAREWELL, MY LOVELY	
MURDER ON APPROVAL	BARBADOS QUEST	
MURDER ON MONDAY	HOME AT SEVEN	
MURDER WILL OUT (VALERIE HOBSON)	VOICE OF MERRILL, THE	
MUTINEERS, THE	PIRATE SHIP	
MY BROTHER, THE OUTLAW	MY OUTLAW BROTHER	
MY NAME IS IVAN	YOUNGEST SPY, THE	
MY OLD MAN'S PLACE	GLORY BOY	
MY OUTLAW BROTHER	MY BROTHER, THE OUTLAW	
MY SEVEN LITTLE SINS	I HAVE SEVEN DAUGHTERS	
MY TEENAGE DAUGHTER	BAD GIRL (ANNA NEAGLE)	TEENAGE BAD GIRL
MY WORLD DIES SCREAMING	TERROR IN THE HAUNTED HOUSE	
MYSTERY OF THE BLACK JUNGLE	BLACK DEVILS OF KALI, THE	
MYSTERY SUBMARINE (JAMES R. JUSTICE)	DECOY	
NABONGA	GORILLA	
NAKED CHILDHOOD	ME	
NAKED NIGHT, THE	SAWDUST AND TINSEL	
NASTY RABBIT, THE	SPIES A-GO-GO	
NAUGHTY ARLETTE	ROMANTIC AGE, THE	
NAUGHTY GIRL	MAM'ZELLE PIGALLE	
NAVY BORN	MARINERS OF THE SKY	
NAVY HEROES	BLUE PETER, THE	
NAVY VS. THE NIGHT MONSTERS, THE	MONSTERS OF THE NIGHT	
NET, THE	PROJECT M-7	
NEVER GIVE AN INCH	SOMETIMES A GREAT NOTION	
NEVER TO LOVE	BILL OF DIVORCEMENT (MAUREEN O'HARA)	NOT FOR EACH OTHER
NIGHT, THE	LA NOTTE	
NIGHT AMBUSH	ILL MET BY MOONLIGHT	
NIGHT HEAVEN FELL, THE	HEAVEN FELL THAT NIGHT	
NIGHT OF THE DEMON	CURSE OF THE DEMON	
NIGHT OF THE QUARTER MOON	FLESH AND FLAME	
NIGHT THEY KILLED RASPUTIN, THE	NIGHTS OF RASPUTIN	
NIGHTS OF CABIRIA	CABIRIA (GIULIETTA MASINA)	
NIGHTS OF RASPUTIN	NIGHT THEY KILLED RASPUTIN, THE	
NO ESCAPE (DEAN JAGGER)	I ESCAPED FROM THE GESTAPO	
NO ESCAPE (LEW AYRES)	CITY ON A HUNT	
NO HIGHWAY	NO HIGHWAY IN THE SKY	
NO HIGHWAY IN THE SKY	NO HIGHWAY	
NO MAN IS AN ISLAND	ISLAND ESCAPE	
NO PLACE LIKE HOMICIDE	WHAT A CARVE UP	
NOBODY RUNS FOREVER	HIGH COMMISSIONER, THE	
NONE BUT THE BRAVE (RICHARD BASEHART)	FOR THE LOVE OF MIKE	
NORTH STAR, THE	ARMORED ATTACK	
NOT FOR EACH OTHER	BILL OF DIVORCEMENT (MAUREEN O'HARA)	NEVER TO LOVE
NOTHING TO LOSE	TIME, GENTLEMEN, PLEASE	
NOTORIOUS GENTLEMAN (REX HARRISON)	RAKE'S PROGRESS, THE	
NOVEL AFFAIR, A	PASSIONATE STRANGER, THE	
NUDE IN A WHITE CAR	BLONDE IN A WHITE CAR	
O.S.S. 117 – MISSION FOR A KILLER	MISSION FOR A KILLER	
OBSESSION (ROBERT NEWTON)	HIDDEN ROOM, THE	
OCTOBER MAN, THE	HANGMAN'S NOOSE	
OLIVIA	PIT OF LONLINESS	
ON ANY STREET	LA NOTTE BRAVA	
ON OUR MERRY WAY	MIRACLE CAN HAPPEN, A	
ON THE FIDDLE	OPERATION SNAFU	OPERATION WARHEAD
ONCE UPON A THURSDAY	AFFAIRS OF MARTHA, THE	
ONE BORN EVERY MINUTE	FLIM-FLAM MAN, THE	
ONE CENT	BOOT POLISH	
ONE FATAL HOUR	TWO AGAINST THE WORLD	
ONE FOR THE BOOK	VOICE OF THE TURTLE	
ONE HORSE TOWN	SMALL TOWN GIRL (JANET GAYNOR)	
ONE PLUS ONE	SYMPATHY FOR THE DEVIL	
1,000 PLANE RAID, THE	THOUSAND PLANE RAID, THE	
ONE WOMAN'S STORY	PASSIONATE FRIENDS	
ONIBABA	HOLE, THE	
ONLY THE FRENCH CAN	FRENCH CAN CAN	
OPERATION CONSPIRACY	CLOAK WITHOUT DAGGER	
OPERATION CROSSBOW	GREAT SPY MISSION, THE	
OPERATION DISASTER	MORNING DEPARTURE	
OPERATION MERMAID	BAY OF ST MICHEL	
OPERATION SNAFU	ON THE FIDDLE	OPERATION WARHEAD
OPERATION WARHEAD	ON THE FIDDLE	OPERATION SNAFU
ORACLE, THE	HORSE'S MOUTH, THE (ROBERT BEATTY)	